HISTORY

GENERAL EDITORS
DR BIANCA JACKSON AND JONATHAN MORTON

HISTORY

A CASSELL BOOK

An Hachette Livre UK Company

First published in the UK 2008 by
Cassell Illustrated, a division of
Octopus Publishing Group Ltd.
2–4 Heron Quays,
London E14 4JP

A CIP catalogue record for this book is available from the
British Library.

ISBN-13: 978-1-844-03591-5 (UK Edition)

Distributed in the United States and Canada by
Sterling Publishing Co., Inc
387 Park Avenue South, New York, NY 10016-8810

ISBN-13: 978-1-844-03639-4 (U.S. Edition)

10 9 8 7 6 5 4 3 2 1

Commissioning Editor: Laura Price
Project Editor: Jenny Doubt
Editors: Ruth Patrick, Bianca Jackson
Assistant Editors: Sally Mesner, Fiona Kellagher
Production: Caroline Alberti

Creative Director: Geoff Fennell
Designer: John Round

Publisher: Mathew Clayton

Printed in Hong Kong

CONTENTS

CONTRIBUTORS

Demir Barlas is a Ph.D student in Theater at Cornell University, USA. He specializes in Turkish and Iranian performance history and folk Islam.

David Anderson is a Master of English student at the University of British Columbia, in Vancouver, Canada.

D. Larraine Andrews is an award-winning Canadian freelance journalist and author of the historical guidebook entitled *The Cowboy Trail A Guide to Alberta's Historic Cowboy Country*.

Ned Beauman is Web Editor at *Dazed & Confused* magazine and writes for the *Guardian* and the *Financial Times*.

Andrew Blades is a research student and tutor at Oxford University. He writes for *The Stage* and *English Review*.

Rosamunde Bott is a freelance writer and novelist with a specialist interest in history. She has had several articles published in family history publications.

Lorraine Brownbill A Scotland-based factual writer for over 25 years, Lorraine has an astonishingly varied client base and portfolio including tourism to training, wildlife to walking.

Bethonie Butler has written for *Entertainment Weekly*, EW.com, *The Washingtonian Magazine*, and *The Providence (R.I.) Journal*. She lives in Queens, NY.

Denis Casey graduated from University College Dublin (B.A. History, M.A. Medieval Studies) and is currently a Ph.D candidate at the University of Cambridge studying medieval Irish kingship.

Alexandra Coghlan took undergraduate degrees in English and Music at Balliol College Oxford, before moving to Trinity College Cambridge where she studied for an MPhil in Criticism and Culture.

Alex Cummings is a doctoral candidate at Columbia University who writes about missionaries, music, newspapers, pirates, planning, and research triangles.

Laura Davies is currently completing a Ph.D on eighteenth-century cultural history at Cambridge University.

Kerry Duffy is a writer and copywriter, contributing to www.britishboxing.net.

David Dunning is a full-time, freelance writer, specializing in creative non-fiction.

Rachel Eley studied English Literature at Oxford before defecting to the social sciences for an MA in Environment and Development. Romance and pragmatism led her to California where she hopes to find a rewarding career in sustainable development and lots and lots of gold.

Carly Fabian was born in South Africa and studied English and Philosophy at the University of Cape Town. She is currently reading Law at King's College, London.

Jeremy Fialko is a Food Manufacturing analyst at an investment bank, covering stocks such as Nestlé and Danone. He previously read Economics at Cambridge.

Hannah Furness is a recent graduate from Oxford University, where she studied History.

Karen Garner teaches U.S., Asian, and Women's History at SUNY Empire State College. In 2003, she was a Fulbright Scholar at the University of Vilnius Gender Studies Centre in Vilnius, Lithuania, and has published a book titled *Precious Fire: Maud Russell and the Chinese Revolution* (University of Massachusetts Press).

David Greenwald is a Los Angeles-based freelance writer whose work has appeared in *Entertainment Weekly* and *Billboard*.

Michael Hallam is a freelance writer living in Brighton. He is currently completing a Ph.D at Sussex University on British literature and the 1940s.

James Handley was educated in London and at Pembroke College, Oxford. He lives and works in Niigata City, Japan.

Helena Hewson is a freelance writer with a keen interest in social history and amateur artist specializing in charcoal.

opposite **The Allies divide Berlin after World War II.**

Michelle Higgs is a freelance writer of articles for a wide variety of publications. She is also the author of three social history books.

Anne Hsu received her graduate degree in Physics at UC Berkeley. She is currently a scientific researcher in cognitive science.

Roger Johnson is an American Studies D.Phil student at the University of Sussex, working on the Reagan presidency and its developing historical meanings.

Martin L. Johnson is a doctoral student in cinema studies at New York University. His dissertation research is on the production and exhibition of local film in the United States from the 1920s to the 1950s.

Mark Juddery is an Australian writer, journalist, and historian. His books include *1975: Australia's Greatest Year* (John Wiley & Sons) and *Debunked! The 50 Most Overrated Things* (Random House).

Mariko Kato is a freelance writer for various publications including the *Japan Times*, with B.A. Honors in English and M.Sc in Comparative and International Education from Oxford University, UK.

Fiona Kellagher studied English Literature at Warwick University. She has taught English as a second language and works as an editorial assistant in London.

Frieda Klotz studied Greek and English at Trinity College Dublin and then completed a doctorate at Oxford University.

Eric Kohn graduated from NYU with a degree in cinema studies and journalism. His writing appears in the *New York Press*, *The Hollywood Reporter*, and other publications.

Andrea Korda is an art historian working towards a doctorate at the University of California, Santa Barbara. Se holds a Master's degree in Art History from Concordia University (Montreal, Quebec) and a Bachelor of Arts degree from Queen's University (Kingston, Ontario).

Sonja Kudeljnjak is a freelance writer and illustrator. She obtained her Master's at Sussex University in 2007.

Brian Ladd, a historian, is the author of three books on Germany and a new history of cars and cities.

Colette Leisen is a Vancouver-based artist, writer, and mother who is currently working on a book of personal essays titled, *Shiksa in the Schtedl*.

Keith A. Leitich is an independent researcher and consultant based in Seattle, WA. His research focuses on ethnic conflict and migration in the former Soviet Union within the larger context of globalization of Central Asia.

Fred Lindsey is Assistant Professor of Cultural Studies at John F. Kennedy University in Pleasant Hill, California.

Terence McSweeney is lecturer in film history. He is the co-editor of an upcoming volume entitled *Millennial Cinema: Representations of Memory in Contemporary Film*.

M. E. Powell is a freelance journalist, writer, and photographer based in Regina, Saskatchewan, Canada. Scholastic recently published her first book, *Dragonflies are Amazing!*

Heather K. Michon is an independent writer and historian living near Charlottesville, Virginia.

Ian Morley is a Postdoctoral Fellow based at the Department of History, Chinese University of Hong Kong. He specializes in Urban History, principally nineteenth-century Britain.

Ben Morton works for the British Columbia Ministry of Aboriginal Relations and Reconciliation as a Senior Advisor for Aboriginal Education and Culture. He received his Masters in Indigenous Governance from the University of Victoria, Canada in 2005.

Jay Mullins is a freelance writer and website editor who recently completed a degree in broadcasting at Ravenbourne College. He thinks Genghis Khan did a lot for world history.

Justin Norris is a scholar, writer, and critic, and has written widely on numerous topics, primarily English Literature. He currently lives in Vancouver, Canada.

J. Owen read History at the University of Southampton. He now works as a policy advisor for a UK Government Department in London.

opposite The fall of the Berlin Wall.

Laura Charlotte Pechey studied at the Universities of KwaZulu Natal, Leeds, and Cambridge. She is writing her doctoral thesis on animals in nineteenth- and twentieth-century South African writing.

Leith Peterson, MLIS, is a London, Ontario writer, researcher, and archives consultant. Her published articles and produced plays have covered a wide variety of topics.

Greg Pittard graduated with a degree in film studies from the University of Kent, and is currently a writer for an established publication in London and a voluntary contributor to webzines and film festivals.

Duncan Proudfoot studied English and History at the University of Cape Town before working as a teacher and writer. He is now a commissioning editor n London.

Dr Elizabeth Purdy is a political scientist and freelance writer who is involved with women's issues. She has also published articles in other fields.

Carolyn Purnell is currently a Ph.D student at the University of Chicago, and her academic interests are in eighteenth-century French leisure and the history of science.

Dr Anna Marie Roos is a research associate at the Wellcome Unit, Oxford University. She is a historian of science and medicine.

opposite A young survivor of the Beslan school siege.

Martin Sayers is a history graduate and freelance writer whose work has appeared in numerous magazines, newspapers, and books.

Chris Schonberger graduated from Harvard University with a B.A. in English Literature. He has written for a variety of publications, including *Entertainment Weekly* and *Let's Go* travel guides. He would argue that the greatest moment in history was when England defeated West Germany in the 1966 World Cup Finals.

Todd Scribner is a Ph.D student currently studying at The Catholic University of America and has a forthcoming dissertation on neoconservative Catholic thought during the Reagan era.

Lynn Shepherd worked in business for fifteen years before returning to Oxford for a doctorate. She is now a corporate copywriter, with clients ranging from Acas to Zurich.

Geoffrey Shullenberger is pursuing a Ph.D in Comparative Literature at Brown University in Providence, Rhode Island.

Yvonne Sims is an Assistant Professor of American and Ethnic Studies in the Department of American Studies at The Pennsylvania State University-Harrisburg.

Ben Snook is a London-based writer and researcher who, as well as working freelance, writes for www.bitsofnews.com. He will shortly submit his Ph.D in tenth-century history at Selwyn College, Cambridge.

Josh Spero is an arts and features journalist, contributing to the *Guardian*, *The Times*, and several magazines, and a Classics tutor.

Julie Sutherland completed her Ph.D at Durham University and now teaches at Kwantlen University College in Canada. She also manages a professional theater company (Pacific Theatre) in Vancouver, British Columbia.

Hedley Paul is a UK-based freelance writer with an M.A. in Modern History, who also writes scripts and music for TV and film animations.

David Thorley is a Stoke-on-Trent-born journalist, now based in Oxford. In 2007 he was awarded Arts Council funding to support his first novel.

Maxime Turcotte practices corporate law in Montreal, Canada. He holds an M.A. in political economy from the London School of Economics and sits on the Board of the Insitut du Canada Moderne.

Claudine van Hensbergen is currently completing a doctorate exploring the significance of courtesan narratives within English Literature, 1660–1725.

Annie Wang lives in Vancouver, Canada working in television news and freelance writing. Her online blog www.cayenne andchocolate.blogspot.com follows her "foodie" experiences around the world.

Christina C. Welsch is a Robert W. Woodruff Scholar at Emory University pursuing a Bachelor of Arts in European History.

Charlotte Whittle is pursuing a Ph.D in Hispanic Studies at Brown University in Providence, Rhode Island.

Sally Percival Wood is a Research Fellow at Deakin University, Melbourne. Her doctoral research on the 1955 Asian-African Conference at Bandung, Indonesia, focused on India and China, and the evolution of their cultural and diplomatic interactions with the West. She is also interested in Australia's relationships with Asia and the Middle East.

Michael Wodzicki has a background in Canadian politics and works in international development. He's been published on human rights, foreign policy, and democracy.

INTRODUCTION

It is typical in a book of this kind that some type of disclaimer is offered in the introduction, an apology for what has been left out or underrepresented. Indeed, we could spend pages lamenting the absence of an entry on the invention of the zipper in 1913 or the fact that certain countries, like Trinidad and Tobago, are only mentioned in relation to horrific massacres or despotic rulers, leading the reader to believe that bloodshed is the only significant event that has occurred in these nations. However, we refuse to apologize because despite the name of the book, this is obviously not the definitive list of key events in world history in the last hundred years. There is no such thing. Rather, it is a list informed by our place and time in the history we seek to represent, not to mention our own views of what is historically relevant. A right-wing fundamentalist, for example, might not have included the first male-to-female transsexual surgery as a key event in world history, just as a Marxist historian might not see the pertinence of the discovery of Botox to the struggle of the people.

In fact, it is this lack of cohesive historical narrative that makes this book so unique and exciting. Pick up any history book on the shelf at your local bookstore and you will usually find a carefully crafted "story" in which all the inevitable discrepancies and non-sequiturs have been ironed out. This allows the historian to create a comprehensive chronicle of times past or to provide evidence for a particular theoretical standpoint. However, history, as this book highlights, is not one single, seamless trajectory. We have chosen to present the last century as a series of events so that history may be approached instead as a jigsaw puzzle. Events rub up against one another, but also exist independently in their own right. This allows the reader to draw his or her own conclusions about how the past has shaped the present and to construct his or her own historical narrative, facilitating the creation of multiple histories rather than one decisive "History."

This focus on the multiplicity of history is also why we decided to include not only politically historical events, but also social, scientific, cultural, and even meteorological events from across the world. Where there is either academic debate or a number of possible dates for an event, we have chosen to let the reader to decide for him/herself when the key "moment" happened. Some events can be pinpointed to almost the exact second of their occurrence; others simply refuse to be pinned down and, as such, we have left them floating within the year. This has made for some strange bedfellows: the invention of the mini-skirt by Mary Quant is presented alongside the formation of the Viet Cong and Nigerian independence in 1960; AIDS is first identified in 1981 at the same time that MTV is launched in America and the IRA ends its hunger strike at Maze prison in Ireland. But it is these unexpected juxtapositions that allow the reader to re-think what history is and how it should be understood. What does it mean, if anything, that some of what may be considered the most frivolous occurrences transpire during times of great political unrest? Do the events in developing countries shape what happens in the so-called First World, and vice versa? While this book provides a myriad of historical tidbits that may be familiar or completely foreign to the reader, one of its most exhilarating characteristics is that it prompts as many questions as it answers.

These questions are further complicated by our desire to represent as many countries as possible, in both the book itself and by our choice of contributors. Our writers consist not only of historians and assorted academics, but also lawyers, artists, civil servants, freelance writers, and even a food-manufacturing analyst. They live in America and Britain, Australia and Canada, Japan and South Africa. Our own prejudices as editors, which are there despite how hard we try to be objective, are therefore interrogated and undermined by the multiplicity of voices and experiences that comprise this collection. As we ourselves have learned throughout the creation of this book, a singular event may be understood and described in an infinite amount of ways, with all ways being "correct." These varied articulations of history prevent the book from becoming a static narrative and instead allow for a truly global and fluid approach to the past.

Before we leave you to discover all of the gripping, horrifying, and often magnificent events we have included in this text, we would like to thank a number of people who worked tirelessly on this project with us. Our writers were of an exceptional caliber, and their enthusiasm for the project was unparalleled. In particular, we would like to thank Demir Barlas who saved us too many times to count and whose ability to write so articulately under numerous time constraints was amazing (and frankly disturbing). We would also like to thank Laura Price for giving us the opportunity to work on this wonderful project, and her unwavering belief that we could do it properly. Lastly, we do not have enough space for the tribute that our senior editor, Jenny Doubt, deserves, but we hope that she knows what a great supervisor (and friend) she has been throughout. She held our hands every step of the way and is as much a part of this book as we are.

Dr Bianca Jackson and Jonathan Morton

Key Discovery
The birth of genetics rediscovered

Although seemingly puttering in the monastery garden, in 1856, a monk named Gregor Mendel began experiments crossing different strains of pea plants. He was trying to understand how physical traits could be passed down from parent to offspring. Peas were good for genetic experiments because they rapidly germinate and have easily identified characteristics, such as flower color and seed textures, that can be observed and counted. After observing thousands of crosses, Mendel discovered that the color of pea flowers and the texture of pea seeds are inherited in mathematical ratios. He also realized that some genetic traits are dominant and others are recessive, linking the external appearance of the plant to its genetic inheritance. This is the key idea behind heredity, and why Mendel is known as the "father of genetics."

This "father" was on the very margins of the scientific community, and his work generally ignored until 1900 when Carl Correns (1864–1933) and Hugo de Vries (1848–1935) independently rediscovered his achievements. By this point, scientists had detected chromosomes under the microscope, and it was understood that when sex cells (eggs and sperm) divided, their chromosomes were equally parceled out to daughter cells. Correns realized that Mendel's genetic traits resided on chromosomes, an idea known as the chromosome theory of heredity. The achievements of a reclusive Austrian monk in a garden led to our understanding of genetics, covering everything from inherited susceptibility to disease to eye color.
Anna Roos

Date January 25, 1900

Country Austria (Mendel); Germany (Correns); Netherlands (de Vries)

Why It's Key Mendel's work resulted in the birth of the idea of heredity, the genetic inheritance of traits.

Fact Mendel sent the results of his experiments to Charles Darwin (1809–1882), who did not recognize their significance as a driving force behind natural selection and evolution.

Key Cultural Event
Kodak introduces the Brownie Camera

In February 1900, the Eastman Kodak Company announced a new camera that would revolutionize photography. The Brownie Camera was simple to use and affordable, costing only US$1. It was an immediate popular success, bringing photography within the reach of a far wider section of the population than ever before and ushering in a new era in picture making. While photography had previously been a specialized pursuit reserved for the privileged or professional, the Brownie Camera transformed photography into a popular tool and a staple of North American social life. Armed with their Brownies and other dollar-cameras that followed in its wake, families could finally document their own milestones and fill albums with pictures of birthdays, holidays, and other moments of daily life.

The Brownie's advertising was directed specifically toward children and families, with the tagline "so simple they can easily be operated by any school boy or girl." The camera's name and the illustrations on its packaging also targeted children by association with the Brownie characters of Palmer Cox's popular children's stories. The original Brownie was made from jute board and wood, covered with imitation leather, and measured 12.5 x 8.1 x 7.9 cm. For just US 15c, Brownie owners could buy film for six small square pictures. Kodak sold a line of Brownie Cameras until the 1960s, when it was discontinued due to increasing demand for 35mm cameras that used Kodak's newer color films, such as Kodachrome.
Andrea L. Korda

Date February 1, 1900

Country USA

Why It's Key The Brownie created a revolution in social documentation, making photography accessible to the majority of Americans.

Fact George Eastman of the Eastman Kodak Company was the first to mass market photography. He introduced the Kodak Camera in 1888 with the slogan "you press the button, we do the rest."

opposite The Brownie in action.

Key Cultural Event
The World's Fair opens in Paris

The 1900 World's Fair in Paris, or the *Exposition Universelle* as it is known in French, attracted a colossal number of visitors, estimated to be about fifty million people in total, from the time it opened in April until November 10, 1900, when it closed. With more than 70,000 exhibitors and incorporating the second modern Olympic Games as well, the fair was a grandiose carnival celebrating human endeavors, while concurrently granting an optimistic look to the future and the potential of technology.

Despite attracting huge numbers of visitors, the enormity of the event meant it was a financial loss, which the national government of France ultimately covered, although in broad cultural terms, the significance of the event was colossal. In the realm of architecture, for example, intricate art nouveau was promoted, as were new technological innovations. These included the world's first movies that projected simultaneous sounds and images, the debut of a moving floor known as an escalator, and Rudolf Diesel's showing of a primitive version of a motor engine.

In Paris itself the event led to major construction projects on a scale not undertaken since the activities of Georges Haussmann in the mid-nineteenth century, including the erection of monumental edifices like the *Petit Palais*, *Grand Palais*, the *Pont Alexandre III*, train stations such as the *Gare de Lyon*, and *Gare d'Orsay*, and the city's first underground metro line. The new century had begun.

Ian Morley

Date April 14, 1900

Country France

Why It's Key The World's Fair in Paris celebrated past human achievements, while ushering in the start of a new century.

Fact The exposition was where the world's first talking movies were unveiled.

opposite The Eiffel Tower, built between 1887 and 1889 as the entrance arch for the *Exposition Universelle*.

Key Cultural Event
Olympic Games welcomes women athletes

The 1900 Summer Olympics, officially known as the Games of the II Olympiad, was only the second of the modern international Olympic Games, after its revival in Athens, Greece, in 1896. It was held in Paris as part of the 1900 World's Fair (*Exposition Universelle*), and as a result, was spread over five months, with no opening or closing ceremonies. The two events merged to such an extent that some athletes were not even aware that they were participating in the Olympics.

Yet the 1900 Games remain a key historical event as the first modern Olympics to allow female competitors. On July 11, British tennis player Charlotte Cooper, already a three-time Wimbledon champion, became the first female Olympics gold medalist, winning the women's singles and the mixed doubles. Other female competitors included French croquet players Madame Despres, Madame Filleaul Brohy, and Mademoiselle Ohnier, and American golfer Margaret Ives Abbott, an arts student from Chicago, who died in 1955 without ever knowing that she was the first American female Olympics champion.

The 1900 Games were also controversial for the decision to hold events on a Sunday, provoking protests from many American athletes who, as representatives of their colleges, were expected to withdraw rather than compete on the Sabbath. Nevertheless, over 1,000 competitors took part in 19 different sports, including some unusual one-off events, such as the equestrian high and long jumps, swimming obstacle race, two-day cricket, and live pigeon shooting.

Mariko Kato

Date May 14, 1900

Country France

Why It's Key Women were allowed to compete in the Games for the first time since their modern makeover.

Fact The first female Ancient Olympics champion was a Spartan princess called Kynisca, in 392 BCE.

Key Political Event
The Boxer Rebellion ends

European Christian missionaries established a presence in China during the Ming Dynasty (1368–1644), but it was not until the late Qing Dynasty (1644–1911) that the Chinese started to actively resist their presence. Significant changes in China's relationship with the West began with the Treaty of Nanjing signed by Britain and China on August 29, 1842, at the end of the Opium Wars (1939–1842). This marked the first of a series of "unequal treaties" that encroached to an ever-increasing degree upon Chinese sovereignty. The treaties opened up greater access and freedom of movement to European and American missionaries, so that the number of missionaries in China more than doubled from 1870 to 1899.

In 1898, a secret revolutionary society, I-ho-Ch'uan, meaning Righteous and Harmonious Boxing Order, began a campaign of animosity toward foreigners in northwest Shandong Province. Posters denouncing Christians and their "tricky techniques to deceive people" called the Chinese to rise against them. Fed up with foreign demands, the Dowager Empress Cixi proclaimed her support for the uprising, but after the death of some 200 foreigners and 30,000 Chinese Christians, a united foreign force of about 20,000 troops crushed the rebellion. China, and the Qing Dynasty, was left further weakened by the Boxer Rebellion. The Boxer Protocol of 1901 extracted exorbitant compensation, which, by the time it was fully repaid in December 1940, amounted to almost 1 billion taels (US$739 million).

Sally Percival Wood

Date May 31, 1900

Country China

Why It's Key The Boxer Rebellion was a disastrous movement against the presence of foreigners in China that further debilitated the Qing Dynasty.

Key Cultural Event
First flight of the Zeppelin

On July 2, 1900, a small crowd gathered on the shores of Lake Constance in Germany to watch the first flight of the new airship designed by Count Ferdinand von Zeppelin. The expectant onlookers saw the huge inflatable take flight for around eighteen minutes before being forced to land on the lake.

Although airships were already in use, Count von Zeppelin's design was groundbreaking in that it was the first to have a skeleton constructed around the bags of gas that lifted it off the ground. Von Zeppelin reasoned that this would make it more durable and capable of long-range missions.

Despite early problems that resulted in numerous crashes, the Count was proven right, and by the time World War I broke out fourteen years later, the German military were using Zeppelins to further the war effort.

During the course of the conflict, regular Zeppelin raids dropped bombs over London and the east of England, resulting in deaths and causing widespread panic.

The use of Zeppelins by the military came to end with Germany's defeat in 1918, but this was not the end of the airship. Their civilian potential in carrying people was enthusiastically pursued, and by the 1930s, Zeppelins were making regular transatlantic passenger flights. However, competition from airplanes began to eat into the Zeppelin's market share, and the disaster of 1937, when the Hindenburg airship caught fire after docking and killed thirty-five passengers, effectively signaled the end of the Zeppelin's widespread use.

Martin Sayers

Date July 2, 1900

Country Germany

Why It's Key The development of the Zeppelin was a significant step in the history of human flight, encouraging further developments in military and civilian air transport.

opposite The Graf Zeppelin airship at rest.

Key Cultural Event
Death of Friedrich Nietzsche

More than eleven years after a mental collapse, probably caused by tertiary syphilis, the renegade classical philologist and self-proclaimed "Antichrist" met his end in his home in Weimar. It was no coincidence that he died in the city of Goethe and Schiller. His sister Elisabeth Förster-Nietzsche, who during the philosopher's madness had made herself his exclusive guardian and literary executor, moved him there in 1897, probably in a deliberate attempt to reserve for him a place in the pantheon of German high culture. It is unclear how Nietzsche would have felt about this arrangement; although he intensely admired Goethe, he spent much of his adult life in voluntary exile from Germany and lambasted the Teutonic cultural chauvinism of the circle of proto-fascists presided over by Elisabeth and her husband, Bernhard Förster.

Nietzsche's death as a mad, lonely prophet propelled him into iconic status throughout Europe. The solitude and silence of his final years would signal for many the absolute estrangement of the authentic visionary in modern society. Meanwhile, his most quotable phrases about the death of God and the "*Übermensch*," parroted by the would-be disciples he deplored as "Zarathustra's apes," would convert Nietzsche, for many, into a proponent of facile individualistic amoralism, military aggression, and fascist brutality. Only decades later would his monumental and nuanced interrogation of the West's philosophical traditions begin to receive the broad recognition it now enjoys.
Geoffrey Schullenberger

Date August 25, 1900

Country Germany

Why It's Key Nietzsche died on the cusp of the century in which he would become possibly the most influential and certainly the most notorious of philosophers.

Fact Some of Nietzsche's books sold fewer than ten copies in his lifetime, but his fame grew steadily after his descent into madness, and exploded following his death.

Key Cultural Event
Death of Oscar Wilde

Oscar Wilde's life was one of artistic success marred by personal conflict. Although married, he had various homosexual encounters, most famously with Frank Miles, Robert Ross, and Lord Alfred Douglas (whom he knew affectionately as "Bosie"), despite the fact that homosexuality was illegal in Britain.

Having achieved celebrity through the popularity of his plays and witticisms (many renowned during his lifetime), Wilde found himself in court facing charges of having committed "homosexual acts amounting to buggery." The trial, along with the many lewd accusations and exposés of the particulars of Wilde's private life, were widely reported and raised his profile yet further. While Wilde vehemently defended homosexuality, many other high profile homosexual men of his circle fled Britain, fearing a similar fate.

Having been prosecuted, Wilde was sentenced to two years' hard labor, after which he too left Britain, spending the final two years of his life penniless in Paris, where he resumed his homosexual lifestyle. When he died in 1900, rumors were rife that the meningitis which had killed him had been brought on by syphilis. Though this is now seen as unlikely, the connection of venereal disease with homosexuality was common at the time and added to the sense of fear and paranoia in the homosexual community.

Wilde contributed significantly to "the Cause" of reforming the homosexuality law and was a member of the clandestine Order of Chaeronea, an underground society promoting homosexuality and campaigning against its suppression.
Ben Snook

Date November 30, 1900

Country France

Why It's Key Wilde's high-profile imprisonment and death scared many other homosexuals into remaining "in the closet," yet simultaneously brought same-sex sexuality into the limelight.

Fact Wilde was received into the Roman Catholic Church on his deathbed.

Key Discovery
Quantum mechanics proposed

Quantum mechanics is a branch of physics that describes elementary particles, which exhibit simultaneous wave-like and particle-like properties. German physicist Max Planck first presented the quantum hypothesis in 1900 while describing the problem of black body radiation, the thermal radiation emitted from an object that absorbs all light. Planck posited that energy was absorbed and radiated in packets. This led Albert Einstein to hypothesize that light itself is also quantized into discrete packets, which he called photons.

French physicist Louis de Broglie first proposed the wave-like nature of particles, which was later developed into a theory of particle behavior based on wave mechanics by Austrian physicist Erwin Schrödinger in the 1920s. However, at the same time, German physicist

Werner Heisenberg produced a mathematical equivalent to Schrödinger's theory without waves, using only linear algebra. English physicist Paul Dirac unified the wave-particle theories, and incorporated them with the theory of relativity. This led the way for U.S. physicist Richard Feynman to formulate the modern theory of quantum mechanics known as quantum electrodynamics, which explains how charged subatomic particles interact within electric and magnetic fields.

Quantum mechanics is one of the two fundamental theories of modern physics, the other being general relativity. While these two theories are not directly contradictory, they still elude unification. Current particle theory research focuses on attempting to combine these two theories under one cohesive model.
Anne Hsu

Date December 14, 1900

Country Germany

Why It's Key This is the first proposition of the revolutionary theory that energy comes in the form of quantized packets, paving the way for modern theories of elementary particles.

Key Cultural Event
Freud publishes *Interpretation of Dreams*

Human fascination with dream interpretation dates back as far as 3000-4000 BCE, when primitive peoples recorded them on clay tablets, and dreams have been valued as a form of prophecy throughout the ages. However, in the early nineteenth century dreams were dismissed as reactions to anxiety or even bad digestion, and it was Sigmund Freud's *Interpretation of Dreams* that helped dream interpretation to re-emerge as a new scientific theory.

First published in German in 1899, *Interpretation of Dreams (Die Traumdeutung)* introduced the theory of the unconscious in relation to the concept of dreams as forms of "wish fulfillment." According to Freud, during sleep the unconscious attempts to resolve a conflict or cause of anxiety from the past. In waking hours, the preconscious "censors" the often disturbing information

volunteered by the unconscious, and it is only when we are asleep that this barrier is lowered and our true "wishes" reveal themselves. Drawing on patient case studies, literature, and even Freud's own dreams, *Interpretation of Dreams* is also the first text in which Freud mentions the Oedipus complex – the psychosexual theory that children regard their father as a competitor for the mother's love.

Not all psychoanalysts agree with his theories. In the third edition, Freud explores more literal interpretations of dreams, causing some psychoanalysts to argue that his dream interpretation is predominantly a search for sexual or phallic symbols. However, Freud remained unperturbed, claiming of this work, "insight such as this falls to one's lot but once in a lifetime."
Mariko Kato

Date 1900

Country Austria

Why It's Key *Interpretation of Dreams* transformed our understanding of the unconscious and is widely considered to be Freud's most important contribution to psychology.

Key Discovery
Oil discovered in Texas

Spindletop, Texas, just south of the town of Beaumont, was a salt dome that had been suspected of containing oil since 1865. The first group to look for oil at Spindletop was an oil company named Gladys City, formed by Patillo Higgins. After several failed attempts, the company partners began to lose faith and Higgins left the project. Over thirty years later, in 1899, Captain Anthony Lucas arrived to drill at Spindletop. At 10:30 a.m. on January 10, an oil spray six inches across rose over 200 feet above the ground. It could be seen for over ten miles.

Over the next three months, Beaumont transformed from a small, run-down town to a booming industrial center. Land values skyrocketed; plots of land, once barely worth a few hundreds of dollars, suddenly were being sold for tens to hundreds of thousands of dollars. The promise of oil attracted herds of investors and the population of around 10,000 rose quickly to approximately 50,000.

Over six hundred companies were chartered to drill at Spindletop. These included the beginnings of many well-known brands such as Texaco, Chevron, Mobil, and Exxon. Production of oil at Spindletop rose to 100,000 barrels a day at its peak, significantly boosting America's oil production.

After its initial boom, Spindletop's oil production dwindled over the next decades until the Yount-Lee Oil Company found a second gusher of oil. This second production lasted for a decade before trickling to a close. Spindletop was officially closed in 1950.

Anne Hsu

Date January 10, 1901

Country USA

Why It's Key The discovery of one of the most famous oil fields in the United States, Spindletop Hill near Beaumont, Texas, caused a small town to boom in population and prosperity, and changed the face of the U.S. oil industry.

Key Person
Queen Victoria

Victoria was born at Kensington Palace, London, on May 24, 1819, and, on the death of William IV in 1837, she became Queen aged eighteen. She reigned over what was seen as a triumphant age of industrial expansion and economic progress. The British Empire became the dominant global power, to such an extent that by the time of her death it was said that Britain had an empire on which the sun never set.

In 1840, she married Prince Albert, who is best remembered for his conception of the Great Exhibition of 1851. Victoria was a busy mother as well as the reigning monarch, bearing nine children between 1840 and 1857. Their marriages into other royal families helped to spread the influence of Victorian Britain.

Victoria's popularity grew in tandem with increasing imperial sentiment and what would now be described as racism and xenophobia. Nevertheless, it was during her reign that political power gradually diffused to the electorate, and the modern concept of the constitutional monarch as a more nominal figure above political parties was born. However, Victoria herself would not waive the opportunity to voice her opinions, if sometimes in private, and never distanced herself from political life. She continued her duties until her death at Osborne House on the Isle of Wight, on January 22, 1901. Her reign lasted almost sixty-four years, currently the longest in British history.

Mariko Kato

Date January 22, 1901

Born/Died 1819–1901

Nationality British

Why It's Key Queen Victoria's death marked the end of the Victorian era.

Fact Queen Victoria is the longest reigning British monarch, and was the last British monarch of the House of Hanover.

Key Person
Vincent van Gogh

Born in Groot-Zundert, Holland, in 1853, Vincent van Gogh was a serious and introspective boy. He tried his hand at several professions, including teaching and preaching, before deciding to paint in 1880. Though he studied art in Belgium, in 1886 he went to Paris to join his brother Theo, who managed Goupil's Gallery. While in Paris, he met painters Degas, Pissarro, and Gauguin, and began to paint in the short brushstrokes of his Impressionist contemporaries. Though this greatly influenced him, van Gogh quickly moved toward a freer and more expressive technique, which would place him in the genre known as Post-Impressionism.

However, van Gogh's life was both economically and personally disastrous. Suffering from mental illness, he broke away from his friends, and cut off a piece of his left ear (the only painting he sold during his lifetime, *The Red Vineyard*, was created around this time). Though under a doctor's care, he shot himself in the chest in July 1890, and died two days later, aged thirty-seven.

It was not until eleven years later, on March 17, 1901, that seventy-one of van Gogh's paintings caused a sensation at the Bernheim-Jeune gallery in Paris. He had produced all of this work (approximately 900 paintings and 1,100 drawings) during the ten years before his death. His influence on Expressionism, Fauvism, and early abstraction proved great, and the seventy-one paintings, with bold brushstrokes and expressive colors, were rapturously praised. His paintings now rank among some of the most expensive in the world.
Mariko Kato

Date March 17, 1901

Born/Died 1853–1890

Nationality Dutch

Why It's Key Though van Gogh saw little success during his lifetime, the exhibition caused him to find fame posthumously and to be regarded at the greatest Dutch artist after Rembrandt.

Fact van Gogh became a preacher in a mining town in Belgium but was dismissed for being "overzealous."

Key Cultural Event
Britain launches its first submarine

Dismissed by Admiral Sir Arthur Wilson as being "underhand, underwater, and damned un-English," Britain was the last major maritime nation to investigate the use of submarines, launching the *Holland I* in 1901. Although at least seventeen submarine designs were recorded between 1578 and 1763, it was not until metal was used in shipbuilding that further progress could be made. From the 1860s the United States and France produced a number of models.

John Philip Holland, an Irish-born American, designed the first truly effective submarine with funds from Irish Nationalists seeking liberation from Britain. Holland's submarine was the first to be formally commissioned by the U.S. Navy, who accepted Holland's Type 6 design in 1900, described by one American newspaper as "Uncle Sam's Devil of the Deep."

Britain's first five submarines were also based on Holland's designs. These early petrol-driven submarines were basic and dangerous. Some vessels kept three white mice on board to warn of potentially lethal petrol exhaust fumes. Germany decided to wait until the much safer diesel engine had been perfected before developing the first of their U-boats.

The early years of the twentieth century saw the rapid development of the submarine service in navies around the world, spurred on by pioneering new technology such as the diesel engine, the Whitehead torpedo, and the electric motor. By the beginning of World War I, there were around four hundred submarines distributed across sixteen navies.
Michelle Higgs

Date October 2, 1901

Country UK

Why It's Key Britain's launching of its first submarine meant that all the major maritime powers now had at least a rudimentary submarine flotilla, setting the stage for future underwater warfare.

Key Discovery
Hearing aid patented by Hutchinson

Hearing loss has been a problem with hundreds of attempted solutions, but until Miller Reese Hutchinson's Acousticon hearing aid, developed in 1901, none fit the bill. Existing devices such as the ear trumpet and speaking tubes were bulky and impractical, and the consensus was that if people were going to use something to improve their hearing, it would need to be at least somewhat aesthetically pleasing.

After working as an engineer in the U.S. Light Service and serving in the American-Spanish war, Hutchinson set up a laboratory in New York where he started working on an electrical hearing aid (and also, ironically, the klaxon auto horn). Previously the ear trumpet was the common form of hearing aid. It directed the desired sound into the ear by filtering out unwanted noise.

Hutchinson took this idea further with the electric analogue hearing aid. Set according to the individual's level of hearing needs, it worked by converting all acoustic input to electrical impulses that were sent to a carbon receiver, which then converted the amplified impulses back into sound for the ear. Not only did it set the standard for future developments in hearing aids – paving the way for even smaller and, more recently, digital aids – but the small size and easy application also made it very popular with people who had previously chosen to turn a deaf ear to their deficiency rather than use unsightly and cumbersome devices, doubtless making many dinner table conversations much less challenging than they might have been before.

Fiona Kellagher

Date November 15, 1901

Country USA

Why It's Key The hearing aid was a popular and practical solution to a problem affecting millions of people.

24

Key Cultural Event
First Nobel Prize awarded

Alfred Nobel was born on October 21, 1833 in Stockholm, Sweden. Though an avid reader and fluent in five languages, he was principally known during his lifetime for his work in chemistry. In October 1863, he received a Swedish patent for his percussion detonator – the "Nobel lighter."

His experiments with nitroglycerine proved highly dangerous; an explosion in his factory in 1864 killed several people, including his younger brother, Emil. Yet, Nobel maintained his optimism. When he invented dynamite in 1866, he rather naïvely thought it would end all wars and bring peace to the world. However, when his brother Ludvig died in 1888, a French newspaper mistakenly ran an obituary for Alfred, dubbing him "the merchant of death." Not wanting to be remembered for this, Nobel decided to dedicate

94 percent of his money for the establishment of the Nobel Prizes.

When Nobel died on December 10, 1896 from a cerebral hemorrhage, he left a will that assigned his enormous fortune of 31 million Swedish kronor to be awarded to "those who, during the preceding year, shall have conferred the greatest benefit on mankind." This was initially met with many obstacles, including outraged relatives and the practical difficulties of establishing the prizes, and it was only five years after his death that the first prizes were awarded. They were conferred in five subjects: chemistry, physics, physiology or medicine, literature, and peace. A sixth subject, economics, was added in 1969.

Mariko Kato

Date December 10, 1901

Country Sweden

Why It's Key The Nobel Prizes are arguably the world's most famous international awards and a benchmark for genius and the betterment of humanity.

Key Discovery
Marconi broadcasts across the Atlantic

The beginning of the twentieth century would see the first steps of an innovation that would eventually evolve to revolutionize worldwide communications.

Guglielmo Marconi, an Italian inventor, had been investigating the possibility of completely transmitting a wave broadcast signal across the Atlantic in order to progress further from and compete with the transatlantic telegraph system. Marconi built upon the ideas of his contemporaries by using a two-circuit system and then adding a kite-supported 400-foot high antenna to receive signals.

On December 12, 1901, Marconi announced to the world that he had indeed picked up a message in St. Johns, Newfoundland in Canada from a power station in Cornwall approximately 2,100 miles away. The message was simply a constant Morse code letter "S" intermittently heard against a wall of interference. Frantic research ensued, and within six years the radio wave could be electronically detected and amplified, resulting in an established medium used by the military, the shipping industry, the entertainment industry, and the radio, which would become an essential household item.

Many fellow scientists raised doubts about Marconi's claim, as well as questioning his debt to the work of Nikola Tesla, with whom the radio patent was first registered in 1900. Nevertheless, Marconi is credited with successfully recording the first ever transatlantic radio signal, and in 1909 went on to accept a joint Nobel Prize in Physics for his discovery.
Greg Pittard

Date December 12, 1901
Country Canada/UK

Why It's Key The breakthrough of receiving a cross-Atlantic transmission would lead to rapid advancements in world radio technology.

Key Person
Helena Rubenstein

Like her beauty products, there are many elements of Helena Rubenstein's life story that remain unproven; much of the mythology about her is self-promulgated. What is true, though, is that Rubenstein's establishment of a beauty salon in Melbourne, Australia, in 1902, marked the beginnings of the multi-billion dollar beauty industry.

Rubenstein was born in Krakow, Poland, probably in 1870, and was the eldest of eight children. She moved to Australia in 1894, possibly to avoid a marriage that her father had arranged. There, she began to produce a quasi-medical concoction that she called "Crème Valaze." Rubenstein maintained that it was made from a rare mountain herb, and her own peachy complexion aided its popularity. She soon set up a beauty salon, which had an "operating theater," and claimed to cure everything from warts to double chins, as well as poor skin. The business was successful from the start.

In 1905, Rubenstein went to Europe to study skin treatment with European specialists. Her business continued to prosper. She lived first in London and then in Paris, marketing her products in each city. When World War I broke out, she left Paris and traveled to New York. Her rivalry with Florence Nightingale Graham (Elizabeth Arden) and Charles Revson, who founded Revlon, was well known.

In 1964, Rubenstein published a memoir entitled *My Life for Beauty*. She died soon afterwards. At that time, her business was worth more than US$60 million.
Frieda Klotz

Date January 5, 1902
Nationality Australian

Why It's Key Rubenstein's first beauty salon marked the start of a hugely successful business venture and sparked the development of the beauty industry.

Key Cultural Event
China bans foot-binding

Foot-binding was practiced in China for more than 1,000 years. The exact date it began is difficult to pinpoint; however, references to China's partiality for tiny feet extend back as far as 500 CE. One story tells of the last Empress of the Shang Dynasty (1700–1027 BCE) who had a clubfoot. She persuaded the Emperor to rule that all young girls' feet should be compressed so that hers would be accepted as a sign of beauty. Then there was the sovereign-poet Li Yü (southern Tang Dynasty, 618-907 CE) who made a huge golden lotus for his concubine Lovely Maiden to dance inside with her feet bound in white silk so they would appear as dainty blossoms. While foot-binding has traditionally been associated with dance, its more prosaic purpose is found in the poem: "Why must the foot be bound? To prevent the barbarous running around!"

It was widely accepted that foot-binding was designed to confine women indoors. Her dependence upon servants would then prove that her husband was sufficiently well-off not to require her physical labor or financial contribution. But it also had its erotic connotations. Women's restricted footsteps were believed to keep their bodies firmer and men loved to fondle tiny feet as a prelude to sex. The practice started to wane with foreign influence, and was officially denounced by the Qing Court on February 1, 1902, as part of the Boxer concessions. Nevertheless, right up until the 1920s, some girls were still forced to have their feet bound.

Sally Percival Wood

Date February 1, 1902

Country China

Why It's Key A landmark change in sexual politics, the announcement of the edict officially concluded years of women's physical confinement.

opposite An x-ray of the hobbling deformity caused by foot-binding.

Key Political Event
Lenin's "What is to be Done?" published

The paradox of Marxist Communism was that it sought to achieve complete freedom, but could only do this through organized and disciplined action. This is the problem Vladimir Ilyich Lenin outlined in "What is to be Done?," a pamphlet that he published in 1902. The tensions and disagreements within the revolutionary movement frustrated Lenin. In "What is to be Done?" he writes that "we are walking in a small, tight group along a steep and difficult path, firmly joining hands. We are surrounded by enemies... " Discipline was required.

Critics have often argued that the view of the working classes, which Lenin outlines in the pamphlet, is a negative one. The working classes could not be the source of social democracy, but Lenin suggests that it could be brought to them from outside; The bourgeois intelligentsia would bring it to them, after the educated intelligentsia has worked through the philosophical questions. On the other hand, though, the pamphlet has been seen as providing a positive model for an organized party. Without such organization, the revolution that ultimately took place in 1917 could not have succeeded.

The concept of freedom that Lenin delineated in "What is to be Done?" was influential, but also inherently problematic. Stalin drew on it to validate his actions, as did other Communist governments, arguing that the masses could not lead themselves, but needed to be led by those who knew better.

Frieda Klotz

Date March 1,1902

Country Russia

Why It's Key Lenin outlined his views on how an organized party should operate, with an educated elite leading the working classes. The idea has continued to influence Communist party policy (and be manipulated by it) ever since.

Key Cultural Event
Circuit Court ends Edison's monopoly on cinema

In 1891, Thomas Edison registered two patents with the U.S. Patent Office – one for a machine called the kinetograph, a camera that captured images on celluloid film, and another for the kinetoscope, a device that allowed viewers to peer through a peep-hole and see a series of images lit up in rapid succession. Two years later, at the Brooklyn Institute of Arts, the Edison Company presented the first moving pictures to a public audience. With the subsequent invention of the Edison Projector, which accommodated group viewings on large screens, the technology of modern cinema was born just in time for the turn of the century.

In the first decade of motion-picture production, Edison and his team dominated the burgeoning silent film market – for them, cinema was more about mastering the technology than crafting an art form.

However, other independent film companies began to compete with Edison's company, the most popular of which was Biograph. To protect his inventions and eliminate the competition, Edison began suing rival film producers for patent infringement. Initially he was successful, but on March 10, 1902, a U.S. Circuit Court of Appeals in New York overruled Edison's claim that he held patent rights to all aspects of motion picture technology. The Edison Company no longer held a monopoly on the technology of cinema. Though Edison would remain relevant in filmmaking into the next decade, independent producers brought diversity to the novel medium. A new type of cinema was on its way to sweeping the nation.

Chris Schonberger

Date March 10, 1902

Country USA

Why It's Key The court's decision effectively ended Edison's monopoly on motion picture technology, allowing independent cinema to flourish.

Key Political Event
Independence for Cuba

The official ceremony wasn't until noon, but the streets of Havana were alive with people early on the morning of May 20, 1902. The sun was shining, the parks and gardens were ablaze with tropical flowers, Cuban flags fluttered from virtually every rooftop, and the city was "arrayed like a queen to await the coming of her lord," in the words of one correspondent.

Celebrations had been going on since the previous day, with thousands attending memorials to fallen rebel leaders and firework displays. Groups of schoolchildren congregated in the Plaza de Armas to sing songs.

Inside the colonial palace, General Leonard Wood and his men prepared for their departure. Ships lay at anchor in the harbor, ready to take them home. These were the final moments of a troublesome chapter in American history. Cuba had been governed by the U.S.

military since the end of the Spanish-American War in 1899 – a situation that pleased neither the Cubans nor many Americans, but the U.S. government was loath to relinquish control of the strategic island. Cubans had little choice but to agree to a permanent U.S. base at Guantanamo and other concessions.

The ceremony in the Audience Room of the palace was simple: General Wood read the "Documentary Transfer" and ceded control to President-Elect Tomas Estrada Palma and his government. As the crowds thundered outside, Wood and his staff quietly departed. After 410 years of colonial rule, the Republic of Cuba was born.

Heather Michon

Date May 20, 1902

Country Cuba

Why It's Key The country emerged from centuries of Spanish rule to form the Republic of Cuba.

Key Political Event
End of the Second Boer War

The Second Boer War was initially fought conventionally. Utilizing trench systems and barbed wire, the Boers funneled the highly regimented British soldiers into traps and ambushes, using tactics which had been developed during the American Civil War and which would be used again to devastating effect on the battlefields of World War I.

Having laid siege to a number of cities and scoring several high-profile victories over the British, the Boers suffered a series of heavy defeats and the remnants of the conventional Boer army in the field was defeated in 1900. However, the Boers fought on, resorting to guerrilla warfare and attacking soft targets and supply lines in actions, and that predicted the tactics of later insurgencies in the twentieth century (such as those in Vietnam and Korea).

The British, under Lord Kitchener, fought back with a "scorched earth" policy (popularized in Malaya fifty years later), depriving the land of all that could be of use to the Boer guerrillas, including women and children, who were interned in concentration camps. Concentration camps had been used before by the Americans and Spanish, though not on the same scale. Conditions were poor and as many as 25 per cent of those interned (who also included black Africans) died of disease and malnutrition.

The Boers surrendered in 1902 and the war ended with the Treaty of Vereeniging. This brought the Transvaal and Orange Free State into the British Empire and laid the foundations for the formation of the Union of South Africa.

Ben Snook

Date May 31, 1902

Country South Africa

Why It's Key The Boer War was the first "modern" war of the twentieth century and provided a number of important precedents, including the use of concentration camps.

Fact Up to 40 per cent of British conscripts were considered unfit to fight due to poor health.

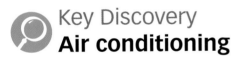

Key Discovery
Air conditioning

For centuries, humans developed various means of sparring with heat. Romans draped wet mats across their doorways so that evaporation would cool the wind; Greeks included cold water in their bathing regimens, and numerous peoples across the world found fanning an indispensable technique.

However, it wasn't until 1902 that the elements were truly conquered. Willis Haviland Carrier, who would later be known as the "father of air conditioning," graduated with a Master's degree in engineering from Cornell University in 1901 and began working at the Buffalo Forge Company in upstate New York. One of his first assignments was to assist a Brooklyn printing company that, because of heat and humidity fluctuations, was having trouble with color ink alignment. After noting that cold air absorbs humidity

from warm air, Carrier devised a method of moving air over cooled pipes, consequently dehumidifying and cleansing the air, and solving the printers' problems.

But although Carrier birthed air conditioning at the beginning of the century, the technology didn't receive its moniker until 1906 when Stuart H. Cramer used the term in a patent application for a machine that added water vapor to the air in textile factories. Yet, it took several decades for air conditioning to catch on as a cooling system for people rather than machinery.

In 1919, the first air-conditioned movie theater opened in Chicago, Illinois, and the first cooled department store, Abraham and Straus, appeared in New York City. Air conditioning only lost its luxury status after World War II.

Carolyn Purnell

Date July 17, 1902

Country USA

Why It's Key The invention and development of air conditioning presented a solution to the age-old problems of human and mechanical over-heating, resulting in increased comfort and improved efficiency in industry.

Key Cultural Event
The Aswan Dam is completed

The completion of the Aswan Dam in 1902 was a key step in the development of the British Empire's flood management legacy in Egypt. For centuries the Nile's erratic seasonal flow had caused floods and droughts, destroying farmland and spreading famine throughout the country.

As well as controlling the river, the new dam would generate electricity and provide water for agriculture. Construction began in 1899 and the dam was officially opened on December 10, 1902.

Built largely by John Aird & Company, the structure was a rock-fill gravity dam 1,900m long and 54m high. However, the original design by Sir William Wilcocks proved to be inadequate, and between 1907–1912 and 1929–1933, the dam was raised twice to cope with the Nile's flood patterns.

When the dam almost overflowed in 1946, a second dam was finally built four miles further upstream. Opened in 1970, this became known as the Aswan High Dam. Today it forms Lake Nasser, a reservoir that extends 300 miles from the First to the Third Cataract. However, its construction had a long and troubled history. Political disagreements led to Britain and America withdrawing a US$270 million loan for the financing of the dam in July 1956. This prompted the Egyptian government to raise funds by nationalizing the Suez Canal, creating a major international incident – the Suez Crisis – that saw Britain, France, and Israel temporarily invade the region.
Jay Mullins

Date December 10, 1902

Country Egypt

Why It's Key The Aswan Dam generated significant economic growth in southern Egypt, enhancing trade with Sudan.

opposite The Aswan Dam under construction across the Nile River.

Key Person
Isadora Duncan

American dancer Isadora Duncan is often known as the mother of modern dance. Wearing loose flowing, seductive tunics while dancing barefoot, she rejected the conventions of traditional schools of ballet and dance to develop her own philosophy based on the writings of German philosopher Friedrich Nietzsche. Duncan applauded Nietzsche's focus on creativity and health, and his belief in affirming the realities of real life rather than the afterlife.

In 1903, Duncan delivered a speech in Berlin called "The Dance of the Future." Here she outlined her philosophy of dance, stating that it should be more like that of the ancient Greeks, emphasizing natural movements and rhythms to express both human forms and emotions. Though initially received with critical reviews in America, by 1909 Duncan was internationally acclaimed for her dance performances and choreography.

Duncan founded three dance schools for girls based on her philosophy in France, Germany, and Russia. Preferring simple scenery and costumes over elaborate ones, she maintained that the dancer should be the focus of attention, and was the first to suggest that dance deserves a place among the high arts.

Duncan also became known for her exciting, unconventional, and tragic personal life. This included scandalous romances, the accidental death of both her children, frequent public drunkenness, and financial troubles. In 1927, Duncan was killed when one of her famous long scarves became entangled in the wheel of her motorcycle.
Anne Hsu

Date February 1, 1903

Born/Died 1877–1927

Nationality American

Why It's Key Isadora Duncan pioneered the modern dance movement when she abandoned traditional ballet for a more expressive, emotional style that is danced barefoot.

Key Person
W. E. B. Du Bois

Born in 1868 in Great Barrington, Massachusetts, William Du Bois first became involved in civil rights when he taught in rural Tennessee schools during his summer vacation to help pay for his university tuition. Experiencing the Jim Crow laws firsthand, Du Bois developed a strong interest in African-American history, and went on to become the first black man to receive a PhD from Harvard University, for his dissertation on *The Suppression of the African Slave Trade*.

Yet the work that Du Bois became most renowned for was *The Souls of Black Folk*. Published on April 5, 1903, it is a collection of fourteen essays that is partly autobiographical, partly a social documentary, and partly an African-American history that examines race relations in the United States. Topics range from Reconstruction to the role of religion in the black community; however at the center of every piece is the question of race. Written largely as a response to the racial accommodation policies of Booker T. Washington, *The Souls of Black Folk* claims that, "the problem of the twentieth century is the problem of the color-line," and criticizes Washington for not doing more to further African-American civil rights.

Reprinted twenty-four times between 1903 and 1940 alone, the work is Du Bois' most widely read text, and earned him the title of the "Father of Social Science." As Du Bois' biographer Manning Marable noted, *The Souls of Black Folk* became one of the "foundation texts for the movements and struggles of an entire people."
Fred Lindsey

Date April 5, 1903
Born/Died 1868–1963
Nationality American

Why It's Key The publication of *The Souls of Black Folk* in 1903 prophetically heralded a turn to protest and self-assertion as a major tactic in the struggle for "Negro" betterment.

Key Political Event
Russian pogroms

As Russia expanded during the eighteenth and nineteenth centuries, large numbers of Jewish people suddenly found themselves under the anti-Semitic rule of Tsarist Russia, creating mass conflicts. These clashes frequently erupted into anti-Jewish riots, known as pogroms, during which Jews were forced from their homes and often killed. One of the most notorious of these pogroms took place in Bessarabia on April 6, 1903, when a mob fueled by anti-Semitic superstition ran riot, killing and raping Jewish people and setting fire to their homes.

The violence fed into a deep-rooted distrust of the Jewish people among ordinary Russians, and trouble flared elsewhere in the country. The authorities did little to stop this; indeed it is believed that the Okhrana – the Tsarist secret police – was instrumental in encouraging the violence. The higher echelons in Russia were convinced that the Jewish people were involved in spreading the new ethos of socialism and stirring up trouble against the government. Violence against the Jewish people persisted for the next two years, culminating in a riot in Odessa, during which as many as 800 Jews were murdered and 5,000 injured.

The pogroms were instrumental in persuading tens of thousands of Jewish people to emigrate to Western Europe and North America. The violence also encouraged the fledgling Zionist movement, which looked to establish a Jewish homeland in Israel. Significant numbers of Russian Jews settled in the Middle East, sowing the seeds of conflict between the Jews and Arabs that still shows no signs of abating.
Martin Sayers

Date April 6, 1903
Country Russia

Why It's Key Anti-Semitic violence led to widespread Jewish emigration from Russia and encouraged early Zionists to settle in the Middle East.

Key Cultural Event
New York Stock Exchange unveiled

The world of finance moved boldly into the twentieth century on April 22, 1903, when the New York Stock Exchange (NYSE) was unveiled at its new home at 18 Broad Street. By the close of the nineteenth century, New York had established itself as the world's leading financial center. Trading in stocks had risen six-fold between 1896 and 1901; however, such an expansion in trade left the existing exchange building sorely inadequate, and eminent architect George B. Post was commissioned to design its successor.

Despite building delays and a final bill amounting to four times the original US$1 million estimate, many heralded the result as a masterpiece of neoclassic architecture. Twenty thousand people attended its unveiling to take a tour of the building and to see such marvels as the ornate ceiling, the grand trading floor, and a 15-meter-high window overlooking the city. One of the most iconic aspects of the new NYSE building was John Ward's "Integrity Protecting the Works of Man": six huge marble figures standing over the Broad Street façade. Each awe-inspiring 7-meter-high statue (Integrity, Mining, Agriculture, Science, Industry, and Invention) represented a different cornerstone of America's prosperous economy and served as a constant reminder of the country's heritage.

In the century following the building's construction, further space was required for trading. Extensions included the 23-storey "garage" built onto the main building in 1922, the "Blue Room" in 1965, and most recently a new high-tech trading floor located at 30 Broad Street.

Jay Mullins

Date April 22, 1903

Country USA

Why It's Key The NYSE expanded and modernized with a fit-for-purpose trading hall, which confirmed its dominance in world finance.

Key Political Event
Morel's account of Belgian Congo atrocities

King Leopold II of Belgium colonized a large area around the Congo River in the 1880s. The Congo Free State (later the Belgian Congo) was his personal fiefdom, controlled ruthlessly by a private army. A relatively unknown shipping clerk, E. D. Morel, noticed strange financial anomalies in transactions between his company, Elder Dempsey, and the Congolese government. He deduced that the Congo's thriving ivory and rubber exports could only be operable with a massive system of forced labor. Morel's dedication to exposing the truth of Leopold's regime helped forge one of the first formally organized human rights movements.

Morel founded his own newspaper, *West African Mail*, in 1903, to help propagate the Congolese slavery exposé to a wider audience. Momentum was building. The House of Commons, influenced by Morel's ceaseless agitation, passed a resolution on the Congo, which led to the diplomat Roger Casement (later famously executed for treason due to Irish Republican activities in World War I) being sent to investigate the country firsthand. His damning report, published in 1904, graphically confirmed Morel's accusations, describing acts of bodily mutilation and coercion. Public outcry to "The Casement Report" was great and swelled the ranks of the recently formed Congo Reform Association, of which Morel was secretary. In 1908, international pressure became too great and the Belgian government ended Leopold's reign. In 1924, Morel was nominated for the Nobel Peace Prize, in large part due to his zealous desire to help the oppressed people of the Congo.

Michael Hallam

Date May 20, 1903

Country Belgian Congo

Why It's Key The Congo Reform Association made the Congo the most infamous of the exploitative European colonies in Africa and contributed significantly to growing awareness of issues of human rights.

Key Political Event
Serbian monarchs assassinated

On June 10, 1903, a group of nationalist officers invaded the royal palace in Belgrade, and assassinated the Serbian King Alexander and Queen Draga. King Alexander, the last of the Obrenovic dynasty, had been unpopular among the Serbian public because of his pro-Austro-Hungarian policy. A week before the assassination, Alexander suspended the Liberal Constitution, introduced unfavorable election reforms, and abolished the freedom of the press. After the assassinations, the parliament decided that the new king would be Prince Peter of the Karageorgevic dynasty, who was living in Geneva. One of the first things King Peter did after coming to the throne was to grant indemnity for all of the conspirators against Alexander and offer the assassins top civil and military positions in the new government.

The assassination of King Alexander and its aftermath had an immense impact on Serbia's foreign policy. Europe was shocked by the murders and Britain broke off diplomatic relations with Serbia, not reinstating them for the next three years.

Some of the effects of the regicide were even more far-reaching. King Peter's rejection of the Obrenovic dynasty's pro-Habsburg policy and his shift toward a more nationalist agenda led to Austria-Hungary's implementation of various economic measures with the aim of preventing Serbia from becoming too independent. The rivalry between Serbia and Austria-Hungary, followed by Austria-Hungary's annexation of Bosnia and Herzegovina in 1908, ultimately resulted in World War I.
Sonja Kudeljnjak

Date June 10, 1903

Country Serbia

Why It's Key The assassination of King Alexander created tensions between Serbia and Austria-Hungary, which would lead to World War I.

Fact King Alexander, who was twenty-six at the time of the assassination, was ten years younger than Queen Draga, who had been a lady-in-waiting to his mother.

34

Key Cultural Event
Telegraph sent around the world

The first message to travel around the world was sent at 11:23 p.m., July 4, 1903, from President Theodore Roosevelt to Clarence MacKay, president of the Commercial Pacific Cable Company, and said, "Congratulations and success to the Pacific cable which the genius of your lamented father and your own enterprise made possible." Mackay, who was with Roosevelt in Oyster Bay, New York, received it within twelve minutes. The message was transmitted by the Postal Telegraph Company's land wire from Oyster Bay to San Francisco. Then Commercial Pacific's undersea cables transmitted the message through to Honolulu, Midway, Guam, Manila, Hong Kong, Azores, Canso, New York, and back to Oyster Bay.

The message passed through many sections of wire through which other historic messages were sent, such as the first telegraph message by Samuel Morse and the first audible speech message by Alexander Graham Bell. Notable transmission of electricity had also passed through these wires, including the first trolley circuit, the first vacuum tube lighting, and the first current of hydro-electricity transmitted from the Niagara Falls power plant.

The Commercial Pacific Cable Company, founded in 1901, provided the first direct telegraph route between America and the Philippines, China, and Japan. They remained in operation until the 1950s, when old cables became in need of extensive repair or replacement. These repairs would cost millions of dollars and were too expensive for the company to maintain. The company closed down in 1951.
Anne Hsu

Date July 4, 1903

Country USA

Why It's Key The first message telegraphed around the world was a breakthrough in global communications.

Key Cultural Event
London's first petrol-driven taxi

Before petrol came the electric cab. In August 1897, The London Electric Cab Company rolled out the capital's first motorized taxis, known as Berseys after their designer C. W. Bersey. Running on eight-volt batteries, they ferried passengers around the city at a top speed of nine miles per hour; the high-pitched whir of their motors earning them the nickname "Humming Birds." They were deeply unreliable and the cause of many an accident, including one fatality; in 1897, a nine-year-old was killed trying to steal a ride by jumping onto a passing Bersey's springs. By 1900 the taxis had been withdrawn from service.

In 1903 they were replaced by London's first petrol-driven taxi, the Prunel. These cabs were French built, and had been operating in Paris since 1899. In London, they were run by the Express Motor Service Company. Effectively they were modeled on the design of the horse-drawn Hansom cabs, but the horse was replaced by a chain drive transmission. The carriage had two seats, and like the Bersey, the driver sat on a platform above and behind the carriage, operating the steering column instead of horse reins. The engine was a twelve-horse-power Aster, trebling the capacity of the Bersey's motor.

Early passengers found the experience discomfiting – traveling at high speed with no driver in sight – and by the end of 1903, new taxis were beginning to take a more familiar shape with the driver seated at the front.

David Thorley

Date August 1, 1903

Country UK

Why It's Key Petrol-driven taxis have become a cornerstone of London's transport system, as well as a part of its identity.

Fact There are now over 21,000 taxis operating in London, which account for 0.4 per cent of the capital's carbon emissions.

35

Key Political Event
The creation of Panama

From the outset, the Isthmus of Panama played a pivotal role in the history of imperialism in the Americas. Vasco Nuñez de Balboa chose it as the site for the first permanent European settlement on the American mainland in 1510. Three years later, he and a group of fellow adventurers hacked their way through the jungle and stumbled upon the Pacific Ocean. Nuestra Señora de la Asunción de Panamá, a city founded on the Pacific coast in 1519, became a crucial gateway: from there, Francisco Pizarro would launch the expeditions down the coast of South America that culminated in the conquest of Peru.

Nearly four centuries later, another burgeoning imperial power, cognizant of the area's immense strategic importance, inserted itself aggressively into Panama's affairs. The United States had supported Colombia's control of the region and generally favored Nicaragua as the site of a transoceanic canal throughout the nineteenth century, but 1902 marked a drastic policy shift for the rising superpower. Theodore Roosevelt, determined to seize control of the unfinished canal begun by French engineers in the 1880s, persuaded Congress to pass the Spooner Act, which authorized the completion of the canal under U.S. supervision. Frustrated by Colombia's reluctance to accept his terms, Roosevelt encouraged the Panamanian oligarchy to declare independence from Colombia, and sent military backing to their cause in the form of the gunship U.S.S. Nashville. November 3, 1903, marked Panama's transformation into a nominal republic and de facto protectorate of the United States.

Geoffrey Schullenberger

Date November 3, 1903

Country Panama

Why It's Key Having driven Spain out of Cuba and Puerto Rico in 1898, the United States strengthened its grip on the Western hemisphere by forcing Panama's independence from Colombia, thus permitting the completion of the Panama Canal under U.S. control.

Key Cultural Event
The Wright brothers fly

The weather forecast for December 17, 1903, suggested that Kitty Hawk, North Carolina, would provide the most favorable weather conditions for a day of flying. After spending the previous three years experimenting with gliders and kites, testing their various models in wind tunnels they had created themselves, Orville and Wilbur Wright took their bi-plane, *The Flyer*, to the calm fishing hamlet of Kitty Hawk and prepared for takeoff.

At 10:30 a.m., Orville took the first flight of the day and remained airborne for just twelve seconds, covering a distance of 36 meters. Despite the brevity of their first attempt, history had been made: it was the first sustained, power driven flight.

Alternating piloting duties between them, the Wright brothers made three more subsequent flights, the fourth and most impressive of which lasted for 59 seconds and covered 259 meters.

The Wright brothers had spent years researching flight, and their passion and interest resulted in additions that would change air travel forever. Studying everything from birds to gliders, Orville and Wilbur focused their sights on the extremities of the airplane, realizing the importance of controlling the wings, nose, and rudder in order to navigate safely through the elements. For additional power, they also designed a petrol engine, which was built into the fuselage.

The brothers continued their research into flight and making important advancements in aviation. In 1909, the U.S. government accepted the Wright flying machine for army use.

Kerry Duffy

Date December 17, 1903

Country USA

Why It's Key The flight marked the birth of air travel. The "three-axis control" theory – comprising the ability to *roll* the wings from right to left, *pitch* the nose up or down, and *yaw* the nose from side to side, enabling the pilot to maintain control – remains true to this day.

opposite *The Flyer* takes off with Orville Wright at the controls, while his brother looks on.

Key Cultural Event
The tea bag is invented

In 1908, New York tea merchant Thomas Sullivan sent samples of tea to some of his customers in small silk bags rather than in the more expensive tins that he had been using up until then. Some of the recipients assumed that these were intended to be used in the same way as existing infusers such as the tea ball, a perforated metal container that was filled with loose leaves and immersed in boiling water before being removed by means of an attached chain. Some of those who tried to use the silk bags in this way complained to Sullivan that the mesh was too fine for the tea to infuse properly. So Sullivan used gauze to develop the first purpose-built tea bags.

In the United States, people took rapidly to this new invention, while many British travelers expressed horror at coming across these new-fangled tea bags sitting alongside cups of tepid water. In the UK, wartime shortages of materials stalled the widespread adoption of the tea bag, and as late as the 1960s, less than 3 per cent of tea sold in the UK came in bags; by 2007, however, this had grown to a staggering 96 per cent. As tea bags could be filled with very broken leaf or even dust, the days of finely grading tea had come to an end on most estates and the once-formal ritualized drink became a drink of universal convenience.

Duncan Proudfoot

Date 1904

Country USA

Why It's Key Tea, once an expensive, ceremonial drink, became a convenience drink, and its popularity increased enormously as a result.

Key Political Event
The Russo-Japan War

The Russo-Japan War was a conflict between the imperialist ambitions of two fast-growing empires. Since the 1868 Meiji Restoration, Japan had been adopting Western ideas and modernizing industrialization at a phenomenal pace. Meanwhile, Russia was looking to increase its influence in the East, and had agreed with China that it would occupy Port Arthur in southern Manchuria. As it is the only warm-water port on the Pacific Ocean, Port Arthur was a prized territory. Japan refused to allow Russia to occupy Manchuria, and on February 10, 1904, Japan declared war on Russia.

By the end of April, Japan had occupied Korea, and headed on to Manchuria. After many fierce confrontations, conducted primarily by sea, the Japanese seized Port Arthur in the decisive Battle of the Yellow Sea on August 10. The Russian navy finally fell to Japan on January 2, 1905, and the Japanese continued north to conquer Mukden, the capital of the Liaoning province in northeast China. The war finally ended with the signing of the Treaty of Portsmouth in Portsmouth, New Hampshire on September 5, 1905.

The number of casualties in this war is considered to be between forty and eighty thousand on each side. Japan's military strength was a surprise to external observers, and had a resonant effect on rebalancing power in East Asia. Japan emerged as the new Great Power, while the Russian Tsarist government faced increasing dissatisfaction from its people, ultimately leading to the 1905 Revolution.

Mariko Kato

Date February 10, 1904

Country Korea/China

Why It's Key This war resulted in the first major victory of an Eastern country over a Western one in the modern age.

opposite A popular print showing the attack of Japanese 1st infantry on Russian position at Nanshan near Port Arthur.

Key Cultural Event
Kaiser Wilhelm II makes a recording

Thomas Edison developed his cylinder phonograph as a result of working on two other inventions – the telegraph and the telephone. He started by experimenting with a needle and diaphragm that was able to transmit sound vibrations to indents on paper. These indents could then be played back repeatedly as sound. This initial concept developed into the cylinder phonograph, the first machine for recording and playing back sounds.

By the 1900s, a standard model of the phonograph could be affordably bought on the market for US$20, significantly less than its earlier price of US$150 in 1891. Edison first exhibited his cylinder phonograph in Europe before Emperor Wilhelm II of Germany. Wilhelm showed keen interest in learning about how it worked: he had the phonograph taken apart and reassembled, and paid great attention to the scientific principles behind its operation. Wilhelm then presented a lecture to his court that evening on the Edison phonograph.

Several years later, in 1904, Wilhelm was asked to make a recording of his voice for posterity, which would be deposited in the Harvard University archives. Wilhelm asked all other people to leave the room, and stood alone as he spoke on the career of Frederick the Great into Edison's phonograph. He then recorded a second essay on "Fortitude in Pain" for the National Museum in Washington. These became the first political recordings in history.

Anne Hsu

Date March 3, 1904

Country Germany

Why It's Key This is the first recording of a political document ever made.

s.Ko

Key Person
Major Francis Younghusband

In March 1904, Major Francis Younghusband embarked on a political mission to Tibet that was to spark a massacre and become a virtual invasion by the British Empire. Frustrated in his attempts to secure concessions with Tibet, the viceroy of India Lord Curzon authorized Younghusband to enter the country with a military escort and negotiate trade and frontier issues with the local authorities.

Younghusband's attempts to bargain were met with indifference, prompting a British contingent under the command of Major General James Macdonald to slaughter six hundred people at Guru. This extreme show of force did not have the desired effect, and Younghusband once again failed to reach an agreement at Jiangzi before marching into Lhasa, the Tibetan capital.

Backed up by an occupying British force, Younghusband finally forced the Dalai Lama to sign the Anglo-Tibetan Treaty on September 6, 1904. This action secured trading rights with Britain and warded off the threat of Tibet's annexation by Russia, easing the period of imperial rivalry known as "The Great Game." Younghusband received a knighthood later that year.

Despite his involvement in the bloody events in Tibet, Younghusband is primarily known for his contributions to geographical research. A renowned mystic and explorer, he pioneered the use of the long-abandoned Muztag Pass of the Karakoram Range in order to establish the water divide between India and Turkistan.

Jay Mullins

Date March 31, 1904

Born/Died 1863–1942

Nationality British

Why It's Key Younghusband's expedition caused a massacre in Tibet that enabled the British Empire to ruthlessly expand its economic influence.

40

Key Cultural Event
St. Louis World's Fair

In 1904, St. Louis, Missouri, was the location of both the World's Fair and the Olympic Games. These two events brought St. Louis to international attention. As well as viewing magnificent exhibits from all over the world, visitors could immerse themselves in culture, sports, and entertainment. All kinds of refreshments were sold at the fair, including the hugely popular hamburger and equally popular ice cream cone.

The origins of the hamburger and the ice cream cone are debatable. While the Menches of Akron, Ohio, claimed to invent the hamburger in Hamburg, New York, in 1885, the Bibly family insisted that they were the first to serve hamburgers on a bun in 1891. Similarly, the patent for the ice cream cone was filed by a number of inventors at the beginning of the 1900s. But while both the hamburger and the ice cream cone

were invented elsewhere, the St. Louis World Fair is regarded as the site at which they became popular and where the controversy over their origins began as the "inventors" met each other for the first time. According to some sources, Texan Fletch Davis (1864–1941) sold ground beef patty sandwiches from a concession at the amusement area, and his "invention" was commented on in various newspapers. With over fifty ice cream stands scattered around the fair, companies emerged in 1904 to produce machines that could be used to bake the cones. News of the hamburger and the ice cream cone had spread and this quintessential "American" cuisine began to be sold worldwide.

Michelle Higgs

Date July 1, 1904 (sometimes April 30, 1904)

Country USA

Why It's Key The hamburger and the ice cream cone were both popularized at the World's Fair, making them famous worldwide.

Fact The World's Fair was also known as the Louisiana Purchase Exposition, so named to commemorate the centennial of Louisiana's purchase from France.

Key Person
Hertha Ayrton

Sarah Phoebe Marks was educated with her cousins, who first introduced her to mathematics and science. She took the Cambridge University examination for women and from 1877–1881 read mathematics at Girton College – co-founded by her friend Barbara Bodichon as a women's college – where she changed her name to Hertha.

Back in London in 1884, Hertha attended evening classes on electricity run by Will Ayrton, an electrical engineer. His wife, a pioneering woman doctor, had died the previous year, and Hertha and Will were married in 1885. As well as giving lectures to women about electricity and its potential to change their domestic lives, Hertha also took over Will's experiments on the electric arc, demonstrating a linear relationship between arc length, pressure, and potential difference, known as the Ayrton equation. Hertha's analysis, presented in twelve papers in *The Electrician*, established her unique reputation as a brilliant female electrical engineer. She was elected a member of the Institution of Electrical Engineers, the only female member until 1958. Her lecture to the International Electrical Congress in Paris in 1900 helped persuade the British Association to allow women onto their committees.

Although proposed as a candidate for the Royal Society in 1902, she was ineligible as a married woman with no standing in the law. Yet, in 1904, she became the first woman to read a paper of her own work to the society. In 1906, Hertha was awarded the society's prestigious Hughes medal for her scientific work, the only female recipient to date.

Michelle Higgs

Date June 16, 1904

Born/Died 1854–1923

Nationality British

Why It's Key Hertha Ayrton was the first woman invited to read a paper at the Royal Society, the world's oldest scientific academy.

Fact Hertha was well-known in her support of militant suffragists such as Emmeline Pankhurst, who recovered from hunger strikes at Hertha's home before returning to prison under the "Cat and Mouse Act."

Key Political Event
Herero genocide

Germany annexed South West Africa (now Namibia) in 1884, but it was not until 1894 that *Schutztruppe*, crack imperial troops, were sent to enforce Berlin's rule. They built stone forts enabling German settlers to penetrate ever more deeply into the territory, levying taxes and dispossessing the Herero and Nama peoples. Towards the end of 1903 the Nama, under Hendrik Witbooi, rebelled and a few months later the Herero joined them.

After an uprising in the town of Okahandja on January 12, 1904, Kaiser Wilhelm II sent 14,000 troops to the region under the leadership of Lieutenant-General Lothar von Trotha, who had suppressed the Boxer Rebellion in China with ruthless efficiency. At Hamakari on August 11, the Herero were surrounded on three sides and decisively defeated. The open fourth side led to the Omaheke area of the Kalahari Desert where waterholes had either been poisoned or were patrolled and survivors bayoneted. Most of those who attempted to cross the desert into Botswana died. In the words of von Trotha's *Vernichtungsbefehl* ("annihilation order") of October 2: "Inside German territory every Herero tribesman, armed or unarmed, with or without cattle, will be shot."

This campaign of extermination, which had reduced the Herero from a population of 80,000 to around 15,000, was eventually halted and survivors were placed in slave labor concentration camps – all Herero over the age of seven had to wear metal discs around their necks designating them as free labor.

Duncan Proudfoot

Date 1904–1908

Country German South West Africa (now Namibia)

Why It's Key The Herero were the first ethnic group to be subjected to genocide in the twentieth century in a way that directly foreshadowed the Nazi Holocaust.

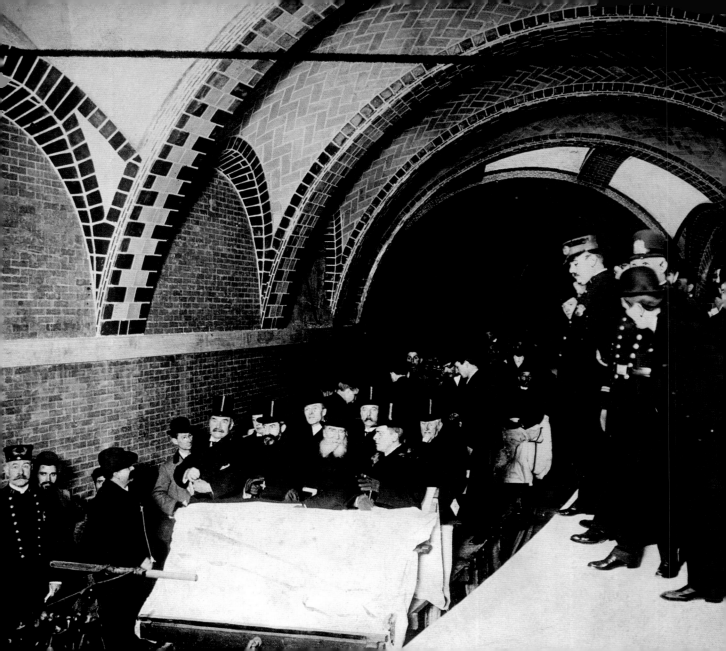

Key Person
Ivan Pavlov

Born on September 14, 1849, in Ryazan, Russia, Ivan Petrovich Pavlov received his doctorate in natural sciences from the University of St. Petersburg in 1879. It was over a decade later, at the Department of Physiology at the Institute of Experimental Medicine, that Pavlov noticed that dogs tended to salivate before food coated with chili powder was delivered to their mouths. He called this phenomenon "psychic secretion," and after a series of experiments, classified the dogs' behavior as "conditional reflexes," reflexes that occur as a reaction against specific previous experiences.

Pavlov had proved that the nervous system plays the dominant part in regulating the digestive process, and made it possible to study psychic activity objectively and scientifically. After further developments to this discovery, he was awarded the Nobel Prize on October 12, 1904, and he collected fans from across genres, including the British philosopher Bertrand Russell, who praised the importance of Pavlov's work for the study of philosophy of the mind.

Partly due to his international status as Nobel Laureate, Pavlov was highly valued by the Soviet government, and was able to continue research throughout his life. He later examined the use of conditioning to establish an experimental model of the induction of neuroses. Even when he died in Leningrad on February 27, 1936, his priority was science: he asked his student to record the circumstances of his last moments, so that there would be evidence of this terminal phase of life.

Mariko Kato

Date October 12, 1904

Born/Died 1849–1936

Nationality Russian

Why It's Key Pavlov's research forms the basis of the modern physiology of digestion, and his concept of the conditioned reflex was groundbreaking in both science and psychiatry.

Fact Russian physiologist, psychologist, and physician Ivan Petrovich Pavlov was awarded the Nobel Prize in Physiology or Medicine in 1904.

Key Cultural Event
New York subway opens

By the start of the twentieth century, New York was a vast city of three and a half million people, and the question of how to get to work had become problematic. Most people lived in Manhattan, which was extremely densely populated, while few lived in Brooklyn and Queens. A range of steam trains catered to Brooklyn, which the middle classes inhabited, but more was needed.

In 1900, work began on a new underground railway that would be powered by electricity. The New York subway system opened on October 27, 1904. Its first line ran from City Hall to 145th Street and Broadway, and it had four tracks, which meant that local and express trains could run in each direction at the same time. It had taken four years and 10,000 men to build. The subway was soon extended into the Bronx, and lines were built to reach Brooklyn and Queens. It was the fastest and most complex city transportation system in the world.

After the building of the subway, New York City expanded rapidly. In 1900, the Bronx had been a leafy suburb; by 1923, a million people lived there. By the 1940s, the combined underground systems were carrying eight million people. The development of the subway system has continued. In 1968 the state created the Metropolitan Transport Authority (MTA), and from the 1980s onwards, the MTA had made the subway system safer and more disability friendly.

Frieda Klotz

Date October 27, 1904

Country USA

Why It's Key The New York subway was the fastest and most efficient urban public transport system in the world.

opposite Financiers, city officials, and policemen ride New York City's first subway.

Key Discovery
The Cullinan Diamond

Until 1985, the 530.20-carat Star of Africa cut from the Cullinan Diamond was the largest cut diamond in the world; it is set in King Edward's scepter and can be seen in the Tower of London along with the rest of the Crown Jewels of Great Britain. In 1985, however, it lost its record to the 545.67-carat Golden Jubilee, found in the same Premier Mine in South Africa (a carat is 0.2 grams). This was presented to the King of Thailand in 1997 on the fiftieth anniversary of his coronation. The original, uncut Cullinan Diamond, though, remains the largest gem-quality stone ever found.

When Willem Prinsloo, the owner of Elandsfontein Farm near Pretoria, died, Thomas Cullinan quickly bought the land. He registered the Premier Diamond Mining Company and mining began shortly afterwards. On the evening of January 26, 1905, superintendent

Frederick Wells spotted something catching the light, only nine meters from the surface. He pried it loose and, thinking it worthless, sent it for analysis. It turned out to be a perfectly clear and colourless diamond, weighing 3,106.75 carats, twice the size of any previous find. The diamond was presented by the Transvaal Republic to King Edward VII for his sixty-sixth birthday on November 9, 1907. The second largest diamond cut from the original stone, the Lesser Star of Africa, is a 317.40-carat cushion-shaped diamond, which is set in the front of the Imperial State Crown of Great Britain.

Duncan Proudfoot

Date January 26, 1905

Country Transvaal Colony of Britain (now South Africa)

Why It's Key The Cullinan Diamond remains the largest uncut diamond ever found.

Fact In 2007, several news stations reported that a diamond more than twice the size of the Cullinan Diamond had been found, however, this proved to be a hoax.

opposite A miner holds the Cullinan Diamond shortly after it was found.

Key Cultural Event
"SOS" signal adopted

Before radio communication was available, ships far from shore had no way of communicating with land. In 1899, Guglielmo Marconi developed wireless telegraphy. This was radio communication using Morse code, which allowed contact between land and ships at sea. The first International Radiotelegraphic Conference was held in 1903 in Berlin, Germany, and the issue was raised of establishing common operating procedures, especially standard calls for ships in distress.

On April 1, 1905, the German government decreed a set of national radio regulations. One of these was that the Morse coded sequence "··· --- ···" which stands for "SOS," would be the signal for a ship in distress.

There has been some speculation about the origins of this sequence. Some believe that "SOS" originated from "SOE," which was the German signal

for a general inquiry call. Some claim that the Morse code for the letter "E," being a single dot, was considered to be too difficult to decipher in a static filled signal.

"SOS" was adopted as the international signal of distress at the second International Radiotelegraphic Conference in 1906. Marconi's telegraphy company proposed a second popular distress signal of the time, "CQD." This combined "CQ," which was a general call, with "D" for "distress." For over a decade, both "SOS" and "CQD" were used in distress calls. However, the need for a consistent standard eventually resulted in "CQD" being replaced entirely by "SOS."

Anne Hsu

Date April 1, 1905

Country Germany

Why It's Key The "SOS" signal was the precursor for standardized radio communications worldwide despite national differences and rivalries between competing radio companies.

Key Political Event
Bloody Sunday

At the beginning of 1905, Russia was losing the war against the Japanese, and discontent was growing among her workers, who were suffering from starvation and increasingly harsh working conditions. Nevertheless, the call for liberalism by marginal political groups was deemed too radical, and many still looked to Tsar Nicholas II as their leader who would deliver peace and wealth.

On January 22, 1905, a group of around 200,000 protestors marched through the snow to the Winter Palace in St. Petersburg, with a petition demanding food, better working conditions, and an end to the Russo-Japanese War. The crowd consisted largely of women and children who believed that the Tsar would hear their pleas if he could see their suffering. For the protestors, it was supposed to be a peaceful, patriotic, and exciting day during which they would get to see their "Father." However, the Imperial Guard met them at the entrance and, after initial warning shots, opened fire. By the end of the day, several hundreds were dead or wounded as they were directly shot or trampled in the ensuing panic.

Worried by the Bloody Sunday massacre, the Tsar responded with the *October Manifesto*, which marked Russia's first move into democracy with the establishment of an elected parliament, the Duma. This at first seemed to be an answer to the people's prayers. Yet, in reality, the manifesto was calculated to placate the opposition, and the Tsar soon manipulated the laws to ensure that he retained autocratic power over the Duma.

Mariko Kato

Date January 22, 1905

Country Russia

Why It's Key Regarded as the beginning of the Russian Revolution of 1905.

Fact The Tsar's Winter Palace became the location for another milestone in Russian history when, in October 1917, the Bolsheviks overthrew the Provisional Government.

opposite Soldiers shooting at fleeing protesters in Palace Square.

Key Cultural Event
First movie theater opens

Moving pictures had been adapted as a storytelling format over a decade earlier, but when Harry Davis and his brother-in-law John P. Harris, a pair of Pittsburgh-based businessmen, opened the first theater to exclusively screen films in the town's commercial district, the profitability factor was obvious. The decision to capitalize on the medium arose from its earlier popularity in penny arcades, where patrons could view movies in the back for five cents. Combining the price of admission with the Greek term for ancient theaters, the attraction was dubbed the Nickelodeon. These primitive movies utilized a developing twenty-four-frames-per-second technology that Thomas Edison had appropriated for his kinetoscope, but the stories were hardly composed of simple gags. Single reel films introduced audiences to suspense, drama, and comedy on the big screen. As a result of their appeal, Nickelodeon programs ran all day, containing multi-genre programs that repeatedly screened from morning until midnight.

With the emergence of the movies' entertainment value came the desire to make more money. Records indicate that the theater accommodated a sizable crowd of 450 viewers on its first day. On its second, that number increased to 1,500. A year after the Pittsburgh store opened, hundreds of Nickelodeons flourished across the East coast. Historians have contested that Davis and Harris were officially the first owners of a movie theater over the years, but its success marked an indisputable turning point in the history of cinema, as the official union of art and industry had fully materialized.

Eric Kohn

Date June 19, 1905

Country USA

Why It's Key The success of the first American movie theater solidified the fate of the cinema as a significant commercial art form.

Fact Early movie screenings typically included simple documentaries, travelogues, and short stories.

Key Discovery
Einstein's special theory of relativity

After graduating from the Swiss Federal Polytechnic School in 1901, Albert Einstein could not find academic work and instead took an unfulfilling job at the Swiss patent office. His personal difficulty was science's good fortune; the office's monotony let him work on theoretical problems that had first occurred to him as a teenager.

In 1905, he generated what was arguably the greatest output of scientific theory ever – history has even labeled 1905 Einstein's *annus mirabilis*, his Miracle Year. During this time, he published four hugely influential papers. One, "On the Electrodynamics of Moving Bodies," presented what is now known as the special theory of relativity. In it Einstein argued that firstly, light traveled at a constant speed, regardless of one's position relative to the light, and secondly, that nearing light speed causes time itself to slow down. The influence of this argument is difficult to overestimate. It, along with Einstein's earlier work, led directly to his famous equation of mass and energy, $E = MC^2$. These new ideas completely reversed the classical physics Newton had developed centuries earlier.

While largely unimportant in day-to-day functions, relativity has incredible effects in astronomical calculations. Our foundational understanding of the universe was reworked by these discoveries, and its practical consequences were hardly less dramatic: Einstein's work led to the development of the atomic bomb. The "Miracle Year" began a scientific and philosophical revolution; one so far-reaching that Einstein would be named *Time*'s Person of the Century in 2000.
Christina Welsch

Date September 28, 1905 (The theory appears in *Annalen der Physik*)

Country Switzerland

Why It's Key Einstein's theory of relativity, first appearing in its "special" form, completely revolutionized the field of physics, radically shifting perceptions on subjects from space and time to morality.

Key Political Event
The Aborigines Act

The Aborigines Act of 1905 was conceived as a solution to what British settlers in Australia saw as the problem of a "dying race" that had no hope of adapting to modernity. The act was particularly aimed at "half-caste" children who, owing to the measure of white blood running through their veins, held some potential as future citizens. In order to "protect" them from the squalid camp conditions of indigenous Australians, children below the age of six were removed without parental consent. Basic education and training for menial employment, such as laboring and domestic work, was the objective, after which half-castes would integrate into "white" society and "breed out" their Aboriginality. Chief Protectors of Aborigines, such as A. O. Neville, made famous by the film *Rabbit Proof Fence* (2002), had complete control over Aboriginal lives, every aspect of which was at their sole discretion. This included control over the money they earned and whom they could marry.

The term "Stolen Generation" was coined by historian Peter Read in 1981 when he found that enormous gaps in record-keeping made it impossible to calculate the number of Aborigines affected. It is estimated that from one child in three, to one in ten, was removed, and that not one Aboriginal family was untouched by this policy. The *Bringing Them Home* report of 1997, an inquiry into the impact of the policy of removal, sought to reconcile the damage done through acknowledgment, compensation, rehabilitation, and an apology.
Sally Percival Wood

Date December 23, 1905

Country Australia

Why It's Key The removal of Australian Aborigines' rights over their children opened the way for a program of family separation, known as the "Stolen Generation," which would last until the 1960s.

Key Political Event
Japanese anti-aboriginal campaign

Ceded to Japan after victory in the Sino-Japanese War of 1895, Taiwan was to be the showpiece of the world's newest imperial power. After early success in subduing the ethnic Chinese majority, the new military government, seeking to classify and exploit the entirety of the island's natural and human resources, turned their attention to the timber-rich mountains of the east and their indigenous aboriginal tribes.

In April 1906, Tokyo appointed military commander Sakuma Samata the island's Governor-General, with a specific mandate to consolidate and extend control over the aboriginal population. His brutal campaign peaked with his "Five-Year Pacification Plan." Confiscating tribal land and forcibly relocating whole villages, the army displaced up to half of the mountain aborigines from their homelands. Resistance was mercilessly crushed by collective punishment; eastern Taiwan became a testing ground for increasingly elaborate methods of "pacification" including the use of nerve gas, aerial bombardment of villages, and the quarantining of aborigines behind electric fences.

As early as 1923, when the visiting Crown Prince Hirohito declared that the aborigines had been civilized and need no longer be labeled "barbarians," Japanese propaganda claimed that the natives had been subdued by means of an enlightened imperial education. The episode, elements of which pioneered the Japanese Army's later atrocities in continental Asia, remains one of the twentieth century's "forgotten massacres," and activists among the aborigines' modern descendants continue to campaign for its wider public recognition.
James Handley

Date April 11, 1906

Country Taiwan

Why It's Key Japan's bloody policy in the mountains of east Taiwan foreshadowed the later oppression of its colonial subjects throughout East Asia.

1900–1909

49

Key Cultural Event
Pentecostalism starts to catch on

The LA Times declared that a "Weird Babel of Tongues" could be heard at William J. Seymour's Azusa Street Revival, during an outbreak of religious ecstasy. An African-American preacher, Seymour united white and black Christians in a new outpouring of the sensual religious fervor that had surged before in America during the "Great Awakenings" of the eighteenth and nineteenth centuries. The movement drew its inspiration from the story of Pentecost in the Bible, which told of the Holy Spirit visiting the apostles of Jesus and causing them to erupt in unintelligible exaltation. Pentecostals followed the scriptural example by "speaking in tongues" during vibrant services filled with singing and celebration, even though other denominations considered the practice inappropriate. The congregants were largely migrants from rural America who sought refuge in the shared values of a traditional religious community. Eccentric evangelists like Aimee Semple MacPherson, who pioneered the use of radio to reach followers, ministered to their needs. In due time the Pentecostal movement splintered into numerous denominations, and it was gradually eclipsed by the worldly pop culture of the 1920s and subsequent traumas of economic depression and war. The spirit revived, however, in response to the social tumult of the 1960s; organizations like the Assemblies of God, which advocate passionate worship and conservative positions on social issues, have grown rapidly ever since. Missionaries have also spread Pentecostalism throughout the world, and have found many converts among Latinos in the United States.
Alex Cummings

Date April 14, 1906

Country USA

Why It's Key One of the most vibrant new spiritual movements of the twentieth century burst onto the scene in Los Angeles in 1906.

Key Disaster
San Francisco earthquake

It began at 5:12 a.m. when a foreshock hit with enough force to be felt throughout the whole San Francisco Bay area. The main thrust of the earthquake, with its epicenter near San Francisco, came with terrifying force less than 30 seconds later and lasted between 45 and 60 seconds. The ground shook, buildings collapsed, gas mains broke, and devastating fires broke out. The fires, which burned for three days and nights, destroyed the central business district and caused more devastation than the earthquake itself.

The rupturing of the northernmost 290 miles of the 800-mile long San Andreas Fault caused the earthquake. While those living between Los Angeles in the South and Oregon in the north would have felt the earthquake, it was San Francisco where the damage and loss of life was most severe.

At the time it was estimated that around 700 people were killed but later research puts the death toll closer to 3,000. More than half the city's 400,000 population were left homeless.

The San Francisco earthquake marked the beginning of scientific study of earthquakes in the United States and, as a result, the "elastic-rebound" theory was formed, explaining how the earth's crust stretches and the accumulated stress is released and rebounds causing an earthquake.

Although the Richter Scale was not devised until 1935, scientists today estimate that the San Francisco earthquake probably measured between 7.7 and 8.3 on the Richter Scale.

Lorraine Brownbill

Date April 18, 1906

Country USA

Why It's Key It marked the beginning of the scientific study of earthquakes in the United States and resulted in the "elastic-rebound" theory, which still serves as a model for understanding earthquakes today.

opposite Horse-drawn wagons amid rubble after the San Francisco earthquake.

Key Political Event
Finland gives women the vote

On June 1, 1906, Finland became the first country in Europe to adopt a parliamentary system that enabled women to vote and run for parliamentary elections. Finland, which had been a Grand Duchy of the Russian Empire since 1809, had previously only had a parliament with limited powers, consisting of upper-class men. Russia's defeat in the war against Japan in 1905, which led to social unrest in Finland, was an opportunity for Finland to gain more independence. In order to ease the unrest, the Russian Tsar issued a manifesto establishing a parliamentary system in Finland based on universal suffrage. The first elections took place in spring 1907 and had a 70.7 per cent turnout. Of the 62 women that ran for the elections, 19 were elected to the first parliament, most of them as representatives of the Social Democratic Party.

Other Nordic countries soon followed suit. Norway gave women the right to vote in 1913, Denmark in 1915, and Sweden in 1921. Changes were starting to happen in the rest of Europe as well. Some countries, such as Germany and Poland, introduced female suffrage in 1918, but in most other European countries the struggle for female suffrage lasted longer. After granting limited female suffrage in 1918, the U.K. gave women voting rights equal to men's in 1928; France gave women the vote in 1944, and Italy in 1945. In Switzerland women were not allowed to vote until 1971.

Sonja Kudeljnjak

Date June 1, 1906

Country Finland

Why It's Key Female suffrage was the first major step toward gender equality.

Fact The first country to give women the vote was New Zealand, in 1893.

Key Cultural Event
Coke replaces cocaine with caffeine

The precise formula for making Coca-Cola is a notorious trade secret. Reading the ingredients column on the side of a Coke can will only take you so far: carbonated water, high fructose corn syrup, caramel color, phosphoric acid, natural flavors, and caffeine. After that, you need to track down one of the two company executives entrusted with the recipe.

Less secret is the tale of Coke's inception. In the 1880s, John Pemberton, a dispensing chemist in Atlanta, Georgia, used to mix tonics to soothe his customers' complaints. The most effective turned out to be an experimental concoction of caffeine, cocaine, and alcohol. Its taste was bitter, so the blend was diluted in the caramel syrup, which is still an ingredient today. Pemberton instructed that his syrupy preparation – "a precious brain toner and reliever against nervous troubles" – should be taken with carbonated water, which he provided at his counter.

Exactly how much cocaine the original formula contained is impossible to guess, but it was only a decade or so after the drink's invention that a debate about the safety of cocaine use began to gain momentum in the United States. By then, Pemberton was dead, and Asa Candler, another druggist, controlled the company. Candler was reluctant to exorcise cocaine altogether, as he believed the drink should live up to its name and contain at least some by-product of the coca plant. Nevertheless, he reduced the content to 1/400 of a grain per ounce of syrup before it was eventually eliminated.

David Thorley

Key Political Event
Dreyfus rehabilitated by the French army

In July 1906, a review by the French War Ministry quashed, without retrial, a conviction of treason against Captain Alfred Dreyfus. The Dreyfus affair, "the crime of the century," caused deep divisions in late nineteenth-century French society.

Alfred Dreyfus was an Alsatian Jewish artillery officer who had seen his home annexed by the newly formed German Reich during the Franco-Prussian war of 1870–1871. He joined the French army and rose to the rank of captain. Although possessed of a disagreeable personality, he appeared to have a bright future ahead of him when, in 1894, he was arrested and charged with treason on suspicion of supplying information to the German army.

Dreyfus was found guilty and sentenced to life imprisonment. Information continued to be leaked to the German army, and it became apparent through the investigations of Colonel Marie-Georges Picquart that another officer, Marie-Charles Esterhazy, was the guilty party. French opinion was deeply split between the anti-Dreyfus right and pro-Dreyfus left, whose case was magnificently expressed by Émile Zola in his legendary open letter *J'Accuse!*. Those responsible for Dreyfus' conviction had both suppressed and forged evidence, and after a retrial in 1899 (which again found him guilty), he was pardoned.

The affair shook the social fabric of the Third Republic and only truly ended when Dreyfus was officially declared innocent in 1995.

Denis Casey

Date 1906

Country USA

Why It's Key The Coca-Cola Company became one of the largest companies in the world with 55,000 employees and a turnover in excess of US$23 billion.

Fact Coke's effect on the health of its drinkers is still a hotly debated question. Its inventor John Pemberton used to assist the state of Georgia in prosecuting salesmen of fake chemicals.

Date July 12, 1906

Country France

Why It's Key The rehabilitation of Dreyfus marked the end of a controversy that had rocked France in the 1890s.

Key Political Event
All India Muslim League founded

The first seeds of partition were planted in India in 1905 when Viceroy Lord Curzon partitioned Bengal. Though the British claimed this was an administrative move, the underlying intention was to quell Hindu nationalism in the region, and so separate Hindus from Muslims. Hindus violently opposed the partition, but Bengali Muslims, who shared a strong sense of unity particular to this eastern pocket of India, agitated for its retention. In 1906, an All India Mohammedan Educational Conference was convened in Dhaka. The meeting was principally organized to draw support for the partition of Bengal and to combat anti-partition agitation; however, such was the mood of political confidence that the All India Muslim League was born.

To safeguard political representation for Muslims, the league demanded separate communal electorates in areas of Muslim minority, and this was delivered under the Indian Councils Act of 1909. In 1913, Mohammad Ali Jinnah joined the league, and it set its sights upon self-government. This was a more radical political position than any previously taken by the Hindu-dominated National Congress, which at that time advocated India as a member of a British Imperial Federation. Although the league formed an alliance with Congress, and Jinnah proclaimed "this great communal organization" to be a powerful factor for a united, independent India, Jinnah was bitterly opposed to Gandhi's *satyagraha* movement. Under Jinnah's leadership, Muslim minority organizations were brought into the fold of the All India Muslim League, and in March 1940, it voted for an independent Pakistan.

Sally Percival Wood

Date December 30, 1906

Country India

Why It's Key The founding of the Muslim League officially denoted the beginning of communalism in India's independence movement, and would lead to the bloody partition of 1947.

Fact Satyagraha was Gandhi's policy of non-violent resistance as a means of pressing for political change.

53

Key Cultural Event
The electric washing machine is invented

Prior to the electric washing machine, cleaning clothes was arduous and time-consuming. Before the introduction of the scrub board in 1797, people used a combination of stream-washing and rock-scrubbing, and while William Blackstone's 1874 hand-cranked washer certainly improved the process, the one-shirt-at-a-time method was still lengthy.

The invention of the electric washing machine is often attributed to Alva J. Fisher, who was issued a patent on August 9, 1910. However, his priority cannot be claimed with any certainty because machines entered manufacture several years earlier. Fisher's "Thor," a drum-type machine with a galvanized tub and electric motor, was produced by the Hurley Machine Company around 1907, but the company may have started producing electric washers as early as 1906.

Regardless of who actually invented the machine, its popularity was immense and variations numerous. During the nineteenth and twentieth centuries, over 2,000 patents were issued for various types of electric washing machines. Of all the cleaning mechanisms offered by these patents, only two are prevalent in washing machines today: the agitator system introduced by the Maytag Company in 1922, which forces water through clothing, and the cylinder system, in which the clothes are washed by moving about inside a rotating tub. In the 1930s, John W. Chamberlain invented a machine that could wash, rinse, and wring, making electric washers even more time-efficient, and 1947 ushered in the ever-popular top-loading washer.

Carolyn Purnell

Date 1907

Country USA

Why It's Key The electric washing machine allowed for more time-efficient, less labor-intensive, and more frequent (and consequently hygienic) laundry.

Key Cultural Event
Klimt paints *The Kiss* (*Der Kuss*)

Probably Klimt's best known painting, *The Kiss* is a representation of a moment of passion between a man and a woman. Both wear golden, richly decorated robes, they kiss upon what appears to be a patch of colorful flowers. The painting's sensuality is typical of Klimt's erotic style, but interpretations of its meaning vary. On first glance, it seems to express a mutual joy in the kiss, but many people have suggested that the woman is resisting it, or that she remains detached while the man seems wholly involved.

Born in Baumgarten, Vienna, on July 14, 1862, Gustav Klimt began his artistic life decorating theaters and other buildings with his brother, Ernst. Later, he became renowned for his paintings of women, sometimes naked or dressed richly in mosaic-like costumes with ornamental backgrounds. The often erotic nature and subject matter of his work caused criticism on grounds of immorality, and it was occasionally banned from exhibition.

The Kiss was painted between 1907 and 1908, and is typical of the emotional and decorative style that was expressed by painters of the Vienna Secession movement, which had been founded by Klimt himself. However, it also shows a departure from Klimt's normal theme of very dominant or powerful women, for example, *Judith* of 1901. The painting has become a popular icon, to be seen on all kinds of merchandise, but it remains a tantalizingly ambiguous work, raising questions about the relationship between the couple and the fine balance of control, particularly sexual, between a man and a woman.

Ros Bott

Date 1907–1908

Country Austria

Why It's Key Klimt's *The Kiss* expressed a new symbolic eroticism, combining the radicalism of the Vienna Secession movement with the new Western movement of art nouveau.

Key Cultural Event
Picasso paints *Les Demoiselles d'Avignon*

When Picasso showed his newly completed *Les Demoiselles d'Avignon* to fellow painters and art critics at his studio, it was met with shock and distaste. Matisse declared it an outrageous attempt to paint the fourth dimension, and Derain suggested that, "one day we shall find Pablo has hanged himself behind his great canvas."

The work, painted on a 2.5 meter-square canvas, initially included male clients – a medical student and a sailor – alongside five prostitutes. Picasso worked through more than a hundred sketches, but finally decided to paint over the clients, leaving the women to gaze out at the viewer. Inspired by prehistoric Spanish sculptures and African and Oceanic masks, the women's faces are drawn with impetuous and violent brush strokes, conveying sexual anxiety. While Picasso, like his contemporaries, regarded Africa as a symbol of savagery, he admired this wildness as a source of vitality.

In depicting sexual freedom in *Les Demoiselles d'Avignon*, Picasso betrayed the traditional middle-class values of his time. He also rejected the current popular artistic style of Impressionism, which concentrated on shades of color and light, choosing instead to draw defined lines. This paved the way for Cubism.

Even before the painting became celebrated as a key masterpiece, Picasso himself declared that it had changed his own understanding of art, calling it his "first exorcism painting." Housed in the Museum of Modern Art in New York, *Newsweek* declared it in July 2007 to be the "most influential work of art of the last 100 years."

Mariko Kato

Date July 1, 1907

Country France

Why It's Key Possibly the most important painting of the twentieth century, *Les Demoiselles d'Avignon* introduced Cubism.

Fact *Les Demoiselles d'Avignon* portrays five prostitutes in a brothel in Barcelona.

Key Cultural Event
Baden-Powell starts the Boy Scouts

Once a famous war hero, Robert Baden-Powell is now as renowned for his interest in the education of young people as for his actions in service to his country. Convinced that certain attributes were not being properly encouraged in education, he wanted to create a curriculum that focused on developing the mind, sympathy for others, and physical health.

In August 1907, Baden-Powell held the Brownsea Island Experimental Camp, the first scout camp based on his ideas for educational reform. This was the beginning of the Boy Scout movement.

These ideas were captured in the first part of *Scouting for Boys*, which he published in 1908. The qualities of leadership, responsibility, cooperation, and comradeship were ingrained in young Boy Scouts by organizing members into troops and patrols. Baden-Powell also believed in the importance of adventure and encouraged scouts to be open to new experiences.

Much of Baden-Powell's structure for Boy Scouts was inspired by Ernest Seton's vision of camping and woodcraft. Seton had developed his own movement of camping for boys known as Woodcraft Indians, which he described in the book *The Birch Bark Roll of the Woodcraft Indians*. Baden-Powell incorporated several aspects of Seton's vision into the Boy Scouts. These included the small group units, the uncompetitive system of badge earning, and the use of an animal to identify each patrol group. Some tensions eventually arose between Seton and Baden-Powell as Seton felt that credits conferred to Baden-Powell as the inventor of Scouting were significantly based in Seton's ideas.
Anne Hsu

Date August 1, 1907

Country UK

Why It's Key The Boy Scouts is a program for developing self-reliance, initiative, courage, helpfulness, and integrity in boys, which still thrives today.

Key Cultural Event
Bakelite

The story of plastic begins with the story of Velox, a photographic paper that could be developed in artificial light. Leo Baekeland, a Belgian native, developed the product in 1893 and sold the rights to George Eastman of the Eastman Kodak Company in 1899 for US$1 million. The sale of Velox allowed Baekeland to move to Yonkers, New York, where, in 1904, he turned his attention to the rising cost of shellac, a resinous varnish used as an electrical insulator. He dreamed of creating a cheaper, durable, and moldable substitute. By 1907, Baekeland had developed the first synthetic plastic, formally known as "polyoxybenzylmethylenglycolanhydride." Luckily Baekeland simplified things by calling it "Bakelite."

Bakelite, the result of the combination of formaldehyde and phenols, is a nonconductive, hard plastic that does not soften when heated, making it ideal for electrical uses. However, Bakelite's applications didn't stop there. It was integrated into phonograph records, billiard balls, and cameras, and during the Great Depression of the 1930s, its low cost made it possible for families to purchase radios and other goods at significantly cheaper prices. In addition, Bakelite's fade-resistant colors and durability made it perfect for jewelry and decorative goods.

Baekeland's patent on phenol-formaldehyde resin expired in 1927, opening the market to new competitors and formulas. By 1945, over 400,000 tons of plastic were being produced each year in the United States alone, a number that has increased to over 47 million tons in 2007.
Carolyn Purnell

Date 1907

Country USA

Why It's Key The invention of plastic opened the door to a wide range of new products, inventions, and technologies that have had a major impact on our daily lives.

La triple détente.

Key Political Event
Triple Entente formed

Even if the countries of the Triple Entente (France, Britain, and Russia) had never become embroiled in World War I, the creation of such an alliance would have merited the attention of history.

The Triple Entente ultimately owed its existence to the unification of Germany during the Franco-Prussian war of 1870–1871. The mastermind of the unification, Chancellor Otto von Bismarck, followed a policy of portraying Germany as a "satiated" state. Declaring Germany void of territorial ambitions or desire for empire, Bismarck skillfully played state against state with the aim of keeping France internationally isolated. In this he was eminently successful, courting imperial Russia and Austria-Hungary, and relying on Britain's "splendid isolation" from European affairs. After Bismarck's fall, German policy failed to consolidate the Iron Chancellor's gains. France, isolated for over twenty years, grasped the opportunity and wooed Russia, which resulted in the formation of an alliance. The addition of Britain was the surprising element, as it reversed nearly a hundred years of British policy. In the previous century, Britain had fought with the Germans against France and against Russia in the Crimea. Now, fear of a bellicose Germany (especially its expanded navy) led Britain to make common cause with its old enemies.

The creation of this power bloc (with a mirror opposite in the Triple Alliance of Germany, Austria-Hungary, and Italy), increased international tensions that would eventually lead to World War I.

Denis Casey

Date August 31, 1907

Country France/UK/Russia

Why It's Key The creation of this formal alliance was an important step on the road to World War I.

opposite French postcard by Paul Dufresne showing a caricature of German Emperor Wilhelm II being kicked by the boots of the Triple Entente armies.

Key Person
Florence Nightingale

Florence Nightingale was named after the Italian city in which she was born on May 12, 1820. As a young woman she was widely admired, considered highly intelligent, and was thus expected to make a good marriage. But in 1837, Florence had what she described as her "calling" from God. She undertook nurse training in Germany, which led to her appointment as Superintendent of the Establishment for Gentlewomen in 1853.

When Britain, France, and Turkey declared war on Russia in 1854, Nightingale arrived at the Barrack Hospital in Scutari, a suburb in Asian Constantinople, with 38 nurses. Although doctors did not instantly welcome the introduction of female nurses to military hospitals, the nurses were soon crucial in attending the continuous arrival of wounded soldiers. In addition to devoted nursing, Nightingale wrote home on behalf of the soldiers, sent their wages to their families, and introduced reading rooms to the hospital.

After the Crimean War, Nightingale became a central figure in the campaign for a Royal Commission to investigate the health of the British Army. She also contributed to Army and hospital statistics, leading her to become the first woman to be elected a fellow of the Statistical Society in 1860. In the same year, she established the Nightingale Training School for nurses at St Thomas' Hospital, and published her best known work, *Notes on Nursing*. In her final years, Nightingale received many honors, becoming the first woman to receive the Order of Merit, in 1907. She died on August 13, 1910, aged ninety.

Mariko Kato

Date November 29, 1907

Born/Died 1820–1910

Nationality British

Why It's Key Nightingale was a legend in her lifetime, and became the first woman to receive the Order of Merit.

Fact Florence Nightingale, known as "The Lady with the Lamp," was a pioneer of modern nursing, a writer, and a recognized statistician, celebrated for her contribution to nursing in the Crimean War.

Key Cultural Event
Sorel's *Reflections on Violence* published

*R*eflections on Violence (*Réflexions Sur La Violence*) has been a touchstone of radicalism for a hundred years. First published in 1908, Georges Sorel's book is one of the most controversial modern contributions to political philosophy.

Sorel has been described as a "wild Marxist." He railed against the infiltration of bourgeois ideology into the working class, as this would dismantle ideas of revolution. He believed in syndicalism, supporting direct action and all forms of proletarian agitation, such as strikes, boycott, and industrial sabotage. *Reflections on Violence* achieved some of its notoriety because of Sorel's prolonged engagement with the role of violence, which could, he suggested, be positive in the arena of class struggle. Sorel also proposed that social change requires a conceptualized "myth" to animate the masses. This myth, an overarching ideology that could maintain revolutionary momentum, could not be judged in terms of truth; it had an ethical legitimacy if it inspired working-class mobilization.

Sorel's theorizing was profoundly prescient of the political and social upheaval of the decades that followed its publication. "Energizing myths" were sold across Europe by the clamorous demagogues of both the left and right. Some commentators have suggested that European fascism drew direct inspiration from Sorel. The popular success of Nazism, for example, depended on its mythic treatment of Hitler (the Führer) and the all-powerful state (The Fatherland, The Third Reich). In truth, *Reflections on Violence* was a provocative text for radical thought in its myriad forms.
Michael Hallam

Date January 1, 1908

Country France

Why It's Key *Reflections on Violence* is a controversial and seminal text that presaged the methods of twentieth-century totalitarianism.

Key Political Event
Turkish revolt in the Ottoman Empire

The ailing Ottoman Empire was dealt a mortal blow on July 24, 1908, when Sultan Abdul Hamid II, reacting to extreme pressure from reformers and Turkish nationalists, announced the restoration of the 1878 constitution he had himself suspended.

For years organizations had been founded to put an end to the Sultan's alleged mishandling of the Empire's affairs. Formed in 1899 by Istanbul students, the Committee of Union and Progress (CUP) was one such group. Although its leaders fled to Paris when their plans were uncovered, many of the so-called "Young Turks" continued to exert their influence from afar.

The catalyst for the revolt was provided by Ottoman troops based in Macedonia under the command of Major Ahmed Niyazi. The Major had been a long-term conspirator against the Sultan, and fearing his discovery, he staged a revolt on July 3, 1908, along with 200 supporters, demanding that the Empire return to a constitutional government. The rebellion spread quickly, leaving Abdul Hamid with no choice but to restore the constitution on July 24.

However, the victory for the Young Turks was short-lived, as deep-rooted internal differences prevented them from taking charge of the new government until 1913. Despite a successful handling of domestic matters, the new government's foreign policy failed dismally when it formed the Ottoman-German Alliance at the outbreak of the Great War. By October 9, 1918, with the war all but lost, the CUP resigned from government, effectively signaling the dissolution of the Ottoman Empire.
Jay Mullins

Date July 24, 1908

Country Turkey

Why It's Key The rebellion against Sultan Abdul Hamid II and the formation of a new government sounded the death toll for the Ottoman Empire.

opposite Illustration from *Le Petit Journal*, May 2, 1909. Sailors faithful to the Sultan shoot their Young Turk commander who wanted to shell the palace.

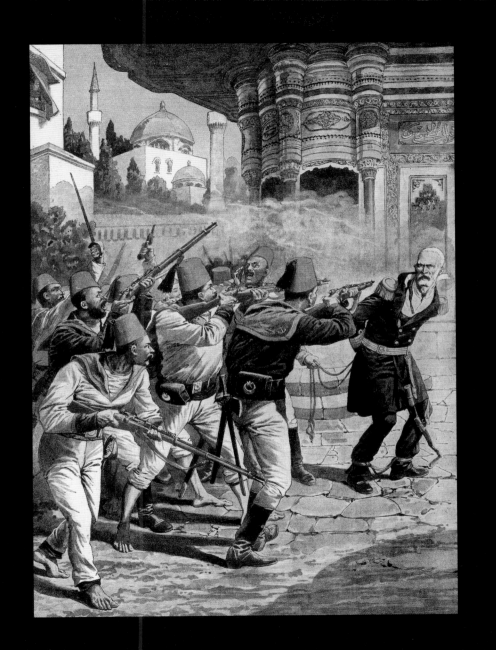

Key Political Event
The birth of the FBI

In 1908, U.S. Attorney General Charles Bonaparte, appointed by President Theodore Roosevelt in 1905, created a corps of special agents that would be in charge of conducting investigations on the federal level. The establishment of a federal investigative agency was highly controversial at the time because Americans were still used to the nineteenth-century tradition of having government services organized at the municipal level. However, Bonaparte realized that the Department of Justice would benefit from having its own investigative force, instead of having to hire external operatives. For this reason, on July 26, 1908, Bonaparte ordered the Special Agents of the Department of Justice, appointed in June 1908, to report to Chief Examiner Stanley W. Finch. That event is now considered to be the beginning of the FBI.

The organization did not initially have a name and was referred to as a "special agent force" until March 1909, when Bonaparte's successor, Attorney General George Wickersham, named it Bureau of Investigation. It was not until 1935 that the name Federal Bureau of Investigation was introduced. Since then, the FBI has been involved in the investigation of all the major crimes and political threats pertaining to the United States, and has gained even more authority after the passing of the Patriot Act in 2001, which enables law enforcement agencies to tap telephone conversations, screen e-mails, and access financial, medical, and other kinds of records.
Sonja Kudeljnjak

Date July 26, 1908

Country USA

Why It's Key The FBI has become the main investigative and intelligence agency of the United States.

Fact The motto of the FBI is "Fidelity, Bravery, and Integrity."

Key Cultural Event
Ford introduces the Model T

Automobiles were originally luxury items accessible only to the very rich. But, in 1908, Henry Ford changed this by producing the Model T, the first automobile designed for the middle classes, which was so popular that Ford workers were unable to fill the orders that poured in. Between 1909 and 1927, Ford sold 15,000,000 Model Ts.

Often referred to as the "Tin Lizzie," the Model T had a four-cylinder water-cooled engine and could reach 40–45 miles per hour on smooth roads. The steering wheel was set on the left to provide a better view of oncoming traffic. Headlights, a folding top, a windshield, and a spare tire were considered optional. The Model T originally sold for US$850, but the introduction of the assembly line allowed Ford to reduce the price to under US$300.

Ford opened plants in England, France, and Germany, and around the world the Model T helped to transform economies and societies. Automobile-related industries flourished as manufacturers sought to meet the needs of automobile production. Tourism became a major industry, and gas stations, motels, and camp grounds sprang up as consumers hit the road. A real estate boom developed when families moved to the suburbs, and when automobile manufacturers began selling cars on credit, other businesses followed suit.

By 1927, Chevrolet was challenging Ford's dominance of the automobile industry, so Ford converted his plants and began manufacturing the Model A. Within three years, the new model was outselling Chevrolet two to one.
Elizabeth R. Purdy

Date September 30, 1908 (first Model T manufactured)

Country USA

Why It's Key The Model T transformed the world, creating mobile societies and helping to launch consumerism, while making Henry Ford into the richest man in the world.

Key Political Event
Bulgaria claims independence

October 5, 1908, saw Ferdinand, Tsar of Bulgaria, declare independence for his nation, signaling the beginning of the end for the once mighty Ottoman Empire. Bulgaria had been under Ottoman rule since the late 1300s, but a renewed desire for independence swept the population during the latter half of the nineteenth century. The Bulgarian people revolted against their rulers in the April Uprising of 1876. Widespread fighting broke out between civilians and Ottoman soldiers, who ruthlessly crushed the revolt. Villages caught up in the uprising were pillaged and as many as 12,000 people were killed, mainly in the Plovdiv region.

For the next thirty-two years, Bulgaria's fate lay in the hands of the European superpowers: Great Britain, Russia, Germany, and the Ottoman Empire. Russia's desire to usurp the Ottomans led to the Russo-Turkish War of 1877–1878. The victorious Russians had designs for a large Bulgarian state, including Macedonia, Moesia, Thrace, and Dobrudja, much to the displeasure of Britain who saw this as a threat to its interests in the Balkans. A compromise in the form of the Treaty of Berlin was signed in 1878 with a new Tsar of Bulgaria installed: Alexander II.

Dissatisfied with Alexander's liberal tendencies, Russia staged a coup in Bulgaria resulting in the Tsar's abdication in 1886 and the instatement of the more conservative Ferdinand of Saxe Gotha. By 1908 the European powers were moving toward inevitable conflict, and Ferdinand used the opportunity to declare Bulgaria fully independent on October 5.
Jay Mullins

Date October 5, 1908

Country Bulgaria

Why It's Key The loss of Bulgaria from the Ottoman Empire was evidence of its imminent collapse.

Key Political Event
Austria-Hungary annexes Bosnia and Herzegovina

On October 6, 1908, Austria-Hungary announced the annexation of Bosnia and Herzegovina, wresting control of the two Balkan nations from the grip of the crumbling Ottoman Empire.

The official annexation was already a formality since the European superpowers had awarded administration of the provinces to Austria-Hungary in 1878, even though the Ottomans retained the legal title. It was thought that this compromise was simply a temporary solution to cool rising tensions in Europe, with many nations seeking to add Bosnia and Herzegovina to their own territories. Similarly to Bulgaria, a number of the region's Slavic population desired full independence, whereas neighboring Serbia saw the instability in Bosnia and Herzegovina as an opportunity to extend its influence.

The already ailing Ottoman Empire was dealt a mortal blow in 1908 when the Committee of Union and Progress (the so-called Young Turks) staged a rebellion against Sultan Abdul Hamid II and his government. Austria-Hungary took advantage of Turkey's weakened state to officially bring Bosnia and Herzegovina under their rule. This caused outrage across Europe, especially amongst Serbs and pan-Slavic nationals, while Russia, Austria-Hungary's main political rival, was also furious that its authority in the region had been undermined.

These tensions did not ease in the following months, and by 1909, Germany reaffirmed its allegiance to Austria and promised to stand shoulder-to-shoulder with them against Russia and its allies in any future conflict. The wheels were in motion for World War I.
Jay Mullins

Date October 6, 1908

Country Bosnia and Herzegovina

Why It's Key The Austro-Hungarian Empire's aggressive expansion angered many parts of Europe, setting the continent on course for war.

Key Political Event
Death of Empress Cixi

The Empress Cixi (also Tz'u-hsi) was born in Beijing on November 29, 1835, into an illustrious Manchu lineage. She became the concubine of the Emperor Xianfeng, who ruled from 1851–1861, in her teens and was elevated to favorite in 1856 after she gave birth to his only son, Tongzhi. Although Cixi was of a lower status as the mistress, or concubine, of the Emperor, as his favorite she held some status in the Imperial bureaucracy and became a consummate conspirator. After Xianfeng's death, Tongzhi became Emperor at the age of only five and Cixi was granted the co-regency until 1873 when her son died. Following Tongzhi's death, Cixi plotted to have her infant nephew Guangxu ascend the throne, which ensured her position as regent. Although she nominally relinquished her position in 1889, after a palace coup in 1898 Cixi resumed power and her nephew was imprisoned.

As Dowager Empress, Cixi was a conservative and ruthless ruler. But she dithered over reforms that were urgently needed to modernize the Qing Dynasty, unwisely abandoning the program of the "Hundred Days' Reforms" only to reinstate them later. Her political instincts were also misplaced in her support of the Boxer Rebellion, which would be disastrous for the Qing Dynasty. As the only female ruler of the Qing Dynasty, Cixi was largely blamed for its collapse. Before her death on November 15, 1908, she ordered that her imprisoned nephew Guangxu be poisoned. He died the following day.
Sally Percival Wood

Date November 15, 1908

Country China

Why It's Key The death of the Dowager Empress Cixi signaled the final collapse of the Qing Dynasty, which officially ended in 1911.

Key Political Event
Belgium annexes the Congo

The infamous Berlin Conference of 1884–1885, where European countries began their colonial division of Africa, had one particularly notorious result. There, Leopold II's ownership of the Congo was validated. Leopold was the Belgian king, but his control of the newly, and highly inaptly, named Congo Free State was personal. Within a few years, his greed for rubber profits and his apathy toward the Congolese led to some of the worst atrocities of European imperialism. Some estimate that the country's population decreased by 10 million.

Missionaries, merchants, and reporters who revealed these horrors generated international outrage. By the early twentieth century, the protests were impossible to ignore. When the U.S. government joined the British in demanding major reforms in the Congo, Leopold decided to sell his colony. The Belgian government, humiliated by its depraved figurehead, bought it for more than 200 million francs. Ceremonies of annexation were held at Boma, the Congolese capital, on November 15, 1908. Unfortunately, the change in ownership was less influential than many had hoped. Cruelty continued, though at a lesser pitch than under Leopold. Furthermore, the Belgian approach to the Congo was highly paternalistic; no Congolese was allowed to hold any position of power in administration, and tribal chiefs were forced either to accept Belgian policy or be overthrown. Belgium's failure to develop the colony in any substantial way in preparation for independence, finally won in 1960, may have significantly contributed to the country's recent political troubles.
Christina Welsch

Date November 15, 1908

Country Congo Free State (now Democratic Republic of Congo)

Why It's Key The annexation of the Congo by the Belgian government was the result of a massive international protest against the atrocities perpetrated in the colony under Leopold II, its former sovereign.

Key Political Event
NAACP founded

The National Association for the Advancement of Colored People (NAACP) has been instrumental in improving the legal, educational, and economic lives of African-Americans. Historically, the NAACP has its roots in the "abolitionist movement," and in the struggle for freedom and equality initiated when President Abraham Lincoln issued the Emancipation Proclamation.

The organizational model for the NAACP was the Niagara Movement, an association founded in 1905 by a small band of educated radicals, including W. E. B. Du Bois, as the first significant black protest movement of the twentieth century. It challenged the then-dominant accommodation theories of Booker T. Washington, and advocated higher education, voting rights, and first class citizenship for black Americans. To do so, the Niagara Movement agitated the courts and demonstrated a willingness to be defiant in its fight against racism. It was in this spirit that the NAACP was founded. Dismayed at the violence that was committed against African-Americans, a group of multi-racial activists, including Du Bois, William English Walling, Mary White Ovington, and Oswald Garrison Villard – grandson of the abolitionist, William Lloyd Garrison – issued a call for racial justice, "and the renewal of the struggle for civil and political rights." Though the ensuing activist group was originally called the National Negro Committee, it was renamed the NAACP. It became a mixed and formal organization of sixty people pledged to focus on Du Bois' Niagara Movement philosophy, and to secure for all people the rights guaranteed in the Thirteenth, Fourteenth, and Fifteenth Amendments to the United States Constitution.

Fred Lindsey

Date February 12, 1909

Country USA

Why It's Key The NAACP became one of the most powerful interracial organizations devoted to civil rights and racial justice in the world.

Fact Though their relationship with the African-American community has been notoriously contentious, the Jewish community contributed greatly to the founding and continued financing of the NAACP.

63

Key Cultural Event
Selfridges department store opens in London

Selfridges was the vision of Henry Gordon Selfridge, an American who had made his fortune in retail as a partner in the famous Marshall Field Store in Chicago, Illinois. In 1906, at the age of forty-nine, he moved to London and sought to replicate his success in the capital. Selfridge decided to build a large department store on Oxford Street, which he intended to become not merely a shop, but also an institution that would feature in the social and commercial life of London.

The store, which took just a year to build, cost UK£400,000 and covered six acres of floor area with one hundred separate departments. With an absence of dividing walls and partitions, the vast range of wares for sale were displayed to great effect in bright and airy show rooms. This was completely foreign to the British eye, which was more used to smaller shops.

The Times called Selfridges "London's Greatest Store" and Selfridges' imaginative advertisements at the time proclaimed its motto of "Dependable Qualities Only, at London's Lowest Prices – Always."

The store's goal of making shopping "more recreative and pleasurable" was evident in the building's design with a luxurious smoking lounge for gentlemen, a suite of restaurants connected with a roof garden for al fresco dining, and a series of rest and reception rooms. With such innovations as shopping by telephone and positive encouragement to browse without any obligation to buy, Selfridges quickly became a household name.

Michelle Higgs

Date March 15, 1909

Country UK

Why It's Key The opening of Selfridges revolutionized the modern department store.

Fact When Selfridges first opened, the building included an interpreter's room, a silence room, a bureau de change, a library, and a hairdressing salon as well as railway, steamship, and theater ticket offices.

Key Cultural Event
Diaghilev introduces modern ballet to Europe

In 1909, expectant audiences of the Théâtre du Châtelet in Paris witnessed a new touring Russian ballet ensemble and were shocked and captivated by what they saw. The success of the first *Ballets Russes* performances ensured Sergei Diaghilev's place in the modernist radicalizing of artistic practice.

Diaghilev wanted to break from established European ballet with its emphasis on method, precise execution, and formulaic setting. This offended his symbolist and anti-rational sensibility and under his direction the *Ballets Russes* rebelled against every element of classical ballet. Avant-garde artists like Léon Bakst painted striking, colorful, asymmetric sets and exploited European fantasies of the East with stylized Asian designs (the celebrated *Scheherazade* of 1910 transformed tastes in fashion and interior design). The choreography and dancing was also entirely exotic to Western spectators. Diaghilev assembled a troupe of superlative ability, including Tamara Karasavina, Vaslav Nijinsky, and Anna Pavlova. Nijinsky's performances were incendiary, impassioned, vigorously athletic, and highly sexualized. By violently exceeding the established techniques of ballet, Nijinsky seemed to transgress too the conventions of Western genteel society (augmented by the fact he lived openly as Diaghilev's lover) triggering fascination from the European intelligentsia.

Diaghilev's pursuit of artistic abstractionism anticipated and influenced modernist developments in theater, writing, and painting. His belief that dance could and should embody intense emotion continues to energize the practice of expressive modern dance.
Michael Hallam

Date May 19, 1909

Country France

Why It's Key Diaghilev's innovative *Ballets Russes* laid the foundations for modern dance and influenced experiments in the whole spectrum of the arts.

opposite Vaslav Nijinsky photographed as principal in the first season of Diaghilev's *Ballets Russes* in Paris, 1909.

Key Political Event
Prince Ito of Japan assassinated

Smiling and bowing to the crowd, Prince Ito Hirobumi stepped from his train car onto the platform of the station at Harbin, China at 9 a.m. on October 26, 1909. As he made his way past an honor guard assembled to welcome him, a series of shots rang out without warning. The platform became bedlam. When the crowd was cleared, the 72-year old Japanese statesman was found lying on the ground, mortally wounded. He died moments later.

The assassination of Prince Ito shocked the world community. The popular, affable politician had been one of the driving forces behind Japanese modernization in the late nineteenth century, and had served as his country's first prime minister. In 1905, he was appointed Resident-General of Korea, which had been made a Japanese protectorate after the Russo-Japanese War.

Ito was a proponent of gradual annexation in Korea, and it was this position that led to his death. Although he had resigned months earlier, Korean nationalists still saw him as a symbol of Japanese dominance. His assassin, a young man named An Jung-geun, did not flee the scene: "I came to Harbin for the sole purpose of assassinating Prince Ito to avenge my country."

Ito was carried home to Japan and honored with a state funeral; An Jung-geun was tried and executed. In 1910, using Ito's assassination as a pretext, the Japanese government forcibly annexed the Korean peninsula.
Heather Michon

Date October 26, 1909

Country China

Why It's Key The assassination of Prince Ito gave Japan a pretext to annex the Korean peninsula.

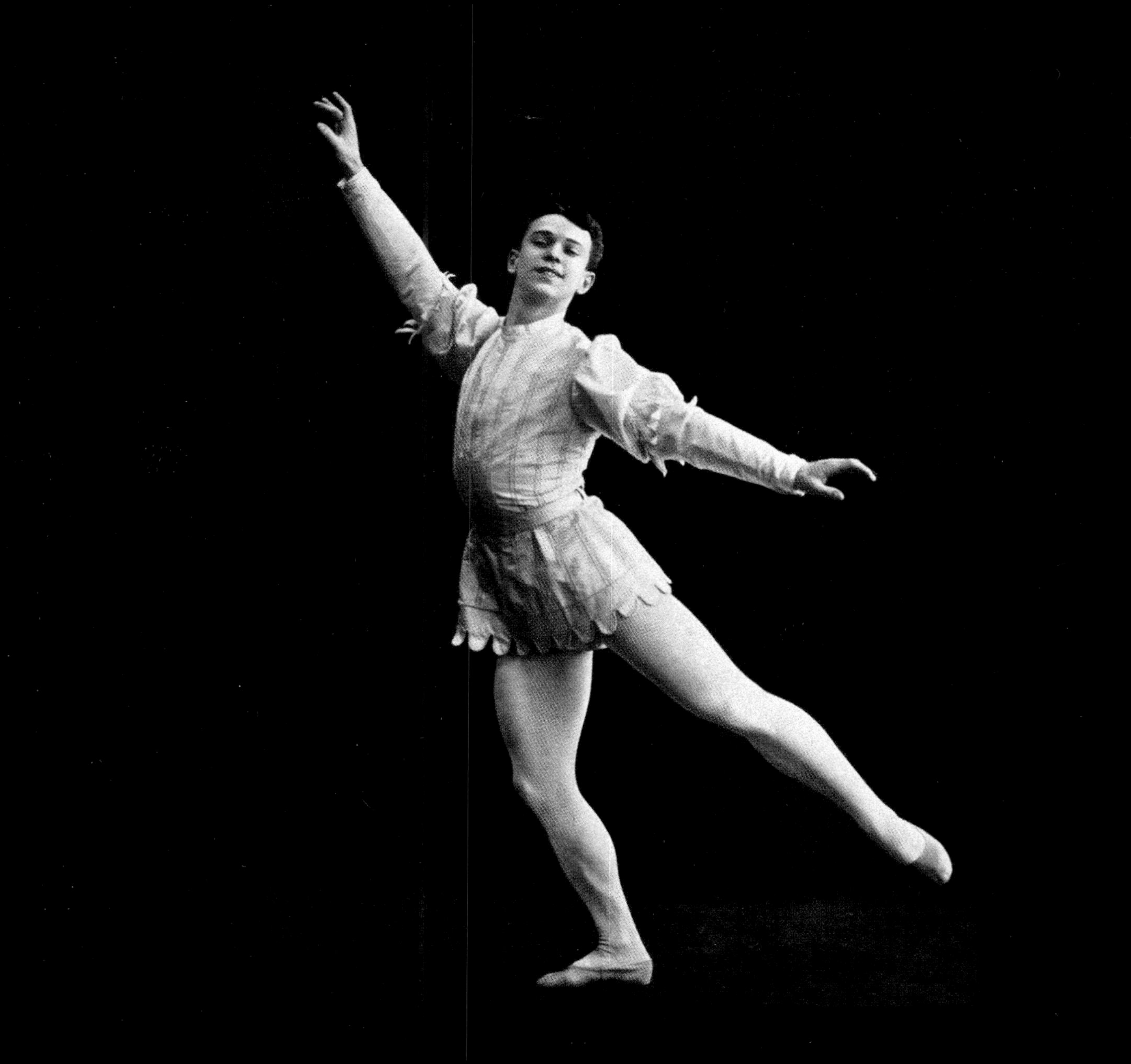

Key Political Event
United States sends warships to Nicaragua

Having flexed its hemispheric muscle by facilitating Panama's secession from Colombia in 1903, the United States once again asserted its hegemony in Central America. Nicaragua, like Panama, had long been coveted as the potential site of an inter-oceanic canal that would shorten trade routes between the eastern U.S. and California. Moreover, U.S. companies had invested massively in the country since the nineteenth century and held a large stake in its economy. Nicaragua's instability under the liberal government of José Santos Zelaya provided a pretext for direct military action. In October 1919, several hundred armed rebels associated with conservative opposition groups, which had long received covert aid from the U.S., were captured and executed by Zelaya's government; among them were two American mercenaries. In response,

president William Howard Taft suspended diplomatic relations and sent gunships to force Zelaya's resignation.

It was neither the first nor the last time the United States would approach Nicaraguan affairs with force. In a bizarre episode, Tennessee-born adventurer and privateer William Walker had undertaken a "conquest" of Nicaragua in 1856 with the backing of a private army, briefly establishing himself as president. More sustained involvement in Nicaragua would quickly follow the 1909 intervention: the Marines occupied the country permanently between 1912 and 1933, shoring up the conservative government and protecting U.S. economic interests. The northern superpower subsequently installed Anastasio Somoza as president, creating a hereditary puppet regime that ruled for over forty years.
Geoffrey A. Schullenberger

Date November 18, 1909

Country Nicaragua

Why It's Key The decision to take sides in Nicaragua's civil conflict initiated a pattern of U.S. intervention in the country's affairs that would continue throughout the century.

Key Cultural Event
First kibbutz initiated

The rampant anti-Semitism that plagued Russia at the beginning of the twentieth century made daily life difficult for the Jews living there, but the unrest led to a promising new beginning. While many of the refugees that fled to Israel during the Second Aliyah didn't stick around, the ones responsible for creating kibbutz life forged a revolutionary mentality. In 1909, a dozen Jews traveled on horseback to a southern region of the land near the Sea of Galilee and initiated a community that flourished on farming and self-preservation. They called the settlement "Kvutzat Degania," borrowing the name from local grains they thrived on. The Jewish National Fund purchased land owned by a neighboring Arab settlement, and Degania quickly turned into a commune of farmers. In its first year, 320 people joined. Later, hundreds of kibbutzim

spread throughout the Jewish state, especially after it became official in the middle of the century.

Signaling the arrival of communist ideals to Jewish settlements in Israel, the kibbutz provided an essential ingredient in the formation of modern Zionism. Residents lived off the land and exclusively made group decisions, not even individually nurturing the children that lived there. While Orthodox Jews believed in a spiritual need for members of their religion to live in Israel, kibbutz dwellers took a secular approach, supporting the necessity for the Jews to remain close to the land, but not the rituals. Today, kibbutzim are no longer sheer havens for socialist ideology, but the farming mentality still dictates their existence.
Eric Kohn

Date 1910

Country Palestine/Israel

Why It's Key It marked the beginning of a fresh secular wave of Jewish life in Israel.

Fact Aliyah refers to the immigration of Jewish peoples to the land of Israel.

Key Person
Marie Curie

Marie Curie (*née* Maria Sklodowska) was born in Poland in 1867, and is famous for her work in the investigation of radioactivity and her pioneering status as an acknowledged female scientist. Outstandingly intelligent, she studied physics and mathematics at the Sorbonne (University of Paris), and graduated with a first place in physics and a second place in math.

In 1895, she married Pierre Curie, and together they explored radioactive emissions from certain elements, building on the work of Henri Becquerel and his discovery of radioactivity in uranium. Their research led them to the source of radiation, and they were able to demonstrate that radioactivity is an atomic property, rather than a property of interaction between elements. They subsequently discovered polonium and radium, and Marie's work on the isolation of radium earned her the first science doctorate to be awarded to a woman in Europe. In 1903, she was awarded, along with her husband and Becquerel, the Nobel Prize for Physics.

Tragically, Pierre Curie was killed in a street accident in 1906, but Marie continued to research, taking her husband's chair at the Sorbonne, as well as bringing up her daughters. Her *Treatise on Radioactivity*, published in 1910, was an explanation of her research on radioactivity, and helped earn her the Nobel Prize for Chemistry the following year. She later worked on medical applications for radium with her daughter Irene.

Due to her constant exposure to radiation before the dangers were known, Marie Curie developed leukemia in the 1920s, and died on July 4, 1934.
Ros Bott

Date 1910

Born/Died 1867–1934

Nationality Polish

Why It's Key What we know about radioactivity stems from the research carried out by Pierre and Marie Curie, explained and detailed in this fundamental publication.

Fact Marie Curie is sometimes known as the "Mother of Modern Physics," and it was she who coined the word "radioactivity."

Key Cultural Event
China abolishes slavery

In 1906, Chou Fu, viceroy at Nanking, submitted an initiative to the Emperor of China calling for the end of slavery. At the time, the inhabitants of China were divided into four classes: banner men (the ruling class), free Chinese subjects, outcasts, and slaves. The law stipulated careful classification of everyone in the Chinese population into one of these four classes, and those who tried to avoid the duties of their class were severely punished.

Fu argued his case for emancipation of the slave class on several grounds. He referred to edicts presented during the Manchu Dynasty, which argued for better treatment of slaves, and pointed out the inconsistency between slavery and the program of reform that the Chinese government was currently implementing. Fu also cited the abolition of slavery in Europe and America as an example to follow. He reminded the Emperor that many foreign nations would regard China as barbarous for its toleration of slavery.

The recommendations of Fu were finally accepted and slavery in China was abolished on January 31, 1910. The Chinese commission in charge of the abolition ruling supported emancipation in theory; however, the actual eradication of the tradition was difficult, especially because of opposition from Manchu nobles. Though no longer classified as slaves, former slaves of Manchu nobles were still required to remain with their masters for the rest of their lives.

Yet, despite its slow implementation, the edict of 1910 did allow all of the slaves in China to eventually become free laborers.
Anne Hsu

Date January 31, 1910

Country China

Why It's Key This was a significant victory for the abolitionist movement.

Key Cultural Event
Griffith films in Los Angeles

When movies first became a popular form of entertainment in the United States between the last decade of the nineteenth century and the first decade of the twentieth, their production was limited to the east coast. The earliest film studios took root in New York City. Over time, however, filmmakers realized the technical advantages of moving to the other side of the country. The sunny weather allowed for natural lighting all year long, and the comparatively spacious marketplace permitted plenty of room for new businesses to set up shop.

The revolutionary silent film director D.W. Griffith, a rising star at the Biograph Company, traveled to Hollywood for the period piece *In Old California*. The movie, which featured a Latino storyline, would become known as the inaugural Hollywood production, followed three years later by Cecil B. Demille's *The Squaw Man*.

Griffith's motivation for shooting in the area was one of practicality and aesthetics: the director wanted to avoid the rigidity of studios by taking his productions into natural environments to create a sense of realism. But the ultimate result of this sojourn, which would become annual for Griffith and his team of actors, was the emergence of a commercial entity. Griffith and the filmmakers that followed him were opening the floodgates for the evolution of Hollywood. Over the next ten years, with major studios like Paramount Pictures reigning over the town and hundreds of films in production, movies became the dominant industry.
Eric Kohn

Date March 10, 1910

Country USA

Why It's Key By taking the first film shoot to the west coast, Griffith created a new, permanent home for commercial filmmaking.

Fact Since Griffith's name was not attached to many of his projects, decades passed before he was truly recognized as the first Hollywood filmmaker.

opposite D.W. Griffiths on set.

Key Political Event
Union of South Africa formed

In 1886, gold was discovered on the Witwatersrand, which was to become the source of 40 per cent of all gold ever mined. The resulting gold rush led directly to the Jameson Raid on the Transvaal Republic in 1895 and the Second Anglo-Boer War, which began in 1889. The 1902 Treaty of Vereeniging, which ended the war, made the Transvaal and Orange Free State colonies of the British Empire. It took a further eight years for the two former Boer republics and the Cape Colony and Natal to be united in the Union of South Africa, under a governor-general with former Boer general Louis Botha as its first prime minister.

Britain wanted to establish a unitary, strong, self-sufficient state rather than a federation along the lines of Canada and Australia. Although the Cape Colony's existing, limited, non-racial franchise, which was restricted to property owners, was entrenched in the act of union, so too was the color bar of the former Boer republics, betraying the political aspirations of the roughly 40,000 black South Africans who had fought on the side of the British in the Anglo-Boer War. A delegation to London of black and white South Africans, led by former Cape Prime Minister William Schreiner, to protest against this entrenchment of the color bar met with no success. In 1931, the Union became a Commonwealth Realm, meaning that Britain could no longer legislate on behalf of South Africa, and on May 31, 1961, South Africa became a republic.
Duncan Proudfoot

Date May 31, 1910

Country South Africa

Why It's Key By granting self-government and allowing its constituent states to retain their color bar, the union laid the groundwork for the Republic of South Africa's subsequent policy of apartheid.

Key Political Event
The outbreak of the Mexican Revolution

In November 1910, Francisco Madero issued his rallying cry for rebellion against the corrupt and repressive regime headed by Porfirio Díaz. The insurrection he planned did not take shape, but other symptoms of unrest were soon to follow. An agricultural laborers' movement appeared in Chihuahua led by Pancho Villa, while in the south, indigenous groups clamored to reclaim their lands in a movement led by Emiliano Zapata. Madero's proclamation thus coincided with the inception of the revolutionary careers of the two men who would become the iconic figures of the period.

In 1911, Madero returned to Mexico from exile in Texas and established a provisional government on the border. Aided by progressive factions in the Díaz regime, he came to power by popular election toward the end of that year. But the electoral victory, far from ushering in a period of stability and democracy, did little to address a mass of claims that had emerged out of multiple elements of Mexican society. A mere month later, Zapata unveiled his Plan of Ayala, advocating the restitution of land to the Mexican Indians. By the time Madero was assassinated in 1913, after two failed coups by different factions of the opposition, Victoriano Huerta had emerged as the strongest new figure in the political landscape. Huerta's unconstitutional government allowed some reactionary factions to believe that they had found a replacement for Porfirio Díaz, but his government, like that of Madero as well as several of their successors, would prove short-lived and cataclysmic.

Charlotte Whittle

Date November 20, 1910

Country Mexico

Why It's Key Francisco Madero's ill-fated attempt to supplant dictator Porfirio Díaz as president of the Mexican Republic served as the catalyst for a twenty-year civil war, which would be considered the cultural and political watershed of Mexican modernity.

opposite **Mexican painter Diego Rivera's** *Agrarian Leader Zapata*.

Key Person
Ekra Agiman

Ekra Agiman – commonly known under his English name, Joseph Ephraim Casely-Hayford – was not a novelist by trade, though he wrote several books. Born in Ghana (at the time, the British Gold Coast colony) to wealthy parents, he was well educated and served as a teacher and journalist before becoming a lawyer after a stay in London. Dismissed from his teaching duties because of his political leanings, he spent time as a newspaper editor for the *Gold Coast Echo* and the *Gold Coast Chronicle* and would continue to hold such positions for most of his life. As a political activist and legislator, Agiman was a staunch advocate for the pan-African movement and founded the National Congress of British West Africa. In 1920, he addressed the League of Nations and represented the Congress in London.

Ethiopia Unbound: Studies in Race Emancipation, published in 1911, reflects many of his concerns. The novel is set in both England and Africa, featuring a philosophical discussion between an African and an English counterpart. While a fictional text, it asserts the very real African desire for emancipation and relies on both historical and contemporary events. Drawing on his background as a teacher, it called for a national university with an Africanized curriculum. *Ethiopia Unbound*'s political agenda represented an important perspective, but more significant was that it was written in English, allowing its message to reach a new audience and calling attention to the relevance of African writers.

David Greenwald

Date 1911

Born/Died 1866–1930

Nationality Ghanaian

Why It's Key Agiman's *Ethiopia Unbound: Studies in Race Emancipation* was the first African novel written in English.

Fact Agiman's correspondence with Booker T. Washington influenced the United States pan-African movement.

Key Cultural Event
First airmail delivery

The first airmail delivery was an international affair: a French pilot flew a British aircraft from Allahabad to Naini, India, in a fundraising stunt authorized by the British government.

In 1910, the Humber Motor Company was invited to exhibit its products at the Industrial and Agricultural Exhibition being held in the United Provinces of India, and a team was sent from England for the exhibition. Led by Walter George Windham, an aviation visionary who founded the first British aero club, the team travelled to India by ship, bringing along dismantled aircraft parts. Upon arrival in India, they reassembled their planes in a field near the exhibition grounds.

One day, the Vicar of Holy Trinity Church in Allahabad asked Windham if he would use his planes to raise money for a nearby student hostel. Windham

agreed, and suggested the idea of carrying specially postmarked mail by air to Naini for a surcharge of 6 annas. The proceeds would be donated to the Oxford and Cambridge Hostel for Indian students. The Indian Government approved the idea, and over 6,100 pieces of mail from all regions of India arrived for the flight. All of the mail was marked "First Aerial Post, U.P. Exhibition Allahabad 1911." Frenchman Henri Pequet was chosen to fly a plane known as the Sommer biplane for the delivery.

On February 18, 1911, Pequet flew the 13 km across the Ganges River. Upon landing, the local postmaster received the mail, and delivered it by ground transportation to destinations around the world.
Anne Hsu

Date February 18, 1911

Country India

Why It's Key The first airmail delivery offered a new and faster method of delivering mail over long distances.

opposite Preparing for the first airmail flight.

Key Discovery
Rutherford discovers the structure of the atom

"It was almost as incredible as if you fired a 15-inch shell at a piece of tissue paper, and it came back and hit you!" The disbelief expressed in this pronouncement by the New Zealand-born scientist Ernest Rutherford was entirely understandable. At his lab in the University of Manchester, he had just discovered that the majority of the mass and charge of an atom resided in a small nucleus, which was surrounded by a large volume of empty space. This overturned the atomic model proposed by J. J. Thomson (the discoverer of the electron), whereby an atom was analogous to a plum pudding: solid, with electrons embedded in it like plums.

Rutherford's experiment involved bombarding a sheet of gold foil only 0.00004 cm thick with alpha particles, with detectors placed around the sheet. These

registered that some particles passed straight through, some were deflected through at angles, and a few even bounced directly back. Rutherford and his collaborators concluded that the particles that did not pass through must have met a strong central resistance and so the concept of the nucleus was born.

Rutherford made many important discoveries during his career and his work is fundamental to modern science. Prior to the discovery of the nucleus, he had already received the 1908 Nobel Prize for Chemistry. This was somewhat ironic as he once famously declared that, "all science is either physics or stamp collecting."
Denis Casey

Date March 7, 1911

Country UK

Why It's Key Rutherford's discovery of the atomic nucleus was one of the greatest scientific discoveries of the twentieth century.

1910–1919

Key Political Event
The Supreme Court busts the Standard Oil trust

Founded in 1870, Standard Oil was one the largest businesses in American history. Under John D. Rockefeller's leadership, Standard Oil expanded rapidly. By 1875, the Ohio-based company had opened forty other facilities in the United States. In 1882, Rockefeller and his associates signed a trust agreement that gave Standard Oil control of 75 per cent of American refineries, 90 per cent of pipelines, and 15 per cent of crude oil products. Standard Oil also owned gas, copper, iron, steel, shipping, banks, and trust companies as well as railroads.

The State of Ohio challenged the monopoly in court, and Standard Oil responded by moving its base of operations to New Jersey where the company was identified as a holding company with a nationwide operation. When competition within the petroleum company increased in response to the introduction of the automobile in the United States, Standard Oil earned a reputation for ruthlessly buying out competitors.

In 1890, Congress passed the Sherman Anti-Trust Act, giving the national government the authority to regulate corporate trusts that extended across state lines. The issue of monopolistic trusts became a decisive issue in the 1904 presidential election, and Theodore Roosevelt launched a trust-busting campaign. After years of court battles, the United States Supreme Court ordered Standard Oil to dissolve its trust in 1911, dividing the company into thirty-four smaller companies, including Mobil Oil, Chevron, and Exxon. Despite international growth, Standard Oil never regained the status it had enjoyed before 1911.
Elizabeth R. Purdy

Date May 15, 1911

Country USA

Why It's Key The trust-busting cases served as a death toll for uncontrolled big business in the United States and alerted other countries to the threat that unchecked industrial greed posed to capitalism.

Key Political Event
The Agadir Crisis

France's desire to control Morocco had been contributing to a rise in tension between the European empires since the turn of the century. A secret pact between France and Spain, with the agreement of Britain, had led to Morocco becoming a virtual French protectorate. This rankled with the Germans, who were unhappy about their economic interests in the country being threatened. The situation eventually resulted in the "First Moroccan Crisis," when the German Kaiser visited Morocco and made an inflammatory speech arguing against French influence in the country. Although eventually resolved, the crisis escalated to the point where France moved extra forces to the German border.

The "Second Moroccan Crisis," also called the "Agadir Crisis," took place when the German warship *Panther* was sent to the Moroccan port of Agadir in July 1911 with the stated intention of protecting German businesses from a local uprising. However, the underlying reason of this classic piece of gunboat diplomacy was to press German claims for rights in Morocco, in light of an increased French military presence in the country.

The crisis ended peacefully but it inflamed existing tensions between Britain and France on one hand, and Germany on the other. The British suspected Germany of planning to locate a naval base on Morocco's Atlantic coast, and this pushed the alliance of Britain and France closer together. The slow progression toward a war between the Great Powers was starting to gather pace.
Martin Sayers

Date July 1, 1911

Country Morocco

Why It's Key Tensions between the European powers in North Africa served to deepen the divisions that would eventually lead to World War I.

Key Cultural Event
Theft of the *Mona Lisa*

Vincenzo Perugia became a national hero in his native Italy when he admitted to stealing the *Mona Lisa* from the Louvre in Paris, where he had once been a trusted employee. Unaware that Leonard da Vinci had presented his painting to Francis I when he moved to France, Perugia felt duty-bound to return the masterpiece to Italy, from where, he wrongly believed, Napoleon had stolen it during his occupation.

Familiar with the Louvre from his time as a carpenter there, Perugia concealed himself within the depths of the vast museum, and prepared for his task. He emerged from his seclusion in the early hours, calmly removing the "enigmatic lady" from her security box (which Perugia himself had made), detached the frame, and tucked the painting under his smock, walking nonchalantly into the night.

The next day, August 21, 1911, the *Mona Lisa* was of course missing, yet it was wrongly believed to have been taken away to be photographed. It wasn't until August 22 that the police were called and a thorough search of the museum was conducted. By this time Perugia was long gone and had taken his loot to Florence, Italy where it remained until December 10, 1913. Seemingly fed up with holding onto the painting, Perugia answered an ad placed by art dealer Alfredo Geri, who was looking for work to exhibit.

Upon the discovery, Perugia was promptly arrested and sentenced to just over a year in prison.
Kerry Duffy

Date August 21, 1911

Country France

Why It's Key The Louvre officials were more concerned about vandalism than theft, and Vincenzo Perugia's success sent shockwaves around the art world.

Fact Pablo Picasso was questioned about the disappearance of the *Mona Lisa*.

Key Political Event
Chinese Revolution

The final decades of China's Manchu rulers, in power since 1644, were marked by tumultuous uprisings and foreign intrusions. After the death of Dowager Empress Cixi, and the imprisoned Emperor Guangxu the following day, the Qing Dynasty was close to collapse. Cixi had proclaimed the two-year-old Puyi her successor, leaving in place a coterie of now-despised Manchu regents. The revolution began with an accidental bomb blast in the Wuhan tricity – Hankou, Wuchang, and Hanyang – on October 9, 1911. The makers of the illicit bombs were discovered and immediately executed by Qing police. In the days that followed, arsenals were raided and a series of military mutinies quickly spread beyond Wuhan to Shanxi, Hunan, and Jiangxi Provinces where Qing loyalists were slaughtered.

By the end of November, fifteen provinces had been won by the revolution. Qing forces fought on until Nanjing, China's former capital, fell to the Revolutionary Alliance in December. Sun Yat-sen was in the United States raising funds for the revolution when it began. He arrived home on Christmas Day and was voted provisional president of the Chinese Republic, a role he assumed on January 1, 1912. The infant Emperor Puyi was forced to abdicate that February on condition that he would continue to live in the imperial palace. The Chinese Revolution was swift, bringing to an end one of the world's most enduring empires that had survived more than two millennia.
Sally Percival Wood

Date October 9, 1911

Country China

Why It's Key China's revolution in 1911 brought to an end more than two millennia of imperial rule. In a country that had known no other form of governance, this resulted in political chaos until the founding of the People's Republic of China in 1949.

Key Cultural Event
First aerial bomb dropped in war

The Italo-Turkish war was of relatively minor global importance; however, opposition to the Ottoman Empire sparked fierce nationalism in the Balkans, which led to the two Balkan wars which, in turn, led to the assassination of Archduke Franz Ferdinand in Sarajevo, and the outbreak of World War I.

Although aircraft and hot air balloons had been used since the eighteenth century as surveillance platforms, the idea of actually attacking the enemy from the air was all but unheard of. Indeed, the purpose of the flight in October 1911 had been to survey Turkish positions; explosives were dropped only as a secondary objective. Furthermore, aerospace technology was, at this time, at a nascent stage (the Wright Brothers' famous flight took place only nine years before the Italo-Turkish war). Aircraft were often made from fabric, paper, wood, and string, and could not carry enough fuel to stay airborne for long. They did not, at this stage, make satisfactory war machines.

Nevertheless, the concept of an aerial assault was one which gained popularity during World War I, as airships and bombers on both sides bombarded opposing positions. The practice of aerial warfare begun at this time continued throughout the twentieth century. Within nine years of the first bomb being dropped, the Italian General Giulio Douhet published his seminal work, *The Command of the Air*, outlining tactics for strategic aerial bombardment. The imprecise nature of aerial bombardment, even when it was not deliberately aimed at civilians, often led to horrendous collateral damage.

Ben Snook

Date October 23, 1911

Country Libya

Why It's Key First use of aircraft in war as weapons (rather than as surveillance devices) predicted a revolution in warfare.

Fact The Turks lost as many as 14,000 men in the war. It is uncertain, however, if any of them died as a direct result of the October 23 airstrike.

Key Discovery
Amundsen reaches the South Pole

On December 14, 1911, close to the South Pole, Helmer Hanssen asked South Pole expedition leader Roald Amundsen to take over his position at the front of their team. Hanssen, an accomplished skier, normally led the dog-pulled sleds, but with the pole so close, Hanssen felt that Amundsen should be the first to reach it. When they arrived, a Norwegian flag was hoisted on two ski poles, and Amundsen insisted that each of the five men present share in the accomplishment by holding it as it was planted. Amundsen spent the next two days recalculating their position and traveling within a short radius of their original stop to ensure that they had indeed achieved their goal.

By the time his team returned to their expedition base at the Bay of Whales, they had been travelling for ninety-nine days and covered over 2,250 kilometers. Although Amundsen had only informed his crew of the plan to reach the pole when their ship, *Fram*, was well underway, careful planning was nonetheless crucial to their success. This can be seen in the utilization of dog-pulled sleds as opposed to the pony-led sleds of the failed Scott expedition.

Amundsen's death in 1928 was in keeping with his heroic life; he died in a plane crash attempting to reach an SOS call from a former teammate, and the newly independent Norway had lost its first great national hero.

Denis Casey

Date December 14, 1911

Country Antarctica

Why It's Key Amundsen's trip was the first successful expedition to the South Pole.

opposite **Norwegian explorer Roald Amundsen in Antarctica.**

Key Disaster
Titanic sinks

British ocean liner the RMS *Titanic* was the largest passenger steamship to be built in her day, accommodating a total of 3,547 passengers and crew. She was the pinnacle of luxury and supposedly unsinkable, fitted with a double-bottomed hull that was divided into sixteen watertight compartments, four of which needed to be flooded before the liner's buoyancy would be endangered. However, her maiden voyage in 1912, from Southampton, England to New York City, ended in disaster.

At 11.40 pm on April 14, at approximately 400 miles south of Newfoundland, the *Titanic* struck an iceberg. It sank two hours and forty minutes later. There was dispute over the number of deaths – the United States quoted 1,517 and the British 1,490. Only the arrival of the Cunard liner *Carpathia* 1 hour and 20 minutes after the *Titanic* sank prevented further deaths in the ice-cold water.

The disaster provoked change in maritime safety measures, including the establishment of the International Ice Patrol and a mandate requiring that every ship have lifeboat space for each person (the *Titanic* had 1,178 boat spaces for 2,224 passengers and crew). Also, since another liner, the *Californian*, had not heard the distress signals of the *Titanic* due to the absence of a radio operator, a 24-hour radio watch became compulsory. The glamor associated with luxury liner mythologized the tragedy, and intrigue continues about the victims and the events on the ship in the hours before she sank. Interest was further renewed when the wreck was discovered in 1985.
Mariko Kato

Date April 14, 1912

Country USA

Why It's Key The disaster is one of the worst peacetime maritime disasters in history.

Fact Ocean liner *Titanic* struck an iceberg at 23:40 (ship's time) on Sunday April 14, 1912, sinking at 02:20 on Monday, April 15, causing a loss of approximately 1,500 lives.

opposite News of the *Titanic* disaster reaches the newspapers.

Key Political Event
War begins in the Balkans

In March 1912, an alliance of Balkan states including Serbia, Bulgaria, Greece, and Montenegro formed the Balkan League. The league demanded the independence of its states from the Ottoman Empire and aimed to seize all her territory in Europe. On October 12, 1912 the league declared war on Turkey.

The league had the support of the Great Power Russia, though she was reluctant to get directly involved, and was watched with alarm by Austria-Hungary. Austria-Hungary felt particularly threatened as there were many ethnic Serbs living within its borders that might be encouraged to revolt. In any case, neither power wanted to see the interests of its rival advanced.

At the end of November, the Balkan League defeated Turkey and in May 1913, the "Treaty of London" divided almost all of the Balkan League's territory in Europe among league members. However league members fell out over the spoils of the conflict and a Second Balkan war began on June 29, 1913. One month later it ended and the "Bucharest Peace" brokered in August 1913 once again settled all territorial claims. However, dissension remained as the interests of smaller states conflicted, and tension continued to mount between Russia and Austria-Hungary.

These wars demonstrated that the Balkan States had the capability to act independently, and uncovered a dangerous rivalry between the Great Powers of Russia and Austria-Hungary. Moreover, the rise of Balkan nationalism earned the region a reputation as the "powder keg of Europe," whose instability threatened the very survival of the great multinational empires.
Helena Hewson

Date June 29, 1913 (second Balkan war)

Country Balkans

Why It's Key The Balkan Wars destabilized the great empires of Europe and threatened military conflict between Russia and Austria-Hungary.

Key Cultural Event
Schoenberg concert causes scandal

Arnold Schoenberg was active at a time when many intellectuals and artists in Vienna were growing anxious to revolutionize artistic expression. Schoenberg himself was eager to move away from late nineteenth-century Romantic music, and, together with his students Webern and Berg, he formed the "Second Viennese School." Provoked by his wife's infidelity in 1908, his musical experimentation grew more adventurous, producing some works without any reference to tonality. In 1910, he wrote *Theory of Harmony* (*Harmonielehre*), which became one of the most influential texts on music theory in history. Some of his music was well received in his time. In February 1913, the Viennese audience gave the premier of his *Gurrelieder* a standing ovation, and the composer received a laurel crown. However, a few weeks later, on March 31, a concert including works by

Schoenberg, Zimlinsky, and Mahler caused a scandal. One contemporary newspaper reported that, after Schoenberg's Chamber Symphony No. 1 in E major, "one could hear the shrill sound of door keys among the violent clapping and in the second gallery the first fight of the evening began." When audience members clambered onto the stage to box the conductor's ears during Berg's *Alternberg Lieder*, Schoenberg interrupted the performance and threatened them with police interference. Fights broke out, and the concert had to be canceled. It became known as *Watschenkonzert* (ear-boxing concert). Unperturbed, Schoenberg went on to create the twelve-note composition technique (also known as serialism), which became one of the most polemic systems in the music world.

Mariko Kato

Date March 31, 1913

Country Austria

Why It's Key Despite infuriating the audience with its experimental nature, the program of this concert paved the way for a new era in twentieth-century music.

Fact Austrian (and later American) composer Arnold Schoenberg (1874–1951) is known as the pioneer of the atonal motivic development in music.

Key Cultural Event
Stravinsky's *The Rite of Spring* premier causes riots

Born in 1882 in Oranienbaum, Russia, Igor Stravinsky established himself as an avant-garde composer, fusing folk song-inspired melodies with exuberant orchestration and primitive rhythms. After the ballet *The Firebird* was rapturously received in 1910, Stravinsky became more audacious and innovative, and completed another ballet, *The Rite of Spring*, three years later, whose premier became one of the most notorious scandals in musical history. As the first notes rang out in the highest register of the bassoon, French composer Camille Saint-Saens walked out, outraged by the misuse of the instrument. Catcalls and fights erupted and the auditorium lights were flicked on and off in an attempt to calm the crowd. It was not only the revolutionary music that shocked the audience, but also the uncomfortable theme of pagan sacrifice

illustrated by outrageous costumes and choreography. Yet, the music stoically survived to the end of the performance. As the commotion increased, conductor Pierre Monteux carried on unperturbed. Stravinsky later commented: "It is still almost incredible to me that he actually brought the orchestra through to the end."

Despite news of the riots spreading ahead of subsequent performances, the ballet began to be received more warmly. After its first concert performance almost a year later, an ecstatic crowd carried Stravinsky through the auditorium and into the Place de la Trinité. The work marked the beginning of modernism in music, and as the audience's ears adapted to it, its name became synonymous with musical reinvention and avant-garde masterpiece.

Mariko Kato

Date May 29, 1913

Country France

Why It's Key The premier of *The Rite of Spring* (*Le Sacre du Printemp*) at the Théatre des Champs-Elysées in Paris is considered the most notorious event in musical history.

opposite Scenes from the groundbreaking ballet *The Rite of Spring*.

Key Political Event
Davison dies under the King's horse

Emily Wilding Davison was educated at Royal Holloway College and in 1895, achieved a first class honors in English at the Oxford University entrance examination for women. Oxford degrees were closed to women so she could not graduate, but she became a teacher and continued to study, gaining a degree from London University in 1908.

In 1906, Davison joined the militant Women's Social and Political Union (WSPU) and two years later acted as a steward for the union's first major procession to London's Hyde Park. By 1910, she had given up teaching to work full-time for the WSPU. Davison undertook numerous illegal activities to publicize the cause, including assault and setting fire to pillar-boxes. During her eight separate spells in prison, she resorted to hunger strikes and was subjected to solitary confinement, force-feeding, and had a hosepipe turned on her in her cell.

At the age of forty, Emily Davison came to public attention when she stepped in front of the King's horse at the Derby while it was in mid-race. The jockey could not avoid hitting her, leaving her unconscious, and she died four days later. It is unclear whether Emily intended to commit suicide or simply to attach the union's tricolor ribbon to the horse's bridle as a form of protest.

Thousands of suffragettes lined the streets when her coffin was transported through London before its final journey to the family grave in Northumberland. Davison's epitaph of "Deeds, Not Words" is the motto of the WSPU.

Michelle Higgs

Date June 4, 1913

Country UK

Why It's Key Through her defiant act, Emily Davison became a martyr for the suffragette movement, but failed to sway political or public opinion to her cause.

opposite Emily Davison killed by King George V's horse, Anmer.

Key Political Event
Formation of the Ulster Volunteer Force

The blood used by some to sign the Ulster Solemn League and Covenant was barely dry when the Ulster Volunteer Force (UVF) was inaugurated to coordinate armed resistance to Home Rule (a measure of autonomy) in Ireland. As the likelihood of the introduction of Home Rule increased, so too did the concerns of a substantial minority in Ireland. This (largely Protestant) minority, located mainly in the northeast of Ireland, were concerned that the introduction of a Home Rule parliament in Dublin, dominated by a Catholic nationalist majority, would be detrimental to both their economic well-being, and religious and civil liberties.

Allied with the Conservative party in Britain, the UVF drilled and armed, but were uncertain whether their efforts would ultimately be directed against nationalist or government forces. Nevertheless, their preparations (with the aid of ex-members of the British Army) were impressive. The acquisition of approximately twenty thousand rifles and two million rounds of ammunition, and the founding of cavalry, ambulance, and motorcycle corps all contributed to the creation of a serious potential fighting force capable of plunging Britain and Ireland into civil war.

Nationalists responded by setting up the Irish Volunteer Force along similar lines. The threat of large-scale bloodshed in Ireland was averted with the outbreak of World War I. The majority of both forces enlisted in the British army in the hope that the government would reward their loyalty by supporting their respective political aims.

Denis Casey

Date September 28, 1913

Country Ireland/UK

Why It's Key The founding of the Ulster Volunteer Force exacerbated divisions in British society over Irish demands for independence.

Key Cultural Event
Ford institutes the assembly line

In the early twentieth century, "scientific management" took hold in industrialized nations in response to the ideas of mechanical engineer Frederick Winslow Taylor (1856–1915). Taylor speeded up manufacturing by timing worker actions to eliminate wasted movements and redesigning tools to work quickly. Although Henry Ford (1863–1947), the world's leading automobile manufacturer, was not an advocate of Taylorism, he understood the importance of increasing production to fulfill consumer demands and maximize profits.

By December 1, 1913, Ford had turned his plant into an assembly line. At designated work stations, employees remained in place while automobiles and parts came to them at waist level. As a worker completed a designated task, the automobile moved to the next worker. The introduction of the assembly line cut production time from 12.5 to 1.5 work hours, and Ford boasted that his workers could turn out a Model T every 24 seconds. In the first year of operation, production rose from 82,000 to 189,000. By 1923, Ford was producing 2,000,000 Model Ts a year.

Assembly lines did not call for skilled workers because employees became expert through repetition. The monotony of the work and the loss of individual control led to major problems with employee morale, including excessive absenteeism and high turnover. However, within two years of Ford raising wages to an unprecedented US$5 a day, turnover dropped from 48 to 6.4 per cent. In 1926, Ford introduced the eight-hour, five-day workweek, giving employees more leisure time to enjoy their new Fords.
Elizabeth R. Purdy

Date December 1, 1913

Country USA

Why It's Key The introduction of the assembly line revolutionized the manufacturing process, allowing workers around the globe to increase production and profits to unprecedented levels.

opposite The final assembly line at the Ford Motor Company's Highland Park plant.

Key Cultural Event
First successful non-direct blood transfusion

Blood transfusions were by no means a new idea prior to 1914. Indeed, a blood transfusion was recorded as early as 1492, when it was carried out in Rome on Pope Innocent VII, who had suffered an apoplectic stroke. Though unsuccessful, this was the start of a long, varied exploration for success.

Early experiments carried on in the 1600s used animals in blood transfusions. In 1665, Oxford physician Richard Lower successfully transferred blood from one dog to another. However, in 1678, transfusions from animals to humans were deemed unsuccessful when, after numerous experiments, it became patently clear that the two diverse fluids could not mix.

In 1818, James Blundell, a British obstetrician, carried out the first successful human-to-human transfusion on a post-partum mother who was hemorrhaging, taking blood from her husband's arm and injecting it into the woman. He performed a further ten transfusions around this period with a success rate of 50 per cent, and published his results.

One of the main problems with human-to-human blood transfusions during the nineteenth century was the clotting of blood. However, the discovery in 1914 that sodium citrate could be used as an anti-coagulant allowed for the longer preservation of blood. Blood could theoretically be taken from a donor in one location and administered in another. On March 27, 1914, with the knowledge of these findings, Belgian doctor Albert Hustin performed the first successful non-direct blood transfusion, which eventually led to the storage of blood and modern blood banks.
Kerry Duffy

Date March 27, 1914

Country Belgium

Why It's Key The first successful non-direct blood transfusion meant that transfusions could occur without the donor having to be present, and allowed for the blood banking system that is used today.

Fact Hustin's non-direct transfusion led to R. Weil's demonstration of the feasibility of refrigerating and storing anti-coagulated blood in 1915.

Key Political Event
Third Home Rule Bill

While the great W. E. Gladstone publicly declared "my mission is to pacify Ireland," his political successor and Liberal Prime Minister, H. H. Asquith, simply snarled "wait and see" when questioned regarding his Irish policy. Asquith, however, came closer to solving the "Irish Question" than his former chief ever did.

For over thirty years, Home Rule (a measure of autonomy) was the demand of Irish nationalists. Gladstone twice failed to secure it, but the breaking of the Lords' parliamentary veto during the "People's Budget" controversy removed a major stumbling block to Irish and Liberal aspirations.

The arming of both unionists and nationalists, coupled with the polarization of British politics over Home Rule, brought Britain closer to civil war than any period since the eighteenth century. Asquith's cool political acumen led him to play for time and a settlement was finally reached as the storm clouds of war were breaking over Europe in the summer of 1914.

A compromise was enacted whereby Home Rule was introduced for all of Ireland, but an undefined Ulster was temporarily excluded and each Ulster county entitled to opt in or out at the end of the exclusion period. The bill was immediately suspended for the duration of the upcoming war, which was expected to be over by Christmas.

The war dragged on for over four years by which time Asquith's government had fallen and Home Rule was no longer enough to satisfy Irish demands.
Denis Casey

Date May 25, 1914

Country Ireland/UK

Why It's Key After more than thirty years of political campaigning, Irish constitutional nationalists seemed to have secured a measure of independence for Ireland, but were overtaken by political events.

Key Political Event
Assassination of Archduke Franz Ferdinand

In June of 1914, Archduke Franz Ferdinand, heir to the Austro-Hungarian Empire, visited the Bosnian capital of Sarajevo to observe military maneuvers and open a museum. Bosnia was then an official part of the Austro-Hungarian Empire, having been annexed in 1908. However, the desire for political independence remained strong among Bosnia's large Serb population, which led to the formation of nationalistic societies devoted to the liberation of Slavic peoples from Austro-Hungarian rule. One such group, the "Black Hand," plotted to assassinate the archduke during his visit.

In the morning of June 28, an attempt to attack the archduke's motorcade with a hand grenade failed. The conspirators dispersed, and the archduke's party continued to their destination. But later that afternoon, in an amazing coincidence, the archduke's car made a wrong turn and stopped directly in front of conspirator Gavrilo Princip, who was eating at a local delicatessen. Princip acted swiftly and fired two bullets into Ferdinand's car, killing both the archduke and his wife.

The event sparked outrage throughout Europe. Austria-Hungary, already looking for an opportunity to undercut the increasingly powerful Serbian state, blamed Serbia for the assassination and quickly mobilized its army. Germany, an ally of Austria-Hungary, rushed to its defense, while France and Russia, wary of German and Austro-Hungarian aggression, mobilized their forces in response. The Great Powers of twentieth century Europe, bound by a web of treaties and fearful of preemptive strikes, were all swept up in the gathering conflict. Open war broke out in July of 1914.
Justin Norris

Date June 28, 1914

Country Bosnia

Why It's Key This assassination was the direct cause of World War I and one of the most significant geo-political events of the twentieth century.

opposite Gavrilo Princip under arrest following the shooting.

Key Political Event
Alliance system leads to war

At the beginning of the twentieth century, political control of Europe was divided among a small group of "Great Powers": nations – often empires – that culturally, militarily, and economically dominated the continent. These heavyweights maintained a fragile alliance system, characterized by a continual shift of allegiances, and diplomatic and military maneuvering. Motivated by geography, colonial ambitions, historical enmities, and internal political concerns, each nation strategized to extend its own sphere of influence while limiting and minimizing that of its opponents.

Germany, Austria-Hungary, and Italy were mutual allies – forming the so-called "Triple Alliance." On the opposing side, Russia, France, and England formed an alliance in an effort to counter growing German influence. Ambitious and mistrustful of their neighbors,

the Great Powers began a race to industrialize, to stockpile arms, and to build complex war-strategies, creating an extremely unstable political climate.

The assassination of Archduke Ferdinand (heir to the Austro-Hungarian Empire) by Serbian nationalists destroyed this delicate balance. Austria-Hungary was eager for an opportunity to limit growing Serbian influence. Germany backed Austria-Hungary, while Russia mobilized in Serbia's defence. Germany declared war on Russia, and France, Russia's ally, was soon in the conflict as well. Finally, Germany invaded Belgium, and Great Britain, having sworn to protect Belgian neutrality, declared war on Germany in return. The race toward war, once commenced, proved impossible to stop, and a conflict began that would take 20 million lives.
Justin Norris

Date July 28, 1914

Country France, Germany, Austria-Hungary, Russia, UK

Why It's Key The geo-political climate of nineteenth century Europe set the stage for one of the bloodiest conflicts of the twentieth century.

Key Political Event
Opening of the Panama Canal

After decades of toil and as many as 30,000 deaths from yellow fever, malaria, and other hazards endemic to the swampy tropical region, the 82-kilometer Panama Canal opened to traffic on August 15, 1914. The Spanish had considered building a canal near the same site as early as the sixteenth century, but the enterprise remained a pipe dream until 1881, when a French team led by Ferdinand de Lesseps, renowned architect of the Suez Canal, began work on what was originally to be a sea-level inter-oceanic channel. Unprepared for the vicissitudes of climate and terrain and ravaged by illness, the French-run project floundered and had to be abandoned in 1889. Authorized by the Spooner Act to take control of the unfinished canal, U.S. president Theodore Roosevelt played a key role in forcing Panama's independence

from Colombia in 1903, and immediately negotiated the Hay-Buneau-Varilla Treaty, which established U.S. control "in perpetuity" over the canal zone.

Having assessed the failure of the French effort, Roosevelt's engineers decided on a lake-and-lock type canal. Meanwhile, medical professionals took precautions to reduce the incidence of mosquito-borne illnesses that had decimated Lesseps' work crews. At its height, the canal project employed as many as 40,000 laborers, most of them drawn from Martinique, Guadeloupe, and other Caribbean islands. The canal transformed international shipping routes and remained under the firm grip of the United States until the 1977 Carter-Torrijos treaty arranged for its transfer to Panamanian control on December 31, 2000.
Geoffrey Schullenberger

Date August 15, 1914

Country Panama

Why It's Key The completion of the canal fulfilled the centuries-old dream of a "middle passage" connecting the Atlantic and the Pacific oceans, and affirmed the commercial, political, and military dominance of the United States in the western hemisphere.

Key Political Event
German Zeppelins bomb British towns

Zeppelins were huge 190-meter-long airships, named after their inventor, Count von Zeppelin, who had built his first successful model in 1900. Before World War I, they were used as luxurious, civilian airships. However, when war broke out, Germany recognized the potential of Zeppelins for reconnaissance and employed them from the outset to gather information from the enemy.

With the deadlock on the Western Front, Germany stepped up its use of the airships to bomb British towns and cities. The first air raid by German Zeppelins took place on January 19 around the east coast of Britain. Bombs were dropped on Great Yarmouth, King's Lynn, Cromer, and Sheringham. This first raid caused structural damage and a number of civilian casualties, including the deaths of four people.

Zeppelin raids continued until 1917, by which time they had killed 556 people and injured a further 1,357. Despite these casualties, 77 of the total 115 Zeppelins had been put out of action; Explosive shells could destroy the airships when the hydrogen that powered them was set alight.

While Zeppelins posed a very real threat to civilians, the accuracy and success of their bombing raids was hampered by problems with navigation, bad weather, and poor night visibility. Their small bombs were never intended to hit military targets, merely to cause panic in the population and jeopardize the war effort. Although minor disruption was caused, the Zeppelins never succeeded in weakening the morale of British civilians.

Michelle Higgs

Date January 19, 1915

Country UK

Why It's Key Zeppelin air raids during World War I brought death and destruction to ordinary British civilians in their own homes.

Key Cultural Event
First transcontinental telephone call

Using a replica of the first telephone he invented almost forty years earlier, Alexander Graham Bell made the first transcontinental telephone call from the offices of the American Telephone and Telegraph Company (AT&T) at 195 Broadway, Manhattan, New York City. He called his assistant, Thomas A. Watson, who was in San Francisco. They replicated the first telephone conversation they had in March 1876 with Bell saying "Mr Watson, come here. I want you." Watson replied saying it would take him a week as he was so far away.

Bell had established AT&T in 1885 specifically to build and operate a long-distance telephone network. The first line between New York and Philadelphia was completed by the end of that year. Seven years later, the company opened its first long-distance line

connecting New York and Chicago. The circuit could only handle one call at a time and cost US$9 for the first five minutes.

Although AT&T had completed the construction of the first transcontinental telephone line linking America's east and west coasts in June 1914, the historic telephone call by Bell to Watson on January 25 was timed to coincide with the Panama Pacific International Exposition in San Francisco.

The new transcontinental service was available to all AT&T's customers, but at US$20.70 for the first three minutes, it was too expensive for the majority. AT&T continued at the forefront of telecommunications, developing the first transatlantic service in 1927 and a transpacific service in 1934.

Michelle Higgs

Date January 25, 1915

Country USA

Why It's Key This milestone in telecommunications allowed individuals to speak to each other across the country, and led to further important developments, such as transatlantic and transpacific services.

Key Cultural Event
Birth of a Nation released

Silent film director D. W. Griffith was an essential creative force in the early history of cinema. Rejecting theatrical conventions, Griffith pioneered the use of close-ups and cross cutting between multiple events to heighten viewers' emotional involvement. He was an established filmmaker at the age of forty, with hundreds of titles to his name, when he made *Birth of a Nation*, the historic achievement for which he is best remembered and, in many circles, denounced. Based on the novel *The Clansmen* by Thomas Dixon, Griffith's film takes place during the American Civil War, following storylines featuring the north and south. Ultimately, the accomplishment of Griffith's directorial finesse has been overshadowed by the movie's blatant racism. The Ku Klux Klan represent the main protagonists of the film, portrayed as heroes for their victory over the Black Reconstruction. Consequently, the African-American characters come across as rapists and savages, utterly devoid of any redeemable qualities.

While various progressive groups sought to ban the film, its success was inevitable. The story appealed to white, upper class Americans as the movies, which were previously popular among working-class citizens, had never done before. In terms of production scale, it was the first epic movie, shot on a budget of US$60,000 and running two-and-a-half hours, which was unheard of at the time. Griffith tried to make penance for the outrage caused by *Birth of a Nation* with his next film, the sprawling social drama *Intolerance*, but the damage to his legacy was irrevocable.
Eric Kohn

Date March 3, 1915

Country USA

Why It's Key D. W. Griffith's monumental epic revealed the power of the movies as a supreme storytelling format, but its racist plot showed the danger of their mainstream appeal.

Fact Prior to directing *Birth of a Nation*, Griffith made nearly 450 films for the production company Biograph.

Key Political Event
Poison gas used at Ypres

At around 5 p.m. on April 22, 1915, German troops began another in a series of bombardments over the French trenches in the ongoing Battle of Gravenstafel, the second of four battles that made up the campaign known as Second Ypres. An English soldier, watching from a distance, noted something curious: "a low cloud of yellow-gray smoke or vapor, and, underlying everything, a dull, confused murmur."

The "confused murmur" was the sound of French troops dying from the yellow cloud of chlorine gas that the Germans had packed into more than 5,700 artillery shells – 168 tons in all. It floated over four miles of trench lines. In ten minutes, half of the 10,000 French troops in those trenches were dead.

The use of poison gas in warfare had been forbidden by the Hague Convention of 1899 and 1907, but once the gates were opened at Second Ypres, all sides turned to chemicals to advance their military goals. Chlorine, phosogene, and mustard gas led to 1.2 million casualties between 1915 and 1918, and were responsible for more then 91,000 battlefield deaths. In 1925, with the horrors of the Great War still fresh in their minds, the international community again came together to ban the use of chemical weapons. Most nations still abide by the convention.

Ironically, the gas attack at Ypres failed. Surviving French troops broke and ran for safety, but the Germans were worried about the remaining gas cloud. By the time the air cleared, English and Canadian troops had regained almost all the abandoned territory.
Heather Michon

Date April 22, 1915

Country Belgium

Why It's Key The first use of poison gas in warfare allowed countries to kill large numbers of soldiers with very little effort.

Key Cultural Event
McCrae writes "In Flanders Fields" at Ypres

Canadian physician John McCrae fought on the Western Front in 1914, but later served as a surgeon attached to the First Field Artillery Brigade in Belgium. An author of several medical texts, Lieutenant Colonel McCrae spent seventeen days treating injured soldiers in the Ypres salient, his patients including Canadians, British, Indians, French, and Germans. He later wrote of this ordeal: "I wish I could embody on paper some of the varied sensations of that seventeen days... Seventeen days of Hades!"

The day after witnessing the gruesome death of a friend and former student, Lieutenant Alexis Helmer, in a shell burst on May 2, 1915, McCrae composed "In Flanders Fields" in an ambulance beside the Canal de l'Yser, north of Ypres, looking out onto wild poppies growing in the nearby cemetery.

He showed it to a young soldier who was with him, who declared that the poem was "exactly an exact description of the scene in front of us." Despite this, McCrae himself was dissatisfied with it. The poem was only published after another officer sent it to a number of English newspapers, and *Punch* printed it on December 8, 1915.

McCrae died of pneumonia while on active duty in 1918, and *In Flanders Fields and Other Poems* was published the following year. Today, most Remembrance Day ceremonies feature this poem in some form, and its reference to poppies has made them a symbol of World War I.

Mariko Kato

Date May 3, 1915

Country Belgium

Why It's Key "In Flanders Fields" is the most anthologized poem about World War I.

Fact "In Flanders Fields," a fifteen-line poem written in memory of soldiers who died in World War I, is composed in the form of a French rondeau.

Key Disaster
The sinking of the *Lusitania*

The sinking of the British Cunard line's *Lusitania* by the German submarine U-20 is considered to have been a major contributory factor to United States' entry into World War I. The vessel, a 32,000-ton passenger liner, was launched in 1906, and won the Blue Riband for the fastest transatlantic crossing the following year. With the outbreak of war the British Navy requisitioned many civilian ships, but *Lusitania* continued to act as a passenger liner between Britain and the United States.

On May 7, 1915, a single torpedo from the U-20 sank the *Lusitania* off the south coast of Ireland. Some survivors were rescued by two nearby fishing boats but despite this and the heroic efforts of the local Courtmacsherry lifeboat, whose crew bravely rowed to the scene in vain, almost 1,200 of the 2,000 on board perished.

A second explosion, following the initial torpedo blast, and the rapid sinking of such a large vessel in less than twenty minutes, have given rise to numerous conspiracy theories. Chief among these was that the *Lusitania* was transporting large quantities of materials in aid of the British war effort. Although the *Lusitania* was carrying some ammunition, the second explosion probably originated from the steam propulsion system, while flaws in the ship's design also contributed to its rapid demise.

Numerous dives have resulted in the deterioration of the *Lusitania* and the wreck is now designated a national monument by the Irish government.

Denis Casey

Date May 7, 1915

Country Ireland

Why It's Key The deaths of U.S. citizens on the *Lusitania* helped contribute to the entry of the United States into World War I.

Key Political Event
Japan presents Twenty-One Demands to China

Through its victories in the First Sino-Japanese War and the Russo-Japanese War, Japan had become the latest Great Power, and now extended its territorial interest to China. With the establishment of the new Chinese Republic, Japan saw the chance to secure influence over its mining and metallurgical potential.

On January 18, 1915, Japanese Prime Minister Shigenobu Okuma and his Foreign Minister Takaaki Kato drafted a list of twenty-one demands and presented it secretly to Chinese President Yuan Shih-kai. The demands included the confirmation of Japan's domination over the Shandong Province and southern Manchuria, with rights to settle and control transport systems, and the appointment of Japanese political, financial, and military advisors to the Chinese government. They also bound China against conceding further coastal or island control to any power except Japan. If achieved, the demands would reduce China to a Japanese protectorate. Shih-kai leaked the content to the European powers, hoping that they would protest, and initially rejected the proposal. However, he was forced to accept a revised version when Japan posed an ultimatum, threatening war. Final treaties were signed on May 25.

The Twenty-One Demands sparked condemnation from other major powers and acute anti-Japanese sentiments in China. It led to the May Fourth Movement four years later, when university students stirred a mass political movement against the Treaty of Versailles, which transferred Germany's rights in Shandong to Japan.

Mariko Kato

Date January 18, 1915

Country China

Why It's Key The unfair demands – made in secret – ignited Chinese hostility toward Japan.

Fact At this time, Western powers were heavily involved with the war in Europe, and Japan had declared war on Germany in August 1914.

Key Political Event
Armenian genocide begins

In 1914, some two million Armenians were living within the sprawling, faltering Ottoman Empire. Three years later, their numbers had fallen by 1.5 million, victims of a systematic genocide.

Christian Armenians had long been seen as a problem in the Muslim-dominated Ottoman Empire. Like other ethnic minorities, Armenians were subject to discrimination and occasional pogroms. However, the beginning of World War I gave Ottoman leaders the opportunity to vilify Armenians as enemies within, supporters of the Russians, while good Ottoman citizens supported the Germans. On May 29, 1915, the Ottoman government passed the Tehcir Law, giving it authority to deport anyone deemed a threat to national security.

Had it been only the deportation of a few malcontents, the Armenians might have suffered, but survived. Instead, the Tehcir Law, along with the Law of Expropriation and Confiscation, gave the Ottomans the power to round up hundreds of thousands of Armenians, seize their property, herd them into concentration camps, and dispose of them en masse, either by forced deportation or by wholesale killing. The Nazis would later adapt their techniques of mass gassing, poisoning, and drowning.

Nearly a century after the fact, the event Theodore Roosevelt called "the greatest crime of the war" remains a source of international contention. Despite all evidence to the contrary, the Republic of Turkey still rejects any labeling of the event as a genocide. Twenty-three countries and forty U.S. states have adopted resolutions acknowledging it as such.

Heather Michon

Date May 29, 1915

Country Turkey

Why It's Key One of the first modern genocides displaced or massacred an estimated 1.5 million Armenians during World War I.

opposite Armenian refugees fleeing from their oppressors in Syria, 1915.

Key Political Event
Invention of the Fokker E1

World War I initiated a rapid development of the airplane as a military tool. Planes were initially unarmed and used strictly for reconnaissance. Tales are told of enemy pilots smiling and waving as they passed each other in the air. However, airmen soon began attacking each other with bricks, handguns, and grenades, and efforts to design armed planes quickly followed. A major limitation on early warplanes was the difficulty of combining an accurate weapon with a front-mounted propeller; in order to avoid shooting off the propeller, machine-guns had to be angled sideways, which made them notoriously difficult to aim. In 1915, a French engineer developed a solution: a synchronizing device that allowed bullets to be fired through the blades of a propeller. This device was used successfully on a French plane, until mechanical failure forced the plane to land in enemy territory. Despite the pilot's attempt to burn his aircraft, the Germans captured the new technology. Anthony Fokker, a Dutch airplane designer working for Germany, replicated the interrupter mechanism and fitted it to a plane of his own design: the Fokker E1.

The new design gave Germany a season of overwhelming air superiority – the so-called "Fokker Scourge." The allies eventually responded with improved designs of their own, and consequently, the air progressively became more than a place for gathering information; it became a new battlefield. The technological and tactical innovations of World War I set the course for future conflicts, where air superiority would increasingly become the deciding factor.
Justin Norris

Date July 1, 1915

Country Germany

Why It's Key Technological innovations paved the way for the rapid growth of aerial combat and the modernization of military tactics.

Key Cultural Event
Leo Frank is lynched

At 3 a.m. on April 27, 1913, the body of a thirteen-year-old worker named Mary Phagan was found in the elevator shaft of the National Pencil Factory in Atlanta, Georgia. She had been raped and murdered earlier in the day, while outside, the city was celebrating Confederate Memorial Day holiday with parades and parties.

Suspicion focused on Leo Frank, the co-owner/manager of the factory. He was the last one known to have seen Phagan that day, when she came to his office for her pay: $1.20 for 10 hours work. Frank was a thin, nervous-looking New Yorker. As a Yankee and a Jew, it was easy for investigators to believe the tale told by a black workman named Jim Conely: that Frank had forced him to help carry the girl's lifeless body to the basement that day. He was arrested on April 29.

Frank was sentenced to death on October 10, 1913, but public outcry convinced the governor to commute the sentence to life imprisonment on June 21, 1915. Less than two months later, a group of twenty-five men seized Frank from the Millegeville Work Farm. He was found hanging dead from a tree near Marietta the next morning.

In 1982, 82-year old Alonzo Mann admitted that he had seen Jim Conely – alone – dragging Mary Phagan's body to the basement on the day of the murder. Conely had threatened the then thirteen-year-old Mann with death if he told. Leo Frank was officially pardoned on March 6, 1986.
Heather Michon

Date August 17, 1915

Country USA

Why It's Key Frank's death led to the founding of the Jewish Anti-Defamation League and the reinvigoration of the Ku Klux Klan.

Key Cultural Event
The gasoline-electric hybrid car

Buyers of gasoline-electric hybrid cars at the very end of the twentieth century may have thought they were acquiring a cutting-edge technology. In fact, the new hybrids were merely refined versions of an old idea. During the first years of the automobile boom, around 1900, makers of steam, electric, and petroleum-powered cars competed for customers' favor. Several inventors in Europe and North America pursued the idea of combining gasoline and electric propulsion, in order to minimize the vibrations, smell, and noise of the former while improving on the limited power and range of the latter.

The Woods Motor Vehicle Company of Chicago, an established producer of electric automobiles, unveiled its Dual Power car in 1916. It was a full hybrid, able to run on its four-cylinder gasoline engine, its 48-volt DC electric motor, or both, and it had a battery recharged by regenerative braking. Unfortunately, at US$2,650 it was priced far above many gasoline-only rivals, it was heavy, not especially reliable, and its top speed of thirty-five miles per hour failed to impress customers. Nor did they much care about its lower exhaust emissions or its impressive fuel economy at a time of cheap petroleum. Both the car and the Woods Company were gone from the market by 1918. Propitious circumstances for a hybrid car would not return for another eight decades.
Brian Ladd

Date 1916

Country USA

Why It's Key Hybrid cars were nothing new in the year 2000!

Key Political Event
Battle of Verdun

Verdun, like so many of the battles of World War I, saw enormous loss of life, yet had an uncertain effect on the course of the war itself. One million casualties were accrued and forty million shells fired during the ten-month engagement. The savage fighting became a symbol of French endurance, yet it resulted in almost no change to the position of the combatants' front lines.

The talismanic nature of Verdun was central to the battle, as its strategic importance was minimal, a point recognized by both sides. The true aim of the Verdun offensive, launched by General Erich von Falkenhayn in February 1916, was to induce a massive attrition of French forces: France was to be bled dry on the banks of the Meuse. Although Verdun's military value was negligible, its psychological significance was clear to all. It had been a military camp since Roman times and recently had been the last great French fortress to fall during the Franco-Prussian war of 1870–1871. It was felt that if Verdun was captured again, history would repeat itself. Consequently, von Falkenhayn knew that the French would defend Verdun at all costs.

The French realized that Verdun was a trap but nonetheless felt obliged to pour reinforcements into its defense, at enormous cost. The spirited French resistance led by Marshal Pétain succeeded in repelling the Germans but the mutual slaughter was devastating.
Denis Casey

Date February 21, 1916

Country France

Why It's Key The battle of Verdun was a battle of attrition intended to break the French army but which became a symbol of French defiance.

Key Political Event
Svkes-Picot Agreement

Long before the conclusion of World War I, it was clear to Western powers that the vast Ottoman Empire – corrupt and over-extended – would not survive the conflict. The fate of the entire Middle East, rich with oil and strategic ports, lay in the balance, and control of these lands was of great interest to leaders across Europe.

Beginning in November 1915, French diplomat François-Georges Picot and British diplomat Mark Sykes began a secret correspondence that attempted nothing less than to redraw the map of the Middle East. Under the resulting Sykes-Picot Agreement, formalized on May 16, 1916, Britain would claim modern-day Jordan, most of Iraq, and the port at Haifa. France would gain control of southeast Turkey, northern Iraq, Syria, and Lebanon. Palestine would be jointly administered, and Russia would be granted the city of Constantinople and several Armenian-dominated districts.

Portions of the Sykes-Picot Agreement would later be annulled by other diplomatic correspondences, the Russian Revolution, and the negotiations over the Treaty of Paris at the end of World War I, but it deftly illustrated the complexities of Western interest in Arab lands; a theme that would play out countless times throughout the twentieth century, and continues to be of critical importance in modern geopolitical thought.
Heather Michon

Date May 16, 1919

Country UK/France

Why It's Key An early attempt by the West to redraw the map of the Middle East and exert control over the Arab world.

Fact The agreement conflicted with the promise that the British had already made to Husayn ibn Ali, Sharil of Mecca, which was that the Arabs would receive a significant share of the territory won if they launched a revolt in Hejaz against the Ottoman rulers.

Key Political Event
Battle of the Somme

Perhaps more than any other event, the Battle of the Somme has come to epitomize the stationary slaughter of World War I. In the space of five months, between July and November 1916, the battle produced over one million casualties along a fifty-kilometre line between Péronne and Amiens, with no appreciable gain for either side. Although 1916 as a whole was a year of unimaginable slaughter, the Somme holds a particular place in British history due to the heavy losses they incurred.

Although an Anglo-French operation had originally been planned, the enormous French losses at Verdun meant that when bombardment of German lines began on June 23, the Somme offensive was essentially a British affair. During the course of a single week, over 1.5 million shells were rained down on German positions before the first wave of British troops advanced. The vast quantities of shells fired were intended to obliterate the German positions, enabling the British army to merely walk unopposed across no-man's land. It failed.

As 100,000 heavily laden British soldiers advanced on July 1, they were met with a murderous hail of machine gun fire from the German lines. During that day alone the British army suffered 60,000 killed or wounded. Intense slaughter continued on both sides for five more months, and the Somme fittingly became known to the German army as *das Blutbad* (the blood bath).
Denis Casey

Date July 1, 1916

Country France

Why It's Key A futile attempt to break the stalemate of World War I – which resulted in enormous casualties.

Key Cultural Event
Ball recites the first Dada manifesto

The Dadaist movement began at the same time as World War I, its participants reacting against bourgeois values – which they believed to be the cause of the war – and the the barbarism of the human atrocities committed in the name of war. They dismissed the concept of conformity, both in society and in art – hence making the classification of Dadaism as an organized movement an inherent paradox. Dadaism was "anti-art," embracing chaos and irrationality, and rejecting all traditional aesthetics and coherent sensibilities in visual arts, literature, and music. The term Dada itself is believed to be a nonsensical word.

On July 14, 1916, German author and poet Hugo Ball recited the first Dada manifesto at the Dadaists' nightclub *Cabaret Voltaire* in Zurich. In the manifesto, read to an audience of fellow Dadaists, Ball outlined Dadaist philosophy in three points: "1. Dada is international in perspective and seeks to bridge differences; 2. Dada is antagonistic toward established society in the modern avant-garde, Bohemian tradition of the *épater-le-bourgeois* posture; and 3. Dada is a new tendency in art that seeks to change conventional attitudes and practices in aesthetics, society, and morality." His manifesto was the first of other important Dadaist manifestos, including that of Romanian poet Tristan Tzara in 1918.

Even though the movement had died away by the beginning of World War II, it is regarded as the starting point of postmodernism in art, influencing later styles such as surrealism.

Mariko Kato

Date July 14, 1916

Country Switzerland

Why It's Key It was the first official declaration of the Dadaist movement, paving the way for other important manifestos.

Fact Dadaism is a cultural movement that began in Zürich, Switzerland, during World War I.

Key Political Event
First use of tanks

By 1916, the Western Front had become a stagnant but deadly war of attrition. Both sides had established well-fortified trenches defended by barbed wire, artillery, and machine guns. Even massive attacks against these defensive lines brought only minimal territorial gains at a cost of thousands of casualties.

Both sides sought a technological advantage to end the stalemate and breach the enemy's defensive line. In concept, the tank was a perfect solution: a self-propelled armored vehicle, capable of traversing treacherous terrain, breaching barbed wire, and withstanding the machine guns that were proving so deadly against infantry assaults. The British Army was the first to transform this concept into a battlefield reality, fielding forty-nine Mark I tanks on September 15, 1916, at the Battle of Flers-Courcellette. The results of this experiment were both impressive and disappointing. While mechanical failure prevented all but fifteen of the units from entering the field, those tanks that did engage in battle contributed to significant advances by the Allies, including the capture of several German-held villages.

The tank did not single-handedly decide the fortunes of World War I, as the British High Command had hoped it would. The technology was too new and the science of tank warfare still undeveloped. However, the eventual advances in technology and strategy that followed the birth of the tank would also end the age of static trench warfare altogether – bringing in a new era of swift-moving, mobile combat that would come to characterize World War II.

Justin Norris

Date September 15, 1916

Country France

Why It's Key Despite initial unreliability, tanks would lead to a paradigm shift in the nature of modern warfare, rendering the trench-style fighting of World War I obsolete.

Fact The name "tank" comes from the fact that the British Army listed the pieces being shipped to the continent as being "Water Tanks" in order to maintain secrecy.

Key Person
Margaret Sanger

Margaret Sanger, who opened the first birth control clinic in the United States, is considered one of the most important figures of the twentieth century. As a nurse in New York City, Sanger often saw women from poor families who could not support the children they had year after year, and who died or grew old before their time from repeated pregnancies. Sanger realized that women would never be free until they could control their reproductive lives; however, most states prohibited the dispensing of birth control information and devices.

After several physicians refused to help establish a birth control clinic, Sanger launched it with only her sister, Ethel Byrne, and her secretary. The clinic opened on October 16, 1916, in a curtained storefront window in Brooklyn, New York. By 5 p.m., 140 women had arrived. Over the next several days, 464 women sought help. On the tenth day, a well-dressed woman was immediately identified as an undercover policewoman. The next day, the women were arrested, and the clinic was closed.

When American women were given suffrage rights in 1920, Sanger was allowed to operate in a less hostile but still precarious environment. In 1924, she opened the Birth Control Clinical Research Bureau where women were seen by a licensed physician. In 1942, the name was changed to Planned Parenthood Federation of America. Planned Parenthood became an international organization in 1953, and, thanks to Margaret Sanger's efforts, most governments now recognize the importance of women's rights and family planning.
Elizabeth R. Purdy

Date October 16, 1916
Born/Died 1879–1966
Nationality American
Why It's Key Sanger's birth control clinic brought public attention to the fledgling birth control movement and paved the way for the recognition of the constitutional rights of American women to control their own bodies.

Key Political Event
Assassination of Grigori Rasputin

Characterized alternately as saint and heretic, renowned for his healing and reviled for his debauchery, Grigori Rasputin remains an enigmatic and fascinating figure in Russian history. As a young Siberian peasant, he was rumored to possess supernatural or psychic powers, and after a conversion experience at the age of eighteen, he developed a reputation as a self-proclaimed holy man and a skilled healer. Rasputin's name also became entwined with a heterodox sect called the *Khlysty*, whose rites were rumored to involve self-flagellation and even orgiastic practices.

Rasputin attracted the attention of the Russian Tsarina in 1908, when he was summoned to use his reputed healing powers on the young heir to the Russian throne, who suffered from hemophilia. His success began his rise to power and influence.

Rasputin became an intimate member of the imperial family and a wielder of inordinate power in the royal court. He remained a saintly figure in the eyes of the royal couple, but outside of court, rumors of his promiscuity brought increasing scandal onto the monarchy. A group of nobles plotted a now-legendary assassination. They reported that, despite ingesting enough cyanide to kill five men, receiving numerous gun wounds, and being brutally beaten, Rasputin remained alive and struggling until he was thrown into a river, where he eventually died from hypothermia. This story is difficult to authenticate, but the assassination of Rasputin marked a decline in the authority of the Russian monarchy and heralded the bloody changes to come in the Russian Revolution.
Justin Norris

Date December 16, 1916
Country Russia
Why It's Key The assassination was an assault on the power of the Russian monarchy and a herald of the political instability to come.

opposite Russian mystic and self-styled holy man Grigory Yefimovich Rasputin surrounded by his court followers.

Key Cultural Event
Duchamp creates *Fountain*

Born in Normandy, France in 1887, Marcel Duchamp studied at the Académie Julian in Paris, where he soon found himself losing interest in painting. Art, to Duchamp, was more about having an idea than about physically making something, and he viewed skilled craftsmanship or beauty of technique as almost meaningless. Allying himself with the Cubists, the young artist became a New York sensation after his fractured oil *Nude Descending a Staircase, No. 2* was exhibited at the historic Armory Show, where skeptics famously compared it to "an explosion in a shingles factory." He then moved permanently to the United States, founding the New York outpost of the Dada movement with Man Ray and Francis Picabia.

Fountain, still his most famous work, consists simply of a urinal turned ninety degrees and signed "R. Mutt." Unlike an *objet trouvé*, or "found object," which would usually be chosen for its accidental beauty, a "ready-made" like *Fountain* is a mass-produced article selected completely at random, isolated from its functional context, and displayed as a work of art. In 1917, when Duchamp anonymously submitted the urinal to the Society of Independent Artists, on whose board he sat, his colleagues barred it from exhibition. However, *Fountain* subsequently became one of the most famous and influential works of the twentieth century, an ancestor of everything from Pop Art to Minimalism to Tracey Emin's *My Bed*. It is also an enduring puzzle for philosophers attempting to answer the question "What is art?"

Ned Beauman

Date 1917

Country France

Why It's Key Duchamp's invention of the "ready-made" was the most provocative contribution of the Dada movement to modern avant-garde art.

Key Cultural Event
First jazz recording

Since its inception, jazz has typically been associated with black American musicians, particularly those hailing from southern states – notably New Orleans. Still, the first jazz recording is believed to be *Livery Stable Blues*, which was recorded by the all white, Original Dixieland Jass Band (ODJB). The group, which later changed its name to the Original Dixieland Jazz Band, were marketed as "The Creators of Jazz," an assertion that was certainly false considering the earlier contributions of black American musicians to the budding genre.

All of the musicians had at one time played in the New Orleans-based Papa Jack Laine bands, which performed in parades and street festivals in Louisiana. A Chicago promoter approached two of the musicians about assembling a New Orleans-style band that would perform in Chicago. They eventually landed performing gigs in New York, where other New Orleans musicians had found success as part of vaudeville acts.

Livery Stable Blues is also reported to be the first album to sell more than one million copies. However lacking the group may have been in authenticity, their performances, culminating in the fateful recording of *Livery Stable Blues*, launched an energetic new genre and brought jazz's upbeat tempo to the masses.

Bethonie Butler

Date February 26, 1917

Country USA

Why It's Key Despite controversy surrounding the launch of jazz by a white band, the 1917 recording established a new genre of music and a sizable jazz following.

Key Political Event
USA enters World War I

War had raged in Europe for three years when the U.S. decided to join the fray. President Woodrow Wilson had won reelection in 1916 with the slogan, "He Kept Us Out of War." However, repeated attacks on American ships by German submarines outraged many citizens, leading Wilson to mobilize an immense war machine never before seen in American history. New government agencies regulated big business, millions of young men were drafted, and war critics were imprisoned through the nation's first anti-sedition laws since 1798.

Although troops did not land in Europe until 1918, American industrial might and manpower helped break a grim stalemate that had kept European soldiers tied down in trenches for years. America's impact was not only military, however. Wilson called for all people of the world to enjoy self-determination, or the right to choose their own government. Although the victorious Allies failed to follow through on this pledge for their own colonies, the message inspired later movements against colonialism. Wilson also proposed a League of Nations, the forerunner of today's United Nations, although he could not win support for the organization in the U.S. Senate.

On the home front, the war provided the occasion for the passage of alcohol prohibition and women's suffrage. Ill will over America's involvement also inspired a spirit of isolationism that persisted until the nation joined World War II in 1941.

Alex Cummings

Date April 6, 1917

Country USA

Why It's Key The United States helped turn the tide in a protracted conflict, marking the country's debut as a major player in world affairs.

Key Political Event
Lenin's Finland Station speech

On the night of April 16, 1917, the prominent political activist Vladimir Lenin arrived by train to thunderous applause at the Finland Station in Petrograd (now St. Petersburg), Russia. Lenin had become a prominent figure within the Bolshevik party, writing influential pamphlets and organizing anti-Tsarist demonstrations. However, fearing for his safety, he wrote in self-imposed exile until the revolutions of 1917.

When Lenin heard the news of the 1917 February Revolution and the overthrow of Tsar Nicholas II, he was in Zurich, Switzerland. He was taken by surprise, as he had not expected a revolution within his lifetime, and decided to return to Russia immediately. Having negotiated with the German government to travel through Germany on a "sealed train," and possibly funded by a German military keen to encourage any agitators that would help take Russia out of the war, Lenin arrived at Petrograd. He gave a speech on the Finland Station platform, emphasizing his disgust at the bourgeois Provisional Government, and calling for the immediate withdrawal of Russia from the imperialist war. His radical declarations shocked the more moderate Bolsheviks who at the time supported the government, but by the end of the month, Lenin had achieved a majority in the party and secured the leadership in a fast-growing movement.

The speech formed the basis of the revolutionary April Theses published in the Bolshevik Party newspaper a few days later. In October that year, Lenin would overthrow the Provisional Government and emerge as the country's new leader.

Mariko Kato

Date April 16, 1917

Country Russia

Why It's Key Lenin's return from exile marked the beginning of the last, successful revolution against the Provisional Government.

Fact The Russian revolutionary Vladimir Lenin (1870–1924) was the main leader of the 1917 October Revolution, and in 1922, became the first de facto leader of the Soviet Union.

Key Political Event
The German Revolution

The popular uprising that came to be known as the German Revolution started on October 29, 1918, when sailors at the German naval base in Kiel refused to sail into battle against the British navy. Within days, the unrest had spread across Germany and reached soldiers fighting on the Western Front.

The German establishment crumbled in the face of the widespread rioting and demonstrations, and the Kaiser was eventually forced to abdicate and flee the country. Germany was declared a republic on November 9, 1918, and German forces accepted terms of surrender two days later.

Hitler and other extremists later seized upon the revolution as proof of the "stab in the back," that they believed was responsible for Germany's defeat in the war. In their eyes, the German war machine was heading toward victory against the allies until traitors and cowards betrayed it on the home front. This fed into the unhappiness felt by many disaffected World War I veterans, who made up a large part of Hitler's early support.

In reality, the war was effectively over by the fall of 1918 and the sailors' mutiny was merely a reaction to an order that would bring about more meaningless death and destruction. Germany had no chance of winning the war of attrition that World War I had become and food shortages, in particular the famous "Turnip Winter" of 1917–1918, had been causing unrest for the last year.

Martin Sayers

Date October 29, 1918

Country Germany

Why It's Key The German Revolution swept away the old imperial order in Germany and paved the way for the Weimar Republic.

Key Political Event
The Wielkopolska Uprising

The Wielkopolska Uprising, also known as the Greater Poland Uprising, took place against the backdrop of the end of World War I and the fragmentation of the German empire.

Poland had effectively ceased to exist as a nation state at the end of the eighteenth century and since then, the empires of Russia, Germany, and Austria-Hungary had divided the country up between them. The defeat of Austria-Hungary and Germany in the war and the revolution in Russia meant that the Polish people once again saw the chance to exist as an independent nation.

After the signing of the armistice, the allies agreed that an independent Polish state should be created; however, the exact shape of the new country was unclear. Poles in what was still Germany were fearful that they would remain under German rule and took the opportunity to rebel against German authority. The uprising started on December 27, 1918, after a rabble-rousing speech by Ignacy Paderewski, a famous Polish pianist who would later become the first head of state of the new country.

The insurgents were very successful against a German army devastated by World War I, and by the time the Treaty of Versailles was signed in 1919, the Polish people held a significant amount of what had been German territory. This demonstrated the vigor of the new Polish identity and had a significant impact on drawing the western boundary of the new Polish nation.

Martin Sayers

Date December 27, 1918

Country Poland

Why It's Key The successful fight for Polish independence fueled the sense of injustice felt by Adolf Hitler.

Key Person
Anton Drexler

Anton Drexler was a fervent nationalist well before the Nazis rose to power. When he was declared unfit to serve in World War I, he joined the pro-war Fatherland Party. Yet, as the war drew to a close, Drexler yearned for an alternative to the middle-class political parties, one that was both nationalistic and listened to the masses. On January 5, 1919, Drexler co-founded the German Workers' Party in Munich. Initially, it had about forty members, most of whom were Drexler's work colleagues from the rail depot in Berlin where he worked as a locksmith. However, the party quickly began to take shape, and it welcomed a certain Adolf Hitler in October.

On February 24, 1920, Drexler was persuaded by Hitler to re-name the GWP the National Socialist German Workers' Party, to more clearly outline its vision. Drexler and Hitler also published its first program, later known as the "Twenty-Five Points," in which the party refused to accept the terms of the Treaty of Versailles. To appeal to the nationalists, they declared that equal rights should only be given to German citizens, and for the socialists, they advocated such ideals as profit-sharing in industries and free education.

By the end of 1921, Hitler's persuasive influence over the party, supported by his powerful oratorical skills, made his rise to power inevitable and Drexler stepped down as the party leader. He left the party in 1923, and was largely forgotten by the time of his death in 1942.

Mariko Kato

Date January 5, 1919

Born/Died 1884–1942

Nationality German

Why It's Key Drexler's German Workers' Party was the predecessor of the Nazi Party.

Fact Born in Munich, Anton Drexler was a German Nazi leader who would ultimately be overshadowed by Adolf Hitler.

Key Political Event
Irish War of Independence begins

The Irish War of Independence is traditionally considered to have begun with an ambush in Co. Tipperary on the same day as Sinn Féin MPs (abstaining from Westminster) held their own assembly in Dublin. Until the cessation of hostilities in July 1921, the Irish Republican Army (IRA) employed highly successful guerrilla tactics, which culminated in the development of small bands of highly mobile troops known as "flying columns."

The early phase of the war consisted of attacks against RIC (Royal Irish Constabulary) barracks, particularly in outlying areas. The British government responded to RIC impotency by recruiting two auxiliary police forces drawn largely from World War I veterans. The brutality of some members of these reinforcements did much to aid the IRA's public appeal. The British army, however, was never fully employed in the conflict, as it was felt that doing so would bestow legitimate military status upon the IRA.

The war mainly consisted of attacks by the IRA and reprisals by British forces. The most infamous of these was "Bloody Sunday" (November 21, 1921) when, following the assassination of a number of British intelligence agents, the auxiliary police forces killed twelve spectators at a football match in Dublin.

IRA military successes, coupled with Sinn Féin's ability to paralyze civil administration, led to the Anglo-Irish negotiations that resulted in the creation of an independent Irish state.

Denis Casey

Date January 21, 1919

Country Ireland (now Republic of Ireland)

Why It's Key The war was the beginning of an armed struggle, which led to the creation of an independent Ireland.

Key Political Event
Founding of Mussolini's Fascist organization

Less than six months after World War I ended, the Italian Fascist movement was founded at a meeting in a hall in the Piazza San Sepolcro in Milan. This gathering was an inauspicious affair, which was later deliberately enshrouded in myth, in an attempt to cover up many facts embarrassing to Mussolini and his collaborators.

Although only approximately fifty people attended the meeting, the official roll call of *Sansepolcristi* (the name given to founder members) eventually swelled to many hundreds, due to the benefits early membership later provided when the Fascists came to power.

A remarkable diversity existed in the political beliefs of the small crowd that were actually present. Anarchists, communists, republicans, and varying shades of liberals, among others, were all represented.

The opinions of most did not resemble anything that would later be recognizable as characteristically Fascist. This is unsurprising as Mussolini did not possess a definite ideology and was wont, then as later, to adopt and jettison policies with frequent abandon in the interests of short-term gain. His newspaper, *Il Popolo d'Italia*, falsely claimed that a political program had been adopted at the meeting and trumpeted the event. The national press, in contrast, took little notice.

From this unfavorable beginning, the Fascist organization grew until, two and a half years later, King Vittorio Emanuele III invited Mussolini to become prime minister, marking the genesis of the world's first Fascist dictatorship.

Denis Casey

Date March 23, 1919

Country Italy

Why It's Key The founding of the world's first Fascist party paved the way for the first Fascist dictatorship.

Key Political Event
Massacre at Amritsar

World War I divided Indian public opinion: while some – notably Mohandas K. Gandhi – actively supported the British in the hope that India would be granted Home Rule, Indian nationalists continued their calls for revolution.

Tensions between the government and nationalists came to a head on April 10, 1919, when the authorities ignored calls for the release of two popular leaders who had protested against emergency powers conferred by the Rowlatt Act. Banks, railways, and government buildings were set alight; at least eight Europeans died; and British troops killed eight to twenty Indian civilians. Martial law was declared on April 13, and Brigadier Reginald Dyer was sent to curb unrest. Since this was also the day of a Sikh festival, tens of thousands had gathered around the Sikh shrine in Amritsar's city park. A small group of Indian nationalists, protesting against the conscription of Indians and war taxes, had also congregated. Although not many of the crowd, not even the nationalists, would have known about the ban, Dyer's troops surrounded the park without warning, and fired for ten minutes into the unarmed assembly, killing between 379 and 1,000 people, and injuring 1,000-2,000.

While former British Prime Minister H. H. Asquith condemned the massacre as the worst atrocity in British history, Dyer was feted in the British press as the savior of empire, who had prevented a second "Indian Mutiny." In India, however, many were radicalized by the massacre, including Gandhi, who began to use mass civil disobedience in the fight for independence.

Laura Pechey

Date April 13, 1919

Country India

Why It's Key While many Indians had supported, at the very least, partial British rule, the massacre precipitated a mass shift to Indian nationalism and calls for full independence.

Key Cultural Event
Traffic light patented

In the early years of the twentieth century, Detroit, Michigan was a popular place for the innovations of traffic signals. In 1917, Detroit installed the first traffic tower in the United States. In 1920, it became the first city to use red, green, and yellow lights to control traffic, and later that year, a Detroit police officer, William L. Potts, invented the four-way, three-color signal light.

Although the story of the modern electric traffic light is historically tangled because various people have laid claim to its assorted parts, one inventor's concept, in the early 1900s, helped make the "first-ever traffic signal." Oscar A. Erdman issued a patent on June 24, 1919, in Detroit for an automatic signal with the capacity of operating without requiring human control or vehicle activation. Touted by Erdman as an improvement in signal lights, the invention was for signal lights to be used at street crossings to regulate the movement of traffic at each of the four corners of two intersecting streets. Two signaling devices were positioned to be observed by traffic on one of the streets and on opposite sides, as well as opposite sides of the cross street, while two others were to provide a similar arrangement for the intersecting street. The object of the invention was to have one pair of signals indicate "go," while the other pair would indicate "stop" and vice versa. Unfortunately, it was considered too complicated to produce, but Erdman's ideas were later modified for use.

Fred Lindsey

Date June 24, 1919

Country USA

Why It's Key Erdman's invention, while not adopted entirely, paved the way for the modern traffic light.

Key Political Event
Treaty of Versailles

The Treaty of Versailles was a peace agreement between the Allies and Germany at the end of World War I. Signed at the Palace of Versailles in Paris, it was intended to secure peace, satisfy the strategic interests of the Allies, and meet public demands that Germany be severely punished.

The terms of the treaty against Germany were very harsh. The country lost a considerable amount of her territory and all overseas colonies. Other lands occupied by Germany were to be given the opportunity to decide their own fate by a vote. Military measures restricted the numbers of German armed forces and forbade the possession of an air force. Most controversially, Germany had to take full responsibility for causing the war and make substantial reparation payments to the Allies for damages caused, later agreed at £6.6 billion annually. To ensure that payments were made, all territories west of the Rhine were to be occupied by Allied forces for fifteen years.

The treaty had a profound impact in Germany; it became known as *Das Diktat* ("dictated peace") because the German delegation was not allowed to negotiate terms with Allied representatives. Resentment grew among Germans, particularly because their nation had to take the blame for the war. Many Germans felt humiliated and "stabbed in the back" by their own government's acceptance of the terms at Versailles. This rejection became the dominant theme of German politics throughout the 1920s and encouraged a nationalist backlash that became a future source of international tension.

Helena Hewson

Date June 28, 1919

Country France

Why It's Key The Treaty of Versailles was intended to safeguard the future of Europe; but its terms had disastrous effects on Germany that led eventually to the outbreak of World War II.

Key Cultural Event
The White Sox fix

The team of the Chicago White Sox fix is better known, unsurprisingly, as the "Black Sox." The 1919 World Series against the Cincinnati Reds appeared to be keenly contested; only one home run was scored all series and the games were close and intense. Eight of Chicago's players, however, were throwing the game. Baseball, America's national sport, had reached its lowest ebb.

The conspiracy is still shrouded in doubt. The chief instigator appears to be First Baseman Arnold "Chick" Gandil. The idea of underperforming for payment from criminal gamblers backing the opposition might not have been his, but Gandil played a prominent role in establishing links to the gangster fraternity and recruiting players. The most famous player involved was "Shoeless" Joe Jackson, a prolific hitter. It was he who hit the solitary series home run, and, according to supporters attempting to rehabilitate his reputation, attempted to get "benched" for the series after realizing the ramifications of the fix. He might even, as some accounts suggest, have told club owner Charles Comiskey about the plan before the series began. Comiskey's parsimony, legendary in the game, alienated many of his players and motivated the conspirators. The stars of the World Series believed they should have pay packets commensurate with their glorified status, but the plan they hatched contravened the ethos of a game sacred in American cultural life. Acquitted in the judiciary due to lack of evidence, all eight players were banned from professional baseball for life.

Michael Hallam

Date October 1, 1919

Country USA

Why It's Key The White Sox fix shocked America, and remains the biggest scandal in U.S. sporting history.

opposite The 1919 White Sox line-up.

Key Cultural Event
Frost's "The Road Not Taken" published

With twenty lines and four stanzas, Robert Frost gave America a startling declaration of personal independence. On a literal level, "The Road Not Taken" tracked the travails of a person confronted with two paths in a forest, and the outcome of deciding to take "the one less taken." But throughout the following verses, the narrator contemplates what might have happened if he had taken the other road, and by the end he's reminiscing on the experience as though looking back over his entire life. In this way, "The Road Not Taken" posits a universal declaration of choosing to be unconventional, but leaves it up to the reader to decide whether or not it's a wise choice.

Frost, raised in New England, often immersed himself in the woodsy surroundings suggested by his poem. An English teacher with one acclaimed book to his name when "The Road Not Taken" was published in his second collection, Mountain Interval, Frost had fallen into a prestigious literary crowd, including the poet Edward Thomas, whose difficulty in choosing routes on their regular forest strolls, Frost claimed, inspired the poem. The ambiguity of its language, however, opened it up to various interpretations, and Frost himself offered many over the years. Whatever its true meaning, the poem came to define Frost's ability to grapple with abstract social themes without negating the sheer beauty of the written word. That skill won him the Pulitzer Prize four times.

Eric Kohn

Date 1920

Country USA

Why It's Key The poem came to define a sense of creative freedom in the United States and the archetypical expressive poem.

Fact Although generally associated with the New England community of artists, Frost was actually born in California.

Key Political Event
Nationalism grips Japan

After joining the victorious Allies in World War I, Japan enjoyed unprecedented global prominence. At the 1919 Versailles conference, it was officially recognized as one of the "Big Five" of the military and industrial powers, and granted a permanent seat on the League of Nations council. However, Japan also faced urgent problems of post-war inflation, influx of Western ideologies, and a growing labor movement. National debt and lack of governmental reform gained support for new socialist and communist parties, and Prime Minister Hara Takashi was assassinated in 1921, followed by other coalition politicians.

Fearing the growing strength of left-wing powers, the government passed the Peace Preservation Law in 1925. This was a direct defense against communist ideas filtering from Russia. It denied change in political structure or private property, and demanded moral obligations to the emperor and the state. With the 1928 Great Depression, Japan turned to fascism, and cultivated strict militarization and a prosperous industrial sector. The rapidly expanding Imperial Army, accountable only to the emperor, commanded disproportionate influence over foreign policy. In 1932, Japan was censured by the League of Nations for invading China-ruled Manchuria, and withdrew from the organization the following year.

By World War II, Japan had signed anti-communism treaties with Germany and Italy. Nationalist sentiments had been strongly implemented in the Japanese consciousness, to ensure great nationwide endeavor and sacrifice fighting in the emperor's name.

Mariko Kato

Date 1920

Country Japan

Why It's Key Japan's extreme nationalism bought enemies in both neighboring countries and the disapproval of its Western allies from World War I.

Fact Since the 1868 Meiji Restoration, extreme nationalism had been the enduring essence of right-wing politics in Japan, and has since been the backbone of pro-war politics.

Key Political Event
Formation of the League of Nations

In January 1918, Woodrow Wilson unveiled his Fourteen Points: a popular, idealistic outline for peace after World War I. Wilson wanted nations to interact through diplomacy, not war. His last Point was most important to him: it proposed a "general association of nations" to dissolve conflicts. At the Paris Peace Conference, Wilson focused on this "general association" to the extent that he ignored many of his other points. On January 10, 1920, Wilson, with support from political leaders in the U.K. and France, succeeded: the League of Nations was officially established. In its Covenant, members promised to avoid war and to protect other nations.

The League enjoyed a few modest successes. Its sub-organizations, like the International Labor Organization, prompted social reform around the world. It also defused some conflicts, like the 1921 territorial dispute between Finland and Sweden. However, the League was ultimately a failure. It had no military, so its decisions were unenforceable. More importantly, it had little political power. The U.K. and France were the only great powers always in the League; Germany was not invited until 1926 and left in 1934. The United States, despite Wilson's campaigning, never joined. That decision was made by domestic politics: the Republican-controlled Senate refused the League because it would have undermined U.S. independence.

The League's structural weaknesses and its relative insignificance stopped the organization from responding to Italian, German, and Japanese aggression in the 1930s. It was replaced on April 8, 1946, with the stronger, more inclusive United Nations.

Christina Welsch

Date January 10, 1920

Country USA/UK/France/Germany/Italy/Japan

Why It's Key Leaders at the Paris Peace Conference after World War I created the League of Nations to avoid future conflict, but problems in its design and the United States' failure to join made the League incapable of avoiding World War II.

Excessive alcohol consumption had been seen as a problem in western civilization since the eighteenth century, but early state prohibition laws in the U.S. proved ineffective. By the end of the American Civil War, drunkenness, gambling, prostitution, and violence were common occurrences in many saloons.

In response, temperance groups were formed, and by 1900, the Anti-Saloon League was demanding the introduction of anti-saloon laws. Twenty-three states complied, and in 1917, Congress submitted the 18th Amendment, prohibiting the "manufacture, sale, or transportation of intoxicating liquors." This was passed as the National Prohibition Act (or popularly as the Volstead Act, having been introduced by Congressman Andrew Volstead), and it came into effect at midnight on January 16, 1920.

The law restricted any liquor that had an alcoholic content of over 0.5 percent, though liquor that was for medicinal, religious, or industrial purposes was allowed. As a result, consumption reduced by nearly two thirds, but the law was difficult to enforce. Criminal gangs took over the control of alcohol production and distribution, making huge profits, which allowed them to bribe public officials, and competition between gangs often resulted in murders. Previous supporters of prohibition recognized that the problems were worse than before and, during the Great Depression, many argued that the law restricted employment and the national economy. The public were now strongly in favor of repeal and on December 3, 1933 the 21st Amendment brought an end to national prohibition.
Ros Bott

Date January 16, 1920

Country USA

Why It's Key Prohibition had a great impact on American society during the 1920s and is believed to have been the cause of increased criminal activity, bribery, and corruption within the big cities.

119

Key Cultural Event
Agatha Christie publishes her first novel

Agatha Christie is best-known today for the eerily engaging whodunit mystery novels *And Then There Were None* and *Murder on the Orient Express*, but these are only two samples of her prolific writing that came to define the crime novel for a variety of reasons. Christie's ongoing character, the detective Hercule Poirot, starred in her first novel, *The Mysterious Affair at Styles*. Drawing on a tradition put forth by Arthur Conan Doyle with his Sherlock Holmes stories, Christie followed Poirot through many adventures over the years, building up a personality marked by keen investigatory skills.

The British author created situations littered with clues leading up to conclusive finishes. Christie's books often featured enigmatic narratives that readers could treat as crime documents, following the events surrounding a murder and drawing their own conclusions about the culprit. In ... *Styles*, she laid out the framework: several people drawn together at an isolated manor, all whom could be suspects in a murder. Told in first person by Captain Hastings, a close friend of the detective, the novel lays out the events and lets Poirot put everything together at the end. This classic structure came to define the golden age of detective fiction. As a result, it's also responsible for the timeless board game "Clue"/"Cluedo."
Eric Kohn

Date February 27, 1920

Country USA

Why It's Key Christie's storytelling provided the archetype for the modern crime novel.

Fact The novel was initially printed in several newspapers as an eighteen-part serial.

Key Political Event
Hitler renames the German Worker's Party

In 1919, when the German Army heard of the new German Workers' Party (DAP), they sent Adolf Hitler, then a young corporal, to spy on a meeting. However, on arrival, Hitler discovered that the party's visions were very similar to his own. He identified with its nationalism and its anti-Semitism; as he later recalled in *Mein Kampf*, his hatred toward the Jews had grown during his homeless years in Vienna. When a point was raised by a DAP member with which Hitler disagreed, he stood up and argued passionately against him. Hitler's enigmatic skills as an orator impressed the group, and he was invited to join the party. Hitler became its fifty-fourth member, and became the propaganda manager and main speaker.

Hitler's influence in the party grew, and on February 24, 1920, he changed its name to the National Socialist German Workers' Party (NSDAP). This allowed the party to use nationalistic concepts to appeal to the right wing, and pseudo-socialist ideas to attract the workers. Hitler had always disliked socialist doctrines, particularly those that advocated racial equality. Yet he knew that since World War I, socialism was popular among the German people and so he redefined socialism to favor equality only for those who had "German blood." The blend of nationalism and socialism advertised in the new name attracted much support, and it became the country's largest political party.

In 1921, Hitler replaced Anton Drexler as leader, and became the new head figure of the NSDAP – nicknamed the Nazi party.
Mariko Kato

Date February 24, 1920

Country Germany

Why It's Key The change was a clear announcement of the party's visions, and reflected Hitler's growing control over the party.

Fact Austrian Adolf Hitler (1889–1945), orphaned at eighteen, struggled to succeed as a painter and became homeless in Vienna in 1909.

Key Political Event
Gandhi preaches non-violence

On August 11, 1920, Mohandas Gandhi wrote an article for his weekly journal, *Young India*, entitled "The Doctrine of the Sword" in which he called upon his countrymen to practise non-violent methods in the struggle for national independence. Although he stressed that violence is preferable to the non-action of cowardice, he strongly asserted that non-violent resistance and self-sacrifice are superior to violent methods, which ultimately cause more problems.

Born in 1869, and trained as a lawyer, Gandhi began his political career in South Africa campaigning against racial prejudice. His passionate belief in non-violent methods to fight injustice led to the creation of the word, *satyagraha*, joining two Sanskrit words meaning "truth" and "firmness" and this philosophy became the force behind his campaigns.

Gandhi's involvement in the fight for Indian independence began when the British broke their promise to free India after World War I. He began to campaign for passive resistance, but after the Amritsar massacre of 1919 he launched the Non-Cooperation Movement on August 1, 1920, including a boycott of British products.

Gandhi's beliefs about non-violence were never to do with submission or acceptance; it was a philosophy of conscious suffering, and the courage to take action in a non-violent way, even though that might mean injury to the self. His teachings created a large following in India and ultimately led to Indian home rule, although this was not without its violent outbreaks.
Ros Bott

Date August 11, 1920

Country India

Why It's Key Gandhi's philosophy of non-violent resistance was a major factor in the struggle for Indian independence from British rule and made him one of the greatest humanitarians in world history.

Key Political Event
United States grants women the vote

It was March 3, 1913, the day before his inauguration as the United States' president, when Woodrow Wilson's train arrived in Washington, D.C. to silence. On Pennsylvania Avenue, an estimated half million people were watching a woman's suffrage parade, organized by activists Alice Paul and Lucy Burns, in an attempt to turn the nation's attention to their cause, gaining the vote for American women through a federal suffrage amendment.

Up to 8,000 women marched in rows of three across, dressed in white, past hundreds of thousands of onlookers made up of both supporters and opponents of suffrage. Army troops would later be called in to curb the violence that ensued when local police disregarded their obligation to ensure a peaceful march. The women were ridiculed, spat on, and beaten. The public outcry against the police and their failure to protect the women resulted in the firing of the police chief, but more importantly, generated even more support for the suffrage movement. In New York, several weeks later, another march drew 10,000 participants.

"Paul's Forces," the "shock troops" of the American suffrage crusade, gained attention in the next seven years through massive demonstrations, hunger strikes, confrontations with the police, pickets, and boycotts, and many were jailed or committed. Their efforts, however, were not in vain. After over seventy years of protest by countless women, the 19th Amendment to the Constitution was finally passed on August 26, 1920, granting American women the right to vote.

Colette Leisen

Date August 26, 1920

Country USA

Why It's Key The creation and mobilization of various women's groups secured women the right to vote in the United States, giving them greater political power.

Key Discovery
Insulin

At 2 a.m. on October 31, 1920, a London, Ontario doctor jotted down twenty-five words that would lead to a medical breakthrough for people with diabetes. Dr Frederick Banting's technique for isolating the anti-diabetic component of the pancreas was considered crude by some. However, it prompted him to continue his research at the University of Toronto in the spring of 1921. There, Professors J. J. R. Macleod, C. H. Best, and Dr J. B. Collip worked with Banting on refining his research.

The result of their efforts – an extract called insulin – was first successfully administered in 1922. Banting and Macleod were awarded the Nobel Prize for Physiology or Medicine in 1923; Banting shared his prize with Best, and Macleod with Collip. The quartet decided not to seek a patent for insulin, but instead sold the rights to the University of Toronto for CA$1. This selfless gesture ensured that insulin could be affordably manufactured for years to come.

Banting died tragically in a plane crash in 1941, but he has not been forgotten. In 1994, he was inducted into the Canadian Medical Hall of Fame, and insulin was chosen number one in the Canadian Broadcasting Corporation (CBC)'s Greatest Canadian Inventions contest, in January 2007. The Flame of Hope, first kindled in 1989, still burns in a cairn outside Banting House National Historic Site, in London, Ontario. The Flame is a reminder that insulin is only a control for diabetes and not a cure. When a cure is found, the Flame is to be extinguished.

Leith Peterson

Date October 31, 1920

Country Canada

Why It's Key Banting's initial technique led to the development of insulin, a control substance for people with diabetes. Insulin has extended the lives of millions of diabetes sufferers around the world ever since.

Key Cultural Event
Russia allows abortion

In 1920, only a few years after the Bolshevik Revolution, Russia became the first country in the world since late antiquity to both tolerate and legalize induced abortion. Russia's leader, Vladimir Lenin, insisted that legalized abortion would not only prevent the many deaths and injuries caused by amateur abortions, but also empower Soviet women. The decision was partly pragmatic, as it opened the way for an increasing number of women to join the workforce, but was ultimately equivocal. Russian women took advantage of the new laws in large enough numbers to worry the Soviet leadership that the supply of new bodies, hence new workers, was in peril. By some estimates, there were three abortions for every new birth in Moscow in the 1930s. Despite some retrospective regret on the part of Soviet officials, the state was never able to stem the tide of abortions, and to this day Russia retains one of the highest abortion rates in the world.

Regardless of its ultimate outcome and reception within Russia, Lenin's 1920 decision heralded the future of reproductive rights in the West and manifested the ongoing connection between progressive politics and a woman's rights to choose. The United States, which during the Cold War portrayed itself as a beacon of individual liberties standing in contrast to the oppressive Soviet system, did not itself follow Russia's suit on abortion until as late as 1973.
Demir Barlas

Date November 14, 1920

Country Russia

Why It's Key Modern reproductive rights for women began in the Soviet Union, whose legalization of abortion anticipated the more liberal laws of the West.

Key Cultural Event
First use of "robot"

The play *R.U.R.* (*Rossum's Universal Robots*), written by the Czech playwright Karel Capek, was first performed on January 25, 1921, in the National Theater in Prague, and is renowned for containing the first ever use of the term *robot*. The expression *robot* stems from the Czech word *robota*, meaning "forced worker," "slave," or "drudgery." Capek's choice of that particular word is connected to the robots' initial role in the play, in which they are used as labor for mechanical tasks that nobody else wants to do. The robots in *R.U.R.* are not robots in the traditional sense of the term, but are biological machines assembled out of genetically engineered tissue. At the end of the play, the robots destroy the whole of humanity except for one person, a scientist who in the end comes up with a formula to create more robots.

The concept of a robot has existed for centuries, starting from the bronze giant Talos in Homer's *Iliad*; but it was the introduction of the term *robot* in *R.U.R.* and the ideas associated with it that gave the concept of a robot its full modern meaning. Furthermore, the ethical issues touched upon in *R.U.R.*, such as whether an artificially created humanoid entity has the same rights as a real human, and the possible consequences of creating machines with the same abilities as humans, are vital for the course of the future development of robotics.
Sonja Kudeljnjak

Date January 25, 1921

Country Czechoslovakia (now Czech Republic)

Why It's Key The play *R.U.R.* had an immense impact on the modern concept of the robot.

Fact One of the first people to design a humanoid robot was Leonardo Da Vinci.

Key Political Event
Lenin announces new economic policy

The Bolsheviks sustained their forces through the bloody civil war by confiscating the goods they needed. Some of them saw this "war communism" as a step toward their ultimate goal of abolishing private property, but it provoked fierce opposition, especially from peasants, and led to a catastrophic decline in agricultural production. After the civil war, Lenin's response was the "New Economic Policy" (NEP). While the state would control the "commanding heights" of the economy – heavy industry, wholesaling, banking, transport – NEP legalized private trading for profit. Peasants could sell their produce, subject to taxation rather than the earlier grain requisitions.

Some of Lenin's fellow Bolsheviks saw NEP as a step backward, but it proved to be a sound practical measure. NEP solidified Bolshevik control of Russia, unleashing small-scale private enterprise to repair the damage of war and revolution. By 1927, the last year of NEP, industrial and agricultural production finally surpassed the levels of 1913, before the outbreak of World War I. What Lenin would have done thereafter cannot be known: shortly after he launched NEP, his health began its rapid decline. Certainly he intended NEP as a temporary step on the way to establishing Communism, but his colleagues disagreed about the rate of transformation. While some of them saw no need for sudden change, others shared the widespread resentment of the "speculators" who made fortunes (most of them modest) under NEP. This discontent, along with grain shortages, encouraged Lenin's successor, Stalin, to revoke NEP.

Brian Ladd

Date March 8, 1921

Country Russia

Why It's Key Lenin slowed the pace of his revolution in order to consolidate power.

Key Political Event
Bulhoek Massacre

The 1913 Native Land Act had increased pressure on the Union's black population, driving sharecroppers from white farms and restricting black ownership to less than ten per cent of the country. Into an already overcrowded Ntabelanga, in Bulhoek (now Whittlesea), near Queenstown, came the followers of Enoch Mgijima, the millenarian Israelites, who believed in African-American William Crowdy's claim that black people were descended from the lost tribes of Israel. A face-off between the dispossessed, in the form of the Israelites, and a white government made jittery by black resistance was all but inevitable.

Halley's Comet, which had blazed overhead in 1910, had led Mgijima to prophesy that the world would end in 1920. Three thousand Israelites arrived for the 1919 Passover celebration and squatted on Crown land where they resisted removal, saying they accepted no authority but God. After a prolonged stand-off, the Union government sent Colonel Theodore Truter with over a thousand officers, three machine guns, and artillery. Opposing him were 500 Israelites who had been told by Mgijima that the bullets of the government forces would turn to water. They were armed with *assegais* (short, stabbing spears) and *knobkieries* (wooden clubs). An ultimatum on May 20, 1921, for the illegal squatters to destroy their homes and leave the area went unheeded, and, in the ensuing massacre, 163 Israelites were killed, 129 wounded, and 95 taken prisoner, including Mgijima and his brother who were sentenced to six years.

Duncan Proudfoot

Date May 24, 1921

Country South Africa

Why It's Key The Bulhoek Massacre was the first of many atrocities perpetrated in support of white domination in a unified South Africa; it foreshadowed the 1922 Bondelswarts Massacre in South-West Africa, Sharpeville in 1960, and many other incidents.

Key Political Event
Chinese Communist Party founded

After the collapse of the Qing Dynasty in 1912, the Chinese were left with the challenge of establishing a new form of governance after two millennia of imperial rule. China had been in political disarray for decades and though compelled to modernize, it was still searching for an ideological framework that could resist the old. Chinese intellectuals had not taken much notice of Marxism until after Russia's Bolshevik Revolution in 1917. It was Li Dazhao of Beijing University who was the first to apply Marx's principles of the urban proletariat to the Chinese experience of foreign imperialist aggression, exploitation of the peasant class, and capitalist oppression. Li Dazhao's followers, one of whom was Mao Zedong who worked under him at the Beijing University library, were electrified by Marx's socialist ideas, which they recognized as a solution to China's political turmoil.

The May Fourth Movement, a gathering of some 5,000 students in Tiananmen Square, Beijing, in 1919, was primarily in protest of the Versailles treaty, which transferred former German leaseholds in China to Japan. However, it was also the first public articulation of Marxist intellectual ideas as a means of modernizing China and regaining its territorial integrity. With the support of Russia, the student unions established in the wake of May Fourth took the reform movement across China, spreading the Marxist doctrine. Founded by Li Dazhao, Chen Duxiu, and Mao Zedong, the Chinese Communist Party was born, and held its first congress, in Shanghai in 1921.

Sally Percival Wood

Date June 1, 1921

Country China

Why It's Key The Chinese Communist Party would reunify China as the People's Republic in 1949 after a century of war and political upheaval. It would also send China into decades of isolation during the Cold War years until America's President Nixon reopened diplomatic channels with his visit in 1972.

Key Cultural Event
Vasconcelos initiates the Mural Program

After the immense and violent upheaval brought by the Mexican Revolution, José Vasconcelos was determined to implement a revolution in education, which he saw as a vital tool for the emancipation of the masses. He was responsible for an unprecedented initiative of state sponsorship of the arts, which included funding the work of three men who determined the course of Latin American art in the twentieth century.

Committed to transforming society through art, the muralists painted in public spaces such as schools and government buildings, embracing the mural as a medium for reaching the masses. The three great muralists, Diego Rivera, José Clemente Orozco, and David Alfaro Siqueiros, portrayed indigenous cultures and sufferings in their work. While Siqueiros' work was profoundly rooted in the revolutionary struggle (he suffered imprisonment and exile for his political affiliation), Orozco focused on historical and pre-Hispanic sources. Diego Rivera – whose fraught relationship with the Communist Party and with his capitalist patrons made him a perpetually controversial figure – depicted the workers' struggle and Mexico's chaotic history, while envisioning the role of technology in the future of mankind. He is also credited with the revival of Italian fresco painting techniques. In 1929, he began the Presidential Palace mural whose notoriously epic narrative sweep begins in pre-Hispanic times and encompasses the peak of Aztec civilization, the Spanish conquest of Mexico, industrialization, and the Mexican Revolution. His boldly colorful murals have become emblematic of Mexican art and continue to influence artists worldwide.

Charlotte Whittle

Date June 1, 1921

Country Mexico

Why It's Key The muralist movement represents a pinnacle of Latin American art in the twentieth century as well as one of the most ambitious public art projects of the modern era.

Fact Rivera's mural of Mexican history at the Presidential Palace in Mexico City took twenty-two years to complete.

Key Cultural Event
Inkblot test published

Even as a child, the Swiss psychiatrist Hermann Rorschach (1884–1922) was so fascinated by the images perceptible in apparently random inkblots that he was nicknamed "*Kleck*" or "inkblot" by his school friends. Though he did not develop his eponymous test until 1921, Rorschach began as early as 1911 to experiment with inkblots as a way of analyzing personality disorders and the functioning of the unconscious mind. These types of tests are known as "projective" tests, and work by eliciting spontaneous responses to words, phrases, or ambiguous images. The ambiguity is key, because it allows people to project their own unconscious desires, wants, and fears onto what they hear or see.

It was during his time as director of the asylum at Herisau that Rorschach developed what has become one of the most famous and widely used of these tests, which he published as a monograph titled *Psychodiagnostik*. He created ten different symmetrical inkblot cards, five in color and five in black and white. During the test, patients were presented with each card in turn, and a detailed scoring system assessed every aspect of their response, from their attitude to color and form to the shapes they perceive, whether bats or birds, monsters or mountains.

Like many projective tests, the Rorschach inkblots have provoked considerable controversy, and the test has been condemned as not only unreliable, but also as overly dependent on the way it is administered. Nevertheless, it remains in widespread use to this day.
Lynn Shepherd

Date June 10, 1921

Country Switzerland

Why It's Key One of the first psychometric tests to achieve widespread acceptance, which is still in use across the world today.

Key Political Event
Lisbon Massacre

Portugal had entered the twentieth century as a pre-industrialized agrarian society, in turmoil both economically and politically. Led by Machado Santos, the country's popular republican movement finally overthrew the monarchy in 1910 and established the democratic First Republic. But apart from measures against the old order – especially anti-clerical laws – the new republic lacked unity, and was further hampered by general strikes, government corruption, a growing monarchist opposition, and the disastrous economic effects of World War I. Mounting civil unrest came to a head in October 19, 1921, when elements of the army and navy in Lisbon revolted against the government of the Liberal Prime Minister, António Granjo.

In what became known as the infamous Night Of Blood (*A Noite Sangrenta*), Granjo and several other prominent republicans including Santos, the founder of the republic, were arrested and killed. The country, and the world, was shocked by the bloody turn of events and, despite the coup's leaders alleging that the massacre was against their orders, it marked the beginning of the end for parliamentary democracy in Portugal. The First Republic struggled on until 1926. It was then brought down by a successful military coup, which paved the way for the rise in power of António Salazar who led the country into a repressive, right-wing dictatorship for forty years. It wasn't until after another military coup in 1974 that Portugal became a democracy again and truly entered the modern era.
Hedley Paul

Date October 19, 1921

Country Portugal

Why It's Key The assassination of leading parliamentary politicians symbolized the republic's impotency in the face of growing military and anti-democratic opposition.

Key Political Event
Irish Free State proclaimed

The Anglo-Irish treaty signed on December 6, 1921, by representatives of the British government and the Irish revolutionary government concluded the Irish War of Independence and recognized the creation of an Irish Free State (*Saorstát Éireann*) within the British Empire. The preceding conflict was a guerrilla campaign conducted by the Irish Republican Army (IRA), which sought to establish an Irish republic. It erupted in January 1919 on the same day as Irish MPs, who had refused to take their seats in Westminster, held their own legislative assembly (Dáil Éireann) in Dublin.

The treaty granted dominion status, comparable to that possessed by Canada, to a twenty-six county unit of southern Ireland. The six counties of Northern Ireland similarly gained a measure of independence.

A split in the Irish government between extremist and moderate nationalists quickly followed. Dáil Éireann narrowly approved the settlement in January 1922, and in the subsequent general election a substantial pro-treaty majority was elected. Despite this, the IRA and much of the country were deeply divided and a civil war broke out between pro and anti-treaty forces, which ended in victory for the former in 1923.

Successive Irish governments sought to expand Irish independence by redefining the role of the British Commonwealth of Nations, of which Ireland was then a member. This process culminated in the declaration of an Irish Republic in 1949.

Denis Casey

Date December 6, 1921

Country Republic of Ireland

Why It's Key The treaty marked the birth of an independent Ireland.

Key Cultural Event
Joyce's *Ulysses* published

Begun in 1914, the avant-garde novel *Ulysses* took James Joyce seven years to complete. The work is a modern version of Homer's *Odyssey*, and chronicles the unexpected events that befall protagonists Leopold Bloom and Stephen Dedalus on one day in 1904 in Dublin.

The novel's ambitious scale remains unmatched in literary history. Each of its eighteen episodes features a different theme written in varying technique, weaving an elaborate labyrinth of allusions and interconnections, as well as puns and word-play, and experimenting with the stream-of-consciousness narrative. Its plot is ambitious and colorful, including a birth, a funeral, adultery, drunkenness, and sexual encounters.

Ulysses was first serialized in the American journal *The Little Review* in 1918. However, when it came to the sexually explicit *Nausicäa* episode, in which Bloom masturbates with a girl to fireworks, the work was put on trial for obscenity and consequently banned in the United States. It was eventually published in its entirety in Paris in 1922, in the same year as T. S. Eliot's "The Waste Land." While this signaled a new era in literature, *Ulysses* still remained illegal in the United States and the United Kingdom until the 1930s. When it finally became universally available, *Ulysses* gained iconic status for its range of styles, sparkling humor, and epic length, and is now widely recognized as a touchstone for the start of modernism.

Mariko Kato

Date February 2, 1922

Country France

Why It's Key One of the twentieth century's greatest novels, *Ulysses* epitomizes the stream-of-consciousness writing of the modernist movement.

opposite James Joyce and Silvia Beach, the American who eventually published *Ulysses*, standing in the doorway of Shakespeare & Co. in Paris.

Key Cultural Event
Semana de Arte Moderna de São Paulo

The coalition of like-minded iconoclasts involved in organizing this watershed event in Latin American cultural history together formed an extraordinary generation that included composer Heitor Villa-Lobos, painter Anita Malfatti, poet Oswald de Andrade, and polymath Mário de Andrade. United in their desire to shake the foundations of Brazil's official cultural establishment, these *enfants terribles* chose to showcase their creative audacity in one of the most visible venues of São Paulo, the country's bustling economic and cultural capital. The eclectic group were determined to put the arts in Brazil on par with the most radical innovations in Europe, while at the same time proclaiming the country's creative autonomy by drawing on Brazil's vital and diverse indigenous traditions. This fusion of cosmopolitanism and nationalism gave the event its unique character and proved fertile for the subsequent development of the arts in Brazil.

The week's programming featured daily performances of works by Villa-Lobos, poetry readings, round tables, and art displays. Mário de Andrade read out the first of a series of manifestos that would define the literary tasks of his generation, and Malfatti and other artists offered workshops for the city's youth, hoping to unleash their spontaneous energies. The exposition's *succès de scandale* gave unprecedented publicity to these and other artists, and provoked the ire of the loathed establishment: the Brazilian Academy of Letters summarily expelled one of its founding members, Graça Aranha, in retaliation for the laudatory address he delivered at the week's opening event.
Geoffrey Schullenberger

Date February 11, 1922

Country Brazil

Why It's Key The "modern art week" held in São Paulo's municipal theater spearheaded the Brazilian avant-garde revolution in literature, music, and the visual arts, and featured contributions from the majority of the country's most notable artists.

Key Political Event
Foundation of the *Suiheisha*

For the classes that had labored for centuries under its burden, the abolition of feudalism – which saw the dispossession of Japan's samurai warrior class in 1872 – offered the promise of a new, more equitable social order and a share in the nation's wealth. Among those hoping to benefit were the *Tokushu Burakumin* ("People of Special Villages"): a segregated, hereditary class of slaughterers, executioners, and tanners forced to perform work deemed unclean by Buddhist tradition. Fifty years into Japan's modern era however, new generations of *Burakumin* continued to suffer the persistence of their historic abuse, facing discrimination in housing, employment, and education.

In 1922, over a thousand militant young *Burakumin* convened in Kyoto to found the *Suiheisha* (National Leveler's Association). Their platform, published as the "Suiheisha Declaration," was Japan's first appeal for political freedom to be justified in terms of universal human rights. Announcing "*Burakumin* of Japan, unite!" and elaborating their mission to restore humanity's "divine dignity," the declaration's language drew upon both the radical and the religious, as did their flag: a blood-red crown of thorns set against a black background. The *Suiheisha*, which eventually grew to over 40,000 members and become notorious for its practice of kidnapping and subjecting to mock-trials those alleged to have discriminated against *Burakumin*, was ultimately to share the fate of many of the era's radical liberal and leftist movements. Finding it impossible to operate under growing ultranationalist pressure, it dissolved in 1940.
James Handley

Date March 3, 1922

Country Japan

Why It's Key The founding assembly of former outcastes in Kyoto led to Japan's first declaration of human rights.

Key Person
Trixie Smith

The roots of rock 'n' roll stretch across genres, instruments, and even continents, but its powerful allure to listeners is impossible to pin down or explain. However, etymologists have traced the term itself back to Trixie Smith, a little-known African-American singer who was the first person to record the words "rock 'n' roll" in a song.

Born in 1895, Smith moved to New York at the age of twenty, where she quickly found work singing in nightclubs. It wasn't until 1922, though, when she won that year's Manhattan Blues contest as the only African-American competitor, that Smith became known for her trademark "railroad blues," with stories of women on the move.

"My Man Rocks Me (With One Steady Roll)" was not Smith's best-known song, but it showcases her thin, mournful voice in a piece with strong sexual overtones. The themes of sex and rebellion would later be played out in rock 'n' roll, even if the song did not foreshadow the genre.

Smith wasn't able to capitalize on her brush with fame in 1922, as she recorded fewer than fifty songs between 1923 and 1939. Similar artists, like Ma Rainey and Bessie Smith, used the same formula as Smith with greater success. Yet, in the 1930s, strong blues women lost their favor with audiences, and by the 1950s, it seemed as if rock 'n' roll was a men's genre. However, Smith's 1922 song shows that rock has always had a feminine side, and it's not a soft one.

Martin Johnson

Date September 1, 1922

Born/Died 1895–1943

Nationality American

Why It's Key Although Trixie Smith's utterance of the term didn't give birth to the genre "rock 'n' roll," it suggests the genre's rich history.

1920-1929

129

Key Cultural Event
"The Waste Land" published

Thomas Stearns Eliot was born in St. Louis, Missouri, and attended Harvard University, but in 1914 he moved to England to become a visiting Fellow at Merton College, Oxford University. He resided in England for the rest of his life, becoming a British citizen in 1927. With his notoriously difficult marriage to Vivien Haigh-Wood putting him under severe financial pressure, he worked as a teacher, a lecturer, and later took up a post at Lloyd's Bank.

Nevertheless, with the advice and support of his contemporary Ezra Pound, Eliot's reputation in the literary world grew. Published in the wake of World War I, "The Waste Land" reflected the disillusionment of the post-war generation of artists, juxtaposing and fusing many different styles. It combines the form of the dramatic monologue, as employed in his earlier successful poem "The Love Song of J. Alfred Prufrock," with the structure of a musical fugue. Its collage of contrasting voices and abrupt disjunctions, as well as lines in foreign languages and diverse literary allusions, made the poem one of the most controversial literary works of his time. It also gave birth to some of the most quoted poetic lines, such as "I will show you fear in a handful of dust."

Despite receiving mixed reactions when first published, "The Waste Land" became the forerunner in the modernist movement, and established its writer as the most dominant figure in modern literature. T. S. Eliot won the Nobel Prize for Literature in 1948.

Mariko Kato

Date October 1, 1922

Country UK

Why It's Key A 434-line modernist poem, "The Waste Land" is one of the most influential and controversial poems of the twentieth century.

Key Political Event
Mussolini leads March on Rome

The concept of a March on Rome, whereby fascists would descend on the Italian capital and seize power, was probably first proposed by the charismatic poet Gabriele D'Annunzio in 1919. The actual march was a triumphal parade by Mussolini's blackshirt militia on October 30, 1922, in response to King Vittorio Emanuele III's request of the previous day that Mussolini form a government. Mussolini's appointment as prime minister was the result of increased instability in post-World War I Italy. A succession of short-term governments seemed unable to deal with Italy's social and economic problems, though much of the unrest that was to lead Mussolini to power was actually caused by his militiamen (*squadristi*) themselves.

Attempted insurrection by fascists in late October mostly ended in subdued failure. However, successes in Milan, coupled with advice from various prominent figures, may have proved crucial in the king's decision to ignore Premier Facta's belated request for the imposition of martial law, and he appointed Mussolini in Facta's stead.

The myth of the March on Rome, whereby hundreds of thousands of Blackshirts seized power after the death of three thousand *squadristi* during an insurrection, developed quickly. In reality, only thirty thousand arrived in Rome a day after Mussolini was appointed prime minister. The March, accompanied by genuine spontaneous acts of public approval and the fascists' trademark violence and political murder, celebrated the beginning of the world's first fascist government.
Denis Casey

Date October 30, 1922

Country Italy

Why It's Key The March on Rome celebrated the beginning of the world's first fascist government.

opposite Mussolini on the March on Rome.

Key Political Event
Atatürk founds modern Turkey

Descended from *Kocacik* nomads, Mustafa Kemal Atatürk was born in Salonica (now Thessaloniki, Greece) on March 12, 1881, and became a prominent Turkish army general and political activist. After serving in the Balkan Wars and World War I, he led a successful nationalist revolution in May 1919 in Anatolia against the Islamic Sultan, who ruled the crumbling Turkish Empire. The Turkish War of Independence, as the revolution became known, was focused on resisting the peace settlement imposed on Turkey by the victorious allies, and preventing the Greeks from claiming Smyrna and its hinterland as their own. After establishing a provisional government in Ankara in 1921 and formally abolishing the Ottoman Sultanate the following year, Atatürk proclaimed the Turkish Republic on October 29, 1923, and became its first president.

The laws of Islam had long governed Turkey and Atatürk believed that this held back the development of democracy in the country. Once in power, he sought to modernize and westernize Turkey by changing the political structure, creating a secular state that separated the concerns of government from religion. Over the next fifteen years, Atatürk introduced radical and wide-ranging reforms to Turkish life, including the extension of legal rights for women, adoption of the Roman alphabet, the introduction of Western style dress, a European legal system, and secular schools. Though he was often dictatorial and ruthlessly crushed any opposition to reforms, Atatürk remained popular and in power until his death in 1938.
Helena Hewson

Date October 29, 1923

Country Turkey

Why It's Key Mustafa Kemal Atatürk created the modern secular state of Turkey, which is strategically important as the gateway between East and West in Europe.

Key Discovery
Excavation of Ur

Ur of the Chaldees, a city mentioned in the Bible as the birthplace of the patriarch Abraham, was systematically excavated between 1922 and 1934 by the British archaeologist Sir Charles Leonard Woolley. Ur, a prominent city of the ancient Sumerian civilization, is now located in the south of Iraq, which was part of the British Mandate of Mesopotamia at the beginning of Woolley's dig. Sponsored by the British Museum and the University of Pennsylvania, the Woolley excavation discovered nearly two thousand tombs, including some spectacular royal burial places. One of these, the tomb of Puabi – possibly a queen, priestess, or both – contained hundreds of breathtaking and excellently preserved artifacts that illuminated the faded history of Sumer.

The Woolley excavation rediscovered a city and civilization that had been lost for thousands of years, and made a strong case for the power and glory of the ancient Sumerians. Perhaps more importantly, thanks to the extreme antiquity of the city, the excavation disclosed fascinating details of human life at the very dawn of civilization. For example, by finding criminal codes, numerous other examples of writing, technological artifacts, weapons, and art, the excavation of Ur provided scientists with the tangible means of understanding the earliest truly settled human beings. While Ur itself has long since disappeared into the sands of Iraq, the 1922–1934 dig preserved many of its invaluable relics for posterity.

Demir Barlas

Date November 2, 1922

Country Iraq

Why It's Key The systematic excavation of Ur shed light on the dawn of human history and uncovered fabulous tombs.

Key Cultural Event
Wittgenstein's *Tractatus Logico-Philosophicus*

Born into a wealthy Vienna family in 1889, Ludwig Wittgenstein planned to become an engineer but soon became fascinated by the foundations of mathematics. An extraordinary thinker but also a practical man, he studied at Cambridge University under Bertrand Russell from 1911 until 1914, when he returned to Austria to fight in the Austro-Hungarian Army. At the same time he was laboring over a treatise that would express his deep skepticism about the nature of philosophy.

In just eighty pages of numbered propositions, Wittgenstein argues that the world consists not of things, but of facts, which are combinations of simple objects, and that all this is reflected in the hidden logical structure of human language. But what are these objects, combinations, and facts actually like?

Wittgenstein leaves that ambiguous, and consequently the work has been the subject of great confusion and dispute ever since its publication. Even more troubling, however, is the *Tractatus'* conclusion: that all claims of ethics, aesthetics, and philosophy are meaningless, including those contained in the *Tractacus* itself, and anyone who really understood the book would have no choice but to discard it as nonsense. After writing the famous closing sentence, "Whereof we cannot speak, thereof we must be silent," Wittgenstein abandoned philosophy and became a schoolteacher, only returning to the field in 1927 when he began to wonder if he had been mistaken in some of his beliefs.

Ned Beauman

Date November 11, 1922

Country Germany

Why It's Key In one the most audacious and disorienting works in the history of philosophy, Wittgenstein posed a challenge that all who followed him would have to answer.

Key Cultural Event
Discovery of Tutankhamun's tomb

Against the prevailing view that all the major pharaonic sites of the Valley of the Kings had already been discovered and cataloged, Howard Carter was determined to uncover the burial chamber of a king whose nine-year reign barely figured in the historical record. He had reason to believe that the tomb he sought was well hidden enough to have been spared the periodic looting perpetrated in most of the pharaohs' tombs since ancient times. With backing from his aristocratic patron, Lord Carnarvon, Carter and his team of archaeologists and Egyptian laborers had toiled for six years in the Valley of the Kings, with nothing to show for it. However, on November 4, excavators uncovered the entrance to a staircase. Twenty-two days later, Carter and his team had reached the tomb's antechamber and verified the abundance of treasures that had remained untouched for over 3,000 years. It would be another three months before the archaeologist and his team had fully surveyed the antechamber and penetrated the royal burial chamber containing Tutankhamun's opulent sarcophagus. By this time, curious travelers were arriving from around the world to visit the site of the dig. Although he griped bitterly about the presence of tourists, Carter was nothing if not a brilliant publicist: his book-length account of the discovery and international lecture tours played a major role in lodging Tutankhamun's name in the popular imagination. Meanwhile, the sudden death of Carnarvon five months after the tomb's discovery helped generate the legend of the "mummy's curse."
Geoffrey Schullenberger

Date November 26, 1922

Country Egypt

Why It's Key Carter's discovery captured the imagination of the world, inspiring a wave of "Egyptomania" in areas of popular culture ranging from architecture to film.

Fact "King Tut's" prominence in the modern imagination stands in disproportion to his brief and relatively inconsequential rule from 1333 to 1324 BCE.

1920-1929

133

Key Cultural Event
First general release Technicolor movie

Contrary to popular belief, color films have been made since the beginning of cinema in the 1890s. In the early years, films were hand-colored, a time-intensive process that dyed images or particular characters in vivid reds, blues, and yellows that were used to signify times of day and moods, or to highlight certain characters.

But making full-color films wasn't possible with hand coloring so in 1915, Herbert Kalmus and Donald Comstock formed the Technicolor Motion Picture Corporation, which labored for years before developing a complicated color process. After many false starts, they found that one could film an event with two cameras, one filtering out the red light, and the other filtering the blue. These two prints were glued together, producing the illusion of full color.

This two-strip Technicolor method didn't last long, but the success of *The Toll of the Sea* helped Technicolor maintain its lead in producing color technology. In 1928, an improved method was developed that used three cameras and didn't require the gluing of the filmstrips. By 1935, the technology was advanced enough that Hollywood sound films could be produced in Technicolor. The company maintained close control of the technique, and required that studios use the company's own technicians on set. By the 1960s, Technicolor was replaced with Eastman Kodak's Eastman Color, a technology that didn't require three cameras but lacked Technicolor's vibrancy. Although there are still fans of Technicolor, it is no longer used in film production.
Martin Johnson

Date November 26, 1922

Country USA

Why It's Key Technicolor became the dominant color film process from the 1920s until the 1950s, making it the color technology of many classic Hollywood films.

Key Political Event
Russia renamed the USSR

When the Soviets met in Moscow in late 1922 to announce the unification of fourteen autonomous states into a single body to be called the Union of Soviet Socialist Republics, or USSR, the world community by and large viewed it as a positive development. Russia and her neighbors were struggling in the aftermath of war, violent revolution, and crop failures, which had left tens of millions of people on the brink of starvation. The creation of the USSR seemed to promise stability to a very troubled region.

The Soviet Parliament adopted their new constitution in Moscow on December 30, 1922, to thunderous applause. Some commentators likened the creation of the new nation to the birth of the United States, as the colonies had been drawn into a powerful whole. "It is not intended to use force anywhere," wrote a Moscow-based correspondent for the Chicago *Tribune*, although other autonomous regions were expected to join.

Vladimir Lenin was appointed as head of the new government, but it became clear he would not hold the post for long. Ten days before the announcement of the USSR, Lenin suffered the latest in a series of strokes. By January, he was bed-ridden. Long before his death on January 21, 1924, Lenin's power had been passed to Josef Stalin. Stalin set the USSR on the road to becoming a superpower, but at the cost of millions of lives.
Heather Michon

Date December 30, 1922

Country USSR (now Russia)

Why It's Key The establishment of the Union of Soviet Socialist Republics created a unified Soviet state and had profound implications on the development of the Cold War.

1920-1929

Key Political Event
Invasion of the Ruhr Valley

After Germany's failure to pay for the World War I reparations, on January 11, 1923, French and Belgian troops occupied the industrial Ruhr River Valley, the center of the German coal, iron, and steel production. The Ruhr workers initially responded to the invasion by following the policy of passive resistance. Backed by the government, the workers went on strike in order to stop France from taking Ruhr's coal and steel. However, coal had been the driving force of the German economy and without it, the already deteriorating economy collapsed. Furthermore, the government was paying the striking workers in order to prevent potential social unrests, which only led to a greater deficit and inflation. Faced with a total economic disaster, the government called off the strikes in September 1923.

The occupation of the Ruhr eventually ended in August 1925, after the French accepted the Dawes Plan of 1924, according to which the reparation payments were supposed to be 1 billion gold Marks in the first year, rising to 2.5 billion by 1928. The Dawes Plan was subsequently reformulated in 1929 as the Young Plan, which reduced the reparation payments and ended foreign control of the German economy. However, Germany was still unable to pay the reparations, due to a global economic depression. When Adolf Hitler was elected Chancellor in 1933, he renounced the Treaty of Versailles, including Germany's obligation to pay reparations.
Sonja Kudeljnjak

Date January 11, 1923

Country Germany

Why It's Key The French occupation of the Ruhr made obvious the harshness of the reparations demands imposed on Germany by the Treaty of Versailles, and further worsened the economic climate, which would benefit the Nazi Party.

Fact The Ruhr invasion was initiated by the French Prime Minister Raymond Poincaré.

Key Cultural Event
Chanel No. 5 launched

When asked about her nighttime attire, the actress Marilyn Monroe famously quipped that she wore Chanel No. 5 to bed. Since it was created in 1921, the perfume has remained a classic fragrance and a representation of what keeps the Chanel fashion house at the top of the industry – Gabrielle "Coco" Chanel's trademark affinity for simplistic, yet modern style.

The creation of Chanel's signature scent arguably contains as much rumor as fact, which perhaps adds to the allure of the perfume. It is said that when Chanel commissioned Russian perfumer Ernest Beaux to create a fragrance for her, she chose the fifth sample he presented. It has also been claimed that Chanel believed in numerology, and named the fragrance after her lucky number – a theory further supported by Chanel's decision to unveil the perfume on the fifth day of the fifth month. Chanel No. 5 was also notable because of its composition – Chanel wanted to create a synthetic perfume that would last, as opposed to the short-lived natural fragrances women commonly wore at that time. Taking his inspiration from nature, Beaux created the crisp, floral aldehyde fragrance layering notes of ylang-ylang, jasmine, rose, neroli, and vanilla, among other scents.

The perfume's sleek bottle was a design triumph of its own, having been immortalized on silkscreen prints by the artist Andy Warhol in 1985. The bottle is also believed to have established the first appearance of Chanel's unmistakable logo – two interlocked letter "C"s.
Bethonie Butler

Date May 5, 1923

Country France

Why It's Key No. 5 was one of Coco Chanel's highest-grossing ventures, one that, along with the "little black dress" and her famous Chanel suit, remains a Chanel brand staple. It was also the first completely synthetic fragrance.

Key Political Event
Hyperinflation in Germany

After the end of World War I, Germany's economy started deteriorating rapidly. The 1919 Treaty of Versailles crippled the country's trade and imposed on it severe reparations payments. The amount that Germany had to pay for the reparations, combined with the debts from the war, exceeded their GDP. This situation caused an increasing devaluation of the German Mark, which the government responded to by printing more money. Soon gold and dollar reserves diminished and only paper money was being issued. The government could not decide how to pay the reparations; in the meantime, the value of the German Mark against the dollar continued to plummet.

In January 1923, US$1 was worth 9,000 Mark and on July 25, 1923, the exchange rate for US$1 was already 600,000 Mark. The situation was so bad that workers were given their wages each morning in baskets. Then they had to spend the money as soon as possible because at the end of the day it would be worthless.

Germany managed to stop the inflation in November 1923, but the negative impact of the inflation and the reparations was already taking shape. Hitler's National Socialist Party, which denounced the Berlin government and the economic burden imposed on Germany by the Allies, was starting to gain increasing support from the public. Hitler manipulated public opinion and blamed the economic crisis onto those he wanted to represent as enemies, which eventually helped him take power.
Sonja Kudeljnjak

Date July 25, 1923

Country Germany

Why It's Key Hyperinflation led to increased support for the Nazi Party.

Fact In November 1923, a loaf of bread in a German shop cost 580 billion Mark.

Key Person
Antonio Gramsci

Before November 8, 1926, Antonio Gramsci was an activist who abandoned his promise as an intellectual for a life where he engaged directly with immediate political questions. He helped start the Communist Party in Italy in 1921, and by 1924, he was the party head and one of the leaders in the fight against the country's Fascist government. In November of 1926, the government cracked down on the country's left political movements, and Gramsci was immediately jailed for his opposition to Mussolini.

Receiving notice that his jail sentence was extended to twenty years in 1928, Gramsci was transferred to a new prison in Rome, where he began one of the most sustained intellectual efforts of the century. Collectively called the *Prison Notebooks*, Gramsci filled thirty-three workbooks with his theory of cultural hegemony, the process by which working classes take on the values and interests of the upper and middle classes. Unlike other Marxists, who argue that the working classes are kept in place by coercion, Gramsci proposes that the working classes need to develop their own culture before a true revolution is possible. Organic intellectuals, who come from the working classes, are able to make this change possible, and according to Gramsci, intellectual life should not be separate from political struggle.

When Gramsci died in prison in 1937, his sister-in-law, Tatiana, smuggled his notebooks out of the jail and sent them via diplomatic bag to Moscow to be published. However, his writings were not released until after World War II.

Martin Johnson

Date November 8, 1926

Country Italy

Why It's Key The arrest turned the Italian political leftist into a philosopher, and in prison he produced one of the most thorough analyses of politics and society in the twentieth century.

Fact Gramsci died in prison before any of his intellectual writings were published.

1920–1929

151

Key Cultural Event **Heidegger publishes *Being and Time* (*Sein und Zeit*)**

Born in Messkirch, Germany in 1889, Martin Heidegger wrote and published *Being and Time* while teaching at Marburg University. Over several hundred pages, he argues that philosophers since Plato have made the mistake of thinking of "being" as nothing but a property or essence enduringly present in things, overlooking the metaphysical background conditions that make this possible. To investigate "being" properly, we must examine what it is about human existence, or *Dasein*, that makes reality intelligible to us.

However, Heidegger, who died in 1976, is not often read today. Firstly, his reputation has never recovered from his enthusiastic support of Hitler in the 1930s. The French Occupation Authority forbade him from teaching after World War II, though this decision was overturned in 1951 and he was made Professor Emeritus by the Baden government. Secondly, *Being and Time*, his greatest work, is difficult to the point of total impenetrability; few people have finished it, and even fewer can claim to understand it. Yet, it remains an awe-inspiringly profound and ambitious work, which has taken its place in the canon of Western thought. Although Heidegger's most obscure claims – for example, "The Nothing itself nothings" – were often mocked and dismissed by Anglo-American philosophers, his influence has been felt strongly on subsequent French thinking, especially on existentialism and deconstruction.

Ned Beauman

Date 1927

Country Germany

Why It's Key Heidegger hoped to explain the very nature of existence, and in the process, to correct the errors of every philosopher since Plato.

Key Cultural Event
Lindburgh flies the Atlantic alone

At 7:52 a.m. on May 20, 1927, Charles Lindburgh coaxed his plane, the *Spirit of St. Louis*, down the muddy runway of Roosevelt Field in Long Island, New York. To win the US$25,000 Orteig Prize, the 26-year-old pilot had to cross 3,600 miles of ocean without landing for refueling or directions. Carrying four sandwiches, two canteens of water, a compass, and 451 gallons of fuel, he turned toward Nova Scotia.

Lindburgh was used to finding his way across unfamiliar territory. At home, he would see someone on the ground, fly low, shout out his question, and then glide until he received his answer. When he saw a man aboard a fishing boat on the morning of May 21, he decided to give it a try. "Which way is Ireland?" he shouted. The man just stared up at him with his mouth open. The young pilot decided it was futile,

and headed on his way. He found the Irish coast not long after.

Hugging the coasts of Ireland and England, he winged across the English Channel at about 1,500 feet, and soon saw the coast of France. "I first saw the lights of Paris a little before 10 a.m.," he said, "and a few minutes later, I was circling the Eiffel Tower at an altitude of about 4,000 feet." Twenty-one minutes later, he landed at Le Bourget airport, to the cheers of thousands of spectators. "Lucky Lindy" had won his US$25,000 and his place in the record books.

Heather Michon

Date May 21, 1927

Country USA/France

Why It's Key It was the first non-stop, solo transatlantic flight in aviation history.

Key Political Event
Chinese War of Liberation

When Sun Yat-sen died in 1925, the unity of the Chinese Communist Party (CCP) and the Nationalist People's Party (the *Guomindang*) started to unravel. Sun Yat-sen founded the *Guomindang* in 1912, the year he became the first (provisional) president of the Republic of China. Two years after his death, Chiang Kai-shek assumed the leadership of the *Guomindang* and set about purging it of its Communist elements. On August 1, a series of CCP insurrections sought to regain Communist authority in the city of Nanchang, the capital of Shanxi Province. Known as the Nanchang Uprising, the episode established the Communists' military organizational capacity and an army of core CCP troops, which became the Red Army, later the People's Liberation Army. Under the leadership of Mao Zedong, Zhou Enlai, and Zhu De, the Red Army gained

enormous support, and by 1933 boasted a contingent of 200,000. As bitter conflict raged between the *Guomindang* and the CCP, Japanese forces started bearing down on China from Manchuria where in 1932 it had installed Emperor Puyi as head of the puppet state, Manchukuo. More intent on destroying the CCP, Chiang Kaishek resisted fighting the Japanese until 1937. By this time the nationalist forces, despite U.S. sponsorship, had lost domestic support, were depleted, and disorganized, while the PLA continued to gain momentum through the organization of peasants into guerrilla forces. After an interlude of eight years (1937–1945) when China defeated the Japanese, the civil war resumed, ending in 1949.

Sally Percival Wood

Date August 1, 1927

Country China

Why It's Key The Chinese war of liberation defined the irrevocable split between Chiang Kai-shek and the nationalists, and the Communist Party led by Mao Zedong. The conflict would last until 1949 and the formation of the People's Republic of China.

Key Political Event
Murphy and the Famous Five "Persons Case"

You might not be able to fight City Hall, but social activist Emily Murphy and the Famous Five managed to knock Canadian legislature into the twentieth century.

Born Emily Gowan Ferguson on March 14, 1868 in Cookstown, Ontario, Murphy came from a prominent legal family and became a self-taught legal expert. Settling in Edmonton, Alberta in 1907 with her husband Arthur Murphy, she wrote four books and multiple articles under the penname Janey Canuck, and worked to bring about the Dower Act (1911) securing women a share of their husband's property.

In 1916, the same year that Alberta women won the vote, Murphy became the first woman Police Magistrate in the British Empire. On her first day, a lawyer challenged her appointment because she was not a "person" under Canadian law – a law that also prevented women from being appointed to the Senate. Murphy's thirteen-year struggle to have women declared persons under the British North America Act of 1867 included spearheading the Famous Five (including Nellie McClung, Irene Parlby, Henrietta Muir Edwards, and Louise McKinney). On August 27, 1927 the women petitioned the government, and less than a year later, on March 14, 1928 the question of whether the definition of "persons" included women was brought to the Supreme Court of Canada.

On April 24, the Court decided against the women. Undaunted, the Famous Five took their case to the British Privy Council, where they finally won on October 18, 1929. Murphy died of diabetes in 1933.

Marie Powell

Date August 27, 1927

Country Canada

Why It's Key As a result, Canadian women are considered legal persons and can be appointed to the Senate.

Fact Canadian women first got the vote in 1916, though different provinces introduced the legislature at different times.

1920-1929

153

Key Discovery
Heisenberg's Uncertainty Principle

In essence, the Uncertainty Principle states that when attempting to measure the movement of subatomic particles, it is impossible at the same time to know both their position and their momentum. Werner Heisenberg arrived at this conclusion through another seemingly illogical assumption, but nevertheless, one that lies at the heart of the broader theory of quantum mechanics: at this subatomic level, physical objects can be described in terms of both waves and particles, rather than as one or the other.

The Uncertainty Principle made a significant contribution to an important developing field of physics, the leading proponent of which, Niels Bohr, Heisenberg had worked for and was a personal friend of. The work of these two men came to form what is known as the Copenhagen Interpretation, and stimulated many important later advances. But this interpretation also came under considerable challenge, particularly from those who rejected its conception of a system of possibilities rather than determinations. Over the succeeding decades, however, it has been shown to accurately reflect, and to predict, experimental data, despite the fact that even those physicists who employ it cannot fully explain why it works. Furthermore, although it is grounded in complex mathematics, the paradox at the heart of quantum mechanics has a broad, non-specialist appeal. The more controversial element of its history, the contribution made by the work of Heisenberg and Bohr to the construction of nuclear bombs, has also ensured its prominent public attention.

Laura Davies

Date September 1, 1927

Country Germany

Why Its Key Heisenberg's Uncertainty Principle is a foundational theory of modern theoretical physics.

Key Cultural Event
Philo T. Farnsworth demonstrates a television

In 1922, a fourteen-year-old farm boy from Utah had the idea that by transmitting and deflecting a series of electron beams he could create a moving image; less than ten years later he built the machine and called it a television.

From an early age Philo T. Farnsworth had displayed a natural affinity for all things mechanical, though he knew little about electronic theory. One evening, when his family was trying to figure out why a generator on the farm had stopped, Farnsworth surprised everyone by fixing it, and his parents allowed him to turn an attic room into his own science lab.

When his high school chemistry teacher, Justin Tolman, discussed with him the principles of electricity, Farnsworth was inspired and drew many prototype sketches of a machine that could receive and display

moving images. Five years later, after just two years of university education, Farnsworth demonstrated a working model to the press, then in 1934 to the public at the Franklin Institute in Philadelphia.

Farnsworth later became embroiled in a legal dispute over patents with the Radio Corporation of America acting on behalf of Vladimir Zworykin, who claimed to have invented a similar machine in 1923. The patent was ultimately decided in Farnsworth's favor, when his teacher Tolman produced those original drawings given to him from years before. RCA were forced to pay Farnsworth substantial royalties, before he sold his patents to them for a considerable sum some years later.

Terence McSweeney

Date September 7, 1927

Country USA

Why It's Key Television is one of the defining inventions of the twentieth century.

Fact Philo Farnsworth was named one of *Time* Magazine's 100 Greatest Scientists and Thinkers of the Twentieth Century.

Key Cultural Event
The Jazz Singer released

By the 1920s, movie stars loomed large and Hollywood was a major commercial industry. It wasn't until the end of the decade, however, that a final technical element would become an intrinsic part of the medium as it exists today: sound. *The Jazz Singer*, a melancholy saga starring famed singer Al Jolson and directed by Alan Crosland, used Vitaphone's sound-on-disc technology to implement six musical numbers into the film. The production, produced by Warner Bros., wasn't the first to utilize the new machinery: a year earlier, Crosland's *Don Juan* included a fully synchronized orchestral score and sound effects. *The Jazz Singer* built on those advancements with scant recorded dialogue and a successful fusion of the gimmick with the storytelling. The plot follows a Jewish boy whose father rejects him for showing interest in

secular show business. Years later, Jolson's character returns home to make amends with his family, setting the stage for a heartbreaking climax as the son sings a prayer for his father shortly before his death.

The movie gained acclaim, but the real star of the show was Jolson's voice. Although silent cinema persisted for a few more years, many popular performers from its heyday, including Charlie Chaplin, ultimately chose to alter their style as an acknowledgment that audiences could hear their voices. Other actors, such as Buster Keaton and Mary Pickford, had a harder time transitioning into the sound era. The career death of silent stars was explored in Billy Wilder's 1950 film *Sunset Boulevard*.

Eric Kohn

Date October 6, 1927

Country USA

Why It's Key The implementation of an audio soundtrack into movies paved the way for a new age of filmmaking, the "talkies."

Fact The plot of *The Jazz Singer* was modeled after lead actor Al Jolson's own experiences.

opposite Al Jolson in *The Jazz Singer*.

Key Cultural Event
Coming of Age in Samoa published

The American cultural anthropologist Margaret Mead (1901–1978) was only twenty-four when she spent nine months in Samoa, observing the sexual experiences of young girls on Ta'u Island. Mead's colorful and highly readable account of her findings became one of the most widely known anthropological texts ever written. It was also one of the most influential. Mead painted a compelling picture of a close-knit and well-adjusted society, where sex was a natural and positive experience, and starkly contrasted this with the repressive social mores that prevailed in the United States at that time. The book had a huge impact on contemporary theories of childrearing and contributed, at least indirectly, to the emergence of far more permissive attitudes to sex in Western society. Yet, *Coming of Age in Samoa* is now one of the most

controversial texts of its time and kind. While Samoans have found her descriptions of their culture misleading and insulting, scientists have questioned the scientific accuracy of Mead's methods. She has been accused of altering or even fabricating the evidence to fit her own preconceived theories. One of her greatest critics was Derek Freeman, an anthropology professor from New Zealand. In various works published after her death, Freeman claimed that some of the girls Mead worked with had admitted to him that the stories they'd told her were either lies or jokes, undermining Mead's hypotheses about Samoan sexuality. However, several of Freeman's conclusions have also been disputed, and the whole debate remains both lively and unresolved.
Lynn Shepherd

Date 1928

Country USA

Why It's Key A famous and groundbreaking book that – rightly or wrongly – challenged the existing perceptions of adolescent sexuality.

156

Key Person
Paul Dirac

Paul Dirac was probably the best physicist you've never heard of. Born in Bristol in 1902, he spent much of his life at the University of Cambridge, before moving to Florida in the 1970s. A deeply thoughtful mathematical physicist, he is best known for developing an equation that describes the behavior of electrons and similar particles. Consistent with both Einstein's special relativity and the then nascent science of quantum physics, this "Dirac equation" explained many properties of particles that had hitherto been mysterious.

According to legend, it was while staring into his Cambridge fireplace that the crucial pieces of the puzzle fell into place in his mind. He believed his equation was correct but there was a problem because it produced solutions not only corresponding

to particles with positive energy – the electrons – but also describing particles with negative energy. Rather than rejecting these latter solutions as nonsense, Dirac predicted that they would correspond to antimatter; the electron would be accompanied by a positron, a particle with opposite (positive) charge to the electron, but identical in all other respects. When Carl Anderson discovered such a particle in 1932, it confirmed Dirac's prediction as one of the great triumphs of theoretical physics and won him a share of the 1933 Nobel Prize for Physics. Dirac spent the next fifty years working on problems in quantum mechanics, but he will always be remembered for his equation. Engraved on his memorial, it is the only equation in Westminster Abbey.
Laura Davies

Date February 1, 1928

Born/Died 1902–1984

Nationality British

Why It's Key The discovery of antimatter was a crucial advance in theoretical physics, drawing us nearer to an explanation of the structure of the universe, and a discovery that often features in science fiction.

Key Political Event
Turkey becomes a secular state

Out of the ashes of the Ottoman Empire – which was defeated in World War I and carved up by the Treaty of Sevres (1920) – rose a state made in the forward-thinking vision of its founder, Mustafa Kemal Atatürk. As leader of a new democratic parliament based in Ankara – as opposed to the Islamic Caliphate run from Istanbul – he launched the War of Independence, which led to Turkey's statehood in 1923.

Atatürk, Turkey's first president, molded the country into a western-style democracy, a liberal republic based on European law codes. A founding principle was secularism, and on March 3, 1924, the powers of the Caliphate were transferred to the new government. By the time the state religion was disestablished on April 10, 1928, Islamic schools had been closed, Islamic law abolished, headscarves banned in public buildings, and a wider religious tolerance encouraged.

Since the 1960s, Atatürk reforms have been known as "Kemalism" and are regarded as the ideological foundation of modern Turkey. However, Turkey's history since Atatürk's "revolutions" has not always been that of the democratic, stable polity he desired – there have been several coups and periods of military rule. The country's presence in Cyprus has met with international disapproval and it faces internal instability with Kurdish rebels in its eastern regions. Nevertheless, Atatürk built a bridge between Europe and Asia, a modern state based on principles of equality and tolerance, which cast off a millennium of history to look to the future.

Josh Spero

Date April 10, 1928

Country Turkey

Why It's Key Under Atatürk, Turkey turned toward Europe by abandoning Islam as the state religion, adopting the Roman alphabet, and instituting equality for women.

1920–1929

157

Key Political Event
Kellogg-Briand Pact

In June 1927, the French Prime Minister, Aristide Briand, proposed to the then American Secretary of State, Frank B. Kellogg, that they enter into an agreement expressing their mutual renunciation of war. Concerned that the pact would place the Americans in an indirect alliance with the French, Kellogg instead suggested a multilateral treaty, which rejected war as an instrument of national policy or solution to international disputes and included multiple nations. Briand accepted and on August 27, 1928, the Kellogg-Briand Pact (otherwise known as the "Pact of Paris") was signed in Paris in a new spirit of conciliation, initially by fifteen, but eventually sixty-five, independent nations, including Germany.

However, the Pact was fundamentally flawed. In practice, it was interpreted as allowing war in the case of national defense, and individual nations reserved the right to act to protect "special interests." A more profound problem was that there was no provision for any kind of enforcement and the pact was powerless against threats from aggressive nations, as the Italian invasion of Ethiopia in 1935 ably demonstrated. Indeed, within twelve years of the signing of the Pact, all of the signatories became invoved in World War II.

But while the treaty was useless as a practical instrument in preventing war, it was important in redefining war as a an act perpetrated upon a victim state by an aggressor state. Its legacy may be seen in current international law, which requires any military action to be justified as self defence.

Helena Hewson

Date August 27, 1928

Country France

Why It's Key The Kellogg-Briand Pact was an international attempt to prevent a recurrence of the horrors of World War I by signing an agreement that condemned and renounced war as a part of national policy and method of solving international disputes.

Key Discovery
Fleming discovers penicillin

Before his career as a research scientist, Alexander Fleming served as a physician in World War I and witnessed many soldiers dying from septicemia, or blood poisoning. He and other scientists at the time knew microbes caused diseases from Louis Pasteur's Germ Theory of Disease, and they were searching for a substance that would kill germs without killing the patient. Joseph Lister (1871), William Roberts (1874), Pasteur (1877), and André Gratia and Sara Dath (1920s) had all previously observed that bacterial growth was inhibited by the presence of fungus, but it was Fleming that brought these observations to fruition.

Experimenting with the bacteria *staphylococci*, Fleming noticed his culture plates were contaminated with mold, which in itself was nothing novel. Yet, he then noted that bacterial growth was inhibited in a zone around the fungus. Extracting the mold, he named it penicillin, and published his results in 1929. In 1938, a biochemistry team at Oxford University headed by Dr Florey and Dr Chain produced a stable antibiotic product from the mold extracts. Penicillin was experimentally injected into patients at the Radcliffe Hospital, and cured strep throat, scarlet fever, syphilis, meningitis, and many other deadly diseases. In 1945 Fleming, along with Florey and Chain, was awarded the Nobel Prize. Fleming, however, correctly predicted that bacteria would over time become resistant to the new antibiotic, and indeed by 1952, three-fifths of all *staphylococci* infections had become antibiotic-resistant. Scientists today are still searching for new wonder drugs to outwit microbes.

Anna Marie Roos

Date 1928

Country UK

Why It's Key Fleming's discovery and isolation of the antibiotic penicillin from the fungus *Penicillium notatum* saved countless lives from disease-causing microorganisms.

Fact Fleming was hired at St Mary's Hospital not only because of his skills as a physician and scientist, but because he was a crack shot. The hospital administrators wanted him on their rifle team.

158

Key Political Event
Stalin introduces the first Five-Year Plan

Born in 1879 into a peasant family, Joseph Stalin rose to power through a brutal combination of manipulation and strength of will. When he succeeded Lenin as leader, the legacy of the Civil War left a confused mix of Communism and capitalism that remained disorganized throughout the country.

As the new dictator, Stalin visualized the end of any form of market-driven economy. Unlike his predecessor, he dismissed internationalism, and sought "socialism in one country." However, he feared falling further behind the West and, claiming that "either we make good the difference in ten years or they will crush us," he launched his first Five-Year Plan on October 1, 1928.

The Five-Year Plan aimed to quickly industrialize the Soviet Union and collectivize farms, setting strict production quotas. It placed goals that were clearly unrealistic – a 250 per cent increase in overall industrial development and a 330 per cent expansion in heavy industry alone. The first plan was declared successful in 1932, although two more were introduced in 1933 and 1938, and those who feared punishment for not meeting the targets often falsified their reports. Many skilled workers, as well as those who openly resisted, were executed or exiled, and protesting farmers who burnt their crops and refused to work led to horrific famines.

In his second Five-Year Plan of 1933, Stalin increased steel production to rival other foreign powers and Russia's growing industrial strength was a key factor in the defeat of Nazi Germany.

Mariko Kato

Date October 1, 1928

Country USSR

Why It's Key The ruthless goals set in Stalin's Five-Year Plans shaped Communism in the Soviet Union, and established it as a new global superpower.

Fact "Stalin" was an adopted name, meaning "man of steel." His real name was Joseph Dzhugashvili.

opposite A tribunal of two farmers who failed to make the required targets to meet the Five-Year Plan.

Key Cultural Event
Disney creates Mickey Mouse

Animation character Mickey Mouse, the most famous creation of the Walt Disney Company, was born in Walt Disney's imagination in early 1928 on a train from New York to Los Angeles. Disney had attended a meeting in which financial supporters had rejected Oswald the Rabbit – an earlier cartoon character – and, concerned that he would disappoint his staff, he decided to replace him with a mouse. Disney later claimed that the reason for choosing a mouse was because "a mouse is sort of a sympathetic character." He initially invented a mouse in red velvet pants and named him "Mortimer," but his wife, Lilian, suggested "Mickey."

Back in the studio, animator Ub Iwerks developed the character, designing his physical appearance and animating the first three Mickey shorts. His source of inspiration was English comedian Charlie Chaplin: "We wanted something appealing, and we thought of a tiny bit of a mouse that would have something of the wistfulness of Chaplin – a little fellow trying to do the best he could."

Mickey Mouse made his screen debut on November 18, 1928, at the Colony Theater in New York, as the star in *Steamboat Willie*, the first movie to be played with a synchronized soundtrack. This date later became known as his official birthday. Mickey's shy, falsetto voice was recorded by Disney himself. Since then, Mickey Mouse has become one of the most recognized and loved characters in the world and also brought phenomenal success to the Walt Disney Company.

Mariko Kato

Date November 18, 1928

Country USA

Why It's Key It marked the birth of one of the most internationally recognized cartoon characters.

Fact Mickey Mouse is an Academy Award-winning cartoon character that is now an icon for the Walt Disney Company.

opposite Walt and Mrs Disney with a stuffed Mickey Mouse.

Key Cultural Event
Tampon with applicator and string

Although women have used disposable tampons since Ancient Egypt, the modern tampon with applicator and string was not developed until 1929. Dr Earle Cleveland Haas, a general practitioner who also dabbled in Depression-era real estate, decided to reinvent the tampon after witnessing the discomfort his wife and his female patients experienced from wearing diaper-like pads during their periods. Haas was already an accomplished medical inventor; he had successfully patented a ring for the contraceptive diaphragm that earned him US$50,000.

On a visit to California, a friend told him that she often inserted a piece of sponge internally instead of using the more popular sanitary napkins. Haas quickly realized that the same function could be accomplished using compressed cotton. Yet, Haas knew that women would want to be able to insert and remove the tampon without having to touch it. Though he initially thought about introducing a metal applicator, he instead decided to use a set of cardboard tubing he had on his shelf, which could be flushed down the toilet after use.

Haas patented his tampon on November 19, 1931; however he referred to it as a "catamenial device" from the Greek for monthly menses. Soon afterwards, he registered the trademark "Tampax" for his invention. Tampax went on to become one of the most successful tampon companies in the world, and in 1986, the editors of *Consumer Reports* magazine voted tampons one of the fifty most revolutionary inventions.

Bianca Jackson

Date 1929

Country USA

Why It's Key The invention of the tampon with applicator and string offered women an easier, cleaner, and more comfortable way of dealing with their monthly periods.

Fact According to Haas, the name "Tampax" came from the combination of the words "tampon" and "vaginal pack."

Key Political Event
Yugoslavia created

Ever since the forming of the Kingdom of Croats, Serbs, and Slovenes in December 1918, the country was being internally divided by the struggle between Serbs and Croats. The Croats were boycotting the Belgrade Parliament since June 1928, after the leader of the Croatian Peasant Party, Stjepan Radic, had been assassinated on the floor of the parliament by a Serbian MP, Punisa Racic. As a result, Croatian MPs refused to return to the parliament until Croatia was given more autonomy.

The ruler of Yugoslavia, King Alexander Karageorgevic, chose a radical way to end the crisis. On January 6, 1929, he abolished the constitution and introduced a personal dictatorship. Alexander also changed the name of the country to the Kingdom of Yugoslavia and abolished the borders of Croatia, Serbia, and Slovenia. The new borders were based on nine regions, *banovinas*, which were named after the principal rivers, so as to avoid regional patriotism and try to promote a Yugoslav national identity. Most of the members of the new cabinet were Serbs.

King Alexander was assassinated in October 1934 by political dissidents and tensions continued to increase. Yugoslavia was occupied by the Axis forces on April 6, 1941, and capitulated less than two weeks later. Its territory was divided into several entities, including the Independent State of Croatia and a Serbian rump state under General Milan Nedic. Yugoslavia would not be reconstituted until November 1943.
Sonja Kudeljnjak

Date January 6, 1929

Country Yugoslavia

Why It's Key The January 6 Dictatorship exacerbated the internal conflict between Croats and Serbs, which would ultimately lead to the breakup of Yugoslavia.

Fact During the dictatorship, King Alexander introduced the death sentence for anyone planning to overthrow the new regime.

1920-1929

163

Key Cultural Event
Bourke-White's career launched

Margaret Bourke-White began her career as an industrial and architectural photographer, but turned to photojournalism in 1929 when her photographs caught the attention of publisher Henry Luce. In May of 1929, Luce invited Bourke-White to work for his newest publication, *Fortune* magazine. Her earliest photographs for *Fortune*, published in the first issue, exhibited characteristics of the picture essays that she would later help pioneer at *Life* magazine.

When Luce decided to start a new publication that would cover the week's news in pictures, Bourke-White was a natural choice for one of the first four staff photographers. Her photographs were chosen for the cover and lead story of *Life*'s first issue, published on November 23, 1936. The ten-page article deals with the construction of the Fort Peck Dam in Montana and documents the lives of the workers building the dam. Not only do the pictures represent an early example of an American picture essay, they were also among the first examples of social documentary photographs to reach wide circulation. Bourke-White continued to contribute to *Life* for approximately thirty more years, traveling around the world and producing iconic photographs of significant events. By the end of the 1960s, the circulation of *Life* began to decline as televised images increasingly displaced the photographic essay. Bourke-White passed away in 1971, one year before *Life* ceased publication.
Andrea L. Korda

Date May 8, 1929

Country USA

Why It's Key Her photographs for *Life* created a novel form of reporting where photographs take center stage.

Fact Bourke-White was the first female photographer for both *Fortune* and *Life* magazines, as well as the first female official photographer for the United States Army Air Corps.

opposite Bourke-White on the Chrysler Building.

Key Cultural Event
Wall Street crashes on "Black Thursday"

The economic boom of the 1920s lured Americans into investing large sums of money in the stock market, often buying on margin. When the stock market crashed on "Black Thursday," 1929, the loans were called in. Former American millionaires sold apples on street corners. Others committed suicide. Three million Americans lost their jobs and more businesses collapsed every day. Banks closed, leaving families with no means of support, and the Great Depression spread around the world.

President Herbert Hoover, however, refused to believe that the Depression was more than a temporary setback. As a conservative, Hoover was opposed to government interference in the economy, but he proposed tax cuts and asked businesses to reduce wages. In response, three thousand companies slashed wages, and thousands of others instituted mass layoffs. By 1930, unemployment had risen 149 percent. When state and city governments became unable to offer relief, Hoover encouraged private charities to offer assistance, exhausting their resources. Families stood in line at soup kitchens. One million people traveled the United States, looking for food and work.

Hoover's failure to react aggressively to the problems of the Great Depression led to his defeat in 1932. His successor, Democrat Franklin D. Roosevelt, launched the New Deal, turning the United States into a social welfare state. Countries around the world followed suit, conceding that nations have a responsibility to ensure a basic standard of living to all who reside within their borders.

Elizabeth R. Purdy

Date October 29, 1929

Country USA

Why It's Key The Great Depression led to the redefinition of American politics and economics and turned the United States into a social welfare state, serving as a model for similar reforms around the world.

opposite Customers from local brokerage houses swamped the exchange on Wall Street in an effort to gain entrance.

Key Cultural Event
Sliced bread introduced nationally in the USA

In 1912, Otto Frederick Rohwedder of Davenport, Iowa, sold his jewelry stores to finance his idea for a machine that would slice bread. Unfortunately, a factory fire destroyed his first prototype, and it was not until 1927 that he was able to fund another attempt. His commercial bread slicer and wrapping machine was completed in 1928, and he began to market it despite the warnings from bakers that pre-sliced bread would go stale too quickly.

Records suggest that it was the Chillicothe Baking Company in Missouri that first used the slicer commercially on July 7, 1928. The product was called "Kleen Maid Sliced Bread." Other sources suggest that the first commercial use was made in Battle Creek, Michigan, but there is very little evidence for this. However, it was not until two years later that sliced bread was made commercially viable. Gustav Papendick, a St. Louis baker, invented a machine that would wrap the bread and keep it fresh, and in 1930, the Continental Baking Company introduced sliced bread under its already established "Wonder Bread" brand, which went on sale nationally. Although sales were slow to start with, it grew in popularity until in 1933 it outnumbered sales of unsliced bread. It was also the Continental Baking Company that introduced the now ubiquitous saying: "the best thing since sliced bread" as part of its campaign to advertise sliced bread in the 1930s.

Ros Bott

Date 1930

Country USA

Why It's Key The invention of pre-sliced bread was a technological innovation that revolutionized the way people eat bread, and helped to popularize the toaster.

Fact Charles Strite invented the electric toaster in 1926.

Key Political Event
Stalin temporarily halts forced collectivization

Communists shared the ultimate goal of "collectivizing" agriculture. They believed that peasants needed to pool their land and livestock in order to adopt mechanization and improve productivity, and also to ensure their control by the ruling party. Stalin decreed collectivization in 1928, but it proceeded slowly until late 1929, when he declared that it was necessary to destroy the class of rich peasants he called "kulaks," a label soon applied to anyone resisting collectivization. During the next frenzied months, Communist Party activists spread across the countryside, demanding that peasants join the new collectives. Many peasants slaughtered their few animals rather than surrender them. Soldiers surrounded recalcitrant villages and mowed down peasants with machine guns. Thousands of kulaks

were deported to the remote labor and prison camps of the "Gulag."

Stalin halted the growing chaos with a newspaper article entitled "Dizzy with Success," published on March 2, 1930. In it he blamed overzealous subordinates for the excesses of collectivization, and he gave most peasants the chance to withdraw their lands and livestock from the collectives. The lull was brief; soon collectivization and coercion resumed. The worst suffering was yet to come, as the disruptions unleashed one of the worst famines in history, in which millions died. Within a few years, the Soviet Union had collectivized its agriculture, and sent millions of surplus peasants to work in its new factories – a remarkable economic transformation achieved at a terrible price.
Brian Ladd

Date March 2, 1930

Country USSR

Why It's Key Stalin blamed subordinates for the horrors of agricultural collectivization.

168

Key Political Event
The Salt March launches civil disobedience movement

In 1930, Mahatma Gandhi issued a round of demands to British Viceroy Lord Irwin in the National Congress's program of agitation for Indian independence. The demands included the prohibition of alcohol, protection for Indian cloth manufacturers, and the abolition of the salt tax. Salt, Gandhi declared, was essential to the human diet and the inalienable right of all Indians to enjoy free of tax. In the eighteenth century, the East India Company had acquired the monopoly over salt trade, and the British had since enjoyed the revenue from the salt tax. Though the tax was small per capita, it amounted to 4% of annual revenue. More importantly it was a matter of deep resentment for Indians, every one of whom required salt.

Gandhi mobilized this resentment when conceiving the Salt March. Commencing on March 12, 1930, at his

ashram near Ahmadabad, the protest march concluded 241 miles away, and 24 days later, at Dandi on the Gujarat coast on April 6. Arriving at the beach with his seventy-eight hand-picked followers and with the international media recording the event, Gandhi scooped up a handful of salt and famously declared the beginning of India's satyagraha ("non-violent") Civil Disobedience Movement. The Salt March was followed by raids on the Dharasana Salt Works over several weeks when some 1,329 satyagrahis were successively beaten by the colonial police. Gandhi was imprisoned until January 1931, after which a truce was reached, the Gandhi-Irwin Pact, signed in March 1931.
Sally Percival Wood

Date March 12, 1930

Country India

Why It's Key The Salt March launched Gandhi's satyagraha ("non-violent") movement of civil disobedience in India, which ultimately resulted in Indian independence. It came to symbolize the power of peaceful protest, which inspired, most famously, Martin Luther King Jr. and the American Civil Rights Movement of the 1950s and 1960s.

Key Cultural Event
Hitchcock releases his first talkie, *Blackmail*

Alfred Hitchcock was a mere thirty years old when he made *Blackmail*, but certainly the right person to deal with the new technology of sound recording. Hitchcock already had a wife and child in addition to an international reputation as a rising talent. The British director's first hit, a silent thriller called *The Lodger* (1927), brought him immediate prestige, but *Blackmail* helped solidify his directorial skill.

British International Pictures had commissioned the filmmaker to shoot the film, a streamlined tale of murder and detective work with a trim budget, using occasional sound. Eager to experiment, Hitchcock instead chose to make two versions of the film – one silent and the other with sound. The studio was content with the latter version, which proved the director's ability to adapt. *Blackmail* offered a smooth representation of Hitchcock's burgeoning abilities. It marked the first time he would conclude a movie with a chase scene at a public location (in this case, the British Museum, London).

Ever the innovator, Hitchcock implemented the use of sound directly into the plot. The story follows a woman who kills a man after he tries to seduce her. Her paranoia about getting caught climaxes when she overhears a conversation and the word "knife" stands out amid gibberish. Such clever devices caught the attention of Hollywood producers, and Hitchcock soon became a popular filmmaker overseas. Over the course of the decade, his reputation would continue to blossom, but he was still going strong thirty years later when he made *Psycho* (1960).

Eric Kohn

Date October 6, 1930

Country USA

Why It's Key The film solidified Hitchcock's reputation as an extremely innovative filmmaker.

Fact Anny Ondra, whose heavy Polish accent was difficult for English speakers to understand, played the main character. The problem of her accent was resolved by having another actress speak Ondra's lines off-camera.

1930–1939

169

Key Person
Haile Selassie, Emperor of Ethiopia

Haile Selassie I, Emperor of Ethiopia from 1930 to 1974, was perhaps the most famous – and fascinating – African leader of the twentieth century. His remarkable career and long reign began with the death of Empress Zewditu in 1930, paving the way for the man who was styled "Conquering Lion of the Tribe of Judah, King of Kings of Ethiopia, and Elect of God" to come to a throne said to date back to Solomon. Selassie presided over the framing of a constitution and plunged himself into other modernizing projects that were cut short by the Italian invasion of Ethiopia in 1935. Selassie went into exile and became a global symbol of his embattled country, particularly after a moving speech to the League of Nations. The emperor became *Time* magazine's "Man of the Year" and remained the most visible symbol of anti-colonial resistance in the world during his exile. Selassie's increasing celebrity contributed to his status in the doctrine of the Rastafarian religion, adherents of which claimed that the emperor was actually God incarnate. While Selassie largely fell off the European radar after the Italian surrender of 1941, his fame in Jamaica and other centers of Rastafari practice kept growing, especially after reggae superstar Bob Marley introduced the world to the doctrine that Selassie was Jah, or God. After Selassie's death in 1975, Rastafarianism continues to keep him alive.

Demir Barlas

Date November 2, 1930

Born/Died 1892–1975

Nationality Ethiopian

Why It's Key Ethiopia's penultimate emperor became a twentieth-century icon, particularly for progressives, anti-Fascists, and Rastafarians.

Key Person
Dietrich wears pants in *Morocco*

A sound film star with silent star looks, Marlene Dietrich's role as "Lola Lola" in the 1930 Josef von Sternberg film *The Blue Angel* made her famous overnight. Playing a nightclub singer whose performance is so spectacular that an aging professor leaves his career to follow her, Dietrich helped define the femme fatale role that was a staple of Hollywood films in the 1930s and 1940s.

But as Dietrich showed in *Morocco* – her follow-up to *The Blue Angel* – she was more than just a character type. Working again with von Sternberg, who collaborated with her on seven films in five years, Dietrich established herself as an actress willing to flout convention. In its most famous scene, she wears a pantsuit – the first time an actress had done so in a Hollywood film – and kisses another woman on the lips. While she could barely speak English when she appeared in the film, Dietrich's acting was nominated for an Academy Award, and she laid the groundwork for a star image that still resonates today.

Not surprisingly, Dietrich was as shocking off camera as she was when she was in front of it. Having affairs with men and women – including some of her fellow actors – in the early 1930s was too scandalous to be widely reported, but in the decades that followed, she has become an icon for queer individuals, who were inspired by her sexual independence.

Martin Johnson

Date December 6, 1930

Born/died 1901–1992

Nationality German

Why It's Key By refusing to accept traditional parts for women, Dietrich led the way for other female actors to set role models for women.

Fact In her earlier films, Dietrich often played the part of a demure housewife.

opposite **Marlene Dietrich** in the film *Morocco*.

1930–1939

Key Cultural Event
First male-to-female transsexual surgery

The first recorded sex reassignment surgery was performed in 1931 in Berlin, transforming male Einar Wegener to female Lili Elbe after a series of five surgeries that eventually and tragically resulted in her death. Born in Denmark, Wegener built a career as a successful artist, working alongside Gerda Gottlieb whom he married in 1904. Dressing in female clothing with increasing regularity to model for Gottlieb's paintings, Wegener adopted the name Lili Elbe and began to socialize as a woman, being introduced initially as Wegener's sister. Engaging and attractive, Lili received wide acceptance as a woman, and even an offer of marriage from an unsuspecting suitor, before undergoing experimental surgery to alter her sex organs from male to female. This operation, conducted by famous sexologist Dr Magnus Hirschfeld, was the first of its kind, and was apparently successful in removing the male sex organs.

Dr Warnekros performed Elbe's subsequent surgeries in Dresden, with a second operation transplanting ovaries into her body, and a third and fourth requiring their removal after dangerous complications arising from their rejection. In 1931, a fifth operation was performed, with the aim of eventually allowing Elbe to become a mother, but she died shortly afterwards. Although sex reassignment surgery resulted in the death of Lili Elbe, it allowed her to live as a woman and was the pioneering example of this now well-established procedure.

Hannah Furness

Date 1931

Country Germany

Why It's Key It pioneered the procedure that now allows individuals to correct what they believe to be the misalignment of their gender and physical sex.

Key Cultural Event **Dali paints *The Persistence of Memory* (*La Persistencia de la Memoria*)**

Though he drew heavily on the realism of the Pre-Raphaelites and French nineteenth-century painters, Salvador Dali (1904–1989) is known principally for his contributions to Surrealism. Pioneering methods such as the "paranoiac-critical method," in which he would deliberately induce psychotic hallucinations to inspire artistic expression, Dali created works that gave dreams a surreal yet disturbingly credible nature.

Painted in 1931, *The Persistence of Memory* portrays the eternality of time, and our limited existence within its boundaries. In a bleak landscape, ants crawl toward a larger-than-life watch, but are inflicted with death and decay on contact. The watch itself drapes over the surface edge, and other watches melt over a tree branch and a head. The head is said to be the approximation of Dali's own profile, and the long eyelashes on the closed eyes evoke sexual symbolism.

In this work, Dali wanted "to systematize confusion and thus to help discredit completely the world of reality." Nevertheless, the reality of the objects, as well as the realistic portrayal of the coast of Catalonia, Dali's home, in the background, contributes to its disturbing attraction. It is also recognized as the graphic illustration of Einstein's theory of relativity, as well as the transitional piece between Dali's Freudian phase and his growing interest in science. The painting is now celebrated as one of Dali's best works, and has been exhibited at the Museum of Modern Art in New York since 1934.
Mariko Kato

Date 1931

Country Spain

Why It's Key It is one of the most famous examples of surrealism in art.

Key Cultural Event
Empire State Building constructed

It was no accident that the newly constructed Empire State Building held the title of tallest building in the world. Standing 1,454 feet above the New York City streets, it was built to impress, and businessman John J. Raskob spent good money ensuring it would rise high above the competition.

Work began on March 17, 1930, when America was in the grip of the Great Depression, but no such circumstances were going to limit the ambitions of Raskob. William Lamb, an architect from the firm Shreve, Lamb & Harmon, was responsible for its Art Deco style, and on May 1, 1931, ahead of schedule, President Hoover officially declared the Empire State Building open.

Construction of the skyscraper was always going to be fraught with danger, and while not officially recorded, around five construction workers lost their lives in the pursuit of grandeur. This, however, was lower than estimated, as it was believed that more than a hundred workers would die.

The Empire State Building held the title as tallest building in the world up until the construction of the World Trade Center in 1972, and while it no longer retains that title today, it remains an arresting prominence on the New York skyline.

Millions of people have left their fear for heights at the door and marveled at the amazing views from the Observatory located on the eighty-sixth floor. It remains to this day a popular tourist attraction, and has been immortalized in music, art, and film.
Kerry Duffy

Date May 1, 1931

Country USA

Why It's Key One of the most familiar buildings in the world, the Empire State Building was built during the Depression, and has become an enduring symbol of hope.

Fact The Empire State Building has been named one of the seven wonders of the modern world by the American Society of Civil Engineers.

opposite The Empire State Building under construction.

Key Political Event
Japanese conquest of Manchuria

During the modernizing decade of the 1920s, Japanese leaders waged ideological and political battles to define Japan's role in world affairs. Elected civilian leaders in the Japanese Diet, who promoted constitutional democracy, a world market economy, and some accommodation with the global security interests of the western world powers, faced-off with nationalistic leaders in the Japanese army, who put forward their imperial aspirations in East Asia in the name of Japan's divine Emperor Hirohito.

Long-established "unequal" relationships with weak Chinese governments had already yielded a favorable trade position for Japanese businessmen in the northern Chinese province of Manchuria, but the army hoped to lay formal colonial claim to the strategic territory. Japanese army officers tried to destabilize the

Chinese Nationalist government by assassinating the Nationalists' Manchurian Warlord ally, Zhang Zuolin, in 1928. However, the Nationalists arranged an uneasy truce with the Diet, and the army's plans to gain jurisdiction over Manchuria temporarily failed. On September 18, 1931, the army tried again, on the pretext of restoring "peace" after a supposed Chinese attack on the South Manchurian Railway Company. Japan's modern army easily overpowered Chinese forces and occupied all of Manchuria by December. In the League of Nations forum, western powers and China issued ineffective diplomatic protests and formed an international committee to investigate the causes of the incident, but failed to dislodge the occupying army. Japan left the League of Nations in 1933.

Karen Garner

Date September 18, 1931

Country China

Why It's Key The incident established Japan's imperial policy, and inspired Nazi German leader Adolf Hitler to reject diplomatic pressures to curtail German imperial ambitions in Europe by the League of Nations.

Key Cultural Event
Coca-Cola introduces the modern Santa Claus

In December 1931, the Coca-Cola Company's holiday advertising campaign introduced the United States to a fresh take on the Santa Claus mythology. As a blend of influences including Father Christmas, a British figure dating back to the seventeenth century, and the Dutch Sinterklaas, based on St. Nicholas, the gift-giving Christmas character was ripe for reimagining (and commercial appropriation). The cheery, fireside images of the bushy-bearded, red-and-white-suited man captured the public imagination and quickly became his definitive rendition. Though this particular portrayal of Claus wasn't entirely original – rival company White Rock Beverages used a similarly attired version of the character in advertisements as early as 1915 – it was Coca-Cola's campaign that popularized it.

Swedish-American artist Haddon Sundblom painted the advertisements in 1931, and initially used his friend Lou Prentiss as a model. They debuted in *The Saturday Evening Post* and went on to appear in such magazines as *Ladies Home Journal*, *National Geographic*, and *Collier's*, with portraits of Claus rosy-cheeked and smiling, Coca-Cola bottles (or logos) close at hand. Santa Claus remains an element of the company's holiday marketing, but though the two have become synonymous, Claus' depiction has taken on a life of its own. He's a frequent figure in pop culture, including films such as 1947's *Miracle on 34th Street*, but his real dwelling place – other than the North Pole, of course – lies in the imaginations of wishful children on Christmas Eve.

David Greenwald

Date December 26, 1931

Country USA

Why It's Key The image of Santa Claus as a jolly old man has become a beloved cultural standard.

Fact Beginning in the 1920s, Coca-Cola used early versions of Claus to alter the beverage's reputation as a warm-weather drink.

opposite Haddon Sundblom painting showing red Santa Claus figure enjoying a Coke.

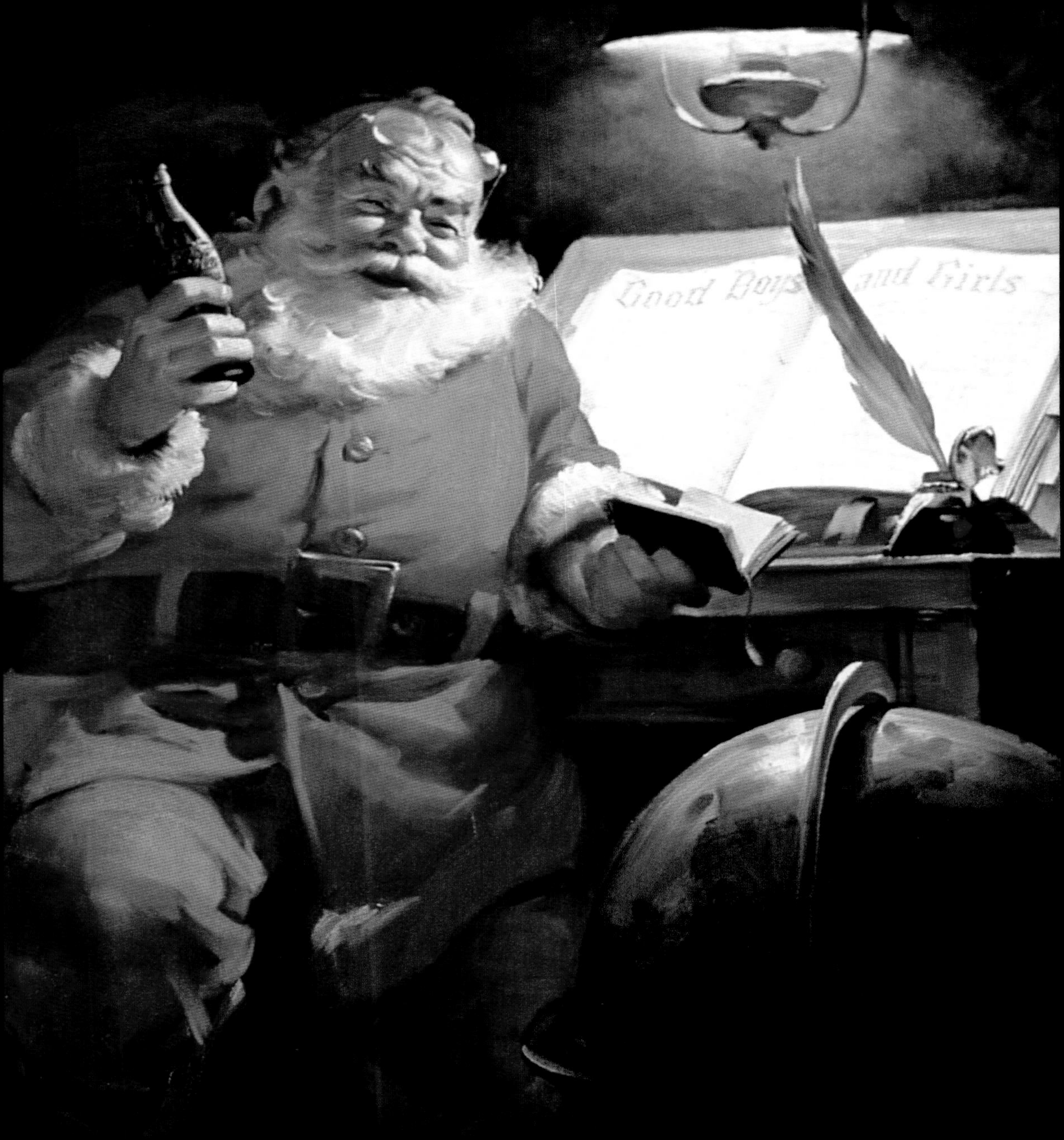
Good Boys and Girls

Key Cultural Event
Huxley's *Brave New World* published

When Aldous Huxley published *Brave New World* in 1932, he was already a best-selling writer and social satirist, with four satirical novels to his name, including *Point Counter Point* (1928). However, his fame became stratospheric with the release of *Brave New World*, which questions the effects of international warfare and industrial revolutions on mankind.

In his time, Huxley had seen the moral chaos of World War I and hysteria of mass production, witnessing cultural changes at their most drastic. Intended as a parody of H. G. Wells' utopian work *Men Like Gods* (1923), *Brave New World* depicts a "negative utopia," in which personal identity has been sacrificed. London, in the year 2540, is free from war and poverty, and its inhabitants are protected by advanced health and technology. However, these come at a cost of all

things human – culture, art, philosophy, religion – and are sustained by sex and drugs.

Throughout his works, Huxley vocalized his skepticism about the abusive power of science and technology, provoking criticism from his readers. In later years, he turned to Eastern mysticism, reaching the idea that humans should be like amphibians, capable of surviving in different environments. The solution to mankind seemed, as Huxley admitted, to be tolerance and adaptability: "It is a bit embarrassing to have been concerned with the human problem all one's life and find at the end that one has no more to offer by way of advice than 'Try to be a little kinder.'"
Mariko Kato

Date 1932

Country UK

Why It's Key *Brave New World* is one of the most popular and controversial works of science fiction alongside George Orwell's *1984* (1949).

Fact *Brave New World*, a novel by author and critic Aldous Leonard Huxley (1894–1963), took its ironic title from Miranda's famous speech in Shakespeare's *The Tempest*.

Key Political Event
Thousands killed in peasant uprising

As in most of Latin America, the Depression had a disastrous effect on El Salvador. In a country where a small number of rich families owned the vast majority of wealth, the collapse of coffee prices boosted an already-strong Marxist movement among the impoverished peasants. It also sealed the fate of the recently-elected progressive government of President Arturo Araujo, who was deposed late in 1931 by a military coup and replaced by General Hernández Martínez. Incensed at the downfall of Araujo, who had pledged to help the poor, an alliance of peasants and indigenous Pipil Indians was galvanized into action by the Salvadoran Communist Party on January 22, 1932. Armed mainly with machetes, the rebels occupied several towns, ransacked government offices, cut supply lines, and

attacked a military garrison, killing fewer than a hundred people in the three-day uprising.

The military's response was the indiscriminate massacre of 30,000 peasants and Indians, most of whom had nothing to do with the uprising. *La Matanza* – "the slaughter" – was one of the worst atrocities perpetrated by a modern Latin American country against its own people and had a profound effect on the Indians who, fearing further persecution, abandoned their Pipil culture in favor of westernization. However, subsequent regimes played down the massacre, instead hailing Martínez as the country's anti-Communist savior and using the threat of further left-wing revolt to justify the role of the military in the eyes of the business and landowning classes.
Hedley Paul

Date January 22, 1932

Country El Salvador

Why It's Key The first Marxist revolt in the Americas was brutally suppressed by the military, setting El Salvador's political agenda for the next fifty years.

Key Discovery
Splitting of the atom

New Zealand scientist Ernest Rutherford theorized that the atom consisted of a tiny nucleus orbited by a cloud of electrons. In the Cavendish Laboratory in Cambridge, British physicist John Cockcroft and Irish physicist Ernest Walton were urged by Rutherford to slam particles at atoms with a high enough speed to break apart the atom's nucleus. In order to move particles at speeds sufficient for bombarding the nucleus, industrial-sized equipment was built and the laboratory soon looked more like a factory than a lab.

In 1932, Cockcroft and Walton succeeded in splitting the atom using their high-speed accelerator. The process involved shooting protons at a lithium atom target to produce two atoms of helium and energy. They were awarded the Nobel Prize in physics for the work in 1951.

In 1939, German physicists Otto Hahn and Fritz Strassmann, along with Austrian physicists Lise Meitner and Otto Frisch, succeeded in splitting uranium through the process of nuclear fission. The process of nuclear fission allowed the atom to be transformed into a powerful source of energy. It paved the way for many future developments, including the atomic bomb and nuclear energy supplies. These scientific achievements also marked a fundamental change in the nature of particle physics research. Atoms were no longer examined on small laboratory tables, as had been done by Rutherford and his predecessors. Instead, scientists began building huge accelerators. Today accelerators are miles in length and cost many billions of dollars.

Anne Hsu

Date April 14, 1932

Country UK

Why It's Key The splitting of the atom allowed the atom to be transformed into a new powerful source of energy, which could be used to produce atomic bombs.

1930–1939

177

Key Political Event
Salazar becomes leader of Portugal

Antonio de Oliveira Salazar joined the Portuguese government in 1926 after a military coup overthrew the existing administration. He served as finance minister for some years before becoming head of state in 1932. As premier, he introduced a new regime, the Estado Novo (New State), which promised his people a strong, incorruptible Portugal.

On the outbreak of the Spanish Civil War in 1936, Salazar supported Franco's nationalists, fearing that victory for the left-wing republicans would threaten his regime, and Franco's eventual victory further bolstered his position. In common with his new neighbor, Salazar carefully proclaimed neutrality throughout World War II.

Even for a dictator, Salazar took a remarkably firm hold of the country. He was unhappy with delegating and obsessively supervised his ministers' work. He was also a fiercely authoritarian ruler and dealt harshly with dissenting voices, sending many opponents to concentration camps in Africa.

The post-war years saw a decline in Portugal's strength and influence. Salazar was fiercely protective of Portugal's overseas colonies, unwilling to enter into the process of decolonization that countries such as Britain were starting. This resulted in a series of colonial wars that weakened Portugal and isolated Salazar on the world stage.

Despite this, Salazar's shrewd judgment and populist appeal enabled him to hold on to power until being disabled by a stroke in 1968. He died in 1970 and tens of thousands thronged the streets of Lisbon to watch his funeral procession.

Martin Sayers

Date July 5, 1932

Country Portugal

Why It's Key Salazar's elevation to head of the Portuguese state ushered in a period of dictatorship that would last until the 1970s.

Key Cultural Event
Braille – the world's standard alphabet for the blind

Born in France in 1809, Louis Braille lost his sight in both eyes after a childhood accident. He was an intelligent child and went to school with his sighted friends for two years, learning purely by listening. When he was ten, he won a scholarship to the Royal Institution for Blind Youth in Paris, one of the world's first schools for the blind. At the school, children were taught to read through a raised-print system, but not to write.

Louis Braille refined and developed the system that is named after him but he did not invent it. Originally devised as a form of "night writing" for soldiers in the trenches, the inventor was an army captain named Charles Barbier. His sonography system used raised dots for tactile reading and writing. It represented words according to sound, not their spelling, and was based on twelve dots. The system was too complicated for the army and in 1821, realizing that it might be useful to the blind, Barbier visited Louis Braille's school.

Within a short period, Louis Braille recognized the potential of sonography. He worked hard to simplify it and within three years, at the age of fifteen, he had devised his own system using six dots, based on spelling rather than sound. Crucially, Braille could be written with a simple stylus as well as read. At first, the system was not widely adopted but after Louis Braille's death in 1852, its simplicity and practicality became increasingly recognized.

Michelle Higgs

Date September 1, 1932

Country Worldwide

Why It's Key Braille allowed blind and partially sighted people to read and write, giving them some independence and control over their own lives.

opposite Blind workers at the Institute for the Blind transcribing the Bible into Braille.

Key Political Event
Iraq becomes independent

Iraq, the seat of the Abbasid Caliphate at the high tide of Arab domination of the Middle East, passed out of the hands of Arabs in the pre-modern era, when Mongols and, more enduringly, Turks took over and dictated the administration of the area. It was not until the Arab Revolt against the Ottoman Turks that Iraq glimpsed an Arab future. However, in repudiating Turkish rule, Iraqi Arabs aligned themselves with the British, who had fought the Turks throughout World War I and were more concerned about their regional interests than the niceties of Arab self-rule. As a result, Iraq was first placed under a British mandate and granted independence in 1932, with King Faisal – the leader of the Arab revolt – installed as monarch.

Britain left an independent Iraq isolated from the Persian Gulf and safely divided against itself, consisting as it did of three disparate Ottoman provinces with little shared national, cultural, or religious character. This Iraq was guaranteed to remain a puppet of British interests – at least until 1958, when the Iraqi Army staged a coup and removed itself from the British orbit. Shortly afterwards, Iraq and Britain clashed again over the question of Kuwait, which Iraq claimed as a province. This resentment, one of the birth pangs of Iraq, manifested itself in the Iraqi invasion of Kuwait three decades later. This folly, coupled with the spectacular disunity of Iraqis following the 2003 U.S. invasion, gestures toward Iraq's independence as a moment of trauma rather than liberation.

Demir Barlas

Date October 3, 1932

Country Iraq

Why It's Key The messy circumstances of Iraq's liberation from Turkish and British rule helped spark many Mesopotamian crises to come.

Key Cultural Event
The BBC's World Service begins transmission

The Empire Service was originally established to broadcast to the far-flung countries of the British Empire. Listeners were advised not to expect too much as given the lack of finances, the programs would be "neither very interesting nor very good." The first program was a two-hour transmission to Australia and New Zealand with four later broadcasts to other parts of the empire.

Early transmissions were targeted at five areas: Australia and New Zealand, India, East and Southern Africa, Canada, and the West Indies. All the programs were intended for evening listening. As transmissions crossed over to other regions, after 1933, the BBC stopped describing the transmissions by region.

With the outbreak of World War II, there was a rapid expansion of programs for overseas transmission. As a result, the number of staff increased dramatically from 103 in 1939 to 1,472 in 1941, and the European Services section transferred to Bush House near Fleet Street. By 1940, the BBC was broadcasting 78 news bulletins per day in 34 different languages including Icelandic, Albanian, Hindi, Burmese, and the dialect of Luxembourg. Refugees were used for the new services but they had to be fast, accurate translators and good English speakers.

By the end of the war, programs were being broadcast in 45 languages and the BBC had established itself as the world's largest international broadcasting organization. The World Service became the model for broadcasting services in the former empire and elsewhere in the world.
Michelle Higgs

Date December 19, 1932

Country UK

Why It's Key The World Service took on a new significance during World War II as it continued to broadcast to occupied Europe, and through its post-war broadcasts to countries with press censorship.

Fact Originally called the Empire Service, its name was changed to the Overseas Service in 1939 and again to the World Service in 1965, to emphasize world affairs.

1930-1939

Key Political Event
Hitler becomes Chancellor of Germany

The effects of the Great Depression resulted in the violent polarization of German politics between the extreme left and right during the early 1930s. By 1932, the Nazis had been transformed from an insignificant right-wing movement into the largest party in Germany, holding over one third of the national vote.

The Nazis were anxious for power as their popular appeal had slipped by the November elections of that year and their financial support was drying up. However, the aging Paul von Hindenburg, who had narrowly defeated Hitler in the 1932 presidential election, proved to be their main obstacle.

The political program of the incumbent chancellor – von Schleicher – alienated many, including Hindenburg. In response, Franz von Papen, a former chancellor and favorite of Hindenburg, attempted to regain power by manipulating the Nazis. Although von Papen desired the chancellorship himself, he acquiesced in Hitler's demand for that post, provided that he became vice-chancellor and Nazi representation in cabinet was minimal.

Hindenburg distrusted Hitler but was persuaded by von Papen and others that Hitler would be a mere puppet for the aristocratic old guard. Hindenburg finally assented and appointed Hitler chancellor in January 1933. Von Papen, utterly lacking in foresight, boasted of "hiring" Hitler. Hitler, however, having sought office for so long, had no intention of being von Papen's pawn, and the Third Reich was born.
Denis Casey

Date January 30, 1933

Country Germany

Why It's Key The beginning of Nazi rule in Germany resulted in the outbreak of World War II.

Key Political Event
Burning of the Reichstag

At about 9.30 on a Monday evening, the alarm was raised that the Reichstag was on fire. Although the fire gutted the building, the consequences were more politically than architecturally severe. Hitler, who had been dining with Joseph Goebbels at the time of the fire, described it as a sign from heaven and used it as an excuse to convince Chancellor Hindenburg to pass the *Reichstagsbrandverordnung* ("Reichstag Fire Decree"), which suspended many civil rights and, more importantly, outlawed the Communist Party, which was a significant force in the German parliament.

The Nazis claimed immediately that the fire had been part of a communist plot to overthrow the Weimar republic. In July 1933, Marinus van der Lubbe, a Dutch communist, was indicted for the crime (along with four other men: Ernst Torgler who was German; and Georgi Dimitrov, Blagoi Popov, and Vassili Tanev who were all Bulgarian). Having confessed, van der Lubbe was sentenced to death. The other men, who claimed that the fire had been started by the Nazis, were found innocent and released. It is generally agreed that van der Lubbe was involved in the fire but the extent of the damage and size of the fire make it seem unlikely that he was acting alone.

The fire and the removal of the communists from the government following the *Reichstagsbrandverordnung* allowed the Nazis to capitalize upon national concerns about Bolshevism, significantly increasing their popularity and share of the vote in elections held only days after the fire.
Ben Snook

Date February 27, 1933

Country Germany

Why It's Key The Nazis used the fire as evidence of a communist plot, the reaction against which helped them to seize power.

Fact As many as 4,000 leading communists were arrested as a result of the fire.

1930-1939

181

Key Political Event
FDR Starts the New Deal

When Franklin Delano Roosevelt, the Democratic Governor of New York, won the presidential election of 1932, the U.S. had been floundering in a painful economic depression for three long years. His predecessor, Republican Herbert Hoover, was a champion of business who believed in the ideals of individualism and self-help, convictions that prevented him from taking drastic measures to tackle the nation's crisis.

In 1933, no one knew exactly what to do about the problems plaguing the U.S. economy, let alone the failure of the world market, and Americans considered solutions that ran the gamut from business self-regulation to radical socialism. Roosevelt initially leaned toward the first option, asking businesses to agree to voluntary codes for wages, prices, and treatment of labor. When these measures seemed to fall short – many companies signed on to participate but did not actually follow the regulations – Roosevelt saw that Americans were listening to more radical solutions, like Louisiana Senator Huey Long's plan for redistributing wealth or the organizing drives of newly militant labor unions.

The government launched a second wave of reforms around 1935, which created pensions for the elderly, welfare for single mothers, and organizing rights for unions. The popularity of these programs endured for years, changing the way Americans looked at what their government could do to aid citizens in need and regulate the economy.
Alex Cummings

Date March 4, 1933

Country USA

Why It's Key Although conceived as a cure for economic ills, the New Deal revolutionized the function of government in America.

Key Political Event
First concentration camp in Germany

Less than two months after Hitler came to power in 1933, the first concentration camp opened in the suburbs of Dachau, a town outside Munich. The concentration camp (a concept first invented by the British during the Boer War) was initially intended by the Nazis to be a tool of political oppression, not systematic murder. Its first inmates were opponents of their regime, such as left-wing members of the Reichstag. Although the prisoners were given no fixed sentence, most were released after approximately a year. Thus, this camp differed from later purpose-built death camps (such as Treblinka) or work-death complexes (such as Auschwitz).

Much of the later barbarism of the concentration camp system was present at Dachau, which served as a model for future camps. Beatings, torture, murder,

horrendous medical experiments, and the notoriously abusive *Kapo* system (whereby individual prisoners were selected as overseers of prison labor details), were all features of Dachau.

Dachau also served as a training ground for future camp commandants. Rudolph Hoess, who spent nearly four years as a guard at Dachau, took the infamous motto *Arbeit Macht Frei* ("Work Shall Set You Free") from Dachau and had it emblazoned over the gate of his own camp at Auschwitz.

Of approximately 200,000 inmates, roughly 30,000 died in Dachau during its 12 years in operation. The remainder were transferred to other camps (where they were almost certainly killed) or released.
Denis Casey

Date March 22, 1933

Country Germany

Why It's Key Dachau was the first in a system of Nazi camps that would result in the deaths of millions across Nazi-occupied Europe.

182

Key Cultural Event
King Kong the movie is released

Few images from the early years of the Hollywood sound film have retained the cultural significance of King Kong straddling the Empire State Building. In the giant ape's eponymous big screen debut, a new generation of movie audiences was born, one with the opportunity to see their dreams come to life. Financed by RKO Pictures for roughly US$600,000, the movie made a fast profit and then some, breaking box office records with a cumulative gross of US$10 million. Audiences all over the world responded to *King Kong*.

One of the first sound films to include a full orchestral score (by Max Steiner, the eventual composer for *Casablanca* [1942]), the movie featured some of the strongest special effects moviegoers had seen. Although the stop motion technique used to animate Kong and various other monsters was

employed a few years earlier in *The Lost World* (1925), the visuals in *King Kong* complemented its distinctive plot. Directors Merian C. Cooper and Ernest Schoedsack helmed anthropological films prior to making *King Kong*, contributing to the movie's exotic vibe. That it has been remade twice, once in 1976 and again in 2006, speaks to its endearing story, and the script's summation that "'twas beauty that killed the beast" reveals its literary source material. This melding of special effects and intricate filmmaking devices signaled a new form of escapism. *King Kong* provided a primitive outline of what was to transpire, forty-five years later, when another landmark achievement combined suspense with special effects. It was called *Jaws* (1975).
Eric Kohn

Date April 7, 1933

Country USA

Why It's Key The movie's success and technical ingenuity paved the way for Hollywood's ongoing love affair with the fantasy genre.

Fact The bloated budget almost caused the studio to declare bankruptcy.

opposite The famous Empire State Building scene from *King Kong*.

Key Cultural Event
Mandelstam writes "Stalin Epigram"

When Osip Mandelstam wrote his "Stalin Epigram" in November 1933, it was only a matter of time before the authorities knocked on his door. The poem, a mere sixteen lines, was a courageous indictment of Josef Stalin, the "Kremlin mountaineer" who left a mountain of corpses in his wake. With fingers like "thick worms" and a mustache like "huge laughing cockroaches on his top lip," the poem depicts Stalin as surrounded by "a scum of chicken-necked bosses" who whistle, meow, and snivel at his bidding.

In May 1934, Mandelstam was arrested, subjected to a vicious interrogation, and exiled, along with his wife, Nadezhda. He was released in May 1937, but arrested again the following year and deported to a camp near Vladivostok. He was never heard from again. However, efforts to silence the poet were thwarted by Nadezhda. She saved his work by memorizing and preserving it for publication after Stalin's death, as she and others did with many of the most important poets of the period.

Mandelstam, along with Boris Pasternak, Marina Tsvetaeva, and Anna Akhmatova, formed a core of writers who tried to write through and against the regime, under the threat of terrible punishment. Tsvetaeva eventually hanged herself on August 31, 1941, and Akhmatova lost her husband and her son but survived through terrible hardships until 1966. Pasternak, however, was saved by the personal whim of Stalin, who seems to have had an unexpected, and rather hypocritical, fondness for his poetry.
Larraine Andrews

Date November 1, 1933

Country USSR

Why It's Key The "Stalin Epigram" demonstrated the power of the written word and the fear it created in Stalin's brutal dictatorship.

Key Political Event
Political parties banned in Bulgaria

The 1917 revolution in Russia had a striking effect on Bulgaria, leading to a rise in anti-monarchist sentiments. Bulgaria had a largely agrarian economy and found itself crippled by huge reparations following World War I. In 1923, a coup removed the left-wing Prime Minister Aleksandur Stamboliyski, who had been allied with the Communists, and beheaded him. A right-wing administration under Aleksandar Tsankov took power, backed by Tsar Boris and the army, and a campaign of oppression aimed at left-wing elements in Bulgaria ensued.

Communist and agrarian factions fought back, making two attempts on the Tsar's life. Although an amnesty was declared in 1931, the effects of the Great Depression led to widespread discontent across the country and increased support for the Communist Party. In 1934, a second right-wing coup was launched against the moderate government, which enabled the Tsar to take power personally (ruling through puppet prime ministers Georgi Kyoseivanov and Bogdan Filov). The immediate banning of all other political parties enthroned the Tsar as an absolute ruler. As such, he was able to promote Bulgarian relations with Nazi Germany and Fascist Italy unopposed. In 1941, Bulgaria signed the Tripartite Pact, officially becoming a German ally and entering the war on the Nazis' side.

Tsar Boris died suddenly in 1943 and resistance to the Germans became widespread throughout the country. Bulgaria was occupied by the Soviet Union in 1945 following a Communist coup, and true democracy was not restored until February 1990.
Ben Snook

Date June 12, 1934

Country Bulgaria

Why It's Key The banning of political parties enabled a pseudo-fascist regime to take power in the region, which was friendly to Nazi Germany.

Fact Bulgaria was one of only three countries allied to or occupied by Germany that resisted sending its Jewish population to Germany in the Holocaust (the other two were Denmark and Finland).

Key Political Event
Night of the Long Knives

In 1934, Adolf Hitler was still in a precarious position. His hold on power was growing tighter but he faced threats from the army, sections of big business, and the more radical members of his own party. His three closest and most powerful officials, Hermann Goering, Joseph Goebbels, and Heinrich Himmler (leader of Hitler's personal bodyguard force, the S.S) decided to play on Hitler's paranoia in order to strengthen their own positions. They manipulated rumors of a potential second revolution from the Nazi paramilitary group called the S.A. ("Storm Battalion") and its leader Ernst Röhm.

With over three million members, the S.A looked increasingly threatening to Hitler, and its competition with the German Army was forcing him to choose between them. However, Röhm had been one of

Hitler's earliest and most dynamic supporters, and the S.A. under Röhm's leadership had played an important role in destroying Hitler's opposition during elections.

Nevertheless, Röhm's socialist views were unpopular, as were his demands for revolution and his open homosexuality. On June 30, 1934, encouraged by Goering and Himmler, Hitler personally arrested Röhm in Munich. During the next 24 hours, several hundred other senior S.A. officers were arrested, and many were shot upon capture. Following initial hesitation, Hitler also had Röhm killed.

After participating in the event, the army was now obliged to swear loyalty to Hitler personally, rather than to the nation, tying them to him with a "blood oath" and ensuring that they were no longer a threat.
Mariko Kato

Date June 30, 1934

Country Germany

Why It's Key The purge was a turning point in Nazi Germany, consolidating Hitler's supreme power as judge and jury over the lives of the German people.

Fact The phrase "Night of the Long Knives," used by Hitler to refer to the purge, was taken from a popular Nazi song.

1930–1939

185

Key Political Event The Long March consolidates the leadership of the Communist Party in China

In October 1934, Chiang Kai-shek's *Guomindang* forces surrounded the Red Army's base at Yudu in the province of Jiangxi. To evade the *Guomindang*, Zhou Enlai, one of the principal leaders of the Chinese Communist Party (CCP), orchestrated its decampment to both confuse the *Guomindang* and avoid an all-out battle. The year-long, 6,000 mile trek, which started out with around 100,000 people, is famously known as the Long March. Winding through mountains and dangerously crossing rivers along the way, thousands died either from intermittent battles with *Guomindang* forces, from illness and exhaustion, or from starvation. Among them were two of Mao Zedong's children and his brother.

The Long March is a central episode in the founding of the People's Republic of China. En route

the CCP were ordered not to harm or show disrespect to the peasants they encountered, and therefore garnered enormous support from China's rural population. It was also the defining moment when Mao Zedong assumed leadership of the CCP. The pivotal roles of Mao Zedong and Zhou Enlai would form a power-sharing partnership – Mao as Chairman and Zhou as Premier – that would last until the end of their lives in the 1970s. When the Red Army arrived at what would be its new headquarters at Yenan in the northern Shanxi Province in October 1935, it was half its size. Once established in Yenan, however, the Red Army, isolated from the *Guomindang*, was able to regenerate with strong proletariat support.
Sally Percival Wood

Date October 16, 1934

Country China

Why It's Key The Long March, while devastating in terms of the number of lives lost, consolidated the leadership of the Chinese Communist Party. It also drew crucial widespread support among the rural peasants, who made up the majority of China's population.

Key Political Event
The murder of Kirov

In the early 1930s, Sergei Kirov was a leading light of the Soviet Union's Bolshevik government. He had become close friends with Stalin after the death of the leader's wife, and was one of the few members of Stalin's inner circle who dared to criticize him. Kirov's willingness to express disapproval, coupled with his popularity within the Bolshevik party, became dangerous under Stalin's increasing paranoia. On December 1, 1934, Leonid Nikolaev, a young Bolshevik party member, shot Kirov dead in his office.

Although Nikolaev's actual motive is uncertain, it seems likely that Stalin was behind the killing in some way. Stalin took immediate action in turning the murder to his own advantage. Without investigation, he quickly declared that the killing was part of a counter-revolutionary plot against the Bolshevik government.

This was obviously spurious, but in the pretence of dealing with the murder, Stalin laid down laws that enabled the swift arrest and trial of anybody suspected of being a "terrorist." The maximum penalty for those convicted was death, with no possibility of appeal.

Stalin was an admirer of how Hitler had dealt with opponents during political mass execution "The Night of the Long Knives" earlier that year, and the new laws gave him the excuse he needed to purge his party of opponents, real or imagined. This task was undertaken with murderous zeal and within four years "The Great Terror," as it became known, resulted in more than two million people being executed or deported to labor camps.
Martin Sayers

Date December 1, 1934

Country USSR

Why It's Key The killing of a key member of Stalin's government was the start of a murderous purge of opponents that resulted in the deaths of millions.

Key Cultural Event
Monopoly board game patented

Monopoly is the best-selling board game in the world. Over 200 million copies have been sold, and it's produced in twenty-six countries. But like any good game of Monopoly, the history of the popular pastime is filled with tricky deals, fortunes won and lost, and maybe a little bit of cheating.

The popular history of the game put forward by publisher Parker Bros., as well as its parent company Hasbro, credits the invention of Monopoly to Charles B. Darrow, an American salesman who lost his job during the Great Depression. As the story goes, Darrow thought jobless Americans needed a way to pass the time and came up with the idea for Monopoly after a trip to Atlantic City. Parker Bros. rejected the first version that he presented to them in 1934, citing fifty-two flaws in the game. However, he was awarded a patent on January 5, 1935, after impressing the company with his independent sales.

But while Darrow reaped the financial rewards of the game's success, many critics – most notably Ralph Anspach, inventor of the Anti-Monopoly game – attributed the idea to a Quaker woman named Elizabeth Smith. In 1904, she developed a game called The Landlord's Game to demonstrate the tax theory of Henry George. Her game was later bought and distributed on a small scale by Parker Bros., who didn't end its legal wrangling over the trademark of Monopoly until mid-1980s. While the Darrow story is still prevalent, most historians consider him one of the final developers, not the inventor, of Monopoly.
Chris Schonberger

Date January 5, 1935

Country USA

Why It's Key In spite of legal disputes, Monopoly would go on to become the best-selling board game in the world.

Key Cultural Event
Kodachrome film goes on sale

Kodachrome film, the first commercially successful color film, went on sale on April 15, 1935. The three-color positive film was sold with the price of development included, with the processed film returned to the customer as mounted slides. The film spawned a new American cultural phenomenon: the family slideshow. Treasured memories were now projected in full color in living rooms across America. The Eastman Kodak Company introduced a printing service for Kodachrome in 1941, though the added cost of printing certainly contributed to the fad for slide projection. The use of Kodachrome film declined in the 1960s, as people increasingly chose color prints over slides and used Kodak's newer color negative films.

The name Kodachrome was coined in 1914, when Kodak first began devising a color film process. A two-color process suitable for professional use resulted, but was a resounding commercial failure. The story of the successful Kodachrome film had its start three years later in 1917 when the inventors, Leopold Mannes and Leopold Godowsky, Jr, were just teenagers and better known as musicians than as aspiring scientists. After seeing an early color movie they were inspired to improve on the process in their school's science laboratory. Mannes and Godowsky began receiving Kodak's support for their experiments in 1922, but it was only after relocating to the Kodak headquarters in Rochester, New York, in 1930 that they were finally able to create the easy-to-use, three-color film known as Kodachrome.

Andrea L. Korda

Date April 15, 1935

Country USA

Why It's Key Kodachrome film brought color to the family photograph and popularized the home slide show.

Key Cultural Event
Keynes proposes a new economic theory

In *The General Theory of Employment, Interest and Money*, John Maynard Keynes created an entirely new approach to macroeconomics. His innovation was to realize that the total demand for goods is the driving factor in any economy, especially in times of economic decline. Therefore, he suggested that to rescue an economy from recession, the government must spend rather than save. This, in turn, would encourage citizens to spend more (as there would be more money in circulation). More spending would lead to more investment, which, in turn, would increase the economy, reversing the effects of a recession. At the same time, Keynes went against the central tenets of classical economics, in which it was understood that an economy would inevitably and automatically work toward a state of full employment and optimum level of production. Keynes accepted that full employment and maximum production were achievable, but argued against the assumption that they were natural states, automatically achieved. Rather, he saw them as temporary stages in an ongoing series of economic situations.

Despite the fact that few economists initially accepted Keynes's ideas in the United States, his theory was proved successful by Roosevelt's "New Deal," which had at its core many of the principles laid out by Keynes (although there is disagreement as to the extent to which Keynes's work directly influenced Roosevelt). After World War II, Keynes's work became the standard against which almost all subsequent economic theories were measured.

Ben Snook

Date February 1, 1935

Country UK

Why It's Key Keynes' book, *The General Theory of Employment, Interest and Money* created modern macroeconomics.

Fact John Maynard Keynes was an avid bibliophile who accumulated a sizable collection of Isaac Newton's papers.

Key Political Event
The Nuremberg Laws

By 1935, anti-Semitism was becoming an increasingly dominant ideology in the Nazi Party, though ministers feared Party action against the Jewish people would unsettle the economy. At a conference on August 20, however, high-ranking official Adolf Wagner argued that such danger could be avoided if a firm policy was imposed. The following month, several such policies were announced at the annual Party Rally at Nuremberg. These denaturalization laws, later called the "Nuremberg Laws," were based on an arbitrary theory to discriminate against the Jewish people. Those with four German grandparents were considered of "German blood," while those with three or four Jewish grandparents were classified as Jews.

The first of the two laws, The Law for the Protection of German Blood and German Honor, prohibited marriages and sexual relations between "Jews" and "Germans," while the second, The Reich Citizenship Law, excluded Jews from German citizenship. Other laws demanded that Jews carry identity cards, and the government assigned new middle names to those who did not have recognizably "Jewish" first names. Ownership of Jewish businesses was reallocated to non-Jewish Germans, Jewish lawyers were forbidden to practice, and Jewish doctors could not treat non-Jews. In a special session during the rally, the laws were passed unanimously by the German Parliament, although the votes were largely irrelevant, since Hitler had already given himself the power to pass laws without parliamentary approval, as declared in the Enabling Act of 1933.

Mariko Kato

Date September 15, 1935

Country Germany

Why It's Key The Nuremberg Laws formalized unofficial discrimination against the Jewish people.

Fact Previous to the Nuremberg Laws, Hitler declared intermarriages as a threat to "Aryan" superiority in the book *Mein Kampf*, which he wrote while in prison in 1924.

Key Political Event
Italy invades Abyssinia

From 1932, Fascist dictator Benito Mussolini planned to invade Abyssinia in his quest to create an Italian Empire in East Africa. Italy already occupied territory on either side so the addition of Abyssinia was a logical step that would boost Mussolini's popularity at home. Unsurprisingly, the Abyssinian government was increasingly worried about border disputes with Italian forces and, in 1934, appealed for help from the League of Nations in dealing with them. The league were still considering what to action to take when, in January 1935, Emperor Haile Selassie of Abyssinia, fearing an imminent Italian invasion, asked again for immediate assistance. His plea was ignored.

Mussolini's army marched confidently into Abyssinia on October 3, 1935. The League of Nations reacted immediately; the occupation was condemned and economic sanctions proposed. However, Italy and Abyssinia were both members of the league, and other member states, anxious not to alienate Italy in case of future conflict and conscious of their own interests, found it difficult to agree on sanctions, which were postponed until November 1935. But the sanctions were only half-heartedly applied, having little effect. In May 1936 Emperor Selassie of Abyssinia went into exile. The Italian occupation of Abyssinia was short-lived but the League of Nations was fatally wounded. Their failure to act decisively and their betrayal of a fellow league member destroyed public confidence, and other leaders, Hitler in particular, were encouraged in the belief that in the future they could pursue expansionist policies unhindered.

Helena Hewson

Date October 3, 1935

Country Abyssinia (Ethiopia)

Why It's Key The invasion of Abyssinia demonstrated the inability of the League of Nations to act decisively to protect a member state. Hereafter, its reputation was destroyed and its presence ignored by the Great Powers.

opposite Italian artillery on the march during the war with Abyssinia.

Key Political Event First "Per Se" law defines "Driving Under the Influence" (DUI)

The problem of drunk driving predated the automobile age: cities worried about intoxicated carriage drivers, and the railroads had to crack down on drunken employees. Automobiles, though, proved to be particularly lethal weapons, and governments in the early twentieth century grappled with the difficulty of identifying and prosecuting drunken motorists. Policemen judged whether suspects were "driving under the influence" of alcohol (DUI) based on the smell of their breath, erratic driving, slurred speech, or the inability to walk a straight line – none of which could be guaranteed to ensure a conviction in court.

By the 1930s, scientific studies linked the measurable alcohol content of blood to the slowed reflexes and impaired coordination of drunk drivers. Norway was the first country to respond with a "per se" DUI law – that is, one that declared a driver in violation of the law simply for having too much alcohol in his or her blood, regardless of visible impairment. In 1941, Sweden followed suit. So did most other governments, but not until decades later, because fears about the invasion of motorists' privacy trumped the desire to protect the public against drunk drivers. Norway established a blood alcohol content of 0.05 per cent as the threshold of legal intoxication, and it typically imprisoned violators. Many places chose a higher level (and lesser punishments) at first, but in recent years most governments have settled on either 0.08 per cent (or 0.8 milligrams per milliliter, which is essentially the same thing) or 0.05 per cent, sometimes less, as the legal limit.

Brian Ladd

Date June 16, 1936

Country Norway

Why It's Key The offense of drunk driving acquired a legal and measurable definition.

Key Political Event
Outbreak of the Spanish Civil War

Francisco Franco and his allies launched their rebellion against the Spanish Republic amongst explosive tensions. Subsequent to the declaration of the Second Republic in 1932, the rising political fortunes of socialist, communist, and anarchist factions had alarmed the ruling institutions of traditional Spain, especially the Catholic Church and the army. After the victory of the left-leaning Popular Front in the elections of February 1936, assassinations, skirmishes, and vigilante actions on the part of paramilitary groups had made violence an everyday reality. July 12 witnessed the murder of socialist official José Castillo; his allies retaliated the following day by assassinating José Calvo Sotelo, parliament member and devout monarchist.

After declaring his revolt from exile in the Canary Islands on July 17, Franco quickly established control there, using the islands as a base for incursions into the Iberian peninsula via Spanish Morocco. His nationalist forces quickly made significant advances, and Franco was named head of state of an alternative government on October 1, 1936. The drawn-out and often brutal struggle between republicans and nationalists that raged over the subsequent three years became a proxy war for the forces that would later clash in World War II: Franco received support from Fascist Italy and Germany, while the Soviet Union as well as International Brigades composed of U.S., Latin American, and European volunteers assisted the republic. The conflict was a cultural watershed, inspiring important works by Pablo Picasso, George Orwell, Ernest Hemingway, and others.

Charlotte Whittle

Date July 17, 1936

Country Spain

Why It's Key An iconic ideological struggle, right-wing general Francisco Franco's successful insurgency against Spain's elected Republican government initiated one of the twentieth century's longest-lasting dictatorships.

opposite Anarchist militia from the National Confederation of Labor in Barcelona during the Spanish Civil War.

Key Cultural Event
German Olympics broadcast

The history of television is said to be one of the more important stories of the twentieth century. However, few people realized that the 1936 German Olympics in Berlin marked the first live television coverage of a sports event in world history.

As Adolf Hitler was not a sports fan, he was convinced to use television by Joseph Goebbels, who served as his propaganda minister. Goebbels explained to Hitler that the presence of large television cannons at the side of the stadium could not help but attract international public attention, and that the Olympics could therefore be exploited to benefit the advancing Nazi cause, both inside and outside the country. Using the Olympics and television to his advantage, Hitler and Goebbels hoped to demonstrate to the world that the Aryan race was superior to others.

The German firms Telefunken and Femseh were put in charge of televising the 1936 Olympics using American equipment from RCA and Philo Farnsworth, inventor of the first electric television. Although the picture quality of these broadcasts was poor, the Germans used three cameras placed at strategic positions, and the transmissions went over the airwaves to twenty-one special viewing booths. Over 150,000 Germans followed the Olympic Games via television, and its viewing was substantial enough to maintain seventy-two hours of coverage.
Fred Lindsey

Date August 9, 1936

Country Germany

Why It's Key The filming and live broadcast of the 1936 Berlin Games (Olympics) inaugurated many of the techniques used in recording sports in the twenty-first century.

Fact The 1936 Games were also made into a film titled *Olympia* (1938) by Leni Riefenstahl, a prominent German filmmaker and a favorite of Hitler's.

Key Cultural Event
Owens wins at the German Olympics

Adolf Hitler had high hopes for the 1936 Olympic Games, which were being hosted by Germany in the city of Berlin. Awarded to Germany before Hitler came to power, the Führer took full advantage of the prestige that such an event would present. Investing huge amounts of time and money into preparations for the greatest show on earth, Hitler looked forward to welcoming the world to Germany and of displaying the superiority of his "Aryan" race.

However, Hitler was not to know that far away in the United States, a little-known black athlete by the name of Jesse Owens was quietly making his mark on amateur track and field. On May 25, 1935, Owens broke three world records and equaled a fourth in one afternoon at the low-key Big Ten meet in Michigan. His inclusion in the American squad for the Olympics was

assured and so in August 1936, he represented his country in the most stunning fashion by being the first American to win four gold medals in the Olympics.

Victorious in the 100m, 200m, and 4 x 400m relay, Owens saved his most dramatic triumph for the long jump, in which he beat popular German athlete Luz Long in a highly contested final.

Jesse Owens' resounding victory ensured the 1936 Berlin Olympics was remembered for the right reasons and Hitler's belief that the "Aryan" people were the dominant race was spectacularly shown up. In 1955, President Eisenhower named Owens the "Ambassador of Sports."
Kerry Duffy

Date August 9, 1936

Country Germany

Why It's Key Jesse Owens made a mockery of Adolf Hitler's belief in a supreme race.

Fact Popular with the Germans, in 1984, a street in Berlin was named after Jesse Owens.

opposite Jesse Owens assumes his controversial pose atop the podium in 1937.

Key Cultural Event
Debut of the Volkswagen car

At the Berlin motor show in 1933, Hitler announced his intention to encourage car ownership. Hitler knew that most Germans could only dream of owning a car; he wanted to develop a small, economical car, the *Volkswagen* ("people's car") that was cheap enough for the working masses to afford. In 1934, Ferdinand Porsche was commissioned to design it and a working prototype was launched just a year later.

After the commercial debut of the Volkswagen on October 21, 1936, the development of the car was transferred to the Nazi German Labor Front (DAF). It was financed by the compulsory contributions of German workers to the "*Kraft durch Freude*" (KdF), or "strength through joy" program, which organized approved leisure activities. A new savings stamp scheme was introduced to allow workers to save up

for a car, and the DAF took over the development of the new car to be known as the "KdF-Wagen." On May 26, 1938 Hitler ceremoniously laid the cornerstone for a purpose built factory, which would mass produce the cars beginning in September 1939.

During World War II, mass production stopped and the flagship factory was used for military construction. However, production restarted in 1949, expanding rapidly with its VW "Beetle," so named because of its distinctive curved hood design. By 1965, over a million Beetles were produced annually.

Sales of the original Beetle declined during the 1970s, but the iconic value of the brand was so strong that Volkswagen relaunched an entirely new Beetle in 1998.

Helena Hewson

Date October 21, 1936

Country Germany

Why It's Key From its idealist origins in Nazi Germany, the Volkswagen Beetle grew to become one of the most iconic car designs of the twentieth century.

Key Person
Robert Johnson, blues guitarist

All of Robert Johnson's recorded music was laid down in two Texas sessions, one in San Antonio on November 23, 1936, the other in Dallas on June 19, 1937. Forty-one songs, none of them longer than three minutes, are the legacy of a rambling musician whose life and character has always been shrouded in myth. Even during his lifetime, Johnson was an ellusive character, known to few and always on the move. Martin Scorsese said about him: "The thing about Robert Johnson was that he only existed on his records. He was pure legend."

The legend is certainly better known than the life. The folklore has it that as a young man on a Mississippi plantation, Johnson yearned to become a bluesman. On instruction, he took his guitar to a crossroads one midnight, and was met by the devil who tuned it so he

could play anything he wanted. The devil's price for this service was the young man's soul.

In fact, the folklore belongs to another bluesman, Tommy Johnson, and was appropriated by Robert, but he got his wish. His recording sessions produced eleven albums: the complete works of the most influential bluesman of all time. His microtonal shifts transformed blues guitar. Keith Richards' first impression of listening to Johnson was that he "was hearing two guitars, and it took me a long time to realize he was doing it all by himself." He recollects thinking to himself: "This guy must have three brains."

A year later, Johnson died from poisoning, aged twenty-seven, again standing at a crossroads.

David Thorley

Date November 23, 1936

Born/Died 1911–1938

Nationality American

Why It's Key Johnson's guitar playing changed the sound of American music forever.

Fact In 1938, John Hammond, Sr put on a concert at Carnegie hall celebrating the roots of African-American music. Johnson died shortly before, so Hammond played two of his records from the stage.

Key Cultural Event
King Edward abdicates the throne

In 1931, Edward, then Prince of Wales, met Wallis Warfield Simpson, an American divorcee, at a house party. A few months later Edward and Wallis – at the time married to her second husband Ernest – met again, and in January 1932, Wallis spent a weekend with Edward at Fort Belvedere, his country retreat.

Edward succeeded to the throne in January 1936 when his father, George V, died, but by this time Edward was deeply in love with Mrs Simpson. Wallis and Ernest divorced in October 1936 and the following month Edward, now King Edward VIII, broke the news to Prime Minister Stanley Baldwin that he wished to marry Mrs Simpson. The Prime Minister advised him that the British people would never accept the American divorcee as their queen. When Edward suggested a morganatic marriage, where he would be

King and Wallis merely his consort, this was rejected by both the British Cabinet and the governments of the British dominions. This news left Edward with three choices – to finish his relationship with Mrs Simpson, to marry against the advice of his ministers who would then resign, or to abdicate.

On December 10, 1936, Edward signed the Instrument of Abdication and broadcast the news to the nation the following day. Immediately, Edward's brother, Albert George (Bertie), who was married to Elizabeth Bowes-Lyon, was proclaimed King George VI. Edward took the title Duke of Windsor and left the country for Austria. The following year Edward and Wallis Simpson married in France.

Lorraine Brownbill

Date December 10, 1936

Country UK

Why It's Key When King Edward abdicated, King George VI succeeded him and Princess Elizabeth, King George's daughter, became heir presumptive, thus changing the natural course of the British monarchy.

Key Political Event
Switzerland legalizes euthanasia

Euthanasia, the practice of humanely assisting in the death of a terminally ill patient, is a highly contentious moral issue, with religious, medical, and ethical considerations heightening its controversy. Deriving from the Greek terms *eu* and *thanatos* to mean "good death," euthanasia most commonly refers to causing the death of a patient either by administering lethal doses of medication or failing to intervene when it could be possible to prevent her death.

In 1937, the criminal code of Switzerland was changed to state that suicide was not considered a crime and that it could legally be assisted. This assistance was restricted to instances where altruism was the only possible motive; any assisted suicide with a negative incentive, such as financial gain, remained a

crime. This legislation made Switzerland the first country to legalize euthanasia and was followed by high profile and emotive cases in the UK and United States to allow terminally ill patients the same option of a more dignified and painless death. In 1977, California became the first U.S. state to support the right of a mentally competent patient to leave a "living will," outlining their wish to die without medical intervention, and in 1993, the Netherlands decriminalized voluntary physician-assisted suicide in the terminally ill. This was extended to seriously ill patients in 2002, the same year that euthanasia was also legalized in Belgium.

Hannah Furness

Date 1937

Country Switzerland

Why It's Key The legalization of assisted suicide gave the terminally ill the choice of ending their lives when they were no longer able to function.

Key Cultural Event
Nylon

When the scientists at the DuPont chemical company in Wilmington, Delaware, were working on the fiber later known as nylon, they could have had no idea just how wild the world would go for it. The first true synthetic fiber, made from nothing more than coal, water, and air, was developed by Dr Wallace Carothers in the 1930s as an alternative to silk stockings. It took off immediately since it was much stronger than silk, just as lustrous, and far less expensive, bringing quality hosiery to the American public. Though it was patented on February 16, 1937, commercial production did not start until 1939, and – in an early example of clever marketing – the name "nylon" was never trademarked, sending it loose into the popular vocabulary.

Yet, nylon went on to have much wider uses than simply stockings. The fiber proved to be indispensable to the war effort, taking up silk's slack in parachutes, and being used in ropes, tires, and uniforms. Since the war, it has also become a common component of everything from carpets and guitar strings to automobile parts. Silk stockings have been banished to the extremity of luxury, while nylon is a household product in countless forms.

Clouds hover over the origin of the word "nylon." Some say it comes from the combination of "New York" and "London," while DuPont themselves say it was a largely arbitrary coinage, along the lines of cotton and rayon.

Josh Spero

Date February 16, 1937

Country USA

Why It's Key The invention of nylon changed the face of science – and the legs of the world.

Key Disaster
Hindenburg explodes

On the evening of May 6, 1937, the Zeppelin *Hindenburg* was arriving in the United States on the first of eighteen scheduled trans-Atlantic flights between Frankfurt and Lakehurst Naval Air Station, New Jersey. With a top speed of 132 kilometers per hour, it took just over fifty hours to make the westbound journey. Radio broadcaster Herbert Morrison described the sun on the windows of the observation deck "sparkling like glittering jewels on a background of dark velvet." Eight minutes later, as the *Hindenburg* caught fire, he could be heard shouting for the ground crew to get out of the way, before crying, "Oh, the humanity!" as the Zeppelin was completely destroyed in less than forty seconds.

Dying Ernst Lehmann, the senior officer on board, blamed a bomb, but an eye-witness had seen the airship's skin "fluttering" before it caught fire. The *Hindenburg* had been delayed by bad weather and it is thought that as it made an unusually sharp turn, a bracing wire snapped, tearing open a hydrogen cell (surviving crew testified that the craft had become heavier toward the back, suggesting a gas leak). Landing ropes wet by rain conducted static and sparks probably ignited the hydrogen. Although Germany had been denied non-flammable helium following World War I, the U.S. government had offered to sell it some, but this had been rejected as too expensive. Of the thirty-six passengers and sixty-one crew on board, twenty crew and thirteen passengers, along with one member of the ground crew, died.

Duncan Proudfoot

Date May 6, 1937

Country USA

Why It's Key The *Hindenburg* disaster destroyed public trust in airships and brought an abrupt end to the Zeppelin era.

Fact The Zeppelin *Hindenburg*, at over 800 feet long and weighing 242 tons, was the largest aircraft ever built. Thirty-four people died when it burst into flames and crashed.

Key Political Event
Picasso's *Guernica* first exhibited

Picasso's mural *Guernica*, first exhibited on May 23, 1937, at the Paris International Exhibition, is arguably the best known painting of the twentieth century. The event that inspired Picasso's painting took place on April 26, 1937, when the Nazi Luftwaffe bombed the ancient Basque town of Guernica, killing about 1,500 residents and wounding 800. Picasso had already been commissioned to paint a huge mural for the Paris World's Fair, and the painting had been ready in a different version before the bombing of Guernica took place. However, on learning of the bombing, Picasso renamed the painting *Guernica* and adjusted it so as to express the horror of the carnage.

The painting has become a universal symbol of the violence of war and the resistance to oppression. Its innovative monochrome imagery is open to interpretation and there is no agreement on its ultimate meaning. Picasso intended *Guernica*'s meaning to be fluid and individual, which he expressed in his own words: "A painting is not thought out in advance. While it is being done, it changes as one's thoughts change. And when it is finished, it goes on changing, according to the state of mind of whoever is looking at it." After the Paris International Exhibition, the painting was sent to New York, and Picasso requested that it remain there until the end of Franco's regime in Spain. *Guernica* was finally returned to Spain on September 10, 1981, eight years after Picasso's death.
Sonja Kudeljnjak

Date May 23, 1937

Country Spain

Why It's Key *Guernica* is one of the most representative paintings of the twentieth century and a symbol of the horrors of wartime destruction.

Fact The Nazi attack on *Guernica* was not ordered by Hitler, but by Franco.

Key Cultural Event
Opening of the Golden Gate Bridge

Measuring some 2.7 kilometers in total length, weighing almost 900,000 tons, designed with two monumental towers measuring in excess of 225 meters, and supporting a roadway 67 meters above the high water mark, the monumental scale of the Golden Gate Bridge makes it an instantly recognizable landmark in the San Francisco Bay area.

Completed and opened in 1937, the Golden Gate Bridge's significance extends beyond its monumental size, for it is a globally recognizable symbol of San Francisco and the Pacific Coast of the United States. The Golden Gate Bridge was the end result of a vast engineering project, one of the largest undertaken in America at the time. It was also one of the most complex, due to issues of wind, strong water currents, and earthquakes, which necessitated groundbreaking engineering techniques. In so doing it has become a potent icon of America's ability to overcome once seemingly insurmountable environmental challenges. With its distinct design, scale, and color, the American Society of Civil Engineers have hailed it a modern wonder of the world.

Constructed at a cost of almost US$37 million, the Golden Gate Bridge has established itself since opening as a major traffic artery that links the San Francisco Peninsula to nearby Marin County. Nevertheless, with its enormous scale, distinct design, and the picturesque backdrop of the San Francisco Straits, the bridge attracts tourists from across the world for the purpose of marveling at its splendor and technological sophistication.
Ian Morley

Date May 27, 1937

Country USA

Why It's Key An important highway across San Francisco Bay, the bridge is a major feat of modern engineering.

Fact Once the world's longest suspension bridge, the Golden Gate Bridge is constructed in a seismically active zone, and was born from an idea by Joseph Strauss, an engineer who designed vast numbers of bridges in the United States.

Key Cultural Event
Amelia Earhart disappears

Had things gone according to schedule, Amelia Earhart would not have been flying across the blue expanse of the Pacific on July 2, 1937. The original plan had envisioned completing the Pacific first, but an accident during takeoff from Pearl Harbor caused a lengthy delay, and the seasonal weather patterns changed. When Earhart and her navigator, Fred Noonan, took off from California on May 21, they headed east.

By June 29, they had crossed North America, Africa, Southeast Asia, and Australia, and reached Lae, Papua New Guinea. Ahead of them lay the most daunting leg of the journey: the 2,566 miles of open water between Lae and Howland Island. Earhart's Lockheed Electra rolled down the runway at 10 a.m. on July 2.

Over the next twenty hours, Earhart was in sporadic radio contact with her support ship near Howland. For most of that period, things seemed to be on track. But sometime during the night, Earhart and Noonan drifted off course. The last faint transmission came at 8:43 a.m. Then there was silence

For sixteen days, ships and planes canvassed a Texas-sized piece of the Pacific without finding a single sign of the plane or crew. Tragically, she is now remembered more for her disappearance than her record-shattering career in aviation or her tremendous spirit. "She was," said one eulogist "in rebellion against a world which had been made, for women, too safe, too unexciting. She wanted to dare all that a man would dare."

Heather Michon

Date July 2, 1937

Country USA

Why It's Key The loss of a pioneering female aviator initiated one of history's greatest mysteries.

Key Political Event
Japan invades China

Japan and China had fought incessantly since 1931, when Japan falsely accused Chinese dissidents of dynamiting a section of railroad in Manchuria near Mukden (known as the Mukden Incident). Imperialist Japan had long been aiming to dominate China and gain control of its resources, and used this dispute as an excuse to occupy Manchuria.

From such localized "incidents" grew a full-scale war, triggered by the Marco Polo Bridge Incident, after which Japan had occupied the North China Plain by the end of 1937. China's weak military strength forced the nationalist party *Guomindang* and the Chinese Communist Party to cooperate. However, both parties were wary, and the breakdown of the alliance was one of the reasons for Japan's territorial victories. The Battle of Shanghai, one of the bloodiest battles of the war,

began in August 1937. The Chinese government resisted Japanese attack of the large industrial city for three months, hoping vainly for intervention from western powers. Japan ultimately broke through, but the resistance of the Chinese defense had unnerved the Japanese forces, and encouraged the Chinese. The atrocities inflicted and the great number of deaths helped only to increase the nationalist sentiments on both sides.

When Japan attacked Pearl Harbor in 1941, the conflicts merged into World War II. With aid from the United States, China was better equipped, and by 1945 had liberated large areas of Japanese-occupied territory. The war finally ended with the surrender of Japan in August 1945.

Mariko Kato

Date July 7, 1937

Country Japan

Why It's Key The Second Sino-Japanese War was the largest Asian war in the twentieth century.

Fact The First Sino-Japanese War was fought in 1894–1895 over the control of Korea, which Japan won.

Key Political Event
The Parsley Massacre

Perejil. It's a Spanish word for parsley, and for one terrible week in October 1937, it was the most dangerous word in the Dominican Republic. With brutal efficiency, soldiers went from person to person, holding up sprigs of parsley and demanding that they say the word. If the person pronounced *perejil* without the proper trilling of the "r," they were summarily gunned down, struck with a machete, or clubbed to death. Between October 2 and October 8, anywhere from 15,000 to 35,000 had failed the test.

The Parsley Massacre, as it was later called, targeted people of Haitian ancestry; people with a Creole-speaking background. Rafael Trujillo, the dictatorial ruler of the Dominican Republic, had ordered their deaths. Trujillo was a racist, a Dominican who hid his own Haitian background with makeup. But he was a pragmatist, as all dictators must be. The Dominican Republic covered two-thirds of the island of Hispaniola, with Haiti confined to the remaining third. The Dominican Republic was sparsely populated, especially in the borderlands, and the largely empty territory along the Massacre River was tantalizing to Haitian farmers working the played-out fields of their country. Trujillo wanted to solidify the border, and there seemed to be no better way to do that then to clear the Haitians out of those lands.

International mediators pressured Trujillo to pay reparations to Haiti for the massacre, eventually settling on the rather paltry sum of US$750,000. Of this, the Dominican Republic paid only US$525,000.
Heather Michon

Date October 2, 1937

Country Dominican Republic

Why It's Key The Parsley Massacre was an incident of massive ethnic cleansing in the Caribbean.

Key Political Event
Rape of Nanking

In the summer of 1937, the Chinese forces shocked and frustrated the Japanese army by showing stubborn resistance when the latter attacked Shanghai. After an eventual victory in December, the Japanese soldiers moved on to Nanking.

Unlike the troops at Shanghai, the forces at Nanking were poorly organized and were soon defeated. After conquering the city, the Japanese soldiers were ordered to kill all captives. Reportedly told by superiors to inflict maximum pain and show no mercy, the young men brutally murdered the prisoners of war. Eyewitness accounts state that, for the next six weeks, Japanese troops slaughtered over half of the citizens in Nanking, and raped and murdered tens of thousands of women and girls. Many victims were beheaded, mutilated, burned, buried alive, or disemboweled.

Opium was allegedly distributed following the massacre to pacify those that had survived horrific atrocities, and the army also established the Comfort Women system, in which girls became slave-prostitutes to the Japanese soldiers.

The details of these weeks are still extremely controversial and much debated. Some Japanese officials have admitted to crimes, while others have denied involving any citizens, although surviving photographs suggest otherwise. Nevertheless, the evidence is varied, and the number of victims asserted range from several hundred to tens of thousands. The massacre continues to be a point of acute contention between the two countries.
Mariko Kato

Date December 13, 1937

Country China

Why It's Key It is considered as one of the single most horrific cases of genocide in history.

Fact The Rape of Nanking took place at the height of the Second Sino-Japanese War.

Key Cultural Event
Bíró files patent for his pen

American inventor John J. Loud filed the first patent for a ballpoint pen in 1888. The "ballpoint" was a tip incorporating a tiny ball bearing which, when rolled over a surface, automatically became coated with ink. Loud's pen was impractical because it leaked and was slow to dry, causing smudges, and his patent was commercially unexploited.

In the 1930s, László József Bíró, a Hungarian journalist, and his chemist brother Georg, developed Loud's invention further using a viscous oil-based ink, which dried quickly. On June 15, 1938, they filed a patent in Britain and registered another in 1940.

Immigrating to Argentina in 1940, the Bíró brothers, registered an Argentine patent for their Biro pen on June 10, 1943, forming the Eterpen Company to manufacture it. The pen was regarded as a success because it could write for a year without needing to be refilled. During World War II, the British government purchased the licensing rights as the Royal Air Force needed a pen that would not leak at high altitude, raising the pen's profile.

By the late 1940s, a number of companies were manufacturing ballpoint pens including Eversharp (formerly Eterpen) in Argentina, Martin Brothers in Britain, and Reynolds in the United States. Martin Brothers registered the name "biro" in 1947. Yet, ballpoint pens did not become truly popular until the mid-1950s when BIC and Parker started manufacturing better quality versions. Today, the pen is known as the Biro in Britain and the ballpoint pen in the United States.

Michelle Higgs

Date June 15, 1938

Country UK

Why It's Key The Biro ballpoint pen was the first commercially available writing instrument that was both portable and reliable.

Key Cultural Event
Development of Nescafé

Nescafé was launched on April 1, 1938, in Switzerland. It was not, however, the world's first instant coffee. In 1903, a Japanese chemist named Dr Kato patented a process for manufacturing soluble coffee powder, and an Englishman named George Washington commercialized it in 1909. These early incarnations generally involved brewing a batch of high-strength, concentrated coffee and then boiling it dry. However, when reconstituted with water, the resulting concoction tasted unpleasant, with little resemblance to coffee, and did not catch on.

Then, in 1930, the Brazilian Coffee Institute approached Nestlé and asked the company to develop an instant coffee that retained its flavor, as it hoped that the additional demand created would help address Brazil's huge coffee surplus. After seven years of research Nestlé's team of scientists, led by Max Mortgenthaler finally achieved the desired results using a process of spray drying, with the new product named Nescafé.

Nescafé was an immediate success. So popular was it during World War II that the entire U.S. production was earmarked for the armed forces. Since its launch, the freeze-dried Gold Blend was developed in 1984, and a decaffeinated range in 1986. Nescafé is by far the world's most popular coffee, with an estimated 3,000 cups consumed every second. Nescafé is the second most valuable food and beverage brand behind only Coca-Cola, and its exceptional strength has been key in making Nestlé the world's largest food and beverage company.

Jeremy Fialko

Date 1938

Country Switzerland

Why It's Key The development of Nescafé popularized instant coffee, and its success helped Nestlé become the world's biggest food and beverage company.

Key Political Event
The Munich Conference

As a result of the Treaty of Versailles, Germany lost a considerable degree of territory to its neighboring states at the end of World War I. One of these, the newly formed Czechoslovakia, was given an area called the Sudetenland, which contained three million ethnic Germans. The multinational composition of many of the eastern European states created by the Paris peace treaties led Mussolini to quip that Czechoslovakia itself should more properly be designated "Czecho-Germano-Polono-Magyaro-Rutheno-Romano-Slovakia."

With the rise to power of the Nazis, German foreign policy used the threat of war to throw off the shackles of the Treaty of Versailles, and by 1938, their focus was on the repossession of lost territory such as the Sudetenland. In an effort to diffuse a potentially explosive situation, the British Prime Minister, Neville Chamberlain, attempted to reach a compromise. A four-power conference consisting of Germany, France, Britain, and Italy (to which the Czechoslovakians were not invited) was held in Munich in 1938 and the Sudetenland was ceded to Germany.

Despite his success, Hitler later claimed that he had been "robbed" of his war, and in 1939, Germany overran the remainder of Czechoslovakia. Despite his "Peace for our time" speech, German behavior at Munich convinced even the arch-appeaser Chamberlain that conflict was inevitable. When Hitler made further territorial demands (against Poland) in 1939, France and Britain were no longer inclined to accommodate him.

Denis Casey

Date September 28, 1938

Country Germany

Why It's Key Although the Munich Conference marked the high point in the appeasement movement, it signaled to Britain and France that war with Nazi Germany was fast becoming inevitable.

Key Cultural Event
Welles causes panic with *War of the Worlds*

America had already fought one world war, but so far their foes were solely terrestrial. When Orson Welles went on the radio on the eve of Hallowe'en to announce that Martians were invading New Jersey and attacking civilians, listeners in nearby areas reacted with immediate panic. Over a million people thought mankind was under attack.

Of course, the aliens hadn't really landed. The broadcast, a segment in CBS radio's weekly "Mercury Theater on the Air" program, was adapted by Welles and his colleagues as a highly experimental revision of H. G. Wells' 1898 science fiction novel, *War of the Worlds*. The program's keen structure certainly intended to trick people. Welles took on the role of a reporter at the scene of the alien landing, as updates on the increasingly hostile event continually interrupted regular programming. Hence, many listeners tuning in after the introduction heard the announcement as if it were an authentic dispatch. Nevertheless, Welles later claimed that "the extent of our American lunatic fringe had been underestimated."

Although hoodwinked audiences threatened the network with lawsuits, the controversy eventually receded, leaving only amazement at the elaborate prank Welles had devised. The attention helped his program gain sponsorship and paved the way for his Hollywood career (two years later, he made the landmark film *Citizen Kane*). But Americans didn't forget the experience; in 1941, some radio listeners were skeptical about announcements of the Japanese attack on Pearl Harbor.

Eric Kohn

Date 1938

Country USA

Why It's Key Audiences' susceptibility to the false reports demonstrated the power of the media to influence public awareness.

Fact Welles was twenty-three years old at the time of the broadcast.

Key Cultural Event
Kristallnacht ("Night of Broken Glass")

Adolf Hitler had spouted plenty of anti-Semitic vitriol since becoming the Chancellor of Germany in 1933, but it wasn't until a sudden act of violence that the full extent of his oppressive intentions began to take shape. When a Parisian man named Herschel Grynszpan assassinated a member of the staff in the German Embassy in retaliation for the Party's cruel treatment toward his family, Hitler and the rest of the German leadership used it as an opportunity to begin their first widespread attack on the Jews. A decree to the Gestapo that filtered down throughout the Third Reich ordered the invasion of Jewish households, and the destruction of temples and Jewish-owned storefronts. As a result of the massive obliteration, the night this order became a reality was known as *Kristallnacht*, or "Night of Broken Glass." Hundreds of Jews were killed or imprisoned at the hands of Nazi storm troopers, while most German residents kept to themselves.

Kristallnacht was no secret to the rest of the world. Newspapers in other countries took note of the pervasive violence and pointed out the extensive anger-fueled behavior of the Nazi Party. For the party itself, *Kristallnacht* provided an excuse to begin the plan to eliminate Jewish presence in German society. Jewish property was transferred to German ownership, and Jewish residents began getting deported to concentration camps. The violent spiral of genocidal intent had reached terminal velocity.

Eric Kohn

Key Political Event
Franco becomes dictator in Spain

Born on December 4, 1892, Francisco Franco pursued a successful career in the Spanish military before gaining dictatorial control of the country and building a formidable reputation as a powerful twentieth century leader. On October 1, 1936, Franco – an able military general – became head of the opposing nationalist regime in Spain as protests against the newly elected left-wing Popular Front government escalated. Conducting a gradual but successful advance alongside valuable assistance from German and Italian forces, Franco negotiated a resounding victory for the nationalists on April 1, 1939, seizing complete control of Spain and bringing the Spanish Civil War to a brutal conclusion. As he ordered the execution of tens of thousands of his leftist opposition and imprisonment of many others, Franco quickly established a dictatorship, dissolving the Spanish Parliament and remaining in authoritarian control until his death in 1975.

Franco's early rule was shaped by the need to restore the war-torn country and was influenced greatly by the ongoing World War II. While he made efforts to ensure Spanish neutrality, Franco's sympathy with Hitler's Germany and Mussolini's Italy was evident, although he later established an alliance with the United States in opposition to Communist regimes. While contemporary world leaders recognize the legitimacy of Franco's dictatorship, his legacy is controversial and overshadowed by the deplorable violence and repression that characterized much of his rule.

Hannah Furness

Key Cultural Event
World's Fair first live televised event

Promising its 45 million visitors a glimpse into the future, the New York World's Fair unveiled exciting new technology at the opening ceremony on April 30, 1939, as Franklin D. Roosevelt's welcoming speech was broadcast to television audiences for the first time. Aiming to showcase new innovations and developments, the fair displayed original inventions such as electric calculators and keyboards, a voice synthesizer, and a display of cars alongside the Radio Corporation of America's (RCA) exhibition of the television.

Previously unknown to audiences, the television presented at the New York World's Fair cost US$600 – approximately the same amount as a new car – and would stun its limited number of viewers with its innovative technology. The speech delivered by President Roosevelt at the opening ceremony was attended by around 200,000 visitors and viewed by several hundred others, watching from inside the RCA pavilion at the fair itself and transmitted via the Empire State Building to a receiver installed on the sixty-second floor of Radio City in Manhattan. The television exhibition impressed visitors by displaying moving pictures of audience members on the small screen built within a transparent set intended to preempt accusations of trickery. The display also demonstrated how the unfamiliar new technology would fit into American homes, and was the beginning of what would soon become a multi-billion dollar industry stretching across the globe.
Hannah Furness

Date April 30, 1939

Country USA

Why It's Key The first television broadcast introduced this new and seminal piece of technology to the general public.

Key Discovery
Sutton Hoo ship

In the mid 1930s, Mrs Edith Pretty, owner of Sutton Hoo House and an enthusiastic spiritualist, claimed that she had seen an apparition of a mailed warrior atop the largest of the mounds in her garden. Through the Ipswich Museum, she employed Basil Brown, a local archaeologist, to investigate. Brown began work and, guided by Mrs Pretty, eventually discovered the remains of a boat buried in the main mound. Charles Philips, an archaeologist from the University of Cambridge, soon arrived to take over the excavation. During this investigation, numerous artifacts came to light, including the iconic helmet by which the site is best known.

Excavations ceased during World War II and the site was used as a training ground for tanks. In 1983, a team led by Martin Carver of the University of York returned to the site and conducted a thorough investigation of the remainder of the mounds. The work was published in its final form in 2005.

Finds from Sutton Hoo have thrown considerable light on the earlier Anglo-Saxon period and demonstrated links with the continent, the Mediterranean, and even the Islamic world. The artifacts found in the main mound have led some to believe that it was Rædwald, king of East Anglia (mentioned by the Venerable Bede), who was buried there. Although this is a conclusion born from convenience rather than evidence, it is an attractive prospect. Parallels have been drawn between Sutton Hoo and the discovery of another high-status burial mound in Southend-on-Sea, Essex, in 2003.
Ben Snook

Date May 11, 1939

Country UK

Why It's Key The discovery of the Sutton Hoo ship was one of the most significant archaeological finds in England.

Fact No definite evidence of a body was found in the main burial mound, which led to speculation that it could have been a cenotaph rather than a tomb.

Key Cultural Event **First live televised transmission of a sporting event**

On the afternoon of May 17, 1939, just eighteen years after the first live radio transmission of a sporting event, the National Broadcasting Company (NBC) broadcast a live baseball match on television.

The game was the second match of a double header between rivals Columbia University and Princeton University at Baker Field in Manhattan, New York. Compared with today, the technology used was rudimentary and the coverage of the action was poor. Only one camera filmed the match and the quality of the images was not comparable to the high definition quality we now enjoy; the players were clearly visible but it was hard to follow the small white ball as it moved quickly across the ball park. However, those who watched the action on the four hundred sets all over the United States became a part of sporting and television history.

While Princeton went on to win the game 2–1, the real winner was NBC. Three months later, the first professional match was televised between the Brooklyn Dodgers and the Cincinnati Reds. After this, live sporting events became a large part of primetime television schedules, ratings winners, and an extremely lucrative market for advertising. NBC became a towering force on American television and held the rights to show Major League baseball from 1939 to 2000, when Fox Broadcasting Company purchased the rights for a total of US$2.5 billion.

Terence McSweeney

Date May 17, 1939

Country USA

Why It's Key Sport begins its enduring relationship with television.

Key Person
Ambroise Vollard

While the genius of artists working at the turn of the twentieth century lives on through the innumerable canvases and sculptures housed in museums and private collections – Maillol's bronze nudes, Picasso's *Guernica* – the man who first recognized the worth of many of these artists is not as often remembered. Ambroise Vollard died on the cusp of the outbreak of World War II. Yet despite the political disquiet to which his years bore witness, he passed away knowing he had been instrumental within the development of a new world view of art – incorporating the post-impressionist, avant-garde, and modernist movements.

Vollard opened his gallery on Paris' Rue Laffitte, at the heart of the Parisian art world, in 1893; here he displayed and commissioned works, nurturing the talent and financial needs of, amongst others, Cezanne, Degas, Matisse, Picasso, Rouault, and van Gogh. Vollard bought the early work of these men when no one else would, and further promoted them through his publishing associations. Vollard's ability to foresee and influence contemporary artistic movements helped to shift the forum of art from the purview of the established salons of the nineteenth century, to that of the individual, commercial dealer. An enigmatic figure, Vollard remains today the man of many faces with which Picasso, in his *Portraits of Vollard* (1937), envisaged him; a man, whose significance Picasso further testified to, in remarking that "the most beautiful woman who ever lived never had her portrait painted, drawn or engraved any oftener than Vollard."

Claudine van Hensbergen

Date July 21, 1939

Born/Died 1866–1939

Nationality French

Why It's Key Ambroise Vollard's professional support was crucial in developing the reputation of many of the most famous artists of the twentieth century.

Key Political Event
The defense of the Polish Post Office

The Polish Post Office was Polish sovereign territory in Danzig, a free city that lay at the top of the "Polish Corridor" (territory that had been ceded to Poland after World War I). The strip of land gave Poland access to the Baltic Sea, but in doing so split Germany into two, separating East Prussia from the rest of the country.

Hitler used this reviled clause of the Treaty of Versailles as a pretext for war, demanding the return of Danzig and for strips of German territory to run over Polish land to reconnect East Prussia to the Fatherland. Poland refused, and secured guarantees from Britain and France to act against any German aggression.

Hitler knew that any move against Poland would lead to conflict but on September 1, 1939, German forces moved across the border, triggering World War II.

One of the first German targets was Danzig and the Polish Corridor.

Polish militia mounted a heroic defense of the Post Office and held off the attackers for some considerable length of time before being overrun. After the battle, instead of freeing the surviving defenders or interning them as prisoners of war, Nazi authorities put them on trial as partisans and shot them after they were found guilty. The incident showed that the Germans were capable of appalling atrocities and that the coming war would be brutal in the extreme.

Martin Sayers

Date September 1, 1939

Country Poland

Why It's Key The defense of the Polish Post Office was one of the first battles of World War II and an early demonstration of German brutality.

Key Political Event
Evacuation begins in British cities

In the months before the outbreak of World War II, the British government planned the evacuation of 3 million people from industrial areas to the safety of the countryside. This included schoolchildren with their teachers, children of pre-school age with their mothers, expectant mothers, invalids, and blind people.

"Operation Pied Piper" was never compulsory. Parents had to register their children for evacuation, and children under five could only be evacuated if accompanied by their mothers. This meant the break-up of the family unit, which a high proportion of parents were reluctant to do.

Evacuation from England and Scotland began on September 1 and was mostly completed by September 3, the day the war broke out, but there was no evacuation from Wales. The actual number

of evacuees was approximately 1.5 million, not the planned-for 3 million. Children left the towns and cities with their schools by train and were billeted with households in the countryside who had volunteered to take them in. Evacuation was a culture shock for both parties. Many of the evacuees came from areas of severe poverty and had never seen the countryside before. Nevertheless, the operation was hailed a "triumph of preparation, organization, and discipline."

By January 1940, more than half the evacuated children had returned home. After the Blitz started in August 1940, a further evacuation program took place but on a much smaller scale over a period of weeks.

Michelle Higgs

Date September 1–3, 1939

Country UK

Why It's Key The mass evacuation of children and other vulnerable people was a very real sign to the British population that World War II was imminent.

opposite **Police help evacuate children from Ealing Station, London in 1939.**

Key Political Event
Start of Nazi euthanasia policy

The Nazi "euthanasia" policy was rooted in an ideology that promoted the pseudo-Darwinian ideal of Germanic mental and physical perfection and the inferiority of other "lesser" races and individuals.

From 1933 onward, the Nazis promulgated "racial hygiene" laws, including measures such as the compulsory sterilization of the mentally ill. An official euthanasia policy was not introduced until October 1939, after the outbreak of war. This policy (which was not euthanasia in the normal, voluntary sense), initiated the killing of adults and children who suffered from mental and physical defects. The program was headed by Dr Karl Brandt, Hitler's personal physician, and camouflaged with euphemisms such as the "Charitable Foundation for Institutional Care," the name given to the policy's overseers.

People selected for death by doctors, often on the most arbitrary of examinations, were usually administered lethal injections or gassed. Many of the developments in gassing (and the perpetrators) were later utilized in concentration camps. Although officially ended in 1941 due to opposition from some sections of the public, the killings continued in secret throughout the war, even as the allies were overrunning Germany.

The willing participation of the medical profession in the murder of the most vulnerable members of society, often children, adds to the moral repugnance of these crimes. As many as 150,000 may have been killed but few perpetrators were brought to account. Brandt, however, was tried and hanged in 1948.
Denis Casey

Date October 20, 1939

Country Germany

Why It's Key The systematic killing of the mentally ill resulted in the deaths of over 100,000 people and fed directly into the development of the concentration camp system.

Key Cultural Event First advertising jingle broadcast nationally in the United States

Throughout the 1930s, Pepsi-Cola was overshadowed in sales and popularity by its arch-rival Coca-Cola. However, despite the ever-present threat of bankruptcy, the company did have one clear selling point: its bottles were twice the size of Coca-Cola's for the same five-cent cost, an obvious attraction to Americans hard-hit by the Depression. But with only a tiny advertising budget, Pepsi had to look for news ways of competing with Coca-Cola as traditional methods, such as billboards, were too expensive.

In 1939, the company introduced two popular cartoon characters, Pepsi and Pete, whose comic strip capers were cheaply and effectively syndicated in newspapers across the country. Continuing the "Twice As Much For A Nickel" advertising theme (or campaign, as it would be known now), the catchy "Nickel Nickel" jingle was commissioned and recorded, unusually, to song-length. Other products had been advertised, usually live and as spoken commercials with only a brief musical jingle on the end, on local stations as commercial radio exploded during the 1920s and 1930s. But in 1940 the memorable Pepsi recording took advertising to a whole new level, as it was played coast-to-coast on network radio. The jingle was a huge radio and jukebox hit, both nationally and internationally, becoming the cornerstone of Pepsi's advertising strategy for the next decade. Its popularity also immediately translated into sales as Pepsi mounted a serious challenge to Coca-Cola for the first time. Advertising would never be the same again.
Hedley Paul

Date 1940

Country USA

Why It's Key Pepsi-Cola's hugely popular "Nickel, Nickel" song used the growing medium of national radio to great success, and became an advertising phenomenon.

Fact Later known as "Pepsi-Cola Hits The Spot," the tune went on to be recorded in fifty-five different languages with over 1 million records produced.

Key Cultural Event **Benjamin writes** *Theses on the Philosophy of History*

The *Theses on the Philosophy of History* were German philosopher and literary critic Walter Benjamin's last composed writings. Benjamin, a Jew and a critic of the Nazi Party, was attempting to immigrate to the United States via Spain when he died in September 1940. He was ill from traveling, but he also overdosed on morphine; in all likelihood he took his own life, fearing he could not escape the persecutory grasp of Hitler's regime.

Benjamin left behind an extraordinary body of work and a unique contribution to modern thought. His eighteen brief "theses" are poetic but lucid meditations on history that also reflect keenly on an understanding of present time (Benjamin uses the term *Jetztzeit*, or "time of the now"). Benjamin was an unorthodox Marxist – his writing involves less a critique of fascism rather than a challenge to the hierarchies of thought that allow fascism to flourish. Benjamin also questioned dominant historicist conceptions of time (including some Marxist theory) that sees history purely as a sequence of events connected "like the beads of a rosary." Benjamin argues for a historical approach that understands more profound or mystical connections through history, in which the present era forms a "constellation" with an earlier one. In synthesizing different traditions, including the theological and the Marxist, Benjamin created compelling and original theses. His work, most importantly, influences rarefied developments in critical thought while addressing the nature of present-day reality, as it did the ferment of 1940.

Michael Hallam

Date January 1940

Country France

Why It's Key Benjamin's exceptional exploration into Marxism and Jewish mysticism continues to influence the understanding of history.

1940–1949

213

Key Cultural Event **McDaniel wins an Academy Award**

Despite their many contributions to the arts in the first half of the twentieth century, African-Americans found little success in mainstream motion pictures, where they experienced systematic racism and discrimination. In many Hollywood films, African-Americans only appeared in secondary roles – servants, cooks, porters, maids, and shoe shiners – and were paid less for their work than their white counterparts. Moreover, movie theaters were often segregated in this period, particularly in the South. If filmmakers wanted to utilize black actors in roles that better reflected the African-American experience, they could only produce so-called "race films," films created for an all-black audience.

Given this, it is not surprising that Hattie McDaniel's role as a maid in *Gone With The Wind*, and her subsequent Oscar win, had a mixed reception by black audiences. McDaniel's best-known line from the film, "I don't know nothing about birthing babies," was derided by many African-Americans, who saw the phrase as emblematic of the patronizing way black people were treated by Hollywood.

However, some African-Americans regarded McDaniel's victory as a source of pride, despite their problems with the role itself. Today, McDaniel is viewed as both a symbol of the way Hollywood treated African-Americans before the civil rights movement of the 1960s, and a pioneer for the African-American actors that followed her.

Martin Johnson

Date January 29, 1940

Country USA

Why It's Key By winning the Oscar, McDaniel proved that African-American actors were as talented as white actors, even though they were restricted to secondary roles in Hollywood film.

Fact Despite her Oscar win, McDaniel was paid far less than the other actors in the film.

Key Political Event
Formation of the Home Guard

On May 14, 1940, Anthony Eden, the Secretary of State for War, broadcast an appeal to the public to join a new force for home defence called the Local Defence Volunteers. Their purpose was to guard against possible landings by German parachute troops in Britain, which had been very successful in Belgium and Holland. The appeal was particularly aimed at men in "small towns, villages, and less densely inhabited suburban areas" aged seventeen to sixty-five who could undertake the job on a part-time basis.

The public response was overwhelming. By the end of the following day, a quarter of a million men had enlisted at their local police stations. This increased to over 1.5 million by the end of the summer. At first, there was a lack of organization, training, and equipment for the more than one thousand battalions formed. They were forced to arm themselves with private firearms and other makeshift weapons.

In July 1940, the Local Defence Volunteers were renamed the Home Guard by Winston Churchill. By the winter, they had standard-issue army uniforms and World War I rifles supplied by the United States. Throughout 1941–1942, army-style ranks were introduced and sub-artillery and other weapons were provided together with regular training.

Even after the danger of invasion had passed, the Home Guard, or "Dad's Army" as it was affectionately called, continued with its war work by manning anti-aircraft batteries and undertaking dangerous bomb disposal. However, the Home Guard stood down in early November 1944.

Michelle Higgs

Date May 14, 1940

Country UK

Why It's Key Although ineffective as an anti-invasion force, from 1942 the Home Guard's role on anti-aircraft sites freed up 100,000 regulars for other duties.

214

Key Political Event
The evacuation of Dunkirk

On May 10, 1940, the German army invaded the Low Countries and France. Despite valiant resistance, the German troops marched relatively smoothly through the region. Soon, the bulk of the Allied forces were trapped in a shrinking circle near the port of Dunkirk in the north-east of France, and on May 25, the British War Office decided to launch Operation DYNAMO, a mass evacuation of the British Expeditionary Force (BEF) from Dunkirk.

The operation began on May 26 and ended on June 4, and it rescued 338,226 British and French troops. On May 31 alone, 68,014 men were saved. The evacuation has been called "near-miraculous," and much of its success was due to British effort. The Royal Air Force (RAF) fought against the much larger German air force – the Luftwaffe – to give the evacuation cover.

When the British navy found its numbers insufficient, hundreds of civilians took their own ships to Dunkirk to help, some in tiny rowboats and fishing boats. These small vessels transported about 99,000 men. Their actions succeeded in part because the weather and the geography of Dunkirk allowed both the perimeter's defense and the evacuation's speed. However, DYNAMO could not have worked without Hitler's inexplicable decision on May 24 to halt his ground troops, giving the British time to begin the evacuation. DYNAMO saved some of the best of the Allied forces and fostered a spirit of determination among the British. Many have argued that, without Dunkirk, Hitler would have won World War II.

Christina Welsch

Date May 26, 1940

Country France

Why It's Key The evacuation of more than 338,000 troops out of Dunkirk ahead of the German army saved the Allied forces' core of experienced soldiers, and provided them with a source of pride and determination throughout World War II.

opposite The evacuation scene at Dunkirk, 1940.

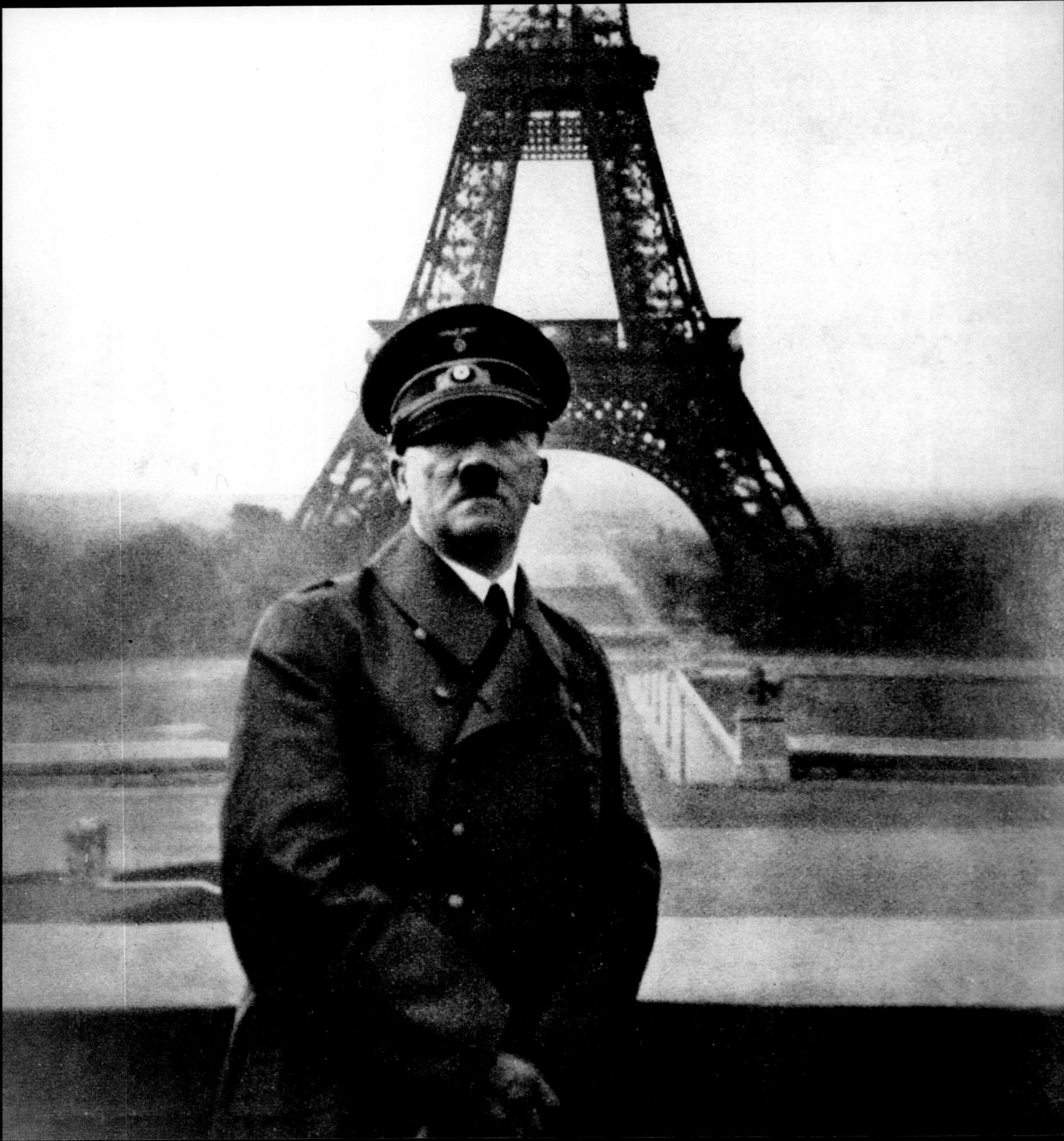

Key Political Event
Churchill makes "Finest Hour" speech

On the day that Britain and France declared war on Germany on September 3, 1939, Winston Churchill was assigned as First Lord of the Admiralty by Prime Minister Neville Chamberlain. As the war gained momentum, Churchill vocally condemned Nazi Germany in letters and speeches.

When Churchill made the "Finest Hour" speech, he had taken over as British Prime Minister for five weeks. France had fallen to Germany earlier that month, and Britain faced the real possibility of invasion. At this dark hour for Britain, Churchill did not disguise the imminent danger ("Hitler knows that he will have to break us in this Island or lose the war"), but used this sense of urgency to rally the people, calling on them to rise to the challenge, and reassuring them that the British military forces would deliver. The famous final sentence of the speech predicts confidently the healthy future of the British Empire for many years to come: "Let us therefore brace ourselves to our duties, and so bear ourselves that, if the British Empire and its Commonwealth last for a thousand years, men will still say, 'This was their finest hour'."

This inspirational, well-crafted speech was aired on the radio later that day, and instilled hope in the British people. A few months later, the German invasion failed due to lack of air command, prompting Churchill to declare gleefully in October: "We are waiting for the long-promised invasion. So are the fishes."

Mariko Kato

Date June 18, 1940

Country UK

Why It's Key The speech is one of most famous oratorical pieces by Sir Winston Churchill, and widely ranked among the world's most powerful political speeches.

Key Political Event
The fall of France

After a long period of relative inactivity dubbed the "phony war" in Britain, World War II began to gather pace in May 1940 when German forces attacked the Low Countries of Belgium, Holland, and Luxembourg. Victory was swift and enabled Germany to bypass the heavily fortified Franco-German border, arriving on France's Northern flank by late May. Despite desperate rearguard action by French and British troops, they were no match for the superior German army. An advance guard of Panzer tanks moved quickly through northern France, punching a hole through allied lines and encircling huge numbers of troops. By June 4, the British Expeditionary Force and a significant number of French soldiers had pulled back to the beaches of Dunkirk where they managed to retreat across the channel.

Hitler's forces continued moving through France and by June 14 had entered Paris, where German soldiers marched triumphantly up the Champs Élysées. Italian troops attacked southeastern France on June 20 and the final humiliation took place on June 22 when French generals signed terms of surrender in the same railway carriage where the Germans had accepted armistice terms in 1918.

Germany occupied three-fifths of French territory, with only the rump puppet-state of Vichy France, led by the aging General Petain, left in the south. In defiance of the French surrender, General Charles De Gaulle proclaimed himself leader of Free French forces from his base in London.

Martin Sayers

Date June 22, 1940

Country France

Why It's Key The surrender of France to Germany marked the apex of Hitler's *Blitzkrieg* (Lightning War) campaign across continental Europe.

opposite Hitler by the Eiffel tower after capturing Paris.

Key Political Event
Battle of Britain, "The Hardest Day"

By the end of June 1940, Poland, Denmark, Norway, Holland, Belgium, Luxembourg, and France had all fallen to Nazi Germany, and Hitler contemplated a plan to invade Britain, code-named *Seelöwe* (Sea-Lion). For this to have any hope of success, however, the Royal Air Force would have to be destroyed (though any German invasion force would still have had to contend with the Royal Navy). At the beginning of July, the RAF had 754 fighters, mostly Hurricanes and Spitfires, and the Luftwaffe a total of 3,272 bombers and fighters combined.

During the first phase of what came to be called the Battle of Britain, the Luftwaffe bombed shipping, radar stations, and coastal towns. The subsequent *Adlerangriff* (Eagle Attack) was intended to destroy the RAF, both in the air and on the ground – *Adler Tag* itself on August 13 utilized practically every aircraft the Luftwaffe had. After a few days' lull, on August 18, a first wave of 108 bombers and 483 fighters launched another enormous assault. Successive raids attempted to destroy fighter command airfields, notably at Kenley and Biggin Hill, both home to sector operations rooms directing the defense.

"The Hardest Day" is also significant in that it saw the Ju 87 Stuka, the Luftwaffe's main precision bomber, withdrawn from the battle, as it had proved too vulnerable to fighter attack. Subsequent major assaults took place in September, after which the Luftwaffe switched to night-time raids on London, and Hitler turned his attention to the east.
Duncan Proudfoot

Date August 18, 1940

Country UK

Why It's Key On no other day of the battle would either the Luftwaffe or the RAF have more planes put out of action; the Luftwaffe had 69 planes destroyed and 31 damaged, while Fighter Command had 34 destroyed and 39 damaged (the RAF as a whole lost an additional 29 planes destroyed and 23 damaged on the ground).

Key Cultural Event
Bugsy Siegel goes to Las Vegas

Benjamin "Bugsy" Siegel was born in Brooklyn, New York, in 1906. Involved in criminal activity from an early age, he quickly became an important figure in the New York underworld. Although Jewish, Siegel developed strong links to the Italian-American Mafia, which at that time was growing in power across the United States.

In the 1930s, he arrived in Los Angeles to develop Mafia activities on the American west coast. Yet it was the small desert town of Las Vegas in Nevada that really captured his imagination. Gambling had been legal in the state since 1931 and Siegel first visited Las Vegas in 1941 to review operations at the existing small-scale casinos. Seeing potential, he singled it out as the location of a proposed gambling empire. Mafia bosses, excited by the amount of profit Siegel was predicting, agreed to back his venture.

Despite his grand ambitions, bad planning and poor workmanship thwarted Siegel's plans. His first casino, The Flamingo, opened at the end of 1946, but it actually managed to lose money in its first few months of existence. The Mafia quickly lost patience and on June 21, 1947, Siegel was shot dead at his mansion in Beverley Hills.

Siegel's legacy was extraordinary; after his death, money began to pour into Las Vegas and casinos mushroomed. Today, Las Vegas is the Hollywood of the gambling industry, generating billions of dollars each year.
Martin Sayers

Date 1941

Country USA

Why It's Key By effectively creating Las Vegas, Bugsy Siegel laid the foundations for today's multi-billion dollar gambling industry.

Key Cultural Event
Death of Virginia Woolf

On April 18, 1941, a group of teenagers cycling near Lewes, East Sussex in England, found a body floating in the River Ouse. Leonard Woolf was called to identify his dead wife, and an inquest was held the following day, which concluded that Virginia Woolf, novelist and Bloomsbury *grande dame*, had committed suicide "while the balance of her mind was disturbed." Twenty-one days earlier, she had left Monk's House with a stone in her pocket, after writing a note to her husband: "No one could have been so good as you have been."

Though these few facts of Woolf's death are set down solidly in the coroner's report, the mythology they have sparked continues to develop. For some, the suicide was prompted by wartime fear, which appears to be corroborated in some of her writings; for others, it is metonymic of the fate of the trapped woman writer, a prototype for subsequent literary suicides such as that of Sylvia Plath.

With all these versions of Woolf's death to hand, it is tempting to read her fiction for clues to her "disturbed" mind, but that would miss the universal applications of her work. Her stock has never been higher; she is now a staple of English syllabuses and an icon of both academic and popular culture. In turn, her ascendancy has opened up a whole new "modernism" for readers, beyond Proust, Joyce, and Mann, of writers gradually surfacing after decades of relative neglect; geniuses salvaged from the wreckage of the twentieth century.

Andrew Blades

Date March 28, 1941

Country UK

Why It's Key Woolf's death was the first step in the posthumous recognition of Woolf as a key writer of the twentieth century.

Fact Both Woolf's husband Leonard and her sister Vanessa were famous in their own right, as a journalist and a painter respectively.

Key Cultural Event
First public lending rights in Denmark

On June 17, 1918, Thit Jensen, a Danish novelist, made a speech to the Danish Library Association. She argued that Danish libraries should remunerate authors for the loan of their books. Librarians and publishers strenuously objected. Although the controversy eventually died down, she revived it with the support of her colleagues in the mid-1920s.

Jensen gained a major ally in 1929, when Danish author and arctic explorer Peter Freuchen joined the fray. Freuchen convinced the publisher of his latest book to put a clause in that would prohibit public loans without some kind of financial compensation. The Danish High Court ruled he could do this.

Freuchen had already established himself as an outstanding individual before the Danish Court ruling. From 1913 to 1920, he served as colony governor in Thule, Greenland. The first of his three wives, Navarana, was an Inuk he married in 1911. Navarana accompanied him on many of his arctic travels and bore him two sons before the 1921 influenza epidemic.

Jensen and Freuchen's lobbying efforts paid off. In 1942, the Danish government introduced an amendment to the Libraries Act that granted remuneration for the use of authors' works in public libraries. Word War II delayed implementation until April 1, 1946, when a section to the existing Libraries Act came into force. Although various changes have been made to the original scheme over the years, the public lending rights program still remains in effect in Denmark, as well as in twenty-two other countries.

Leith Peterson

Date April 1, 1941

Country Denmark

Why It's Key Denmark was the first country to establish a public lending rights system.

Key Cultural Event
Citizen Kane is released

No film in history has been showered with the ubiquitous praise leveled at *Citizen Kane*. The world has accepted it as essential viewing for casual movie buffs and cineastes alike. Why the histrionics? The first movie directed by radio and stage star Orson Welles, a mere twenty-five years old when he transitioned into the movie business, it showcased brilliantly insightful storytelling. The plot focuses on the morally ambiguous life of a fictional newspaper tycoon, Charles Foster Kane (played by Welles). Media magnate William Randolph Hearst, whose life influenced the vitreous character, attempted to blacklist the film and basically succeeded. Although Welles won an Oscar for Best Original Screenplay, the movie flopped. Over the years, however, critical acclaim paved the way for its legendary reputation.

Citizen Kane made a radical break with traditional models of filmmaking. Welles' cinematographer, Gregg Toland, used deep focus to capture extensive action in single shots. The narrative was equally complex, employing tactics like fake newsreels to place Kane into history, and make-up so that the actors appeared to age over the course of the story. The mystery behind Kane's last word, "Rosebud," sustains the movie's sense of wonder, but good filmmaking couldn't sustain Welles' career. His follow-up, *The Magnificent Ambersons*, was altered by the studio and, in later years, the director had to independently finance his increasingly experimental productions. "I started at the top and worked my way down," Welles once said. "An artist has always to be out of step with his time."
Eric Kohn

Date May 1, 1941

Country USA

Why It's Key Welles' unconventional storytelling methods revolutionized the art of filmmaking.

Fact Facing poor box office predictions, Welles offered to buy the movie from RKO and distribute it himself.

opposite **Poster for *Citizen Kane*.**

220

Key Political Event
Hitler decides to attack the USSR

By 1941, Adolf Hitler had virtually eliminated all opposition in western Europe; Britain alone remained unconquered, and Hitler began to dream of a campaign in the East. Although Germany and Soviet Russia had signed a non-aggression pact in 1939, Hitler's plan of world domination dictated an eventual conquest of the USSR; the enormous resources of these territories would provide fuel for the German war machine and a territorial base for German expansion. For this campaign, code-named "Operation Barbarossa," Hitler assembled a force of over 3 million men, 3,000 tanks and 7,500 artillery pieces. It was the largest invasion force in history.

Facing unprepared and disorganized Soviet resistance, the Germans made swift gains and by August were within reach of Moscow. However, poor German planning, needless delays, and underestimation of

Soviet troop strength led the Germans into a dreaded winter campaign. Lacking proper equipment for winter fighting, the German ranks were crippled by the devastating Russian winter; by November they had suffered almost 750,000 casualties. Distracted by fresh Allied assaults from the west, the Germans eventually capitulated and were forced back by the Red Army.

The consequences of Hitler's eastern attack were profound. Its failure cost vast amounts of men and resources, and opened a disastrous second front to the war. It also emboldened the rest of the Allies, who prepared their own counter-offensives and began to press on Germany's western border. The defeat of the German war machine – once thought unstoppable – became assured.
Justin Norris

Date June 22, 1941

Country Germany/USSR

Why It's Key Hitler's decision to attack the USSR drained vital resources from his campaign on the Western front, and Russia's eventual repulsion of the attack contributed to the defeat of Nazi Germany.

Key Political Event
Pearl Harbor

Images of dive-bombing Japanese planes and U.S. battleships exploding in flames have been seared into the collective American consciousness, by history and Hollywood alike. But the real historical impact of Japan's attack on the United States' Pacific Fleet has been no less significant.

Tensions between Japan and the United States had been deteriorating since the 1920s, and they worsened with Japan's invasion of Manchuria and alliance with Nazi Germany during World War II. In 1941, the United States was still technically a non-combatant, and a significant contingent of American isolationists tended to view the conflict as only "Europe's war." However, in the early morning of December 7, 350 Japanese aircraft launched two waves of attacks on the United States' Pacific Fleet, as well as nearby airfields and other military targets. Five American battleships and 188 American planes were destroyed, along with thousands of personnel killed and wounded. Japan lost only 29 aircraft and a handful of midget submarines. It was conceived to be a monumental victory for the Japanese Empire.

The surprise attack mobilized U.S. public opinion in favor of retaliation, and virtually ensured the United States' entry into the conflict. President Roosevelt declared war the next day, famously characterizing December 7 as "a date which will live in infamy." In the long term, the attack proved disastrous for the Axis countries; it succeeded in waking the "sleeping giant" of America's industrial might, revitalizing the Allies and leading to Japan's total defeat.

Justin Norris

Date December 7, 1941

Country USA

Why It's Key The attack on the U.S. fleet at Pearl Harbor led to the American entry into World War II, contributing to the eventual Axis defeat.

opposite Huge columns of smoke go up from the USS *West Virginia* and the USS *Tennessee*, crippled at Pearl Harbor.

Key Political Event
Wannsee conference

Contrary to popular opinion, the Wannsee Conference, held in a former Interpol office outside Berlin, was not the scene of the decision to eradicate the Jewish people. Nazi policy had previously focused on encouraging Jews to emigrate, duly robbing them in the process. This approach changed to one whereby Jews judged capable of labor would be worked to death and those incapable killed immediately. Even before Wannsee, gassings were already underway at locations such as Chelmno in occupied Poland. The conference was intended to discuss the implementation of the "final solution" to the "Jewish question," which in essence had already been decided upon.

The secretaries of various government departments attended the meeting, chaired by Reinhard Heydrich. Much of the proceedings were taken up with arguments over the legal definition of a Jew. Among the fifteen highly educated men present (over half of whom held doctorates), the question of the morality of mass murder was never raised.

The minutes of the meeting (recorded by Adolf Eichmann) were reworked repeatedly as they were designed for a reasonably wide circulation among the Nazi elite. They are characterized by the usual Nazi employment of euphemisms, of which "final solution" has become the most infamous.

Popular misconception aside, the conference did play an important role in the establishment of the SS's primacy in the Nazi's Jewish policy, which led to the deaths of millions of people.

Denis Casey

Date January 20, 1942

Country Germany

Why It's Key The Wannsee Conference was a key event in the administration of Nazi murder policy.

Key Cultural Event
Singapore falls to Japan

The fall of Singapore in February 1942 to the Japanese was nothing short of a humiliation for the British Empire. After nine days of fierce fighting, 80,000 British Commonwealth troops surrendered to General Tomoyuki Yamashita's vastly inferior force of 30,000. It was the single largest capitulation of British military personnel in history, and came only five days after Churchill had insisted to General Wavell that the "battle must be fought to the bitter end at all costs," because the "honor of the British Empire... is at stake."

On February 8, 4,000 Japanese landed at Sarimbun Beach in the north-west of the island and made progress inland despite heavy resistance from Australian troops. Hopelessly outnumbered, Singapore's meager air force was evacuated to Sumatra, leaving the skies clear for Japanese bombers to terrorize the island. The island's large-caliber coastal guns, designed for penetrating the hulls of battleships, offered little defense against Japanese air raids.

General Yamashita viewed Singapore as a strategic port in Southeast Asia, but the Japanese were also motivated by a desire to defeat the island's prominent Chinese community, who had offered economic support to China in the Sino-Japanese war. Ironically, Singapore surrendered on February 15, the first day of the Chinese New Year, and during the three and a half years of Japanese occupation that followed, the Chinese, Malayan, and Indian citizens were brutally repressed.

Jay Mullins

Date February 15, 1942

Country Singapore

Why It's Key The loss of Britain's stronghold in Southeast Asia during World War II exposed the empire as militarily weak.

Fact General Yamashita chose Singapore's Ford Motor Factory as the location for Lieutenant-General Arthur Percival to receive the island's terms of surrender.

Key Cultural Event
Gas chambers become operational in Auschwitz

The climax of the film *Schindler's List* (1993) shows a crowd of terrified Jewish people getting shepherded into a large barren room, only to have their tension relieved as water begins raining down on them. Unfortunately, most people incarcerated in Auschwitz-Birkenau, the massive concentration camp built by the Nazi Party in the south of Poland, met a far worse fate than showers. While the Nazi Party had employed gas chambers as an extermination technique in the late 1930s, their use in Auschwitz became the camp's central horrific device. Auschwitz was comprised of three distinct areas: one for administrative work, another for forced labor, and the third for extermination. Auschwitz II contained the gas chambers, large rooms that roughly 20,000 prisoners were forced into on a daily basis as the lethal gas Zyklon-B was filtered into the room. Elderly prisoners and women with children almost always got sent to Auschwitz II, although some were subjected to grotesque experiments before they were killed.

The implementation of the gas chambers in Auschwitz illustrated the sheer systemization of the Nazis' genocidal intentions. There was no accident in the design; the gas chambers were created for a single purpose and there was no way to disguise it as otherwise. Hence, the evidence put forth at the Nuremburg Trials and elsewhere could not be disputed. Word of the massive slaughter leaked out of the camp via escaped prisoners in 1944, but liberation didn't arrive until one year later with the arrival of Soviet troops.

Eric Kohn

Date March 20, 1942

Country Poland

Why It's Key The gas chambers marked the beginning of the Nazi's most prevalent extermination technique in the infamous concentration camp.

Fact About 7,600 survivors were discovered in Auschwitz II at the time of its liberation.

Key Political Event
Roosevelt issues Executive Order 9066

Citing the need for protection against "espionage and sabotage," on March 21, 1942, President Franklin D. Roosevelt signed Executive Order 9066, authorizing the removal of citizens living within an exclusion zone stretching 50–60 miles inland along the west coast.

Technically, the order allowed for the removal of *any* citizen, but practically, it meant Japanese-Americans. In all, 120,000 citizens of Japanese descent – 62 per cent of them legal, native-born Americans – were ordered to report to "Civilian Assembly Centers" all over the west coast in the months after the order was issued. They were allowed to bring only what they could carry. Most were then sent on to one of ten War Relocation Centers, or WRCs, spread across the American West: Gila River and Poston, Arizona;

Amache, Colorado; Heart Mountain, Wyoming; Jerome and Rohwer, Arkansas; Topaz, Utah; Minidoka, Idaho; and Manzanar and Tule Lake, California. More "troublesome" detainees could be sent to federal or military prisons or camps.

American internment camps were not designed to inflict punishment or cause death, but they were far from comfortable. Prisoners suffered from extreme temperatures, fell ill from infectious diseases common to any communal living situations, and had to suffer the indignities of life under guard.

In December 1944, the Supreme Court ruled in *Ex parte Endo* that detentions were illegal, and on January 2, 1945, the exclusion order was rescinded. Each internee was given US$25 and a train ticket home.
Heather Michon

Date March 21, 1942
Country USA
Why It's Key The order was the largest forced relocation of citizens in U.S. history.

Key Political Event
Gandhi launches "Quit India" campaign

World War II provided a turning point in India's movement to end British rule. Mahatma Gandhi, leader of India's National Congress and advocate of non-violent resistance (*satyagraha*), had been opposed to Britain's approach to the war. Of the Munich Agreement signed in 1938 by Adolf Hitler and Neville Chamberlain he wrote: "The peace that Europe gained at Munich is a triumph of violence." Even worse was Britain's declaration of war without consultation with India, which committed thousands of Indians to fight on its behalf. The program of civil disobedience launched in 1930 was escalated in an attempt to dislodge the British, and by 1941, had resulted in the imprisonment of thousands of *satyagrahis*.

In 1942, Gandhi was anguished by India's increasing vulnerability to Japanese attack. The

Congress Party insisted that India be declared neutral and in August endorsed the new "Quit India" campaign. Within hours, Gandhi and his fellow leaders were arrested and imprisoned without trial for two years. The campaign went ahead, but without Gandhi's guidance, his insistence on non-violence strayed. Strikes, boycotts, and the sabotage of railways and telegraph lines frequently resorted to the use of bombs. The British were alarmed but realized, with some international pressure, that a post-war British Raj was untenable. Though the "Quit India" campaign achieved its aim, as Congress leaders languished in prison the Muslim League's agitation for a separate Pakistan gained momentum, ultimately delivering a splintered, brutalized independent India.
Sally Percival Wood

Date August 8, 1942
Country India
Why It's Key The "Quit India" campaign was the final phase in Gandhi's campaign of civil disobedience to dislodge the British. Ironically, however, it delivered a partitioned India, wracked by communal violence, which opposed all that Gandhi's movement of non-violence had symbolized.

Key Political Event
Battle of Stalingrad begins

Stalingrad, on the Germans' left flank, was of vital strategic importance as Russia's center for both manufacturing and communication. That it bore the name of the USSR's leader added a personal dimension to the struggle for both sides. German "Army Group South" (consisting of the 6th Army under Friedrich Paulus, the 4th Panzer Army, and their Romanian and Hungarian allies) had surrounded Stalingrad (defended by the Russian 62nd Army under Vasily Chuikov) by early August. Vicious fighting ensued. To minimize the effectiveness of German *blitzkrieg* tactics, Russian commanders ordered their troops to engage the enemy as closely as possible, denying the Germans vital air and artillery support lest they killed their own men.

Late in 1942, the Russians launched a counter attack codenamed Operation Uranus. Focusing on the German flanks, defended by poorly trained Hungarian and Romanian troops, the Russians encircled the Germans so that the besiegers became the besieged. The Russians then began to advance on the Germans, gradually closing the pocket. In January 1943, more than 91,000 starving, demoralized Germans surrendered, though small-scale resistance continued for another month or so.

As many as two million soldiers and civilians were allegedly killed during the battle. Although casualties were horrific on both sides, the massive loss of men and machines struck an irreversible blow to the German army. Stalingrad was, in every sense, a turning point of World War II.

Ben Snook

Date August 21, 1942

Country Russia

Why It's Key The battle resulted in massive casualties from which Germany could not recover and marked a turning point in World War II.

Key Political Event
The Beveridge Report

The *Report on Social Insurance and Allied Services* by Sir William Beveridge was a momentous government document published in Britain and popularly known as "The Beveridge Report." It contained the revolutionary idea that post-war Britain could be organized to defeat the five "giants" of society, which Beveridge identified as "disease," "ignorance," "squalor," "idleness," and "want," through a system of social security. The British "welfare state" would be responsible for the care of all of its citizens, from "cradle to grave," ensuring that familial incomes did not fall below a certain level. A financial safety net would look after people irrespective of income when life events made it impossible for them to look after themselves, such as during illness, unemployment, and old age, and the government would also guarantee improvements in education and housing, as well as a free health service. These developments in social welfare would be achieved through a system of insurance, the cost of which would be shared between the state and the individual.

The proposals of the Beveridge Report were revolutionary as they recommended a significant extension of the state's responsibility in its attempt to eliminate poverty. Following the report, Britain introduced family allowances in 1945, while in 1946, National Insurance and the National Heath services were enacted. Together, these policies formed a powerful blueprint for social and economic policy in Britain and abroad, and redefined the notion of the "welfare state."

Helena Hewson

Date Dec 1, 1942

Country UK

Why It's Key The Beveridge Report established the principles of the British welfare state and influenced the development of welfare systems in other countries.

Key Cultural Event **Cousteau and Gagnan develop scuba diving gear**

The name Jacques Cousteau – or as he's called in his native France, *le commandant Cousteau* – is synonymous with the ocean. While he's famous for documenting the secrets of underwater life in his book *The Silent World* and various television series, one of his greatest contributions was made years prior. Beginning a lifelong love affair with the ocean, he entered the French Navy in 1930 as head of the underwater research group. In 1943, he and engineer Emile Gagnan developed the "aqua-lung," a new breed of diving suit. The key was the invention of the demand valve, or regulator, which would allow for the easy management of air supply under the duress of the ocean's shifting pressures.

This, along with a high-pressure diving cylinder, resulted in the first SCUBA (short for Self Contained Underwater Breathing Apparatus) gear. It was based on an open-circuit design, in which gas is released from the suit upon the diver breathing out; previous, closed-circuit designs were based on a potentially dangerous oxygen recycling system, which Cousteau and Gagnan's invention rendered obsolete. But it was Cousteau's later role in the public eye that captured imaginations, and his explorations on board his ship, the *Calypso*, opened a window to a previously unseen world. He remains a part of popular culture today; he is gently satirized in the 2004 film *The Life Aquatic with Steve Zissou*, which follows a Cousteau-like character played by Bill Murray.

David Greenwald

Date 1943

Country France

Why It's Key Cousteau and Gagnan's "aqualung" technology enabled lengthy underwater excursions and exploration.

Key Cultural Event
Sartre's *Being and Nothingness* published

When Jean-Paul Sartre published *Being and Nothingness* (*L'Etre et le Néant*) in 1943, Paris was under Nazi occupation, and the young socialist had no choice but to submit the hefty manuscript to the authorities for approval. It's clear, though, that the censors did not actually read it, for if they had, they would have banned it; the book is not only one of the founding texts of existentialism but also a profound tribute to human liberty.

Sartre was born in Paris in 1905. After publishing several works of psychology and fiction, including the influential *Nausea* (*La Nausée*, 1938), he joined the army at the start of World War II and then spent a few months in a German prison camp. *Being and Nothingness* attracted few readers beyond a small circle of professional philosophers, but it was enough to make his name, and start him on the path to becoming perhaps the best-known philosopher of the twentieth century. In the difficult 600-page work, Sartre argues that the world is divided into being-for-itself – human consciousness – and being-in-itself – everything that remains, including the material world, the past, the body, and so on. We wish to turn other humans into objects, while remaining ourselves a subject, and others wish to do the same to us. This struggle, Sartre says, is the basis not only of open conflict, but also of love and sex. Consciousness gives us true freedom as well; a great but terrifying gift.

Ned Beauman

Date 1943

Country France

Why It's Key This masterwork marked the beginning of French existentialism.

Key Political Event
Members of the White Rose executed

Between June 1942 and February 1943, German intelligence was desperate to discover the identity of a resistance group known as *die Weisse Rose* – "the White Rose." During those months, six pamphlets written by the group had been distributed across the country, urging resistance to Adolf Hitler and the Nazi movement.

On February 18, 1943, two students were found distributing the latest pamphlets on the campus of the University in Munich. Hans and Sophie Scholl, a brother and sister in their early twenties, were at the center of the small White Rose organization. Within hours, all the other members were arrested for treason. Most were students who had once supported the Nazi cause, but had become sickened by the atrocities of Hitler's war.

Four days later, the first trials began. "You know the war is lost," Sophie Scholl told the court. "Why don't you have the courage to face it?" The verdict was swift: they were found guilty and told that the execution would take place that day. To discourage followers, Hitler's government had decided on public beheadings. Sophie and Hans Scholl and Christoph Probst went to the guillotine that evening, followed by two others in July, and the final member in October.

The executions did not lead to popular support for resistance in Germany; in fact, their deaths were essentially ignored until the 1970s, when they were rediscovered and became folk heroes. Their rallying cry – "We will not be silent" – has become a mantra for critics of war.

Heather Michon

Date February 22, 1943

Country Germany

Why It's Key The execution of the German resistance fighters demonstrated Hitler's intolerance to dissenting opinions in his country.

Key Political Event
The Warsaw ghetto uprising

The Warsaw ghetto, built as a result of Nazi determination to exterminate the Jewish people through segregation and imprisonment, contained approximately 400,000 inhabitants forced into cramped, unsanitary, and inhuman conditions. With an average of seventy deaths per day from starvation and disease, further brutality was inflicted upon ghetto members in the summer of 1942, as 300,000 Jews were transported to their deaths at the Treblinka extermination camp.

Faced with the inescapable reality of further executions, the remaining ghetto inhabitants formed a resistance group named the *Zydowska Organizacja Bojowa* (Z.O.B), or Jewish Fighting Organization. After a limited victory in January 1943, in which twelve Germans were killed and the deportation of further

ghetto inhabitants delayed for several days by fighters armed with smuggled weapons, the Z.O.B prepared for a final resistance. On April 19, 1943, German forces entered the Warsaw ghetto, aiming to transport the remaining inhabitants to be executed at Treblinka. Armed Jewish insurgents met the German soldiers, driving away 2,000 German troops and resisting further attack for nearly one month. An act of desperate resistance against relentless Nazi anti-Semitism, the Warsaw ghetto uprising was officially defeated on May 16, 1943, although it took many months to be put down irreversibly. An estimated 14,000 Jews were killed or executed, with the remaining 42,000 being deported to labor camps near Lublin.

Hannah Furness

Date April 19, 1943

Country Poland

Why It's Key The Warsaw ghetto uprising is a rare example of organized, armed resistance to Nazi anti-Semitic brutality.

opposite Jewish civilians being marched out of Warsaw during the destruction of the ghetto by German troops.

Key Discovery
Hoffman writes about LSD

The first LSD trip was an accident. Dr Albert Hoffman, a Swiss chemist working for Sandoz Laboratories, brushed his fingertips against LSD-25, a synthesized lysergic acid he had created in 1938 and spent two hours entranced. Initially intended as a circulatory and respiratory stimulant, Hoffman's exposure revealed psychedelic properties. Three days later, on April 19, 1943, Hoffman took the world's first intentional LSD trip, this time ingesting a hefty 250-milligram dose. He experienced vivid colors and changes in perception that he considered mind-expanding. On April 22, he prepared a report of his findings and presented it to the lab's pharmaceutical department, depicting the drug's effect as "an uninterrupted stream of fantastic images" – the first documentation, scientific or otherwise, of the uses of LSD.

He became a staunch promoter of the drug, writing that users would able to "develop a new awareness of reality" in *Insight – Outlook* (1989). He would also refer to it as "my problem child." Used initially in psychological research and treatment, LSD, of course, went on to play a major role in United States 1960s counterculture and was eventually demonized by the establishment. This was an unfortunate setback for the scientist, who considered it a valuable tool. Hoffman made further advances in psychedelic drugs, isolating the chemical properties of Mexican magic mushrooms in 1958 and, now at over one hundred years old, he continues to push for LSD's medicinal use through his foundation.

David Greenwald

Date April 22, 1943

Country Switzerland

Why It's Key Hoffman's report documented the first-ever LSD trips.

Fact The Albert Hoffman Foundation, founded in 1988, gathers records of the use of mind-expanding substances to study their relationship to both individual and collective consciousness.

232

Key Political Event
The Dambusters Raid

Operation Chastise, "The Dambusters Raid" of 1943, constituted only one night of bombing, but was destined to be the most famous and audacious raid of World War II.

The Ruhr Valley was the industrial engine room of the Nazi war machine. Its giant dams provided hydro-electric power, water, and control of canal levels. The dams were considered, by the allies and Nazis alike, impervious to attack; the water would suppress the impact of conventional bombs, and tight air and land defenses and inaccurate bombing techniques made getting a direct hit almost impossible. Barnes Wallis, a designer of airplanes for the Vickers Company, began developing a radical new concept – a spherical bomb, delivered at the right height and imparted with back spin, could bounce across the water. The ricochet effect

would mean dams could effectively be attacked from a distance. The idea met initial trepidation, but Wallis' perseverance and stringent testing finally persuaded Arthur "Bomber" Harris, head of Bomber Command.

On the night of May 16, 1943, 617 squadron, flying in specially modified Lancaster bombers led by Wing Commander Guy Gibson, used the "bouncing bomb" to seriously breach the Möhne and Eder dams. The raid was dangerous, requiring very low flying and a full moon to illuminate their maneuvers. The squadron lost fifty-three men. Germany's industrial output was ruptured – power stations and railway lines became engulfed in water. Most importantly, the striking originality of the raid provided Britain's war effort with an enduring story of indomitable and daring spirit.

Michael Hallam

Date May 17, 1943

Country Germany

Why It's Key The Dambusters Raid made a powerful strike at the industrial production of the Third Reich and accelerated innovation in bombing technology.

Key Cultural Event
Term "teenager" is first used

The Oxford English Dictionary traces the hyphened word "teen-ager" back to 1941. Common consensus, however, holds that both the term and the concept of the "teenager" were born in 1944, with the advent of *Seventeen* magazine, the first mass-market publication designed exclusively for that age group. Many consider the "bobby soxer" fans of Frank Sinatra around this time to be one of the first distinct teenage groups. Sometime in the 1950s, it was established enough to drop its hyphen and become central to popular culture.

The birth of the teenager in the 1950s started in the United States, with the collision of several new fashions and movements. At one end there were the bright skirts and visceral thrills of rock 'n' roll; at the other, the ennui and angst of James Dean and J. D.

Salinger. By the 1960s, the term "generation gap" was being used by sociologists to denote this new phenomenon, whereby adolescents no longer behaved as neither-quite-adult-nor-child, and instead developed distinct subcultures, identities, and opinions. Thanks to movies, commercials, books, and music, the teenager could now be found all over the world.

By the 1970s, teenage culture had evolved so rapidly that a nostalgia industry established itself around the 1950s and 1960s version; films like *Grease* and television shows like *Happy Days* catered for the original teenagers who had now grown up. Mods, rockers, punks, and more recently, goths, and "Generation X" kids are all direct descendants, proof that youth subcultures show no sign of slowing down.
Andrew Blades

Date 1944

Country USA

Why It's Key It created a new social group that arguably defined the second half of the twentieth century.

Key Political Event
Stalin deports the Chechen people

The multinational mosaic of the Russian Empire permitted Stalin to manipulate old enmities to help ensure his control. In the nineteenth century, the Russian Empire had conquered the territory of the Chechen people, in the northern Caucasus, but most Chechens' refusal to assimilate had led to lasting friction. When the Soviet Union retook Chechnya from Nazi Germany, Stalin accused the Chechens of collaboration, although few of them had aided the Germans. The accusation appears to have been mainly a pretext to uproot any remnants of Chechen autonomy. In February 1944, Stalin approved deportation plans drawn up by his secret police chief, Lavrenti Beria, and police units were dispatched. On February 23, Chechens were ordered to gather in their local squares, where they were arrested and packed

onto sealed trains bound for remote and desolate areas of Kazakhstan. Within weeks, nearly 400,000 Chechens were deported under such brutal conditions that tens of thousands of them died on the way.

The Chechens fate was all too typical. Already in 1941, ahead of the German advance, Stalin had deported the ethnic Germans who had long lived along the Volga River. As territories were retaken in 1943 and 1944, dozens of smaller ethnic groups suffered fates similar to that of the Chechens. Chechen culture did survive the deportations, as most Chechens re-formed their communities in Kazakhstan. In 1957, the year after Stalin's death, they were permitted to return home.
Brian Ladd

Date February 23, 1944

Country USSR

Why It's Key Stalin used the pretext of wartime collaboration to carry out ethnic cleansing.

Key Political Event
The World Bank and the IMF created

In the summer of 1944, 730 representatives from 44 nations met in Bretton Woods, New Hampshire, to develop methods for stabilizing the economies of countries that had been devastated by World War II. Consequently, on July 1, conferees created the International Bank for Reconstruction and Development (the World Bank) and the International Monetary Fund (IMF). While the IMF was designed to promote international monetary cooperation and world trade, the World Bank was established to distribute low-interest and no-interest loans. Once industrialized economies were stabilized, attention shifted to developing countries, particularly in Africa, Asia, and South America. Due to the focus on eradicating poverty and the goal of making developing countries self-supporting, developing nations have been able to build electric power plants, roads, railways, bridges, ports, and natural gas pipelines, and make improvements in education, health, telecommunications, agriculture, industry, water supplies, and employment.

Although they are separate organizations, the World Bank and IMF work together. In fiscal year 2005, the World Bank awarded US$22.3 billion in loans and grants for 278 projects ranging from fighting HIV/AIDS in Brazil to doubling the income of rural residents in Turkey. In response to criticism that loans were being used to enrich corrupt politicians, the World Bank and IMF have instituted stringent anti-corruption policies and practice strict oversight. Loan applications from countries with established histories of corruption may be turned down.
Elizabeth R. Purdy

Date July 1, 1944

Country USA

Why It's Key The World Bank and the International Monetary Fund have become the chief promoters of economic stability and technological advancement in developing countries, dispensing roughly US$1 trillion to nations around the globe since 1944.

Key Cultural Event
Miller reports the first use of napalm

Although there are different variants of napalm, essentially a mixture of fuel and gelling solution, the version popularized during the Vietnam War was developed at Harvard University in 1942. Led by Louis S. Fieser, whose previous work in organic chemistry had led to the synthesis of cortisone, a team of chemists mixed napthenic and palmitic acids to form bombs and flame-throwers. The first use of napalm in war occurred on July 23, 1944; however, it was not until journalist Lee Miller captured on her camera the use of the deadly incendiary at the Battle of St. Malo that the world witnessed the devastating effects napalm could have.

Originally a model and fashion photographer, Lee Miller became a renowned war correspondent and photojournalist during World War II. While she initially applied to work for the British government as a war reporter, they did not allow women to cover the war, much less the front line. Instead, Miller became an official correspondent for the U.S. government and covered the war for American *Vogue*, combining war reporting with a fashion sensibility in such comments as: "I sheltered in a Kraut dugout, squatting under the ramparts. My heel ground into a dead detached hand... "

Miller's astonishing work covers many other aspects of the war. She sent images from Dachau back to *Vogue*, accompanied by a cable that said, "I implore you to believe this is true." Her ethos was to capture the lives of ordinary people in extraordinary situations.
Frieda Klotz

Date October 10, 1944

Country France

Why It's Key Though napalm is generally associated with warfare during the Vietnam War, Lee Miller's photographs captured the devastating effects it had during World War II.

Fact Miller did not initially know that she had photographed the effects of napalm; the censors immediately confiscated her photos after she filed them.

Key Political Event
The Battle of Leyte Gulf

In October 1944, U.S. armed forces initiated invasion of the crucial Japanese strategic bulwark of the Philippine Islands. Attempting to intercept, the Japanese Navy was decimated in four ferocious confrontations.

In a key engagement, Clifton Sprague and his comparatively tiny shore support unit, Taffy 3, were cast as David against the Goliath of Admiral Kurita and the Imperial 2nd Fleet, including *Yamato*, the largest battleship in the world. After a destructive air assault in the Sibuyan Sea, Admiral William Halsey, believing Kurita's damaged fleet was in retreat, sailed north to engage the Japanese Northern Fleet. This was a decoy presence deployed precisely to weaken U.S. defense of landing stations at Leyte Gulf. Simultaneously, Kurita had unexpectedly rerouted to near the exposed unloading American transports and beachhead.

Destroy them and the invasion would be over before it began. Taffy 3, outmatched, courageously attacked Kurita's colossal battleships. Admiral Sprague's audacity, hazy weather, and poor reconnaissance led Kurita to believe he was facing the full fleet of Halsey, and, in a fateful decision, he disengaged.

Attritional land combat through the Pacific Theater would follow, but Leyte Gulf represented a terminal blow to Japanese naval involvement. Indeed, the era of the dreadnought battleship was over, superseded by carrier-borne aircraft. A devastating new tactic was also pioneered in this battle: suicide attack. *St. Lo*, of the heroic Taffy 3 group, was the first military vessel sunk by a Kamikaze pilot – the first of many in the remaining ten months of war.

Michael Hallam

Date October 23, 1944

Country Philippines

Why It's Key The largest maritime battle of World War II ended Japan's challenge to U.S. naval supremacy.

Key Cultural Event
Third pandemic of bubonic plague controlled

When the third pandemic of the bubonic plague was finally quelled in 1945, it brought to an end ninety years of suffering that had engulfed both hemispheres, decimating populations in Russia, North Africa, Western Europe, and South America. Although the last major outbreak occurred in Peru and Argentina, the disease remained active until 1959, when fatalities were reported to have fallen to less than two hundred a year.

The first deaths were discovered in the Chinese province of Yunan in 1855, before spreading to Canton and Hong Kong by the 1890s. Overseas trade extended the plague throughout the Far East, and by the time the disease had run its course, over twelve million people had died in India and China alone.

The third pandemic coincided with a major breakthrough in plague research. In 1894, the bacteriologist Alexandre Yersin succeeded in isolating the plague bacterium (*Yersinia pestis*). Scientific evidence proved that the disease was transmitted to humans by fleas carried on infected hosts such as black rats. Following this, the manufacture of new insecticides, antibiotics, and vaccines in the first half of the twentieth century played an important role in halting the third pandemic. Outbreaks of the plague are extremely rare today and are largely restricted to remote areas of the world, such as the Mongolian steppe, where humans and wild animals continue to live in close proximity.

Jay Mullins

Date 1945

Country Peru/Argentina

Why It's Key The end of the third pandemic marked mankind's mastery over an ancient infection.

Fact It is widely believed that the Mongol Jani Beg brought the Black Death to Europe by catapulting infected corpses into a Crimean city he was besieging.

Key Political Event
Bombing of Dresden

Arthur "Bomber" Harris, head of RAF Bomber Command from February 1942, believed that "area bombing" of entire cities and towns could break German morale. This tactic, while adopted partly because of the inaccuracy of existing technology, has justifiably been called "terror bombing," estimated to have killed up to 600,000 German civilians. The Allies had developed a tactic of dropping incendiary bombs to create "firestorms" in which superheated air rose above a target, sucking in cold air in the form of 150 mph winds, literally sucking people into the flames and suffocating others. Operation Gomorrah had targeted Hamburg in this way in 1943, killing an estimated 40,000 people.

In 1945, Dresden – known as Florence on the Elbe – was Germany's largest built-up area that had not yet been bombed. Filled with refugees fleeing the rapidly advancing Red Army, it also had practically no anti-aircraft defences. On the night of February 13, just over 800 aircraft, mainly Avro Lancasters, bombed Dresden in two waves to divide the nightfighter defense. Unusually, the briefing had given aircrews no strategic aiming point, telling them simply to bomb any built-up area. In the ensuing firestorm, Dresden was almost entirely destroyed, one airman describing how he had "seemed to fly for hours over a sheet of fire." On the following two days, 527 planes of the U.S. 8th Air Force continued to bomb Dresden. In the aftermath it was impossible to count the dead, but recent research has suggested that around 35,000 died, though other estimates are considerably higher.

Duncan Proudfoot

Date February 13–15, 1945

Country Germany

Why It's Key The bombing of Dresden remains a key incident in any discussion of the limits of justifiable conduct in prosecuting a war.

Key Cultural Event
Photograph of U.S. flag being raised on Iwo Jima

Joe Rosenthal, who died in 2006, was thirty-three when he captured his 1945 Pulitzer Award-winning image, commended as "a frozen flash of history." Ironically, he had been rejected for military service on account of poor eyesight, but, using a Speed Graphic camera and a shutter speed of one four-hundredth of a second, he took what is perhaps the most famous photograph of World War II. It appeared on at least 3.5 million posters for a war-bond publicity campaign and on a Marine Corps commemorative stamp, as well as later serving as the model for the 100-ton, bronze Marine Corps Memorial in Arlington, Virginia.

Despite its fame, Rosenthal was suspected of having posed the shot, a claim he always denied. As a photographer who had been alongside Rosenthal pointed out, if it had been posed the men's faces would probably have been facing the camera.

Rosenthal was in one of the first waves of 70,000 Marines sent to seize the island, about 660 miles south of Tokyo, for use as an airbase. He took the photograph on the fifth day of the thirty-six-day battle, during which one in three Marines was injured or killed – of the men in the photograph, only three survived. They were ordered home by President Roosevelt and sent on a nationwide tour to promote war-bond sales, which raised US$26.3 billion. Rosenthal always downplayed his role, saying, "What difference does it make who took the picture? I took it, but the Marines took Iwo Jima."

Duncan Proudfoot

Date February 23, 1945

Country Japan

Why It's Key One of the iconic images of World War II and probably also the most widely reproduced photograph in U.S. history.

Fact The flag-raising on top of Mount Suribachi did not mark the end of the battle for Iwo Jima; of the men in the photograph, four would be among the 6,621 U.S. servicemen who died. 19,217 were injured, and, of 22,000 Japanese defenders, only 1,083 survived.

Key Political Event
The liberation of Belsen

The liberation of Bergen-Belsen concentration camp, in north-western Germany, is one of the most singularly emotive operations the British Army has ever undertaken. The unparalleled media access to the event relayed devastating realities of the German camp system. The newsreels, replete with heaps of emaciated corpses, disturbed the British population and permanently entered its psyche, sometimes erroneously, as an emblem for the entire Holocaust. Belsen is occasionally given the incorrect title of an extermination camp, such as existed at Auschwitz, when its original purpose was as a holding camp for a Jewish contingent that could be used as leverage in plans of diplomatic exchange.

This was tragically altered in March 1944. The administration decided Belsen was underused and sick prisoners arrived from across the hemorrhaging camp system. Typhus and tuberculosis ravaged the inmates. SS Captain Josef Kramer, formerly at Auschwitz-Birkenau, was made the new camp commandant in December of 1944. Prisoners were now sent to Belsen to die, not from systematic extermination, but starvation and disease. The extermination camps liberated in Eastern Europe by Russian forces were previously evacuated, their infrastructure dismantled. In contrast, Belsen held an estimated 60,000 seriously ill prisoners when British personnel first entered it on April 15, 1945. The photographs and reports this generated, along with survivor testimony of the liberation, have created its symbolic status in the world's understanding of Nazi inhumanity.

Michael Hallam

Date April 15, 1945

Country Germany

Why It's Key The liberation of Belsen graphically exposed Nazi brutality to a global audience.

Key Political Event
Red Army begins attack on Berlin

In the spring of 1945, the British and American armies invading western Germany received orders to stop short of Berlin, in deference to delicate diplomatic agreements with the Soviet Union. Stalin had assured his Western allies that he, too, did not see Hitler's capital as a strategic objective, but in fact, he was determined to take it, and he had over two million soldiers lined up along the Oder River, just fifty miles away. On April 16, the Red Army launched its massive final offensive.

Even then, daily life plodded on in Berlin, with the Nazi newspapers and radio still filled with lies about great military successes. It was on April 20 that Berliners got their first inkling of what was to come. As Hitler observed his fifty-sixth birthday in a cursory ceremony, before retreating to his bunker, Red Army commanders realized that their advance units were within artillery range of the city, and shells began raining indiscriminate death and destruction on it. The next day, Russian soldiers reached the eastern suburbs. By April 25, the city was surrounded. Diehard Nazis fought the invaders from street to street, pausing to hang deserters from lampposts with signs around their necks declaring, "I am a traitor" or "I am a coward." Tens of thousands of soldiers and civilians died by April 30, when Hitler, by his own hand, joined them. His generals surrendered the city two days later.

Brian Ladd

Date April 20, 1945

Country Germany

Why It's Key Russia's attack on Berlin dealt the deathblow to the Third Reich.

Key Political Event
Death of Mussolini

Following the fall of Sicily in July 1943, the Fascist Grand Council backed Galeazzo Ciano's plan to make a separate peace with the Allies. Mussolini was dismissed and imprisoned in a hotel in the Abruzzi Pennines. Rescued by commandos in gliders led by Otto Skorzeny, Mussolini established the Salo Republic in German-occupied northern Italy – one of his first acts was to execute Ciano and four other opponents.

In April 1945, Parma and Verona fell, and uprisings occurred in Milan and Genoa. Mussolini attempted to escape with his mistress, Clara Petacci, to Switzerland, but, in Dongo, he was recognized and arrested. There are conflicting accounts of what happened next. According to one, partisan Walter Audisio pretended to rescue the couple, but outside the Villa Belmonte in Mezzegra, overlooking Lake Como, as he attempted to shoot them, his gun jammed and Pettacci grasped the barrel. Mussolini then asked to be shot in the chest; Audisio killed Pettacci before complying. In another, Petacci grabbed the gun of one of the partisans escorting the couple to Milan for public execution; shots were fired, Mussolini was hit, and they were both killed.

Their bodies were displayed in Milan, along with those of thirteen other Fascists, at an Esso gas station on the Piazzale Loreto, where fifteen partisans had been executed and their bodies displayed. Mussolini was posed "holding" his scepter, his head on Pettacci's breast. They were then hung, upside down, along with five others. Mussolini was buried the following day, in Predappio.

Duncan Proudfoot

Date April 28, 1945

Country Italy

Why It's Key Mussolini's death marked the end of Fascism in Italy, and the treatment of his body after death is said to have left Hitler determined to have his and Eva Braun's bodies burned following their suicide, which took place just two days later.

Key Political Event
Hitler's marriage and suicide

As Soviet troops closed in on what remained of the German Reich Chancellery in Berlin, Adolf Hitler decided to marry his long-term mistress Eva Braun and then commit suicide. At this stage, the war was hopelessly lost and Hitler, a physical and mental wreck, had been deserted by all but a few of his closest comrades.

Braun, over twenty years Hitler's junior, had been his mistress for more than a decade. However, she was kept hidden from public view and often treated with contempt by Hitler among his inner circle. In contrast, her loyalty to him was absolute, and she traveled to Berlin in April 1945 in order to be with him when the end came.

Their marriage took place shortly after midnight on April 29 in the bunker of the Chancellery building, officiated by a city councillor, with Bormann and Goebbels acting as witnesses. The silent and surreal atmosphere of the post-wedding party was noted by one of Hitler's secretaries who dryly commented that the guests were not in a position to toast the couple's future.

The honeymoon was indeed short, as Hitler and Braun committed suicide on the afternoon of April 30 when Braun took cyanide and Hitler shot himself. Amidst the constant Red Army shelling, their bodies were set alight in the Chancellery garden and Hitler's corpse, like that of many of his victims, was ignominiously consumed by fire.

Denis Casey

Date April 30, 1945

Country Germany

Why It's Key Hitler's suicide spelled the end of a twelve-year rule which had plunged the world into war and marked a new low in human behavior.

Key Political Event
The United Nations is founded

In the summer of 1945, the delegates of fifty nations signed the United Nations Charter, and the United Nations Organization (UN) officially came into existence. It has a number of principal organs, the two most important being the General Assembly and the Security Council. The General Assembly makes recommendations on issues such as human rights and the environment, while the Security Council has primary responsibility for maintaining peace and security. The Security Council has at its disposal military forces provided by member states and can call on UN members to impose economic sanctions to reinforce its decisions.

From the beginning, the UN has worked to prevent disputes between and within states escalating into war, and has helped bring existing conflicts to a permanent end by monitoring ceasefires, occupying buffer zones, and reinstating democratic processes. Many other agencies under the auspices of the UN such as the World Health Organization (WHO) and the World Food Program (WFP) work all over the world to alleviate the effects of natural disaster, disease, war or other crises.

United Nations membership has expanded since 1945, currently standing at 192 members, and its primary concern has been with peacekeeping military operations; it has ongoing commitments in Europe, West Africa, and the Middle East. The UN continues to play an important role in resolving conflicts and consolidating world peace; however in recent years humanitarian concerns have become more central. One of the greatest recent achievements has been the creation of a universal Code of Human Rights.
Helena Hewson

Date June 25, 1945

Country USA

Why It's Key The United Nations is an international organization that promotes global peace and security through international cooperation.

Fact United Nations day is celebrated each year on October 24.

241

Key Political Event
Potsdam Conference creates tension for the Cold War

From July 16 to August 2, 1945, British Prime Minister Winston Churchill, U.S. President Harry Truman, and Soviet leader Joseph Stalin met at Potsdam, Germany, to discuss the conditions of the end of World War II. The main topic of the conference was what to do with Germany, which had surrendered on May 8, 1945. There were few things the negotiators agreed on – the main issue of dispute being German reparations – but in the end, several agreements were reached. Germany was to be completely disarmed and demilitarized under four occupational zones controlled by the Allies. The Soviet Union was entitled to reparations from its occupational zone in Germany. The judicial and educational systems were to be purged of Nazi influences to make way for a democratic German society and Nazi war criminals were to be prosecuted.

Finally, a controversial decision was made to allow Poland to deport German residents from the part of the German territory Poland had received after the adjustment of the Soviet-Polish border.

During the conference, the U.S., Great Britain, and China also released the Potsdam Declaration, threatening Japan with "prompt and utter destruction" unless it surrendered immediately. Japan only agreed to a conditional surrender, which the United States responded to by dropping nuclear bombs on Nagasaki and Hiroshima. The U.S. possession of the atomic bomb caused distrust between the United States and USSR. The western Allies were already suspicious of Stalin's motives. The Allied leaders never convened again and were soon engaged in the Cold War.
Sonja Kudeljnjak

Date July 16, 1945

Country Germany

Why It's Key Potsdam Conference introduced the main players, tensions, and disputes of what would become known as the Cold War.

Fact During the conference, Clement Atlee replaced Winston Churchill, after Churchill was defeated in the British elections.

Key Political Event
Atomic bomb is dropped on Hiroshima

When the United States dropped the atomic bomb on Hiroshima at 8:15 a.m. on August 6, 1945, it marked the beginning of the end of World War II. Colonel Paul Tibbets, commander of the 509th Composite Group, flew the B-29 aircraft named "Enola Gay" at a low altitude on automatic pilot before climbing to 31,000 feet. Across from Ota River, over the T-shaped Aioi Bridge, whose distinct structure made it the ideal target, Tibbets dropped a 9,700-pound uranium bomb. "Little Boy" detonated 1,900 feet above the city, directly killing 80,000 people and another 60,000 in the following months from injuries and radiation exposure. The yield of the explosion was later estimated to be fifteen kilotons of TNT.

It is generally accepted that U.S. President Harry Truman issued the official bombing order on July 25 in an attempt to avoid a potential Japanese invasion after Japan would only agree to a conditional surrender, choosing Hiroshima for its plethora of military establishments. Yet the accuracy of this prediction is challenged by those within the U.S. Army, including Henry Arnold, commanding general of the air forces, who declared in his 1949 memoirs that "[it] always appeared to us, atomic bomb or no atomic bomb, the Japanese were already on the verge of collapse." A forty-page memorandum was allegedly delivered to Roosevelt in January, which outlined surrender terms offered by Japanese officials that were virtually identical to those ultimately accepted after the atomic bomb attacks on Hiroshima, and three days later, Nagasaki. The circumstances surrounding the event remain buried in doubt and controversy.

Mariko Kato

Date August 6, 1945

Country Japan

Why It's Key It was the first time (of only two) that a nuclear bomb was used in warfare.

Fact The Atomic Dome, the only surviving building near the epicenter of the bomb blast, is now a World Heritage site.

opposite The huge mushroom cloud above the devastation in Hiroshima.

Key Discovery
First digital computer

Commissioned by the U.S. Army's Ordnance Department to calculate ballistic trajectories during World War II, the Electronic Numerical Integrator and Computer, or ENIAC, was begun in 1943 and completed two years later. Despite the vast size of the computer and its reliance on delicate vacuum tubes, the ENIAC worked well and so proved that the theory behind electronic computing was correct. In the UK, Alan Turing, whose team went on to build and use the top-secret Colossus machine to help break German codes, had made many of the great advances in the theory of computing before the war. Important foundations in programming had also been made by engineer Konrad Zuse in Germany, and his Z3 machine, which was destroyed in an Allied air raid in 1945, can lay claim to be the first program-controlled processor.

Nevertheless, the ENIAC was arguably the most advanced electronic computer up to that date with a flexibility that the other machines lacked – it was possible, for example, to later turn it into a stored-program computer, which greatly reduced the manual rewiring necessary for each program change. Taking only thirty seconds to complete a calculation that previously took a person twenty hours, its initial calculation was for the first hydrogen bomb, and the ENIAC contained most of the fundamental concepts and components from which modern computers have evolved. But after 1952, the ENIAC gradually became obsolete and what was once the world's fastest computer was shut down for good in 1955.

Hedley Paul

Date October 1, 1945

Country USA

Why It's Key Although British and German scientists had also made huge strides in computer technology, the American ENIAC is commonly accepted as the world's first electronic general-purpose digital computer and the prototype of all subsequent computers.

HIROSHIMA (ATOMIC) STRIKE

Key Political Event
War of Liberation breaks out in China

Following the sudden end of World War II in Asia with the defeat of Japan in August 1945, China's bitter political rivals, the Nationalist Government led by Chiang Kai-shek and the Communist Party led by Mao Zedong, scrambled to position themselves for the coming internal struggle for national leadership. Despite being officially allied against imperial Japan since 1937, the "united front" of Chinese Nationalist and Communist forces was an alliance in name only. The ideologically and politically opposed forces rarely collaborated on military strategy. After Chiang Kai-shek launched a series of attacks on Communist armies by Nationalist Government forces in January 1941, the anti-Japanese alliance became a fiction maintained for political purposes by the Nationalist's American allies who also fought against imperial Japan in Asia and the Pacific.

As the war ended in 1945, the Americans hoped to prop up the Nationalist Government with economic aid, military equipment, and logistical support, and to forestall a civil war that, the Americans believed, would be exploited by its Cold War rival, the USSR. American emissaries General Albert Wedemeyer and General George C. Marshall advised the Nationalist Government to agree to a ceasefire and form a coalition government to incorporate the Chinese Communist Party into a Nationalist-led regime, but Chiang Kai-shek and Mao Zedong resisted American formulations. Instead, Nationalist and Communist armies battled openly in Manchuria in June 1946, vying for control over territory recently recovered from Japan, and the final phase of China's long civil war began.
Karen Garner

Date June 26, 1946

Country China

Why It's Key The final phase of China's civil war broke out despite American efforts to forestall it, and marked the culmination of the Chinese Communist Party's rise to governing power and the establishment of the People's Republic of China in 1949.

Key Cultural Event Dr Spock's *The Common Sense Book of Baby and Child Care* published

On July 14, 1946, the American pediatrician Dr Benjamin Spock published *The Common Sense Book of Baby and Child Care*, a book that would have a huge influence on how parents treat their children and cause a major change in expert opinions. Before Spock's book was published, the common belief had been that the priority of children's upbringing should be discipline and that parents should not be too lax because that might spoil the children. Parents were advised to feed their children on a regular schedule and not to be too affectionate because that would not prepare children to be strong adults capable of surviving in a cruel world. Spock's book, on the other hand, encouraged parents to treat their children as individuals and to trust their instincts, rather than following some preestablished rules of child rearing.

His message to mothers was "you know more than you think you do."

The result of Spock's philosophy was the development of a modern, more permissive, style of childrearing. The book has remained relevant because each new edition was revised to accommodate new social trends. For example, one of the controversial claims from the first edition, that mothers should always be there for their children and give up their careers for them, was updated in the 1998 edition, which advises that both parents should have equal responsibility for the child's upbringing.
Sonja Kudeljnjak

Date July 14, 1946

Country USA

Why It's Key The book has become one of the biggest bestsellers of all time and has popularized a modern approach to parenting.

Fact By 1998, Dr Spock's book had been translated into 39 languages and had sold over 50 million copies.

Key Person
Mother Teresa receives the "Call from God"

Thirty-six year old Sister Teresa was sitting in her seat aboard a train traveling from Calcutta to Darjeeling, on her way to her annual spiritual retreat when, "in a quiet, intimate prayer with our Lord, I heard distinctly, a call within a call. The message was quite clear: I was to leave the convent and help the poor whilst living among them. It was an order."

The former Agnes Gonxha Bojaxhiu of Skopje had long been guided by her faith. In September 1928, she had left her family in Macedonia to join the Sisters of Our Lady of Loreto, and took the name Teresa in honor of Saint Teresa of Lisieux, patron saint of missionaries. In 1929, she traveled to Calcutta, where she took her final vows in May 1937. For nineteen years, she was a beloved teacher and principal at St Mary's School for Girls, but in 1948, she left her order to follow the Lord's call, calling her departure "my greatest sacrifice." By 1950, she was running her ministry in the slums of Calcutta, known as the Missionaries of Charity.

For the next forty-seven years, Mother Teresa helped feed and comfort the poor, the sick, and the dying, and building an order of more than 5,000 people who feed more than 500,000 families worldwide each year. She died on September 5, 1997, just five days short of the fifty-first anniversary of her "call within a call," a day now celebrated by her order as "Inspiration Day."

Heather Michon

Date September 10, 1946
Born/died 1910–1997
Nationality Albanian
Why It's Key The "call" resulted in the creation of a great humanitarian leader.

Key Political Event
The Havana Conference

Charles "Lucky" Luciano was one of the most dominant personalities in organized American crime. Less famous than Al Capone, his impact on the mob was more far-reaching; he was a force through the 1930s, transforming old-fashioned Italian Mafiosi culture into an America Mafia with global reach. By 1946, Luciano had been deported from the United States, but covertly made base in pre-revolution Cuba. In an effort to reassert his waning influence, Luciano called together a conference in Havana of all the major players: every big Italian and Jewish mobster family was represented. Drugs were a principal talking point. Mob history is surrounded by myth and apocrypha: some writers suggest Luciano wanted to contract the Mafia narcotics trade to ingratiate himself with U.S. authorities and end his exile. More likely, Luciano advanced plans for a massive heroin distribution network. It would be cultivated in the Far East, refined in France (the "French Connection"), fronted by the Italian export industry, and distributed from Cuba.

The conference is infamous for several reasons: the proposed killing of legendary gangster Bugsy Siegel; Luciano's upbraiding of rivals to his position of de facto "Boss of Bosses"; the Frank Sinatra concert that performed as a too convenient reason for the Mafia fraternity to be on the island. But Havana was the originating moment of a global market for illegal narcotics and this was its lasting legacy. Mob crime would no longer be about parochial gang feuds or rigging the slots in a casino: it was big, ruthlessly efficient international business.

Michael Hallam

Date December 22, 1946
Country Cuba
Why It's Key The Havana Conference changed the emphasis of organized crime and laid the framework for a global business in illegal narcotics.

Key Cultural Event
Tezuka creates *New Treasure Island* (*Shin Takarajima*)

Although humorous pictographs in Japan can be traced back to the twelfth century, the word "manga," used to denote Japanese comics, was first coined in 1815. Katsushika Hokusai, a leading woodblock printmaker, used two Chinese ideographs – *man* (whimsical) and *ga* (picture) – to describe his illustrated doodles. However, the modern manga evolved from the U.S. comic strip, which was popularized by publishing mogul Joseph Pulitzer in the 1920s. Pulitzer was the first person to give comics regular attention when he introduced them into his newspaper, *New York World*, as a diversion from the seriousness of the headlines. In Japan, they were used both as entertainment and as a vehicle for propaganda until the end of World War II, when they were transformed into an amusement directed solely at children.

The publication of Osamu Tezuka's first comic, *Shin Takarajima* ("New Treasure Island"), changed the face of the Japanese comic and ushered in the "golden age" of manga. Born in the Osaka Prefecture, Tezuka was studying to be a doctor when he penned his first comic at the age of nineteen. As the name of the book suggests, Tezuka took Robert Louis Stevenson's *Treasure Island* (1883) as the inspiration for a story about a rabbit who finds a map to pirate treasure. Despite the miserable economic conditions of postwar Japan, this work became an immediate bestseller. It sold an unprecedented 400,000 copies and was read by both adults and children alike. Since the publication of *Shin Takarajima*, the manga industry has become a multi-billion dollar global market.
Bianca Jackson

Date 1947

Country Japan

Why It's Key *New Treasure Island* transformed manga from a children's pastime into a multi-billion dollar industry enjoyed by adults and children alike.

Fact Katsushika Hokusai – who coined the term manga – is best known as the creator of the woodblock print series *Thirty-Views of Mount Fuji*, which includes the iconic print, *The Great Wave off Kanagawa*.

1940–1949

251

Key Discovery
The Dead Sea Scrolls

The initial discovery of the Dead Sea Scrolls has been heavily mythologized and exists in multiple, contradictory versions. The most popular account is of a young Bedouin shepherd who threw stones into a cave to drive out an animal under his care. The sound of shattering pottery caught his attention and he searched on his hands and knees in the darkness until he found several ceramic pots containing leather and papyrus scrolls. He sold them to a local antiques dealer who split up the find and sold three to a scholar at Hebrew University and four to the Archbishop of Syria. These four were eventually sold in 1954 through a classified ad in *The Wall Street Journal* where they came to the attention of the wider archaeological community. Subsequent expeditions found scrolls in eleven more caves and the findings include parts of

almost every book in the Hebrew canon as well as commentaries on the law, rulebooks of the community, descriptions of war conduct, hymnic compositions, and liturgical writings. Archaeologists believe that a Jewish sect called the Essenes wrote the scrolls during the period from about 200 BCE to 68 CE and that they are the oldest existing works of their kind. The texts are written from right to left with no punctuation and often without spaces between the words. This fact, and the fragmentary nature of the parchments themselves, has led to significant difficulties of translation and interpretation. Much of the debate has been about the relationship between the scrolls and traditional, canonical writings, but there have also been claims of Vatican cover-ups and even alien authorship.
Jonathan Morton

Date February 1 1947

Country Palestine

Why It's Key The Dead Sea Scrolls are the only surviving copies of biblical documents and reveal various details concerning many aspects of Judaism practiced during the Second Temple period (516 BCE to 70 CE).

opposite An archaeologist studies sections of the scrolls.

Key Cultural Event
Kalashnikov designs the AK-47

After the end of World War II, Lieutenant General Mikhail Kalashnikov, dismayed by the inferiority of Soviet assault rifles, wanted to build a weapon that surpassed its German and U.S. counterparts in efficiency and accuracy. The result was the AK-47, its name taken from its creator and the year in which it was first produced.

Since its invention, the AK-47 has become much more than a weapon; it has entered popular culture as a revolutionary icon, referenced countless times in film, literature, and music. Such is its power as an image that it can even be seen on the flag of Mozambique and the coat of arms of East Timor and Zimbabwe. While not the most accurate assault rifle, it has become successful due to its reliability, durability, cheapness to manufacture, and ease of use. Many regard it as a superior weapon to the American-made M16.

In the years since it was first manufactured, the Soviet Union (now Russia) has supplied the AK-47 to governments from Asia to Africa, South America to the Middle East. While primarily manufactured in Russia, variations of the weapon have been made all over the world. It has been suggested that over 100 million AK-47s have been distributed since the 1940s. While Kalashnikov has been twice decorated by the Russian Federation for his invention, he has never received a rouble in royalties; yet his name is known around the globe.

Terence McSweeney

Date 1947

Country USSR

Why It's Key The AK-47 is the most widely used assault rifle in the world.

Key Cultural Event
Christian Dior introduces the "New Look"

In 1947, fashion designer Christian Dior unveiled his Spring "*Corolle*" collection, and with it changed not only the direction of contemporary couture, but also introduced a new philosophy of postwar fashion.

World War II had come to an end, and with it the need for the aggressively practical and economical utility designs. Dior's was the first collection to be shown postwar, and after years of restrictions and privations, its newly luxurious and elegant styles caused an international sensation.

The style of the collection, dubbed by influential *Harper's Bazaar* editor Carmel Snow, the "New Look," focused on the female silhouette, exaggerating the hourglass shape with tiny waists, spreading out into a full skirt and bust. Replacing the severe masculine-style tailoring of wartime were more softly curving shapes, with rounded shoulders and skirts that fell to mid-calf, further enhanced in their elegance by the use of layers of petticoats. The result was both feminine and opulent, and in an early Paris photo shoot, women attacked models on account of the extravagant wastefulness of designs that employed so much excess material.

As society adjusted to the move away from wartime frugality, however, the designs were enthusiastically adopted and copied across the world. Paris was established irrevocably as the international fashion capital, as women learned once again to celebrate and enjoy their femininity.

Alexandra Coghlan

Date February 1947

Country France

Why It's Key Dior's "New Look" collection pioneered the development of postwar fashions and started the international industry of fashion branding.

Fact The "*Corolle*" collection was named after the French botanical term for the soft inner petals of flowers.

opposite A French model wears the "New Look" in Paris.

Key Cultural Event
The Diary of Anne Frank published

The world knew about the atrocities of the Holocaust long before the end of World War II, but the legacy of Anne Frank provided an individualistic sense of tragedy to the genocidal events. A German-Jewish teenager whose family hid in Nazi-occupied Holland before getting shipped off to concentration camps, Frank kept a candid diary that combined the standard observations of a fifteen-year-old girl with the harsh reality of oppressive times. While Anne Frank died of typhus at the Bergen-Belsen concentration camp in 1945, her father, Otto, survived the war and discovered her personal musings. Frank's transcription of the diary caught the attention of a historian and landed a mention in the newspaper *Het Parool*. A publication deal followed in 1947, and its English translation in 1951 brought the phenomenon of the diary into full swing. A Broadway play entitled *The Diary of Anne Frank* opened in 1955, and five years later, the Anne Frank House in Amsterdam became a museum, and one of the city's most popular tourist attractions.

Over the years, Anne Frank's story has captivated readers (and audiences of its film and stage adaptations) due to the startlingly insightful perspective of its young protagonist. While Frank mused on typical family issues, her existentially poignant scrutinizing of the Nazi occupation put a human face on the massacre. "It's a wonder I haven't abandoned all my ideals," she wrote. "Yet I cling to them because I still believe, in spite of everything, that people are truly good at heart."
Eric Kohn

Date June 25, 1947

Country Holland

Why It's Key The book put a human face on the Holocaust, and became one of the most distinct twentieth century literary achievements.

Fact The book has sold over 25 million copies in 67 languages.

opposite An extract from Anne's diary.

Key Political Event
Creation of the CIA

Although the United States has carried out intelligence activities since the presidency of George Washington, the CIA (Central Intelligence Agency) was officially formed in 1947 under the National Security Act. Its forerunner, the Office of Strategic Services (OSS), was the brainchild of New York lawyer and war hero William J. Donovan, who had been approached by President Franklin D. Roosevelt to draft a plan for a new intelligence organization. Established in June 1942, the OSS collected and analyzed strategic information, and conducted special operations not assigned to other governmental agencies. However, the OSS never received total jurisdiction over all foreign intelligence, and was subsequently dissolved at the end of World War II, transferring its functions to the State and War Departments.

When Harry S. Truman succeeded to office after Roosevelt's death in 1945, he quickly recognized the need for a postwar centralized intelligence system. Drawing on a proposal that Donovan had submitted to Roosevelt eleven months earlier, Truman planned to introduce an espionage organization run by civilians and directly supervised by the president, which would coordinate all intelligence services. The proposal faced extreme opposition from the military services, the State Department, and the Federal Bureau of Investigation, all of which were reluctant to relinquish their own authority. Yet, Truman soon abandoned his attempts to assuage the dissenting governmental factions. Congress passed the National Security Act in 1947, establishing America's first independent source of foreign intelligence.
Bianca Jackson

Date July 26, 1947

Country USA

Why It's Key The CIA became the first independent U.S. agency responsible for supplying national security intelligence to the U.S. policymakers.

Dit is een foto, zoals ik me zou wensen, altijd zo te zijn. Dan had ik nog wel een kans om naar Holywood te komen.

Annelrank.
10 Oct. 1942

1940-1949

(translation)
"This is a photo as I would wish myself to look all the time. Then I would maybe have a chance to come to Hollywood."
Anne Frank, 10 Oct. 1942

Key Political Event
The partition of India

After a nationalist struggle that lasted over three decades, the Indian subcontinent finally gained independence from colonial rule at midnight on August 15, 1947, ending 350 years of British presence in India. However, autonomy was achieved at a high cost. Under the provisions of the India Independence Act, India and Pakistan were established as separate dominions, with predominantly Hindu areas allotted to India and Muslim areas allotted to Pakistan. While the Indian National Congress and the Muslim League agreed to a partition of India along religious lines, Cyril Radcliffe, a British lawyer who had little knowledge of Indian conditions, hurriedly drew up the division of the country using out-of-date maps and census materials. India received most of the subcontinent's 562 scattered polities – or princely states – the majority of the British provinces, and parts of the three remaining provinces, while Pakistan consisted of a western wing, with the boundaries of what is now Pakistan, and an eastern wing, with the boundaries of what is now Bangladesh.

Though the end of imperialism in India was widely celebrated, partition was one of the most violent upheavals of the twentieth century. Twelve million people were uprooted from their homes; hundreds of thousands of people were killed or disappeared; thousands of women were raped or abducted; and countless people were forced into religious conversions as they found themselves on the wrong side of the border. In hindsight, it was ethnic cleansing on a grandiose scale – "temporary" camps still exist housing refugees who fled from the brutality of partition.
Bianca Jackson

Date August 15, 1947

Country India/Pakistan

Why It's Key The birth of India and Pakistan as autonomous countries also resulted in massive bloodshed, ethnic cleansing, and forced religious conversion.

Key Cultural Event
Yeager breaks the sound barrier

Ending with a sonic boom rather than a whimper, the breaking of the sound barrier marked the end of a host of problems that had long plagued aircraft. Approaching supersonic speeds – faster than the speed of sound – caused manifold issues with early, propeller-driven planes. Concerns such as air flow and wing flexing made reaching the barrier (in flight parlance, a speed of Mach 1) out of the question, and while certain propeller tips could reach supersonic speeds, this created disruptive turbulences for the rest of the plane. With the propeller inadequate, research began on the jet engine. During World War II, the German V-2 ballistic missile broke the barrier, but piloted aircraft remained a more complicated matter.

In 1942, the UK's Ministry of Aviation and Miles Aircraft began work on a supersonic-ready prototype, the Miles M.52, but it wouldn't be until after the war in the United States that the barrier was finally broken. On October 14, 1947, at California's Muroc Air Force Base, test pilot Charles "Chuck" Yeager reached Mach 1.07 in the experimental Bell X-1. Yeager, a West Virginia-bred former mechanic and fighter pilot, almost didn't make the historic flight: two days prior, he'd broken two ribs while horseback riding and hid the injury from military doctors. It wasn't his last record-breaking flight – he would later fly planes reaching more than double the speed of sound – but it was certainly the most important: the advances made on the Bell X-1 soon became jet aircraft standards.
David Greenwald

Date October 14, 1947

Country USA

Why It's Key Breaking the once-impermeable sound barrier was an important step for aeronautics.

Key Cultural Event
Meet the Press is launched

Meet the Press began on radio on June 24, 1945, produced by its creator Lawrence Spivak and noted journalist Martha Rountree. It moved to television on November 6, 1947, where it has remained a staple of Sunday television.

It first aired in color in 1960 and began broadcasting satellite interviews in 1966. Transcripts and videos of the show are now available via Internet. Guests are interviewed by a moderator before facing a panel of noted journalists who ask probing and insightful questions. John Kennedy recognized the show's influence on American politics and culture by referring to it as the "fifty-first state." Britain's Prince Philip managed to win a substantial raise for the royal family by joking on *Meet the Press* that the royals would soon be in the red.

Every American president since Harry Truman (1945–1953) has appeared on *Meet the Press* at some point, and many have used the show to send messages to the world as when President Jimmy Carter announced the American boycott of the 1980 Olympic Games after the Soviets invaded Afghanistan. Foreign politics and policy have always been a part of the show, which has sometimes influenced the course of political events. World leaders such as Fidel Castro, Indira Gandhi, Golda Meir, Mikhail Gorbachev, Anwar el-Sadat, Menachem Begin, and Tony Blair have appeared. The list of American guests encompasses icons from all fields, including baseball giant Jackie Robinson, civil rights leader Martin Luther King, evangelist Billy Graham, poet Robert Frost, and feminist leader Gloria Steinem.

Elizabeth R. Purdy

Date November 6, 1947

Country USA

Why It's Key The news show became a forum for interviewing major political and cultural figures from all over the world.

Fact Some five million viewers regularly watch *Meet the Press*, the longest-running and most quoted television program in the entire world.

1940–1949

259

Key Discovery
The first successful transistor is invented

After World War II, William Shockley (1910–1989), a solid-state physicist who is considered the father of the transistor, returned to his position with Bell Labs, adding physicists John Bardeen (1908–1991) and Walter Brattain (1902–1987) to his team. Postwar advances in semiconductor technology were largely a result of the discovery that artificial crystals could be created for use as semiconductors by adding impurities to natural crystals such as silicon. On December 16, 1947, Bardeen used a foil-wrapped three-dimensional prism that he had opened on one side and filled with wax to amplify sound 100 times. The new device was called a "transistor," and over time, the term became synonymous with all semiconductor amplifiers. Shockley, Bardeen, and Brattain were jointly awarded the Nobel Prize in Physics in recognition of their work

"on semiconductors and their discovery of the transistor effect."

Within five years of the discovery of the transistor, Bell Labs began licensing its technology for use in products such as radios and telephones. By 1956, European and Japanese companies had joined the industry. Early research into transistors was financed predominantly by the United States government, which contributed US$50 million between 1952 and 1964. The "super information highway," otherwise known as the internet, was made possible by the invention of microchips containing millions of transmitters that were first used in computers designed to facilitate military communication. In the digital age, transistors have become a billion dollar industry.

Elizabeth R. Purdy

Date December 16, 1947

Country USA

Why It's Key The discovery of the transistor was an essential ingredient in the technological revolutions of the early twentieth century and ultimately led to the development of the silicon chip and the dawning of the computer age.

Fact "Transistor" is a combination of the words "transfer" and "resistor."

Key Cultural Event
The Kinsey Report causes scandal

2004 saw the release of Bill Condon's film *Kinsey*, with Liam Neeson in the role of Alfred Kinsey, the sexologist. It followed in the footsteps of the off-Broadway musical *Dr. Sex* (2003). Few famous scientists can claim Hollywood hits to their name; even fewer go on to feature in musical theater. It is a mark of our fascination with sexual matters that Alfred Kinsey remains one of the most infamous men to have ever worn a lab coat.

Kinsey's first report, *Sexual Behavior in the Human Male*, was published in 1948. *Sexual Behavior in the Human Female* followed in 1953. Both reports came out of interviews, which included questions about sexual orientation, extramarital intercourse, masturbation, and sadomasochism. The conclusions pertaining to homosexual incidence were the most controversial. Kinsey claimed that 37 per cent of adult males had had at least one same-sex experience to the point of orgasm. He also concluded that 4 per cent of the white male adult population was exclusively homosexual, though his figures were misinterpreted and it was widely reported to be 10 per cent.

Much has been made of the potentially biased samples that Kinsey used. For example, a sizable proportion of his findings came from prison inmates and sex offenders, and whether this was decisive in the resulting figures is still a matter of much debate. Nevertheless, the Kinsey Reports were among the few "scientific" books to become bestsellers; an unmistakeable sign of the sexual revolution to come.
Andrew Blades

Date January 3, 1948

Country USA

Why It's Key The Kinsey Report suggested that what were previously thought of as "deviant" sexual acts were more common than people imagined.

Fact The first Kinsey Report sold over 200,000 copies in its first two months in the United States alone.

opposite The only four people to have access to case studies used in the Female report.

Key Political Event
Gandhi is assassinated

Mohandas Karamchand Gandhi, dubbed "the Mahatma" meaning "Great Soul" in Sanskrit, was born in Porbandar, Gujarat, on October 2, 1869. After studying law at University College in London, he was admitted to the British bar in 1891. In 1894 Gandhi accepted a position with a law practice in Durban, South Africa, where he remained for twenty years. It was in South Africa that he first encountered the violence of racism and conceived his philosophy of non-violent resistance, which he called *satyagraha*. Returning to India in 1914, Gandhi revitalized the National Congress Party with his philosophy of *satyagraha*, instigating a program of non-violent resistance to British rule. Also central to his vision for an independent India was unity among Hindus and Muslims.

After launching the "Quit India" campaign of 1942, Gandhi and senior congressmen were imprisoned. This saw the All India Muslim League's agitation for a separate Muslim state gain momentum. By 1948 communal violence had intensified to the extent that, on January 13 that year, Gandhi began a protest fast. He soon realized, however, that partition was inevitable and urged India to honor a debt of 550 million rupees to Pakistan. This enraged more zealous Hindus and on January 30, just days after terminating his fast, fellow Hindu Nathuram Godse fired three bullets into Gandhi at a prayer meeting. Gandhi's death inspired a universal outpouring of grief. Even Gandhi's nemesis, Britain's King George VI, described his death as an "irreparable loss" not only to India, but to mankind.
Sally Percival Wood

Date January 30, 1948

Country India

Why It's Key The death of Gandhi caused India, and indeed the world, to lose one of its most charismatic and proactive spokespersons for non-violent resistance.

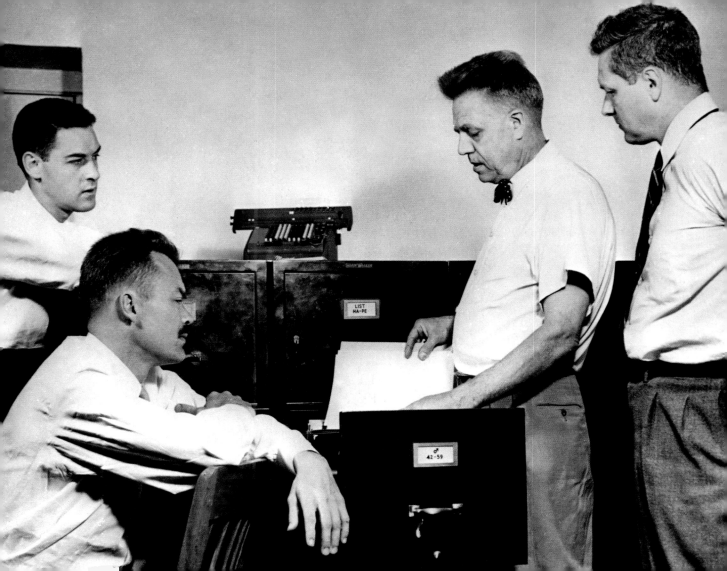

Key Cultural Event
Big Bang theory is proposed

The paper entitled "The Origin of Chemical Elements" by George Gamow and Ralph Alpher, published in the journal *Physical Review* on April 1, 1948, was the basis of a breakthrough theory, which advanced the modern understanding of the origins of the universe. Gamow and Alpher's theory, called the Big Bang Theory, states that the universe began about 10 to 20 billion years ago, when a giant explosion initiated the expansion of a singularity, an unthinkably small primordial zone of extreme temperature and infinite density, whose origins are still unknown. As the universe cooled, nuclear reactions took place that led to the creation of matter. The theory also claims that the expansion started by the Big Bang is a never-ending process. Edwin Hubble's 1929 discovery that galaxies are moving away from us at speeds proportional to their distance is considered the most convincing proof of the expansion.

The introduction of the Big Bang Theory has given modern cosmology a direction for further research. In 1965, Arno Penzias and Robert Wilson detected cosmic background radiation, a possible residue of the Big Bang explosion. In June 1995, NASA scientists detected primordial helium in the remote parts of the universe, which is potential proof of the aspect of the Big Bang Theory stating that hydrogen and helium were created during the initial moments of the universe. The research on the origins of the universe is still ongoing and might never be able to offer a definite answer.
Sonja Kudeljnjak

Date April 1, 1948

Country USSR/Belgium/USA

Why It's Key The Big Bang Theory has become the dominant theory about the origin of the universe.

Fact In 1927, the Belgian priest Georges Lemaître proposed that the beginning of the universe was the explosion of a primeval atom.

1940-1949

264

Key Political Event
World Health Organization is established

First proposed during the 1945 United Nations Conference on International Organization, it would take several more years of planning before the UN's vision of an international health agency would be realized. On April 7, 1948 – now celebrated as World Health Day – the World Health Organization's (WHO) constitution formally came into effect, with the agency inheriting the mandate and resources of its predecessor, the League of Nations' Health Organization. Based in Geneva, the organization has since become the world's leading authority on global health issues, making significant strides in areas of epidemic control, immunization, quarantine response, and international drug standardization.

Since its establishment, WHO has been a leader in global vaccination initiatives, achieving a significant milestone when, in 1978, it declared the successful eradication of the smallpox virus. Its aim to eliminate the poliovirus appears well on its way to success – the number of diagnosed cases has fallen by over 99 per cent since 1988 when WHO led a global effort aimed at eradicating the disease. The agency has spearheaded a number of high profile campaigns, ranging from raising public awareness of the HIV/AIDS virus to its 2006 Worldwide Stop Smoking Initiative.

In 2003, severe acute respiratory syndrome (SARS) swept across the world, infecting thousands and ultimately killing almost eight hundred people. It is widely recognized that the swift response efforts by WHO contributed largely to the rapid containment of the disease.
Annie Wang

Date April 7, 1948

Country Switzerland

Why It's Key The WHO was instrumental in establishing global healthcare initiatives, and the worldwide eradication of the smallpox virus can be largely credited to the organization's efforts.

Key Political Event
The founding of Israel

The land of Israel has held a sacred significance as a Jewish homeland since biblical times. However, since the Roman conquest, Israel – or Palestine – has been ruled by a multitude of other powers. In the seventh century, Muslims conquered the territory, and in the sixteenth century, it was absorbed into the Ottoman Empire; after World War I, the British controlled it.

The re-creation of a Jewish homeland in Palestine had been a long-held dream for numerous Jews, forming the basis of the political movement called Zionism. From the end of the nineteenth century, a steady stream of Jews migrated to the Holy Land, often fleeing religious persecution in other countries. Then, in 1947, the newly formed United Nations approved a partition plan to create neighboring Arab and Jewish states – a plan the Arabs rejected. However, on May 14, 1948, when the British mandate on Palestine came to an end, the State of Israel was unilaterally declared, and the new country quickly recognized by nations such as the United States and the Soviet Union.

Chaim Weizmann, a Russian-born chemist and leader of the Jewish Agency, became the first president of Israel, with David Ben-Gurion, leader of the Mapai Labour Party, as prime minister. Of the 880,000 population, over 790,000 were Jewish. Although Weizmann and Ben-Gurion would achieve economic growth for Israel through industrial and agricultural reform, in those early days the focus was on contending with, and defending their people from, attacks from their Arab neighbors.

Justin Norris

Date May 14, 1948

Country Israel

Why It's Key The controversial founding of the Jewish homeland led to a war in the Middle East, and laid the foundations for a deep and bitter conflict that continues to this day.

Key Political Event
Arab-Israeli War

Hours before the British Mandate governing the Middle Eastern territory known as Palestine was set to expire, a group of politicians, including Prime Minister David Ben-Gurion, gathered at a Tel Aviv museum and realized a long-held dream by proclaiming the establishment of the State of Israel. Within hours, an army made up of forces from Egypt, Lebanon, the Transjordan, Iraq, Syria, Yemen, Saudi Arabia, and Libya, launched an attack, and quickly occupied eastern Palestine and the Old City of Jerusalem. Many believed that the Jewish state would die in infancy, but over the course of seven months, the new Israeli Defense Forces (IDF) steadily pushed back the Arab invaders. The war was fought with arms and aircraft left over from occupying European armies during World War II, and although not cutting-edge, the damage was extreme. A total of 4,000 Israeli soldiers and 2,400 civilians were killed in the fighting – about 1 per cent of the total Israeli population. Unofficial estimates placed the number of Arab deaths at between 10,000–15,000.

By the time an armistice was negotiated in 1949, the Arabs had been strategically and tactically routed, and Israel was in control of 8,000 square miles of land. But the real losers were the 1.3 million Palestinians who suddenly found themselves a stateless people. At least 350 Palestinian towns had been razed in the fighting. Between 500,000 and 1 million were displaced, with hundreds of thousands ending up in temporary refugee camps that nearly six decades later are permanent refugee cities. It remains one of the world's most unsolvable political problems.

Heather Michon

Date May 16, 1948

Country Israel

Why It's Key Victory over the Arabs gave the new Jewish state a powerful image on the world stage.

Key Political Event
Berlin Airlift

By June 1948, the United States, Britain, and France reached an agreement to merge their respective occupational zones in Germany into a single state, and to work toward economic recovery. The Western Allies' first plan was to introduce a new currency for the western sectors of Berlin, which the Soviets would have no control of. The USSR, which did not want Germany to recover economically and become a potential threat once again, reacted by introducing its own new currency in the Soviet-controlled East Berlin just 24 hours before the West's mark was supposed to go into circulation. On the morning of June 24, 1948, the Soviets also imposed a blockade on West Berlin and closed all rail and land routes into the three western sectors. The United States responded by organizing an airlift of food and basic provisions, which started being flown to Berlin daily from July 1, 1948. Soon the airlift, led by General Curtis LeMay, was providing the city with about 5,000 tons of supplies each day.

The Berlin blockade not only turned out to have been a futile effort for the Soviets, but it also had several unexpected political repercussions. Instead of preventing the creation of West Germany, the blockade made the Western Allies accelerate their plans to set it up. Furthermore, the Berlin Airlift presented the United States as a generous superpower financially superior to the USSR. On May 11, 1949, Stalin finally decided to lift the blockade.
Sonja Kudeljnjak

Date June 24, 1948

Country Germany

Why It's Key The Berlin Airlift was America's first major victory in the Cold War.

Fact The Berlin Airlift was nicknamed "Operation Vittles."

Key Cultural Event
Candid Camera becomes the first reality TV show

From its early days as *Candid Microphone* to its long-running success on television starting in 1948, *Candid Camera* is now widely recognized as the archetypal reality show.

For most of its existence, *Candid Camera* was the only show like it on television. The gag was always the same: an ordinary situation – a day at the office, a walk down the street, an afternoon in the park – becomes disrupted by something unusual. Someone responds like any person would, only the situation becomes more absurd for no apparent reason. Just at the point that something is about to go wrong, the show's host emerges from the background and delivers the show's trademark line, "Smile, you're on *Candid Camera*." With a sheepish grin, the fooled person admits that he or she should have known better, and is allowed to join in the comedy of the moment. This simple set-up, developed by the show's founder Allen Funt, proved to be flexible enough to survive for almost six decades on television as special programming, a major network broadcast, or in syndication. Its most successful decade was the 1960s, when it was regularly rated in the top ten as a CBS program and featured celebrity cameos.

Although the show has been out of production in recent years, it has many imitators, showing that reality television still depends on scripted scenarios or even pranks to make it entertaining. The show also anticipated the widespread use of surveillance cameras, which film people with an eye toward safety, not comedy.
Martin Johnson

Date August 10, 1948

Country USA

Why It's Key The first "reality show" demonstrated that everyday life could be as entertaining as fully scripted shows.

Fact Although the show looked unscripted, it relied on writers, including a young Woody Allen, to keep the stunts interesting.

Key Political Event
The Democratic People's Republic of Korea proclaimed

In the initial aftermath of Imperial Japan's surrender in August 1945, the fate of the Korean peninsula was, to the postwar superpowers, of marginal importance. Ignoring the claims of a native provisional government that had stepped forward, the occupying forces followed a hastily agreed plan to administer the ex-colony under temporary zones of occupation until national elections could take place. The division, no official justification of which was ever delivered, caused frustration and protest throughout Korea.

Stalin had long distrusted the excessive "nationalism" of Korea's native Communist movement and was reluctant to lend it his support. Instead, his secret service introduced an unknown Soviet-trained anti-Japanese guerilla as its candidate for power. Winning a substantial power-base among the peasants with his land-reform policies, Kim Il-Sung and his clique soon became the dominant force in North Korean politics.

Meanwhile, in the southern zone, nationalists who refused to recognize the legitimacy of the U.S.-USSR trusteeship were in the ascendant. The Soviet Union objected to such elements being allowed to stand for election; a ballot held in April 1948, held only in the south and even there boycotted by the left, saw victorious nationalists claim to represent the government of all Korea. In the north, there was no way that Kim Il-Sung's faction would accept unification on anything other than their own terms. Three weeks after the United States handed power to the nationalists, they made a rival claim to government, and the division of Korea became official.
James Handley

Date September 9, 1948

Country North Korea

Why It's Key The DPRK is one of few Stalinist states to survive into the twenty-first century.

Key Political Event
Declaration of Human Rights signed in Paris

On the day the Universal Declaration of Human Rights (UDHR) was signed at the Palais de Chaillot in Paris, Eleanor Roosevelt proclaimed that it "may well become the international Magna Carta of all men everywhere." The former First Lady had chaired the committee that drafted the document. She was the only member of the committee that was not a scholar or expert in international relations, but had approached her job as chairperson with her customary determination. "We wanted as many nations as possible to accept the fact that men, for one reason or another, were born free and equal in dignity and rights, that they were endowed with reason and conscience, and should act toward one another in a spirit of brotherhood," she once said. "The way to do that was to find words that everyone would accept."

But as deliberations over the UDHR began in Paris that winter, it was clear that acceptance was far from universal. Members of the Islamic states argued that the declaration was dominated by western values. Some westerners thought it was too socialist, while Soviet delegates thought it wasn't socialist enough, and the Vatican complained that God was not mentioned. When it finally passed, it was not unanimous. The final vote was 48–0 and 8 abstentions, with the Soviet Bloc, the Saudis, and South Africa refusing to sign on.

Today, the UDHR holds the Guinness Book of World Records title for the "most translated" document, having been published in well over 300 languages.
Heather Michon

Date December 10, 1948

Country France

Why It's Key The declaration was the first global statement on human rights.

Key Cultural Event
de Beauvoir's *The Second Sex* published

Famously, when Simone de Beauvoir took the philosophy exam for Paris' Ecole Normale Supérieure in 1929, only one other student beat her: Jean-Paul Sartre, who would become her lifelong lover. Indeed, de Beauvoir was the only woman to play an important part in existentialism, adding a powerful feminist voice to the movement with books like *The Second Sex* (*Le Deuxième Sexe*), often called "the Bible of Feminism."

Born in 1905 in Paris, where she lived until her death in 1986, de Beauvoir rejected her mother's Catholicism as a teenager, then studied at the Sorbonne and became a teacher. After publishing several novels and essays, she wrote *The Second Sex*, her most famous and controversial work. Synthesized from interviews, literature, sociological research, and de Beauvoir's own experiences, it argues that there is no essence of woman, but rather that "woman" is a category constructed by the institutions, discourses, and practices that make up our society. "One is not born, but rather becomes a woman," writes de Beauvoir. De Beauvoir, like Sartre, hated the bourgeois refusal to look at things as they really are, and, drawing on Marx and Hegel, insisted we admit a painful fact: that women are seen as outsiders, as "the Other," making oppression easy. Applying these harsh insights to sex, abortion, motherhood, marriage, shopping, and work, de Beauvoir's book caused a scandal at the time of its publication and has been required reading for feminists ever since.

Ned Beauman

Date 1949

Country France

Why It's Key *The Second Sex* is a cornerstone of feminist theory that has not lost its power to shock.

268

Key Cultural Event
Postmodernism enters the lexicon

In 1949, Joseph Hudnut, Dean of the Harvard Graduate School of Design, introduced influential segments of the academic world to the term "postmodernism," which he employed in an article republished in his book *Architecture and the Spirit of Man*. Hudnut meant "postmodernism" in a strictly architectural context, specifically to refer to a kind of house. Thirty years later, however, the word – along with its increasingly complex and contradictory meanings – began to find its way into many different academic venues, notably philosophy and literary criticism. By the 1990s, postmodernism entered the popular lexicon, where it came to refer to a hazy constellation of avant-garde, relativist, ironic, and self-reflexive approaches to art, theory, and living.

While the term "postmodernist" had been used by J. M. Thompson in 1914 and B. I. Bell in 1939, and the word "postmodern" by Arnold Toynbee in 1939, Hudnut's usage became common currency in architectural circles, from which perch it had an easier time entering other academic discourses. Postmodernism soon became associated with continental, particularly French, philosophy, whose dense theory and obtuse language is commonly considered the acme of postmodernism. The etymological origins of the postmodern are simpler to understand than the actual significance of the word, which has long eluded any facile understanding. This is largely because the concept of the postmodern itself rejects fixed methods and ideologies, favoring instead a pastiche of tools, approaches, and mindsets.

Demir Barlas

Date 1949

Country USA

Why It's Key The most popular academic buzzword of all time first entered popular circulation in architectural theory.

Key Cultural Event
Death of a Salesman opens in New York

Now that it has become one of the most familiar of all dramas, a staple of high-school syllabuses and stages worldwide, it is difficult to imagine the impact Arthur Miller's *Death of a Salesman* had at the time of its first production in 1949. In a United States shaken by the events of 1939–1945 and preoccupied with the new eastern front of the Cold War, Miller held a mirror up to American achievement and self-confidence, and found it faltering.

The character of Willy Loman, an archetypal salesman getting by on "a smile and a shoeshine," spoke to thousands of middle-aged, middle-American men for whom dreams of prosperity and security had failed to translate into reality. Fearing for his mental health, his wife Linda humors him; relationships with his sons are strained and frequently delusional. He hallucinates a character, Uncle Ben, whose mantra haunts him to the death: "When I walked into the jungle, I was seventeen. When I walked out I was twenty-one. And, by God, I was rich!"

Miller himself found fame, wealth, and critical appreciation, going on to savage McCarthyism (in *The Crucible*, 1953) and chart his marriage to Marilyn Monroe (in *After the Fall*, 1964). His lasting legacy, however, remains *Death of a Salesman*. Its messages have extended well beyond the United States. In the 1980s, it played successfully in China and Japan, and then in 1992 had its first run in Taiwan; it is now, arguably, the most recognizable critique of capitalism in the history of theater.

Andrew Blades

Date February 10, 1949

Country USA

Why It's Key The play questioned the "American Dream" at a vital time in its history.

Fact Since 1949, there has not been a single year when *Death of a Salesman* has not been performed professionally somewhere around the world.

1940–1949

269

Key Political Event
NATO is founded

NATO initially included ten major European States (including Britain and France), Canada, and the United States. It committed its members to peacefully cooperating to resolve conflicts but to come to each other's defense if necessary, because an attack on one NATO member constituted an attack on all.

What bound the NATO alliance together was a common sense of danger from the nuclear capability of the Soviet Union after World War II; NATO's central role therefore was to deter risk of Russian aggression. To this end, the U.S. established missile bases in Europe, some within striking distance of Moscow.

For forty years, the role of NATO remained largely unchanged. However the collapse of the Soviet Union in the 1990s stole from NATO their most important adversary; with the Russian threat gone NATO had to redefine its purpose. This led to the creation of the Allied Rapid Reaction Force (ARRF), which was made available to the United Nations for immediate mobilization in crisis areas, thus confirming NATO's future role in military and peacekeeping operations.

Subsequently, in 1995, NATO took part in its first-ever military operation in the former Yugoslavia. This later developed into a peacekeeping role with forces remaining in Bosnia and Kosovo. More recently NATO has begun peacekeeping operations outside of Europe for the first time, in Afghanistan, Iraq, and Darfur. NATO currently has twenty-six member countries and, in addition to its military forces, continues to be an important forum for discussion on international security issues of common concern.

Helena Hewson

Date April 4, 1949

Country Belgium

Why It's Key The North Atlantic Treaty Organization (NATO) is a regional collective defense organization whose military forces help to provide international security and stability.

Key Political Event
East and West Germany established

After the Potsdam Conference in August 1945, Germany was divided into four occupational zones. The south-west zone was controlled by France, the north-west one by Britain, the south zone by the United States, and the one in the east by the USSR. On May 23, 1949, the three western zones were joined as one state – the Federal Republic of Germany (*Bundesrepublik Deutschland*). The provisional capital of the state, informally referred to as "West Germany," was Bonn. On October 7, 1949, the German Democratic Republic (*Deutsche Demokratische Republik*), i.e. "East Germany," was established on the Soviet zone, with East Berlin as its capital.

West Germany was a capitalist country allied with the United States, Britain, and France. After the currency reform of 1948 and the outbreak of the Korean War in 1950, which created an increase in the global demand for goods, West Germany experienced a long period of economic growth. The country also developed good diplomatic relations with other western countries. In 1954, West Germany regained full sovereignty and opened the way for membership in the NATO and the WEU (Western European Union). East Germany, on the other hand, was an ally of the USSR. It adopted the socialist economic model and became the most advanced country of the Soviet Bloc. Its political structure was that of a centralized, single-party, Communist state. The two countries became one country again on October 3, 1990, when Germany was reunified.

Sonja Kudeljnjak

Date May 23, 1949

Country Germany

Why It's Key The establishment of the two Germanies would cause the two countries to go in opposite political and economic directions.

Fact The United States and numerous other countries did not recognize East Germany until 1972.

opposite East Berliners try to get into West Berlin for food and supplies.

Key Cultural Event
Orwell's *Nineteen Eighty-Four* published

Born in Bengal in 1903, Eric Arthur Blair spent his secondary school years at Eton College in England. After a time in the Indian Imperial Police, he went to Paris to become a writer, but having failed, he made ends meet as a dishwasher. He returned to England in 1929 as a tramp, before eventually taking up a post as a teacher. From 1933, he started publishing under the pseudonym George Orwell, starting with *Down and Out in Paris and London* (1933). He wrote numerous novels and newspaper reviews before *Animal Farm* brought him overnight success in 1945. *Nineteen Eighty-Four* followed suit three years later.

A haunting dystopian novel set in the future year 1984, *Nineteen Eighty-Four* depicts the loss of personal and political freedom in a totalitarian government. It tells the story of Ministry of Truth bureaucrat Winston Smith, who attempts to betray the totalitarian government of Oceania, a fusion of Stalin's Soviet Union with the naval power of a futuristic British Empire. Smith is caught in a deadlock, as personal privacy, truth, and freedom are brutally sacrificed for the sake of state security.

Considered politically dangerous, the novel has been banned by libraries in numerous countries. Nevertheless, it has made a phenomenal impact on the political realm of science fiction, as well as the English language, creating an extensive new vocabulary, including "Big Brother," "Room 101," "thoughtcrime," and "Newspeak." Indeed, Orwell's own name has been transformed into the adjective "Orwellian" to describe political concepts that are characteristic of Oceania.

Mariko Kato

Date June 8, 1949

Country UK

Why It's Key *Nineteen Eighty-Four* is a revolutionary novel that is one of the most famous dystopian works in literature.

Key Political Event
Soviet Union gets the atomic bomb

The nuclear era began in deadly earnest in August, 1945, when the United States dropped two atomic bombs on the cities of Hiroshima and Nagasaki in Japan, effectively ending World War II. This demonstration of apocalyptic firepower did not catch the Soviet Union by surprise. The Soviets had been working on their own nuclear program since 1942, and gave the project the highest national priority once the country had dealt with the remnants of the German Army in Europe. The Soviet atomic program was managed on behalf of dictator Joseph Stalin by his security chief Lavrentiy Beria. The program had as its top scientist the Russian physicist Igor Kurchatov, but also benefited immensely from the phantom contributions of the spy Klaus Fuchs, a British citizen of German background who worked on the Manhattan

Project and passed on information to the Soviets. Due partly to the character of this intelligence, Soviet scientists and engineers hewed closely to American designs that had already proven feasible.

Fuchs, an ardent Communist since his youth, proved to be a vitally important asset for the Soviet nuclear effort, which succeeded far sooner than U.S. scientific and military authorities expected. The Soviet Union detonated its first atomic bomb in Kazakhstan on August 29, 1949, thereby becoming only the second country in the world to acquire nuclear weapons and triggering an arms race that has not abated to this day.

Demir Barlas

Date August 29, 1949

Country USSR

Why It's Key The nuclear arms race officially began when the Soviet Union joined the United States as the possessor of atomic technology.

Key Political Event
China becomes Communist

Since the fall of the Qing Dynasty in 1911, China had been in turmoil. Japan's resolve to occupy China since 1914 had caused ongoing hostility. The conflict between the Nationalist People's Party (*Guomindang*) and the Chinese Communist Party (CCP) followed, which raged from 1927 to 1949. During the Long March (1934–1935), the rural Chinese threw their support behind the CCP, which was imperative for China's defeat of the Japanese. The *Guomindang* had shown little resistance to the Japanese, instead focusing on destroying the Communists. When Japan finally capitulated at the end of World War II, full-scale civil war broke out in China. By this stage, Chiang Kai-shek had lost support from the grassroots Chinese who had lost faith in his commitment to their concerns.

Although Chiang Kai-shek continued to receive external support, principally from the United States, domestic support for the *Guomindang* continued to decline. Not only had the CCP won over the peasants, but captured *Guomindang* officers and soldiers were also joining the People's Liberation Army. In 1949, Chiang Kai-shek was forced into the south-west corner of China. Compelled to either hold this pocket of the mainland or escape to the island of Taiwan, he chose the latter. Taiwan became the nationalist base while the communists proclaimed the mainland the People's Republic of China (PRC) on October 1, 1949, beginning a program of extensive reforms. Though the Chinese were ecstatic to finally be unified, for decades the West refused to recognize the PRC.

Sally Percival Wood

Date October 1, 1949

Country China

Why It's Key The formation of the People's Republic of China (PRC) as a communist state, and its alliance with the Soviet Union, divided the world into two ideological blocs, deepening Cold War tensions. The West refused to recognize the PRC until the 1970s.

opposite Chinese propaganda poster from 1949 showing Chairman Mao and people from the rivers and mountains.

Key Political Event **Costa Rica gives women and people of African descent the vote**

After claiming victory in the bloodiest event in twentieth-century Costa Rican history, the civil war, Jose Figueres Ferrer transformed the sociopolitical and economic chemistry of Costa Rica, stripping away the repressive regime of President Calderon and injecting freedom into the country's bloodstream.

The years preceding the war had been rife with political instability; military intervention and tampered ballots had plagued the Costa Rican elections. After Calderon won the election on March 1, 1948, uprising began across the nation that eventually manifested itself as violence against the government. The civil war lasted forty-four days, and Ferrer succeeded in overthrowing the Calderon administration.

Soon after, Ferrer set up his own junta, gaining emergency powers, and over the next eighteen months, set about turning the country around. On November 8, 1949, Ferrer brought in radical reforms based on constitutions of the previous century, stipulating that a standing army be banned to be replaced by a National Guard so that military involvement in politics would be terminated. Ferrer also allowed voting rights for the first time to women, people of African descent, and illiterates, public education for all, and improved welfare rights.

The improvement in economic infrastructure and quality of life was startling, and although Ferrer handed over power to Otilio Ulate at the end of his junta, he was sworn in as president three times in overwhelming election victories, and is considered the most important political figure in Costa Rica's history.
Greg Pittard

Date November 8, 1949

Country Costa Rica

Why It's Key After years of compromised elections and a bloody civil war, Jose Figueres Ferrer passed 834 reforms that revolutionized the politics, culture, economics, and infrastructure of Costa Rica.

Key Discovery
Carbon dating process developed

In December 1949, an American physical chemist invented a process that changed the face of archaeological and geological research. Willard Libby, a professor at the University of Chicago, developed a radiometric technique for gauging the age of carbon-based materials based on the half-life of the radioisotope C-14.

Libby understood that plants and animals contained the same level of C-14 as the atmosphere in which they perished, therefore making it possible to accurately date organic remains at key archeological sites.

The process is limited to materials up to the age of roughly 60,000 years (about ten half lives of C-14), after which the radioactivity of the C-14 is too low to be registered against background radiation.

However, it remains a valuable dating technique for most archaeological and geological finds. Carbon dating (or radiocarbon dating) has been used to determine the age of the prehistoric fossilized footprints of Acahualinca in Managua, Nicaragua, the controversial Shroud of Turin, and the body of the Kennewick Man.

Libby is also known for his work on the Manhattan Project, where he developed the gaseous diffusion separation and enrichment process for Uranium-235, the radioactive isotope used in the atomic bomb on Hiroshima. In 1960, he received the Nobel Prize in Chemistry for his work on C-14 dating, and also succeeded in pioneering the use of tritium for dating water.
Jay Mullins

Date December 1, 1949

Country USA

Why It's Key Willard Libby's process enabled archaeologists and geologists to accurately date ancient artifacts.

Fact A half-life is the time it takes for half the atoms in a radioactive material to decay.

Key Cultural Event **UN declare forced prostitution "incompatible with human dignity"**

The issue of prostitution is rife with controversy, with attitudes toward it and legislation surrounding it varying widely throughout the world. In 1949, a convention was ratified and published by the United Nations General Assembly regarding prostitution and its link with human trafficking, outlining their consensus that the practice was no longer tolerable. Stating that prostitution and trafficking was "incompatible with the dignity and worth of the human person," and that it endangered the "welfare of the individual, the family and the community," the convention laid down the principle upon which states could base further legislation. The convention included articles requiring the punishment of any individual that "procures, entices or leads away, for the purposes of prostitution, another person, even with the consent of that person," expressly prohibiting the transport of women forced or persuaded into prostitution. It further states that anyone managing or financing a brothel would be punished.

The convention was bolstered by a strong moral foundation, clearly stating that prostitution reduced the dignity of the women involved, and was an important step in recognizing prostitution and human trafficking as serious problems. Underlying the approach of the convention is an understanding of the trafficked woman and sex worker as a victim, while those who facilitate prostitution are criminalized. Eighty-nine countries ratified the convention, with Germany, the Netherlands, and the United States being notable exceptions.

Hannah Furness

Date December 2, 1949

Country Switzerland

Why It's Key The convention clearly stated that prostitution and the trafficking of women for this purpose was incompatible with human dignity, and demanded punishment for those involved in it.

1940–1949

275

Key Political Event
Senator McCarthy begins witch-hunts

When Senator Joseph McCarthy accused 205 members of staff at the State Department of being Communists in a public speech in West Virginia as part of the Lincoln Day celebrations, anti-communist sentiment was already reaching its height in the United States. The *Guomindang* regime in China had just collapsed and a Communist government established. The United States was growing increasingly afraid of the global spread of Communism as the Cold War continued. A month earlier, Alger Hiss, a former senior public servant, had been convicted of perjury, having been.accused of being an accomplice to a member of an underground Communist network.

McCarthy's allegations were immediately and adamantly refuted by Lincoln White, press officer at the State Department, who argued that his claim was "entirely without foundation." Unperturbed, McCarthy told President Harry Truman two days later that he had compiled a list of fifty-seven Communists, and on February 20, he delivered a six-hour speech to Congress in which he indirectly identified eighty-one "traitors." His witch-hunt sparked a frenzy across the country, encouraging blacklists and personal betrayals. Twenty-five states banned Communist activity. McCarthy's public profile had soared overnight, and he had launched one of the most turbulent periods in U.S. history.

McCarthy's reckless methods, founded on intimidation and hearsay, were finally exposed during a televised cross-examination of army personnel. But by that time, an estimated 10,000 people had lost their jobs and their reputations.

Mariko Kato

Date February 9, 1950

Country USA

Why It's Key Senator McCarthy's scandalous allegations fueled the anti-Communist sentiment in the United States to disastrous consequences.

Fact The senate censored McCarthy in 1954 and he died of alcoholism three years later.

Key Cultural Event
First credit card introduced

It was embarrassment that precipitated the invention of the credit card: upon finishing his meal at his local restaurant, businessman Frank McNamara realized he had forgotten his wallet. This wasn't a problem for the well-known client and he left his business card as an IOU. Yet this unfortunate lapse of memory planted a seed of an idea in McNamara's head.

After his faux pas at the restaurant, McNamara realized that the facility of credit could be maximized if it was accepted in more than one establishment. In his line of work as head of a credit corporation, McNamara was well aware that the market was out there, and so he enlisted two business associates and together they pooled their money into this new venture.

The notion of using credit to purchase goods is nothing new, yet at the start of the twentieth century, credit was limited to single stores in order to promote loyalty. This meant that customers would have to carry several cards for separate shops, if they chose to pay by credit. McNamara's vision was realized when the Diners Club Card was introduced on February 28, 1950, with two hundred members. The card was at first accepted at twenty-seven restaurants in New York, but the idea of a credit card soon caught on, and by 1958, the Bank of America and American Express had both launched their credit cards.

Kerry Duffy

Date February 28, 1950

Country USA

Why It's Key The introduction of credit cards had a massive impact on the economy, allowing consumers to purchase goods they previously had to save for.

Key Discovery
Antihistamines introduced as allergy treatment

Histamine, an organic compound made from the amino acid histidine, is found in almost all body tissue. In an allergic reaction, histamine is released from cells in response to foreign substances that enter the body (like pollen). The body attempts to expel the invading substance, and tissues swell, causing the runny nose, itchy eyes, sneezing, and hives usually associated with allergic reactions.

Swiss-born Daniel Bovet, a member of the Pasteur Institute in Paris, along with his assistant Anne-Marie Staub, can be credited with the invention of antihistamines. They sought a natural antihistamine in the human body, but unable to discover one, they succeeded in synthesizing the first antihistamine in 1937. This antihistamine, dubbed F929, protected Bovet's laboratory guinea pigs against high levels of histamine and lessened the symptoms of anaphylaxis, a severe allergic reaction resulting in airway obstruction. F929 proved too toxic for humans, but after thousands of further experiments, Antergan, the first antihistamine to successfully treat humans, was released in France in 1942. Soon, more than 100 antihistamines were developed, most of which were based on Bovet's F929.

By 1950, antihistamines were mass-produced, and many drug companies actually marketed them as a cure for the common cold. While they can't cure a cold, antihistamines can certainly provide relief for some cold symptoms, as well as other afflictions. Dramamine can help sufferers of motion sickness, and other varieties of antihistamines can serve as sedatives or anti-nausea medications.

Carolyn Purnell

Date 1950

Country France

Why It's Key Antihistamines have rid us of sneezing, runny noses, and itchy eyes for years, not to mention preventing even more serious allergic reactions and complications.

Fact Bovet was awarded the Nobel Prize in medicine or physiology in 1957.

Key Cultural Event
Tollund Man discovered

On Saturday May 6, 1950, brothers Viggo and Emil Højgaard were digging peat from a bog near Tollund, Denmark, when they uncovered the preserved body of a man with a rope noose around his neck. Believing the body to be that of a recent murder victim, the Højgaard family informed the police two days later, who brought officials from the nearby Silkeborg Museum. The peat stained body was transported to Copenhagen for study, and returned to Silkeborg Museum, where it has been exhibited since 1952.

"Tollund Man," as the body became known, lived in the early Iron Age and was probably hung in a Celtic sacrificial rite. Numerous bog people have been discovered in northwestern Europe since the late 1800s, many of whom display signs of violent death, such as fractured bones and slit throats. The acid in peat kills bacteria which decomposes organic matter, preserving even the skin texture of bodies. Some important bog bodies include Graubaulle Man (Denmark, 1952), the Windeby "Girl" (later identified as male; Germany, 1952), and Clonycavan Man (Ireland, 2003).

Scientists at first speculated that bog people were punished by their Celtic and Germanic societies for adultery, homosexuality, and bodily deformities. The current theory holds that, although some bodies were deliberately injured, the pressure of the bog itself, and of people walking on the peat, could account for deformed and broken bones. Furthermore, the care with which Tollund Man and other bodies were laid to rest implies the reverence of sacrifice.

David Anderson

Date May 8, 1950 (officially reported)

Country Denmark

Why It's Key Tollund Man is a well-preserved man from the Iron Age (500 BCE–800 CE), a period in European history for which there are no written records as to how people lived.

Fact Tollund Man and Graubaulle Man were inspiration for poems by Irish poet Seamus Heaney, famous for his themes of digging and nostalgia for the ancient past.

Key Political Event
Korean War begins

After the end of World War II, Korean territory was divided at the 38th parallel into the North Korean occupational zone, controlled by the Soviets, and the South Korean one, controlled by the United States. In 1948, rival governments were introduced: the north zone became the People's Democratic Republic of Korea and the south one was set up as The Republic of Korea. The tensions between the two Koreas, incited by Cold War rivalry, was becoming increasingly strained and culminated on June 25, 1950, when nearly 100,000 North Korean troops crossed the 38th parallel and invaded South Korea. The United Nations Security Council immediately condemned North Korea's invasion as an act of aggression, insisted that the North Korean troops withdraw from the South, and invited other UN members to assist South Korea in a "police action" against the aggressor. On June 27, U.S. President Harry Truman authorized the use of U.S. military forces in Korea and appointed General Douglas MacArthur supreme commander.

On September 15, U.S. and South Korean forces under MacArthur started a counter-offensive at Inchon, pushing the North Korean troops all the way to the People's Republic of China border. When victory started to seem imminent, the Chinese entered the war on North Korea's side, prolonging the war until July 1953, when the peace negotiations were concluded. Although the peace agreement ended the fighting, the Cold War tension ignited by the Korean War would remain for the following four decades.

Sonja Kudeljnjak

Date June 25, 1950

Country Korea

Why It's Key The Korean War would cause an explosion of Cold War animosity.

Fact During the war, the United States elected a new president, Dwight D. Eisenhower, who promised the American people an end to the Korean War.

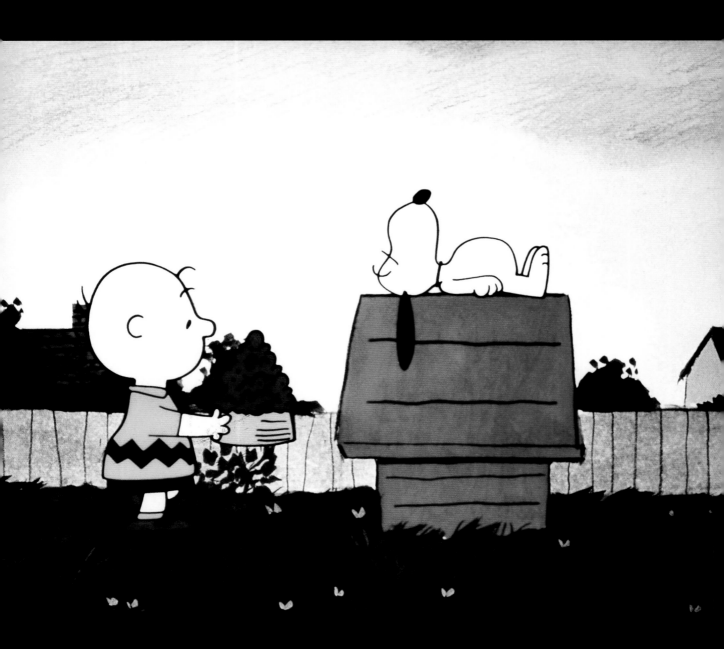

Key Cultural Event
"Peanuts" by Charles M. Schulz is published

Comic strips first became popular in large-circulation newspapers at the end of the nineteenth century, but it wasn't until "Peanuts" that a cartoonist became a celebrity. Charles Schultz, a World War II veteran and Minnesota native, wrote a rough version of the strip called "Li'l Folks" in the late 1940s, which led to the refined version with the famous title being sold to United Feature Syndicate at the decade's end.

Compared to densely serialized strips like "Dick Tracy," "Peanuts" offered a breath of fresh air. Its sweet and simple characters lived in a virtually adult-free world, although strong doses of life philosophy slipped into the four-panel instalments. With Charlie Brown, the artist gave readers a wholly sympathetic character. Charlie, Lucy, Linus, their affable dog Snoopy, and the rest of the gang were instantly appealing, turning "Peanuts" into a virtual overnight success.

Demonstrating the power of mass marketing, the characters became stars of acclaimed holiday television specials and their likenesses would become massive commercial enterprises. When Schultz died in 2000, the strip was appearing in 2,600 newspapers all over the world. Despite the immense popularity of his work, Schultz was fairly publicity shy, leading historians to analyze him through his protagonist; Charlie's parents had the same professions as those of Schultz, and his continual rejection by the opposite sex seemed to reflect the artist's tumultuous romantic life. Regardless, the appeal of the strip testifies to the boundless capacity for pop culture to pervade cultural awareness.
Eric Kohn

Date October 2, 1950

Country USA

Why It's Key The comic strip's popularity demonstrated the commercial viability of the comic medium and gave the United States some of its most iconic characters.

Fact Schultz requested that no future "Peanuts" storylines were written after his death.

opposite Charlie Brown and Snoopy from the Peanuts cartoons.

279

Key Political Event
Occupation of Tibet

On October 7, 1950, 40,000 Chinese troops crossed the Yangtze River into Eastern Tibet, quickly overpowering the much smaller, and poorly equipped, Tibetan militia. The Chinese would defend its actions, declaring that they were "liberating" the Tibetans from oppression and slavery, while Tibetans, and a number of other countries, including India, Britain, and the United States, saw it as an unauthorized "invasion" of the region. Tensions had mounted between China and Tibet when, shortly after the Chinese Revolution in 1911–1912, Chinese forces were expelled from the region, and the Dalai Lama declared Tibet a "small, religious, and *independent* nation." By 1949, China had a new Communist government and, under the leadership of Mao Zedong, quickly moved to reinstate Chinese sovereignty over the region.

Human rights activists consider the "liberation of Tibet" one of China's grossest human rights violations. Thousands of Buddhist monks were tortured and killed during the occupation, over 6,000 monasteries were destroyed, hundreds of thousands were sent into exile, and death estimates range from 400,000 to a staggering 1.2 million.

The 1997 film, *Seven Years in Tibet*, starring Brad Pitt and David Thewlis, garnered heavy criticism from the Chinese government for its negative portrayal of the Communist army over a much more positive depiction of the Dalai Lama. Both starring actors and the film's director, Jean-Jacques Annaud, have since been banned from ever reentering China.
Annie Wang

Date October 7, 1950

Country China

Why It's Key The Chinese occupation of Tibet resulted in the bloody oppression of an entire culture, and is considered one of the country's grossest human rights violations to date.

Key Political Event
Iranian oil nationalized

Iran's abundant oil supply has been a bone of contention for various imperial powers, beginning with Britain's Anglo-Persian Oil Company (APOC) in the early part of the twentieth century. When Iranian prime minister Mohammad Mossadegh came to power in 1951, APOC had been exploiting Iranian oil for years, diverting a small percentage of the profit to Iran and keeping the rest for itself. Mossadegh rightly gauged the voice of the Iranian people as demanding a greater share in their own natural resources, and nationalized the oil industry in 1951. This triggered a three-year crisis at the culmination of which, seeking to resecure Western control of Iranian oil, the Central Intelligence Agency (CIA) of the United States deposed the legitimately elected Mossadegh in a coup and reinstalled the Shah of Iran as that country's ruler.

This flamboyantly illegal act, while guaranteeing the short-term access of Iranian oil to Western powers, created a century of violent antipathy towards the West in Iran.

For twenty-five years after Operation Ajax, as the CIA called its coup, Iranian oil continued to flow to Western companies. In 1979, however, the Islamic Revolution in Iran once more returned Iranian resources to the central government, which returned to the Mossadegh model of nationalization and has retained control of the country's oil and natural gas reserves ever since. As in Mossadegh's day, Iran's control of its oil remains an important motivator of the West's contentious relationship with Iran.
Demir Barlas

Date March 15, 1951

Country Iran

Why It's Key Iran's decision to profit more from its own oil reserves caused the CIA to stage a coup against the country's prime minister, inciting a long cycle of mutual enmity between Tehran and Washington.

opposite The Anglo-Persian Oil Company's refinery at Abadan was the largest in the world.

1950–1959

280

Key Political Event
European Coal and Steel Community created

Among the visionaries who hoped that a lasting peace might be salvaged from World War II, the wisest sought to use international cooperation to restore prosperity. American aid under the Marshall Plan encouraged their efforts. The French economist Jean Monnet was the primary author of the Schuman Plan, after the French foreign minister, Robert Schuman, who guided it through complicated negotiations. The plan called for an international authority to ensure the cooperation of Western Europe's coal and steel industries, which were the core of what was thought of as "heavy industry." Schuman feared that conflicts over access to north-eastern France's iron mines and western Germany's rich coal deposits might derail reconstruction, whereas his plan would make war "not merely inconceivable but physically impossible." The

fruit of his efforts was the European Coal and Steel Community (ECSC), established by treaty on April 18, 1951. Its members were France, Italy, West Germany, Belgium, Luxembourg, and the Netherlands.

The ECSC placed the coal and steel industry under a supranational executive that had the power to direct investments, regulate prices, and allocate raw materials, without interference from the individual member states. The fact that its authority was restricted to one sector of the economy made the member states willing to embark on this daring step away from unrestricted national sovereignty. The ECSC's success laid the groundwork for the broader authority of the European Economic Community (1957) and, later, the European Union with its greatly expanded membership.
Brian Ladd

Date April 18, 1951

Country Europe

Why It's Key European unity took its first step from noble dream to practical reality.

Key Cultural Event
First transmission of color TV

The beginnings of color TV involved serious competition among television manufacturers. On July 11, 1949, the Federal Communications Commission (FCC) began hearings regarding the possibility of introducing a color service. Ten thousand pages of testimony and 256 pages of exhibits were submitted. There were three methods of creating color on screen that were competing for the national standard: the Dot Sequential approach of RCA, the Field Sequential method by CBS, and the Line Sequential proposed by Color Television Incorporated (CTI).

The CBS field system was the simplest. However, it was incompatible with the standard receivers in black and white televisions. On the other hand, RCA and CTI's images were of much poorer quality, so in 1950, the FCC adopted CBS standard.

RCA brought a lawsuit against the FCC in an attempt to stop the beginning of CBS colorcasts, but on May 28, 1951, the Supreme Court ruled in favor of CBS. Yet the delay in CBS broadcasting allowed more CBS-incompatible black and white TV sets to be sold, and when on June 25, 1951, CBS began its schedule of colored commercial programs, over ten million black and white TVs in the U.S. were unable to receive the color channel. The strategic delay by RCA had worked: CBS color broadcasting received disappointing numbers of viewers and advertising sales. In October 1951, CBS showed its last color broadcast. Eventually the television industry banded together under the sponsor of the National Television System Committee to produce compatible color television with high image quality.
Anne Hsu

Date June 25, 1951

Country USA

Why It's Key The first transmission of color TV revolutionized the way the viewing public experienced broadcasting, but ultimately failed because of industry competition.

Key Cultural Event
Salinger's *The Catcher in the Rye* published

When J. D. Salinger transferred an angst-riddled teenage character from the limited domain of his successful short stories to a full-length novel shortly after the end of World War II, the result defined a generation. With the creation of his protagonist, Holden Caulfield, Salinger introduced a fascinating psychological cross-section of the country's burgeoning postwar youth culture. Mixing intelligence with an anti-authority bent, Caulfield was instantly distinctive as the crabby narrator of *The Catcher in the Rye*. Salinger spun a fast-paced metropolitan adventure that tracked Caulfield's expulsion from the haughty private school Pencey Prep to his gradual mental breakdown over the course of several bizarre experiences in his hometown, New York City. Both funny and fraught with a strong component of

melancholia, Salinger's narrative held nothing back: Caulfield addresses readers with maddened honesty.

Throughout its existence, *Catcher* has been viewed as both consequential literature and anathema. It has been frequently banned at religious educational institutes (many of which are in the American South), but the international scholarly community has embraced Salinger's utterly distinct character, whose iconic distaste for "phonies" can be attached to nearly any American countercultural movement from the second half of the twentieth century. Salinger didn't allow the book to become a movie, so the only key to Caulfield's mind is the actual text. Much like his cantankerous protagonist, the author has remained reclusive, refusing to give interviews for nearly thirty years.
Eric Kohn

Date July 16, 1951

Country USA

Why It's Key An essential ingredient in the American canonization of literature, the book's use of explicit language and sexuality remains an object of provocation.

Fact The book continues to sell roughly 250,000 copies a year.

Key Political Event
Assassination of King Abdullah of Jordan

King Abdullah I of Jordan always had a ceremonial dagger in his belt, but the sixty-nine-year-old monarch's volatile temper was such that he didn't fully trust himself not to stab a subject in anger, so he had it soldered into its sheath.

Walking into the al-Aqsa Mosque in Jerusalem for Friday prayers, his prickly nature was in evidence. His bodyguards were crowding him, and he insisted they move back. "This is God's house," he said. "Everyone is safe here."

He and his fifteen-year-old grandson, Prince Hussein, had just stepped into the mosque when a young Arab broke through security and shot Abdullah three times in the head and chest. Prince Hussein grappled with the assailant. He was also shot in the chest, but his life was saved by a medal his grandfather had given him and insisted he wear. Within moments, the assassin and his victim were dead. The West lost one of its staunchest allies, Israel lost one of its only regional supporters, and Jordan's Hashemite Kingdom had lost a revered leader.

Abdullah's eldest son, Talal, suffered from severe mental illness and could not handle the stress of kingship. In August 1952, he abdicated in favor of his son, Prince Hussein. On May 2, 1953, Hussein formally took power, on the same day that his cousin was crowned King Feisal II of neighboring Iraq – two boy kings in charge of six million fractious Arabs. Feisal was killed in a coup in 1958; Hussein ruled until his death in 1999.

Heather Michon

Date July 20, 1951

Country Israel

Why It's Key The assassination of King Abdullah deprived the Middle East of one of its few moderate, pro-Western Arab leaders.

1950-1959

283

Key Political Event
Nehru begins Five-Year Plan

Jawaharlal Nehru, the first Prime Minister of India, inaugurated a tradition of crafting and executing Five-Year Plans that continues to this day. In 1951, the year in which the first such plan was launched, Nehru and his advisers identified and prioritized India's weak points, such as energy and agriculture. After Nehru's death, each successive Five-Year Plan continued to focus upon the most urgent and valuable initiatives available to India. By strategically targeting and mitigating weaknesses, the Indian economy grew to become one of the world's largest, leaving regional archrival Pakistan – whose economic policy is haphazard at best – far behind.

While the Five-Year Plans were socialist in inspiration, India retained the spirit rather than the letter of doctrinaire central planning. Nehru chose a consultative rather than a dictatorial approach toward the Five-Year Plans. He created a Planning Commission in March 1950, and solicited the ongoing input of a broad range of experts. The commission was chaired by the prime minister and administered by the minister of planning, a structure that has remained in place. Further parting ways from the central planning schemes of Communist countries, Nehru envisioned a compassionate and humanitarian rather than a purely materialistic role for the Five-Year Plans, which set out to combat poverty and other social ills in addition to tackling other affairs of policy. The Planning Commission survived Nehru's death and continues to be instrumental in setting India's macroeconomic direction today.

Demir Barlas

Date December 8, 1951

Country India

Why It's Key Jawaharlal Nehru's early planning policies shaped the character of independent India, which blended socialist and free market inspirations to achieve a distinct economic identity.

Key Political Event
The formation of Libya

The birth of Libya as an independent nation state was indicative of the new order being created in North Africa; as the old European empires fragmented, independence was being handed over to the Arabs.

Italy had been the colonial power in Libya, but after the defeat of Italy in the war, Italian colonial possessions came under the temporary control of the British and French. The newly formed United Nations passed a resolution calling for the creation of a Libyan state and this came into effect in late 1951, when Libya was officially recognized as an independent nation.

One man has largely defined the history of independent Libya: Colonel Muammar al-Gadaffi. Gadaffi came to power in a bloodless coup in 1969 that swept away the ruling monarchy, and it was soon evident that he intended to pursue an aggressively nationalistic policy. Gadaffi ordered the removal of British and American military bases from the region and expelled many Italian and Jewish people from Libya. He distanced himself from both of the superpowers and became a passionate supporter of a pan-Arab nation.

Gadaffi has played a significant role on the international stage and has supported several coup attempts in neighboring countries. In the past he has been widely suspected of funding terrorist and revolutionary groups worldwide. This has brought him into increasing conflict with the United States, and in 1986 President Ronald Reagan ordered a retaliatory bombing raid on Libya that killed over sixty people, including Gadaffi's young daughter.

Martin Sayers

Date December 24, 1951

Country Libya

Why It's Key The creation of Libya would eventually lead to the rise to power of Colonel Gadaffi, one of the most controversial figures on the world stage.

Key Cultural Event
Fleming's *Casino Royale* published

Over just two months in early 1952, Ian Fleming wrote *Casino Royale*. He could not have known that his protagonist James Bond, a spy who must beat a Soviet agent called Le Chiffre at poker, would go on not only to sell more than 100 million books, but also to beget the most successful film franchise of all time.

At that time, just married, Fleming was working at the Kemsley newspaper group. He had been born in London in 1908 and, like his famous creation, educated at Eton. In 1939, he joined the naval intelligence division, where, with his charm, social contacts, and gift for languages, he excelled, rising to the rank of commander and becoming one of the few people given access to top-secret Ultra intelligence. However, whereas Bond was a man of action, Fleming did most of his duty at a desk.

After the success of *Casino Royale*, Fleming went to Jamaica every year to write more of Bond's adventures, packing his skilfully plotted books with a heady cocktail of sex, violence, and brand-name luxury. His lean prose was influenced by both detective fiction and his training as a newspaper writer. By 1962, President Kennedy had listed the Bond books among his favorites, and Sean Connery had starred in *Dr No* (1962), making Fleming a worldwide celebrity. Although Fleming, a heavy smoker and drinker, died of a heart attack in 1964, his fictional progeny, an even heavier smoker and drinker, seems to be immortal.

Ned Beauman

Date January 15, 1952

Country Jamaica

Why It's Key In the first of his fourteen books about James Bond, Fleming created one of the twentieth century's most celebrated fictional characters.

opposite James Bond creator, Ian Fleming.

Key Cultural Event
Elizabeth II becomes Queen of England

When Princess Elizabeth was born on April 21, 1926, to the Duke and Duchess of York, it was never anticipated that she would become queen. Her father was the younger son of King George V and, therefore, his elder brother Edward was heir to the British throne. However, following the king's death in 1936, and Edward's abdication that same year due to his relationship with American divorcee Wallis Simpson, Elizabeth's father acceded to the throne, becoming King George VI.

As heir apparent, Princess Elizabeth married her distant cousin, Philip Mountbatten, formerly Prince Philip of Greece and Denmark, in 1947. Upon his marriage he took the title Prince Philip, Duke of Edinburgh. Once married, Elizabeth and Philip traveled widely, and it was while visiting Kenya in February 1952 that she received the devastating news that her beloved father had died of lung cancer. Princess Elizabeth, now Queen, immediately flew home to Britain. She was twenty-five years old.

Her coronation took place in Westminster Abbey on June 2, 1953, in front of more than 8,000 guests, including her son and heir Prince Charles, born in 1948. The streets of London were lined with an estimated three million people waiting to catch sight of the new monarch in the golden state coach. It was the first, and remains the only, British coronation to be broadcast on television and, while few families could afford a television set, those who could were able to watch the moving and ancient ceremony unfold.
Lorraine Brownbill

Date February 8, 1952

Country UK

Why It's Key It marked the start of Queen Elizabeth's long reign during a period of great social and political change.

Key Political Event
Batista seizes power in Cuba

Fulgencio Batista's involvement in politics began in 1933 when he was instrumental in a military coup that took control of Cuba. He was a dominant figure in the island's politics for the next seven years, and in 1940 was elected president. He ruled until 1944 when he lost an election and moved abroad.

Batista returned to Cuba in the 1950s and took part in the 1952 elections. However, his support base was small and before the elections could take place, he initiated another coup, which overthrew the government. Parliament was dissolved and it quickly became clear that Batista intended to rule Cuba as a dictator.

A young attorney named Fidel Castro had been running for a seat in parliament and was disgusted by Batista's abuse of power. Castro presented a petition to Cuba's constitutional court after the coup but, when this was unsuccessful, was forced to flee to Mexico.

Under Batista's stewardship, the Cuban economy thrived and foreign money poured into the country, but he was also corrupt, and embezzled huge sums of money from the country. He took part in brutal suppression as well; opponents were often executed and left hanging in the streets as a warning to others.

The injustices of the new dictatorship caused seething resentment in many parts of Cuba, particularly amongst the poor who saw little of the country's newfound wealth trickle down to them. Fidel Castro would later exploit these tensions on his return to Cuba.
Martin Sayers

Date March 10, 1952

Country Cuba

Why It's Key Batista's determination to rule Cuba as a dictator sowed the seeds of a revolution that would eventually lead Fidel Castro to power.

opposite Dictator Fulgencio Batista speaking to the people.

Key Cultural Event
The Moondog Coronation Ball

The Moondog Coronation Ball is not the most famous of big rock 'n' roll shows – that honor belongs to 1969's Woodstock Festival – but the event in Cleveland, Ohio, does hold the honor of being the first of its kind. Alan Freed, the New York-bound disc jockey often considered to have popularized the term "rock 'n' roll," put the concert together, assisted by Lew Platt, a local concert promoter. Among the top-billed acts were Paul Williams and his Hucklebuckers, Tiny Grimes, the Rockin' Highlanders, the Dominoes, and Danny Cobb.

Tickets ran a mere US$1.50 (US$1.75 at the door) – a bargain compared to today's hefty prices, even with inflation. Nevertheless, several concert precedents were set that night. The Arena usually played home to the Harlem Globetrotters and sporting events, so holding a concert there was a significant step, one that helped pave the way for modern-day stadium tours. Demand was higher than expected, and thanks to organizers losing track of the number of tickets (as well as counterfeiting), the ball was also the first rock show to get shut down. With an estimated 20,000 people angling for about half as many seats in the Cleveland Arena, fire marshals in fear of a riot cancelled the concert after the very first song. All in all, a fitting beginning for a genre that has often provoked teenage excitement and a correspondingly stern adult response.

David Greenwald

Date March 21, 1952

Country USA

Why It's Key The star-studded concert, hosted by influential disc jockey Alan Freed, is considered the first major rock 'n' roll show.

Fact The event was named after Freed's "Moondog Radio Show"; his listeners were known as "Moondoggers."

Key Political Event
Peasants and miners overthrow military regime

Up until 1952, Bolivia's most profitable industry – tin – was controlled by a handful of tin barons. Likewise, over 90 per cent of productive land was owned by a small group of landowners. Both mining and agriculture suffered during the Depression and again, after World War II, as production costs rose, prices fell, and high inflation resulted in economic decline, causing great hardship for Bolivia's peasants and workers. There was also mounting political turmoil when, after the 1951 presidential elections were won by Victor Paz Estenssoro, the candidate of the middle-class progressive National Revolutionary Movement (MNR), a military junta seized control of the government to prevent him taking the presidency.

National outcry turned to peasant-led hunger marches and organized social protest by unionized miners, who were strongly influenced by the revolutionary socialism of Trotsky. Finally, on April 9, 1952, the MNR launched a rebellion in the capital La Paz, distributing arms to peasants and civilians, while the disciplined and armed miners blocked troops from marching on the city. After three days of fighting, during which some six hundred people died, the demoralized army gave up, and Estenssoro became President. True to his word, he overhauled the country by granting universal suffrage, nationalizing the tin industry, raising wages, and redistributing land to the country's peasants and Indians. Despite subsequent upheavals over the next half-century, 1952's National Revolution continues to have a profound and radical effect on the political expectations of Bolivia's people.

Hedley Paul

Date April 9, 1952

Country Bolivia

Why It's Key After Mexico, the coup in Bolivia was the second major revolution in a Latin American country and the first in which the working class, principally unionized miners, played a central role in radically changing the face of Bolivia's future political landscape.

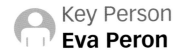

Key Person
Eva Peron

Born the illegitimate child of a poor landowner in rural Argentina, Maria Eva Duarte escaped to Buenos Aires at the age of fifteen to pursue a career as a stage, radio, and film actress. She met Colonel Juan Peron in 1944 at a charity event and they married the following year.

When Peron was elected president, Eva also became involved in politics and a supporter of Peronism, a form of socialism. She developed social programs for the *descamisados* ("the shirtless"), and founded the Eva Peron Foundation for charitable works among the poor. She also created Argentina's first major female political party, the Female Peronist Party. Her beauty, passion, and political achievements earned her huge support when she tried to run for vice president

in 1951, and she was given the official title of "Spiritual Leader of the Nation."

However, on an international level, many accused her of being a fascist and Nazi sympathizer, collaborating with her husband's oppressive propaganda regime that thinly masked fascist tendencies. Her detractors also suggested that she used charity money for her own gain, as she appeared in public in glamorous gowns. At home, the higher classes disliked Eva for her sympathies toward the poor, and both the military and elite opposed her candidacy. She died of cancer aged thirty-three on July 26, 1952, remaining adored and despised in equal measures, making her one of the most controversial women in history.

Mariko Kato

Date July 26, 1952
Born/Died 1919–1952
Nationality Argentinean
Why It's Key Eva Peron was one of the most powerful and controversial women of the twentieth century, rising from a poor, illegitimate child to the First Lady of Argentina.
Fact In 1976, Andrew Lloyd Webber and Tim Rice turned the story of Eva Peron into the smash-hit musical *Evita*.

Key Cultural Event
John Cage's *4'33"* first "performed"

The idea for *4'33"* was germinated in 1951, when John Cage visited the anechoic chamber at Harvard University. He was amazed to hear sounds in a room that was designed to absorb all noise. He later recalled: "I heard two sounds, one high and one low. When I described them to the engineer in charge, he informed me that the high one was my nervous system in operation, the low one my blood in circulation." It was this impossibility of silence that inspired Cage to compose *4'33"*. He wanted to capture the unintentional and unpredictable sounds that the players, the audience, and the surroundings naturally make.

4'33" was premiered by pianist David Tudor on August 29, 1952, in New York. Taylor sat at the piano and closed the keyboard lid, and did not hit any keys for four minutes and thirty-three seconds. To mark the

end of each movement, he opened the piano lid briefly, and timed each with a stopwatch, while turning the pages of the score.

Even though the audience was supportive of contemporary music, some people were not even aware that something was being performed, and grew outraged when they realized that they were going to hear "nothing." Cage had redefined music and silence, and he remained confident of the integrity of his work, writing in 1961: "Until I die there will be sounds. And they will continue following my death. One need not fear about the future of music."

Mariko Kato

Date August 29, 1952
Country USA
Why It's Key The first performance of this notorious work rewrote compositional philosophy in music.

Key Discovery
Crick and Watson discover the structure of DNA

On February 28, 1953, James Watson and Francis Crick announced to the regulars at the Eagle pub in Cambridge that they had discovered life's secret, the chemical structure of DNA – deoxyribonucleic acid. Their mildly inebriated audience for once had heard correctly. Watson and Crick had realized that DNA was a double helix composed of two sugar-phosphate backbones on the outside, with base pairs adenine (A), guanine (G), cytosine (C), and thymine (T) on the inside. These base pairs A, G, C, and T comprise the genetic code.

Watson and Crick had been involved in a race to discover DNA's structure with their rivals, Maurice Wilkins and Rosalind Franklin at King's College, London. Franklin used X-rays to determine the structure of DNA, and thought its structure was helical, giving a talk about her work in 1951 that Watson attended. Franklin's results aided Watson and Crick's realization that the nucleotide base pairs of DNA fit together like pieces in a puzzle, making up the steps of DNA's spiral staircase.

Watson, Crick, and Wilkins were awarded the Nobel Prize for their discovery in 1962. Rosalind Franklin, having been exposed to X-rays most of her professional life before their dangers were known, had by that time died of ovarian cancer. These four scientists' discovery of the language of heredity has subsequently made it possible to sequence the human genome, established DNA as a means of tracking identities, and has furthered our understanding of genetic disease.

Anna Marie Roos

Date February 28, 1953

Country UK

Why It's Key Watson and Crick cracked the genetic code, the chemical structure of life.

Fact DNA's spiral staircase structure appears as a pattern in the door handles of the entrance doors to the Royal Society (the world's oldest scientific institution) in London.

opposite James Watson (left) and Francis Crick with their model of part of a DNA molecule in 1953.

292

Key Political Event
Death of Stalin

On March 6, 1953, the Kremlin announced that one of the most dominant personalities of the first half of the twentieth century and the head of the Soviet Union since 1928 had died. Joseph Stalin, war leader, instigator of repression and terror, had been found five days previously on the floor of his bedroom. He was unable to speak, paralyzed down his left-hand side and convulsing along the right.

Official reports stated that he died of cerebral hemorrhage on the evening of March 5. His daughter, Svetlana, was with him – in the final moments, she reported, he opened his eyes and lifted his left hand as though to pronounce a curse, but no words were emitted. It was a suitably macabre end for a prodigious mass murderer. Some commentators have suggested assassination. Although Svetlana's description corroborates stroke-like symptoms, Stalin had disappeared from public life on February 17, and there were marked inconsistencies in the released medical bulletins. Lavrentiy Beria, the former chief of Soviet security, reportedly admitted poisoning his leader. He had urgent motive: Beria had been earmarked chief victim in Stalin's latest purge of officials. This purge had already included, in an anti-Semitic gesture, the imprisoning of numerous (mainly Jewish) doctors. When Stalin lay on his sickbed, his personal physician for many years was, at Stalin's behest, "in irons."

Following Stalin's death, the Soviet superpower and global politics inevitably changed course. Stalinism did not die with Stalin though, not least in the brutalized psyche of his people.

Michael Hallam

Date March 5, 1953

Country USSR

Why It's Key The death of Stalin was an epochal moment for the people of the Soviet Union and Cold War politics.

Key Cultural Event
The summit of Mount Everest conquered

Edmund Hillary and Tenzing Norgay were members of the 1953 British Everest Expedition, sponsored by the Royal Geographical Society and the Alpine Club. The team was led by Colonel John Hunt, and included a physiologist, a cameraman, and a correspondent from *The Times* newspaper. Hillary and Norgay were no strangers to Mount Everest. In 1951, Hillary had been one of the members of the expedition that discovered the southern route to the summit, and Norgay had reached the record height of 8,599 meters in 1952.

After three weeks' training on neighboring mountains, the team started on their expedition and established camp at the South Col at 7,900 meters. When an initial attempt to reach the top by another pair of climbers failed, Hunt directed Hillary and Norgay to attempt the summit.

They approached it from the southern face, and blessed with good weather, open-circuit oxygen equipment, and their own climbing expertise, Hillary and Norgay reached the peak, at 8,847 meters, at 11.30 a.m. local time. They embraced each other, and Hillary took photographs of Norgay waving flags of Britain, Nepal, the United Nations, and India. Norgay buried some sweets in the snow as a Buddhist offering and Hillary left a crucifix that Hunt had given him. They could only stay there for fifteen minutes because of the oxygen supply.

Their achievement boosted the spirit of the time, when countries were still recovering from World War II. Both men were knighted on their return, and Norgay was awarded the George Medal.

Mariko Kato

Date May 29, 1953

Country Nepal/Tibet

Why It's Key It was the first time that man stood on the highest possible point on the planet.

Fact Edmund Hillary of New Zealand and Tenzing Norgay of Nepal became the first climbers to reach the summit of Mount Everest on the Nepal-Tibet border.

opposite Edmund Hillary ascends Mount Everest for the first time.

Key Political Event
Execution of Julius and Ethel Rosenberg

In the early 1950s, the United States and the Soviet Union vied for technological supremacy and political influence around the world, while Americans worried that communist spies and collaborators were seeking to weaken the "Free World" from within. Politicians like Joseph McCarthy and Richard Nixon made their reputations by trying to root out subversives, often through public hearings in Congress. It was in this climate of fear that Americans learned that Julius Rosenberg, an engineer who worked on the atomic bomb project, might have given secrets to the Soviets.

Most scholars believe that the FBI charged his wife Ethel as a "lever" to make Julius confess, since no solid evidence tied her to espionage activities. Both of the Rosenbergs, however, were electrocuted at New York's Sing Sing prison on June 19, 1953, and debate

over their innocence or guilt has raged ever since. Their supporters claim that the two fell prey to Cold War hysteria, and that the documents that Julius had transmitted to the KGB hardly constituted the "secret of the atomic bomb." Most controversial of all was the use of the death penalty in an unclear case, especially for Ethel.

On the other hand, the Venona Project, a joint U.S.-U.K. operation to decode Soviet spy messages, released documents in 1995 that strongly implicate Julius as an active Soviet agent. Due to this controversy, their execution came to symbolize how the quest for national security can trump due process of law and individual liberty in a time of fear.

Alex Cummings

Date June 19, 1953

Country USA

Why It's Key The electrocution of two alleged spies showed that both the Cold War and anti-communist hysteria were heating up in postwar America.

Key Political Event
Fidel Castro's first attempt at revolution

Few could have predicted that Fidel Castro Ruiz, a graduate of the University of Havana's law school, would come out of nowhere to challenge the legitimacy of strongman Fulgencio Batista's rule. The latter, who had already held the presidency between 1933 and 1944, returned to power in 1952 in a coup, suspending the 1940 democratic constitution and assuming dictatorial powers. In the wake of Batista's coup, Cuba's nationalist opposition was suffering from an acute leadership vacuum after the corrupt and inept rule of Carlos Prío and the suicide of charismatic leader Eduardo Chibás. Into this vacuum stepped Castro, a protegé of Chibás determined to deal a decisive blow to Batista's authority. Along with his brother Raúl and other allies, he chose the Moncada barracks of Santiago de Cuba, one of the country's largest military garrisons, as the target of an audacious assault on the ruling regime.

In military terms, the attack was a catastrophic failure. Poorly armed and badly outnumbered, the rebels were routed: of Castro's approximately 160 companions, 60 were killed in the assault and dozens more were captured and tortured to death by Batista's police. However, the attack would provide Castro with a highly public platform from which to galvanize popular sentiment against Batista. The speech he delivered at his trial ("history will absolve me!") became the manifesto for what was quickly dubbed the July 26 Movement. From prison and later from exile in Mexico, Castro would convert this movement into a full-fledged revolutionary force.

Geoffrey A. Schullenberger

Date July 26, 1953

Country Cuba

Why It's Key The twenty-six-year-old Castro's assault on the Moncada barracks established him as the leader of the movement to overthrow U.S.-backed dictator Fulgencio Batista.

Key Political Event
Korean Armistice signed but never promulgated

After two years of stalemate, agreement to a ceasefire saw the Korean War enter a state of indefinite hiatus. The two sides withdrew two kilometers to positions in which they would remain, facing each other in a state of constant alert, even as their ranks were replaced by second and third generations. The *de facto* new border left the countries in largely the same geographical shape as they were before the war, but with profoundly altered national characters.

For North Korean leader Kim Il-Sung, the armistice was a humiliation on many levels. Not only had he failed in his attempt to unite the Korean peninsula, but his actions had led to the indignity of Korea's destiny, once again, being placed largely in the hands of foreign powers. His authority extremely tenuous, and within three days Kim had begun to order the execution of senior party rivals. In due course, all party factions but Kim's own were purged, the official history of the war completely and crudely rewritten, and a culture of fear and repression created in which critical discussion, of the war or any other matter, became impossible.

On the other side of the Demilitarized Zone, the decades following the armistice saw the political dominance of South Korea by militarist forces which used the threat from the North to justify their authoritarian rule, and it took thirty-four years for a fully liberal democracy to emerge. Meanwhile border skirmishes claimed over a thousand lives – a reminder that the war remained unconcluded.

James Handley

Date July 27, 1953

Country North Korea/ South Korea

Why It's Key Technically no more than a ceasefire, the armistice marked a cessation of hostilities in the twentieth century's longest war.

Key Political Event
Britain suspends Guyana's constitution

After World War II, Britain found itself in a position where it was unfeasible to carry on with a large overseas empire. The 1950s saw the process of decolonization gather pace as Britain's dominions were prepared for independence.

In British Guiana in South America, the move toward independence was started by free elections taking place in 1953. The main winner was the left-wing People's Progressive Party (PPP), led by Cheddi Jagan, which won eighteen out of twenty-four seats in the new parliament. Jagan became prime minister and quickly embarked on a series of radical reforms.

The new government was suspected of encouraging a wave of strikes and demonstrations and Jagan's pro-communist views were causing serious concern in London and Washington.

After just a few months, and despite the government being democratically elected, the British took action. Jagan was deposed, the new constitution was suspended, and British troops were sent to the country to keep order.

The constitution was restored four years later but Guyanese politics continued to be stormy. From 1961 to 1964, severe rioting and fighting between rival political factions and a long general strike led to the return of British troops. Guyana finally achieved full independence in 1966.

Britain's willingness to use force to suppress the Jagan government showed that, despite a willingness to withdraw from empire, regimes that were deemed dangerous to British interests would not be tolerated.
Martin Sayers

Date October 9, 1953

Country Guyana

Why It's Key The incident showed that, while Britain was prepared to decolonize, it would not tolerate unacceptable regimes.

Key Discovery
Link between smoking and lung cancer discovered

In 1950, Sir Richard Doll first posited the link between smoking and lung cancer, which has become commonplace knowledge in the twentieth and twenty-first centuries. Doll, an epidemiologist of considerable reputation, undertook research alongside Austin Bradford Hill to discover the causes behind the noticeable increase in deaths from lung cancer. Initially expecting to find a link between the cancer and pollution, the expansion of the motor industry, or the recently introduced tarmac, Doll and Hill designed a questionnaire to be answered by 650 patients in London suspected to have cancer.

Although the link between lip cancer and pipe smoking had been acknowledged, the prevalence of cigarette smoking meant that any link with cancer was highly controversial. However, the striking correlation between smoking and the diagnosis of cancer demonstrated by Doll's survey provided almost incontrovertible evidence that smoking was a contributory factor to lung cancer. Repeating the study in other English cities brought about identical results; those who smoked were diagnosed with lung cancer while those who had not smoked were not. The British Medical Journal published the results of this investigation in 1950, but the link was not accepted until 1954 when a further study corroborated the results. More recent evidence demonstrates that approximately 87 per cent of lung cancer patients smoked, and the understanding and increasing awareness of the link has undoubtedly saved many lives since 1954.
Hannah Furness

Date 1954

Country UK

Why It's Key The understanding of the link between smoking and lung cancer has enabled people to significantly reduce the risk of contracting the disease.

Key Cultural Event
Golding's *Lord of the Flies* published

In 1954, William Golding, then aged forty-four years old, published his first novel, *Lord of the Flies*. Though he would go on to publish fifteen more books, including novels, essays, and plays, his first remains his most famous.

The novel details the fate of some boys shipwrecked on a beautiful island. They have to fend for themselves, and gradually the group develops its own peculiar and dangerous dynamic. A ship eventually rescues them, but by that time, some are dead and those who survived have lost their innocence. Written just after World War II, the events in the novel can easily map onto what happened in Hitler's Germany, or Stalin's Russia. It has been described as an allegory, a simple story whose wider resonances give it a mythic quality.

Golding had already been a schoolmaster, a lecturer, a sailor, an actor, and a musician when he wrote *Lord of the Flies*, and sent it to twenty-one publishers before succeeding in getting it published. The novel quickly became a bestseller in the United States and Europe. It has since been dramatized for the stage and radio, and was made into a film in 1963 and again in 1990. The novel's success meant that Golding could quit his teaching job and dedicate himself full-time to writing. In 1980, he won the Booker Prize for his novel *Rites of Passage*, and he was awarded the Nobel Prize for Literature in 1983. Golding died of heart failure in 1993 at his home in Cornwall.

Frieda Klotz

Date 1954

Country UK

Why It's Key Written soon after World War II and depicting the darkness of human behavior, *Lord of the Flies* was a bestselling novel worldwide; it also received critical approval.

Fact When Golding died in 1993, he left a manuscript for a novel titled *The Double Tongue*, which was published posthumously.

Key Political Event
The Battle of Dien Bien Phu

After Word War II, France had reinstated its colonial government in Indochina. However, almost immediately they faced a Nationalist Vietnamese independence movement led by Ho Chi Minh.

The French, in an attempt to cut off the supply lines of the Communist Viet Minh forces, set up an Air Base at Dien Bien Phu, in the north of Vietnam. The airbase was located at the bottom of a bowl-shaped river valley, and due to this location, the French were only able to receive their supplies by air from Hanoi.

Ho Chi Minh's forces surrounded the French air base, and on March 13, 1954, began the attack. Within days, France's outlying firebases were overrun, and shortly after, the French airstrip was out of action completely, cutting the base off from the outside world.

The siege continued, with the surrounded French army enduring terrible conditions and severe casualties, until, on May 7, Dien Bien Phu fell to Ho Chi Minh. Over 2,200 French soldiers had been killed and many more thousands were taken prisoner. It was a humiliating defeat for the French that severely damaged the nation's psyche and brought an end to French Indochina.

Following the French withdrawal, Vietnam was divided into a Communist North and a quasi-democratic South. The stage had been set for America's entry into the Vietnam War in 1965.

John Owen

Date March 13–May 7 1954

Country Vietnam

Why It's Key The battle marked the end of French Indochina and paved the way for American involvement in Vietnam a decade later.

opposite Viet Minh troops take Dien Bien Phu, occupied by the French. Parachutists are sent in as support for French troops.

Key Cultural Event
Racial segregation deemed illegal in public schools

The election of Rutherford B. Hayes as President of the United States in 1876 signaled the end of efforts to force the southern states to comply with laws passed during post-Civil War Reconstruction. In response, Jim Crow laws were enacted, segregating African-Americans in all aspects of public life. Legislators attempted to comply with national dictates by instituting the "separate but equal" doctrine to justify segregation in areas such as education, transportation, and public accommodation. Jim Crow laws also prevented African-Americans from voting for politicians who would change discriminatory laws.

In 1954, the Supreme Court bundled five school desegregation cases under the name, *Brown v. Board of Education of Topeka*. In a stunning victory for the civil rights movement, the court unanimously rejected the "separate but equal" doctrine, holding that separate could not be equal and ordering U.S. schools to integrate. Several states reacted with violence, and the National Guard units were called in to protect African-American students and restore order.

The *Brown* decision provided a foundation for a plethora of civil rights cases that eventually overturned legal forms of discrimination throughout the United States. Congress responded by enacting the Civil Rights Act of 1964 and the Voting Rights of 1965, which restored political and economic rights to African-Americans. Although *Brown* initially did little to change entrenched cultural attitudes, the case served as a foundation for reform and propelled the civil rights movement onto the global stage.

Elizabeth R. Purdy

Date May 19, 1954

Country USA

Why It's Key The *Brown* decision opened the door for U.S. courts to find segregation illegal in most aspects of public life and turned the attention of the world to issues of racial discrimination.

Fact After the failure of Reconstruction, many states passed Jim Crow laws that denied rights to African-Americans that had been previously granted.

Key Cultural Event
Tolkien's *The Fellowship of the Ring* published

English writer and philologist John Ronald Reuel Tolkien (1892–1973) was born in South Africa. After serving as a lieutenant in World War I, he worked at the Oxford English Dictionary, and later became an academic at Oxford University, first as Professor of Anglo-Saxon and later as Professor of English Language and Literature.

Known for his expertise in languages and his fantasy fiction, Tolkien wrote *The Lord of the Rings* as a sequel to *The Hobbit* (1937), which, originally written for his children, had become a great success. Set in the Third Age of the imaginary world Middle-earth, the story follows hobbit Frodo Baggins, the unassuming nephew of the protagonist in *The Hobbit*, as he leaves his quiet Shire to destroy the "One Ring" that had been created long ago by the Dark Lord Sauron and whose evil power threatens to conquer the world. With the help of the enigmatic wizard Gandalf and elf, dwarf, and human friends, Frodo embarks on an epic quest for good against evil.

A devout Roman Catholic, Tolkien weaves many theological themes into his work, as well as Norse mythology, philosophy, and fairy tales. Although the initial reviews were mixed, the trilogy won the International Fantasy Award in 1957, and has since sold over one hundred million copies. Tolkien set the tone and found the audience for high fantasy in modern literature, maintained even decades later by other high-grossing writers such as J. K. Rowling and Phillip Pullman.

Mariko Kato

Date July 21, 1954

Country UK

Why It's Key Since its initial publication, *The Lord of the Rings* trilogy has been reprinted several times in many different languages, and remains one of the most popular works in literary history.

Fact The trilogy consists of the novels *The Fellowship of the Ring* (published July 21, 1954), *The Two Towers* (November 11, 1954) and *The Return of the King* (October 20, 1955).

Key Discovery
First successful organ transplant

While the concept of transplant surgery can be found in medical textbooks as early as 700 BCE, where Indian doctor Sushruta describes rebuilding a patient's nose by skin graft, the reality of a successful transplant was not realized until the twentieth century. While surgeons Hua T'O and Pien Ch'isi recorded transplanting organs between patients in third century China, it was only after extensive experimentation with animal organs and several desperate operations on dying patients that transplant surgery between humans became conceivably possible in the modern era.

Initial attempts at transplanting organs were thwarted by the problem of rejection, with the early 1950s seeing several failed attempts at kidney transplants. But as physician Karl Landsteiner classified four different types of blood and Macfarlane Burnet extended medical understanding of the body's immune response system, organ transplant became possible. In 1954, at the Peter Bent Brigham hospital in Boston, Massachusetts, Dr Joseph Murray successfully transplanted a kidney from twenty-four year old Ronald Herrick to his identical twin brother Richard. The operation allowed Richard to live a further eight years and demonstrated that successful organ transplant was indeed possible. As other surgeons performed a successful pancreas transplant in 1966 and both a liver and heart transplant the following year, the work of Dr Joseph Murray laid the foundations of transplant surgery that now saves thousands of lives each year.
Hannah Furness

Date December 23, 1954

Country USA

Why It's Key The first successful kidney transplant laid the foundations for a life-saving procedure, beginning a new era in modern medicine.

Key Cultural Event
Fats Domino's "Ain't that a Shame" released

When popular music in the American South started to be recorded in the early twentieth century, producers ran into a problem they didn't expect: black musicians and white musicians often sound the same when recorded. But in a segregated society, artists could only sell music to members of their own race. Savvy producers realized this, and started to label music recorded by whites as "hillbilly" records and music recorded by African-Americans as "race" records.

It is no surprise that the racial melting pot of New Orleans was the home of many of the artists who first challenged the race line, and as a result, created a new genre: rock 'n' roll. The smooth-voiced baritone Fats Domino, who began his career in 1947 as a nineteen-year-old singer at the Hideaway Club, worked with the producer and songwriter Dave Bartholomew to record a series of hits in the 1950s, including the path-breaking "Ain't that a Shame" in 1955.

The song took off with white teenagers, many of whom thought Domino was a country singer, and a Pat Boone cover of the song the same year helped make listening to black artists acceptable for whites. Domino went on to score sixty-one rhythm and blues hits, and sixty-six hits on the pop chart, making him second only to Elvis in the first decade of rock 'n' roll. Ironically, Domino became more popular with white audiences than African-Americans, who preferred the harder edge of rhythm and blues.
Martin Johnson

Date April 14, 1955

Country USA

Why It's Key By breaking the color line in popular music, Fats Domino opened the door for other black musicians in search of a wider audience and enabled white musicians to borrow black genres of music.

Fact Unlike Little Richard, Elvis Presley, and other rock 'n' roll stars of the 1950s, Domino was considered to be a clean-cut and respectful young adult by the parents of the period.

Key Cultural Event
Ray Kroc buys McDonald's

The mastermind behind the franchising of McDonald's – Ray Kroc – represents capitalism in its most raw form. Whether you see the Golden Arches as an evil symbol of globalization or a beacon of American industry, it's impossible not to acknowledge the influence of Kroc's entrepreneurship.

A piano player and Red Cross ambulance driver, Kroc was making his living peddling paper cups in the 1930s when he ran into Earl Prince, inventor of a five-spindle blender. Intrigued by the machine's efficiency, Kroc negotiated a deal to distribute the product nationwide. His travels brought him to a new burger joint in San Bernardino, California, owned by brothers Richard and Mac McDonald. Immediately, Ray Kroc was enamored with the McDonalds brothers' business model: they cut the price of burgers, narrowed down the menu to burgers, fries, malts, and soda, and eliminated car hops–plus, they were using eight of the five-spindle blenders at once. He secured exclusive franchising rights and established McDonald's Corp. in 1955. That same year, Kroc opened his first McDonald's in Chicago. In 1961, he bought out the McDonald brothers for US$2.7 million, and by 1963, over a billion hamburgers had been sold. He died in 1984 with a family fortune of over US$500 million.

Stressing quality, service, cleanliness, and value, Kroc built an empire that changed the way Americans eat. Piggybacking on the McDonald's brothers' ingenuity, he was responsible for turning a novel idea into a global phenomenon.
Chris Schonberger

Date April 15, 1955

Country USA

Why It's Key The consummate entrepreneur, Kroc franchised McDonald's and turned the idea of fast food into a worldwide phenomenon.

opposite McDonald's owner Ray Kroc eating hamburger.

304

Key Political Event
The Asian-African Conference in Bandung

In April 1955, twenty-nine Asian and African nations gathered at Bandung, Indonesia, for the Asian-African Conference. The conference was convened by the Colombo Five: Indonesia, Ceylon, Burma, India, and Pakistan. As Indonesia's President Sukarno proclaimed in his opening speech, it was "the first intercontinental conference of colored peoples in the history of mankind," and it marked the end of the era of European imperialism that had steadily encroached upon Asia and Africa since the fifteenth century.

The conference took place against the backdrop of Cold War politics, which saw the world divided into two contending ideological blocs. Though the delegates at Bandung were acutely aware of the communist-capitalist neuroses attempting to permeate the event, this overlooked the deeper currents running through the conference. Black American writer Richard Wright, an observer at Bandung, wrote in his book *The Colour Curtain: A Report on the Bandung Conference* that this was no "mere episode in the Cold War," but "sixty-five per cent of the human race [asking] how shall the human race be organized?"

The twenty-nine delegates at Bandung were there to assert their right to self-determination, to claim their entitlements enshrined in the recent United Nations Declaration of Human Rights, and to denounce racialism and colonialism. Though the conference was hailed a success and it was vowed that the Bandung Spirit would be kept alive, a subsequent conference to be held in Algeria in 1965 never eventuated as many of the nations present fell into conflict.
Sally Percival Wood

Date April 18, 1955

Country Indonesia

Why It's Key The Bandung Conference was the first international gathering of Asian and African nation states. Although there were observers from the West, no "white" nations were invited. The conference marked the beginning of the Non-Alignment Movement, and brought together the nations that would form what was later described as the Third World.

Key Political Event
The signing of the Warsaw Pact

Economic, political, and military ties between the Soviet Union and Eastern Europe, burgeoning in the last year of World War II (often due to the tactical presence of the Red Army) and developed in the immediate postwar, were formally expressed and ratified in Warsaw on May 14, 1955.

The original signatories of the treaty constituted all the then socialist states of Eastern and central Europe except Yugoslavia: Albania (who later withdrew), Bulgaria, Czechoslovakia, East Germany, Hungary, Poland, Romania, and, of course, the USSR. One of the central elements of the pact was, in effect, a military alliance. The states undertook to assist one another militarily in the event of any one state being attacked.

Soviet historiography emphasized that the Warsaw Treaty Organization (WTO) was a response to the inherent threats in the inception of NATO (and especially the admittance of West Germany), but in some areas the ostensibly counterpart organizations were radically divergent. To many Western observers, the WTO was a *de facto* Soviet institution, a means for the superpower to extend its influence and control into Europe and expand its military and diplomatic resources. Article 8 of the treaty, promising no "interfering in one another's internal affairs," did not remain inviolate as Soviet intervention forces entered Hungary (1956) and Czechoslovakia (1968). Nonetheless, the idea of collective decision-making was not entirely a façade, and the WTO provided a platform for European Communism to negotiate strategy throughout the Cold War.

Michael Hallam

Date May 14, 1955

Country Poland

Why It's Key The Warsaw Pact formalized the military division between the two power blocs of the Cold War.

Key Cultural Event
First Disney theme park opens

Although he dreamed up Mickey Mouse, Walt Disney was hardly just an animator. Having achieved success with his own studio and a handful of globally popular family films, Disney began to tap into his real talent as an inventor. Fielding requests from fans to tour the Disney Studio lot, he realized the potential to turn such desires into a commodity. While visiting theme parks with his family, Disney began to visualize one of his own. Originally calling it Disneylandia, the mogul purchased 160 acres in southern California to build his vision. One year and US$17 million in expenses after construction began, Disneyland opened to the public in a frenzy of media attention and fan fervor. The place was filled with rides and attractions of all sorts, with employees dressed up as characters from popular Disney films helping to turn the realm of Disneyland into a wholly distinct realm of fantasy.

Realizing this dream while in his mid-fifties, Disney had reached the climax of his entrepreneurial career (he died in 1966). Surrounding the theme park with the Disneyland Railroad, Disney was able to completely contain the elements of his creation in order to capitalize on their profitability and bring his fantastical conceits to life. To this day, Disneyland and its many manifestations all over the world continue to represent the duality of mainstream entertainment, well funded to the point of creating marvelous amusements, but ultimately sustained by financial prerogatives. It was a dichotomy that Disney knew too well.

Eric Kohn

Date July 17, 1955

Country USA

Why It's Key The concept of a franchise-based theme park revolutionized the methodologies of moneymaking in the entertainment industry by bringing the movies to life.

Fact The park has only made three unscheduled closures since it opened: following the assassination of JFK, a Yippie (Youth International Party) demonstration, and the attacks of September 11, 2001, respectively.

Key Cultural Event
Nabakov's *Lolita* published

Russian-American author Vladimir Nabakov (1899–1977) wrote his first literary works in Russian, but became internationally renowned for his English prose and, in particular, his tragicomedy novel *Lolita*. However, not all of the attention was positive. The publication of *Lolita* was considered scandalous for its controversial theme. Written as a prison memoir, the novel follows the voice of narrator Humbert Humbert, who recalls his pedophilic obsessions. When he becomes fixated with a twelve-year-old girl, Dolores Haze, he marries her mother so that he can remain close to her. When the mother discovers this she flees with Dolores, and a long and anguished chase ensues, to dramatically tragic consequences.

Four American publishers refused the novel before it found support from the avant-garde publisher Olympia Press in Paris. When it crossed the English Channel, it was rapturously received, with prominent English author Graham Greene naming it one of the best novels of the year in an interview with *The London Times*. However, the British Home Office panicked at the novel's popularity and ordered copies to be seized, followed shortly thereafter by French authorities. The ban was not lifted until two years later.

The work remains infamous for its content, but is also celebrated for its innovative style. Although the controversy of its erotic subject is often the overbearing impression of the work, it is significant for its wry critique of American culture and sophisticated use of English, with its elaborate wordplay, puns, and anagrams.

Mariko Kato

Date September 1, 1955

Country France

Why It's Key *Lolita* is one of the most controversial, and most innovative, works in twentieth-century literature.

Key Discovery
George de Mestral forms Velcro SA

In 1943, engineer George de Mestral was on a walk with his dog in the Swiss Alps when the dog got its fur matted with grass burrs. Out of curiosity, de Mestral examined these cockleburs, the plant's seed sacs, under a microscope to understand why they stuck to the dog and to his own trousers. He found that the burrs that tormented his dog have small hooks that adhere to the loops in fur and fabric, giving him the idea for a new clothes fastener – Velcro.

De Mestral had patented his first invention – a toy airplane – when he was twelve years old, so it was not surprising that he made invention his full-time vocation. He quit his job as an engineer and with a US$150,000 bank loan, de Mestral set out to find a fabric that would mimic the "hook-and-loop" fastening power of the grass burr. Partnering with a company from Lyon, a world center for weaving, de Mestral produced a workable prototype in cotton that proved too expensive to manufacture, eventually switching to nylon. In 1951, Velcro was patented in Switzerland, and a few years later, de Mestral formed Velcro SA, a multinational company that offers a range of specialty fasteners, including some composed of resin. Velcro is used for everything from shoe ties, picture hangers, and sewing tape to industrial applications. Nature's brilliant design and de Mestral's keen eye together created a product with real sticking power.

Anna Marie Roos

Date September 13, 1955

Country Switzerland

Why It's Key This unique hook-and-loop fastener has revolutionized the clothing industry.

Fact Velcro is a combination of the words "velour" and "crochet."

Key Cultural Event
Rebel Without a Cause released

Movie stars have been around as long as the movies, but few have retained such iconic resonance as James Dean. When the twenty-four-year-old actor appeared as the angry teenage protagonist in *Rebel Without a Cause*, he was at the height of fame, living like a free spirit both onscreen and off. The movie, directed by Nicolas Ray, follows a troubled outsider (the usual focus of Ray's work), Jim Spark, whose family moves to a new town, forcing the young man to cultivate a fresh social life. With a tough attitude and a smooth swagger, Dean seemed born to play Jim. He was a hunk for the new generation of post-World War II apathy, when the country's self-satisfaction ran diametrically opposite to the angst-riddled youth culture. Wooing a local girl (Natalie Wood) and standing up to local bullies, Jim represented a hardened individualism in the new generation of American nonconformists.

Beyond its social ramifications, *Rebel Without a Cause* offered viewers a vibrant, highly stylized experience. The scene where Jim faces off against other high school students in a car race referred to as a "chicken run" defined filmic suspense mechanisms. The dramatic confrontations between him and his parents had emotional strength that remains potent to this day. Eventually, the movie became Dean's tragic legacy, as he was killed in a car accident later in the year. Eerily enough, the actor's death didn't immediately dampen his success, since he was posthumously nominated for two performances in *East of Eden* (1955) and *Giant* (1956).
Eric Kohn

Date October 27, 1955

Country USA

Why It's Key James Dean's performance introduced the world to a new generation of youth rebellion.

Fact The plot was based on a real case study of a rebellious teenager.

opposite **Poster for *Rebel Without a Cause*.**

Key Cultural Event
Tynan and Hobson review *Waiting For Godot*

Samuel Beckett's *Waiting For Godot* received its London premiere on August 3, 1955, directed by Peter Hall for an audience of barely three hundred people. Originally written in French, the play follows two tramps, Vladimir and Estragon, waiting by the road for a man who will never arrive. It rejected traditional literary naturalism, returning theater to its metaphorical roots and turning doubt and uncertainty into tense action.

At this time, Kenneth Tynan of the *Observer* and Harold Hobson of the *Sunday Times* – two of the twentieth century's greatest critics – maintained a fierce rivalry, but the Sunday following the premiere, they for once agreed: the play represented a turning point in modern drama, a peerless example of European absurdism on the British stage.

Initially, they were almost alone in their view. Although *Waiting For Godot* provoked enough controversy that it was able to transfer from the tiny Arts Theatre Club to the West End's Criterion Theatre, it also attracted great hostility from the "old guard" – most notably from Terence Rattigan, the most successful playwright of the past ten years, who condemned the play for its lack of story and character. Often as much as half the audience would walk out during the interval. But the discussion did not die down, and *The Times* even ended up sending their reviewer a second time, so he might grudgingly reconsider his dismissive first review.
Ned Beauman

Date 1955

Country UK

Why It's Key These rapturous reviews helped Beckett's controversial play become acknowledged as one of the greatest works of twentieth-century drama.

JAMES DEAN

... the
bad boy
from a
good family

WARNER BROS.' CHALLENGING DRAMA
OF TODAY'S TEENAGE VIOLENCE!

REBEL WITHOUT A CAUSE

x

CINEMASCOPE · WARNERCOLOR

1950-1959

also starring **NATALIE WOOD** with **SAL MINEO**

Screen Play by STEWART STERN · Produced by DAVID WEISBART

Key Cultural Event
Rosa Parks arrested

On December 1, 1955, Rosa Parks was catapulted into the spotlight as African-Americans mobilized under the leadership of Dr. Martin Luther King Jr. to force Montgomery, Alabama to revise their policy that allowed white bus riders to sit in the front while African-Americans were relegated to the back of the bus, even when the first ten seats were empty.

After a long day of work as a seamstress, Mrs Parks boarded a bus and sat down in the section reserved for whites only. Late in the afternoon, during peak time for people leaving work, the bus began to fill and when a white man entered, she refused to move. The bus driver alerted police who promptly arrested Parks and fingerprinted her. The eyes of the country were thrust on the dignified, soft-spoken woman whereupon civil rights leaders used her case to spotlight the racial injustice of Montgomery's bus system.

The boycott lasted well into the middle of 1956 when the Federal Court ruled it was unconstitutional to have separate seating for African-Americans on city buses. This marked a significant victory for the civil rights movement, but Mrs Parks' name and face had become synonymous with the boycott in Alabama and across the country. Unable to obtain work, she and her family left Montgomery with the satisfaction that her courageous act provided the civil rights movement with the energy needed to push for the equality of all citizens of the United States.

Yvonne Sims

Date December 1, 1955

Country USA

Why It's Key Parks' arrest provided the catalyst to launch the Montgomery Alabama Boycotts, which lasted from 1955 to 1956.

opposite Rosa Parks sits in the front of a bus in Montgomery, Alabama, after the Supreme Court ruled segregation illegal on the city bus system.

Key Cultural Event
Pop Art begins

Richard Hamilton's *What Is It That Makes Today's Homes So Different, So Appealing?* was first shown at the influential "This is Tomorrow" exhibition held in London in August 1954. It is identified by some art historians as one of the first and seminal works of Pop Art, the artistic movement that borrowed from popular culture and legitimized use of its images as a subject for gallery art.

Hamilton's collage is a kaleidoscope of pop culture: "Zabo," the bodybuilder in the center of the piece, even clutches a lollipop (with POP written on it) to emphasize its approach. A burlesque dancer is transported to a sofa in the strange domestic scene, and the film *The Jazz Singer* is advertised through the back window. Although its 1950s inception was in British galleries, Pop Art was indebted to and reflected Americana, especially Hollywood cinema and mass commercial culture. Unsurprisingly, Pop Art subsequently found an outlet in American art through the 1960s, with the images of Andy Warhol and Roy Liechtenstein becoming the most reproduced and iconic work of the era. Pop Art utilized popular visual rhetoric in all its forms, from billboards and comic strips to supermarket products. Artists like Hamilton were equally prepared to engage with different practical techniques and media, such as photo-collage, silk-screen, and airbrushing. The unrestrained ethos of Pop Art both suited its historical moment, the social changes of the 1950s and 1960s, and helped liberate, in a still discernible trend, the subject matter of modern art.

Michael Hallam

Date 1956

Country UK

Why It's Key The birth of Pop Art transformed the traditional subject matter and expression of visual art, especially in Britain and the United States.

Key Discovery
Flat-pack furniture invented

For thousands of years, people buying furniture were stuck with having to transport it home in its full bulk; Gilles Lundgren made this process simultaneously far more convenient and far more difficult. It sounds like a simple idea, purchasing your beds and chairs in their component parts and then assembling them yourself, but it apparently took an incident akin to Newton and his apple for Lundgren to realize the possibilities of the flat pack. Once he had failed to fit his table into his car, so the story goes, he told his bosses at IKEA that cutting the legs off would make all the difference. Anyone since who has had trouble putting together Plank G with Screw 67 should thank Gilles Lundgren.

The idea of flat-pack furniture revolutionized the fortunes of IKEA, a company founded in 1943 by Ingvar Kamprad, which originally sold pens, picture frames, and watches, among other items. In 1947, they started selling furniture, and in 1955, they began designing their own range. Gilles Lundgren, in pioneering the mass-production of furniture as envisaged by Alvar Aalto and the Bauhaus – simple, well made, cheap – gave IKEA the launch it needed. There are now 260 stores in dozens of countries with nearly six hundred million visitors a year and an annual turnover of €20.6 billion. Moreover, furniture manufacturers from all over the world have adopted the ready-to-assemble furniture designed by Lundgren, flat-packing everything from couches to swing sets.

Ben Spero

Date 1956

Country Sweden

Why It's Key Gilles Lundgren's legendary failure to fit his table into his car led to the meteoric rise of global furniture giant IKEA.

1950–1959

313

Key Cultural Event
Elvis releases "Heartbreak Hotel"

"Well, since my baby left me, I found a new place to dwell. It's down at the end of lonely street, at Heartbreak Hotel."

There would have been few teenagers across America in 1956 not familiar with these opening lines of Elvis Presley's first hit record. Released by record label RCA, "Heartbreak Hotel" sold over 300,000 copies in its first three weeks after release, and topped *Billboard*'s pop singles chart for eight weeks, eventually selling over one million copies.

Elvis grew up in the poorest of circumstances in Tupelo, Mississippi. He moved to Memphis as a teenager where he was influenced by the music of blues, country, and gospel. Signed originally by Sun Records in 1954, he released five singles with the legendary label, attracting a substantial Southern fan base. When Colonel Tom Parker took over his management, he sold Elvis' recording contract to RCA and "Heartbreak Hotel," "Love Me Tender," and "All Shook Up" were released in quick succession. Between 1956 and 1958, Elvis dominated the charts and became an international sensation. His erotic performing style and rebellious image won him millions of fans among white middle-class teenagers, but parents were less than impressed by his swiveling hips and curled lip.

Elvis led the way for a musical revolution, bringing the black music of blues and gospel to a white audience. He played a huge part in establishing rock 'n' roll, and remains one of the most popular and influential performers of the twentieth century.

Lorraine Brownbill

Date January 27, 1956

Country USA

Why It's Key The song introduced a new era of American music, confronting the cultural and racial barriers prevalent at that time.

opposite Elvis Presley holding a framed gold record of "Heartbreak Hotel."

Key Person
Khruschev denounces Stalin

In 1956, three years after the death of Josef Stalin, the Soviet Premier Nikita Khruschev made a secret speech to the 20th Congress of the Communist Party, denouncing his predecessor as a brutal dictator. Throughout his thirty-one years in power, Stalin developed a "cult of personality" to promote his image as a humane, just, and compassionate father-figure; Khruschev's speech laid bare the reality underlying this façade, revealing the climate of "suspicion, fear, and terror" that Stalin's leadership involved.

Khruschev detailed the numerous appalling atrocities carried out under Stalin's orders, including the purges of 1936–1938 (in which 30,000 of the armed forces were killed), the murder of Kirov (for which Stalin had other members of the Politburo tried and executed), and the assassination of 98 out of 139 members of the Central Committee from 1937–1938. Khruschev also revealed that Lenin's last will and testament had explicitly advised against Stalin's leadership of the Communist Party, and accused Stalin of violent nationalism and anti-Semitism. Furthermore, Khruschev criticized Stalin's policy in World War II. The speech created shock within the party members.

Despite wishing to dismantle the cult of Stalin, Khruschev advised that the content of his speech was so damaging to Soviet ideology, it should be released gradually. Nonetheless, the speech's content leaked rapidly; in its aftermath, tens of thousands of political prisoners were set free, and hopes were fuelled in Eastern Europe that Communist rule would soon come to an end.

Claudine van Hensbergen

Date February 24, 1956

Country USSR

Why It's Key Khruschev's speech can be seen as the first step towards "de-Stalinization," a process that involved the national and cultural rejection of former leader Josef Stalin.

Fact The text of Khuschev's speech was not published in Russia until 1988.

314

Key Political Event
Pakistan becomes an Islamic Republic

At its formation in 1947, Pakistan was officially a dominion within the British Commonwealth ruled by a Governor-General as the nominal representative of the British monarchy. Nine years later, Pakistan adopted a constitution and declared itself to be an Islamic Republic. This was a departure from Pakistan's Anglocentric foundations as well as from the political personality of the founder of Pakistan, Muhammad Ali Jinnah, a secularist who defied Muslim law in his daily life and habits. Pakistan's new status as an Islamic Republic did not change the young country's tradition of dictatorial rule. Over the next five decades, Pakistan would be led primarily by military strongmen with neither clerical connections to Islam nor republican credentials. The military tipped its hat to both religion and democracy but, in the end, retained power solely for itself. For example, in the 1980s, Pakistani leader General Zia-ul-Haq convened a parliament whose purpose was to provide religious and political guidance for the country. However, the parliament was handpicked by Zia-ul-Haq, vitiating its power as an independent religious or political organ.

Pakistan's self-identification as a Muslim country put the nation directly at odds with its secular neighbor, India, and signaled the country's intent to abandon the secular ways of Jinnah. Even as an Islamic Republic, though, Pakistan has failed to accommodate Ahmadi or Shi'ite Muslims, indicating that it might be more accurately designated a Sunni Islamic Republic.

Demir Barlas

Date March 23, 1956

Country Pakistan

Why It's Key Pakistan officially abandoned the secular aspirations of its founder, Muhammad Ali Jinnah, in 1956, starting down a road of Islamization that has defined the country's social and geopolitical identity ever since.

Key Political Event
Mao's "One Hundred Flowers" speech

When, in 1956, Krushchev condemned Stalin's use of terror, Mao curtailed arrests and executions, but he felt that the lesson from the 1956 Hungarian Uprising was to eliminate counter-revolutionaries. "We must kill," he declared. "And we say it's good to kill." Mao did, however, take cynical note of de-Stalinization. In his four-hour speech, he criticized Stalin's "excessive" purges and invited criticisms of the Communist Party. "Let a hundred flowers bloom," he said. "Let a hundred schools of thought contend." Given that millions had already been killed for dissent, this was a startling departure. To his inner circle he said, "Let all those ox devils and snake demons... curse us for a few months." Clearly, his intention was simply to expose opponents. As Mao was wary of a popular uprising, dissent was allowed only in the form of posters and seminars. People criticized the Party's monopoly of power and secretiveness; China's involvement in the Korean War was questioned; an independent judiciary was called for, and public denunciations were condemned.

When Mao read speculation that the Party leadership was split and that he was a liberal, he forbade further criticisms and initiated the Anti-Rightist Campaign, using Hunan Province, where 100,000 were denounced, 10,000 arrested, and 1,000 killed, as an example of how the crackdown should work. The campaign lasted a year and resulted in 500,000 people losing their posts. Its ultimate aim was to facilitate harsher extraction of food for export to finance Mao's plans for the rapid industrialization of China.
Duncan Proudfoot

Date May 2, 1956

Country China

Why It's Key Mao's twenty-seven-year rule resulted in the death of 70 million Chinese; this speech was a notably cynical precursor to a significant bout of repression.

Key Cultural Event
Osborne's *Look Back in Anger* performed

"I doubt if I could love anyone who did not wish to see *Look Back in Anger*": these were the words of theater critic Kenneth Tynan, in the *Observer* newspaper, on reviewing 1956's most controversial new British play. John Osborne's tour-de-force has never attracted half-hearted responses. For some, it is responsible for every subsequent British play to go beyond the plush curtains and clipped emotions of Terence Rattigan and Noel Coward; for the menace and irreverence lurking in the work of playwrights as diverse as Harold Pinter, Tom Stoppard, and Joe Orton. For others, the overwhelming Osborne mythology eclipses any artistic merit it might have had.

The fact that these debates begin afresh with every new revival only confirms *Look Back in Anger*'s centrality to post-war English-language theater. But it also stands as a symbol of an emergent social group in 1950s Britain. Initially termed the "angry young men," these were working- or lower-middle-class males who were gaining access to university in record numbers. The rants of Jimmy Porter both epitomized and inspired a whole new generation of previously disempowered people. In time, the "angry" net spread wider. "Kitchen-sink" films and TV dramas of the 1960s gave voice to bored housewives, single mothers, and clerical wage-slaves, and along with the boom in mass-medium satire, ushered in a new Britain prepared to question "traditional" values and embrace its own youth cultures.
Andrew Blades

Date May 8, 1956

Country UK

Why It's Key Osborne's play spawned the term "angry young men" that defined a generation.

Fact *Look Back in Anger* put London's Royal Court Theatre at the center of new writing, and made a star of the actor Alan Bates.

Key Cultural Event
First commercially available stereo recordings

Inventors have been trying to reproduce the stereoscopic nature of our hearing since the technology for recording music was first developed. While creating a rudimentary form of stereo recording would seem easy, reproducing our hearing on record proved to challenge inventors. However, in the 1920s, W. Bartlett Jones discovered that one could record a left and right channel of sound on a single record groove, with one sound recorded vertically and the other recorded laterally.

Starting in the 1930s, experiments were conducted with recording orchestras and musicians, which continued through the 1950s. High-profile experimental recording sessions were conducted at Carnegie Hall and other concert venues, and films like Walt Disney's *Fantasia* used similar technology to produce stereo effects. Alan Blumlein improved on Jones' invention by changing the angle at which the grooves were recorded, and by 1959, companies started to sell stereo equipment and recordings.

With their improved, lifelike sound quality, stereo records quickly became successful, and by the end of the 1960s, stereo sound was standard on many home systems. The improvements also led to the development of the audiophile culture, with fans of music and technology purchasing high-end equipment and designing rooms to maximize the quality of sound reproduction. Although quadraphonic systems were introduced in the early 1970s, it never had the same appeal as stereo technology, which remains the standard today for the reproduction of popular music.
Martin Johnson

Date January 30, 1959

Country USA

Why It's Key The advent of stereo recording revolutionized the sound quality of music recordings.

Fact Stereo creates an illusion of three-dimensional sound, even though it only plays on two channels.

Key Cultural Event
Holiday's performance of "Strange Fruit" filmed

Billie Holiday's famous anti-racism song, "Strange Fruit," was in fact written by Abel Meeropol, a Bronx schoolteacher of Jewish descent, for his union magazine. Originally a poem, the song condemned lynching, which was widely practiced in the South at the time of its composition, and became a popular protest song around New York City when the poem was set to music. But the song's chilling presentation is owed to the famous blues crooner, who first learned the song in the late 1930s. By the time Holiday incorporated it into her live performances, and later recorded it on her album, it came to represent a burgeoning civil rights movement, and a lingering pain from the dying practice of lynching. She performed the song until her death in 1959.

That same year, prior to her death, Holiday was filmed in England performing several of her songs. Her recorded performance of "Strange Fruit" may be the most poignant – the emotional lyrics often moved the singer to tears – and the intensity of the subject is reflected on her face in the rare footage. It's a dramatic performance, most notably because the camera stays glued to Holiday for the duration of her performance, but backs away for the last seconds of the song as Holiday flails her arms and lets out the song's dissident last words: "bitter crop."
Bethonie Butler

Date February 10, 1959

Country UK

Why It's Key "Strange Fruit" was a rare and iconic performance of the legendary anti-racism anthem.

opposite Billie Holiday in concert.

Key Political Event
Fidel Castro takes power in Cuba

The small group of revolutionaries who fought a dogged guerrilla war against the U.S.-supported dictatorship of Fulgencio Batista captured the imagination of the world in their gradual but unstoppable march from the mountains of the Sierra Maestra toward Havana. After the resignation of Batista on January 1, 1959, a wave of euphoria briefly disguised the ideological disunity of the opposition. By the following month, the fractures had come to the surface, and no figure would prove as polarizing as Fidel Castro Ruiz, the charismatic attorney who had led the assault on the Moncada barracks in 1953.

In the aftermath of the revolution, Castro was its undisputed public face due to his high profile in the national and international press. Although he initially assumed the role of Commander in Chief of the armed forces, the sudden resignation of Prime Minister José Miró Cardona led to Castro's elevation to that office on February 16. In power, Castro began to implement an agenda far more radical than many of his former allies had anticipated. While his July 26 Movement had previously advocated the restoration of the 1940 democratic constitution suspended by Batista, Castro made evident his ambitions for the total transformation of Cuban society. Abolishing the state institutions of liberal democracy, indefinitely postponing elections, and nationalizing the property of foreign companies, Castro set Cuba on the path toward socialism. The resulting conflict with the United States would play a defining role in the country's development in subsequent decades.

Geoffrey Schullenberger

Date February 16, 1959

Country Cuba

Why It's Key Castro, revolutionary hero for some and brutal tyrant for others, would largely dictate Cuba's unique path for half a century.

Key Political Event
Tibetan uprising violently quashed

In March 1959, Chinese officials in Lhasa, Tibet, invited Tenzin Gyatso, the fourteenth Dalai Lama, to attend a theatrical performance at their army's headquarters. There was, however, one request: he must come alone, without his bodyguards or any companions.

For almost a decade, the young ruler of Tibet had been forced to walk a fine line with the Chinese, who had laid claim to his country in 1948. Chinese "liberation troops" had entered Lhasa in September 1951 and had steadily exerted control over the people. But they had not made any aggressive moves to depose the twenty-four-year-old religious and political leader. This invitation seemed to indicate a change in policy.

In response, more than 30,000 Tibetans turned out to surround the Dalai Lama's Norbulingka Palace to prevent the Chinese from seizing him. The Lhasa Uprising quickly gained support, and the People's Liberation Army moved in on March 17 to silence the protesters. In the space of ten days, Chinese troops killed at least 10,000 Tibetans.

Fearing even greater bloodshed if he stayed, the Dalai Lama decided to flee for the Indian border. "There was nothing I could do for my people if I stayed and the Chinese would certainly capture me in the end," he has said. He and his bodyguards, mounted on horseback, made the long journey across the highlands. He was granted asylum in India and set up a government-in-exile in Dharmsala, where he was soon joined by over 80,000 Tibetan faithfuls.

Heather Michon

Date March 10, 1959

Country Tibet

Why It's Key The violent end to the Tibetan uprising led to the flight of the Dalai Lama from Tibet to India.

Key Cultural Event
The first Grammy Awards

Presented by the National Academy of Recording Arts and Sciences and held at the Beverly Hills Hotel's Grand Ballroom, the first Grammy Awards sought to highlight the previous year's finest songwriting and recordings. Categories included Record of the Year, Song of the Year (both won by Domenico Modugno for "Nel Blue Dipinto di Blu Volare," beating out Frank Sinatra), and Album of the Year, which went to Henry Mancini's *The Music from Peter Gunn*. Other winners included jazz greats Ella Fitzgerald and Count Basie, and awards were given in genres ranging from rhythm and blues to musicals.

It would be a few years before rock 'n' roll would make a splash at the annual awards ceremony – the first Best Rock and Roll Recording award went to Chubby Checker in 1961 – and other genres would have similar troubles making inroads at the industry event. In 1999, Lauryn Hill's *The Miseducation of Lauryn Hill* won the Grammy for Album of the Year, among other categories – the first hip-hop album to win the award. Indeed, the Grammys have drawn controversy in recent years under accusations of honoring commercially successful acts over more critically acclaimed artists. Still, the ceremony has grown in both size and spectacle since 1959, now featuring upwards of thirty major awards (as well dozens of minor ones) and performances by music's biggest stars broadcast across the globe.

David Greenwald

Date May 4, 1959

Country USA

Why It's Key The Grammy Awards are the music industry's most prestigious honor, the equivalent of film's Academy Awards.

Fact Ross Bagdasarian, Sr won two Grammy awards in 1959 for his work as the voice of the animated characters "David Seville and the Chipmunks" – better known as Alvin and the Chipmunks.

Key Cultural Event
Miles Davis' *Kind of Blue* is Released

On August 19, 1959, Miles Davis released what is considered his most successful album, and arguably the most successful jazz record of all time, *Kind of Blue*. His ensemble was an all-star set, which included Cannonball Adderley on alto sax, John Coltrane on tenor sax, Wynton Kelly on piano, Paul Chambers on bass, and Jimmy Cobb on drums. Though Davis is credited with writing all of the songs on the album, it is widely believed that pianist Bill Evans did the majority of composition for *Kind of Blue*. With its mellow sound and simple melodies, the album remains popular even among those not claiming to be jazz aficionados.

In addition to borrowing from the swing, bebop, and pop standards of music past, the album established many jazz standards of its own, including the album's first track, "So What," and "Freddie Freeloader." The album stood apart from other jazz records of its time because its composition broke away from conventional improvisation, which relied on chords, instead using modal sketches, setting parameters for each musician to follow on a given scale. While Davis had experimented with modal composition prior to releasing *Kind of Blue*, the album was the first completely modal album, which allowed for more creative freedom for each musician. The modal composition resulted in what is likely the biggest reason behind the definitive status of Davis' magnum opus – its simplicity.

Bethonie Butler

Date August 19, 1959

Country USA

Why It's Key *Kind of Blue* is widely considered to be the most popular jazz record of all time.

Key Political Event
Formation of the Vietcong

France's withdrawal from Vietnam in 1954 left an uneasy division between two very different authoritarian regimes: the Communist North and the American-allied South. Communists in the South sought to exploit the growing discontent with South Vietnam's leader, Ngo Dinh Diem. Diem responded with violent repression. To the distress of Southern Communists, the Communist government in the North committed little support to their struggle at first, but in 1960 it resolved to step up its efforts. In January 1960, responding to directives from the North, Southern Communists and other opponents of Diem met outside Saigon, the South's capital, to found the Communist-led National Liberation Front (NLF), dedicated to overthrowing Diem. The NLF denounced Diem's government as a disguised colonial regime controlled by the United States, and called for his overthrow, the expulsion of his U.S. military advisers, and the removal of foreign military bases.

The NLF organized the guerrilla fighters of the South into a unified military command. Diem and his American advisers had already labeled these forces the Vietcong, a derogatory abbreviation of the words for Vietnamese Communists. The name stuck, but lost its negative connotations. Over the next few years, the Vietcong's military activities grew into a large-scale guerrilla war, supported by the North, which, in turn, received increasing aid from the Soviet Union. In response, the United States committed more advisers, and then combat troops, in a futile attempt to give the South Vietnamese government control of its countryside.

Brian Ladd

Date January 21, 1960

Country Vietnam

Why It's Key The Vietnamese Communists made a firm commitment to armed struggle against the U.S.-backed South Vietnamese government.

1960–1969

335

Key Cultural Event
The Rat Pack's "Summit at the Sands"

These days, Las Vegas is no stranger to celebrity, but for three weeks in 1960, the strip encountered Hollywood like never before. In town for the filming of heist movie *Ocean's 11*, stars Frank Sinatra, Dean Martin, Sammy Davis Jr, Joey Bishop, and Peter Lawford descended upon the Sands Hotel for performances that would establish the group as the consummate Vegas entertainers. The so-called Rat Pack's rotating membership included such luminaries as Humphrey Bogart, Lauren Bacall, and Judy Garland, but it was the early 1960s *Ocean's 11* lineup that became the group's most famous incarnation.

According to Davis Jr, the residency came in mock response to a real summit meeting – U.S. President Dwight D. Eisenhower, French President Charles de Gaulle, and the USSR's Nikita Khruschev's Paris Summit Conference. The Rat Pack's "Summit at the Sands" consisted of swinging songs and off-color humor, with the group members playing up their boozy, sophisticated images and their real-life friendships. It drew thousands of people as well as attention to the Vegas strip, which rose to greater prominence as a tourist hotspot. Vegas became a second home to the Hollywood group and the 1960 gigs were far from the last summit – the Rat Pack album *Live at the Sands*, for instance, captures a September 1963 performance. Hollywood is still paying homage today: an *Ocean's 11* remake – starring George Clooney and Julia Roberts – was released in 2001.

David Greenwald

Date January 26, 1960

Country USA

Why It's Key The Rat Pack's first performance with a five-man lineup made headlines – and made Las Vegas a destination.

Fact One story has the group getting its name from Lauren Bacall, who, on seeing them return from a night of partying, declared, "You look like a pack of rats."

opposite Dean Martin, Sammy Davis Jr., and Frank Sinatra with Jan Murray (far left).

Key Political Event
Macmillan's "Wind of Change" speech

In 1960, British Prime Minister, Harold Macmillan visited Africa, his trip culminating in South Africa, which was then a member of the British Commonwealth. There he gave a speech that signaled a change in Conservative Party policy. Due to the famous phrase that it contained, it became known as the "Wind of Change" speech. Up to this point, the Conservative Party had favored minority rule in South Africa. Macmillan's speech was part of a desire to promote decolonization and point Britain in the direction of Europe. He stated that "the wind of change is blowing through this continent, and, whether we like it or not, this growth of national consciousness is a political fact." Internationally the speech was well received, but not so by the South African parliament. The white nationalist party remained completely silent after he had spoken.

Although the speech is remembered for one particular phrase, commentators have observed that it is also significant that Macmillan refers to the change as a "fact," signaling that the change was unavoidable. This is indicative of the speech's intricate rhetoric. It was designed to have an emotive and persuasive effect, which would mollify and appeal to its diverse audience of British Conservatives, the South African Nationalist Party, and black Africans, including the African National Congress.

The speech initiated major developments in South African politics: just one month later, black South Africans staged a protest against apartheid, and sixty-seven were killed.
Frieda Klotz

Date February 3, 1960
Country South Africa
Why It's Key His speech signaled a change in British policy toward South Africa, and marked the start of a violent era for that country, which would ultimately lead to an end of apartheid.

336

Key Cultural Event
Fellini's *La Dolce Vita* names the paparazzi

Federico Fellini was hardly a newcomer when *La Dolce Vita* opened in 1960, but the film certainly offered something new. A hilarious stab at fashion culture and international celebrity, the movie also marked the Italian filmmaker's transition from making stark neo-realistic cinema to crafting innovative work for the burgeoning art-house circuit. Set in Rome ten years prior to its release, *La Dolce Vita* follows cynical reporter Marcello (Fellini mainstay Marcello Mastroianni) through a series of encounters filled with riotous symbolism satirizing the glamorous lifestyles of the rich and famous. Of these, particular attention is paid to American actress Sylvia (Anita Ekberg), depicted as a cartoon send-up of Marilyn Monroe.

A *Palme D'Or* winner at the Cannes Film Festival and one of the most talked about films of the year, *La Dolce Vita* spoke to viewers on different levels. While offering a sweeping view of Rome and plenty of sex appeal, Fellini was truly creating a riotous view of show business in all of its absurdities, particularly American notions of attractiveness.

The character of Marcello's photographer, named Paparazzo, ultimately led to the name now given to photographers obsessed with marketing the celebrity image. The term translates into English as "sparrow," although its current connotations are hardly so quaint: Fellini once said that press photographers clustered around their subjects like starving creatures.
Eric Kohn

Date February 3, 1960
Country Italy, USA
Why It's Key Fellini's satiric take on fame helped invent contemporary notions of celebrity.

Fact The film was nominated for four Oscars and won one for costume design.

opposite **Poster for** *La Dolce Vita*.

THE MOST TALKED ABOUT— THE MOST SHOCKED ABOUT FILM OF OUR YEARS

1960-1969

LA DOLCE VITA

AN ASTOR RELEASE
DIRECTED BY FEDERICO FELLINI

LA DOLCE VITA

FEDERICO FELLINI   MARCELLO MASTROIANNI ANITA EKBERG ANOUK AIMÉE YVONNE FURNEAUX MAGALI NOEL LEX BARKER JACQUES SERNAS ALAIN CUNY WALTER SANTESSO RICCARDO GARRONE NADIA GRAY Produced by GIUSEPPE AMATO and ANGELO RIZZOLI

Key Cultural Event
Olatunji's *Drums of Passion* takes the US by storm

Having won a scholarship to study in the United States, drummer Babatunde "Baba" Olatunji left his homeland Nigeria in 1950 for Atlanta, Georgia, intending to become a career diplomat. Astounded at how little his fellow students in the United States knew about African life, he became active in student politics, where his views on Africa's influence on black American culture struck a deep chord with the growing civil rights movement. He also toured with a dance and drum troupe, setting audiences alight with the power of the group's rhythms and chants. Soon he came to the attention of John Hammond, who later signed Bob Dylan, and in late 1959 recorded an album of traditional Nigerian songs for Columbia called *Drums of Passion*, widely acknowledged as the first African music recorded in a modern stereo studio.

Bringing genuine African music to a Western audience for the first time, *Drums of Passion* was a huge success, selling over five million copies worldwide and staying in the *Billboard* charts for two years. Excited by his complicated polyrhythmic drumming techniques, Olatunji also influenced many American musicians such as free-jazz exponent John Coltrane and Latin rock guitarist Carlos Santana, whose cover of the album's opening track was a 1969 hit. Though he made little money from the groundbreaking record or subsequent ones, Olatunji, who died in 2003, spent his life in music and education, and while he never completed his diplomatic studies, he became a true cultural ambassador who put Africa on the world's musical map.

Hedley Paul

Date April 1, 1960

Country Nigeria/USA

Why It's Key The success of Olatunji's *Drums of Passion* sparked a new interest in African music and rhythms, especially influencing U.S. jazz musicians in the 1960s, and he is now seen as an early pioneer of the later world music phenomenon.

Fact In 1965, Babatunde established the Olatunji Center for African Culture in Harlem, where jazz giant John Coltrane played his last concert just before his death.

Key Political Event
Brasília inaugurated

President Juscelino Kubitschek came to power in 1956 promising the new capital enshrined in Brazil's 1891 constitution, and "fifty years of progress in five" – to complete it during his term. A competition for the Pilot Plan was won by Lúcio Costa, who shared Le Corbusier's belief that it was possible to create an ideal society by building an ideal city. Brasília's architect, the young communist Oscar Niemeyer, wanted his buildings to be "as light as possible, to touch the ground gently, to swoop and soar." He contrasted the curves of his cathedral and the domes of the Congress with the straight lines of twenty identical ministry buildings. From above, the city resembles a bird in flight, with a Monumental Axis bisecting a curved Residential Axis. Six-storey residential superblocks are set in vast green spaces,

while highways stretch to all parts of Brazil, including Belém, 2,276 kilometers to the north-east.

When work began in 1956, the site was over 100 kilometers from any railroad or tarred road, but within forty-one months, Brasília was already a large, functioning city (though many of its buildings were only completed later – the cathedral in 1970, for example). Brasília produced a US$2 billion debt and failed to take adequately into account its human occupants, being built more for automobiles than its majority of pedestrians; but it unified Brazil in pride and hope, and opened it up to the West. Brasília is still a work in progress, having inaugurated a new Niemeyer-designed cultural complex in 2006.

Duncan Proudfoot

Date April 21, 1960

Country Brazil

Why It's Key Brasília's construction was a feat of political will, radical urban planning, and architectural daring: a modernist project on a grand scale, built at breakneck speed.

Fact Brasília was added to the UNESCO list of World Heritage Sites in 1987. One of only two large-scale applications of Le Corbusier's twentieth-century principles of urbanism, the other being Chandigarh, in Punjab, India.

Key Political Event
U-2 incident

O n May 1, 1960, the Soviet military shot down an American U-2 plane near Svedlovsk, USSR. The aircraft, flown by CIA pilot Francis Gary Powers, had been on its way from Peshawar, Pakistan, to Bodø, Norway, as part of a mission to take photographs of several military sites in Russia. Upon learning of the incident, U.S. authorities assumed that the pilot was dead and the plane destroyed in the crash, and tried to cover up the real purpose of the flight by claiming that the plane was a NASA weather aircraft that had accidentally entered Soviet airspace as a result of the pilot's problems with the oxygen equipment while flying over Turkey. However, on May 7, the Soviet Prime Minister Nikita Khrushchev announced that the pilot had been captured and had confessed to being on an intelligence mission in the USSR.

The U.S. President Dwight D. Eisenhower refused to apologize for the U-2 incident, thus causing the cancellation of the Paris Summit between the United States, USSR, Britain, and France – scheduled for May 16 – which further complicated U.S.-USSR relations. Francis Gary Powers was convicted of espionage and sentenced to three years' imprisonment and seven years of hard labor, but was exchanged for the Soviet spy Rudolph Abel on February 10, 1962. As a result of the U-2 incident, the United States sped up the development of the spy satellite Corona, which would become the primary U.S. source of intelligence of Soviet activity.

Sonja Kudeljnjak

Date May 1, 1960

Country USSR/USA

Why It's Key The U-2 incident was a major setback in the U.S.-USSR relations during the Cold War, which reached their lowest point during the Cuban Missile Crisis in 1962.

Fact The U-2, also known as the Dragon Lady, is a high-altitude aircraft that can rise up to 70,000 feet.

1960–1969

339

Key Cultural Event
FDA approves birth control pill

B efore the birth control pill was introduced, sex and pregnancy were integrally linked. The U.S. Federal and Drug Administration's introduction of the birth control pill in 1960 changed this situation remarkably. The pill gave women more control over their bodies and allowed them to enjoy sex without the worry of pregnancy. In 1964, three male doctors writing in the UK medical journal *The Lancet* remarked that it gave their patients "a sense of wellbeing and increased pleasure in sexual intercourse."

The pill also strengthened the growth of the feminist movement that simultaneously took place in the 1960s, as is evident by references to it in popular culture at that time. For instance, the U.S. country and western singer Loretta Lynn wrote a song called "The Pill," which celebrated the liberation that it brought.

But this freedom caused anxiety and reaction in some sectors. Christian groups worried that the pill would lead to increased levels of adultery. In 1968, the Pope banned it (along with contraception more generally) in his encyclical.

By 1965, five million American women were taking the drug. The situation was unique: never before had so many people been on such a strong prescription medication for so long a period. Early forms of the pill were high in estrogen, which could cause blood clots, but in the 1970s and 1980s scientists developed safer versions. Dubbed by *Time* magazine as "The Pill that Unleashed Sex," few medications have had such wide-reaching implications.

Frieda Klotz

Date May 9, 1960

Country USA

Why It's Key The introduction of the pill liberated women and contributed to the growth of the feminist movement.

Key Political Event
Mali and Senegal become independent

The decolonization of French West Africa (Mali was also known as French Sudan) occurred during a particularly traumatic time for French interests in Africa. By 1959, France had been engaged in a bitter conflict in Algeria for five years. Characterized by brutal fighting, terrorism, and the use of torture, the Algerian war (as well as the fallout from the defeat in Indochina) severely drained France's resources as well as its will to resist calls for independence.

Against this background, the Mali Federation was formed in 1959. Modibo Keita (an ex-communist) led the Malian delegation, while Mahmadu Dia and Leopold Senghor (a Catholic) represented Senegal. Despite some constitutional disagreements between the parties, concord was reached and the Mali Federation announced its independence in 1960. Although there was no military involvement, the French tacitly supported factions in each country opposed to the union in an attempt to destabilize the new country.

Partly as a result of this (and because of feelings of inequality amongst the Senegalese faction), Senegal withdrew from the federation in August 1960, expelling many Malians from the country in the following year. Both countries experienced political instability as a result: in Senegal, President Leopold Senghor faced a coup led by his old colleague (and prime minister) Mahmadu Dia, which was put down bloodlessly but led to Dia's imprisonment. In Mali, Keita was deposed in a violent coup in 1968 and democratic rule was not safely re-established until the 1990s. Nevertheless, Mali is currently one of Africa's most stable countries.
Ben Snook

Date June 20, 1960

Country Mali and Senegal

Why It's Key Independence led to violence and political instability.

Fact Before independence, Mali and Senegal formed the entity known as French West Africa.

Key Political Event
Belgian Congo gains independence and Civil War

After fifty years of colonial rule, a series of riots in Leopoldville spurred Belgium to concede the Congo's independence in the country's first free elections. Independence was declared on June 30, with Joseph Kasa-Vubu elected president and Patrice Lumumba as prime minister. However, the historic day ended ominously with Lumumba and King Baudouin I of Belgium exchanging insults over old colonial issues.

On July 5, large sections of the army stationed in Leopoldville began to mutiny against white officers, forcing European settlers to flee the city and creating a power vacuum. Faced by 25,000 leaderless soldiers and fearing a descent into chaos, the states of Katanga and South Kasai promptly declared independence from the new republic. An enraged Lumumba demanded military intervention from the UN to restore control, but General Secretary Dag Hammarskjöld regarded the situation as an internal affair and supplied only limited support.

With the country now divided into four disparate states, President Kasa-Vubu dismissed Lumumba, who was later arrested and executed on January 17, 1961. UN intervention now became inevitable, and the ensuing civil war was further enflamed when Hammarskjöld died in a plane crash en route to ceasefire negotiations in Katanga.

For the next three years, U.S., Belgian, and UN forces strove to reunite the country in a string of lengthy operations, defeating the Katangan leader Moise Tshombe in 1962 and the Simba rebellion in 1964. A year later Mobutu deposed President Kasa-Vubu with help of the CIA, and the disastrous First Republic ended.
Jay Mullins

Date June 30, 1960

Country First Republic of Congo (now Democratic Republic of Congo)

Why It's Key The catastrophic disintegration of the First Republic of Congo underlined the difficulties of rapidly reducing colonial control in Africa.

opposite Congolese women dancers join the festivities in honor of the country's newly declared independence.

Key Political Event
S. Bandaranaike becomes prime minister of Sri Lanka

The people of Ceylon were shocked when a Buddhist monk assassinated the popular prime minister, Solomon Bandaranaike, in September 1959. This was followed by an equally unusual chain of events, as his grieving widow Sirimavo, mother of three, quickly established herself as the undisputed leader of the Sri Lanka Freedom Party founded by her husband. In the general election, the former first lady was elected the world's first female head of government.

At her inauguration, she vowed to continue his "socialist programs which reflect the national aspirations of the people." Despite her lack of experience, she proved to be a formidable politician. Her zealous brand of Buddhist Sinhalese nationalism, however, would inflame ethnic tensions with the Hindu Tamil minority. She changed the national language from English to Sinhala, and changed the university admissions policy to benefit the Sinhalese.

The election of a female prime minister did not exactly start a trend. The next decade saw only two other female prime ministers: India's Indira Gandhi and Israel's Golda Meir. Bandaranaike lost the general election in 1965, but would hold the position on two other occasions. In 1994, her younger daughter Chandrika Kumaratunga was elected prime minister, and became president in another election, only three months later. Ironically, Kumaratunga spent much of her presidency trying to end a long-running conflict with the Tamils, which had been aroused by her mother's policies.

Mark Juddery

Date July 21, 1960

Country Ceylon (now Sri Lanka)

Why It's Key Sri Lankans elected the world's first female prime minister.

opposite Sirimavo Bandaranaike on the campaign trail before her election to prime minister.

1960–1969

345

Key Political Event
OPEC created

The Organization of Petroleum-Exporting Countries (OPEC) cartel was founded in 1960 to represent the individual and joint energy interests and policies of Saudi Arabia, Venezuela, Iran, Iraq, and Kuwait. OPEC, whose founder members were responsible for exporting the majority of petroleum consumed on earth, initially configured itself as a purely economic cartel whose purpose was to set prices and control output. Thirteen years after its formation, however, OPEC became known to the world in another light: as a political player. In the wake of the 1967 and 1973 wars between Israel and numerous Arab states, the Arab members of OPEC decided to embargo oil to the United States, Western Europe, and Japan in punishment of their support of Israel. The resulting oil shock of 1973 was immediate and long lasting,

resulting in waves of inflation, unemployment, and economic weakness in the West throughout the 1970s.

The resolve of the Arab members of OPEC did not continue indefinitely, as the embargo also represented a loss of economic opportunity for them. However, when the embargo was lifted in 1974, it had already transformed much of the industrialized world, having put conservation, energy efficiency, and diversification of energy resources on the agenda in its wake. OPEC never again wielded the oil weapon in this way, but, as the gatekeeper to the indispensable resource that keeps the world running, certainly impressed its existence on the mind of elites and ordinary citizens throughout the world.

Demir Barlas

Date September 10, 1960

Country Iraq

Why It's Key The strategic importance of oil became apparent to the whole world when a cartel of exporters politicized the production, export, and symbolism of this most valuable of commodities.

Key Cultural Event
First Paralympic Games

Running alongside the Olympics every four years, the Paralympic Games is a worldwide competition aimed at celebrating the achievements of participating athletes in overcoming various disabilities to reach sporting excellence. The movement has its foundations in England, and the work of Sir Ludwig Guttman, who in 1948 organized a sports competition for World War II veterans suffering from spinal injuries. Known as the Stoke Mandeville Games, in reference to its location, the competition allowed disabled athletes to compete on equal terms, in addition to fulfilling Guttman's intentions of aiding their rehabilitation and physical recovery.

Coordinating sports clubs and hospitals throughout the country, Guttman designed a competition that would run alongside the 1948 London Olympic Games. The success of this event led to the inclusion of athletes from the Netherlands in the 1952 competition, and the tradition of competing alongside the Olympics was established. The first official Paralympic Games was held in Rome in 1960, with around 400 athletes from 23 countries competing in 8 events. In 1976, further disability groups were included in the competition, and in 1988, it was stipulated that the Paralympics would henceforth always be held in the same host city as the Olympics.

Now involving nearly 4,000 athletes from 136 countries competing in 6 distinct disability groups and 27 different events, the Paralympics is a demonstration of talent, ability, and true sporting excellence.
Hannah Furness

Date September 18, 1960
Country Italy
Why It's Key The Paralympic Games have enabled athletes with disabilities to compete and excel in an international sporting competition.

346

Key Political Event
Nigerian independence

The Allied defeat of Nazi Germany fueled national and international calls for decolonization. In Nigeria, the British colonial government quickly made constitutional reforms, largely to keep in step with the neighboring Gold Coast. Federalism was necessitated by the country's ethnic and regional divides, and by its socioeconomic problems. Three major regional parties fought the first general election (1951–1952): the National Congress of Nigeria and the Cameroons (NCNC) (East); the Northern People's Congress (NPC) (North); and Action Group (AG) (West). Following Northern riots in 1953 – in which thirty-six people were killed – a constitution was drawn up providing each regional government with increased powers.

On independence in 1960, the country's first government coalition was formed between the NPC and NCNC, and three years later Nigeria declared itself a Federal Republic. Northern dominance continued to destabilize this unwieldy federation, leading to secession threats, back-to-back military coups and counter-coups (from 1966 onward), and the secession of the east as the Republic of Biafra (1967–1970). As conflict continued, hopes that the exploitation of natural resources would assist Nigeria's rapid economic development dwindled. Having voluntarily relinquished power to civilian administrators in 1980, the military wrested back control in 1983, 1985, and again in 1993, when major civil and religious unrest led to the annulment of the elections. However, since its 1999 electoral victory, the People's Democratic Party has made significant improvements in human rights.
Laura Pechey

Date October 1, 1960
Country Nigeria
Why It's Key Despite hopes that independence would allow Nigeria to grow economically, the country's ethnic, religious, and regional schisms have continued to hamper its growth, causing political infighting and ongoing communal violence.

opposite Princess Alexandra formally opening the first Nigerian Parliament after the country's independence.

Key Cultural Event
Gagarin becomes the first man in space

In a period of frenzied technological competition between the Soviet Union and the United States, Flight Major Yuri Gagarin became the first man in space on April 12, 1961. Alan Shepard was the first American to enter Earth's orbit, less than one month later.

Gagarin's Vostok 1 mission was an event timed for maximum political leverage. Many details of NASA's prospective manned space program were, in contrast to covert Soviet operations, discussed freely in the public domain. NASA had already launched a chimpanzee into outer space. The head Soviet rocket engineer, Sergei Korolev, also wanted to pursue test flights with primates, but was pressurized by the political hierarchy to accelerate development on human spaceflight and win the "space race" at all costs. By spring 1961, NASA was completing final

testing to ensure Shepard's rocket was "man-rated." Korolev and *Vostok* preempted the Americans just in time. Gagarin, a genial former pilot, orbited Earth in 108 minutes, reaching a maximum speed of 28,090 kilometers per hour. Back in earth's atmosphere, he parachuted safely to a field in central Russia. This was kept secret by Soviet authorities, anxious that the world would view the achievement incomplete if Gagarin was thought not to have "landed" his ship.

Overnight, the cosmonaut shot to international fame. *Vostok 1* was used by the Kremlin to affirm the success and mythos of Soviet Communism. In global prestige, this was the apogee of Soviet cosmonautics, though Gagarin was dead less than seven years later – killed in a plane crash.

Michael Hallam

Date April 12, 1961

Country USSR

Why It's Key Sending a man into space opened up new realms of human exploration and, in the eyes of the world's media, signified the Soviet lead in the Cold War space race.

Key Political Event
Bay of Pigs invasion fails

The Bay of Pigs invasion was intended to overthrow the regime of Communist dictator Fidel Castro. The American CIA established supposedly "secret" camps in Guatemala, where Cuban exiles were trained in guerilla tactics and warfare. The counter-revolutionary forces, comprising 1,500 men in total, became known as "Brigade 2506."

However, press coverage of events in the United States meant that even Castro knew that an invasion was imminent. Indeed, Castro ordered the Cuban Air Force to be camouflaged and dispersed.

Keen to distance the United States from any obvious involvement in the operation, President John F. Kennedy changed the proposed location and timing of the invasion at very short notice. Instead of a daylight landing at Trinidad, Kennedy ordered a landing at the

more obscure Bay of Pigs, at night. This late change of plan was partially to blame for the failure of the invasion. Poor reconnaissance cost the rebel forces valuable time and they were subject to air attacks from the Cuban Air Force as dawn broke. The threat of Soviet intervention also created indecision in the U.S. administration, which reneged on its own promise of air support.

The invasion force, devoid of supplies and air cover, was quickly defeated. Roughly 200 of the rebels lost their lives and 1,200 were captured. Mass trials took place and each captive was sentenced to thirty years' imprisonment. However, following lengthy negotiations, most were released in exchange for a "ransom" of US$53 million, in food and medicine, from U.S. companies.

David Dunning

Date April 17, 1961

Country Cuba

Why It's Key The ill-fated invasion attempt was an acute embarrassment to U.S. president John F. Kennedy and set the stage for the Cuban Missile Crisis, which was to take the world to the brink of nuclear war.

Key Political Event
Assassination of Rafael Trujillo

Born in 1891, Rafael Trujillo joined the Dominican National Guard in 1918, at a time when the United States occupied the Dominican Republic. He rose rapidly in status, and by the time the United States withdrew six years later, he was promoted head of the Guard.

In 1930, Trujillo clinched political power during a revolt against President Vasquez. He took control of the country, and established a secret police force that tortured and murdered any opposition. When the capital city Santo Domingo was wrecked by a major hurricane, Trujillo used this opportunity to impose martial law and renamed the capital Ciudad Trujillo. This became the first of many honors that he granted himself and members of his family throughout his reign.

As well as gaining great personal wealth, Trujillo also had the support of the United States as Latin America's leading anti-communist. It was only when Fidel Castro emerged as Cuba's new prime minister in 1959 that the United States started to fear that the Dominican Republic would follow a similar revolutionary model. The CIA recruited the more unhappy wealthy Dominican exiles to remove Trujillo.

On May 30, 1961, Trujillo's car was gunned down on a quiet highway outside the capital. However, by the following day, Trujillo's son assumed control and conspirators were tortured and killed. When a new president, Juan Bosch, was eventually elected in February 1963, he proved more left-wing than America wanted, and in September, the CIA used the Dominican Army to overthrow Bosch by a military coup.

Mariko Kato

Date May 30, 1961

Country Dominican Republic

Why It's Key Rafael Trujillo presided for thirty-one years over one of the most brutal dictatorships in Latin America.

Fact For a long time, the United States supported Trujillo, the U.S. Secretary of State Cordell Hull claiming, "He may be a son-of-a-bitch, but he is our son-of-a-bitch."

Key Cultural Event
Amnesty International founded

Peter Benenson was moved to action when reading an article about two college students who were incarcerated for toasting to freedom in a Lisbon bar during dictator Salazar's regime. In 1961, British lawyer Benenson wrote the impassioned "Forgotten Prisoners" article, urging readers to launch a one-year appeal with the goal of obtaining amnesty. It was met with overwhelming support and generated a maelstrom of stories outlining similar plights of citizens worldwide. This one-year action rapidly transformed into an international movement, and Amnesty International was born. It continued to grow as a result of its unrelenting public awareness campaign and commitment to three irrevocable principles: the organization must be neutral, impartial, and independent. Aside from publicizing governmental wrongdoings, Amnesty International relies strongly on the global distribution of "adoption groups" – volunteers who take on a number of cases and orchestrate a barrage of letters to the offending government. An effective method of protest, it has also shown compassion and solicitude to the prisoner. Gradually its aim went beyond individual cases, and in 1972, a global campaign targeting banning of the use of torture was launched, followed by a vigorous campaign against the death penalty.

While fear, violence, and acts of terrorism barricade our rights to an "external" peace, Amnesty International, recipient of the 1977 Nobel Peace Prize, upholds the principle that imprisonment because of thought, conscience, religion, or faith obstructs our rights to a life of "internal" peace.

Colette Leisen

Date July 22, 1961

Country UK

Why It's Key The foundation is committed to the defense of human dignity against physical and mental torture, and shines a "torch of hope" into the cell of prisoners of conscience.

Key Political Event
Rise of the Berlin Wall

In the early morning hours of Sunday, August 13, 1961, residents of Berlin awoke to the sights and sounds of their city being, literally, split into two. The Soviets had begun construction of the Berlin Wall, initially a jumble of barbed wire and pavement stones, which by the 1980s had developed into a sophisticated system of 3.6m high, 1.5m wide, concrete walls, extending over 155 km (96 miles), effectively cutting off West Berlin from the rest of Eastern Germany.

After World War II, Germany had been divided amongst the Allied Powers of Great Britain, France, the United States, and the Soviets, into four occupation zones. A similar division of Greater Berlin had resulted in western sectors within the Soviet zone of occupation. In 1948, the Western powers united their zones of Germany together, and implemented a currency reform within the West trizone. As West Germany prospered, East Germany began experiencing a mass exodus of its skilled workers and intellectuals. Between 1949 and 1961, an estimated 2.5 million East Germans fled to western parts of Germany. Desperate, the Soviets erected the Berlin Wall and revoked the rights of Easterners to travel to the West. The divide between the East and West had never been so apparent or so stark.

Overnight, the ideological and political differences had manifested themselves into a material reality – barbed wire, machine guns, and a concrete wall.

Annie Wang

Date August 13, 1961

Country Germany

Why It's Key The Berlin Wall would come to symbolize the great divide between the "free" West and the "iron-fist" communism of the East.

opposite East Berlin police, on the left, repair the Wall, damaged during an escape attempt in an armored car, as West Berlin police and others gather on the right.

1960–1969

355

Key Political Event
Menderes, Turkish P.M., hanged

Adnan Menderes, prime minister of Turkey from 1950 to 1960, finished his political career at the end of the executioner's rope on September 16, 1961. Menderes' death was the natural consequence of Turkey's 1960 military coup, in which a junta of resolutely secular and authoritarian army officers accused Menderes and his political allies of corruption and violation of the Turkish constitution. At issue was the mounting tension between a Turkish democratic process increasingly friendly to the historically Muslim sentiments of the Turkish nation, and the militant secularism of the Turkish Army, a legacy of the anti-clerical character of Mustafa Kemal Atatürk, the Ottoman army officer who became the founder of the Turkish Republic.

Menderes was both sympathetic to Islam and a bitter rival of the Republic People's Party (CHP), the secular, liberal, and nationalist party that had dominated Turkish politics since the founding of the republic in 1923. Menderes' popular mandate was therefore particularly bitter to the CHP and the Turkish Army. Menderes' 1961 execution signaled that the Turkish Army was serious about safeguarding Atatürk's reforms against what it considered anti-liberal interests. Indeed, Turkey experienced three more military coups in the twentieth century, each designed to chasten what the officer class considered illiberal political forces in Turkey, and put the country in the hands of Atatürkist politicians. Menderes' fate, and the recurring interventions of the Turkish Army, thus disclosed the ongoing fragility of the Turkish democratic system.

Demir Barlas

Date September 16, 1961

Country Turkey

Why It's Key The Turkish military crushed a popular prime minister's foray into civil democracy, creating a pattern of coups and martial law that cast a long shadow over the country's modern history.

Key Cultural Event
Heller's *Catch-22* published

Born in Coney Island, New York, to Russian-Jewish immigrants, Joseph Heller volunteered for the U.S. Air Force when he was nineteen years old. Like his characters in *Catch-22*, he flew missions over southern Europe, surviving sixty sorties. After the war, Heller attended various American universities, as well as Oxford University, and wrote his first short stories while he worked as an advertising copywriter in New York.

Catch-22, his first major novel, follows the fate of Yossarian, a U.S. Army Air Forces B-25 bombardier. Rich in paradox and grim irony, the novel is a sharp critique of bureaucracy, the absurdity of patriotism and honor, and the folly of living by seemingly arbitrary and nonsensical rules imposed by others. Yossarian, disillusioned by the simultaneous triviality and profundity of both official and personal rules, concludes paradoxically that the only way to survive and remain sane in an insane system is to become insane.

When it was first published in the United States, *Catch-22* received lukewarm reviews, but found its fans in the UK when it was published there six months later. It eventually gained overwhelming popularity in the United States too with the Vietnam War generation, and has since sold over ten million copies in the United States alone.

Catch-22 also introduced a new concept and popular phrase into the English language. The title was chosen for the duplicate digit, and in the novel the term is used to describe a self-contradictory military rule. The phrase is now commonly used to describe a no-win situation.

Mariko Kato

Date November 10, 1961

Country USA

Why It's Key With its deft use of satire, humorous character portrayal, and sharp exposé of erratic bureaucracy, *Catch-22* is widely considered to be one of the greatest literary works of modern times.`

opposite **First edition American jacket of *Catch-22*.**

Key Political Event
Military coup brings Ne Win to power

When Burma declared independence from the British Empire in 1948, Ne Win was supreme commander of the new Burma Army. Over the next decade, the government faced many uprisings from ethnic minority groups and secessionists, and Ne Win temporarily took over from Prime Minister U Nu, to restore law and order. In 1960, he returned power to U Nu, but within two years he had grabbed it back again, this time by a military coup.

The coup was relatively bloodless, and Ne Win immediately set out to ruthlessly smother democracy in Burma, which was renamed Myanmar in 1989. In July 1962, the army intervened in student demonstrations at Rangoon University, dynamiting the union building and killing hundreds. In the wake of this event, Ne Win made his infamous speech in which he declared, "We will fight sword with sword and spear with spear." All universities were closed for more than two years until September 1964.

A new military junta was established under "the Burmese Way to Socialism" program. Hundreds of political leaders were imprisoned without trial, foreigners were expelled, and trade and industry were nationalized. Ne Win isolated Burma from the rest of the world for the next twenty-six years, black markets and smuggling prospered, and the country's economic prosperity withered. By the time Ne Win formally retired in 1988, Burma had been reduced from one of the most prosperous parts of the British Empire, to one of the ten poorest nations in the world.

Mariko Kato

Date March 2, 1962

Country Burma

Why It's Key Ne Win's controversial rule over Burma plummeted the country into poverty.

Fact At birth, Ne Win (1911-2002) was named Shu Maung, meaning "the apple of one's eye," but he changed his name to Ne Win meaning "brilliant as the sun," when he became an officer in the new Burma Independence Army in 1941.

CATCH-22

A NOVEL BY

JOSEPH HELLER

Key Cultural Event
The Beatles release their first hit single

Before their first hit, The Beatles had already gained some popularity in Hamburg, Germany, and in their hometown of Liverpool, where they played regularly at the Cavern Club. Originally known as The Quarrymen, the founder members were John Lennon, Paul McCartney, George Harrison, and Stuart Sutcliffe (until his death in 1962). After numerous changes, including occasional appearances from Ringo Starr, Pete Best became their drummer in 1960.

Brian Epstein first spotted them at the Cavern Club in 1962 and quickly became their manager. By June, he was signing a recording contract with EMI's producer, George Martin, who later suggested replacing Pete Best (who had difficulty keeping time) with Ringo Starr. By August, the famous line-up was complete.

During a September recording session, they played a song written by Paul McCartney in 1958–1959, which had been added to by John Lennon. The now familiar opening bars of Lennon's harmonica introduced "Love Me Do," which became their first release on October 5. It was a minor hit, reaching No. 17 in the UK charts, but eighteen months later, it reached No. 1 in the United States.

Their second single, "Please Please Me," released in November 1962, reached No. 2 in the official UK charts (though it is often cited as their first No. 1 as it reached this position in the *NME* chart), and their first album of the same name was recorded three months later. By the end of 1963, their popularity had spread and the phenomenon of Beatlemania had begun.
Ros Bott

Date 1962

Country UK

Why It's Key The release of "Love Me Do" marked the beginning of a new musical era, which still influences today's musicians, and launched The Beatles into unprecedented international stardom.

opposite The phenomenon that was the Beatles. Left to right: Ringo Starr, George Harrison, Paul McCartney, and John Lennon.

1960–1969

358

Key Political Event
Algeria gains independence

After seven-and-a-half years of bloody warfare between Muslim nationalists and French colonial forces, the people of Algeria were ready for change. Innocent bystanders, both Muslim and European, had been victims of atrocities by both French troops and the Front of National Liberation (FLN). Almost a million Europeans had left the country. French president Charles de Gaulle, realizing that the French empire was coming to an end, offered a way out: Algerians would be able to vote in a referendum either to stay with France, or to become an independent nation.

The final vote wasn't even close. Of 3,116,497 ballots cast, 2,605,293 voted in favor of independence, and only 6,732 voted to stay with France. Election officials noted that even in some of the most heavily European districts, there was not a single "no" vote cast.

Tens of thousands of Algerians poured into the streets of Algiers when the final tally was announced. The green and white flag of the nationalist movement was everywhere. People danced in long lines through the narrow streets of the ancient Casbah. Those who feared wholesale violence against Europeans still in the city were mistaken; newly liberated Muslims shook their hands, embraced them, and offered to buy them tea. It was a short-lived moment of fraternity for weary Algerians, but for one night at least, there was peace.
Heather Michon

Date July 2, 1962

Country Algeria

Why It's Key Independence ended 132 years of French rule in Algeria.

Key Cultural Event
Rolling Stones make their debut

For most teenagers in the 1960s, it seemed you had to be either a Rolling Stones fan or a Beatles fan. The Rolling Stones, with their grubby, unkempt appearance and air of rebellion, were the very antithesis of the clean-cut Beatles. Their popularity came from the combination of their music, image, and the public persona.

Formed in London, the original line-up, which included Brian Jones, Mick Jagger, Keith Richards, Dick Taylor, and Tony Chapman, took their name from the Muddy Waters' track "Rollin' Stone." Initially the group played their brand of Chicago ghetto blues in west London pubs and clubs. Their first formal gig in July 1962 was at the Marquee Club in central London. By this time Jagger and Richards had introduced the sounds of Chuck Berry and Bo Didley to the band.

By early 1963, bassist Bill Wyman and drummer Charlie Watts had replaced Taylor and Chapman. During an eight-month residency at the Crawdaddy Club in Richmond, the Stones attracted larger and larger audiences, and the attention of Andrew Oldham, who became their manager. They signed to record label Decca in May 1963, and hits like *Come On, I Wanna Be Your Man,* and *Not Fade Away* followed. When the band started to tour, wild concerts and frenzied, injured fans compounded their "bad boy" image.

Gradually the band developed a harder rock sound and went on to global fame and, as a live rock band, outlasted all of their contemporaries.
Lorraine Brownbill

Date July 12, 1962

Country UK

Why It's Key The band achieved global fame, and more than forty years after their debut are still playing live, sell-out concerts in some of the world's largest venues.

Key Person
Marilyn Monroe

When Norma Jeane Mortenson was eighteen years old, a photographer discovered her at a defense plant. Two years later, she signed a contract with the film company 20th Century Fox and "Marilyn Monroe" was born. Rising quickly to iconic fame, Monroe appeared in thirty films, including *Some Like it Hot,* for which she won a Golden Globe for Best Actress in a Comedy.

Monroe's personal life was also in the limelight. She had already married and divorced once as Norma Jeane. She married baseball star Joe DiMaggio in 1954 only to divorce him nine months later, and in 1956 she wed playwright Arthur Miller. However, this marriage also ended in 1961, and afterward she was linked to several men, including President John F. Kennedy.

By 1961, Monroe's commitment to work had become erratic, and in June 1962, two months before

her death, Fox Productions fired her for repeatedly failing to appear on the set of the film *Something Has Got To Give*. However, she was re-hired on August 1, and had planned to re-marry Joe DiMaggio a week later. So when, in the early hours of August 5, she was discovered dead in bed in her home in Los Angeles, the news shocked the world. Doctors found her lying naked next to an empty bottle of Nembutal sleeping pills.

Speculations still continue as to the cause of her untimely death, ranging from suicide to murder. The tragedy only enhanced Monroe's status as one of the world's most famous and endearing icons.
Mariko Kato

Date August 5, 1962

Born/Died 1926–1962

Nationality American

Why It's Key Marilyn Monroe is one of the most popular film stars of all time, and became an icon on her death.

opposite Medical attendents removing the body of Marilyn Monroe from her home.

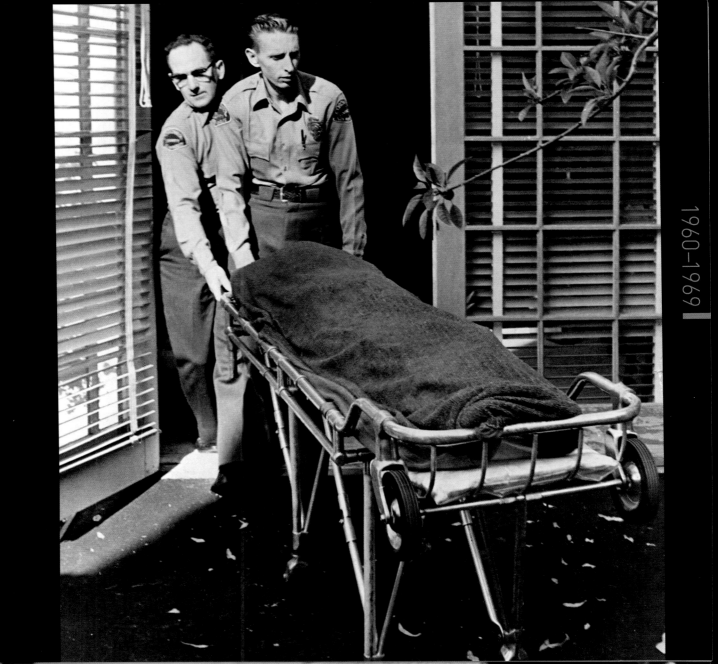

Key Cultural Event
Zapruder films the assassination of JFK

Americans were already reeling from the death of their Commander in Chief when a shocking record of the event kept the image of the assassination in clear focus. As President John F. Kennedy took a fatal ride through Dallas' Dealey Plaza moments before being shot in the back of head, women's clothing designer Abraham Zapruder aimed his 8 mm color camera at the passing vehicle. Zapruder was incredibly close to the car when shots were fired, and the shocking moment was captured in graphic detail. Shortly after the murder, Zapruder handed a copy of the assassination to the Secret Service, where it became an essential document in the investigation of the tragedy. Keeping the original recording to himself, Zapruder sold another copy to *Life* magazine, where black-and-white stills were published several days later. Zapruder himself wasn't interested in exploiting the document for his own gain, and during later court testimonies he broke down in tears when discussing the occasion.

Nevertheless, the Zapruder film gained instant fame as the only recorded document of the entire sequence of events. While nothing in the recording gave reason to discount the culpability of convicted assassin Lee Harvey Oswald, the movie has often been used by conspiracy theorists eager to argue that another gunman must have been present. Its initial television broadcast in 1975, complete with the frightening image of JFK's open head wound, came to be perceived as an iconic moment in the dissemination of violent images in the media.

Eric Kohn

Date November 22, 1963

Country USA

Why It's Key The only complete record of the JFK assassination, its broadcast in 1975 is considered the first time such violent imagery appeared on television.

Fact There were several other filmed documentations of the assassination, although none contained the same amount of detail.

opposite Jacqueline Kennedy leans over to assist her husband just after he is shot.

Key Person
Louis Armstrong

Born into a poor family in New Orleans, Louis Armstrong survived a troubled and unsettled childhood. He started playing the cornet with a local band, before eventually finding fame in Chicago in 1925. He recorded with his famous bands Hot Five and Hot Seven, producing hits with his virtuosic playing on cornet and trumpet.

However, it was his move into singing that established him as an iconic figure in jazz music. Moving away from the style of collective melody playing, he ventured into improvisational solo singing. His simultaneously daring and relaxed style was inspired by his distinctively gravelly voice and rich lower register, and his use of scat singing, a technique that involves stringing nonsensical syllables together, distinguished his music. Armstrong had almost single-handedly invented the role of jazz soloist, and stringed hit after hit, including "Stardust," "When The Saints Go Marching In," and "Ain't Misbehavin'."

By the time Armstrong reached his sixties, his popularity was fading, until he recorded "Hello, Dolly!," a song from a Broadway show of the same name, starring Carol Channing. It was a phenomenal success; it not only knocked the Beatles' "Can't Buy Me Love" off the top of the *Billboard* charts on December 3, 1963, but became the biggest hit of Armstrong's career. It also made him the oldest person to have a No. 1 hit in the United States. Armstrong enjoyed a commercial comeback, and appeared in the film adaptation of *Hello, Dolly!*, starring Barbra Streisand. He died of a heart attack in 1971, aged sixty-nine.

Mariko Kato

Date December 3, 1963

Born/Died 1901–1971

Nationality American

Why It's Key Louis Armstrong is one of the most recognizable and distinctive voices of the twentieth century, and a key innovator in jazz music.

Key Cultural Event
"Simmer Down" causes a sensation

Nesta Robert Marley was born in 1945 in a small village in Jamaica, the son of a white marine officer and a black Jamaican. When his father died, he moved to Trenchtown in Kingston with his mother, and he began to make music with his friend Bunny Livingstone (later Bunny Wailer). Marley (now known as Bob) was also introduced to Joe Higgs, the local reggae star, who became a tutor and mentor to the young singer. He also at this time started playing music with Peter McIntosh ("Tosh").

His first two solo singles, "Judge Not" and "One Cup of Coffee," found little recognition, but he did win a talent contest for his song, "Simmer Down," a melody written as a message to the violent street rebels in the ghettos of Kingston. In 1963, Marley formed a ska band with Livingstone, McIntosh, and others. Originally called The Teenagers, they later changed to The Wailing Rudeboys, and then The Wailing Wailers. At an audition for producer Coxson Dodd, they played "Simmer Down" and it was on the strength of this song that he signed the band. It went out as their first release on December 20, 1963, achieving instant popularity in Jamaica and reaching the top of the charts by February 1964. It is said that 70,000 copies were sold in a few weeks.

The Wailers, as they were now called, were established as a major ska group and the hit launched Marley's career as a singer and songwriter.

Ros Bott

Date December 20, 1963

Country Jamaica

Why It's Key The song launched Bob Marley's career and set him on the road to legendary status with reggae sounds such as "No Woman, No Cry" and "One Love."

Key Cultural Event
Makeba testifies on apartheid

As a baby, Miriam Makeba was once jailed with her mother, who had been arrested for selling home-brewed beer, and as a young woman she worked as a cleaner. In 1959, however, she starred in the hugely successful South African musical *King Kong*, and in Lionel Rogosin's film *Come Back, Africa*, attending its premiere in Venice at the age of twenty-seven. Angered by the resultant negative publicity, the South African government revoked Makeba's passport, even preventing her from attending her mother's funeral the following year. In London, Harry Belafonte helped Makeba to enter the United States, where, initially, she enjoyed great success, even singing at John F. Kennedy's 1962 birthday party. But when she married Black Panther Stokely Carmichael in 1968, she was shunned, and moved to Guinea.

Already high on the UN agenda as a result of African decolonization, racial discrimination rose higher following the 1960 Sharpeville Massacre, in which sixty-nine protesters were killed. As South Africa's principal trading partners were opposing sanctions, the UN launched a campaign against apartheid. At the ANC's request, Makeba testified before the special committee on apartheid in New York, pleading for the release of female political prisoners. She described South Africa as "a nightmare of police brutality and government terrorism," and said that it was time for the world to "act with firmness to stop these crazy rulers from dragging our country into a horrifying disaster." Her records were subsequently banned in South Africa, and her citizenship and right to return revoked.

Duncan Proudfoot

Date March 9, 1964

Country USA

Why It's Key Following the 1960 Sharpeville Massacre, black political opposition in South Africa had been banned; the UN campaign against apartheid initiated an arms embargo as well as other measures.

Fact Revered as Mama Africa, Miriam Makeba was the first South African to win a Grammy, in 1957.

opposite Makeba appears before the UN Trustees Council.

Key Political Event
Sultanate of Zanzibar overthrown

Zanzibar, a small archipelago 25-50 kilometers off the coast of East Africa, was a center of trade from at least the first century BCE. Also known as the Spice Islands, Zanzibar was a major producer of cinnamon, cloves, nutmeg, and peppers. The British took possession of the Arab sultanate in 1890, although the country remained under local rule.

On December 10, 1963, Zanzibar was granted independence. It lasted just thirty-three days. On April 26, 1964, a group of 300 armed men under the control of self-appointed "Field Marshal" John Okello launched a coup that deposed the new democratic government of Sayyid Jamshid bin Abdullah within days. Okello was affiliated with the leftist Afro-Shirazi Party (ASP), and although he began his coup without informing them of his intentions, they quickly rallied to his cause.

Okello targeted Zanzabari Arabs, killing between 5,000 and 20,000 in a few weeks. He would make strange, rambling speeches on the radio, once telling the Arab youth of a town "I will pass through Malindi armed with weapons of which I alone know. I want to see everyone stripped to his underpants and laying down. I want to hear them singing… "

With Okello in control, the ASP moved in. On April 26, 1964, Zanzibar merged with the coastal state of Tanganyika to form the new state of Tanzania. The party soon disavowed Okello, and he disappeared after 1971, the apparent target of an assassination.
Heather Michon

Date April 26, 1964

Country Tanzania

Why It's Key The coup ended in the massacre of up to 20,000 Zanzabari Arabs and led to the creation of Tanzania.

Key Political Event
Mandela sentenced to life in prison

After the Sharpville Massacre of 1960, the African National Congress (ANC), led by Nelson Mandela, was banned. Mandela and many of his other party members concluded that the power of the white nationalists would never be broken with civil action alone, and so they organized the "Spear of the Nation," a guerilla arm of the ANC, to coordinate sabotage against key government installations. With bomb blasts beginning against apartheid, Mandela went underground and eventually overseas to raise awareness of the struggle.

When Mandela returned to South Africa in 1962, he was arrested and was given a five-year prison sentence for encouraging strike action. He decided to handle his own defense and, in order to emphasize he was "a black African in a white man's court," he entered the room wearing beads and a Xhosa leopardskin "*kaross*" (cloak). Though Mandela was found guilty, his bearing and skillful articulation of human rights issues raised his international profile significantly.

While he was in prison, a farmhouse housing ANC weapons and documents was raided, which implicated Mandela and others and allowed the state to seek the death penalty for crimes of sabotage and conspiracy. The Rivonia Trial, as it was known, ended in June 1964, when he was resentenced to life imprisonment for sabotage and attempting to overthrow the state through revolution. Mandela was incarcerated for twenty-seven years in the brutal Robben Island prison. He would not be released until February 11, 1990.
Fred Lindsey

Date June 12, 1964

Country South Africa

Why It's Key Mandela's imprisonment became a rallying cry for the oppressed African nation.

opposite **Nelson Mandela** in the prison yard at Robben Island.

Key Cultural Event
Dylan goes electric at the Newport Festival

The Newport Festival in Newport, Rhode Island, featured heavily in Bob Dylan's early career. His debut performance there in 1963 propelled the then relatively-unknown into a folk hero, leading to worldwide superstardom, bringing folk music to the masses, and influencing many musicians with his socially aware lyrics. His return in to Newport 1965 was highly anticipated, and he was to be greeted like a returning hero. Yet the release earlier in the year of his latest album, *Bringing It All Back Home* should have foretold Dylan's intentions. The record was half acoustic and half electric.

Headlining the Sunday line-up, Dylan came onstage with members of the Paul Butterfield Blues Band, having rehearsed together the day before. The moment he plugged in, the dissent among the crowd was palpable, and after just three songs, the booing and heckling had escalated to such an extent that Dylan walked off. With pleas from the promoters ringing in his ears, Dylan came back onstage and, to presumably appease the hostile crowd, performed two acoustic numbers.

The episode has become an iconic moment in popular music, symbolizing the radicalism of the mid-1960s and its breaking of established cultural boundaries and demarcations. It has since been claimed that the crowd weren't booing Dylan. Rather, it was a reaction to the poor sound quality, and stories of an irate festival organizer threatening to "pull the plug" literally, have been downplayed in recent years.
Kerry Duffy

Date July 25, 1965

Country USA

Why It's Key A folk hero defied expectation, plugged in his electric guitar, and revolutionized popular music.

opposite Dylan plays a Fender Stratocaster electric guitar for the first time on stage at Newport.

Key Political Event
Singapore gains independence

The reasons for Singaporean independence were varied, but the core factors for its separation from the Federation of Malaysia were political and economic. As early as 1953, a commission led by Sir George Rendel allowed an autonomous government beneath a British umbrella. Over the next few years, a new political infrastructure was installed leading to the emergence of several parties and greater public turnout in government elections. However, as Singapore was a tiny nation under colonization for centuries, independence was still a distant hope. In 1959, the country eventually became officially self-governed with the election of the Lee Kuan Yew's Peoples Action Party (PAP).

It was the inauguration of Singapore as part of the Federation of Malaysia alongside Saba, Sarawak, and Malaya that finally forced Singapore toward full independence. Politically and ideologically, the PAP and the government of Kuala Lumpur frequently clashed. As racial tensions increased, it was decided to increase Singapore's economic contribution to the Federation's central government from 40 per cent to 60 per cent. With relations within the Federation becoming unbearable, the PAP sought freedom from the Federation and British control. With its independence finally acknowledged on August 9, 1965, Yusof bin Ishak was appointed president of Singapore. Economically, the decision was a gamble, with the PAP having to tackle huge unemployment and humanitarian issues. However, this arguably led to hard-fought self-sufficiency, which allowed Singapore to become the seventeenth wealthiest nation in terms of GDP per capita.
Greg Pittard

Date August 9, 1965

Country Singapore

Why It's Key Independence was the culmination of months of racial tension within the Federation of Malaysia, and the beginning of the daunting self-sufficiency program.

Key Political Event
Six Day War

On May 23, 1967, the Egyptian navy blocked the Straits of Tiran to all Israeli shipping. This, in itself, was an act of war. In addition, Egypt had accumulated large-scale ground forces on the Sinai Peninsula, and Jordan, amongst other Arab countries, had handed control of its army to Egypt.

In response, Israel launched a pre-emptive attack, under the direction of new Defense Minster, Moshe Dayan, on the morning of June 5. The Israeli Air Force bombed airfields in Egypt, Syria, and Jordan, destroying more than 350 planes – many still on the ground – in just a few hours. An appeal to King Hussein of Jordan, to avoid conflict, was ignored, and Jordan shelled the areas of west Jerusalem and Tel Aviv, forcing Israel to counterattack. In the six days of fierce fighting that followed, Israel occupied the Sinai Desert, Judea and Samaria, the Gaza Strip, the Golan Heights, and the West Bank. These areas afforded Israel the comfort of a "buffer" zone between itself and any potential Arab aggressor. In just six days, Israel had been transformed from a small, vulnerable country to a regional superpower, no longer under threat of attack.

Judea and Samaria was of special significance, since this was actually part of Israel in biblical times. The capture of the Gaza Strip, and the West Bank, however, left Israel with the problem of how to deal with the large Palestinian population under its control, a problem that is still, largely, unresolved.
David Dunning

Date June 5, 1967

Country Israel

Why It's Key The Six Day War was a turning point in the history of Israel.

Key Political Event
Nigerian Civil War (Biafran War)

The Nigerian Civil War was the culmination of decades of political and cultural tension in a nation unified only by name. Over three hundred different ethnic and tribal groups lived in Nigeria; with the north predominantly inhabited by the Muslim Hausa, and the south by the Christian Igbo. After the declaration of independence in 1960, political groups had emerged solely based on the religious and social beliefs of tribes, significantly segregating the nation.

Following accusations of fraud in the election of north and west alliance candidate Abubakar Tafawa Balewa, and increasing anxiety over the discovery of oil in the south, Igbo members of the army organized a military coup led by Johnson Aguiyi Ironsi beginning on January 5, 1966. The coup was largely a failure, and the North executed a counter-coup, placing Lieutenant Colonel Yakubu Gowon into power. Believing there to be no other choice, Colonel Odumegwu Ojukwu announced the separation of the south from the north, proclaiming it the Republic of Biafra. Attempts at peaceful negotiations were ignored, leading the Federation of the north to claim that it would reunite Nigeria by force.

Despite foreseeing a quick end to the war, the south did not surrender until January 13, 1970, as Ojukwu fled by plane leaving his deputy Phillip Effiong to acknowledge the north's impending victory. Three million people are thought to have died through fighting, genocide, and starvation caused by the blockades around Biafra, which denied the south key food and medicine supplies.
Greg Pittard

Date July 6, 1967

Country Nigeria

Why It's Key Three million lives were lost due to bloody violence and starvation.

opposite Ibo soldiers using tugboats as transportation down river during the Biafran war.

Key Political Event
Race riots hasten "Flight to the Suburbs"

White middle-class migration from the inner cities to the suburbs had been occurring steadily since World War II; at the same time, working-class black Americans were moving into the cities to find better industrial employment. But by the 1960s, industrial decline and high unemployment meant many cities were left with large, predominantly black populations crammed into deprived inner-city slums. Despite recent civil rights strides having been made with black suffrage and other anti-racist legislation, blacks were still being denied voting or equal educational rights by white attitudes and resistance. Failure of the authorities to enforce the new legislation caused widespread black disaffection, and riots, often triggered by police incidents, broke out. On July 14, 1967, the National Guard was called onto the streets of Newark when the

arrest of a black taxi driver triggered five days of violence, burning, and looting that left 26 dead and over 700 injured. Newark, together with Detroit, saw the worst of the race riots, which swept across more than 70 U.S. cities in the mid-1960s and greatly accelerated the "flight to the suburbs." As well as losing much of their middle classes to outlying suburbs, populations have continued to shrink in many cities since the riots – Newark's, for example, went from 440,000 in 1950 to today's 280,000. Conversely, the number of Americans living in both urban and rural suburbs in 1950 was 25 per cent, whereas the figure now has doubled to 50 per cent.

Hedley Paul

Date July 14, 1967

Country USA

Why It's Key Slow implementation of civil rights legislation, together with continuing prejudice and deprivation, sparked violence in black inner cities and quickened the trend among whites to leave for the suburbs, thereby rapidly changing the demographics of many U.S. cities.

opposite An African-American assaulted during Detroit's race riot tries to escape from a mob.

Key Cultural Event
Homosexuality decriminalized in Britain

On July 28, 1967, nearly ten years after the Wolfenden Report recommended the decriminalization of homosexual acts, the Sexual Offences bill was given royal assent by the Queen. At the time, it was seen as a further point in the rapid liberalization of laws and mores, both in the UK and around the world.

Prior to this groundbreaking law change, sexual activity between men had been a criminal offence, and could carry a prison sentence of up to two years. However, after the findings of Wolfenden, an increasing number of MPs floated or tabled motions to stop the blackmailing and police intimidation that made life miserable for homosexuals throughout the first half of the twentieth century. Although not all MPs were in favor, and some even warned gay people not to "flaunt"

their sexuality, there was a general sense that justice had been done in parliament; Labour MP Barbara Castle described it as "doing our bit for the boys."

Nevertheless, the age of consent was still unequal; twenty-one, as opposed to sixteen for heterosexuals. Sex also had to be "in private," which excluded hotels, and houses where a third person was present, even if they were in another room. "Buggery" remained illegal in Scotland until 1980, and in Northern Ireland until 1982. It was not until the 1990s and 2000s that the age of consent was equalized and gay people began to be accorded adoption, employment, and civil partnership rights.

Andrew Blades

Date July 28, 1967

Country UK

Why It's Key It was the first liberalizing measure in a process that continues today.

Fact Homosexual offences carried up to two years' imprisonment until 1967.

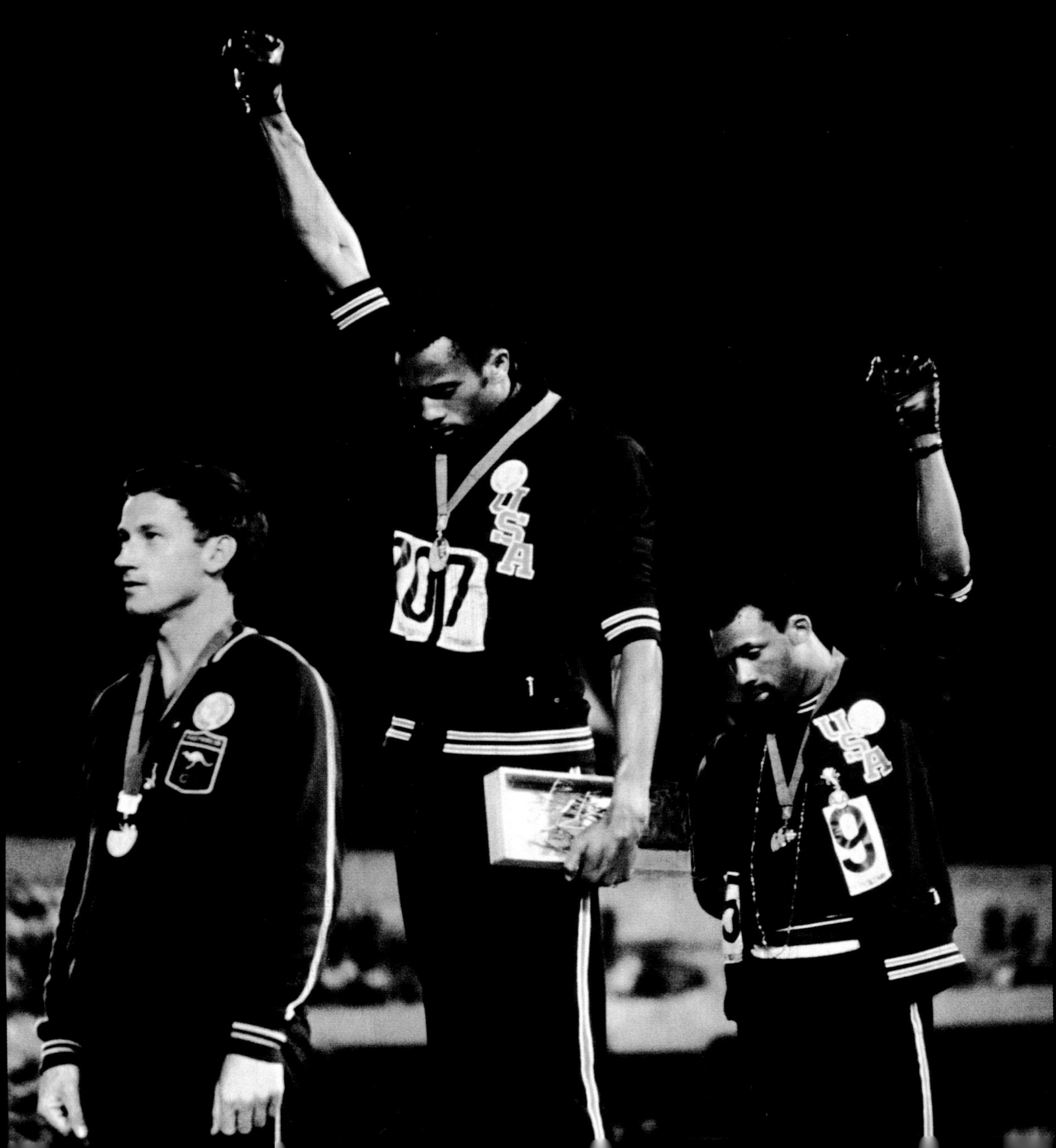
USA
USA

Key Political Event
Massacre at *La Plaza de las Tres Culturas*

Mexico was far from immune to the student protests and general turmoil that consumed the United States and Europe in 1968. In Mexico City, the radicalization of the student left coincided with the run-up to the Olympic Games, that were due to open on October 12 of that year. By September, several months of student unrest in the capital had culminated in the military occupation of Mexico's National Autonomous University and the controversial resignation of the university's rector. The violent confrontations that ensued between students and the military led the ruling PRI to fear for its international reputation at a time when the eyes of the world were fixed on the Mexican capital. In fact, the presence of the international media for the Olympics was part of what motivated the students to protest, in the hope that they would bring their frustration to the attention of the world.

On October 2, 5,000 protesters gathered for a rally at the *Plaza de las Tres Culturas* in Tlatelolco, and the military orchestrated a response that had been secretly planned by the government. Tanks and soldiers surrounded the square, and armed men in plain clothes began shooting from within the crowd. In the chaos that followed, a large number of casualties occurred, but the subsequent cover-up prevents an accurate assessment of the scale of the violence perpetrated against the protesters. The official death toll was reported as 32, but most accounts of the massacre estimate that between 200 and 300 people died.

Charlotte Whittle

Date October 2, 1968

Country Mexico

Why It's Key The massacre planned by the government of Gustavo Díaz Ordaz was a landmark act of brutality by the Institutional Revolutionary Party (PRI), which ruled a nominally democratic Mexico with an iron fist for seventy years.

1960–1969

417

Key Cultural Event
Black Power salute at the Mexico Olympic Games

American athletes Tommie Smith and John Carlos had completed the 200 meter race at the 1968 Olympics and were called to receive their medals; gold and bronze, respectively. They approached the podium wearing black socks, and as the American national anthem played, each held up a black-gloved fist, the symbol for black power. Both men were members of the Olympic Project for Civil Rights, an organization that advocated equality for minority athletes. The organization at one point urged black athletes to boycott the Olympics, but eventually encouraged members to protest racial inequality in their own ways. While some respected the action of Smith and Carlos, others felt the Olympics were the wrong forum for the statement. Smith and Carlos faced fierce opposition from whites and blacks, even receiving death threats. *Time* magazine referred to the demonstration as "effective but petty" and altered the Olympic slogan from "Faster, Higher, Stronger," to "Angrier, Nastier, Uglier."

Another opponent was Avery Brundadge, president of the International Olympic Committee, who asked the committee to suspend the two athletes from the U.S. team. After the committee refused, Brundadge threatened to ban the entire U.S. track team, and Smith and Carlos were expelled from the Olympics.

While many athletes disagreed with the decision to raise the black power salute at the Olympics, several were stunned when the two were expelled, some initially refusing to participate. Three of the pair's teammates – Larry James, Ron Freeman, and Lee Evans – wore black berets to their awards ceremony in protest.

Bethonie Butler

Date: October 16, 1968

Country Mexico

Why It's Key Public reaction to the demonstration was divided, but eventually cost the two athletes their medals and their membership on the United States Olympic Team.

opposite American athletes Tommie Smith and John Carlos protest with the Black Power salute as they stand on the winner's podium.

Key Discovery
The Internet goes online

It is difficult to imagine life without the Internet. So central to twenty-first century existence, the Internet has become invaluable as both a method of communication and a resource of information. First launched in 1969, with the arrival of ARPAnet, the Internet initially sought to revolutionize communication within the military. Named after the Advanced Research Projects Agency, ARPAnet originally linked computer terminals at the University of California in Los Angeles and the Stanford Research Institute. Using the method of packet switching, ARPAnet allowed users to exchange data securely, and new terminals were added at the University of California in Santa Barbara and the University of Utah.

ARPAnet was quickly established as an innovative and useful method of communication, and its network expanded rapidly. Reserved for non-commercial use, ARPAnet connected research institutions and also led to other major technological developments including email, telnet, and file transfer protocol in the early 1970s. ARPAnet subsequently moved beyond military use, and by the mid-1980s, NASA, the National Science Foundation, and the U.S. Department of Energy each developed and launched Wide Area Networks based on TCP/IP. This became known collectively as the Internet, and the international connection first established by ARPAnet with Norway in 1973 was quickly extended worldwide. By 1990, ARPAnet had been replaced by newly developed networking technology, but it had laid the foundations of a worldwide phenomenon that would revolutionize communication technology.

Hannah Furness

Date January 14, 1969

Country USA

Why It's Key ARPAnet was the earliest form of the Internet and revolutionized communication technology.

Key Political Event
Jan Palach sets himself on fire

"Do not be indifferent to the day when the light of the future was carried forward by a burning body." Mourners displayed the slogan on Prague's Wenceslas Square following the horrific suicide of philosophy student Jan Palach. Palach died from burns to 85 per cent of his body when he lit himself on fire to protest the occupation of Czechoslovakia by a Soviet-led invasion on August 20, 1968. His death sparked riots in Prague when police moved in with tear gas and clubs to stop the march of hundreds of demonstrators gathered to pay tribute to Palach's sacrifice. Several days later, an estimated crowd of 500,000 lined the streets in the rain to watch the funeral procession.

Palach and a small group of radicals were outraged at the invasion of their country and the passive reaction of the Czechs. The occupation was Moscow's answer to the "Prague Spring," a brief period of economic and political reform introduced under the leadership of Alexander Dubcek. Dubcek dubbed it "socialism with a human face," but Warsaw Pact countries were worried about the spread of such liberal policies. Czechoslovakia was forced into a period of "normalization," and few reforms survived the Soviet pressure to toe the line. Twenty years later, mass demonstrations were held in Prague over the period called Palach Week, commemorating his death amidst calls for greater freedom. Many were injured and over 1,400 arrested. By November 1989, the Velvet Revolution would herald the end of Communist rule in Czechoslovakia.

Larraine Andrews

Date January 16, 1969

Country Czechoslovakia (now Czech Republic)

Why It's Key Jan Palach became a martyr when he burned himself to death in protest against the Soviet invasion of Czechoslovakia following the brief reform period called the Prague Spring. His death sparked riots but it would be another twenty years before the Velvet Revolution ended Communist control.

Key Political Event
Arafat elected head of PLO

For over thirty-five years, Yasser Arafat – the *nom de guerre* of Muhammad Abdul Rahman Abdul Raouf Arafat Al-Quda Al-Husseini – was the popular face of the Palestine Liberation Organization (PLO), the umbrella group of Palestinian militant groups and political parties that elected him its military leader in 1969, and political leader in 1973. From the late 1960s until his death in 2004, Arafat was scarcely out of the international spotlight.

The first part of Yasser Arafat's career was purely military, featuring numerous guerrilla battles against Israeli forces, and he became known for the pistol worn at his hip and his trademark *kaffiyeh*. Over time, however, the leader of the Palestinians mellowed, and by the late 1980s was ready to talk peace with Israel. Overcoming ingrained Israeli suspicion of his

revolutionary militant past, Arafat nonetheless managed to work together with politicians such as Yitzhak Rabin, the Prime Minister of Israel, for a political solution to the Palestinian problem. These efforts were crowned by Arafat's sharing of the 1994 Nobel Peace Prize. This was the high tide of Arafat's credibility with Israel and reputation in the West. As the Oslo Accords fell apart, Israel and Palestine returned to their previous footing of mutual recrimination, and toward the end of his life Arafat found himself confined to his compound by Israeli tanks and died shortly thereafter. Despite the fact that he had been overtaken by the pace of events, Arafat died as a beloved symbol of Palestine.

Demir Barlas

Date February 3, 1969

Country Palestine

Why It's Key Yasser Arafat, for nearly four decades the face of Palestine, began his rise to prominence as a PLO guerilla but ended as an international statesman.

1960–1969

Key Political Event
USA begins bombing campaign on Cambodian soil

To prevent the North Vietnamese from entering the South, the Nixon administration authorized the bombing of Vietnamese Communist strongholds in Cambodia in March 1969. March 18 was the first day of what would turn out to be a four-year bombing campaign that drew Cambodia into the Vietnam War. Nixon kept the campaign secret from Congress for several months, claiming that the bombings were legitimate. The situation in Cambodia was exacerbated in April 1970, when American and South Vietnamese troops entered Cambodia in order to destroy North Vietnamese and Vietcong sanctuaries and supplies.

The Vietnam War was already the cause of public dissatisfaction and opposition in the United States, which Nixon was trying to appease by promoting the "Vietnamization" of war; promising to bring U.S.

soldiers home and replace them with newly trained South Vietnamese troops. That is why President Nixon's televised announcement on April 30, 1970, in which he declared that the United States had invaded Cambodia, caused shock and anger among the American public. Nixon's address also triggered off a series of massive student protests all over the United States. The culmination of the protests was the shootings at Ohio's Kent State University on May 4, 1970, when four students were killed and nine wounded by members of the National Guard. Nixon ordered the withdrawal of U.S. troops from Cambodia shortly after the Kent State shootings, but the U.S. bombing campaign in Cambodia continued until August 1973.

Sonja Kudeljnjak

Date March 18, 1969

Country Cambodia

Why It's Key The U.S. military involvement in Cambodia caused many violent protests in the United States and damaged Nixon's credibility.

Fact During the bombing campaign in Cambodia, the United States dropped 540,000 tons of bombs and killed between 150,000 and 500,000 civilians.

Key Political Event
The Stonewall Riots

The Stonewall Riots may not have been the first demonstration of powerful resistance against American – or indeed global – homophobia and legalized oppression, but it is fair to say that the dispute that took place there became a point of reference for the gay liberation movement.

When police raided the now-famous Stonewall Inn, a gay bar in Greenwich Village, New York City, and were forcibly resisted by its patrons on June 27, 1969, a precedent was set for rising up against an authority that would indiscriminately persecute an entire cross-section of American people. The raid itself was routine – it was the opposition to the raid that was not. The riots lasted for several days, garnering attention that altered the nation's and the world's perceptions of alternative sexual identities. The women and men who refused to cower under police authority broke a silence that was a *reveille* for other queer people whose fear had stifled them until this moment in history.

Of course the oppression still sits uncomfortably upon the nation's conscience even today – tolerance is an ambiguous word – and certainly the mainstream media did not take well to this gay resistance. But it is true that, as Jerry Lisker pejoratively wrote in the *New York Daily News* on July 6, 1969, "Queen Power" did rear "its bleached blond head in revolt" and the revolution continues into its fourth decade. Today Stonewall is the central symbol of resistance against oppression of peoples with queer orientations.

Julie Sutherland

Date June 28, 1969

Country USA

Why It's Key The Stonewall Riots became a symbol for the gay liberation movement that had gathered momentum in the 1960s.

Fact On the night of the riots, the charge was actually for the illegal sale of alcohol. However, this was a thinly disguised excuse to harass the bar's patrons.

Key Discovery
Man walks on the moon

Neil Armstrong's "one small step" onto the moon's Sea of Tranquillity was the result of an extraordinary commitment made by President Kennedy eight years earlier. Kennedy announced that by the end of the decade an American would have walked on the face of the moon and returned home safely. In order to achieve this, he made the largest peacetime commitment of resources ever known, and the Apollo space program, as it was later called, was born.

At the time of his pledge, only one American had flown in space and no mission had left Earth's orbit. But after a huge research and technological effort, and numerous preparatory missions, *Apollo 11* was ready to make the attempt. The launch and separation of the command and lunar modules were successful, and after a difficult landing on a boulder field, Neil Armstrong, followed swiftly by Edwin "Buzz" Aldrin, became the first man on the lunar surface. Fearing that they might have to take off again quickly, their first task was to collect samples of rocks and soil. The second was to unveil an American flag and erect a plaque bearing the words: "we came in peace for all mankind." This historic event was relayed by satellite and broadcast on television to the waiting world. Although they spent only fifteen hours on the surface, the footprints they made will last for millions of years. Only ten other people have since repeated this feat, and it remains a milestone in human history.

Laura Davies

Date July 20, 1969

Country USA

Why It's Key Armstrong's journey was a pioneering and iconic space mission broadcast around the world.

opposite Edwin "Buzz" Aldrin near Lunar Module *Apollo 11* during the first manned journey to the moon.

Key Cultural Event
Manson Family murders

A self-proclaimed Jesus figure, Charles Manson gathered a group of vulnerable youngsters high on drugs and free love when he moved to San Francisco after his release from prison in 1967. Together they called themselves the "family," and Manson was their leader. Though he quickly established himself as a "spiritual leader," Manson moved the family around the west coast and Mexico, before settling back in Los Angeles, where he preached his beliefs of white supremacy and warned of a race war in a haze of drug-induced certainty.

Upon the release of The Beatles' *White Album* (1968), Manson's fragile grip on reality loosened further as he saw their songs as a vindication of his beliefs. On August 9, 1969, Manson sent his family to the house of Sharon Tate, the young, pregnant wife of Roman Polanski. As Polanski was away in Europe, Tate had invited a group of friends over to keep her company. The family broke into the house in the early hours and slaughtered the five friends, leaving bloodstained messages on the walls and victims. Wanting to ensure his message would not be ignored, the next evening Manson and his family murdered Rosemary and Leno LaBianca.

After their inevitable arrests, the trial was the longest and most expensive in U.S. history, with Manson offering a vociferous defense. But no rhetoric could save him, and he was sentenced to death, along with four of his family. In 1972, when the death sentence was banned, they were given life in prison.
Kerry Duffy

Date August 9, 1969

Country USA

Why It's Key The myth of the summer of love was forever tarnished by the shocking murders committed by Charles Manson and his "family."

Fact Manson had already spent over half his life in correctional facilities when he started the "Manson Family."

Key Cultural Event
Woodstock

When four inexperienced promoters got together to organize the Woodstock Music and Art Fair, they had no idea that their festival was to become a legendary event in the history of rock music. Woodstock became synonymous with the hippie counterculture of the late 1960s, allowing around 400,000 people to enjoy three days and nights of "sex, drugs, and rock 'n' roll." But mostly it was about the music.

Farmer Max Yasgur allowed his land in Bethel, New York, to be used for the festival after the town of Woodstock, 50 miles away, turned it down. The Woodstock name, however, was retained, and organizers anticipated that up to 100,000 people might attend. Approximately four times as many turned up, blocking the roads for miles around. Due to almost non-existent security, most got into the festival for free. The crowds were treated to three days of music from some of the biggest names of the time, including The Who, Janis Joplin, The Grateful Dead, and Crosby, Stills, and Nash. The final act – Jimi Hendrix – closed the festival with a memorable guitar solo of *The Star Spangled Banner*.

Torrential rainstorms hit the event but this only seemed to add to the camaraderie between the festival goers, some of whom danced naked in the sea of mud. Despite the enormous crowds, this monumental event was largely trouble-free and lived up to its billing as "Three Days of Peace and Music."

The following year, Michael Wadleigh's film *Woodstock* became a major box office hit.
Lorraine Brownbill

Date August 15, 1969

Country USA

Why It's Key Woodstock became a symbol for the Hippie culture and "flower power" generation, as well as a milestone in the history of rock music.

opposite The crowd at Woodstock was a phenomenon. The three-day event drew half a million peaceful music lovers.

Key Cultural Event
My Lai massacre reported in U.S. press

One year, seven months, and twenty-eight days had passed between the horrific massacre of several hundred Vietnamese civilians by U.S. forces and the first reports of the event, but the passage of time did little to mitigate public outrage.

My Lai was part of the fallout of the Vietcong's Tet Offensive in January 1968. American military commanders decided to launch a series of raids on several small villages where they believed Vietcong troops were hiding. Charlie Company, a unit of the 20th Infantry's 1st Battalion, was ordered to move against a group of hamlets designated My Lai 1, 2, 3, and 4 on March 16, 1968.

The platoon that entered My Lai 4 found no soldiers or men of military age. But over a few hours, the soldiers led by 2nd Lieutenant William Calley let loose in an orgy of killing. Civilians were beaten, stabbed, tortured, and clubbed, but most were simply shot down. Women were raped, and estimates of the death toll range from 347 to 504. An army helicopter pilot who happened to fly over the scene rescued a few residents.

Calley and twenty-five others were quietly court-martialed for their crimes. The story might not have been told but for Ron Ridenhour, a member of Charlie Company who heard about My Lai 4 from his comrades. Ridenhour wrote to the White House, the Pentagon, and Congress about the massacre, but got no response. Finally, he talked to a reporter named Sy Hersh, who broke the story in November 1969. News of the killing helped further galvanize anti-war critics.
Heather Michon

Date November 12, 1969
Country USA
Why It's Key News of the massacre helped solidify American public opinion against the Vietnam War.

opposite Houses and corpses burned by American soldiers during the My Lai massacre.

Key Cultural Event
Fossey makes the cover of *National Geographic*

In three years of studying the mountain gorilla in the Rwandan jungles, primatologist Dian Fossey had learned that the best way to get close to her skittish subjects was to try to fit in. So when a young blackback named Peanuts approached her one morning, she acted like a gorilla, loudly scratching her scalp and leaning casually back into the dense foliage.

She slowly extended a hand. And then, after contemplating it for a moment, Peanuts did something none of his species had ever done before: he reached out and touched her fingers with his own.

They sat for a moment, holding hands, until "he stood and gave vent to his excitement by a whirling chest beat, then went off to rejoin his group," she wrote in her journal. "I expressed my own happy excitement by crying… "

Peanuts and Fossey were not alone that morning. *National Geographic* photographer Bob Campbell, who had been documenting Fossey's research activities in Rwanda since 1968, was just out of view. His photos became the magazine's cover story in early 1970 and brought enormous public interest to Fossey's cause.

Fossey used her newfound fame to draw attention to the need for conservation and protection of her endangered subjects. But her compassion for the gorilla led to contempt for humans, particularly poachers and government officials who wanted to exploit the animals for financial gain. Fossey was found brutally murdered in her cabin at her Karisoke Research Center two days after Christmas in 1985.
Heather Michon

Date 1970
Country Rwanda/USA
Why It's Key The photograph made primatologist Dian Fossey a household name and introduced people to the plight of the endangered mountain gorilla.

Key Cultural Event
The Beatles break up

When Paul McCartney announced the breakup of The Beatles in April 1970, millions of fans were stunned.

The Beatles' music had been the soundtrack to the lives of a generation of teenagers, but the band had also appealed to children, parents, and even grandparents. After their first hit in 1962, The Beatles' live performances and songwriting skills had quickly taken the world by storm; they seemed universally popular. From the early days of Beatlemania through their progression into experimental sounds and on to the creative masterpiece of the 1967 album, *Sgt Pepper's Lonely Hearts Club Band*, The Beatles revolutionized the popular music scene.

By the end of the decade the band became worn down by the demands placed upon them. They launched their own record label, Apple, in 1968, but personal disagreements crept in and there were signs that the four were increasingly going their separate ways. The divisions were evident during the filming of *Let it Be* (1970), a documentary about the album of the same name. The Beatles recorded *Abbey Road*, their last studio album, in 1969 and gave a last, seemingly impromptu, live performance on the roof of their record company's building in London.

Finally, there were financial problems for Apple, two of the band had married and the disagreements, principally between Lennon and McCartney, intensified. Millions were at stake and Paul filed a lawsuit against John, George, Ringo, and Apple to dissolve the group. Beatlemania was over.

Lorraine Brownbill

Date April 10, 1970

Country UK

Why It's Key It was the end of an era and, probably, the most influential and legendary band of the twentieth century.

opposite The 1969 cover image for the Beatles' *Abbey Road* album.

428

Key Political Event
Kent State shootings

On April 30, 1970, U.S. President Richard Nixon announced that U.S. forces had entered Cambodia. He hoped that this invasion would disrupt North Vietnamese supply lines and end the war, but anti-war Americans saw the strategy as escalation. Reaction was immediate and intense, especially at colleges like Ohio's Kent State University. Anti-war demonstrations were common at that campus. In the late 1960s, the influential Kent State chapter of the radical SDS (Students for a Democratic Society) developed an extremist reputation. The Ohio legislature had passed laws increasing governmental power against such demonstrations, and Ohio citizens had supported Republican governor James Rhodes's harsh responses to past protests. These factors helped define the events that unfolded after Nixon's announcement.

Protests started immediately, and clashes with local police forces occurred on May 1. On May 2, a demonstration resulted in the burning of the ROTC (Reserve Officer Training Corps) building, and the National Guard was called to restore order. Campus administrators canceled a May 4 demonstration, but 3,000 students attended anyway. Attempts to disperse the rally devolved into chaos, and some guardsmen fired at the crowd. In thirteen seconds, sixty-one shots killed four students and wounded nine. Across the nation, campuses erupted furiously, and 80 per cent of U.S. universities were forced into closing by the end of May. That summer, facing such opposition, Nixon had little choice but to hasten the process of withdrawal from Vietnam.

Christina Welsch

Date May 4, 1970

Country USA

Why It's Key The killing of four students at a protest rally against the Vietnam War triggered a massive reaction across the country, which played a major role in forcing U.S. President Richard Nixon to withdraw U.S. forces from the conflict.

Key Cultural Event
Yukio Mishima commits public suicide

Yukio Mishima's first novel, *Confessions of a Mask*, about a young homosexual who hides behind a mask to fit into society, was published in 1949. This semi-autobiographical work established Mishima as one of the most popular writers of his age. His vivid and versatile style, rich in metaphors and aphorisms, was celebrated in his novels, serial novellas, short stories, and literary essays as well as kabuki plays and noh dramas. As his works were translated into English, his popularity spread globally, and he was nominated for the Nobel Prize for Literature three times.

Toward the end of his life, Mishima became outspokenly patriotic to imperial Japan, and was obsessed with the samurai spirit of Japan's past. He organized the Tatenokai, a private army stressing physical fitness and the martial arts.

Feeling increasingly disillusioned by modern Japan, Mishima planned his public suicide as a protest. On November 25, 1970, he and four other Tatenokai members barricaded themselves in the Tokyo headquarters of the Eastern Command of Japan's Self-Defense Forces. After making a speech, calling for the restoration of the emperor to his rightful prominence, Mishima committed *seppuku* (ritual suicide by disembowelment, originally performed by samurais). A Tatenokai member did the duty of *kaishakunin*, beheading Mishima to relieve him of the pain.

Mishima is infamous for his public suicide, but is also admired by critics around the world for his defining role in styling Japanese literature.
Mariko Kato

Date November 25, 1970

Country Japan

Why It's Key Yukio Mishima (1925–1970) is considered to be one of Japan's greatest authors.

Fact Yukio Mishima's real name was Kimitake Hiraokawa.

opposite Appearing on the balcony of the Ichigaya Station, Mishima closed his speach by declaring "Tenno Banzai" ("long live the emperor") before committing *hara-kiri*.

Key Political Event
First law mandating seat belt use

An alarming toll of death and injury accompanied the rapid growth of automobile use around the world. Amid the first major anti-accident campaigns in the 1930s, some American physicians urged auto manufacturers to install seat belts in their vehicles. By the 1950s, a few did so. During the 1960s, under pressure from state and federal governments, the U.S. manufacturers made them standard equipment. Most drivers and passengers did not use them, however, and the highway death toll kept rising.

By then, Australian emergency-room physicians were at the forefront of the arguments for seat belt use. In 1970, which turned out to be Australia's worst year for road deaths, the Australian state of Victoria passed a law requiring motorists to fasten their seat belts. It took effect on January 1, 1971. Within a year,

all the other Australian states had followed suit, closely followed by New Zealand, Japan, and several European lands. Britain, along with most Canadian provinces and U.S. states, eventually fell into line during the 1980s.

Some critics denounced the laws as an infringement on individual liberty. Others questioned their effectiveness in saving lives. Enforcement of the laws, and actual increases in seat belt use, varied greatly. Coming as they did at the same time as other safety measures such as lower speed limits, improved car design, and crackdowns on drunk drivers, their role in reducing the carnage on the highways is disputed, but it has probably been significant.
Brian Ladd

Date January 1, 1971

Country Australia

Why It's Key Governments decided that people had to be forced to protect their lives on the highway.

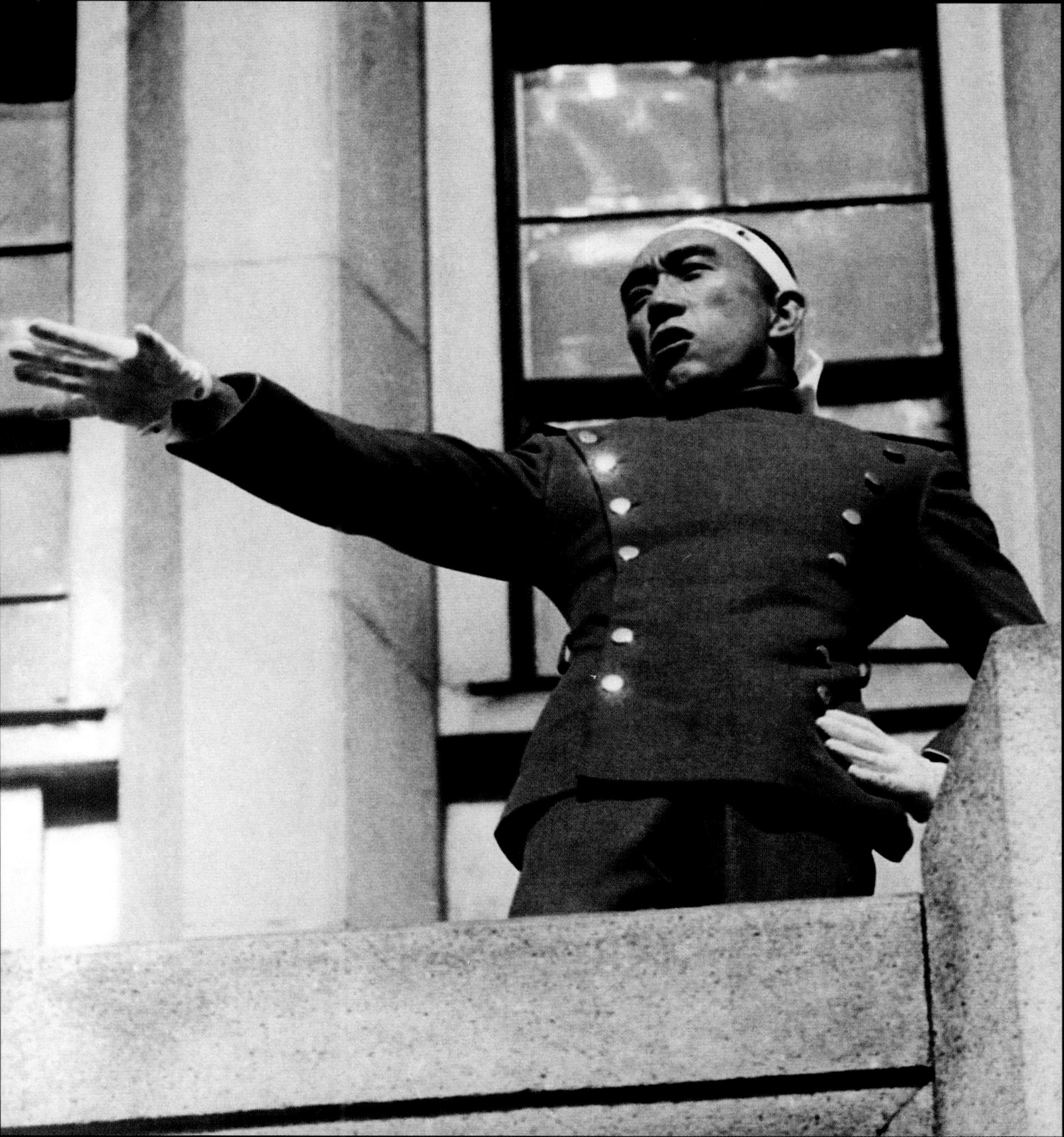

Key Political Event
The Padilla Affair

Heberto Padilla, like many Cuban writers and intellectuals, supported Fidel Castro's revolution during the euphoric years that followed 1959 and initially became a figure in the state-sponsored cultural establishment. By the late 1960s, however, his poems had begun to reflect profound disillusionment with Castro's rule. The awarding of a major national literary prize in 1968 to Padilla for his collection *Out of the Game* (*Fuera del juego*), which featured unabashed attacks on the government's cultural policies, enraged Castro and his cultural commissars. Padilla was promptly placed under surveillance and later house arrest. In 1971, he was accused of "deviationism," imprisoned, and forced to read out a humiliating 4,000-word confession on national television repudiating his former counter-revolutionary attitudes.

Many of the Cuban revolution's most fervent international supporters expressed their dismay and signed petitions criticizing the Cuban government's actions. Fidel Castro launched an aggressive counterattack, denouncing the petitions as the work of effete "bourgeois intellectuals." Some of Padilla's former allies, like novelists Gabriel García Márquez and Julio Cortázar, ultimately re-affirmed their loyalty to Castro and Cuban socialism, while other fellow writers, like Vargas Llosa and Fuentes, became avowed critics. The international left's honeymoon with Cuba was definitively over. Padilla would remain in Havana under surveillance until 1980, at which point he obtained permission to migrate to the United States. He died in Auburn, Alabama on September 25, 2000.
Geoffrey Schullenberger

Date 1971

Country Cuba

Why It's Key The Cuban government's persecution of prominent poet Heberto Padilla caused an acrimonious rift on the Latin American left and did permanent damage to Cuba's image as a culturally open alternative to Soviet Communism.

Fact Padilla's friend Jorge Edwards offers a memorable inside view of the controversy in his memoir *Persona non grata*.

434

Key Cultural Event
Inoue Dainsuk invents the karaoke machine

Before there were prerecorded backing tracks or scrolling lyrics on video monitors, Japanese businessmen in need of relaxation could sing along to hired backing bands in local bars. It was a drummer in one such band, Inoue Dainsuk – the self-confessed worst musician in Kobe, Japan – who first envisaged a machine that would replicate their work. Inoue constructed a number of boxes, each containing a tape deck, amplifier, and coin-slot. He loaded them with pre-recorded accompaniments to popular songs and rented them to local bars.

"Karaoke" means "empty orchestra" in Japanese, and was originally the term for the recorded accompaniments used by professional musicians. Inoue's machine brought karaoke to ordinary people, allowing anyone with enough courage or alcohol to take a turn as their favorite star. The popularity of the karaoke machine received a further boost with the introduction of soundproof cubicles – ensuring privacy for those who wanted to sing, and peace for those who didn't. Since then karaoke has become a pastime to amuse and abuse the ears of millions across the globe.

Inoue never patented his idea and profited little from the million-dollar industry it spawned. Recognition did eventually come. In 1999, *Time* magazine named Inoue as one of the twenty most influential Asians of the twentieth century – alongside Mao Zedong and the Dalai Lama.
Rachel Eley

Date 1971

Country Japan

Why It's Key Japanese technology gives everyone the chance of three-minute stardom, though not everyone is keen to try it.

Key Fact In 2004, the academic journal *Annals of Improbable Research* awarded Inoue the IgNoble Peace Prize: "for inventing karaoke and thereby providing an entirely new way for people to learn to tolerate each other."

Key Political Event
Idi Amin becomes dictator of Uganda

Idi Amin came into power in 1971 through a military coup that overthrew previous Ugandan Prime Minister Milton Obote. Ugandans initially supported this coup, misled by Amin's oaths to abolish secret police, free political prisoners, and re-establish civilian rule.

However, the promised civilian elections were never held and Amin began his rule with a mass execution of officers and troops whom he believed were loyal to Obote, resulting in the murder of around 300,000 people. Less than a year later, in 1972, Amin expelled 40,000–80,000 Indian and Pakistani people from Uganda, in an effort to create an all-black state. Those killed included ordinary citizens, cabinet ministers, chief justices, Supreme Court judges, academics, clergy, medical doctors, business executives, journalists, and foreigners.

Amin continued his oppressive regime by increasing the size of his army, placing military tribunals above civil courts, and dissolving parliament. The economy of Uganda began to collapse as a result of Amin's mismanagement and the expulsion of Indians and Pakistanis who had been significant contributors to the Ugandan economy. Amin's reign of terror continued until 1979 when invading Tanzanian forces took over the city of Kampala. Amin was forced to flee to Libya with his four wives, many mistresses, and about twenty of his children. He lived out the rest of his life quietly in Saudi Arabia, without ever having to answer for the cruelty, bloodshed, and economic ruin that he had brought upon his country.

Anne Hsu

Date February 2, 1971

Country Uganda

Why It's Key Idi Amin was one of the most brutal military dictators to rule post-independence Africa.

Key Political Event
Creation of Bangladesh

The partition of India in 1947 resulted in the formation of India and Pakistan. India was mainly Hindu and Pakistan mainly Muslim. From the outset, the new country of Pakistan faced many challenges. Its people shared the Muslim religion but little else. The country was geographically divided into West and East Pakistan, separated by 1,600 kilometers of India. Significant cultural, ethnic, and language differences existed between the two regions. Although West Pakistan contained a minority of the population, it maintained control over the government, the armed forces, and key parts of the economy. The adoption of Urdu (spoken in the West) as the national language sparked great bitterness in the East, where Bengali predominated. In 1954, following riots in Dhaka, both Urdu and Bengali became national languages.

But resentment continued to escalate in East Pakistan over what were considered unacceptable political and economic inequities. Bengali leaders established the Awami League in 1949 to fight for the independence of East Pakistan and in 1966, under the leadership of Sheikh Mujibur Rahman (generally known as Sheikh Mujib), the league proposed a six-point program to address the problems. When Mujib and the league won an unexpected election victory in 1970, their plan to make the six points the basis of a new constitution eventually led to civil war and the declaration of independence of the new state of Bangladesh. In the process, an estimated one million Bengalis were killed in East Pakistan while another ten million fled to neighboring India.

Larraine Andrews

Date March 26, 1971

Country Pakistan/Bangladesh

Why It's Key The formation of Pakistan, mainly on the basis of religious lines, ignored the fundamental differences of culture, ethnicity, and language that separated West and East Pakistan. Years of conflict and bloodshed led to the creation of Bangladesh as a separate country.

Key Cultural Event **The Soviet Union launches the first manned space station**

The Soviet Union once more led the "Space Race" against the United States by launching the first space station of any kind into orbit around the Earth. The station could serve as a base for scientific research, in addition to supporting human life for long periods in space in comparison to the short journeys that had been commissioned previously.

After the U.S. administration won the battle to land the first men on the Moon, the Soviet Union turned their attention and resources toward the possibility of sustained living in space. The *Salyut 1* space station was launched on April 19, 1971. The station was a modified spacecraft just 15.8 meters long and 4 meters wide that could be habited by up to three crew members.

The first attempt to dock with *Salyut 1* by *Solyuz 10* was a catastrophe, and so a second crew was launched in the *Solyuz 11* mission. Georgi Dobrovolski, Viktor Patsayev, and Vladislav Volkov spent twenty-three days conducting scientific research before a fire on board cut the expedition short.

The success of the station led to further record-breaking stays on improved space stations, and has also continued to influence key areas in mathematics and physics education, present day microtechnology, and food containment; but at a price. The three Soviet astronauts were subjected to a loss of cabin pressure during the reentry of *Solyuz 11*, and tragically died.
Greg Pittard

Date April 19, 1971

Country USSR

Why It's Key For the first time, humans were able to live for long periods in space, as opposed to conducting fleeting missions.

opposite The orbital station *Salyut*.

436

Key Political Event
Formation of Black September

The Palestinian militant group known as Black September, formed in the aftermath of the struggle between its parent Palestine Liberation Organization (PLO) and the Arab country of Jordan, is best known not for its antipathy to the Jordanian government – which the PLO attempted to take over at the end of the 1960s – but for its murder of eleven Israeli athletes and one German police officer at the 1972 Olympic Games in Munich. The Munich affair was the most spectacular act of terrorism to take place outside Israel and Israeli-occupied territories in the history of the Palestinian resistance, but it did not have the result anticipated by Black September. First of all, the militant group took the athletes hostage and asked Israel for the release of hundreds of militant prisoners in exchange for the Olympic delegation. Israel refused. Black September

then panicked and asked for safe passage to Cairo. The West German authorities feigned agreement but lured the terrorists into a trap. Inexpert German handling of what was then a new and confusing scenario in Europe led to the deaths of the hostages and the terrorists alike.

The Israeli response was to hunt down and execute surviving members of Black September while much of the rest of the world united in condemnation of the massacre. The negative publicity surrounding the Munich massacre forced the PLO to abjure foreign terrorism, which spared Europeans such scenes of carnage for another thirty years.
Demir Barlas

Date September 1, 1971

Country Lebanon

Why It's Key The Israel-Palestine dispute drew global media attention at the 1972 Munich Olympics, when the Palestinian splinter group Black September brought terrorism into the heart of Western Europe.

Key Cultural Event
Blue Marble photo of Earth from space

On April 1, 1960, a NASA satellite beamed home grainy black and white television images of Earth, which were useful in weather prediction but failed to capture the popular imagination. On December 24, 1968, *Apollo 8* was the first manned spacecraft to orbit the moon. When the craft rounded the dark side of the moon, an astronaut took a striking photo which captured the moon's gray surface in the foreground and the blue sphere of the Earth in the middle background, a third of it under shadow. Reputed nature photographer Galen Rowell called "Earth Rise" "the most influential environmental photograph ever taken," linking the image to a realization in the popular conscious of the fragility of Earth.

However, "Blue Marble" has seemingly replaced "Earth Rise" as the iconic picture of Earth. On December 7, 1972, astronauts on *Apollo 17* took a full color, crystalline image of the planet from 45,000 kilometers out called "Blue Marble," which became famous for its breathtaking portrayal of Earth as an isolated ecosystem. The photo, taken with the sun behind the spacecraft, illuminating the entire visible surface of the earth, is the most widely published photograph in history.

Since 1972, NASA has used satellite-imaging technologies to record changes to the Earth's surface, including the impact of human populations on natural resources. The European Space Agency launched remote sensing satellites in the 1990s to monitor earthquakes, oil spills, glaciers, and flooding, among other phenomena.

David Anderson

Date December 7, 1972

Country USA

Why It's Key The blue marble photograph is the most iconic image of Earth and, along with other images of Earth from space, has had a huge impact on the green movement.

Fact "Blue Marble: Next Generation" is an ongoing NASA project that uses high-resolution satellite imagery to catalog changes to the Earth's surface over time.

opposite Blue Marble photograph

Key Political Event The Supreme Court grants
women the right to abortion in *Roe v. Wade*

In 1970, lawyers Sarah Weddington and Linda Coffee brought a suit in Texas, challenging a strict abortion law. Because of similar laws in other states, the Supreme Court agreed to hear the case. In 1972, Supreme Court justices directed Weddington toward claiming that the right to abortions was guaranteed by the implicit right of privacy recognized by the court in 1965, in *Griswold v. Connecticut*. When Weddington reargued the case in 1973, the court accepted the privacy argument, holding that women had a constitutional right to obtain abortions, with some limitations according to fetal stage of development.

Roe v. Wade came before the court at a time when rapid social changes were occurring, including the rise of the women's movement and the sexual revolution. Worldwide attention had been drawn to the issue of abortion in response to epidemics of infants born with major birth defects to British, Canadian, and Australian mothers who had taken the French tranquillizer, Thalidomide, and to mothers in the United States who had been exposed to German measles.

The *Roe* decision launched a national debate over the abortion issue. Under several conservative presidents, views on abortion became the litmus test for appointing Supreme Court justices. Consequently, subsequent decisions limited access to abortion while continuing to uphold the basic premise of *Roe*. At the international level, *Roe* focused attention on women's rights and on the need for family planning. Abortion continues to be a divisive issue on moral and religious grounds in many countries.

Elizabeth R. Purdy

Date January 22, 1973

Country USA

Why It's Key The decision gave women the right to control their reproductive lives and opened worldwide discussions on the issue of abortion, leading to major political disagreements over the rights of pregnant women versus the rights of fetuses.

Fact Before the *Roe* decision, some 800,000 abortions still occurred each year in the United States.

Key Political Event
Portugal's Carnation Revolution

After nearly five decades under the firm grip of strongmen António Salazar and Marcelo Caetano, Portugal's drastic, rapid, and peaceful change of political destiny astonished the world. The impulse for regime change came from an unlikely source given the traditionally strong ties of the right-wing leaders to the military: middle-ranking army officers who had served in the seemingly endless counter-insurgency wars directed at crushing independence movements in Portugal's African colonies. Portugal's quixotic efforts to retain its colonial holdings in Africa in the face of the massive process of decolonization that had swept across the continent in the 1960s had mired its armed forces in wars that were despised by most of the population as a drain on the economy and a deathtrap for an entire generation of young men.

The coup began just before midnight on April 24, as rebels took up strategic positions around the country and collaborating radio journalists announced the revolt to the public at large. In the early hours of the morning, multitudes spilled into the streets of Lisbon to express their solidarity with the soldiers. During these euphoric hours, someone began to distribute red carnations among the soldiers, who placed them in the barrels of their rifles. This image would endure as an icon of the momentous events of that day, soon dubbed *A Revolução dos Cravos* (the Carnation Revolution). The progressive military regime that took power centered its program of reforms on "the three D's": democratization, decolonization, and development.
Geoffrey Schillenberger

Date April 25, 1974

Country Portugal

Why It's Key The combined military and popular uprisings that deposed the authoritarian regime, which had governed Portugal since 1926, offered a model of non-violent political change, bringing to an end one of Europe's last remaining fascist dictatorships.

opposite April, 1969: Two Portuguese soldiers seek out inforrmation about the Carnation Revolution.

Key Political Event
Ulster General Strike

The Ulster General Strike took place against a backdrop of increased sectarian violence and political instability in Northern Ireland. A new parliament, the Northern Ireland assembly, had been established in the troubled province in 1973, and in October of that year, mainstream political parties had collaborated with the British and Irish governments to draw up the Sunningdale agreement. This agreement established a basis for power sharing between republican and unionist parties and, controversially, proposed a Council of Ireland that would involve the Republic of Ireland in Ulster's administration.

Hard-line unionists were fiercely opposed to the agreement and feared that it was the first step toward unification with Ireland. The result was a general strike announced by the Ulster Workers' Council, a coalition of hard-line unionists, which started on May 15, 1974. The strike lasted for two weeks and effectively crippled the whole of Northern Ireland, leading to power cuts, food shortages, and limited supplies of petrol and other essentials. The strike was backed by loyalist paramilitaries, and workers were reportedly threatened by armed thugs when they tried to return to their jobs.

Faced with the pressure brought about by the strike, the Sunningdale agreement was discarded and the short-lived Northern Ireland assembly collapsed on May 28, 1974. Ulster reverted to direct rule from London and it would be a further twenty-five years before the province would be self-governing again.
Martin Sayers

Date May 15, 1974

Country Northern Ireland

Why It's Key The strike led to the collapse of Northern Ireland's fledgling parliament and raised serious concerns about paramilitary influence in the province.

Key Political Event
Turkish invasion of Cyprus

The British colony of Cyprus became independent in 1960, after which a long-standing conflict between the Greek-Cypriot majority and the Turkish-Cypriot minority intensified.

Tensions between the two communities came to a head when a coup in July 1974 overthrew the president, Archbishop Makarios. The coup had the backing of the military junta in Greece, and a new leader, Nicos Sampson, a Greek known for anti-Turkish views, was installed.

Turkish-Cypriots feared that Sampson would seek unification with Greece, and appealed to Turkey for help. On July 20, 1974, 30,000 Turkish troops landed on Cyprus, ostensibly to restore order after the coup.

The Turkish forces occupied the northern third of the island, and Cyprus was split into two. The failure to reach a settlement in the months following the invasion also split the island's population – Greeks fled to the south and the Turkish community congregated in the occupied north.

Within days, Sampson had resigned and Makarios had returned, but despite international condemnation, the Turks refused to withdraw. A heavily fortified border, policed by the United Nations, divided Cyprus, and in 1983, the Turkish Republic of Northern Cyprus was declared, although to this day the legitimacy of the state is recognized only by Turkey.

A sign of a thawing of relations occurred in 2004 when the border was opened in places, allowing Cypriots to move freely around the island for the first time in over thirty years.

Martin Sayers

Date July 20, 1974

Country Cyprus

Why It's Key After years of simmering tension between Turks and Greeks, the Turkish invasion led to the division of the small island.

Key Cultural Event
Rumble in the Jungle

The Rumble in the Jungle was so christened by Don King, a numbers runner turned boxing promoter, from Cleveland, Ohio. President Mobuto Sese Seko offered a total purse of US$10 million, to be divided between the fighters, for the fight to be staged in the West African republic of Zaire.

The reigning champion, George Foreman, was – and, indeed, still is – widely considered to be the greatest puncher in the history of heavyweight boxing. In eight bouts leading up to the Rumble in the Jungle, none of his opponents had lasted more than two rounds. Few thought that Ali, at thirty-two, had any chance of interrupting that sequence.

The charismatic Ali did, however, have the support of the Zairian people. The chant of "Ali bomaye," or "Ali kill him," accompanied him wherever he went.

The fight, itself, was famous for the bizarre tactics that Ali adopted. His so-called "rope-a-dope" trick allowed Foreman to land a series of immensely powerful punches to his lower body. All the time, Ali verbally taunted Foreman into wilder, and wilder, attacks.

By the end of the fifth round, Foreman had punched himself virtually to a standstill. The "sleeping elephant," as Ali was later described, awoke. Toward the end of eighth round, Ali landed a right hook, knocking an exhausted Foreman to the canvas. Foreman only just failed to beat the count, but, miraculously, Ali had won.

David Dunning

Date October 30, 1974

Country Zaire (now Democratic Republic of Congo)

Why It's Key Victory in the Rumble in the Jungle made Muhammad Ali only the second man in history to regain the title of World Heavyweight Champion.

opposite Ali smashes a right punch to Foreman's head.

Key Political Event
Haile Selassie I deposed

On September 12, 1974, Halie Selassie I, last emperor of Ethiopia, was forcibly deposed by a military junta following mounting public unrest. Once heralded as the figurehead of African independence for his staunch defiance against the Italian colonial invasion of the 1930s, Selassie suffered an ignominious end to his reign amidst famine and economic collapse.

Between the years 1972–1973 the Wollo region of northeastern Ethiopia suffered a major drought, resulting in one of Africa's worst famines in which 200,000 people died from starvation. The humanitarian crisis was first brought to the world's attention by a BBC documentary, which exposed local Wollo officials as corrupt and guilty of attempting to cover up the famine. This critically weakened Selassie's government and depicted the emperor as being out of touch, seemingly oblivious to his people's plight during his ostentatious eightieth birthday celebrations.

With Selassie's support dwindling, a committee of military officers known as The Derg turned on their emperor and staged a successful coup on September 12, 1974. Haile Selassie was placed under house arrest and his Imperial government dismantled. On November 23, sixty-one former high-ranking officials were executed without trial, including Selassie's grandson and the recently appointed head of state General Aman Michael Andom. Halie Selassie I died on August 27, 1975, aged eighty-two, in his Addis Ababa cell. Respiratory failure was the official cause of death, although some rumors suggest he was smothered in his sleep.

Jay Mullins

Date September 12, 1974

Country Ethiopia

Why It's Key A major humanitarian disaster sparked the downfall of one of Africa's most popular leaders.

Fact Selassie is recognized as the God Incarnate or "Black Messiah" by the Rastafari movement.

Key Discovery "Lucy," a three-million-year-old hominid skeleton is found in Ethiopia

Twentieth-century anthropology was devoted to the question of what evolutionary changes had occurred that made us human. Most anthropologists prior to the discovery of "Lucy" had postulated that walking upright, constructing tools, and growing large brains were developments that all occurred concurrently approximately 2.5 million years ago, separating us from the beasts. The Leakeys, the "first family of anthropology," even argued that there was one line of true man, a larger-brained primate that evolved independently of smaller-brained forms.

However, Donald Johanson and Tom Gray's discovery of the small, hominid skeleton of Lucy in Hadar, Ethiopia, challenged both of these assumptions. Lucy's upright posture indicates that bipedalism was the first step in the development of *homo sapiens*.

Though her long arms suggest that she did climb trees, her ability to walk implies that she literally had a new view of the environment, which may have been the factor that led to bigger brain development in her descendants. Her small stature (she was 3½ feet tall) also meant that it was unlikely she would be able to survive on her own in the savannah, denoting that she was part of a larger social group. Relationships, not tools, seem to have been behind the development of human intelligence.

Johanson and Gray's work also suggests that Lucy seems to be a common ancestor of humans and smaller-brained primates, a "mother" to the human family. Her discovery has led to a reconsideration of how closely related we are to modern primates.

Anna Marie Roos

Date November 24, 1974

Country Ethiopia

Why It's Key Johanson and Gray's discovery showed that human-like creatures were bipedal long before the discovery of stone tools or the development of the "human brain," giving us important clues to our evolutionary past.

Fact Lucy was named after Beatles song "Lucy in the Sky with Diamonds."

opposite Paleoanthropologist Dr Donald Johanson with "Lucy."

Key Political Event
Death of Franco

In his latter years, Franco had appointed Juan Carlos, a Spanish aristocrat and grandson of Spain's last king, to be his successor. After Franco's death in 1975, opposition leaders hoped for a restoration of democracy, but feared that the accession of Juan Carlos would mean a continuation of the fascist regime.

These fears proved to be unfounded as it soon became clear that Juan Carlos was intent on restoring democracy to Spain. However, the young king and his supporters had to walk a political tightrope; mistrusted by left-wingers as being too close to Franco, they also faced opposition from Franco loyalists who were resistant to change.

A government was formed that included large elements of the old regime but democratic protocols were established. In December 1978, a new constitution was ratified by a public referendum and Spain became a constitutional monarchy.

The last gasp of fascism took place in 1981 when parliament was occupied during an attempted military coup led by disgruntled army officers. King Juan Carlos reacted by denouncing the coup on national television and defending the rule of law. The coup had little support in the country and soon collapsed.

The election of October 1982 marked the final break with the fascist regime when the socialist PSOE won a resounding victory and, for the first time since his death, a Spanish government was formed in which none of the members had served under Franco.
Martin Sayers

Date October 29, 1975

Country Spain

Why It's Key The death of one of the twentieth century's most notorious dictators paved the way for the restoration of democracy in Spain.

opposite General Franco's funeral procession heads toward the Valley of the Fallen in Madrid.

Key Political Event Angola and Mozambique gain independence from Portugal

A three-fronted, decade-long battle against its African colonies and their independence-seeking factions came to an end in 1975; after 500 years of Portuguese rule, Angolan factions took arms against their masters and forced the Portuguese to grant independence after a fourteen-year war. Before this "liberation," the Portuguese used Angola as a major slave port. Independent Angola was torn apart by the civil war that ensued, as the ethnically divided MPLA, FNLA, and UNITA armies turned on one another and fought for rule of the country, tearing it to ruins as they went. The MPLA was, and is, the dominant party.

Mozambique also became independent in 1975 when Front for the Liberation of Mozambique (FRELIMO) staged a coup. Four military men took control of the country – Samora Moises Machel, Marcelino Dos Santos, Joaquim Alberto Chissano, and Armando Guebuza – fronting three committees. Together with the Central Committees Executive Committee, and the Political-Military Committee, they determined the direction of independent Mozambique, a one-party state with allies and financiers in the Soviet bloc, although not enough to prevent economic collapse and a decade-long civil war that would claim the lives of a million citizens.

Portugal's postwar foreign policy was out of line with that of the rest of the African colonialists. Holding onto African colonies against resistance movements never likely to be suppressed resulted in the many years of unrest that characterized these two new republics.
Greg Pittard

Date November 11, 1975

Country Angola/ Mozambique/Portugal

Why It's Key The independence of Mozambique and Angola ended Portuguese colonization, but resulted in brutal civil warfare, which continued for decades.

Key Political Event
Soweto riots and massacre

Between 200 and 700 protesters – many of them youths – were killed by the police during riots sparked off by a 10,000 strong student march held on June 16 in Soweto, a black township in Johannesburg. The march in protest against the enforcement of Afrikaans as a medium of instruction in black schools was organized by the South African Students Organisation (SASO), which was informed by both Black Consciousness, as propounded by Steve Biko, and the African National Congress (ANC).

Reports vary as to how the peaceful protest became violent: some claim that students threw stones, others that the police fired shots into the crowd. In any case, when the police fired teargas and bullets at the pupils, they retaliated by burning police cars, and fires raged into the night. Unrest spread nationwide. The government reaction was brutal. By February 1977, more than 575 people, including many teenagers, had been killed. In the following months, SASO and affiliated organizations were banned, and Biko was killed. Violent resistance was increasingly recognized as a necessary evil, and many youths fled to Angola and Tanzania to be trained in the military wings of the ANC and Pan African Congress (PAC), both of which launched armed struggles.

The massacre illustrated the injustice of apartheid, and caused a considerable upsurge in internal and external criticism of the apartheid government, and resistance to it. Throughout the 1980s, June 16 was marked by commemorative protests, and is now symbolically designated as Youth Day.
Laura Pechey

Date June 16, 1976

Country South Africa

Why It's Key The riots and massacre further radicalized the black youth, prompting the older generation of black South Africans to support violent action in the struggle against apartheid, setting in motion years of political violence, which destabilized the apartheid state and ultimately led to its demise.

opposite September 1976: After the Soweto riots, further protests turned violent in Cape Town.

Key Political Event Israeli commandos free hostages
from hijacked Air France Flight 139 in Entebbe

On June 27, an Air France flight from Tel Aviv to Paris via Athens was hijacked by four pro-Palestinian militants, two of them German. They flew to Libya, then to Uganda, where three more militants joined them to demand the release of fifty-three prisoners held in Israel and other countries.

Ugandan president Idi Amin, who had earned his Israeli paratroop wings, had been regarded as Israel's "special African friend," but in 1972, angered at Israel's refusal to supply him with Phantom jets, he had switched allegiance to Libya's Muammar Gaddafi. In Entebbe, the hijackers released 148 hostages, but continued to hold over 100 mostly Israeli or Jewish hostages, including the crew, who had opted to stay.

On July 3, following threats to kill the hostages, Israeli Sayeret Matkal commandos led by Lieutenant-Colonel Yonatan Netanyahu launched a daring rescue mission that depended on surprise. Flying low to evade radar in four C-130 Hercules planes, they covered 2,500 miles to land with loading ramps down. In Land Rovers and a borrowed Mercedes painted black to resemble an official motorcade, twenty-nine commandos sped from the planes to the airport building. Within three minutes of landing, all seven militants had been killed and the hostages freed, though three died, along with Lieutenant-Colonel Netanyahu. The commandos also destroyed eleven MiG fighters to hamper pursuit. A day later, an elderly hostage, Dora Bloch, who had been taken to hospital in Kampala, was dragged from her bed and killed.
Duncan Proudfoot

Date July 3, 1976

Country Uganda

Why It's Key Operation Thunderbolt, later renamed Operation Yonatan, in honor of its leader who was killed, was an audacious success: it humiliated Amin and weakened his regime; two years later he was deposed and exiled.

Key Discovery *Viking I* becomes the first spacecraft to operate on Mars

The crucial phase of NASA's *Viking I* mission to Mars came on July 20, 1976, when the Lander vehicle separated from the Orbiter to begin the longest surface operation of the planet to date.

Launched on August 20, 1975, the Viking rocket took ten months to reach the Red Planet. After an initial orbit to scan for landing sites, the Lander touched down according to plan in western Chryse Planitia, near the Martian equator, and went on to perform a series of experiments to test for biosignatures of life. A range of soil samples were analyzed for the presence of metabolizing organisms, but the results were inconclusive. The debate still continues today as to whether bacterial life exists on Mars, and it is hoped that subsequent missions will build on the Viking program's findings.

The Orbiter was the second key component of the Viking program, and was designed to survey the planet from high altitude and act as a communication relay between Ground Control and the Lander. The Orbiter made a close investigation of Phobos in February 1977 and was forced into a raised orbit in August 1980 when it was discovered that the satellite was running low on altitude control gas and heading for an impact on Mars. Once stabilized, the Orbiter ceased operations on August 17, 1980, after a total of 1,485 orbits.

The Lander continued to operate until November 13, 1982, when software controlling the antenna was accidentally overwritten due to human error. Attempts to regain contact proved unsuccessful.
Jay Mullins

Date July 20, 1976

Country USA

Why It's Key The Viking program probed the question of life on Mars, significantly expanding our knowledge of the planet.

Fact NASA had hoped to land the spacecraft on July 4 to mark the United States Bicentennial, but the first landing site proved to be unsuitable and the date was delayed for over two weeks.

Key Political Event
Death of Mao

In the mid 1970s, China's revolutionary "old guard" was dying. Before Mao Zedong died of Lou Gehrig's (or Motor Neuron) disease at the age of eighty-two, his most bitter rivals and most favored allies had preceded him. PLA founder Peng Dehuai died in November 1974, Chiang Kai-shek in April 1975, and Zhou Enlai in January 1976.

At the time of his death, Mao left behind a mixed legacy, having defined a "people's revolution" that destroyed China's traditional feudal social structures, leading the Communist Party to power and control over national policy, establishing the foundations of a modern industrial economy, and bringing China to nuclear power status.

Mao's brainchild, the 1958 Great Leap Forward development strategy resulted in severe and unnecessary privations for huge segments of the Chinese population. Mao's Cultural Revolution campaign to restore the ideological purity of the Communist Party and government policy unleashed fratricidal violence that resulted in thousands of deaths and millions of purges from the party and ranks of national leaders. The Cultural Revolution weakened state institutions and fragmented a "lost generation" of disillusioned victims of Party power struggles. At the sixth plenum of the Eleventh Party Congress in June 1981, Mao's legacy received the official assessment "his merits are primary and his errors secondary," but those who lived in China during Mao's years in power are less dispassionate in their appraisals of Mao's merits.
Karen Garner

Date September 9, 1976

Country China

Why It's Key Mao Zedong's death at the end of the decade that followed his launch of a devastating and fratricidal Cultural Revolution called forth a national reckoning of his legacy, and, ultimately, a turn toward the more pragmatic and economically driven policies of the post-Mao leadership.

opposite Chairman Mao's body lies in state in the Great Hall of the People, Beijing.

Key Political Event **Violence in El Salvador results in the death of over 3,000 people**

The presidential election of February 20, 1977, followed years of political repression and sporadic unrest in El Salvador. Under the tight control of a small landowning elite and the military, Salvadorans were all too familiar with electoral fraud, coup attempts, and the silencing of dissent, as well as high levels of poverty and unemployment. The UNO, a coalition of leftist and moderate opposition groups, ran against the government under their candidate Colonel Ernesto Claramount. The PCN, the incumbent nationalist party, put up the former defence minister General Carlos Romero, who already had a reputation for the brutal suppression of protest.

Romero unabashedly stole the election through stuffed ballot boxes and violent persecution of UNO voters and officials. The tone was set for his regime on February 28 when government troops fired on a protest in San Salvador led by Claramount, killing and wounding hundreds. Claramount left the scene in an ambulance, declaring: "This is not the end. It is only the beginning."

Resultant disillusionment with the democratic process prompted a rise of radical leftist and communist groups committed to change through more violent means. A spate of kidnappings, bombings, and strikes was responded to not only by severe government crackdowns, but also the formation of paramilitary right-wing "death-squads," who targeted any known or perceived to be involved in the uprising. This erratic violence continued for three years until, after the deposal of Romero by a military coup, the insurgents organized into the FMLN, sparking a full-blown civil war.
Roger Johnson

Date 1977

Country El Salvador

Why It's Key The events following the national election of 1977 put El Salvador on a course for civil war.

Key Cultural Event **Woman sues Dow Corning over malfunctioning silicone breast implants**

Women desiring breast augmentation or needing reconstruction surgery created a demand for devices that simulated the female breast. American manufacturer Dow Corning entered this market in 1962 with a silicone gel-filled implant that was touted as a natural breast implant. In 1977, attorney R. M. Mithoff brought the first successful suit (US$170,000) against Dow Corning on behalf of a woman who charged Dow Corning with manufacturing implants that ruptured, causing health problems. The case had little impact until 1980 when the Washington-based Public Citizen Research Group issued warnings about the dangers of leaking silicone implants. In 1988, the United States Food and Drug Administration exercised its authority to require that breast implant manufacturers provide pre-market demonstrations of product safety.

Pressure on manufacturers increased in 1990 after the news show, *Face-to-Face with Connie Chung*, featured the breast implant controversy. In a multi-million San Francisco case, attorney Dan Bolton produced documents showing that Dow Corning had intentionally kept information about health problems with breast implants from the public. By 1992, the FDA had banned use of silicone breast implants except for breast cancer patients and required that all implants be subjected to strict scientific protocol. In a global settlement, Dow Corning agreed to pay 440,000 claimants US$4.25 billion and filed for bankruptcy. Despite evidence of wrongdoing by manufacturers, some experts still challenge the link between malfunctioning breast implants and medical conditions.
Elizabeth R. Purdy

Date 1977

Country USA

Why It's Key The health of women around the world was affected by faulty silicone breast implants, and the lawsuits called attention to the need for governments to take manufacturers to task and enact measures designed to protect consumers from unsafe medical devices.

Fact 440,000 claimants had filed suit by the beginning of the twenty-first century.

Key Cultural Event
Roots is broadcast on TV

The adaptation of Alex Haley's groundbreaking novel *Roots* into a television mini-series heralded a new era in race relations and television programming. A spectacular and unprecedented success, the twelve-hour series ran over eight consecutive nights, and dispelled the initial fears of television executives regarding its controversial content by attracting the largest audience in television history thus far, an estimated 130 million.

Described as "the single most spectacular educational experience in race relations in America," *Roots* chronicled Haley's family history through seven generations, providing a shocking and often harrowing account of the reality and repercussions of slavery. Beginning with the birth of African tribesman Kunta Kinte, the story followed his capture by slave traders in Gambia and transportation to an American plantation, providing a stark reminder for TV audiences of their nation's involvement in the slave trade. Despite fears that white audiences would find the series irrelevant or that the portrayal of white characters largely as villains would provoke outrage, the story of Kunta Kinte's descendants made a lasting impression upon white and black audiences alike, enhancing historical and racial understanding. While the accuracy of Haley's research is rightly disputed and issues of plagiarism have clouded his achievement, the serialization of *Roots* won nine Emmy Awards from thirty-seven nominations, alongside a Golden Globe and a Peabody Award, and should be considered a seminal moment in TV history.

Hannah Furness

Date January 23, 1977

Country USA

Why It's Key This emotive tale of slavery had an important and lasting impact on American racial and historical understanding.

Key Political Event
The creation of "Charter 77"

When members of the Czech band The Plastic People of the Universe were arrested in late 1976 by Communist authorities, a large section of the left-wing intellectual community in Prague met to discuss a response. Václav Havel, Jan Patočka, Jiří Hájek, Pavel Kohout, and others eventually drafted "Charter 77," a manifesto criticizing the government for failing to meet the standards laid out for it in the Helsinki Accord on Human Rights. It also openly lambasted the regime for breaches of numerous UN Conventions and even its own constitution. It was circulated clandestinely around the country, smuggled abroad, and published in major international newspapers like *The Times* and *Le Monde*.

The regime responded in the official Czech press, describing the manifesto as "an anti-state, antisocialist, and demagogic, abusive piece of writing," and individual signers were described as "traitors and renegades," "a bankrupt politician," and "an international adventurer." Several means of retaliation were later used against the signers, including dismissal from work, denial of educational opportunities for their children, suspension of drivers' licenses, forced exile, loss of citizenship, detention, trials, and imprisonment.

Nevertheless, by 1989 the number of signatories had reached over 1800, and it helped to consolidate the protest movement that would culminate in the Velvet Revolution. Václav Havel was increasingly regarded as the movement's figurehead and became the interim president of the newly liberated Czechoslovakia in December 1989 and president of the Czech Republic in 1993.

Jonathan Morton

Date January 27, 1977

Country Czechoslovakia (now Czech Republic)

Why It's Key The creation of the Charter inspired protest movements in Soviet-controlled Eastern Europe and moved Václav Havel into the political arena.

Key Cultural Event **The Sex Pistols' "God Save The Queen" is released**

Punk offered a fresh alternative to the stagnant music scene of the late 1970s in the UK. The Sex Pistols, with their tattered clothes, spiked hair, safety pins, and brash attitude, were the single most recognizable punk group, and became the iconic figureheads of the movement.

Though they originally recorded "God Save The Queen" while signed to A&M Records, the majority of the 25,000 singles pressed were destroyed when the label decided to drop the band. However, the single was finally released on Richard Branson's Virgin label in May 1977 to coincide with the Silver Jubilee of Queen Elizabeth II. On June 7, in the midst of the jubilee celebrations, The Sex Pistols attempted to play a concert on a boat – the aptly named "Queen Elizabeth" – on the River Thames. The boat was pursued by the police, who cut the power, and arrested a number of those present, including The Sex Pistols' manager, Malcolm McLaren, and his then-wife, Vivienne Westwood.

"God Save The Queen," with its inflammatory lyrics that associated the Queen with a "fascist regime," was seen by many as an affront to the British monarchy and way of life. The BBC and the Independent Broadcasting Authority banned the single, so that it received no airplay, or media exposure of any kind. Nevertheless, "God Save The Queen" reached No. 2 in the pop charts, and there is a suggestion that sales figures were artificially manipulated to prevent it from reaching No. 1.

David Dunning

Date April 22, 1977

Country UK

Why It's Key The alternative national anthem, with lyrics by John Lydon (a.k.a. Johnny Rotten), is widely considered to be a classic of the punk music genre.

Fact An original A&M Records pressing of "God Save The Queen" was auctioned in 2006, for a sum of over GBP12,000.

Key Cultural Event
Star Wars the movie opens

George Lucas wasn't sure if he had a hit on his hands when *Star Wars* burst into theaters. A highly imaginative space opera that combined the thrills of 1940s-era matinee adventure films with state-of-the-art special effects, its prospects with a national audience were uncertain. Although the movie ended up making millions, it was more than just another blockbuster. Its success marked one of the biggest American pop culture frenzies ever. Audiences responded to Lucas' distinctive science fiction vision, which imagined the travails of young Luke Skywalker in "a galaxy far, far away." Populated by bizarre alien creatures, a vastly complicated interstellar culture, and heavy-handed mysticism, *Star Wars* engaged the classic fantasy conceits of J. R. R. Tolkien's *Lord of the Rings* series, although Lucas borrowed more directly from Frank Herbert's popular sci-fi book *Dune* (1965).

Lucas became a major player in Hollywood with the release of *American Graffiti* in 1973, but *Star Wars* provided his entrance to the top tier of commercial filmmakers. The movie and its two sequels birthed a generation of fandom and endless residuals. On its own merits, *Star Wars* had an iconic villain, Darth Vader, and a movie star to help broaden its appeal (Alec Guinness as Jedi guru Obi Wan Kenobi). A quarter of a century later, the director crafted a trilogy of profitable prequels to the *Star Wars* epic, but when the first movie took off, he had other things on his mind: on vacation with his friend Steven Spielberg, Lucas pitched the idea for *Indiana Jones*.

Eric Kohn

Date May 25, 1977

Country USA

Why It's Key The blockbuster film initiated a new generation of fandom for science fiction films.

Fact As of 2007, the entire *Star Wars* franchise has grossed approximately US$4.3 billion.

opposite Darth Vader and his Storm Troopers exert their power in the first *Star Wars* film.

Key Cultural Event
Monumental success of Apple Inc.'s Apple II

Before Apple introduced the Apple I in 1976, most personal computers were sold to consumers as kits, which required hobbyists to assemble them at home using skills learned building amateur radios and reading electronics magazines. After initial success with the Apple I in 1976, Apple Computers released the Apple II a year later, priced at US$1,298, and soon had on their hands the first blockbuster success of the computer industry.

Selling 50,000 units in its first two-and-a-half years of release, the Apple II gave birth to an industry as well as a number of key concepts that remain with us today. The spreadsheet program VisiCalc, the precursor to Lotus 123 and Microsoft Excel, was the industry's first "killer application," so called because it justified the purchase of the computer that ran it. Before the Apple II, no one was sure if computers would ever find a mass consumer and business market. After its success, there was no doubt that the 1980s would be the decade of the computer.

But Apple II was more than a landmark in computer adoption. It was first to utilize color graphics and sound, and featured eight expansion slots that allowed consumers to add disk drives, extra memory, a printer, a modem, and other devices. Even when Apple switched its attention to the development of the Macintosh in 1984, Apple II remained the top seller for the company, and continued to be revised until 1986, when the Apple II GS (graphics and sound) closed out the line.
Martin Johnson

Date June 5, 1977

Country USA

Why It's Key Apple proved that consumers would buy personal computers, giving birth to a billion-dollar industry.

Fact The company prematurely abandoned the Apple line in order to focus their attention on the Macintosh, which failed to find the same success as the Apple II.

Key Cultural Event
Death of Elvis

Elvis Presley had already been dead for three hours before his girlfriend Ginger Alden found him slumped on his bathroom floor. Although rushed straight to hospital, doctors were unable to save him, and at 3:30 p.m. on August 16, 1977, he was pronounced dead. Adored by millions, the world was stunned at the untimely demise of the "King of Rock 'n' Roll" at just forty-two years of age.

Elvis had shocked parents the world over when he burst onto the music scene with his unique brand of rock 'n' roll. His suggestive hip movements and curling lips had done nothing to quell the desires of the new phenomenon of the day, teenagers. They had found their hero.

Elvis was still performing in the year of his death, but he was a shadow of his former self. Clad in his trademark jeweled jumpsuits, the glitter could not distract from the fact he was grossly overweight and equally unhealthy.

The night before his death, he had visited the dentist and was suffering with toothache. He spent much of the rest of the night playing racket ball and bothering his physician with requests for painkillers. At 5 a.m. on the morning of his death, Elvis retired to bed for the last time, breaking his slumber with yet more calls for pain relief.

Elvis' death has been officially attributed to heart failure, but it has been suggested that prescription drug overdose was the more likely cause of death.
Kerry Duffy

Date August 16, 1977

Country USA

Why It's Key The first true icon of rock 'n' roll, Elvis' death left the world in shock.

opposite Hoards of fans wait outside Graceland for the public viewing after Elvis' death.

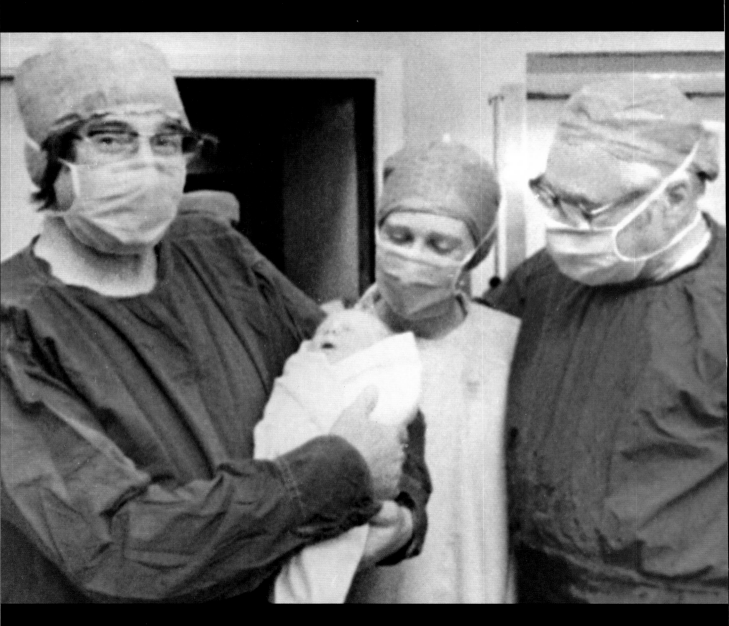

Key Political Event **Control of the Panama Canal transferred to Panama by the year 2000**

In 1903, Panama seceded from Columbia and signed the Hay-Bunau-Varilla Treaty with the United States. The initial treaty allotted US$10 million and an annuity of US$250,000 to Panama, and granted the United States Corps of Engineers authority to build the Panama Canal. The United States gained sovereignty over the Panama Canal Zone, a strip of land on either side of the canal. The project, considered one of the most significant engineering feats in history, was completed in 1914 at a cost of US$336 million. The fifty-mile Panama Canal was built to facilitate transcontinental water traffic. Through a system of water locks and the man-made Gatún Lake, some 1,400 ships a year are lifted back and forth between the Atlantic and Pacific Oceans.

Through treaties signed in 1977 and ratified by the Senate in 1978, the United States relinquished the Canal Zone to Panama on October 1, 1979, and pledged to transfer control of the canal and remaining U.S. military bases to Panama at the end of the century. The transfer of power became effective on December 31, 1999. The United States retained the right of "expeditious passage" for all U.S. warships, and stipulated that the canal remain open, neutral, and secure. Jimmy Carter, who considered the treaty one of the major foreign policy accomplishments of his presidency, was on hand for the transfer ceremony. In 2006, the Panamanian government announced a plan to double the capacity of the canal by the year 2015, allowing larger ships to navigate its waters.
Elizabeth R. Purdy

Date April 18, 1978

Country Panama

Why It's Key For the first time since its founding in 1903, Panama gained sovereignty over its own territory, along with hundreds of millions of dollars in toll fees generated by the canal, thereby illustrating the potential for successful global partnerships.

1970–1979

487

Key Discovery
First test-tube baby

Lesley and John Brown had spent years trying for a baby, and when doctors in their hometown of Bristol could do no more, they were referred to the leading expert in the field of in vitro fertilization (IVF), Patrick Steptoe.

Mr Steptoe, a consultant gynecologist at Oldham District General Hospital, Greater Manchester, and his colleague, Dr Robert Edwards, had spent years researching and refining their techniques before their historic meeting with the Browns.

The method they had perfected involved removing several eggs from the mother and fertilizing them with the father's sperm before implanting the fertilized egg back into the mother, where she would – hopefully – manage to maintain a long-term pregnancy.

Up until November 1977, their pioneering techniques had failed to produce a successful pregnancy, and so with the Browns, they revised their methods a little, implanting the fertilized egg at an earlier stage than they had normally done, and waited with bated breath.

Nine months later Louise Joy Brown was delivered by caesarean section to the delight of not only her parents, but also the millions of childless couples who now saw a light at the end of the tunnel.

Born amid concerns for her future health and fears of what such a procedure would mean for the future, Louise Brown has defied the skeptics and has even given birth to her own, naturally conceived baby boy.
Kerry Duffy

Date July 25, 1978

Country UK

Why It's Key The birth of the first test-tube baby gave hope to millions of childless couples across the globe.

opposite Dr Edwards holds baby Louise shortly after her birth.

Key Political Event **The Camp David Accords begin the Middle East peace process**

Tensions in the Middle East had been steadily building since the United Nations General Assembly created the Jewish State of Israel in 1947, leaving Palestinians without a home. In 1977, Israel's Prime Minister Menachem Begin surprisingly invited Egyptian President Anwar Sadat to Jerusalem. Israel was a strong U.S. ally, and President Jimmy Carter had become friends with Sadat. After peace efforts stalled, Carter invited Sadat and Begin to the United States to continue negotiations. The meeting was held at Camp David, the presidential retreat nestled in the Catoctins of the Blue Ridge Mountain Range. To maintain peace and privacy, Sadat and Begin were assigned to separate lodges. In addition to joint meetings, Carter spent hours hammering out differences in separate meetings.

From September 5 to September 17, Carter labored over twenty-three drafts. His personal notes stated that the final draft was the first Egyptian-Jewish peace agreement since biblical times. The document proposed an Israeli withdrawal from the West Bank and Gaza over a five-year period. Israel was to remain in designated locations to ensure Israeli security, and Egypt agreed to refrain from using force. The accords gave Palestinians a role in future negotiations. The Camp David Accords were signed at the White House at 10:30 p.m. on September 17, and Israel and Egypt signed a peace treaty on March 26, 1979. Sadat and Begin won the Nobel Peace Prize in 1978, but Carter did not win until 2002 when he was awarded the prize for a lifetime of peacemaking efforts.

Elizabeth R. Purdy

Date September 5, 1978

Country USA

Why It's Key President Jimmy Carter's efforts to bring Israel and Egypt to the negotiating table paved the way for settling some of the political, religious, and cultural differences that plagued the highly volatile Middle East.

488

Key Political Event
Vietnam troops invade Cambodia

The crossing of Vietnamese troops into Cambodia signaled the end of Pol Pot's devastating reign in Cambodia, but became the catalyst for years of occupation and genocide. Vietnamese-Cambodian relations had been strained since 1974, after Cambodia demanded that the Mekong Delta be returned to them. Having had settlers there for 300 years, the Vietnamese refused. Since the Vietnamese were allied with the Soviet Union and the Cambodians with the People's Republic of China, the chasm between the countries widened.

The radical policies of Cambodian Prime Minister Pol Pot heightened the tension. In a bid for agrarian utopia, Pol Pot forced urbanites from the cities into the countryside and imposed nationwide collectivization. This drive and the genocide of Vietnamese in Cambodia resulted in the estimated deaths of 1.5 million people.

War became inevitable when the Cambodian army advanced into Vietnamese territory and massacred the populations of bordering villages on April 30, 1977. After last-ditch negotiations broke down, Vietnamese troops engaged Cambodian forces, taking control of key Cambodian cities. Overwhelmed, Pol Pot fled to the Thai border, and a new Vietnamese government was installed under Heng Samrin.

The deaths did not stop there. On February 17, 1979, the People's Republic of China sent troops of their own into Vietnam in response, sparking the month long Sino-Vietnamese war, which killed thousands and devastated Vietnamese infrastructure. A further 1.5 million Cambodians are estimated to have died in the occupational genocide.

Greg Pittard

Date 1978

Country Democratic Kampuchea (Cambodia)

Why It's Key The invasion led to a bloody guerrilla war that caused further cultural genocide and resulted in the defeat of Cambodian Prime Minister Pol Pot.

opposite A Khmer soldier lies dead as a government soldier patrols in Cambodia.

Key Political Event **The second gunman in the assassination of President John F. Kennedy**

In response to public outcry over new evidence that had surfaced about the assassination of President John F. Kennedy in Dallas, Texas, on November 22, 1963, the House of Representatives established the House Select Committee on Assassinations (HSCA) in 1979. Because accused assassin Lee Harvey Oswald had been murdered without being tried, many questions remained unanswered, and many people believed that Kennedy's death had been part of a conspiracy. In 1976, a Senate committee had reported that the Central Intelligence Agency (CIA) had been involved in an unsuccessful plot to murder Cuban leader Fidel Castro at the time of the Kennedy assassination. Two years later, a television appearance by a leading Kennedy assassination scholar had cast doubt on the Warren Commission Report, which represented the official government position on the assassination.

During a period of two years at a cost of US$5.5 million, HSCA launched an investigation into the assassination, and concluded that two assassins had taken aim at President Kennedy, probably Oswald and an unidentified second gunman. HSCA cleared the governments of the United States, Cuba, and the Soviet Union, the CIA, the FBI, the Secret Service, and organized crime of involvement in the assassination but concluded that individuals within any of those groups may have been involved. The hearings focused attention on the issue of trust in government and generated debate on the right of governments to involve themselves illegally in the activities of foreign governments.

Elizabeth R. Purdy

Date March 29, 1979

Country USA

Why It's Key New evidence presented to the House of Representatives raised serious ethical questions about the government's handling of the investigation into Kennedy's death and about the right of governments to engage in political intrigue involving attempted assassinations of foreign leaders.

1970–1979

497

Key Political Event
Zulfiqar Ali Bhutto executed in Pakistan

In 1976, Zulfiqar Ali Bhutto, the charismatic and secularly inclined president (1971–1973) and later prime minister (1973–1977) of Pakistan, nominated General Muhammad Zia ul-Haq to be that country's Chief of Army Staff. Three years later, Zia had his erstwhile benefactor hung in a military barracks in Rawalpindi, Pakistan. In doing so, Zia acted on the verdict of the Lahore High Court as enforced by the Supreme Court of Pakistan, but was the country's strongman at the time and so could have commuted the sentence.

Bhutto's downfall was spectacularly quick, with its proximate cause being his alleged involvement in the murder of a political opponent, but the reality involving the way in which conservative Pakistani Muslims did not favor the egalitarian and indeed socialist directions in which Bhutto was leading Pakistan. Zia, serving as a representative of these Islamists' interests, seized power in a military coup in 1977, and shortly thereafter militated behind the scenes for Bhutto's execution. Zia was diametrically opposed to Bhutto in many ways. Bhutto was born to a wealthy, cosmopolitan, and landowning family while Zia – a teacher's son – clawed his way up the army's ranks and retained a fierce belief in Islam as the organizing principle of Pakistan government. Bhutto's execution was not the last word, however, as his daughter Benazir became the first female prime minister of Pakistan less than a decade after her father's execution.

Demir Barlas

Date April 4, 1979

Country Pakistan

Why It's Key Pakistan's most liberal modern politician was hung by a military dictator, cementing the troubled South Asian country's return to an authoritarian rule from which it has never really emerged.

opposite President Bhutto speaking whilst on a visit to the UK in 1973.

Key Cultural Event
Coppola releases *Apocalypse Now*

Judges at the Cannes Film Festival of 1979 were the first to view – albeit in a rough cut – Francis Ford Coppola's *Apocalypse Now*. They awarded the film the *Palme D'Or* ("Golden Palm") award, the most prestigious available to them. It was the first of many accolades; the film would become one of the most critically applauded of the last twenty-five years.

Apocalypse Now retells Joseph Conrad's novel *Heart of Darkness* (1902) but converts Conrad's Belgian colonial setting (probably the Congo) to American imperialism in Cambodia and Vietnam. It features Captain Willard (played by Martin Sheen), an assassin sent by the American military to eliminate Kurtz, a rogue American officer (Marlon Brando) who has brutally established a personal fiefdom in Cambodia. Kurtz is feared and deified by the local population.

Coppola famously announced at Cannes: "My film is not a movie. My film is not about Vietnam. It is Vietnam." Coppola was highlighting both the deep satirical themes of the film and talking about the problems that beset its filming, which have since become movie legend. Just like touring American soldiers, Coppola suggests, the crew, the actors, and the director himself "were in the jungle... little by little we went insane."

Some critics have pointed to the lack of defined Asian characters in a film claimed to *be* Vietnam. The film acquired its fame and status, nonetheless, because it seems to many viewers a vivid recreation of the psychodrama of the Vietnam War as experienced by the United States and its soldiers.

Michael Hallam

Date May 10, 1979

Country France

Why It's Key After its premiere, *Apocalypse Now* has gone on to become one of the most lauded moments of American cultural self-critique.

opposite Colonel Kurtz's men as Willard approaches the end of his search in *Apocalypse Now*.

498

Key Cultural Event **Akio Morita releases the Walkman to the general public**

When Sony Chairman Akio Morita held up one of the world's first Walkmans and declared, "This is the product that will satisfy those young people who want to listen to music all day. They'll take it everywhere with them... It'll be a hit," he was confident in his vision, even if others had their doubts. Sixteen years and 150 million Walkmans later, Morita had revolutionized the way people listened to music and created a multinational personal music empire.

The original blue and silver Walkman model TPS-L2 was introduced to Japan on July 1, 1979, competitively priced at ¥33,000. It was not the immediate hit Morita had hoped for, and by the end of July only 3,000 units had been sold. Undeterred, Sony began an aggressive marketing campaign. Employees were sent to wander around busy districts offering people the opportunity to listen and test out the device, Walkmans were presented to popular celebrities, and flashy ads were created featuring music pop idols. Sony's efforts paid off and the Walkman label would become a cultural icon. In 1986, the word "Walkman" was added to the Oxford English Dictionary.

As of 2007, Sony had sold over 350 million Walkman-branded devices. These days the Walkman is all but obsolete, eclipsed by newer technology and the rise of the iPod generation. However, it will always be the first, and its cultural impact felt by generations to come.

Annie Wang

Date July 1, 1979

Country Japan

Why It's Key The Walkman revolutionized the way the world listened to music and made Sony into a global powerhouse in the portable music industry.

Fact The Walkman as we know it might never have been – before settling on "Walkman," Morita and his team had contemplated other names such as "Soundabout."

Key Political Event
First modern suicide bomber

The long and vicious Iran-Iraq War gave the world the first ideological suicide bomber of the modern age: Hossein Fahmideh, a 13-year-old Iranian who detonated a number of grenades on his person to destroy an advancing Iraqi tank. Fahmideh was not the first person to sacrifice himself so spectacularly in war, but he was certainly the first fully fledged incarnation of the suicide bomber, both in the nature of his own commitments and the use to which he was later put by Iran.

Fahmideh, despite his young age, was fully indoctrinated in the Shi'ite cult of martyrdom so skillfully manipulated by the Iranian state in its eight-year struggle against Iraq. He saw his death as not merely a civic but also a religious duty and, in the aftermath of his death, the theocratic Iranian state amplified this aspect of the young boy's sacrifice.

Fahmideh was glorified in stamps and memorials, and was singled out for praise by the Ayatollah Khomeini.

While Fahmideh's fame remains largely Iranian, the tactical logic of his suicide bombing has risen to a place of great prominence in the regular and irregular warfare of the past three decades. Suicide bombing, once a novelty worthy of special commemoration or horror, was subsequently deployed not only across the Middle East but also in Europe and the United States.

But whereas Fahmideh attacked a military foe, his successors have not been as selective about their choice of targets.
Demir Barlas

Date 1980

Country Iran

Why It's Key An Iranian child soldier in the Iran-Iraq war laid down the template for generations of suicide bombers to come.

Key Political Event
Boycott of the Moscow Olympics

Although the Olympic games had traditionally been an event where political differences were left to one side, the Moscow Olympics of 1980 were marred by the biggest boycott in Olympic history. U.S. President Jimmy Carter sought to use the threat of a boycott to pressure the Soviet Union into withdrawing its troops from Afghanistan, which it had invaded in 1979.

When it became apparent that the Soviets had no intention of withdrawing from Afghanistan, the United States took action. On March 21, 1980, the Americans announced that none of their athletes would attend the Olympics. More than sixty other countries supported the boycott, including Norway, Canada, West Germany, and China. This seriously reduced the competitive nature of the Games, and Soviet and Eastern European athletes dominated the medal table as a result.

Most Western European nations sent athletes to the Games but they competed on an individual basis under the Olympic flag, rather than their own national flags, and many national anthems were replaced by the Olympic anthem during medal ceremonies.

The Soviets retaliated in similar style when the Warsaw-pact countries boycotted the 1984 Olympics held in Los Angeles. The official reason for this was concern about a lack of security for athletes and officials, but was in effect a direct tit-for-tat boycott. From the Eastern bloc, only Romania defied the Soviets in sending a team to the Games.
Martin Sayers

Date March 21, 1980

Country USSR

Why It's Key The boycott marred the Olympics and led to a retaliatory response at the L.A. Olympics four year later.

opposite The opening ceremony of the Moscow Olympics.

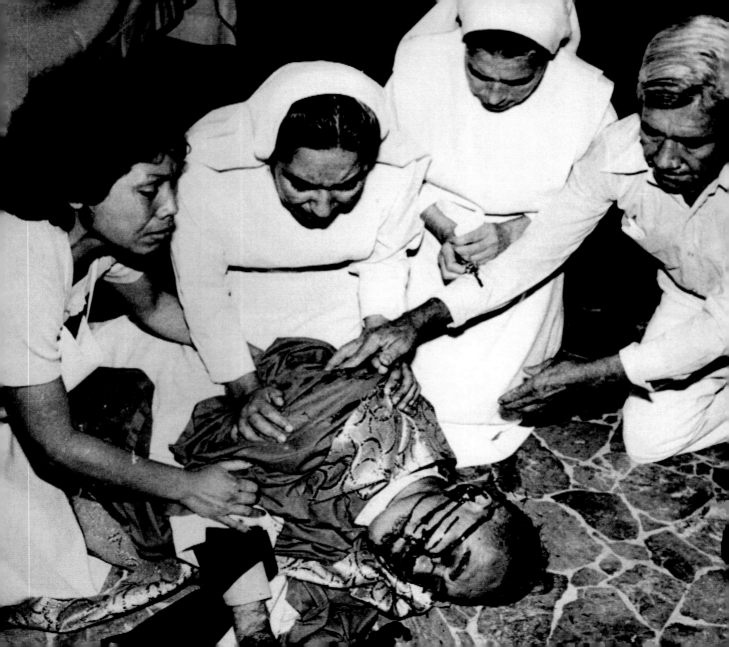

Key Political Event
Assassination of Archbishop Óscar Romero

When El Salvador's widely respected archbishop was gunned down at the altar, it was not difficult to interpret the motives of the gunmen: the murder was a punishment for Romero's public denunciations of the government-sponsored death squads carrying out a "dirty war" against anti-government elements among the rural poor.

The sheer audacity of the killing showcased the no-holds-barred approach of the death squads, many of whose members had been trained in the U.S-operated School of the Americas in Panama. Charged with crushing the armed opposition to the ruling military junta, which had emerged among the rural poor, these paramilitary organizations had already murdered dozens of Catholic clergy in retaliation for their vocal criticisms of violence perpetrated against civilians. Romero, although aware of the risk to his life, had refused to keep silent, and used his authority to express his dissent, even entreating U.S. president Carter to cut off aid to El Salvador's government.

Romero's confrontational attitude was a far cry from the traditionalist and largely apolitical posture he had adopted earlier in his career. It appears that his horror at the assassinations of several friends in the late 1970s convinced him of the need for political intervention on the part of the clergy. Death squads continued to target Catholic priests, Jesuits, and nuns throughout the civil war, which lasted until 1992. In spite of the bad press, the United States continued to support the Salvadoran government, fearful of the rise of another left-wing government in Central America.
Geoffrey Schullenberger

Date March 24, 1980

Country El Salvador

Why It's Key The spectacular assassination of Romero while he celebrated mass at the cathedral of San Salvador stunned the world and drew attention to the prolonged and brutal civil conflict going on in El Salvador.

opposite Nuns attend to the fallen Archbishop Romero minutes after he was assassinated.

513

Key Political Event
Liberian Military Coup

Since its foundation, the Liberian government was largely composed of the country's elite, the descendants of freed slaves. However, by 1980, these "Americo-Liberians" only constituted five per cent of the country's population, and resentment was growing over their dominant social and economic power. In the previous year, riots occurred when the government proposed a sharp increase in the price of rice, the country's staple food.

On the dawn of April 12, 1980, noncommissioned Krahn officers, led by Master Sergeant Samuel Doe, launched a military coup. President William R. Tolbert, Jr was shot dead in his mansion, and the constitution was suspended. In its place, the "People's Redemption Council" was created, and Doe became head of state. Thirteen leading officials, including several former cabinet ministers and the elder brother of President Tolbert, were accused of treason, corruption, and violation of human rights. Only four were condemned to death, but the trial verdicts were overruled by the "People's Redemption Council." On April 22, the 13 men were publicly executed in the capital, Monrovia. They were tied to stakes on a beach next to the army barracks and shot.

Doe's military regime advocated authoritarian policies, banning newspapers and outlawing opposition parties branded as "socialist." In 1985, Liberia held the first post-coup elections, after which Samuel Doe falsely announced that his ruling National Democratic Party had won with 50.9 per cent of the vote, triggering years of coups and civil wars.
Mariko Kato

Date April 12, 1980

Country Liberia

Why It's Key The coup brought an end to Africa's first republic, and resulted in public executions.

Fact The country was named Liberia, meaning "liberty" or "Land of the Free," when it was founded in 1847 by the United States.

Key Political Event
Mugabe wins Zimbabwe election

After years of civil war between black nationalist guerillas and the white minority government in Rhodesia, the country finally held free democratic elections in 1980. A landslide majority elected the guerilla leader Robert Mugabe as prime minister of the newly named Zimbabwe. He initially followed a moderate and pragmatic approach to government. The civil war had been fought by a loose alliance of rebel forces, and out of these he formed an inter-tribal administration to run Zimbabwe. He was also careful not to alienate white landowners and business leaders, who were vital to the economy of the new country.

However, by 1982, Mugabe had fallen out with many members of his cabinet and had dismissed Joshua Nkomo, his chief coalition partner, from the government. This led to widespread anger amongst the minority Ndabele tribe, and a small-scale civil war broke out between Nkomo's supporters and government forces. Mugabe showed his capacity for brutality by sending troops into the Ndabele homeland of Matabeleland, with orders to crush the resistance. Suspected dissidents were executed, and it is estimated that around 20,000 people died as a result.

In 1987, the position of prime minister was abolished, and Mugabe became president, which granted him considerably more power. Nkomo returned to the government as vice-president but with no real authority. Mugabe's re-election in subsequent polls has been accompanied by widespread accusations of vote rigging. Mugabe has effectively created one-party rule in Zimbabwe.

Martin Sayers

Date April 18, 1980

Country Zimbabwe

Why It's Key The rise to power of Robert Mugabe would lead to decades of tyranny in Zimbabwe.

opposite Robert Gabriel Mugabe, first prime minister of independent Zimbabwe, speaks at a press conference.

Key Political Event
Green Party formed

The Green Party of Germany began as a loose group of environmental and peace organizations that officially became the political party "*Die Grünen*" in 1980. Its ideas were based on a statement of principles, the "Four Pillars," which drew on ecology, social justice, democracy, and non-violence. *Die Grünen* enjoyed some independent success in several German governments in the early 1980s, but in 1984 merged with other German "Green" parties to become the Alliance90/The Greens.

By 1994, Alliance90/The Greens was the third most popular political party in Germany, but the peak of its success came in 1998, when it won 8.2 per cent of the vote at elections and formed a coalition government, the Red-Green Alliance, with the German Social Democratic Party, which lasted until 2005. Though it did not secure a place in government in the 2005 elections, it still polled 8.12 per cent of the vote and won fifty-one seats in parliament.

Die Grünen was not the first or the only Green Party in the world. Many countries, including most in Western Europe and the United States have developed Green parties, but the German Green Party remains the most successful and influential. Overall there has been a lack of significant electoral progress for Green parties, but they continue to play an important role, especially in raising the profile of environmental issues worldwide. Furthermore, popular interest in their cause has encouraged other more prominent parties to embrace Green ideas and bring Green policies into the political mainstream.

Helena Hewson

Date 1980

Country Germany

Why It's Key The German Green Party is the most successful and influential of the Green parties worldwide. It has helped to raise awareness of environmental issues in international and domestic politics.

Key Political Event
Shining Path uprising

After its formation in the 1970s by Abimael Guzman, the "Shining Path" became the most formidable rebel movement in Latin America. The Maoist group controlled large areas of the countryside during its heyday in the 1980s and some 70,000 died in the rebellion and counter-insurgency campaign it triggered.

The uprising began in 1980, with the burning of ballot boxes on the eve of the first democratic election in twelve years. Striving to create the perfect communist state, the Shining Path imposed a ruthless and brutal rule on the areas of the country that they controlled, killing villagers they suspected of siding with the government.

The government militia also committed countless atrocities during their attempts to shut down the organization. Some soldiers took to wearing black ski masks to hide their identity during rapes and executions.

The Shining Path carried out a series of high-profile attacks, the worst single incident occurring in July 1992, when two car bombs went off in the middle-class district of Miraflores, killing twenty people and injuring more than 250 others. Guzman was captured in Lima just two months later and sentenced to life imprisonment by a military court.

However, in 2003 this verdict was thrown out and Guzman's re-trial in 2004 ended in chaos after he shouted communist slogans in front of live television cameras. To avoid a repeat performance, tape recorders and cameras were banned from the courtroom for his second re-trial, in 2006, in which he was sentenced again to life imprisonment. Since his arrest the Shining Path has only been sporadically active.

Jonathan Morton

Date May 17, 1980

Country Peru

Why It's Key The Shining Path were one of the most important and provocative revolutionary movements in Latin America.

Key Political Event
Gdansk Shipyard strikes

The sacking of crane driver and activist Anna Walentynowicz on August 7, 1981, was the trigger that began a set of strikes in the Lenin Shipyard in Gdansk, on the Baltic shoreline of Poland. The latest manifestation in an evolving history of Polish worker unrest, the Lenin Shipyard was destined to become the symbolic locus around which the Solidarity anti-communist social movement would foment.

The Communist government of Edward Gierek had, to general dismay, been raising the price of essential commodities (particularly factory-produced meat). Simultaneously, industrial management attempted to preclude protests about the government's actions by denying the authority of state-independent trade unions and the legality of strikes. As editor of an underground union newspaper, *Robotnik Wybrzeza* (*The Coastal Worker*), Walentynowicz was well-known to shipyard authorities. Indeed, she made it her business to be known to them: publicly agitating, and often handing the newspaper directly to her bosses.

When Walentynowicz was sacked, just five months before retirement, it was the martyr moment the union movement needed to galvanize mass support. In the first strike, on August 14, 16,000 workers protested at her dismissal. A little-known electrician called Lech Walesa led the protest, and Walentynowicz was hastily reinstated. On August 31, an agreement was signed that legalized trade unions. In September, the Solidarity party was formed. Walentynowicz, Walesa, and the shipyards would become synonymous with the fall of (Soviet) Communism in Eastern Europe just eight years later.

Michael Hallam

Date August 7, 1980

Country Poland

Why It's Key The Gdansk Shipyard strikes would become a key moment in the struggle for democratic change in Poland and the eventual fall of Communism.

opposite Former Polish president and Solidarity founding leader Lech Walesa speaks to workers during a strike at the Gdansk Shipyard.

Key Political Event
Iran-Iraq War

A 1937 agreement with Iran gave Iraq control over the Shatt al-Arab waterway, its only outlet to the Persian Gulf. In 1975, following an Iraqi-Kurdish rebellion, Iran agreed to stop supporting the Kurds in return for shared control of the waterway.

To Iraqi leader Saddam Hussein, Ayatollah Khomeini's 1979 Iranian revolution was both a threat and an opportunity. When the U.S. Embassy hostage crisis in Tehran increased Iran's isolation, Iraq repudiated the 1975 agreement and invaded. In June 1982, its post-revolutionary power struggle resolved, Iran counterattacked, expelling Iraq and capturing Basra. In May 1984, when Iran responded to attacks on its shipping by attacking both Iraqi and allied shipping, the United States became involved to protect oil shipments (it was also secretly supplying Iran,

channeling profits to the right-wing Contras in Nicaragua). Using costly "human-wave" attacks, Iran captured Al Faw in 1986; Iraq stepped up attacks on cities, oil installations, and shipping.

In July 1987, UN Resolution 598 called for a ceasefire, but Iran, sensing victory, rejected this. Iraq, however, drove the Iranians out of Al Faw, and, in March 1988, attacked occupied Kurdish Halabja with poison gas. Eventually, in August 1988, Khomeini accepted a ceasefire. At least 300,000 had been killed, and many more injured. The total cost to each country exceeded US$500 billion, and both leaders appeared strengthened. The postwar deadlock was broken only when the First Gulf War forced Iraq to agree to withdraw to its 1975 border and exchange prisoners.
Duncan Proudfoot

Date September 22, 1980

Country Iran/Iraq

Why It's Key This extraordinarily long, bloody, and futile conflict contributed to the outbreak of the First Gulf War in 1991; with a strong army and heavily indebted to Kuwait, among others, Iraq invaded its oil-rich neighbor when it refused to forgive Iraq's war debt.

Key Cultural Event
Assassination of John Lennon

John Lennon had spent the evening of his death in a New York recording studio, along with his wife Yoko Ono, arriving back at his luxury apartment in the Dakota building, in the Upper West Side of Manhattan, just before 11 p.m. As he headed into the building, a man called out Lennon's name and as he turned, a .38 revolver was fired five times. Four bullets hit him in the back. He was taken in a police car to St Luke's Roosevelt Hospital Center, where he died.

Lennon had lived in relative seclusion in New York for five years, raising his son, Sean. Ironically, his death came at a time when he was poised to return to his music. He had just completed the *Double Fantasy* album with Yoko Ono, which included the hit track, "(Just Like) Starting Over." News of Lennon's murder was received around the world with disbelief. Quickly

the area outside the Dakota building was transformed into a makeshift shrine while radio stations played some of his best-loved tracks, such as "Imagine."

For people who had grown up with The Beatles, Lennon's assassination had more emotional significance than that of President Kennedy in 1963. His assassin, Mark Chapman, was a drifter who had actually got John's autograph just a few hours earlier. He said he had heard voices in his head telling him to kill the musician. Lennon was honored with a Grammy Lifetime Achievement Award in 1991 and inducted into the Rock and Roll Hall of Fame in 1994.
Lorraine Brownbill

Date December 8, 1980

Country USA

Why It's Key Lennon's senseless murder shocked the world and robbed it of a songwriting genius.

opposite Huge crowds of mourners line the streets outside Lennon's apartment.

Key Political Event
Brixton race riots

The summer of 1981 saw Britain's inner cities ablaze with petrol bombs; the most severe and extensive British riots of the twentieth century.

The July riots took place in Southall (West London) and Toxteth (Liverpool), with smaller outbreaks across many inner-city areas. They followed a weekend of violence over April 10–11 in Brixton, one of London's most ethnically diverse communities. On April 10, a black youth with a stab wound was escorted to a police vehicle by officers. Angry onlookers threw stones at the car in protest at recent increased use of the "Sus" law against the black community; this law allowed police to stop, search, and even arrest a person on suspicion alone.

Tension had been simmering for some time, and after the arrest of another black man on Saturday April 11, the community was plunged into two days of Molotov cocktails, arson, burnt-down shops, and bloodied civilians and policemen. Over three hundred people were injured.

Though race riots have continued to happen sporadically, albeit on a lesser scale, the events in Brixton in 1981 marked a huge turning point in British race relations. It was the first time that Britain's African-Caribbean community had spoken out against police discrimination and intimidation, forcing the right-wing Thatcher government to confront a problem they'd previously ignored. After enquiries and post-mortems, it was concluded that more ethnic minority policemen should be recruited, and the Sus law was written out of the statute.

Andrew Blades

Date April 10–11, 1981

Country UK

Why It's Key The Brixton riots forced a reconsideration of the relationship between issues of race and the law.

Fact The song "Ghost Town," by the multiracial Coventry band The Specials, captured the tenor of the riots, spending three weeks at No.1 during the summer of 1981.

Key Political Event
Shooting of Pope John Paul II

Pope John Paul II was loved by Catholics all over the world but detested by an equal number of influential enemies – including the Soviet Union, whose atheistic sphere of influence in Central and Eastern Europe the Polish Pope spiritually challenged. The Soviets, then, appeared to be likely candidates for engineering the failed assassination attempt on John Paul II in St. Peter's Square on May 13, 1981. The gunman was Mehmet Ali Agca, a Turk with connections to ultra-right-wing Turkish nationalists, the Bulgarian intelligence community, Iran, and international Mafiosi.

Agca succeeded in shooting the Pope, but not in killing him. Surviving the gunshot wounds, John Paul II publicly pardoned Agca and developed a relationship with his would-be assassin over the years, continuing until the Pope's death in 2005. Agca was imprisoned in Italy for twenty years, after which he was extradited to Turkey and imprisoned there for a political murder committed in 1979.

Agca told a number of mutually contradictory stories about the motivation for the assassination attempt on the Pope and, given his complex and shadowy affiliations over the years, the truth of the plot has not emerged. The merciful way in which Agca's intended victim behaved convinced the world of John Paul II's apostolic nature and cemented his high moral standing with believers and nonbelievers alike.

Demir Barlas

Date May 13, 1981

Country Vatican City

Why It's Key Pope John Paul II survived the assassination attempt against him, going on to help destabilize the Soviet sphere of influence in Central and Eastern Europe.

opposite Pope John Paul II lies injured in his jeep in St. Peter's Square after being shot.

Key Political Event
First woman Supreme Court Justice

One hundred and ninety-one years after its founding, the Supreme Court of the United States saw its first woman take a seat on its bench. Sandra Day O'Connor, a fifty-one-year-old Arizona Court of Appeals judge and former State Senator, followed 101 male Justices to the nation's highest court on the nomination of the still-new president, Ronald Reagan, when she was appointed to succeeded Justice Potter Stewart.

The decision generated more controversy amongst the president's supporters than his opponents. The Christian Right saw Justice Potter Stewart's resignation as an opportunity to place on the court a judge who would represent their cause, in particular on the issue of abortion. O'Connor was deemed to be soft on abortion and other essential social issues, and her nomination was immediately opposed by religious figures such as Jerry Falwell, and prominent politicians including Senator Jesse Helms. Other conservatives, however, gave her full support, notably fellow Arizonan Senator Barry Goldwater, who condemned the Moral Majority leader's exhortations to oppose the nomination, declaring that, "every good Christian ought to kick Falwell right in the ass."

The assurances of Ronald Reagan dampened the opposition, and O'Connor was confirmed easily, going on to serve for 24 years. Her career in some ways justified her critics' concerns. Though a conservative who personally abhorred abortion, she saw no place for political activism in the Supreme Court and gained a reputation as a centrist and a moderating "swing vote."

Roger Johnson

Date August 19, 1981

Country USA

Why It's Key O'Connor was the first female Supreme Court Justice.

1980-1989

Key Cultural Event
France launches high-speed TGV trains

The idea of the *Train à Grande Vitesse* (TGV) was first proposed in the 1960s to rival Japan's *Shinkansen* bullet train, which had begun construction in 1959. It was originally designed to be propelled by gas turbines, because of their good power-to-weight ratio, but when the 1973 energy crisis increased oil prices, the turbines were replaced by electricity. The first electric prototype was tested in 1974 and successfully traveled almost 1 million kilometers. In 1976, the French government began to fund the TGV project, and the first high-speed line, LGV Sud-Est (*Ligne à Grande Vitesse*), was laid.

On September 27, 1981, the TGV service opened to the public between Paris and Lyon. It became the world's second commercial high-speed train service after Japan's *Shinkansen*, largely replacing air travel between Paris and other cities in France, as well as cities in neighboring countries. In 1994, a version of the TGV called Eurostar, started running between continental Europe and London through the Channel Tunnel. Traveling at an average of 300 kilometers per hour, the TGV reaches 320 kilometers per hour for over 1,600 kilometers.

On April 3, 2007, a modified version with larger wheels and two engines reached 574.8 kilometers per hour, re-setting the world record for a train running on a conventional railway line. It narrowly missed beating the overall world train speed record of 581 kilometers per hour, set by Maglev, a Japanese magnetic levitation train, in 2003.

Mariko Kato

Date September 27, 1981

Country France

Why It's Key TGV has set records as one of the fastest trains in the world.

Fact TGV stands for *Train à Grande Vitesse*, or "high-speed train."

opposite France's state railway service SNCF presents the high-speed TGV train which first ran between Paris and Lyon in 1981.

Key Political Event
IRA prison hunger strikes

On March 1, 1981, Bobby Sands began a hunger strike in Northern Ireland's Maze Prison, where he was being held for possession of firearms. The aim was to secure special status for prisoners charged with paramilitary, terrorist, or political crimes. The British government had passed legislation removing this designation for political prisoners between 1976 and 1978, resulting in a series of protests by IRA-affiliated prisoners; these included "dirty protests" (refusal to wash), "blanket protests" (refusal to wear prison uniforms), and a prior hunger strike, but they had all failed to produce a satisfactory outcome.

During the 1981 hunger strike, Sands ran for Parliament and was elected by a Catholic district. He died after sixty-six days on strike. As more striking prisoners died, the international media swarmed the prison and Prime Minister Margaret Thatcher finally put her foot down: "Crime is crime is crime," she said. "It is not political." She would not capitulate to the IRA's demands. The remaining protesters ended the strike on October 3, and Sinn Fein saw a drastic surge in popularity over the following years, transforming from a largely militaristic organization into a political force.

The deaths and lack of compromise polarized political groups, and Sands' parliamentary victory demonstrated greater support for the nationalists than many had acknowledged. Strikes broke out in Belfast, and violence spread across Northern Ireland as IRA recruitment increased. Today, murals of Bobby Sands and the other hunger strikers who died remain popular symbols of Irish nationalism.

Chris Schonberger

Date 1981

Country Northern Ireland

Why It's Key Margaret Thatcher's refusal to grant special status to IRA prisoners radicalized politics in Northern Ireland.

Fact Ten people died during the 1981 hunger strike.

528

Key Political Event
Assassination of President Sadat

He had saluted, placed a wreath, and was watching an aerial display by the Egyptian Air Force overhead when two grenades exploded. Then, armed Muslim extremists flew out of the back of a military truck in the procession, raced toward the rostrum where he stood, and opened fire with automatic machine guns. Egyptian President Mohammed Anwar el Sadat, recipient of the 1978 Nobel Peace Prize, fell dead. It was during a parade in Cairo, on October 6, 1981, to commemorate the anniversary of the 1973 Yom Kippur Arab-Israeli war.

Sadat had become something of an Arab hero when he led Egypt and Syria into the war with Israel in an effort to reclaim a section of the Sinai Peninsula. While Israel was successful in counterattacking, Sadat was celebrated as the first Arab leader to actually reclaim territory from Israel. A pragmatist, Sadat then made the historic trip to Jerusalem in 1977 and negotiated the exodus of Israeli troops from the Peninsula; in exchange, Egypt would become the first Arab country to recognize Israel. U.S. President Jimmy Carter mediated negotiations between Sadat and Israeli Prime Minister Menachem Begin, culminating in the signing of a peace treaty on March 26, 1979, the first between Israel and any Arab nation.

The assassination of President Sadat was met with a mixed reaction. While his popularity skyrocketed in the West, he faced isolation and boycotts from the Arab world because of his rapprochement with Israel. His funeral was attended by only one Arab head of state.

Colette Leisen

Date October 6, 1981

Country Egypt

Why It's Key Sadat was the first Arab leader to recognize the State of Israel, and was eventually to pay for this move, which angered Muslim extremists, with his life.

opposite Chaos in the aftermath of President Sadat's assassination.

Key Political Event
OPEC loses monopoly on oil

From the moment it was formed in 1960, the Organization of Petroleum Exporting Countries (OPEC) took control of world oil prices, often raising them by setting production limits. With the thirteen member nations producing a third of the world's oil, the price of crude oil rose from US$1.80 a barrel in 1970 to US$34 in 1981. Faced with such price fixing, Western nations looked elsewhere for their oil. By the early Eighties, a quarter of U.S. oil came from newly discovered oilfields in Alaska. In 1982, for the first time in a decade, OPEC supplied less than half of the non-communist world's oil. To discuss how they could regain control of the market, OPEC delegates had a series of meetings in March 1983 at London's Inter-Continental Hotel. There, they agreed to cut prices for the first time.

The price cut (15 per cent) meant that OPEC lost up to US$100 million a day in income. For the wealthy, less populous nations of the Persian Gulf, this was a minor concern. But developing nations with large populations felt the economic strain – whether OPEC nations such as Indonesia, Nigeria, and Venezuela, or other oil-producing nations, such as Mexico, whose prices were determined by OPEC.

Attempts to establish further production limits were ignored by some of the poorer nations, keeping prices down. OPEC no longer held the reins, with market forces now deciding oil prices.
Mark Juddery

Date March 14, 1982

Country UK

Why It's Key A fall in oil prices led to economic crisis in the developing world.

530

Key Political Event
Falklands War

The Falklands are a group of islands in the South Atlantic Ocean, roughly 480 kilometers (300 miles) off the east coast of Argentina, and some 13,000 kilometers (8,000 miles) from Britain. On March 19, 1982, a group of scrap-metal workmen, accompanied by Argentinean military personnel, arrived on the island of South Georgia and hoisted an Argentinean flag. Residents complained, and the British Foreign Office instructed Royal Navy personnel aboard the ice patrol vessel HMS *Endurance* to remove the flag. This action was deemed sufficiently provocative by the Argentine military junta, led by General Leopoldo Galtieri, to justify military intervention. Argentinean forces began their invasion of the Falkland Islands in the early hours of April 2, 1982.

It became evident within a few days that the recovery of the Falkland Islands would require a major military operation. Admiral Sir Henry Leach, the First Sea Lord, persuaded Prime Minister Margaret Thatcher that he could assemble "Task Force South," a naval armada, to retake the islands. A flotilla of Royal Navy ships and requisitioned merchant ships, including luxury liners the *Canberra* and the *QE2*, duly set sail. By June, the Falkland Islands were back in British hands.

The most striking aspect of the Falklands War was the casualty rate in such a brief period. The official death toll comprises 258 British servicemen, 700 Argentine personnel, and 3 Falkland civilians.

The military junta in Argentina collapsed after its failure to win the Falklands War, highlighting the social and economic fragility of the country at the time.
David Dunning

Date April 2, 1982

Country Falkland Islands

Why It's Key Victory in the Falklands War rescued the Thatcher government from the depths of unpopularity, enabling it to remain in power for another fifteen years.

opposite Troops fighting in the Falklands raise the British flag.

Key Political Event
Boland Amendment

The Boland Amendment and the Iran-Contra scandal that resulted directly from it form a particularly contentious part of the drawn-out history of the U.S. Constitution's division of war powers between the president and Congress.

In early 1982, members of the Democratic-controlled Congress became aware of covert CIA activities in Nicaragua aimed at aiding the "Contra" insurgency against the left-wing Sandinista government. In what was probably more a turf dispute than an expression of support for the Sandinistas, congressmen led by Edward Boland drafted a clause to the yearly appropriations bill (legislation providing funding to the military), which explicitly prohibited aid to the Contras.

Infuriated members of Ronald Reagan's defense and foreign policy team, determined to oust the Sandinistas, went to great lengths to persist in their support for the Contras. Having discovered a loophole in the amendment, which appeared to only prohibit the involvement of "U.S. Intelligence Agencies" in Nicaraguan affairs, they centered pro-Contra activities in the National Security Council, which officially did not qualify as an intelligence agency.

The search for further revenue culminated in a series of bizarre backroom deals by which secret weapons sales to Iran would fund the Contras. According to some investigations, drug money also formed a significant part of the millions of dollars funneled to anti-Sandinista paramilitary groups under Reagan. Scandal did not erupt until details of these and other schemes were leaked to the public in late 1986.
Geoffrey Schullenberger

Date December 8, 1982

Country Nicaragua

Why It's Key The Boland Amendment forced the cold warriors of the Reagan administration to seek surreptitious routes to continue funding the right-wing Contra rebels in Nicaragua – efforts that resulted in one of the biggest political scandals in U.S. history.

opposite A group of Contra Special Forces on a patrol in a remote area of northern Nicaragua.

Key Political Event
The December Murders

In an attempt to quell gathering opposition to the military government of Suriname, fifteen political activists were arrested and allegedly tortured before being shot on the night of December 8, 1982. The victims were mainly Surinamese, but the death of Dutch national Frank Wijngaarde caused outrage in the Netherlands, Suriname's former ruler. The so-called December Murders, or *Decembermoorden*, quickly became an international issue, and both the USA and the Netherlands withdrew offers of financial support to Suriname, resulting in an economic recession.

Although no one has ever gone on trial for the killings, it has long been suspected that the order came from Désiré Delano Bouterse, the chairman of Suriname's National Military Council, who first rose to prominence in the ranks of the Surinamese army after the country gained autonomy from the Netherlands in 1954. He went on to play an integral part in the coup of February 1980, replacing President Henk Arron's democratic government with his own hard-line military rule. The constitution was suspended and Bouterse ruled by decree as the country's de facto leader, sparking civil unrest and the emergence of several political opponents.

Although the Netherlands has issued an international warrant for Bouterse's arrest, he cannot be extradited from his current residence in Suriname because of his former position as head of state. However, Suriname is anxious to put the former dictator on trial for his alleged crimes and legal proceedings are now underway.
Jay Mullins

Date December 8, 1982

Country Suriname

Why It's Key The unresolved murders caused long-term damage to relations between Suriname and the Netherlands.

Key Political Event
Brunei achieves independence

Brunei's declaration of independence in 1984 officially brought to a close a century of British protection. The first written constitution had been introduced in 1959, enshrining Sultan Omar Ali Saifuddin as the source of supreme executive power, the head of both state and government. For the next twenty years, Britain continued to manage Brunei's foreign affairs and defense, helping the Sultan resist overtures to join the Malaysian Federation in the late 1950s and quelling an armed rebellion in 1962. Britain slowly relinquished its influence, eventually signing a new treaty in January 1979 that reaffirmed friendly relations between the countries.

Crude oil and natural gas production make up half of Brunei's GDP. Nevertheless, falling reserves have recently led Brunei to reposition itself as a financial and ecotourism specialist, and in February 2007, the country pledged to conserve a sizable region of the Borneo rainforest. The present Sultan, Hassanal Bolkiah, exercises absolute control over the country's finances, redistributing much of the massive oil revenues to maintain one of the highest standards of living per capita in the world. Education and medical services are free, housing is subsidized, and there is no corporation or personal taxation levied.

Yet with a net private fortune estimated at US$98 billion, the Sultan's extravagant lifestyle is legendary. He owns between 3,000 to 5,000 cars, a private fleet of aircraft including a Boeing 747, a US$3 billion theme park, and a raft of palatial properties in many of the world's major cities.
Jay Mullins

Date January 1, 1984

Country Brunei

Why It's Key Full independence consolidated the power of the oil-rich state's royal family.

1980-1989

545

Key Cultural Event
Macintosh launches computer with mouse

Eight years before the Macintosh computer appeared, Steve Wozniak designed the Apple-1, the first computer to use a typewriter-style keyboard. That was Wozniak's first serious contribution toward making computers accessible to non-computer scientists; his second was the Macintosh, later known as the Macintosh 128K. The Macintosh's innovation was its window-based operating system, which was used with a keyboard and a mouse. The mouse did a lot of the work that previously had to be done by typing in coded command lines to direct a computer to files in its memory. Now each file had a moveable icon that the mouse cursor could simply point to. The system inspired Microsoft's Windows packages.

The computer itself was small and practically cuboid, with a beige casing and a nine-inch monitor. It was equipped with one single-sided 3.5-inch floppy disk drive and had only 128 kilobytes of memory. Even its operating system was disk-based. Its retail price was US$2,495, and 50,000 were sold in the first three months, a moderate performance for a piece of technology which was supposed to revolutionize personal computing.

But in spite of these difficulties, the system received popular acclaim. Lawrence J. Magid wrote in the *Los Angeles Times* that: "The Macintosh is as innovative today as the Apple II was in 1977. It's one of the few computers introduced in the last 18 months that makes no attempt to imitate the IBM PC."

By October 1985, the 128k was replaced by a successor, the 512k.
David Thorley

Date January 24, 1984

Country USA

Why It's Key The Macintosh changed personal computing profoundly, providing the prototype for the size, pricing, and style of all home computers that followed.

Fact The Macintosh launch was marked by the iconic Super Bowl advertisement directed by Ridley Scott and based on Orwell's *1984*.

opposite Steve Jobs and John Sculley with the new Apple Macintosh computer.

Key Political Event
CIA plants mines in Nicaraguan harbors

In the first months of 1984, boats around the coastlines of Nicaragua found themselves in danger from mines floating in main harbors. The surreptitiously placed weapons caused the destruction of five local fishing boats, as well as indiscriminately damaging ships operating under a range of nationalities.

Initially, it was assumed that these attacks were the work of the Contras, the insurgents who had been battling the governing Marxist Sandinistas for three years with the overt moral support, and covert material support, of the Reagan administration. On April 6, however, the *Wall Street Journal* reported that the CIA had been behind the operation (as well as various onshore attacks), sending agents into the harbors on speedboats to lay the mines before returning to mother ships in international waters.

The mines, essentially designed to deter shipping, caused massive damage to the Nicaraguan economy. Protesting the interference as a breach of international law, the Sandinista government took their case to the World Court in The Hague. The United States' actions, both in the specific case and in the broader context, were declared an unlawful use of force.

But Nicaragua's legal success was muted by U.S. refusal to recognize the court's authority. In the United States, the mining was strongly condemned by the public and by the Senate in an official resolution. The operation, which had presidential approval, indefinitely put back any hope of the White House gaining congressional approval for its Central American policy.
Roger Johnson

Date February 25, 1984

Country Nicaragua/USA

Why It's Key The revelation of direct covert intervention in Nicaragua undermined support for Reagan's crusade against the governing Sandinistas, and resulted in condemnation by the World Court.

1980-1989

Key Disaster
Ethiopia famine

Between 1984 and 1985, over one million Ethiopians starved to death. Drought had hit the region in 1981, and in 1984, crop disease and the absence of the spring rains caused another more serious drought. In March, the Ethiopian government warned that crop yield would fall short by one million tonnes. By summer, tens of thousands were dying of starvation and related diseases, and six million were vulnerable.

The West refused to help, claiming that Ethiopia's Marxist-Leninist military government would spend the money arming itself and fighting the 20-year civil war with Eritrea and Tigre. Hoping to shame Western governments into action, Oxfam made a donation of £500,000, the largest single donation in its history. The refusal of Western governments to increase aid forced aid agencies to buy grain at market prices. By October,

with 200,000 dead and eight million threatened, increased media coverage in Western Europe prompted £100 million in public donations. After delays caused by diplomatic problems, foreign aid drops began in November, and Ethiopian military vehicles began to distribute the supplies. Meanwhile, increased internal conflict and heavy storms, which destroyed remaining crops, caused thousands to flee for Sudan daily.

The star-studded releases "Do They Know Its Christmas?" (UK) and "We Are The World" (United States), and two Live Aid concerts, organized by Bob Geldof, helped raise awareness and money. By the end of 1985, the famine was abating, but drought and famine continue to afflict the region.
Laura Pechey

Date March 1, 1984

Country Ethiopia

Why It's Key The severe drought in Ethiopia, which saw hundreds of thousands perish, crucially tested Western commitment to international aid.

opposite Images of the suffering caused by the drought helped to raise awareness and financial aid.

Key Political Event
UK miners' strike

The miners' strike was the most bitter industrial dispute in Britain in recent times. It was triggered by the announcement that a Yorkshire colliery, Cortonwood, was to close. The following day, the Chairman of the Coal Board, Ian MacGregor, announced that Cortonwood was just the first in a program of pit closures, which would ultimately see 20,000 miners lose their jobs.

This revelation led to a nationwide strike, and so-called "flying pickets" were dispatched to collieries around the country to persuade miners to stay away from work. The absence of a national ballot meant the strike was technically illegal, leading to the confiscation of NUM funds, and intervention by the police.

Picket line violence was widespread, particularly in South Yorkshire and Nottinghamshire, and there was much support for the strike from South Wales. At Orgreave coking plant, in South Yorkshire, in June, 10,000 pickets fought a pitched battle against police in riot gear, with police horses, and dogs.

Roughly four months' supply of coal had been stockpiled at pitheads and power stations, and, as the strike wore on, striking miners began to suffer severe financial hardship. In September, a compromise was presented to the NUM leader, Arthur Scargill, by the Coal Board, but he rejected it.

After Christmas, miners started to head back to work in droves, and on March 3, 1985, NUM delegates voted to end the strike. Two days later, many miners marched back to work behind union banners, accompanied by colliery brass bands.
David Dunning

Date March 6, 1984

Country UK

Why It's Key Victory for Margaret Thatcher over the National Union of Mineworkers (NUM) allowed her to complete her pit closure program.

opposite Picket-line tensions during the Yorkshire coal strike.

Key Political Event
Nkomati Accord signed

Mozambique and Angola's 1975 independence deprived South Africa of a buffer, that had protected it from incursions by the African National Congress (ANC). It responded by expanding its military capacity and initiating "détente," a search for allies in Africa. But this collapsed when South Africa invaded Angola in 1975, and brutally suppressed the 1976 Soweto uprising.

B. J. Vorster was deposed by P. W. Botha, who aimed to combat what he saw as a communist "total onslaught" by creating a "constellation" of anti-Marxist southern African states through a combination of military and economic bullying. South Africa cultivated surrogate military forces (UNITA in Angola, and Renamo in Mozambique), disrupted economic traffic, and reduced the number of Mozambicans working in its gold mines from 118,000 to 41,000 in 1977. In 1981, South Africa struck at ANC houses in Matola, near Maputo, and, two years later, facing military strikes, Renamo terrorism, and a terrible drought, Mozambique was forced to negotiate.

In Komatipoort, on the Nkomati River in South Africa, Botha and Mozambican president Samora Machel signed an undertaking not to allow their countries to be used as bases from which to attack each other. Machel expelled the ANC, but South Africa, which increased its military spending by 21 percent in 1984, continued clandestinely to support Renamo. It was only the 1992 Rome General Peace Accord and UN supervision that finally brought the activities of Renamo to an end in 1994, as the ANC took over in South Africa.
Duncan Proudfoot

Date March 16, 1984

Country South Africa

Why It's Key The accord was a cynical diplomatic initiative on the part of an embattled apartheid South Africa to stave off its demise, which was to come, finally, ten years later.

Key Political Event
Gorbachev becomes Soviet leader

When Mikhail Gorbachev became leader of the Union of Soviet Socialist Republics (USSR) in 1985, he wanted to reinvigorate the Soviet system, which was going through a critical period. Old men dominated the Politburo, defense spending was crippling the country, and corruption was rife. However, his radical policies turned out to be instrumental in the demise of the USSR, and he became its last leader.

In 1980, aged forty-nine, Gorbachev had become a full member of the Politburo and the youngest member of the Communist Party's inner circle. When Brezhnev died in 1982, he was succeeded in quick succession by Andropov and then Chernenko. Gorbachev took over the leadership in 1985, and quickly moved younger politicians into key roles, undertook a crackdown on corruption, and began an economic review. However,

he constantly came up against bureaucratic resistance and was frustrated by poor information. In 1986, he introduced a reform program, known as *Perestroika*, aimed at rebuilding society, and declared a policy of *Glasnost* to promote openness in media, government, and Party organizations. It was Gorbachev's *Glasnost* policy and his encouragement of Eastern European countries to fend for themselves that eventually led to the break up of the Soviet Union in 1991.

Gorbachev recognized that Soviet foreign policy also needed overhauling and he began a series of successful meetings with U.S. presidents Ronald Regan and George Bush. He established relationships with other Western leaders, including British Prime Minister Margaret Thatcher, effectively ending the Cold War.
Lorraine Brownbill

Date March 11, 1985

Country USSR

Why It's Key Gorbachev introduced *Glasnost*, which led to a better relationship with the West, the empowering of the Soviet republics, and the eventual break-up of the USSR.

Key Discovery
British Antarctic Survey discovers hole in ozone layer

The British Antarctic Survey (BAS) based in Cambridge, UK, began measuring ozone levels in 1957 at the Halley Research Station in the Antarctic. Ozone in the atmosphere absorbs most of the sun's harmful ultraviolet-B (UV-B) radiation. Over the years scientific teams built up a record of daily, weekly, monthly, and annual measurements. In the early 1980s, according to BAS reports, these measurements showed evidence of a decline in the ozone. In the month of October, for instance, the ozone thinned so much it was almost completely depleted.

BAS scientists Joe Farman, Brian Gardiner, and Jonathan Shanklin published their findings in a report in *Nature* magazine in May 1985, heralded as the first warning of worldwide ozone thinning. NASA scientists had been finding similar results, and in the United

States, Dr Susan Solomon began investigating and reporting on possible causes. Soon these studies pointed to chlorofluorocarbons (CFCs), then used in aerosol cans, air conditioning, and refrigeration. This led to the 1987 Montreal Protocol on Substances that Deplete the Ozone Layer, encouraging countries worldwide to limit the production of CFCs and other ozone-depleting substances. Since then, BAS measurements have indicated the ozone hole is gradually shrinking. Some estimates now suggest it may repair itself by the late twenty-first century.
Marie Powell

Date May 1, 1985

Country UK/Antarctica

Why It's Key The BAS report on ozone depletion causes international accords.

opposite Satellite images of the ozone hole in the spring Antarctic atmosphere.

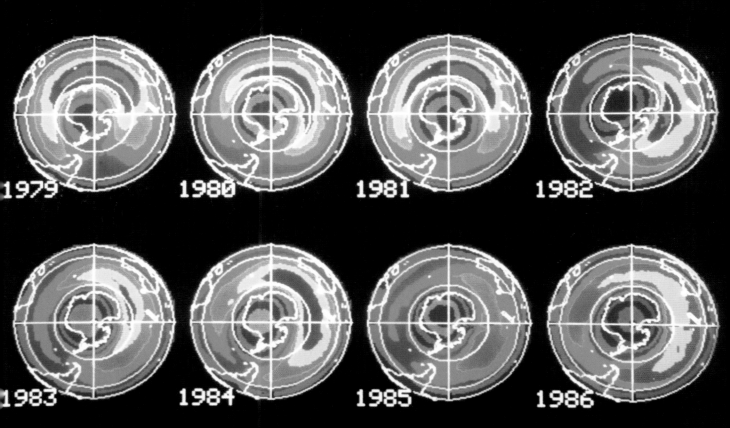

1979 1980 1981 1982

1983 1984 1985 1986

TOMS OCT MONTHLY MEAN

M. R. SCHOEBERL AND A. J. KRUEGER

DOBSON UNITS
130 390 650

Key Political Event
PLF hijack Italian ship

The Italian cruise ship *Achille Lauro* became the unlikely site of an international diplomatic incident when, on October 7, 1985, the ship and all aboard were taken hostage by four men representing the militant Palestine Liberation Front (PLF). The PLF attempted to leverage their hostages to demand the release of fifty Palestinians from Israeli prisons and killed one of the passengers, Leon Klinghoffer of the United States, upon learning that he was a Jew. One of the hijackers shot Klinghoffer, a stroke victim from New York who was confined to a wheelchair, in the forehead, and dumped his body overboard.

After a few days, the PLF agreed to free the hostages in exchange for safe airborne escort out from Egypt, the original destination of the *Achille Lauro*, to Tunisia, then a hotbed of Palestinian militant and revolutionary activity. The U.S. military intervened to prevent the plane carrying the hijackers from arriving at its destination. The plane was diverted instead to Sicily, where the Italian authorities – after a tense jurisdictional dispute with the United States – arrested the four hijackers, although Abu Abbas, the leader of the PLF and probably the mastermind behind the attack, was not located and captured (by the United States) until 2003. The *Achille Lauro* incident hardened anti-Palestinian attitudes not only among Israelis but also in the United States, where a high-profile television movie about the PLF's takeover did little service to the Palestinian cause.

Demir Barlas

Date October 7, 1985

Country Palestine/Italy

Why It's Key The *Achille Lauro*'s hijacking was a precursor of future terrorist takeovers of mass transportation, including the planes employed in the September 11, 2001, attacks on the United States.

opposite The *Achille Lauro* returns to Genoa after the ordeal.

Key Political Event
IWC places moratorium on commercial whaling

Having already banned the hunting of some species (such as blue whales) in earlier decades, the International Whaling Commission (IWC) responded to ever-dwindling whale populations and pressure from "Save the Whales" conservationists by imposing a global suspension on all commercial whaling in 1986. Allowances were made for indigenous people, such as the Inuit, to continue hunting small numbers for their own use. However, the moratorium was opposed by traditional whaling nations, notably Japan, Iceland, and Norway, who continue to find a way around it by controversially hunting some 2,000 whales a year under the guise of "scientific research," which is allowed by the IWC. Japan, which also provokes condemnation for its hunting of dolphins and porpoises, has been trying to overturn the moratorium in recent years by influencing other, often non-whaling, nations on the IWC to vote against it.

Nevertheless, the moratorium and previous bans are helping to reverse the sharp decline in whale numbers, although some species are still on the brink of extinction. Take the world's largest creature, the blue whale: it's estimated there were up to 200,000 of these whales a century ago before industrial-scale whaling took off. Prized for their huge quantities of oil, about 30,000 were killed in 1931 alone, and they were down to a mere 1,500 in the 1960s. Since then, thanks to the IWC ban, the blue whale population has risen to roughly 4,500 today and its slow but gradual rise is mirrored in other endangered species.

Hedley Paul

Date January 1, 1986

Country Worldwide

Why It's Key Despite continuing to be flouted by some whaling nations, the hunting ban has led to a halt in the decline of worldwide whale numbers and is an important landmark in the preservation of endangered wildlife.

Key Disaster
Challenger space shuttle disaster

Embarking on its tenth mission since its maiden flight in 1983, *Challenger* launched from the Kennedy Space Center at Cape Canaveral, Florida. Seventy-three seconds after the launch, and at a height of 14,000 meters, the space shuttle began to break up and veer off course, disintegrating further under the resulting aerodynamic pressure. Liquid hydrogen from the ruptured fuel tank ignited in an explosive fireball as the craft was flung earthward, out of control. The impact as it hit the ocean three minutes later ended any hope of survival for the seven crewmembers inside. A faulty seal in *Challenger*'s right-hand solid rocket booster, unsuited for the cold weather, was found to be the primary cause of the disaster.

Amongst *Challenger*'s crew was Christa McAuliffe, who had won a competition to be the participant in the Teacher in Space project, an idea designed to get American children interested in the space program. This aspect of the mission, and the fact that schools nationwide were broadcasting the launch live, made the disaster all the more poignant. The accident prompted President Reagan to set up the Rogers Commission, which grounded NASA's shuttle program for three years and exposed many of its flaws in design and procedure. Reagan, postponing his State of the Union address, gave the astronauts a televised eulogy, quoting the poet John Magee: "We will never forget them... as they prepared for their journey and waved goodbye and 'slipped the surly bonds of earth' to 'touch the face of God.'"

Roger Johnson

Date January 28, 1986

Country USA

Why It's Key The *Challenger* Seven were the first astronauts to die in-flight.

opposite The fuel tank explodes seconds after launch.

Key Political Event
Revolution in Haiti

In 1986, conditions in Haiti were abysmal. Almost three decades under the dictatorship of the Duvalier dynasty had established a climate of violent political repression. Despite U.S. foreign aid to Jean-Claude "Baby Doc" Duvalier's regime, the Haitian economy remained poor. Tourism, hitherto an important source of revenue, was in freefall as panic mounted over the emerging AIDS epidemic, which some suggested had originally spread to the United States from Haiti.

In the early 1980s both the rural peasantry and the urban middle class were becoming increasingly alienated from Duvalier. Appointed president at nineteen by his father François Duvalier "Papa Doc," Baby Doc's primary interest in the government of Haiti was as a personal slush fund, and his ill-considered marriage to the politically dubious divorcee Michèle Bennet Pasquet further estranged his supporters. Widespread protests began in 1985 in the city of Gonaïves, and by January 1986, much of the country was in open revolt. Duvalier was pressured to leave by members of his own government and by the Reagan administration. After a short-lived struggle to maintain power (declaring that "we are as firm as a monkey tail"), Duvalier was forced into exile in France, where he lives in a small apartment. His departure cleared the way for the short-lived rise of Haiti's first democratically elected president, Jean Bertrand Aristide, who was almost immediately overthrown by a military coup.

Rachel Eley

Date February 7, 1986

Country Haiti

Why It's Key Revolution ends the thirty-year Duvalier regime and clears the way for Haiti's first democratically elected president.

Fact In September 2007, Jean-Claude Duvalier, in exile in France, apologized for the "wrongs" of his regime. President Préval rejected his apology.

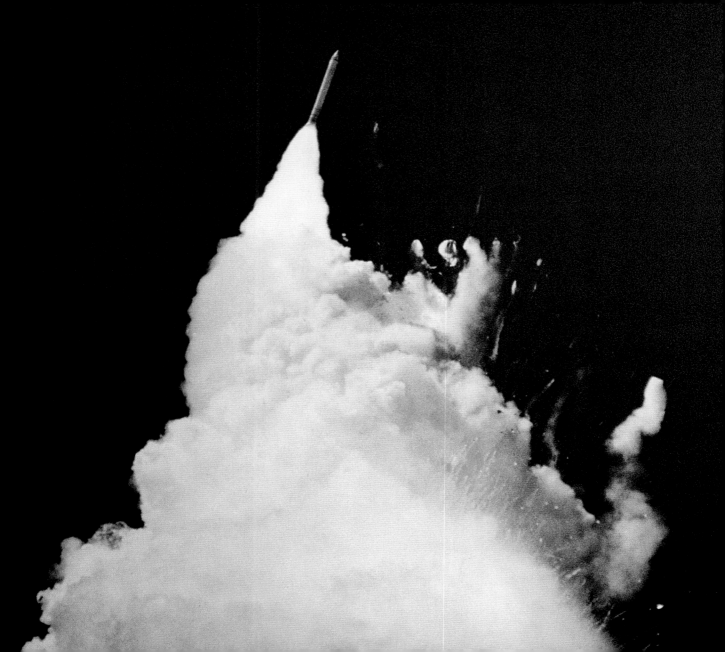

Key Disaster
Explosion at Chernobyl nuclear power plant

Today Chernobyl is almost uninhabited. Over two decades on from the nuclear disaster that made it infamous throughout the world, the area is known as the "zone of alienation."

The incident began on April 25–26, 1986, when a safety test performed on one of the plant's four RBMK-1,000 reactors sparked a runaway reaction. An intense build-up of pressure led to an explosion that destroyed part of the reactor. Faulty radiation readings led plant workers to believe that the reactor was intact, but the graphite core caught fire, causing a partial meltdown and distributing poisonous fallout across Ukraine, Belarus, and Russia.

Thirty thousand people were evacuated under a hasty cover-up operation, but Swedish monitoring stations detected high levels of wind-born radiation,

and the Soviet government was forced to make an embarrassing disclosure. Radioactive waste had to be buried at 800 sites, and a steel and concrete sarcophagus built around the damaged reactor.

Thirty-two people died directly from the disaster, and many more contracted radiation sickness. Despite the evacuation process, thousands of people and millions of acres of land were contaminated, creating a long, grisly legacy of high cancer rates and livestock mutations. The accident provoked an international outcry and fostered opposition to the building of further plants in Russia.

The reactor sarcophagus was later found to be structurally unsafe, leading to a new one being commissioned in 2007.

Jay Mullins

Date April 26, 1986

Country Ukraine (USSR)

Why It's Key It created an environmental crisis that damaged the credibility of both the Soviet Union and nuclear power.

Fact The explosion discharged between 50 and 185 million curies of radionuclides – several times more fallout than experienced at Hiroshima and Nagasaki.

opposite An officer 'protects' himself from the radiation.

Key Cultural Event **West German hacker steals U.S. secrets for Soviets**

Clifford Stoll, an astrophysicist turned systems analyst, had been on the job at Lawrence Berkeley Lab only two days when he discovered that someone had used 75 cents of computer time without paying. Closer investigation revealed that "Hunter," a hacker, had broken into Berkeley computers. Stoll learned that "Hunter" had found a backdoor into the UNIX system, setting up a "Cuckoo's Egg" program that stole passwords and provided super-user privileges, allowing the hacker to search Berkeley computers and use the system to connect to other computers, including MILNET, the system used by the Department of Defense. Stoll set up a program to record the hacker's keystrokes and began tracing the point of origin. No classified military files were stored on networked computers, and authorities were not initially interested.

Stoll followed "Hunter" for a year, contacting German authorities when the hacker was traced to the University of Bremen in West Germany. "Hunter" was Markus Hess, an excitement-seeking employee of a small software firm who had collaborated with a team of hackers to break into computers in the United States, Western Europe, and Japan to steal secrets for the Soviet Union. Hess' major objective had been to gather information on Ronald Reagan's much-touted "Star Wars" weapons system. Congress passed the Electronic Communications Privacy Act in 1986 and updated it as computer technology advanced. Stoll focused worldwide attention on computer hacking in 1989 with the publication of The Cuckoo's Egg: Tracking a Spy through the Maze of Counter Espionage.

Elizabeth R. Purdy

Date 1986

Country USA/Germany

Why It's Key The concept of electronic espionage emerged as experts tracked the hacker's actions, motivating countries around the world to develop tighter computer security measures and enact strict laws and policies on computer hacking.

Key Cultural Event
The "Second Summer of Love"

In August 1987, four young Londoners – Paul Oakenfold, Johnny Walker, Danny Rampling, and Nicky Holloway – went on holiday to Ibiza, where they danced in a club called Amnesia and took ecstasy for the first time. On their return, they were determined to bring some of that lawless energy back to Britain's stagnant dance scene, and within months they found themselves at the center of the biggest youth movement since punk: rave.

Rave began in London clubs, but soon spread to empty warehouses and factories across the UK. MDMA, a synthetic stimulant patented as long ago as 1914 by German pharmaceutical company Merck, was discovered to go beautifully with the dance genre known as "acid house," a messy combination of Detroit techno, New York disco, Chicago house, and European electropop. British youth were smitten, and by the summer of 1988, no club or warehouse was big enough: ravers went out into the fields, where thousands could dance past dawn to a sound system powered by portable generators, undiscouraged by the tabloids' moralistic backlash. Meanwhile, in the north of England, "Madchester" was combining dance with indie rock. The deathblow to the countryside rave movement would eventually arrive with the new police powers established in John Major's Criminal Justice and Public Order Act of 1994. But this could not detract from the enduring vibrancy of Britain's dance music underground, or from the widespread popularity of the ecstasy pill, both established during the Second Summer of Love.

Ned Beauman

Date 1987

Country Ibiza

Why It's Key An entire generation's club and drug culture was brought back from Ibiza and planted in British fields.

opposite Ravers dance at all-night club venue.

576

Key Political Event
Currency devaluation in Burma

On September 5, 1987, the people of Burma were informed that close to 80 per cent of their currency was worthless. In a surprise announcement from the government of General Ne Win, the 25 kyat, the 35 kyat, and the 75 kyat were demonetized. They were no longer legal tender, and could not be exchanged for the few denominations that remained in circulation.

The chaos was immediate. Stores and banks were shuttered. Tourists found themselves holding worthless handfuls of Burmese money that could not be exchanged, even for stable foreign currency. Most people believed that the government's move was directed at black marketeers working along the Thai border, and if that was the case, it did its job. Within days, most illicit trade in goods and currency had stopped. The problem was, the average Burmese citizen suffered far more than the borderland criminals. The demonetization wiped out most people's personal wealth in a single day.

The devaluation of currency also led to the first serious student unrest since 1974. Ne Win had taken power in a coup in 1962, quashing the country's pro-democracy movement with what he called "the Buddhist Way to Socialism." Over the years, the people had fallen into a kind of obedient stupor. But the day after the devaluation, more than 1,000 students rallied in Rangoon, ultimately forcing the government to close the schools. Opposition continued to grow over the next year, culminating in the pro-democratic "8888 Uprising" of August 1988.

Heather Michon

Date September 5, 1987

Country Burma

Why It's Key The devaluation led to the first anti-government riots in over a decade and reinvigorated the country's pro-democracy movement.

Key Disaster
Piper Alpha disaster

The first explosion came at approximately 10 p.m. when a pump blew, allowing gas to escape and ignite. The pump should not have been in use that night at all as its pressure valve had been removed for an overhaul; however, the night crew was unaware of this when the pump was switched on. The resultant fires may well have burned themselves out but they were being fed with fuel from both the Tartan and Claymore Pipelines. At 10:20 p.m., Tartan's gas line burst and a massive fireball engulfed the Piper Alpha platform. Its destruction, and the ensuing loss of life, were now inevitable.

Piper Alpha lay 190 kilometers (120 miles) north east of Aberdeen in the treacherous North Sea and at its peak produced 10 per cent of the UK's North Sea oil. Two hundred and twenty nine men worked on the rig and

167 of them lost their lives that night as explosions and fireballs ripped through it. Most were suffocated by the toxic fumes but some perished in the fires or after jumping from the rig into the freezing sea beneath them.

A major rescue operation swung into force with helicopters and boats being dispatched to the scene. Little could be done. The flames that engulfed the platform reached over 90 meters (300 feet) into the air. The fire was eventually extinguished by famed firefighter Red Adair. In 1990 the official report into the disaster was critical of the safety procedures on the rig owned by Occidental Petroleum and made recommendations to improve offshore safety.
Lorraine Brownbill

Date July 6, 1988

Country UK

Why It's Key It was the world's worst offshore oil disaster and the enquiry that followed it made several recommendations to improve offshore safety.

opposite Firefighters work to extinguish the blaze.

Key Political Event
Mandela's seventieth birthday marked by protests

The banning of anti-apartheid organizations in South Africa in 1960 forced them underground. Internationally, however, a burgeoning anti-apartheid movement focused attention on the plight of black South Africans, in particular political prisoners, such as Nelson Mandela. Following numerous bans, trials, and imprisonments for his political activities, Mandela – the then leader of the military wing of the banned African National Congress (ANC) – was jailed for life in 1964. Mandela's imprisonment testified to the injustice of South Africa's racist regime.

In 1978, Mandela's sixtieth birthday was marked by the launch of the ANC's "Free Mandela" campaign. Ten years on, Mandela's seventieth birthday – June 11, 1988 – which fell during his twenty-fourth year behind bars, was marked by an 11-hour tribute concert at Wembley

Stadium organized by the British Anti-Apartheid Movement (AAM). A star-studded line-up – among them Whitney Houston, Dire Straits, Tracy Chapman, Meat Loaf, Stevie Wonder, Michael Palin, Whoopi Goldberg, and some African acts, such as Hugh Masekela and Miriam Makeba – performed to a capacity audience of 72,000. Around 600 million viewers tuned in to watch in sixty countries worldwide. A march from Glasgow to London and a 200,000 strong rally in Hyde Park, addressed by Archbishops Desmond Tutu and Trevor Huddleston, also marked the occasion.

The event enabled the AAM to pay off its debts, and fund a range of anti-apartheid activities, while also increasing public opinion around the figure of Mandela, now an internationally recognized freedom fighter.
Laura Pechey

Date July 18, 1988

Country South Africa/Worldwide

Why It's Key The celebration of the seventieth birthday of the famous imprisoned anti-apartheid activist prompted renewed international economic and ideological support for the anti-apartheid movement.

Key Cultural Event
N.W.A.'s *Straight Outta Compton* released

By 1988, hip hop was established in America as a varied and popular music genre, if still relatively young. Its occupation of the mainstream was acknowledged that year by MTV's launching of *Yo! MTV Raps*, a regular two-hour show dedicated to hip-hop music. Success did not compromise the genre; rap music instead seemed to become more political and more visceral. In New York, Public Enemy's hectic and revolutionary album, *It Takes a Nation of Millions to Hold Us Back* (1988) was released, while from LA came *Straight Outta Compton* by N.W.A (Niggaz With Attitude), their second offering. Though not delivered with the overt political stance of Public Enemy, the album addressed social realities of impoverished urban life with an aggressive and confrontational urgency. Violent and profane lyrics described the gangland of South-Central Los Angeles against a backdrop of busy, layered drum loops and funk samples.

Tremendously successful, going platinum twice by 1992, it was also highly controversial. It was condemned not only as a glorification of gang violence, but also as a glorification of violence against the police. The album's most notorious track, "Fuck tha Police," prompted a disapproving letter from the FBI to the record company, and the refusal of several police forces to provide security at the group's concerts. *Straight Outta Compton* defined the subgenre of gansta rap, its style and its themes permeating the work of artists even a generation later. It also acted as the bedrock for the divergent, successful solo careers of Ice Cube, Eazy-E, and Dr. Dre.

Roger Johnson

Date August 1, 1988

Country USA

Why It's Key Amid much controversy, *Straight Outta Compton* brought the genre of gansgta rap into the mainstream.

opposite Rap group NWA: DJ Yella, MC Ren, Eazy-E, and Dr. Dre (right).

Key Political Event
The 8888 uprising

For decades, the people of Burma had been living under the repressive and mercurial rule of General Ne Win, who had seized power in a 1962 coup and spent most of his rule isolating the country from the world community.

In the summer of 1988, Ne Win suddenly canceled a portion of the country's currency, pulling from circulation any denomination not divisible by nine, believed to be a lucky number. But it didn't prove so lucky for the thousands of Burmese who suddenly lost their life savings.

The recall of currency sparked unrest among the country's student population, who began staging campus protests. In a demonstration at Rangoon Institute of Technology, police killed a student named Phone Maw, sparking more widespread outrage.

Monks, teachers, and medical personnel were among those who joined the students in calling for greater political freedom, and the pro-democracy movement quickly found a powerful leader in Aung San Suu Kyi, daughter of an early democratic leader.

A major protest was called for August 8, 1988, the date 8-8-88 believed to be a good omen in Burmese culture. But it was not the case: the instability caused by the protests led to the collapse of the Ne Win regime, allowing a military junta under General Saw Maung to take control. The army brutally put down the pro-democracy protesters, killing up to 3,000 in the days following the coup.

Heather Michon

Date August 8, 1988

Country Burma

Why It's Key The 8888 was a popular uprising against political repression, which freed the Burmese people form the oppressive regime of General Ne Win, yet ultimately led to even greater oppression under General Saw Maung.

Key Cultural Event
Ben Johnson fails drug test

For the first time in Olympic history, the three medal winners of the 100-meter final completed the race in less than ten seconds. This feat in human speed was astounding, yet unfortunately for the gold medalist, Ben Johnson, it was proved too good to be true.

Canadian athlete Johnson was making the headlines often in the lead-up to the Seoul Olympics, most notably of all when he broke the 100-meter world record at the 1987 World Championships in Rome. Rumors of substance abuse were filtering through to the sports pages, yet it wasn't until the 1988 summer Olympics that rumor became stark fact.

Ben Johnson lined up against the best athletes in the world on August 29, 1988, and blew the field apart when he came home in world record speed of 9.79 seconds, beating old adversary Carl Lewis to silver.

Walking off the track after a victorious celebration, Johnson was tested immediately for drugs, and a day after making his impact on the Games, he was stripped of his gold medal for testing positive for anabolic steroids. The International Olympic Committee ignored Johnson's excuse of a spiked herbal drink, and he was sent home immediately.

Ben Johnson was banned for two years only to return to competitive running in 1991. However, he was once again found to be guilty of using performance-enhancing drugs in 1993 and was banned for life.
Kerry Duffy

Date August 30, 1988

Country Korea

Why It's Key Johnson's failure of the drug test highlighted the use of performance-related drugs in the highest stages of competition.

opposite **Ben Johnson** sprints to ill-deserved victory.

Key Cultural Event
First Fair Trade label, Max Havelaar, launched

The concept of Fair Trade began in the 1940s with organizations such as "Ten Thousand Villages" in the United States and "Oxfam" in Great Britain. These organizations bought crafts from poor communities in developing countries to sell in wealthier nations. In 1967, the importing organization, *Fair Trade Organisatie*, was established in the Netherlands, and by the 1970s, Non-Governmental Organizations (NGOs), as well as individuals in Asia, Latin America, and Africa, had joined the movement by providing support and assistance to disadvantaged workers and producers.

The first Fair Trade shops opened in 1969. They boosted sales and actively raised awareness for Fair Trading. In the beginning, most Fair Trading consisted of handcrafts, which provided supplementary income to families where women were the heads of household.

The Fair Trade food product appeared in 1973 when *Fair Trade Organisatie* imported coffee from Guatemalan farmers. In the 1980s, a priest collaborating with a Dutch NGO came up with the idea of a Fair Trade label, which would allow Fair Trade products to be identified among ordinary products. This resulted in the establishment of the Max Havelaar label. Within one year, Fair Trade-labeled coffee claimed a three per cent share of the market.

Fair Trade went on to become a global movement. In 2007, over a million producers and workers in over fifty countries were organized under Fair Trade stipulations. The Fair Trade movement had entered into the consciousness of mainstream business, providing awareness of social and environmental responsibility.
Anne Hsu

Date November 15, 1988

Country Netherlands

Why It's Key This was the first appearance of the Fair Trade label, which guarantees that products are from producers that provide decent conditions and stable prices for farmers and workers.

Key Political Event
Benazir Bhutto elected prime minister of Pakistan

Benazir Bhutto's father, Zulfiqar, led the Pakistan People's Party to victory in the 1970s, campaigning on a platform of Islamic socialism. General Muhammad Zia-Ul-Haq overthrew Zulfiqar in 1977, executing the former prime minister on a controversial charge of murder. A period of dictatorship and "Islamization" ensued, as the government tried to conform the economic system to religious law and attempted, with limited success, to reintroduce traditional punishments like stoning and amputation. After Zia's death in a 1988 plane crash, Benazir Bhutto triumphed in Pakistan's first open democratic elections in eleven years. Educated at Harvard and Oxford universities, Bhutto inspired hope in the West that the first woman to lead a Muslim nation would bring progress to Pakistan. Unfortunately, her time in office was marked by

political infighting and sectarian violence, and President Ghulam Ishaq Khan twice removed Bhutto from office in the 1990s on grounds of corruption.

Bhutto came to symbolize two sides of the country; a polished and articulate champion of populism, she could overcome gender barriers in a conservative Islamic society, yet she could not avoid the corruption and instability that have plagued most of Pakistan's civilian governments. Retreating into exile in 1998, Bhutto continued to be the symbolic head of the biggest political party in one of the most populous nations. However, when she returned to Pakistan after being granted amnesty in October 2007, she was assasinated two weeks before the general elections in which she was a leading opposition candidate.
Alex Cummings

Date November 16, 1988

Country Pakistan

Why It's Key Inspiring hope for democracy in Pakistan, Bhutto became the first woman to lead a Muslim state in modern times.

Fact The assasination of Bhutto resulted in a number of riots across Pakistan, and President Musharaf decreed a three-day period of mourning.

opposite Benazir Bhutto among supporters.

Key Political Event
Yasser Arafat rejects violence

Yasser Arafat, the leader of the Palestine Liberation Organization (PLO) began his political career as a guerilla responsible for both planning and executing what his arch-enemy – the Israeli government – considered acts of terrorism. Arafat never shied from calling attention to his own commitment to political violence, as evidenced by the pistol he perpetually wore on his hip, even during his addresses to the United Nations.

For nearly thirty years, Arafat's PLO and Israel clashed on many battlegrounds – including Jordan, Lebanon, and Israel – to resolve, one way or another, the question of Palestine. In the late 1980s, though, an aging and exhausted Arafat decided to renounce the PLO's founding spirit of militancy and pursue avenues to peace. Arafat overcame a great deal of suspicion on

the part of Israel, which implicated him in the deaths of many Israeli citizens, to sit down at the bargaining table with the country's senior politicians. Israel would not engage with Arafat until he recognized its right to exist and publicly renounced violence. Arafat did both, although those who believed in Arafat's unaltered existential commitment to the destruction of Israel met his renunciation of violence with skepticism. Arafat's renunciation of violence was a historic watershed for the PLO but ultimately irrelevant, as the secular and increasingly diplomatic PLO would, within Arafat's own lifetime, lose the battle for the hearts and minds of Palestinians to the influences of militant Islamist groups such as Hamas.
Demir Barlas

Date December 13, 1988

Country USA/Palestine

Why It's Key The PLO leader's mellowing stance and embrace of the bargaining process signaled new potential for a constructive Israeli-Palestinian relationship.

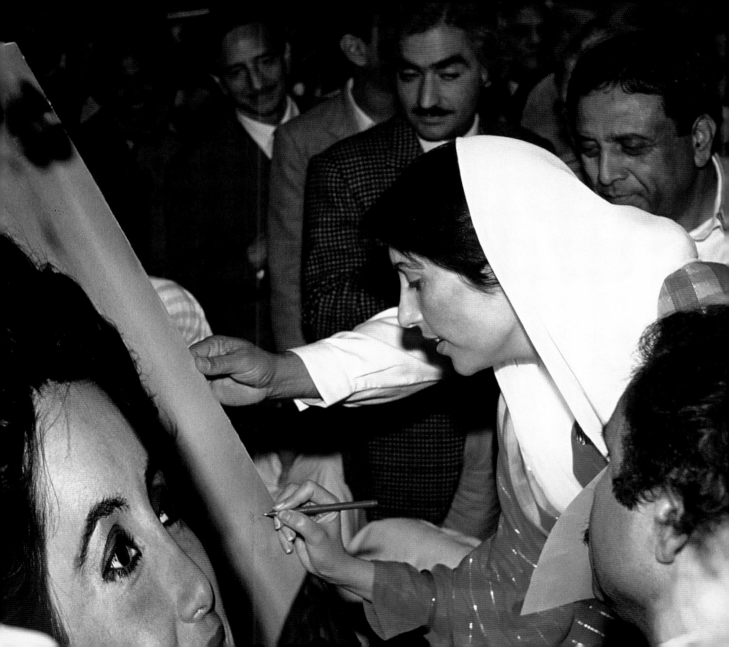

Key Political Event
Terrorist bombing of Pan-Am Flight 103

The New York-bound flight took off from London's Heathrow Airport just after 6 p.m. four days before Christmas. Thirty-eight minutes later and at 31,000 feet, it was blown from the skies above the small Scottish borders town of Lockerbie. All 259 people on board the Boeing 747 were killed, along with 11 people on the ground. Debris and human remains were scattered across 2,000 square kilometers of countryside. Some passengers were found still strapped into their seats.

The victims on the airplane were mainly Americans, including thirty-five students from Syracuse University who had been studying in London, and ten people from Long Island. The 11 Lockerbie residents were killed when parts of the wing section hit Sherwood Crescent at more than 800 kilometers per hour forming a crater 50 meters long.

After intensive searches both on the ground and from the air, 10,000 pieces of debris were found and it became clear that the airplane had been a terrorist target when evidence of a bomb was discovered. In later investigations, forensic experts concluded that about 1 pound of plastic explosive had detonated the airplane's forward cargo hold.

Almost three years after the bombing, American and British investigators indicted two Libyans on 270 counts of murder. Libya handed the suspects over in 1999 after seven years of negotiations and UN-approved economic sanctions. The trial began in May 2000, and in January 2001, Abdelbaset ali Mohmed al-Megrahi was found guilty and given a life sentence, while his coaccused was acquitted.

Lorraine Brownbill

Date December 21, 1988

Country UK/USA

Why It's Key The bombing was a major terrorist atrocity against Britain and the United States, and resulted in economic sanctions being levied against Libya, who eventually admitted involvement in the crime.

1980–1989

opposite A policeman stands by the destroyed nose of the plane.

Key Political Event
300,000 Turkish Bulgarians forced out of Bulgaria

Bulgaria's horrendous assimilation campaign against the country's ethnic Turkish population culminated in May 1989. "Bulgarization" was a desperate attempt to prop up nationalism and the crumbling Communist regime headed by President Todor Zhivkov, yet it amounted to a catalog of human rights abuses and mass emigration that hastened the onset of political change. Nine hundred thousand Turks, approximately 10 per cent of the population, were affected over a six-year period, during which Turkish families were forced to change their names, and Turkish and Islamic education was banned in schools.

The Pomak and Roma communities were the first to be targeted by the government in 1984, who encouraged them to adopt Slavic names with varying degrees of success. In spite of international pressure,

from 1985 onwards, organized militia enforced assimilation, raping, assaulting, imprisoning, and executing those who resisted.

Bulgarian travel restrictions were relaxed on May 10, 1989, and on May 29, Zhivkov asked for Turkey to accept all the Bulgarian Muslims who wished to emigrate. Three hundred thousand people promptly left.

With support from his Soviet allies in terminal decline, Zhivkov's 35-year reign finally ended on November 10, the day after the collapse of the Berlin Wall. He was later sentenced to seven years house arrest for embezzling state funds, but was acquitted by the Bulgarian Supreme Court of inciting racial hatred against the Turks. He died in 1998, but is still revered today by elements of Bulgaria's Slavic majority.

Jay Mullins

Date 1989

Country Bulgaria

Why It's Key Bulgaria's disastrous assimilation policy led to massive human rights violations and a mass exodus of ethnic Turks.

Key Political Event
President Stroessner overthrown

General Alfredo Stroessner ruled Paraguay from 1954, allowing corruption and narcotics to flourish in the small Latin American nation. Though Paraguay maintained economic growth under Stroessner, most of his subjects lived in poverty, with little education. Nonetheless, in a nation that was no stranger to hardship (before Stroessner's ascent, it had endured fifty years of coups, civil wars, and volatile governments), the dictator showed every sign of ruling for life.

In 1989, however, the seventy-six-year-old president was ousted in a surprise rebellion led by his second-in-command, General Andres Rodriquez, and backed by the United States. Despite their close personal and political ties, Rodriguez (who led the largest of Paraguay's three army corps) had sided with a faction that favored democratic reform. Scores of

people, including civilians, were killed in the coup. Stroessner was arrested, but went into exile.

In May, Rodriguez and his party, Partido Colorado (PC), easily won an election that was considered Paraguay's most honest in more than sixty years. Though many were skeptical that the nation could move smoothly into democracy – especially under Stroessner's former deputy – Rodriguez won respect for withdrawing martial law, abolishing the death penalty, and trying and imprisoning senior Stroessner officials. In 1990, he met with President George H. W. Bush in Washington D.C. Stroessner's former assistant, once banned from the United States for profiting from the heroin trade, was now welcomed with open arms.
Mark Juddery

Date February 3, 1989

Country Paraguay

Why It's Key A repressive regime is toppled after a thirty-four-year rule.

Key Cultural Event
Ayatollah Khomeini's fatwa against Salman Rushdie

Although he gained notoriety for the publication of his Booker prize-winning novel, *Midnight's Children*, in 1981, Salman Rushdie is perhaps best known for the furor surrounding the release of his later work, *The Satanic Verses*. Partly inspired by the life of Muhammad, the novel portrays the prophet adding verses to the Qur'an that allow prayers of intercession to be made to three pagan Meccan goddesses.

The publication of the "blasphemous" novel sent shockwaves through the Islamic world, and provoked violent riots. On February 14, 1989, Ayatollah Ruhollah Khomeini, the spiritual leader of Iran, issued a fatwa on Radio Tehran demanding Rushdie's execution. Since then, Rushdie has had to live under police protection.

The novel and the fatwa had far-reaching implications beyond freedom of speech; the

controversy led to broken relations between the UK and Iran in the month following the fatwa. Bookstores were firebombed, and several Muslim communities around the globe held rallies and burned copies of the novel. Those involved in translation or publication were attacked, some killed, and riots in some countries led to deaths. A failed attempt at Rushdie's life was reported in August 1989 in a London hotel.

Despite the controversy, Rushdie remains internationally recognized as a forerunner of postcolonial literature. In addition to the Booker prize and the Booker of Bookers prize, he received the European Union's Aristeion Prize for Literature in 1996, and in 2007, the Queen of England awarded him a knighthood for services to literature.
Mariko Kato

Date February 14, 1989

Country Iran

Why It's Key The fatwa, and subsequent riots against Salman Rushdie, challenged free speech and intimated the power of the written word.

Fact Though it is no longer enforced, the fatwa against Rushdie cannot be lifted as only the person who issued a fatwa may rescind it.

opposite Demonstration and death threats against Salman Rushdie in Beirut.

Key Cultural Event
Madonna releases "Like a Prayer" to outrage

As a song, Madonna's "Like a Prayer" was not especially controversial. In fact, it united critics and fans in praise; many rock journalists still regard it as the very peak of her career, with its astute blend of gospel harmonies and dancefloor drama. It zoomed to No. 1 in the UK, the United States, and Japan.

The video, however, was a different matter. With a plot revolving around a black man wrongly accused of assaulting a young white woman, it was bound to hit the headlines. And with images of Madonna dancing in fields of burning crosses, kissing an effigy of a black saint, and developing stigmata, it became the most notorious pop video in history.

Pepsi had at the time contracted Madonna to appear in a high-profile commercial, which used some of the song. The advertisement aired before the official video for "Like a Prayer" was released, and when the MTV video caused a stir, Pepsi panicked and canceled both Madonna's contract and their sponsorship of her upcoming tour. The adverse publicity did little to dent the public's appetite for pop's most flamboyant female performer; the subsequent album, also called *Like a Prayer* (1989), was another international No. 1.

In 2006, MTV viewers voted "Like a Prayer" "the most groundbreaking music video of all time." Madonna proved that pop videos need not be lightweight or lowbrow, and that women in pop could unite music and image on their own terms.
Andrew Blades

Date February 28, 1989

Country USA

Why It's Key It showed that rock videos could challenge the political, religious, and social establishment.

Key Disaster
Exxon Valdez oil spill

The oil tanker *Exxon Valdez* ran aground on Bligh Reef in Prince William Sound, Alaska, in the early hours of the morning of March 24, 1989. Eight of its eleven cargo tanks were ruptured, releasing more than eleven million gallons of oil. The resulting oil slick was later reported to be eight miles wide.

The *Exxon Valdez* was found to be a mile off course, even though its navigational systems were working correctly. Captain Joe Hazelwood reported that he had encountered icebergs in the shipping lanes, and instructed his helmsman to take evasive action. However, the helmsman failed to correct his course afterwards, and the *Exxon Valdez* struck Bligh Reef.

The oil spill was the largest in U.S. history, and no one was fully prepared to deal with a spill of such magnitude. Efforts at cleaning up did ensue, but much of the wildlife in the region was endangered as a result of the environmental catastrophe. The remote location placed a strain on the ability of government and industry bodies to respond adequately, and severe weather halted initial cleanup efforts.

Predictions that oil pollution would disappear over time have proven to be inaccurate, and the damaged ecosystem is still struggling to recover. The sands around Prince William Sound even to this day contain oil, to a depth of between 10 and 15 centimeters, and only a few of the affected wildlife species have since fully recovered.
David Dunning

Date March 24, 1989

Country USA

Why It's Key The *Exxon Valdez* incident led to the Oil Pollution Act of 1990.

Fact In 2004, Exxon was ordered to pay US$4.5 billion in damages for the *Exxon Valdez* incident.

opposite Exhausted volunteers help in the Alaskan clean-up effort in the aftermath of the spill.

Key Political Event
Voters in USSR elect the Congress of Deputies

Less than a year after proposing a blanket of political reforms, Mikhail Gorbachev reestablished the Congress of People's Deputies (CPD), ushering in a brief period of political transparency enacted through a more democratic electoral process.

Previously known as the Congress of Soviets, the body had once wielded supreme power in the USSR until it was annulled under Stalin in 1936. The rebranded Congress consisted of 2,250 deputies, drawn from across the political spectrum and elected on a competitive, multi-candidate basis.

Enlivened by a refreshing political plurality, the first act of the Congress was to elect deputies to the Supreme Soviet, the Union's permanent legislature for dealing with everyday duties of government. Prior to this, all candidates had been subject to approval of the Communist Party (CPSU). In the middle of the electoral process, Gorbachev was elected the first and only executive president of the USSR on March 15, 1990.

Congress sessions were broadcast to the people in keeping with the spirit of *Glasnost*, ensuring that critics of Gorbachev and the CPSU began to gain higher profiles. Boris Yeltsin used the sessions to undermine Gorbachev's liberalizing agenda, while in contrast, pro-reformers became frustrated that the pace of change was too slow.

Ultimately the CPD highlighted the widening divisions between the liberal and conservative factions in government, as well as growing calls for nationalist independence from across the Soviet bloc. The body's short existence came to an end with the USSR in 1991.
Jay Mullins

Date March 26, 1989

Country USSR

Why It's Key The reintroduction of the Congress of Soviets under a new title illustrated Gorbachev's desire to stimulate political debate about the future of the USSR.

1980–1989

601

Key Cultural Event
Milken indicted on 98 counts of racketeering

During the 1980s, as head of Drexel Burnham Lambert (DBL), financier Michael Milken pioneered the practice of buying "junk bonds" that offered high-yield loans to high-risk companies. By the late 1980s, DBL was valued at US$2 billion on paper, and Milken was earning US$550 million a year. In May 1986, Rudy Giuliani, a reform-minded United States attorney from New York, launched an investigation into the financial dealings of DLB. Two years later, the company was charged with insider trading, stock manipulation, and fraud. In March 1989, Milken was charged with 98 counts of racketeering and securities fraud. DBL declared bankruptcy, and the junk bond industry began to collapse. Milken was sentenced to ten years in prison and banned from the securities industry for life. He paid US$1.1 billion to settle lawsuits filed by government agencies, corporations, service providers, and investors. Milken was released from prison in 1993 when a judge determined that he had been treated unfairly in comparison with others convicted during the securities industry clean-up. After his release, Milken became a philanthropist and established Knowledge Universe, a billion-dollar industry that owns Leapfrog, the manufacturer of educational toys for children.

The investigation into the scandals of the American securities industry had worldwide implications, leading to major financial losses among foreign corporations that had invested in American businesses and among American businesses abroad. Governments around the world began to monitor the activities of big business more closely.
Elizabeth R. Purdy

Date March 28, 1989

Country USA

Why It's Key The conviction of Milken and other businessmen who had engaged in illegal economic practices during the Reagan and Bush administrations were symbolic of a lack of political, economic, and societal controls over the greed that was rampant in the industrialized world.

opposite Despite charges against him, Miliken still had some supporters.

Key Cultural Event
Fraunhofer receives German patent for the MP3

In 1989, the Fraunhofer Society, a German research organization, patented a new audio compression algorithm called MPEG-1 Audio Layer 3, or MP3. Digital music files were too large to be easily downloaded or stored, but the MP3 format succeeded in vastly reducing the size of audio files without a significant loss of sound quality, and the technology was soon grasped by the video games industry. The format's growing popularity with the public from the late 1990s meant the music industry was forced to rethink its distribution strategies, which up until then had all been based on CDs. Now music could be bought and downloaded on the Internet as digital data, with no physical product changing hands, and then thousands of hours of music stored and used on tiny portable MP3 players or mobile phones.

But the ease of sharing the format also means music – specifically in the loss of sales royalties to musicians, publishers, and record companies – is now at greater risk from pirating then ever before, and steps continue to be taken by the industry to regulate illegal downloading and distribution. Meanwhile, others argue that the digital revolution will soon make record companies defunct as musicians can now directly reach a paying global audience with MP3 files and the Internet. Patenting the technology, however, was certainly a financial success for the Fraunhofer Society, which received EUR100 million in MP3 licensing revenue in 2005 alone.

Hedley Paul

Date April 1, 1989

Country Germany

Why It's Key By substantially compressing audio files, MP3 has become the standard digital music format in the computer age, with revolutionary effects on the distribution, storage, and playing of music.

602

Key Political Event
Tiananmen Square protests

A lone man stands in the middle of a wide empty street, barring passage to a line of Chinese military tanks. Dubbed "The Unknown Rebel," it is perhaps the most famous image captured during China's 1989 Tiananmen Square protests – and one of the most widely recognizable of the twentieth century. In the West, it would come to symbolize the struggle of the "little man," and the fight for democracy and political liberation against an iron-fisted, corrupt, Communist government.

The protests began as an expression of mourning after the sudden death of Hu Yaobang, former general secretary of the Communist Party (CCP). On the eve of Hu's funeral, April 21, 1989, an estimated 100,000 students marched across Tiananmen Square in defiance of the CCP. In the following weeks, the protest

escalated exponentially and its message grew more political. The protestors now numbered in the millions, urban workers had joined the students, united by their concern of mounting government corruption, and soon organized protests were being reported in over four hundred cities across China.

At 10:30 p.m., on June 3, the Chinese government rolled out its tanks; protestors were assaulted with tear gas and bullets; thousands were brutally beaten and killed, and by 5:40 a.m. the next day, the bloody crackdown was over. To this day the Chinese government continues to deny any wrongdoing, and censorship has all but erased the Tiananmen Square protests from Chinese history.

Annie Wang

Date April 21, 1989

Country China

Why It's Key The brutal suppression of the student protests would severely damage China's image in the West, and would be a significant strike against the country's already dismal human rights record.

opposite The lone, "Unknown Rebel" facing the tanks of the Chinese military.

Key Political Event
Aung San Suu Kyi placed under house arrest

Aung San Suu Kyi had lived outside Burma for many years, coming home for occasional visits, but living a quiet life as a wife and mother in England. In the summer of 1988, she received word that her elderly mother had suffered a stroke. Suu Kyi hurried to her mother's bedside, but within weeks had been drawn into the political upheaval sweeping the country.

After decades of repressive rule, the Burmese pro-democracy movement was poised for action. Suu Kyi was the daughter of General Aung San, a democratic leader who had been assassinated in 1947, and the family had long been aligned with the democratic movement. The protestors looked to her for leadership. "I could not, as my father's daughter, remain indifferent to all that was going on," she said in August 1988, days after a military junta put down the popular uprising.

She was taken into custody on July 20, 1989. In 1990, she was named prime minister-elect when her NLD party won more than 60 per cent of the vote in parliamentary elections, but has never been allowed to take power. Suu Kyi was awarded the Nobel Peace Prize in 1991, as "an outstanding example of the power of the powerless." She used the US$1.3 million prize to help Burma's poor.

Suu Kyi was held under house arrest continuously from 1989–1995 and imprisoned from 2002–2003 after violating travel restrictions. In 2003, she was returned to house arrest, where she remains today, under guard and isolated from the outside world.

Heather Michon

Date July 20, 1989

Country Burma (Myanmar)

Why It's Key The Nobel Peace Prize winner and leader of Burma's pro-democracy has been held prisoner for nearly two decades.

1980-1989

604

Key Political Event
The Baltic Way

On August 23, 1939, the Soviet Union and Germany signed the Molotov-Ribbentrop Pact. It contained secret protocols that proposed the division of many European countries, including the three Baltic States (Estonia, Latvia, and Lithuania) into "spheres of interest." It was a charter, in other words, for occupation. Fifty years later, to the day, an extraordinary cooperative demonstration took place to mark the occasion and highlight its tyranny.

The "Baltic Way" was one of the (if not the single) longest human chains to have ever been enacted. From Vilnius in the south, through Riga, to Tallinn on the coast of the Gulf of Finland, men, women, and children clasped hands, connecting three capitals over 600 kilometers. This was a monumental and highly visible protest as much about the present as the past.

The illegal annexation of the three countries could be repressed by the USSR no longer. For the Baltic States, this was the watershed symbolic moment to rank with the fall of the Berlin Wall; it signaled a unified and unstoppable desire for independence and autonomy. At 7 p.m. over a million people (it was probably nearer to two) had linked hands. Footage was broadcast around the world – Moscow could not deny it. In December 1989, the Soviet government officially admitted the existence of the secret protocols, and in 1989, Lithuania became the first country to declare independence from the Soviet Union. The Baltic Way had been a unique contribution to the dismantling of the Iron Curtain.

Michael Hallam

Date August 23, 1989

Country
Estonia/Latvia/Lithuania

Why It's Key The Baltic Way heralded the independence of the Baltic States from Soviet hegemony, and constituted a new form of mass, peaceful protest.

Key Political Event
F. W. de Klerk becomes president of South Africa

In 1985, in the face of widespread violence and African National Congress (ANC) calls for South Africa to be made "ungovernable," P. W. Botha declared the first states of emergency – apartheid was becoming increasingly untenable. Four years later, Botha had a stroke, and de Klerk became president. De Klerk, who has always denied that he was simply bowing to historical inevitability, aimed to share power, but without conceding majority rule. In February 1990, he unbanned the ANC and other parties, and released Nelson Mandela.

In December, when negotiations for a new constitution began, Mandela charged de Klerk with heading "an illegitimate, discredited minority regime." It was the start of a bitter feud, largely the result of severe, ongoing political violence that was fomented by a "third force," strongly suspected of being government-backed (during de Klerk's presidency, an estimated 20,000 died in political violence). Mandela did concede privately that he needed de Klerk, and together they won the Nobel Prize for Peace in 1993.

In March 1992, de Klerk won a whites-only referendum to back reform with the slogan, "Vote yes if you're scared of majority rule," but, the following year, out-maneuvered by the ANC, he conceded majority rule. In South Africa's first democratic elections in 1994, de Klerk's National Party won 20 per cent of the vote and he was made a deputy president. He resigned two years later, and, in 2004, having won only 1.7 per cent of the vote, the New National Party merged with its once arch-enemy, the ANC.

Duncan Proudfoot

Date September 20, 1989

Country South Africa

Why It's Key P. W. Botha's replacement by de Klerk made the ultimate and inevitable demise of apartheid considerably more rapid and less bloody than it might otherwise have been.

1980–1989

605

Key Political Event
Hungarian Republic declared

On October 23, 1989, Hungary declared itself a democratic republic, freeing itself from the influence of the Soviet Union and drawing a line under decades of frustrated nationalism.

The end of the Hungarian People's Republic coincided symbolically with the anniversary of the 1956 uprising, in which an estimated 20,000 people were killed by Soviet troops. In the aftermath, the Prime Minister Imre Nagy was executed and replaced by the Soviet loyalist János Kádár, whose first objective was to purge the country of its revolutionary spirit.

Despite these events, Hungary's path toward freedom was relatively untroubled compared with its Eastern Bloc neighbors. Kádár's desire to appease the hostility toward him led to progressive reforms that became known as "Goulash Communism." By the 1980s, political stability and growing competitiveness in the world markets provided a secure platform on which to build a liberal democracy.

In April 1989, the weakening USSR signed an agreement to withdraw its forces from Hungary, and two months later Imre Nagy was reburied with honors, reenforcing national pride. Later that year provisional president Mátyás Szurös declared the Hungarian Republic, ushering in a new constitution that ensured both multi-party and presidential elections.

The first free elections in May 1990 led to the public's rejection of the reformed Communist Party and the formation of a center-right coalition. In May 2004, Hungary was accepted into the European Union after an overwhelming "yes" vote in a referendum.

Jay Mullins

Date October 23, 1989

Country Hungary

Why It's Key Hungary's transformation into a Western-style democracy buried the ghosts of the 1956 uprising.

Key Political Event
Fall of the Berlin Wall

It would be the most brilliant mistake of his political career. During a live broadcast international press conference, Günter Schabowski announced to the world that the Soviets would be opening up its checkpoints between East and West Germany. Further questioning from a journalist prompted Schabowski to declare, "If I am informed correctly, regulation becomes effective *immediately*."

What followed can only be described as sheer chaos of the greatest scale. Tens of thousands of people from both sides immediately began arriving at the border crossings, the guards confused and faced with the chanting mobs stood aside, and East Germany was reunited with the West in a frenzied celebration that would last for four days. Caught up in the euphoria of the moment hundreds of Germans began climbing onto the walls, singing, cheering, and some even hammering and chipping off large chunks of it. The event would be televised and watched by millions around the world. The fall of the Berlin Wall would come to symbolize the collapse of Communism and the end of the Cold War.

Few sections of the original wall remain standing today, and what does remain is rapidly deteriorating and threatened by development. In 2000, conservationists restored several pieces of the wall along the famous East Side Gallery. However, many of the original works are but a shadow of what they used to be, if not covered by graffiti, and slowly fading away.

Annie Wang

Date November 9, 1989

Country Germany

Why It's Key The fall of the Berlin wall was the first step towards the reunification of Germany and was widely regarded as a symbol for the end of Cold War.

Fact Actor and singer David Hasselhoff believes that by singing "Looking for Freedom" on New Year's Eve in 1989 in Germany, he played a pivotal role in the fall of the Berlin Wall.

opposite **Elated Germans reunite.**

Key Political Event
The end of the Cold War

On the March 11, 1985, Mikhail Gorbachev became the last president of the USSR, and his six years in office would precipitate the dissolution of the Soviet Union and the end of the Cold War.

Since the end of World War II, the United States and the Soviet Union had been firmly locked in a tense rhetorical and military game of chess; fueled by paranoid antagonism, geography, territory, and conflicting ideology. Tension had subsided in the late 1970s before the Reagan administration reignited the arms race in 1980 by promising to seek out and nullify Communism, going on to spend over two trillion dollars on the military.

However, although the USSR's army was extensive in numbers, the economy in Russia was deteriorating after the Afghanistan War and the flouting of domestic policies. Gorbachev immediately pushed radical reforms, one of which was *Glasnost*, which allowed media transparency throughout government. The move backfired with revelations of long term problems of housing, food shortages, pollution, and unemployment, leading to a public distrust of the Communist Party.

Concentrating on an internal crisis, Gorbachev was forced to make concessions with the United States, and with the Soviet Union falling apart and no longer able to sustain itself economically, and the fall of the Berlin Wall, George H. W. Bush declared the Cold War over after meeting with Gorbachev in Malta on December 3, 1989. The world's largest Communist entity split into fifteen states on December 31, 1991, with any notion of a Soviet Union extinguished.

Greg Pittard

Date December 3, 1989

Country USSR/USA

Why It's Key The last chapter of the Cold War was effectively over, with the tension over nuclear arms "officially" ending and the Soviet Union dissolving.

Key Political Event
Democratic elections in Chile topple Pinochet

Already reeling from the 1988 plebiscite, which denied him another term as president, Augusto Pinochet weathered a decisive blow when the Chilean public elected opposition leader Patricio Aylwin to the presidency with over 55 per cent of the vote in the first democratic elections in 17 years. To worsen the humiliation, the dictator's anointed successor, former finance minister Hernán Büchi, received a mere 29.4 per cent of votes cast. The opposition also obtained pluralities in both chambers of congress. Against Pinochet's expectations, Chilean voters made clear their desire for a clean break from his divisive authoritarian regime. Although internal and international pressure had forced him into holding elections, Pinochet had underestimated the ability of the opposition parties to capitalize on widespread discontent.

The victorious coalition included a broad swathe of 17 centrist and leftist parties, and featured many candidates who had spent years in exile. Despite their differences, the opposition parties were united by the need to restore democracy. Aylwin was determined to consolidate the country's economic advances while mitigating burgeoning inequalities by investing substantially in social services. Although Chile's transition to democracy was seen as a success, Pinochet still managed to retain influence by altering the constitution and naming himself and several of his closest allies senators for life. As a result of these and other measures taken to protect the military, later efforts to hold the regime accountable for its human rights violations faced major legal hurdles.

Geoffrey Schullenberger

Date December 14, 1989

Country Chile

Why It's Key Free presidential and congressional elections ended Augusto Pinochet's seventeen-year-long military dictatorship.

Key Political Event
U.S. invasion of Panama

After the end of the Cold War, the United States had a seemingly dominant position in Latin America. However, one problem that remained was Panama. The United States wanted the head of the army, General Manuel Noriega, in connection with various criminal activities. Although not the president, Noriega had vast influence, and was effectively the country's dictator

Noriega had previously been a U.S. ally; he had received training from the American military and worked with the CIA But the relationship turned sour, and Noriega had become increasingly involved with Colombian drug cartels. The Panama Canal made the country strategically important to the United States, and the Americans were anxious to displace Noriega.

In 1989, Noriega nullified a general election in the country and attempted to set up his own puppet government. In an astonishing move, he also declared war on the United States. President Bush retaliated by ordering the invasion of Panama, with the stated aim of defending American citizens in the country and restoring Panamanian liberty.

U.S. troops invaded the country on December 20, 1989, and after a series of skirmishes quickly subdued Panamanian forces. Noriega took refuge in the Vatican Embassy where, in an unusual military tactic, the Americans pounded the building with loud rock music for ten days until he finally surrendered.

He was arrested and taken back to the United States, where he was convicted of cocaine trafficking, racketeering, and money laundering, and sentenced to forty years in prison.

Martin Sayers

Date December 20, 1989

Country Panama

Why It's Key The invasion showed that despite the end of the Cold War, the United States was still prepared to intervene in Latin American affairs.

Key Political Event
Execution of Nicolae Ceausescu

The execution of Nicolae Ceausescu brought 25 years of iron-fisted Communist rule to a bloody and ignominious end.

A hardline dictator who remained independent of the Soviet Union during his presidency, Nicolae Ceausescu's reelection in November 1989 angered a population that had long since grown tired of the Communist yoke. In Timisoara, protests against the government's treatment of the Hungarian ethnic population grew into a general anti-government demonstration. On December 17, troops opened fire on the protestors and four days later a mass meeting in Bucharest ended with Ceausescu retreating before a baying crowd. An attempted revolt was put down and hundreds were arrested, but critical damage had already been done to the regime.

As the rebellion spread, the suspicious death of defense minister Vasile Milea led to Ceausescu taking emergency command of the army. On December 22, Ceausescu made another attempt to address the crowds, but they stormed the Central Committee Building, forcing him to escape in a helicopter.

Ceausescu and his wife were eventually caught by police and handed over to the country's new military rulers. The pair were sentenced to death on December 25, and executed by a firing squad in Târgoviste the same day. Before he was shot, Ceausescu proclaimed that history would judge him well, but in reality his downfall sent out a very different message. The days of Communism in Eastern Europe were numbered.
Jay Mullins

Date December 25, 1989

Country Romania

Why It's Key Ceausescu's execution symbolized the weakening of Communism throughout Eastern Europe.

Fact With 1,100 rooms and twelve stories tall, Bucharest's Palace of the Parliament is the world's second largest administrative building after the Pentagon. Built by Ceausescu, some parts have yet to be completed.

1980–1989

Key Political Event
Václav Havel becomes president of Czechoslovakia

Václav Havel was a popular young playwright in Czechoslovakia during the 1960s, satirizing both his Communist leaders and the complacency of his fellow citizens. His plays were banned, however, after he participated in the short-lived Prague Spring of 1968. Refusing to be silenced, he was imprisoned on many occasions over the next two decades, and even when freed, he endured constant surveillance.

Following youth demonstrations and other dissident activity in Prague in early 1989, Havel was again arrested for breach of the peace, inspiring protests both in Czechoslovakia and abroad (he was released within three months). In November, Czechoslovakia's people staged the "Velvet Revolution," a series of peaceful protests and strikes (named after the radical New York rock band the Velvet

Underground, whose music had been an inspiration to Havel and other dissidents).

On November 24, as 500,000 protesters gathered in Prague for the eighth consecutive day, Communist Party head Milos Jakas – finally sensing the demise of Communism – resigned, along with other senior officials. A month later, Alexander Dubcek, the reformer who led the government during the Prague Spring, was elected chairman of a new parliament. Havel, as the most prominent opposition leader, became interim president. Though he initially said that his tenure would be brief, he was elected president at the first post-Communist elections six months later. When Czechoslovakia was divided into separate nations in 1993, he became the Czech Republic's first president.
Mark Juddery

Date December 29, 1989

Country Czechoslovakia

Why It's Key A long-time dissident becomes Czechoslovakia's first non-Communist president.

Key Political Event
Bolivian rainforest to indigenous peoples

Between August and September of 1990, over six hundred indigenous inhabitants of Bolivia's rainforest marched four hundred miles from the city of Trinidad in the country's Beni Department to the capital, La Paz. Their journey, known as the "March for Dignity and Territory," was the dramatic culmination of an indigenous rights movement, which had been gathering force in Bolivia's lowlands for over a decade.

The march was undertaken in protest of the government's disregard for the rights of the country's indigenous peoples at the expense of logging companies and conservationist groups. One of the most controversial areas was the Chimanes Forest, which had been the focus of the world's first "debt for nature" agreement in the late 1980s. Through this agreement, the Chimanes Forest was given over to nature preserves and "sustainable forestry" (logging companies), and the rights of its indigenous inhabitants were largely ignored.

The march generated sympathy for the lowlanders among the rest of Bolivia's indigenous majority. The resulting pressure of public opinion prompted President Jaime Paz Zamora to issue several "Supreme Decrees," which turned over four huge tracts of rainforest, two of them in the Chimanes area, to indigenous Bolivians as communal property.

Though the decrees established an important precedent, multiple factors have vitiated the ability of indigenous coalitions to exercise any real control over their territories, and they continue to be exploited by logging companies and other extractive industries.
Rachel Eley

Date 1990

Country Bolivia

Why It's Key Indigenous Bolivians pressured the government to put vast areas of tropical rainforest under their control.

Fact Bolivia is the largest producer of Brazil nuts.

610

Key Political Event
Niyazov elected chairman of Turkmenistan

The authoritarian and increasingly bizarre regime of Saparmurat Niyazov, self-styled "Turkmenbashi" (Father of the Turkmen), baffled the outside world while dictating the lives of millions in Turkmenistan.

In 1990, when Niyazov was elected to the highest position in the Turkmenistan Communist Party, the Soviet Union was nearing collapse; within a year he found himself the first president of a newly independent nation. As unopposed head of state and head of government, Niyazov's influence reached far into the lives of his people. Opposition parties and independent media were banned, as were beards, ballet, and newsreaders who wore make-up. Niyazov renamed the days of the week and the months of the year, replaced the alphabet, and changed the word for bread to the name of his late mother "Gurbansoltanedzhe." With full control of the country's considerable natural gas wealth, Niyazov ordered the construction of an ice palace in the desert capital while canceling state pensions and dismissing public health workers.

When Niyazov died unexpectedly of a heart attack in 2006 many were uncertain how the isolated and impoverished population would respond. Foreign powers, notably China and Russia, were concerned to preserve and advance their relationships with the country and its increasingly desirable natural gas reserves. Remarkably, the first multi-candidate elections in Turkmenistan's history passed peacefully (if corruptly) and a new president began the task of addressing Niyazov's troubled legacy.
Rachel Eley

Date January 13, 1990

Country Turkmenistan

Why It's Key One of the most authoritarian – and bizarre – regimes in the world begins.

Fact Niyazov's book of spiritual teachings "Ruhnama" was the main component of state education, as well as the Turkmenistan driving test.

opposite A mechanical monument dedicated to the "Ruhnama." Every evening the "book" opens and passages are recited.

Key Political Event
Apartheid laws repealed

Directly translated from the Afrikaans, apartheid means "apartness," and was a system of racial segregation in South Africa that had been fixed as government policy from 1948. Apartheid had aroused widespread censure for decades, both within the country and internationally. However, as sanctions imposed on South Africa became increasingly severe in the 1970s and 1980s, it became clear to the National Party government that the system was no longer tenable. In 1986, the U.S. Congress passed the Anti-Apartheid Act, which banned all investment in, and loans to, South Africa. Soon, many other governments followed suit.

As a result of these significant economic pressures, Prime Minister John Vorster began to relax certain of the "lesser" apartheid laws, such as the ban on inter-racial marriage and the segregation of hotels and public transport. This strategy was continued by his successor, Pieter W. Botha, although Botha balked at the idea of entirely opening up the government to include all races. This hesitation caused huge dissent in the National Party and Botha stepped down after suffering a stroke in 1989. The much younger F. W. de Klerk replaced him, and formally set into motion the final unraveling of apartheid.

On February 2, 1990, de Klerk promised to repeal all the fundamental laws of apartheid, and over a year later, all of the remaining apartheid laws were scrapped on June 17, 1991. A new constitution was drafted, which allowed for South Africa's first democratic elections in 1994 and the country's first-ever representative parliament.

Carly Fabian

Date February 1990

Country South Africa

Why It's Key The scrapping of entrenched racial segregation in South Africa paved the way for the country's first truly democratic process.

1990–1999

613

Key Political Event
The Poll Tax riots

By the spring of 1990, Margaret Thatcher had been prime minister for over ten years and her tenure looked set to continue well into the new decade. However, it was a key pledge in her most recent election manifesto that was to begin a sequence of events that led to her humiliating departure from Downing Street in November of 1990. The Conservatives were committed to replacing the unpopular – and many would argue unfair – General Rates taxation scheme with the new Community Charge (otherwise known as the "poll tax"). The Community Charge was a flat rate fixed payment to be made by all adults to their local authority.

However, as the implementation date for the new tax approached, opposition began to mount. Many of the local councils, who were responsible for setting the level of the tax, had set a rate that was much higher than predicted. As Margaret Thatcher refused to compromise on the tax, the hostility toward her and the government mounted. It culminated on March 31, when riots broke out in central London. What had started as a peaceful demonstration, with over 100,000 people taking part, soon descended into the worst riots the UK had seen for a century. Extensive fighting between protesters and the police took place throughout the West End of London with some of the worst clashes happening in Trafalgar Square. As the unrest raged, shops were pillaged, cars over turned, and buildings – including South Africa House – were set alight.

John Owen

Date March 31, 1990

Country UK

Why It's Key The worst riots in the UK for a century marked the beginning of the end of Margaret Thatcher's tenure as prime minister.

opposite Anti-Poll Tax demonstrators in London.

Key Cultural Event
Hubble Space Telescope launched

Bearing the name of the astronomer Edwin Hubble, this telescope orbits the earth and is serviced by astronauts. Its main task was to accurately measure the rate of the expansion of the universe – something first done by its namesake in the 1920s – but it has done much more than this. It is not the largest telescope in the world, with a mirror just over two meters across, but its images are extremely detailed and acute. From its position in space it is able to pick up ultraviolet light, and its data is not affected by the Earth's atmosphere or from background light, like that from telescopes on the ground. As a consequence, it is a crucial tool for modern astronomers.

Planned for decades before its launch, Hubble suffered many setbacks and difficulties. Funding issues and problems with the space shuttle, including the

Challenger disaster in 1986, all delayed the project. Once in space, it became apparent that the shape of the mirror was slightly flawed and thus the quality of its images was impaired. A space mission resolved the problem in 1993, and since then the telescope has produced such highlights as the Ultra Deep Field, the deepest image of space ever taken, and the discovery of evidence for extra-solar planets. It is now coming to the end of its life, with a number of instrument failures, but its replacement, the James Webb Telescope will not be ready until 2013 at the earliest.

Laura Davies

Date April 20, 1990

Country USA

Why It's Key The Hubble was the first orbital telescope, which has gathered millions of images of previously unexplored galaxies.

opposite Illustration of the Hubble Space Telescope facing the glowing center of the spiral galaxy M100.

Key Disaster
Mad Cow Disease

Mad Cow Disease, or "Bovine Spongiform Encephalopathy" (BSE) to give the disease its scientific name, was first identified in the UK in 1986. The disease causes cattle to exhibit neurological and behavioral symptoms and is, ultimately, fatal.

Mad Cow Disease resides in the brain and spinal tissue of infected animals. Veterinary surgeons discovered that these components were being used in animal feed, and this was how the disease was spreading. The British government therefore imposed a ban on the use of high-risk tissue in cattle feed, and human food, in 1989.

British consumers were, nevertheless, assured that beef was safe to eat. The Minister for Agriculture, John Gummer, famously appeared on television feeding a

beef burger to his young daughter. However, amid plummeting consumer confidence, France imposed a ban on British beef on May 1, 1990, followed quickly by Germany, Italy, and Switzerland. Britain negotiated furiously with the European Union, and the bans were lifted in return for strict health controls on beef exports.

However, the saga began all over again in March 1996, when the British government acknowledged a link between BSE and Creutzfeld-Jacob Disease (CJD). Within one week of this announcement, there was a worldwide ban on British beef products.

In March 2006, the European Union finally allowed Britain to export beef from cattle slaughtered after June 1, 2005, and live cows born after August 1, 1996.

David Dunning

Date May 1, 1990

Country UK

Why It's Key The ban on British beef led to the discovery of a link to Creutzfeld-Jacob Disease, a human form of the disease.

Fact Research into Mad Cow Disease since 1986 has cost in excess of £140 million.

Key Political Event
Burmese democratic elections ignored

B urma's troubled present owes a grievous debt to its colonial past. The country, which stretches down the Thai peninsula, fell victim to the nineteenth-century British conquest of Southeast Asia. It gained independence in 1948 and became a democracy, but resentment and instability endured, allowing a military coup in 1962. Radical socialism was imposed, which drove the economy from a successful exporter of oil and rubies to one of the worst in the region.

The junta's generals, ruling the country with an iron fist, clamped down on freedom of speech and of the press, manifested most horrifically in their violent suppression of pro-democracy protests in 1988. Started by students, they spread to revered Buddhist monks and other groups across the country; 3,000 were killed. Stung by resulting harsh international sanctions, the junta allowed elections in 1990, which were won by Aung San Suu Kyi, leader of the National League for Democracy, but were promptly annulled. The ruling military party won less than 2 per cent of the vote.

These elections were a false glimmer of hope, a thin promise of reform snatched away as soon as it became clear that the junta would not win. Their rule of repression has continued, with Aung San Suu Kyi, now a Nobel Peace Prize laureate for her work promoting democracy, under perpetual house arrest, and protests in 2007 cracked down on with similar ferocity.
Josh Spero

Date May 27, 1990

Country Burma

Why It's Key The junta showed its tenacious determination to hold on to power by overturning the victory of the pro-democracy party.

opposite National League for Democracy supporters with poster of party leader, Aung San Suu Kyi, on election day.

Key Political Event
The Oka Crisis

O n July 11, 1990, the town of Oka, Quebec (population 3,000), about thirty kilometers west of Montreal, became the scene of violent conflict between Quebec provincial police and the Mohawk nation. Media reports that summer burned one image onto the minds of Canadians: Canadian soldiers facing off across a barricade against armed Mohawk warriors with masked faces.

The dispute began when the town proposed expanding a golf course on Kanesatake reserve land, including a cemetery, named in a Mohawk land claim. In March, Mohawk set up a barricade on the disputed land. By July, some two hundred armed Mohawk warriors manned the barricade. Additional barricades were set up at the nearby Kahnawake reserve, blocking the Mercier Bridge into Montreal.

On July 10, Oka's mayor asked provincial police to enforce a court injunction and bring down the barricades. As police stormed barricades the next day, Corporal Marcel Lemay was shot and killed by what later proved to be a Mohawk bullet. Government officials tried to negotiate, but the standoff continued. On August 14, Quebec premier Robert Bourassa called in the armed forces, and on August 30, warriors and soldiers set down their guns and teamed up to take down the Kahnawake barricades. On September 26, 1990 the conflict ended when about fifty remaining Mohawk came out from behind the Kanesatake barricade to be arrested by the army or police.
Marie Powell

Date July 11, 1990

Country Canada

Why It's Key This was the first violent confrontation between the government and the First Nations people, leading to the death of a Quebec provincial police force member.

Key Political Event
Islamist coup attempt in Trinidad and Tobago

Jamaat al Muslimeen is a Muslim group in Trinidad and Tobago, its membership drawn predominantly from the island's population of Afro-Trinidadians. Trinidad has a long-standing divide between its Indo-Caribbean and Afro-Caribbean inhabitants, with the Afro-Caribbeans usually falling into lower social groups. This was important to the popularity of Jamaat al Muslimeen, and their failed coup of July 1990. Also important was the ailing Nation Alliance for Reconstruction (NAR) government's neo-liberal economic policies and the consequent rise in poverty and unemployment.

Yasin Abu Bakr, a former policeman and the leader of Jamaat al Muslimeen, led forty-two insurgents in storming the Red House (Trinidad's parliament building), and taking Prime Minister A. N. R. Robinson captive along with most of his cabinet. Simultaneously, seventy-two other guerrillas occupied the offices of Trinidad and Tobago Television. Bakr appeared on TV that evening to announce that the government had been overthrown. The Trinidad army recaptured the TV station that night, and sealed the area around parliament, while members of the cabinet who were not held set up temporary offices in the Trinidad Hilton.

It took six days of negotiation before Bakr's rebels surrendered. They escaped prosecution for treason under the terms of an amnesty negotiated before they surrendered. Approximately forty died in the coup attempt and millions of dollars' worth of damage was done by looters. The beleaguered government was comprehensively defeated at a general election the following year, winning only two seats.
David Thorley

Date July 27, 1990

Country Trinidad and Tobago

Why It's Key The Jamaat's attempt to take over Trinidad and Tobago in 1990 was regarded by many as the end of the NAR government.

Fact In January 2001, a court ordered the Jamaat to pay the government over US$3 million for damages incurred during the coup. In May, the Jamaat countersued and won US$350,000 for the destruction of its facilities during the same coup.

Key Political Event
Demonstrations force MPRP Politburo resignation

Coinciding with the surge toward national independence in Eastern Europe caused by Gorbachev's liberalizing policies of *glasnost* and *perestroika*, the resignation of the MPRP Politburo signaled the terminal decline of the USSR's influence over one of its most loyal Communist sympathizers.

The Communist Mongolian People's Revolutionary Party was established in 1921, following a period of instability during World War I that saw both Chinese and Red and White Russian regimes established in the country. The death of King Bogd Khan then paved the way for a republic under the control of the Mongolian People's Revolutionary Party (MPRP) to be declared on November 25, 1924. The Politburo followed the conventional Soviet model, espousing collectivization of livestock, the creation of fixed abodes, and the introduction of agriculture in an attempt to marginalize the traditional nomadism of Mongolian life.

During the Cold War, Mongolia acted as a willing buffer for the Soviet Union against China, and the first properly organized political opposition did not emerge until the late 1980s. Demands for faster reforms led to street protests that forced the Politburo resignation and within two months important democratizing changes were made to the constitution. A president and legislative body were introduced, while opposition parties were allowed to stand against the MPRP.

Although the Soviet model had been discarded, the MPRP still claimed 85 per cent of the votes in Mongolia's first free multiparty election on July 29, 1990, remaining in office until 1996.
Jay Mullins

Date July 29, 1990

Country Mongolia

Why It's Key The end of the MPRP Politburo in Mongolia underlined the Soviet Union's weakening grip across Eurasia.

opposite Mongolians gather in huge numbers at a support demonstration for Mongolia's Democratic Union, at Sukhe-Bator square.

Key Political Event
The Iraqi invasion of Kuwait

During the Iran-Iraq war in the 1980s, the United States had backed Iraq, fearing that a victory for the hard-line Iranian regime would threaten oil supplies to the West. This policy included giving nearly US$1billion to Saddam Hussein's regime, enabling him to build a powerful and well-equipped military.

However, the shortsightedness of this policy became apparent on August 2, 1990, when Iraqi forces crossed the border into neighboring Kuwait. The small Kuwaiti defense force was no match for the vastly superior Iraqi army, and Kuwait was quickly occupied. Iraq had a long-standing claim to Kuwait, and Hussein intended to use its vast oil reserves to bolster the Iraqi economy, which were shattered by the Iran-Iraq war.

The invasion caused concern in Washington and around the world, not least because Hussein's armies now directly threatened Saudi Arabia, which controlled more than a fifth of the world's oil supplies. There was widespread international condemnation of the invasion, and Iraq was immediately made the subject of a trade embargo.

A coalition of thirty nations, including Arab countries, was assembled to oppose Iraq's aggression, and vast numbers of troops, mostly American, were sent to the area under the auspices of the United Nations. Hussein was issued with a deadline of January 15 to withdraw his forces from Iraq. By the end of 1990, a multi-national force of 550,000 troops had been built up in the Middle East, and war seemed inevitable.
Martin Sayers

Date August 2, 1990

Country Iraq

Why It's Key Hussein's decision to invade Kuwait threatened to destabilize the whole Middle East and led to decisive action from the UN.

opposite On the Iraqi-Jordanian border, hundreds of displaced refugees wait for food and water from relief workers.

622

Key Political Event
Benazir Bhutto's government dismissed

In 1988, ten years after the execution by hanging of her father, Zulfiqar Ali Bhutto, his young and charismatic daughter Benazir became prime minister of Pakistan, renewing the populist Bhutto legacy and inaugurating a period of civil rule after the decade-long military dictatorship of the Islamist General Zia ul-Haq. At the time of Bhutto's electoral triumph, she was at thirty-five the youngest major head of state in the world and the first female leader of a Muslim country in modern times, and her accession appeared to point the way to a more progressive Pakistan.

Benazir Bhutto's government did not last long, as it was removed from power by Ghulam Ishaq Khan, then the president of Pakistan, in 1990, on charges of corruption. Bhutto alleged that the charges against her were purely political, in the same vein as the charges that had been leveled against her father, but the Pakistani government claimed to have documentary evidence that Benazir and her husband, Asif Ali Zardari, had leveraged their position at the head of government to demand bribes and kickbacks from Pakistanis and foreigners alike. This would have been nothing new in the exceedingly corrupt world of Pakistani politics, but ultimately Bhutto had incurred the wrath of a number of powerful constituencies – including Islamists, landed families, and rivals of her father's party – who wished to see her gone in any case. They got their wish: on December 27, 2007, Benazir Bhutto was assassinated after departing a Pakistan People's Party (PPP) rally in Rawalpindi.
Demir Barlas

Date August 6, 1990

Country Pakistan

Why It's Key The dismissal of Pakistani Prime Minister Benazir Bhutto a decade after the execution of her father further strengthened authoritarian and Islamist forces in Pakistan.

Key Political Event
German reunification

The East German parliament building in the center of Berlin had always been a place of rubber-stamp assemblies. For a few weeks in 1990, that changed, as the newly elected parliament transformed the Communist state. By May, it had agreed to an economic and monetary union with West Germany, and on July 1, East Germany adopted the West German currency, the deutsche mark.

With both German states ready to heal the breach left by the Third Reich's defeat in 1945, the question of reunification was in the hands of the four World War II allies who had occupied Germany and then quarreled over it. Their negotiations in 1990 were intensive and complex, but remarkably efficient. They quickly put aside their fears of the old, militaristic Germany. As soon as Mikhail Gorbachev's Soviet Union agreed to

relinquish its once loyal East German ally, the East German parliament voted to join the Federal Republic of Germany, the state known to outsiders as West Germany and henceforth to be known merely as Germany. The end of German division settled the "German question" that had lingered since 1945, and it was also the first definitive step away from the Cold War partition of Europe.

October 3 was set as the date of unification, and it has been the German national holiday ever since. It turned out to be a rather sober occasion, marking the end of an exhilarating year and the beginning of the painful work of meshing two economies and societies.
Brian Ladd

Date October 3, 1990

Country Germany

Why It's Key The division of Germany, a legacy of World War II and the Cold War, was at an end.

Key Political Event
Lech Walesa elected

Poland, invaded by Nazi Germany in 1939 and rendered a Soviet satellite six years later, recovered some measure of independence in 1990, with the election of Lech Walesa as president of Poland. Walesa, the son of a carpenter, represented the trade union Solidarity and had been a labor activist for at least twenty years before his election, emerging as a seasoned and charismatic organizer at the Gdansk Shipyards. In 1983, Walesa won the Nobel Peace Prize, and in 1989, addressed a joint meeting of Congress, becoming the first non-head of state to do so.

Walesa's rising star resulted in an election victory in 1990, which he construed as a mandate to reorganize the Polish economy on free market lines. His election was a stunning reversal in Polish politics, given that Solidarity had been illegal as late as 1989

and that Communism appeared to be firmly embedded in the country's political culture and institutions. All the same, Poland sloughed off much of its recent Communist past under Walesa, who successfully presided over free elections, economic transformation, and the melting of personal and political taboos.

While Lech Walesa's domestic popularity declined – he lost a re-election campaign in 1995 – his accession to office presaged the end of Soviet influence in Central and Eastern Europe, and indeed the downfall of the Soviet Union itself. Walesa continues to be active in Polish life and politics.
Demir Barlas

Date December 9, 1990

Country Poland

Why It's Key The downfall of Polish Communism presaged the end of the Soviet era of influence.

Key Cultural Event
Wireless technology developed

Contrary to most technological advancements, wireless technology – or Wi-Fi – was effectively initiated by an American government agency. In 1985, the Federal Communications Commission (FCC) decided to allow several bands of wireless spectrum to be used without government licences. These were known as "garbage bands," which were already being used by non-communication equipment such as microwaves. The next step toward Wi-Fi was the establishment of an industry-wide standard. In 1988, the NCR corporation/AT&T (later known as Lucent & Agere Systems) in the Netherlands formed a committee named 802.11 to set up such a standard with Victor Hayes as the chairman. In 1991, Hayes invented Wi-Fi technology, and the first wireless products were brought to market under the name of WaveLAN.

In 1997, basic specifications for international Wi-Fi standards were agreed upon. There were two variants, 802.11b and 802.11a, approved in December 1999 and January 2000 respectively. However, the specifications for these standards filled four hundred pages and were so complicated that many devices still suffered wireless incompatibility. In August 1999, six companies joined together to form the Wireless Ethernet Compatibility Alliance, which would certify compatibility between wireless products. This compatibility standard became known as Wi-Fi. In July 1999, Apple Computer introduced a Wi-Fi slot into its new iBook laptop computers. Other computer companies followed, and Wi-Fi gained consumer popularity, soon being widely used in homes and public places.

Anne Hsu

Date 1991

Country Netherlands

Why It's Key Wireless technology became one of the most widely used technologies at the beginning of the twenty-first century, allowing computer users to access the Internet without having to plug into a telephone modem.

Key Political Event
Operation Desert Storm

Operation Desert Storm was the culmination of the Gulf War, which began with Iraq's invasion and annexation of Kuwait in August 1990. The preliminary phase of the operation, codenamed Operation Desert Shield, began on August 7, 1990, and aimed to deploy UN troops to protect Saudi oil reserves. The UN Security Council gave Iraq the deadline of January 15, 1991 to withdraw from Kuwait peacefully. The Iraqi President Saddam Hussein thought the deadline was an American bluff and decided to ignore it. As a result, on January 16, 1991, the U.S.-led Operation Desert Storm was launched under the command of General Norman Schwarzkopf. Over the following several weeks, the continuous bombing destroyed the Iraqi air defenses, which was followed by attacks on Iraq's roads, communication networks, and other strategic

targets. Iraq responded by launching missile attacks on Saudi Arabia and Israel, hoping to weaken their support for the coalition forces.

On February 24, 1991, the war began to be fought on the ground, and Iraqi soldiers burned seven hundred Kuwait oil wells as they were fleeing from the coalition troops. The allied forces liberated Kuwait on February 26 and two days later Hussein agreed to the UN ceasefire, which officially ended the Gulf War. Tensions between Iraq and the UN continued to increase in the 1990s, as Hussein refused to allow UN inspections of Iraqi weapons. In 2002, Iraq became the target of the U.S. War on Terror and was invaded in 2003.

Sonja Kudeljnjak

Date January 16, 1991

Country Kuwait

Why It's Key The Gulf War increased tensions in the Middle East, which would result in the U.S. occupation of Iraq in 2003.

Fact Operation Desert Storm cost US$53 million.

Key Political Event
Barre ousted from power

Siad Barre was a member of Somalia's Marehan clan, a group representing 1 per cent of the country's 8 million people. Yet he knew how to use tribalism to his advantage: after taking over in an October 1969 coup, he consolidated control by playing majority tribes against one another while favoring his own people with positions of authority. For twenty-two years, it had allowed him to stay in power.

By the mid-1980s, he was facing attacks from rebel groups around the country, including the Somali National Movement, the Somalia Patriotic Movement, and the United Somali Congress in the region around Mogadishu. They had always worked independently, but in the summer of 1990 agreed to come together to oust Barre and his military. Barre was forced to flee his palace, Villa Somalia, on January 26, 1991.

"It's not a government, it's a group of rebels who want to control the city," Barre told Reuters in May. "I am the real legal president of Somalia." The seventy-one-year-old dictator was holed up in a house without water or electricity. He soon agreed to go into exile, first to Nairobi, then in Nigeria, dying in Lagos on January 2, 1995.

Barre's fall did not bring peace. Fighting between the army and rebel groups went on for months. Thousands of Somalis were killed, with hundreds of thousands fleeing the country. The anti-Barre coalition failed, resulting in inter-tribal warfare. Since 1991, at least thirteen governments have fallen, and there is no resolution in sight.
Heather Michon

Date January 26, 1991

Country Somalia

Why It's Key The collapse of Barre's dictatorship led to civil war within the African state.

626

Key Political Event
Largest ever oil slick dumped in the Gulf

The world's largest oil spill occurred on February 26, 1991, when Iraqi troops, fleeing from advancing coalition forces, emptied the contents of several tankers and pumped oil directly into the Persian Gulf from Kuwait's Sea Island terminal. Baghdad later blamed the spillage on U.S. air strikes resulting in the destruction of two Kuwaiti oil tankers. Estimates on the total amount of crude oil spilled range greatly from 42 to 462 million gallons, but it is generally accepted that the spill was at least twice the size of that resulting from the blowout at the Ixtoc I oil refinery, Gulf of Mexico, in 1979.

Coalition pilots attempted to stem the flow of oil by bombing computerized failsafe systems, automatically closing off the pipelines. But this only solved the problem temporarily as the Iraqis resumed pumping by manually opening valves further up the supply line. At its largest, the slick reached a size of 4,000 square miles and a thickness of 4 inches.

The most significant impact of the spillage was on the environment surrounding the Gulf, although establishing the true extent of the damage took many years. Thousands of cormorants died as a result of exposure to the oil, and many species were put at risk, including the endangered hawksbill and the Karan Island green turtles. However, although there was much concern at the time for the region's coral reefs, a study in the late nineties revealed that the damage to the ecosystem was minimal.
Jay Mullins

Date February 26, 1991

Country Kuwait

Why It's Key Saddam Hussein's parting shot crippled Kuwait's oil reserves and damaged the local environment.

opposite Satellite image of the Persian Gulf oil spill.

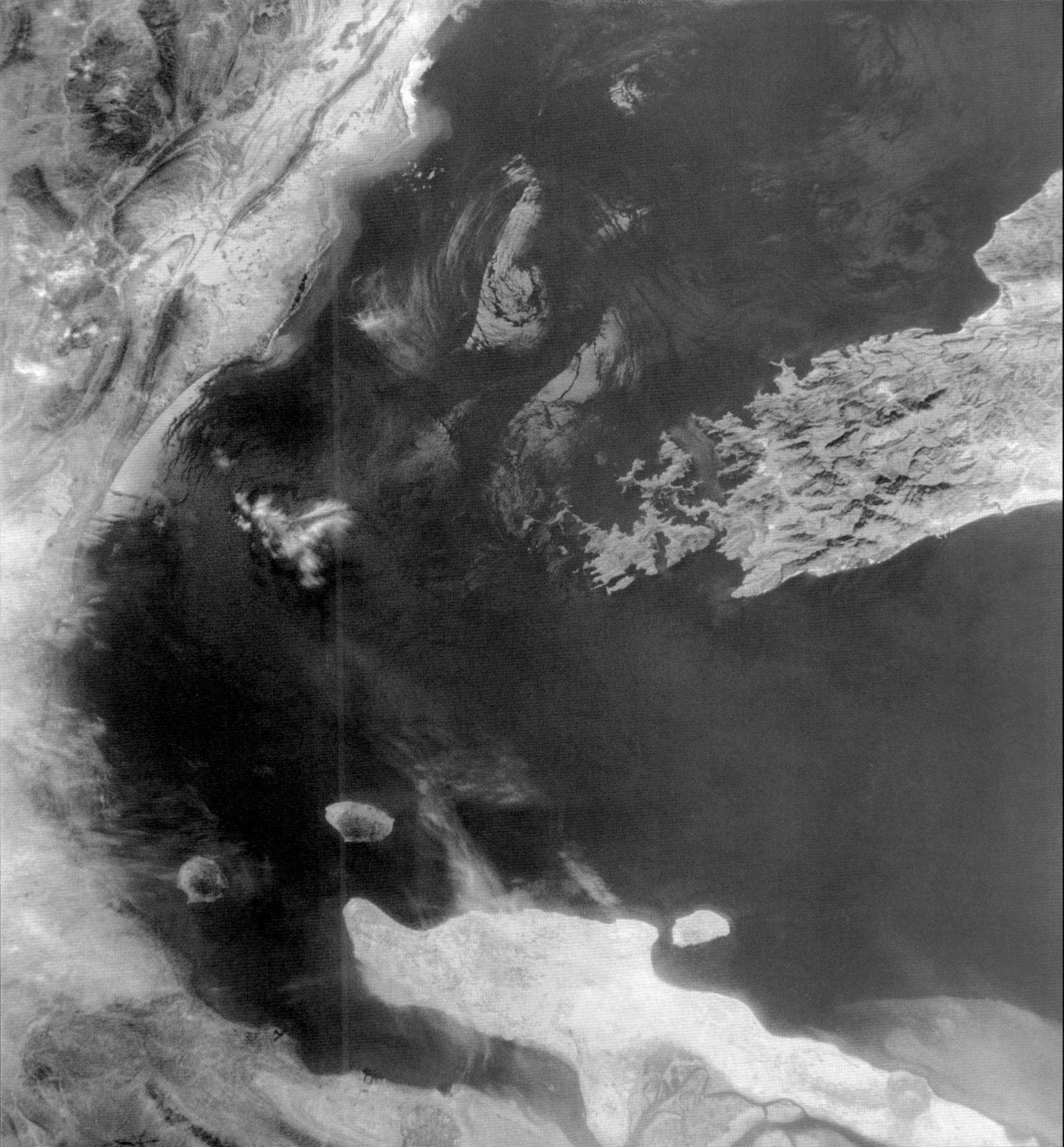

Key Political Event
Civil war in Sierra Leone

On March 23, 1991, Sierra Leone was thrust into a bloody and brutal civil war when Revolutionary United Front (RUF) rebels launched their first attack against government troops in the eastern city of Kailahun. The resulting conflict would last nine years, lead to the deaths of tens of thousands of civilians, and make over two million homeless.

Although lacking any obvious political ideologies, the RUF had a clear objective to usurp Joseph Momoh's corrupt government. Rebel leader Foday Sankoh quickly became popular amongst the people, pledging free public sevices and an equitable distribution of the country's considerable diamond revenues. But the RUF soon reneged on their promises, taking control of many mines by force and using the profits to purchase arms. Conducting a campaign of terror and slaughter against the inhabitants of the capital, Freetown, they kept their enemies in check by means of physical mutilation.

The rebels shocked the international community during the early months of the war when they began recruiting children to aid their campaign. Thousands of youngsters were taken from their homes, many forced to kill their parents as part of their initiation. Guerrillas frequently carved the initials "RUF" on their young soldiers' chests and reportedly rubbed cocaine into open wounds in order to make them frenzied and fearless in battle.

It needed the intervention of private armies, West African peace-keeping troops, the UN, and British forces before a ceasefire was finally signed in Abuja in November 2000.

Jay Mullins

Date March 23, 1991

Country Sierra Leone

Why It's Key The RUF's struggle for power in one of the world's poorest countries was marked by horrendous human rights abuses.

opposite Skull on a stake at a Sierra Leone check point.

628

Key Political Event
Iraqi disarmament crisis begins

Iraq's invasion of Kuwait in 1990 proved to be the eventual undoing of both Iraqi President Saddam Hussein and the Iraqi military establishment. After the rapid and crushing victory of the U.S.-led coalition in the Gulf War, the international community – led by the UN and other multilateral institutions – insisted that Iraq be stripped of the means to manufacture weapons of mass destruction. As a practical matter, Iraq's disarmament proved fraught with difficulties, as Saddam Hussein remained in power after the Gulf War, and his regime regularly interfered with the duties of arms inspectors. Iraq also claimed that it had disarmed as directed, and that the real purpose of arms inspections was to contest the nation's sovereignty.

However, many senior arms inspectors came to believe that, whatever the political demerits of the Hussein regime, Iraq was not in possession of weapons of mass destruction. After September 11, 2001, the United States made the opposite claim, insisting that Iraq was on the verge of triggering a global war. The standoff continued until the U.S. invasion of Iraq in 2003, at which time the United States discovered – much to the chagrin of conservative segments of the political establishment – that Iraq's disarmament had in fact been successful. This discovery put paid to the official *casus belli* advanced by the United States and opened the door to the advance of various alternative theories as to why it had been necessary to invade Iraq.

Demir Barlas

Date April 3, 1991

Country Iraq

Why It's Key Iraq's disarmament was a top international project for almost two decades and was the official reason given for the 2003 U.S. invasion of Iraq.

Key Cultural Event
Mike Tyson charged with rape

Mike Tyson, otherwise known as "Iron Mike," or "The Baddest Man on the Planet," was Undisputed Heavyweight Champion of the World between 1987 and 1990. However, his first loss, to the previously unheralded James "Buster" Douglas, in February 1990, burst his bubble of invincibility, and signaled his descent toward increasingly erratic and violent behavior.

Tyson met eighteen-year-old Desiree Washington, a contestant for the Miss Black America beauty pageant, on July 18, 1991, and took her to his Indianapolis hotel room in the early hours of the following morning. Two days later, Washington filed a complaint against Tyson for rape. The subsequent trial caused a media frenzy, becoming one of the most publicized cases in history and dividing communal

opinion. While feminists struggled to launch an anti-rape campaign, Tyson supporters claimed that the victim was "asking for it" by going up to Tyson's hotel room. The media surrounding the trial often reflected racist and sexist assumptions about rape and rape victims; comments undermining the credibility of black women were made on local black talk radio shows, and expressed by high-profile black men.

Regardless, Tyson was found guilty of rape, and was sentenced to a total of ten years' imprisonment, four of which were suspended. Although he tried to appeal for a new trial in 1993, the Indiana Court of Appeals rejected Tyson's plea. Tyson served only three years of his sentence, with time off for good behavior.
David Dunning

Date July 22, 1991

Country USA

Why It's Key The rape conviction effectively ended the career of one of the most formidable figures in the history of heavyweight boxing, and brought acquaintance rape to the forefront of media attention.

Fact Despite career earnings estimated at US$400 million, Mike Tyson filed for bankruptcy in August 2003.

opposite Mike Tyson leaves the court room during his rape case.

Key Cultural Event
The founding of the World Wide Web

The increasing development of the Internet in the 1980s created a communications tool of enormous potential. But this tool remained relatively unknown outside of a specialized technical community; bringing the Internet to a wider audience, and making it useful to people, required a new vision of the technology.

In 1984, Tim Berners-Lee, a contractor for CERN (a European organization for nuclear research), imagined a method for physicists from around the world to share data without having common hardware or software: a database that blended hypertext with the Internet to create a mutually accessible "web" of information. The first "web-pages" went live near Christmas of 1990; appropriately enough, these pages described the web project itself. On August 6, 1991, Berners-Lee posted a summary of his project on an Internet newsgroup,

explaining it and inviting collaborators; the World Wide Web was born. "Mosaic," a graphical web-browser compatible with home PC and Macintosh computers, became available in 1993. It initiated a revolution of the web project, giving access to anyone with a home computer and Internet connection. The World Wide Web gained increasing popularity for its simplicity, flexibility, and multimedia richness.

Increasing commercialization meant that almost no avenue of the new web was left unexplored. From its initial conception as a database for nuclear physicists, the web expanded to become an essential part of daily life in many modernized societies. A place to shop, learn, socialize, work, and play, the ubiquitous web transformed the fabric of contemporary civilization.
Justin Norris

Date August 6, 1991

Country Switzerland

Why It's Key The World Wide Web would create an information revolution of gigantic proportions, leading to a paradigm shift in knowledge-sharing and commerce.

Key Political Event
Deng Xiaoping picks capitalism

Although China has solidified its role as the world's workshop, the country only chose globally oriented market capitalism under de facto premier Deng Xiaoping, who in early 1992 told audiences in South China that the country should continue to focus on improving its economy, even at the cost of embracing certain capitalistic models and ideas. This was, of course, a radical departure for the largest Communist country in the world, but Deng had long flirted with the idea of accommodating market forces in the Chinese scheme of development. In doing so, Deng parted ways with the hard line of Mao Zedong and encouraged his official successor, Jiang Zemin, to more thoroughly inculcate the market system in China. In particular, Deng pushed for China to engage with the global economy in a way that it had never done.

Deng Xiaoping died in 1997, but China has never looked back from Deng's fateful decisions, which may yet prove to be more important in Chinese history than the country's 1949 embrace of Communism. Today China's economy is the second largest in the world, behind only the United States (which is not growing as quickly as China), and shows few signs of abating. Despite its nominal status as a socialist country, post-Deng China is decidedly in the camp of the capitalist nations and actively flexes its economic power in world markets.

Demir Barlas

Date January 18, 1992

Country China

Why It's Key China got the official blessing for its short march from socialist shut-in to capitalist powerhouse.

opposite Workers take an order from a customer in China's first McDonald's restaurant.

Key Political Event
Coup attempt in Venezuela

Throughout the 1960s and 1970s, Venezuela had been a model of stable democracy, in contrast to the brutal dictatorships that held sway elsewhere in Latin America. The country's two dominant political parties had developed a functional – albeit corrupt – system of power sharing, and had used burgeoning oil revenues to improve the standard of living. Old class tensions resurfaced, however, when plummeting international oil prices derailed Venezuela's prosperity during the 1980s. The austerity measures imposed by the administration of Carlos Andrés Pérez worsened the hardships of the poorest sectors of society, and the widespread dissatisfaction culminated in riots that shook Caracas in 1989. The Pérez government's heavy-handed response led to an even greater loss of confidence in its rule.

Enter Hugo Chávez Frías, a lieutenant colonel from a humble rural background. Convinced that the plight of Venezuela's poor could only be addressed by dismantling the entrenched political establishment, Chávez founded the Revolutionary Bolivarian Movement (MRB), a cohort of like-minded military men named for Venezuela's independence hero, Simón Bolívar. With popular unrest at a high, Chávez decided Venezuela was ripe for regime change. On February 4, MRB-affiliated army units entered Caracas with the intention of occupying key sites and forcing Pérez to resign. By the end of the violent and chaotic day, the coup had failed and Chávez was in prison. Nevertheless, he became a popular hero among the poor and embarked on the path toward victory in the presidential election of 1998.

Geoffrey Schullenberger

Date February 4, 1992

Country Venezuela

Why It's Key A failed effort to overthrow the government of president Carlos Andrés Pérez brought firebrand military officer Hugo Chávez to prominence, and prepared the way for the latter's vertiginous political ascent.

Key Political Event
New Mongolian constitution allows for human rights

In 1992 the People's Republic of Mongolia came to an end, concluding nearly seventy years of unbroken alliance with Moscow. Following the resignation of the Politburo amid the break-up of the USSR, the first free elections in 1990 were won by the communist MPRP. Discussions on a new constitution began in November 1991 and came into effect on February 12, 1992. As well as asserting Mongolia's sovereignty, the new constitution created a single legislative chamber known as the State Great Khural (SGKh) and cemented a range of new human rights and freedoms.

In 1928, the recently installed MPRP began confiscating property from the nobility and organized religion, while private enterprise was strictly prohibited. These measures severely impaired Mongolia's economy, leading to social unrest in the west and south of the country that had to be suppressed. A long-running Sino-Soviet conflict and Mongolia's Communist affiliations had provided the main catalyst for human rights abuses in the preceding years. In 1937, Soviet troops were deployed in Mongolia in response to Japanese military encroachments and the leader Khorloogiin Choibalsan, a staunch supporter of Stalin, ordered a full-scale purge of the Buddhist faith in the army and the party. Lamaism was virtually erased and 30,000 people were killed, approximately 5 per cent of the population.

Between 1989 and 1992 Moscow withdrew its troops from Mongolia in response to the collapse of the Soviet Union, enabling the country to concentrate on building friendly relations with both the Russian Federation and East Asia.

Jay Mullins

Date February 12, 1992

Country Mongolia

Why It's Key Mongolia's new constitution officially ended Soviet control and the religious oppression of previous decades.

Key Political Event
Sarajevo is besieged

It was the longest siege in modern history: from April 6, 1992, to February 29, 1996, the residents of Sarajevo, capital of the former Yugoslavia and site of the 1984 Winter Olympics, were hostages of a bloody civil war. The artillery shells of the Yugoslav National Army, or JNA, fell at an average of 329 a day. On July 22, 1993, 3,777 shells fell within the city limits during a single 24-hour period.

The 420,000 citizens of Sarajevo endured shelling and sniper fire for months at a time, leaving an estimated 12,000 dead and over 50,000 wounded. Much of the city was without power or running water, forcing residents into the streets in search of food and water. Warning signs of "Pazite, Snajper!" ("Beware, Sniper!") appeared in the most dangerous areas. Almost every building in the city sustained some damage, with about 35,000 structures completely destroyed. While much of the damage has been repaired in the decade since the Dayton Accords ended the 44-month long ordeal, there are still vivid reminders of the city's trauma. Among the particularly poignant symbols of the war are the "Sarajevo Roses," scars in concrete made by exploding mortar shells that form petal-like designs. Many of these scars have been filled with red resin to mark those sites where people were killed.

Heather Michon

Date April 6, 1992

Country Yugoslavia

Why It's Key The brutal siege of a modern European city left tens of thousands dead and injured.

opposite A gravedigger buries the bodies of civilians killed during the siege of Sarajevo in the Yugoslavian civil war.

Key Political Event
Rodney King riots

The damage inflicted upon the streets of Los Angeles was unprecedented: 53 dead, over 2,300 injured, and millions of dollars worth of damage. Tensions had been boiling for some time in the predominantly black areas of South Central LA amid low employment, poverty, and claims against the Los Angeles Police Department of institutionalized racism and use of excessive force. The disillusioned community found an outlet for their frustrations when on April 29, 1992, four LAPD cops – Laurence Powell, Timothy Wind, Theodore Briseno, and Stacey Koon – were cleared of the videotaped assault of Rodney King.

It was on March 3, 1991 that petty criminal King was chased by police on suspicion of driving under the influence. Upon stopping the suspect, the four officers were caught on tape beating King mercilessly with batons, while other officers looked on. They claimed self-defense, but as the first few moments of action were not filmed it was hard to prove.

To the black community, this was proof of the racism and the subsequent heavy-handed use of force that were prevalent in the LAPD. Yet at the trial, the police officers seemingly got away with it, prompting the violent riots.

A reluctant political hero, King pleaded, "Can't we all get along?" But it had gone too far, and as LA burned, the LAPD reviewed its practices. In 1994, King was awarded US$3.8 million from the city of Los Angeles, and Powell and Koon were later given a thirty-month prison sentence for their part in the beating.
Kerry Duffy

Date April 29, 1992

Country USA

Why It's Key The videotaped assault of Rodney King and ensuing riots highlighted the racism and excessive force prevalent in the LAPD and caused it to review its policies.

Key Political Event
Abkhazian separatists fight the Georgian government

Georgia gained independence following the dissolution of the Soviet Union in 1991. However, the autonomous republic of Abkhazia, officially recognized as an integral part of Georgia, also desired sovereign status, much to the displeasure of the Georgian government. Tensions in the region had been growing for a number of years before separatist militants attacked government buildings in the Abkhaz capital, Sukhumi, in June 1992.

A month later, the Abkhazian government announced independence, prompting Georgian police and National Guard units to enter the region on August 14 and restore Georgian authority. The separatist forces were steadily beaten back by the Georgian army, which was boosted by the addition of ex-prisoners that had been granted release in exchange for agreeing to fight in Abkhazia. By August 18, 1992, the Abkhazian government had fled the city, and Georgia had regained control of much of the region.

Yet the conflict was to be turned on its head on September 3, 1992, when, following a ceasefire in which Georgian troops pulled out of the Gagra region, Abkhazian militants led by Shamil Basayev launched an offensive against the defenseless Georgian population. They embarked on a horrific campaign of ethnic cleansing, killing as many as 30,000 Georgians and displacing many more. With Russian backing, the separatists laid siege to Sukhumi, which eventually fell on September 27, 1993. The resultant massacre of the remaining Georgians was one of the worst crimes to result from the break up of the USSR.
Jay Mullins

Date August 14, 1992

Country Abkhazia

Why It's Key The Abkhaz-Georgian conflict degenerated into a Russian-backed massacre, becoming one of the worst war crimes in recent history.

Key Political Event
Black Wednesday prompts financial crisis

Several people made a lot of money out of the Black Wednesday crisis; unfortunately, none of them was the Chancellor of the Exchequer, Britain's finance minister. The European Exchange Rate Mechanism was set up in 1979 to allow several countries to create stability in the currency markets, tying various currencies together, but Britain did not join until 1990.

The crunch came in 1992 when the value of the dollar began to fall against the Deutschmark, to which the pound was tied. This meant Britain's exports (many of which were in dollars) were unattractive, which damaged the economy; at some point, there would have to be a correction, where this strong pound would lose its value. Currency speculators (including George Soros) prepared for and precipitated this by selling their pounds and buying strong Deutschmarks, which meant a healthy profit for them and a collapse in the pound.

This stoked Britain's already high interest rates and threw it into a recession, with a housing market crash and businesses failing as a consequence. It completely destroyed the reputation of the Conservative Party for economic competence and led to their landslide defeat in 1997. It also, however, led interest rates to find a natural, sustainable level, giving Britain the economic stability it enjoyed over the subsequent years. This explains the change of name, in some economic circles, from Black Wednesday to White Wednesday.
Josh Spero

Date September 19, 1992

Country UK

Why It's Key The calamitous crash put the British economy into recession and cast the Conservatives out of power, but may have set up Britain's later prosperity.

Key Cultural Event
Catholic Church rehabilitates Galileo Galilei

On June 22, 1633, Galileo Galilei made his way up a spiral staircase to a room and stood before the Holy Office of the Inquisition in Rome. After days of questioning, they were ready to announce their verdict, finding the sixty-nine-year-old scientist and philosopher had "rendered [him]self vehemently suspected of heresy, namely of having held and believed the doctrine which is false and contrary to the Sacred and Divine Scriptures, that the Sun is the center of the world... and the Earth moves and is not the center of the world... "

The punishment was imprisonment, the banning of his book, and recantation of his heretical beliefs. Given the proclivities of the inquisition, it was a modest sentence. Galileo was not tortured or excommunicated; he spent the final nine years of his life in the comfort of house arrest. He was "rehabilitated" by Pope Benedict XIV in 1741 and the prohibition against belief in a sun-centered universe was lifted in 1758, but the trial of Galileo remained a powerful symbol of the gap between science and faith.

It was a schism that Pope John Paul II wanted to heal from the first days of his pontificate. In 1981, he established a panel of experts to reexamine the 1633 case. They found that the court had been well intentioned, but wrong. The Pope made this position plain in a speech on October 31, 1992, declaring Galileo, "a sincere believer," who "showed himself to be more perceptive... than the theologians who opposed him."
Heather Michon

Date October 31, 1992

Country Vatican City

Why It's Key The rehabilitation marked an attempt by Pope John Paul II to reconcile a 350-year old schism between science and faith.

Key Person
Oumou Sangare

Born into a family from Wassoulou in the southwestern historic region of Mali, Sangare grew up with a polygamous father like many Malians of that time. Her mother's pain at being one of several wives was ingrained in her consciousness, and when her father abandoned the family, Sangare helped her singer mother to feed the family by singing herself. At age five, she reached the finals of a contest for the nursery schools in Bamako, the capital of Mali, when she sang in front of 6,000 people at the Omnisport Stadium.

When she was twenty-one, Sangare worked with the great Malian arranger Amadou Ba Guindo to record her debut album *Moussoulou* (meaning "women"), which became a bestseller across Africa. Her unique blend of sounds was inspired by the ancient hunting rituals and traditional music of Wassoulou, and Sangare became the leading female singer-songwriter of African music.

But it was when Sangare signed up with UK label World Circuit that her strong and sensual voice became an international phenomenon. Her second best-selling album *Ko Sira* (meaning "marriage today"), released on October 20, 1993, was voted European World Music album of the Year. Sangare became respected worldwide for her unflinching social criticism and exploration of feminist issues from the perspective of a young African woman, particularly concerning the low position of women in her society and the importance of love and freedom of choice in marriage.
Mariko Kato

Date 1993

Born 1968

Nationality Malian

Why It's Key Oumou Sangare is one of the world's most admired voices, a champion of women's rights, and an ambassador for Wassoulou music.

Fact In many of her songs, Sangare refers to herself as "Sangare kono" meaning "Sangare the songbird."

1990-1999

653

Key Political Event
Clinton's "Don't Ask, Don't Tell" Policy

"Don't Ask, Don't Tell" marked another uneasy point in the American military's history of dealing with minorities. Around the time that a movement was growing for racial desegregation in the military, discrimination by sexuality had just become standard policy. Previously homosexuality had been cause for a dishonorable discharge, but in 1942, it would prevent you from even joining the army. Despite the 1957 Crittenden Report, which found that gay people were no more likely to be a security risk than heterosexual, the laws were not altered.

The brutal murder of Allen Schindler, a U.S. Navy radioman, came at the climax of the 1992 general election campaign, during which Bill Clinton proposed entirely removing the ban on gay people serving. Schindler was murdered in a public toilet in Japan by a fellow soldier for his homosexuality, and the horrific case pushed the issue to the forefront. After Clinton won the election, he tried to pass this complete repeal but was stymied by congressional and popular opposition. The result was the uneasy compromise of Don't Ask, Don't Tell, which treated homosexuality as a secret. If a member of the forces was open, he or she could still be discharged.

Despite current popular opinion in favor of the ban being lifted, the military is still largely opposed. One consequence of Don't Ask, Don't Tell is that dozens of gay Arabic speakers in the military have been discharged, despite the strong need for them during the war in Iraq.
Josh Spero

Date July 19, 1993

Country USA

Why It's Key Clinton tried to steer a path between conservatives and liberals by allowing gay people to serve in the military, as long as they kept their sexuality hidden.

opposite Protesters from the U.S. military demonstrate against the "Don't Ask, Don't Tell" policy in Times Square, New York.

Key Political Event
Arafat and Rabin shake hands in Washington, D.C.

For decades, Yasser Arafat and Yitzhak Rabin had been the worst of enemies. Arafat, the head of the Palestine Liberation Organization (PLO) since 1969, was an avowed enemy to the state of Israel, having vowed to reclaim the entire state on behalf of its Palestinian population. Rabin, the Prime Minister of Israel, had been a soldier for decades, finally becoming Chief of Staff of the Israel Defense Forces (IDF) in time for the Six-Day War against Arab states in the region. After his stint as a soldier, Rabin became the Israeli Minister of Defense. Arafat, meanwhile, was the world's most famous exponent of Palestinian nationalism, which in the PLO charter implied the assimilation or destruction of Israel.

These two diametrically opposed men agreed on one thing toward the close of the 1980s: that decades of war and violence had neither brought Israel closer to security nor the Palestinians closer to independence. As such, Arafat and Rabin began to consider themselves partners for peace and, to this end, began negotiations that would result in the Oslo Accords. As part of this Israeli-Palestinian peace process, Arafat and Rabin publicly met and shook hands on the White House Lawn on September 13, 1993, with a beaming U.S. President Bill Clinton looking on. Although the peace process soon foundered, the Arafat-Rabin handshake was a striking visual reminder of the possibility of rapprochement between even the most entrenched political enemies.

Demir Barlas

Date September 13, 1993

Country USA

Why It's Key The Arafat-Rabin handshake was the epitome of high hopes for peace in the Israeli-Palestinian negotiations that led to the Oslo Accords.

opposite The historic handshake between Rabin (left) and Arafat (right) on the Whitehouse lawn.

Key Political Event
The last Russian soldiers officially leave Cuba

In September 1993, the remaining 1,600 soldiers of what had once been a force of 20,000 left Cuba and returned to Russia, marking the last official act of an intense ideological and economic relationship that had once threatened nuclear war with the United States.

Since the 1960s Cuba had benefited from the exchange of sugar exports for discounted Soviet crude oil, as well as an influx of troops, technicians, and military hardware. At its peak, Soviet aid contributed up to 20 per cent of Cuban GNP via the Comecon, an association set up in 1949 to facilitate economic development throughout the Communist world. Yet by 1991, the collapse of the USSR and the closure of the Comecon had forced an extended depression in Cuba that became known as the "special period." The cancellation of Soviet crude oil shipments caused Cuba's modern industrial economy to grind to a halt. As tractors and refineries lay idle, severe energy shortages crippled the country's agricultural and manufacturing sectors, while imports of consumer goods fell rapidly. Ultimately, the agricultural crisis was eased by the introduction of organic farming techniques and crop diversification, but today Cuban living standards are lower than pre-1991 levels.

Despite the official withdrawal, Russia continued to operate a military intelligence base outside Havana at a cost of US$200 million a year, spying on U.S. communications, until it was closed in January 2002. This was a further blow to the Cuban economy after suffering the side effects of another superpower's economic troubles – this time the slump in the U.S. markets caused by 9/11.

Jay Mullins

Date September 17, 1993

Country Cuba

Why It's Key The withdrawal of Russian forces from Cuba symbolized the end of a powerful Cold War alliance that sent economic shockwaves through Castro's regime.

Key Political Event
Yeltsin suspends parliament and crisis ensues

On September 21, 1993, Boris Yeltsin decreed the dissolution of the Supreme Soviet in response to staunch resistance to his reform program. The declaration split the country's power structure in two and plunged Moscow into the worst street fighting since the October Revolution of 1917.

Following the collapse of the USSR, Yeltsin's reforms were intended to rapidly drive Russia toward a market-based economy, but they instead led to a credit crunch that saw prices soar, savings wiped out, and the selling off of state assets for nominal fees.

On September 22, the Congress of People's Deputies voted to remove Yeltsin through impeachment and install the vice-president Alexander Rutskoy in his place. With the military unsure which side to support, the parliamentarians barricaded themselves inside the White House in an attempt to embolden anti-Yeltsin protests.

The military leaders finally threw their wavering support behind Yeltsin on October 4, and tanks began to shell the White House in an attempt to flush out the defenders. Rutskoy was arrested, and in the days that followed Yeltsin moved swiftly to secure his position, issuing sweeping decrees that undermined the newspapers, political parties, and regional councils that had opposed his reforms. A new constitution was pushed through in a referendum on December 12 that accorded the president a range of executive powers, but Communist successes in the parliamentary elections dealt a huge blow to Yeltsin's hopes of sustaining a neo-liberal economic program.
Jay Mullins

Date September 21, 1993

Country Russia

Why It's Key Yeltsin's confrontation with the Russian parliament led to widespread civil unrest and a new constitution that granted increased presidential powers.

1990–1999

657

Key Political Event
Cambodia becomes a constitutional monarchy

The Cambodian Kingdom had been disrupted in 1970 when it was invaded by U.S. and Vietnamese forces. When Vietnam withdrew in 1989, a new era began. The country's name changed back to Cambodia (from People's Republic of Kampuchea), a new flag was created, and Buddhism was reintroduced as the state religion. However, its political instability still attracted international concern, and in 1990, the UN Security Council endorsed a framework for a comprehensive peace settlement in Cambodia. In the following year, the four main Cambodian political parties signed the Paris Peace Agreements, a political settlement for the restoration of peace, with nineteen other countries and the UN.

The UN was now in charge of enforcing a ceasefire, repatriating over 300,000 refugees who had fled to Thailand, and establishing a pluralistic democracy. As part of this effort, in May 1993, the UN supervised a general election to elect members of a Constituent Assembly that would draft a new constitution.

In September, a coalition government was formed, led by Prince Norodom Sihanouk, who had returned from exile after being deposed in 1970. He immediately ascended the throne, and the pre-1970 Kingdom of Cambodia was restored. Though a kingdom, the country was also a multiparty liberal democracy, and many hoped that peace would be maintained by the sharing of power between political parties.
Mariko Kato

Date September 21, 1993

Country Cambodia

Why It's Key A constitutional monarchy was restored in Cambodia after decades of war and political instability.

Fact Cambodia borders Thailand to the west and north-west, and Vietnam to the east and south-east.

opposite Prince Norodom Sihanouk greets the crowd inside the royal palace in Phnom Penh, Cambodia, on the day he becomes king.

Key Cultural Event
MTV goes to Latin America

When MTV hit the airwaves, it changed the music industry forever. It was a place to find industry news, event information, and different promotions. Artists had the chance to showcase their music through widespread video play and as such music videos that started out as snatched clips became more elaborate as people began to make videos especially for the channel.

In 1993, in response to the Hispanic influences on U.S. culture, MTV Latin America was launched in 19 countries in Central and South America featuring many latino rock and pop artists. Since then it has expanded to MTV En Español – a completely Spanish-language channel, MTV Revolution, and MTV Tr3´s. The global takeover has gone on to include Europe, India, Russia, Pakistan, Australia, and many others.

The early 90s saw more change. In its bid to keep up with the demands of a diverse youth culture MTV branched out to more non-music content. From cartoons for a range of ages – think Nickelodeon to Aeon Flux, Beavis and Butthead, and Daria – to reality TV and celebrity programs to being a voice for youth issues and contemporary culture. In 1992 MTV fronted the Pro-Democracy campaign to encourage young voters and has also targeted topics such as violence, drugs, and crime. Music fans now watch other MTV channels such as MTV Hits, Live, and Total Request. It is a prime example of how media changes and adapts to its audience's ways of absorbing information. Video might have killed the Radio Star but he gave life to a whole new form of music entertainment and culture.
Fiona Kellagher

Date 1993

Country USA, South America

Why It's Key The channel that changed the music industry keeps changing to stay ahead.

1990-1999

Key Political Event
Black Hawk Down incident

The notorious Black Hawk Down incident took place during the battle for Mogadishu, which itself was part of a wider conflict that had been raging within the African nation of Somalia for years. Somalia's government had been overturned in 1991 and the result was anarchy as rival factions fought for control of the country. The fighting had destroyed agriculture in Somalia and famine was widespread. U.S. forces had been sent to the region as part of a United Nations force intended to restore peace to the war-torn nation and ensure that food supplies got through to famine stricken areas.

The battle of Mogadishu took place on October 3, 1993, when U.S. troops participated in a raid on the headquarters of a Somali warlord, Muhammad Farah Aydid. The battle was a disaster for the Americans: during the fighting, militiamen shot down two Black Hawk helicopters using rocket-propelled grenades. This action and the resulting rescue attempt left eighteen soldiers dead and seventy-eight wounded, with captives taken by the Somalis being paraded on television. President Clinton ordered the withdrawal of American forces from the region within six months and the chaos in Somalia continued.

The incident had a profound effect on American foreign policy with the Clinton administration becoming increasingly reluctant to fill the role of the world's policeman. The fear of losing American troops in combat led to many hesitant policy decisions in conflicts around the world.
Martin Sayers

Date October 3, 1993

Country Somalia

Why It's Key The incident had a profound effect on American thinking, leading to a more isolationist foreign policy for many years.

Key Political Event
The Maastricht Treaty creates the European Union

The idea of a unified Europe first gained prominence during World War II, and the Organization for European Economic Cooperation was created after the war to oversee the distribution of American aid under the Marshall Plan. In 1957, six nations established the European Economic Community. In 1991, twelve European leaders met in Maastricht in the Netherlands to negotiate a new agreement. The Maastricht Treaty, also known as the Treaty of the European Union, was ratified on November 1, 1993. In addition to economic integration, the EU pledged its dedication to justice and to common foreign and security policies. Some members adopted the euro, a common monetary unit.

After the dissolution of the Soviet bloc, Eastern European countries began applying for membership. The EU is made up of twenty-seven member nations, encompassing just under five million people, and other nations may join if they meet strict EU requirements. Members must demonstrate a commitment to peace, democracy, law, and human rights. All EU members maintain sovereignty, but citizens of member nations are granted European citizenship and are allowed to vote in local and European elections. Success of the European Union is documented through improved standards of living in member nations, the installation of a frontier-free single market, and the rise of the EU as a major economic power. EU supports foreign studies, provides consumer protections, promotes women's rights, and furnishes aid to developing countries. Polls reveal that 81 per cent of European residents are satisfied with their lives inside the European Union.

Elizabeth R. Purdy

Date November 1, 1993

Country European Union

Why It's Key The EU united much of Europe behind common economic, political, environmental, and humanitarian goals, vastly strengthening Europe's position as an actor on the global scene and promoting global partnerships.

1990-1999

659

Key Cultural Event
Trial for the murder of James Bulger

James Bulger went missing while out shopping with his mother in the Strand Shopping Centre in Bootle, Liverpool, on February 12, 1993. The CCTV footage of James Bulger being led away by the hand was later to become the infamous image associated with the case.

His abductors, Jon Venables and Robert Thompson, both aged ten at the time, escorted the toddler away from the shopping center to an isolated area near the Leeds and Liverpool Canal, where they first assaulted him by dropping him on his head.

They took him on a two and a half mile walk that lasted hours, during which time a number of witnesses later reported seeing the baby being shaken, punched, and kicked. In fact, a total of thirty-eight people saw James in the company of Venables and Thompson, but none saw fit to intervene.

The boys threw paint and stones at James, beat him with an iron bar, removed his shoes and underwear, and left him for dead on a railway line. James' body was discovered two days later, cut in half by a train.

Video stills from the shopping center CCTV footage appeared on TV and in the newspapers, as a result of which an anonymous telephone caller implicated Venables and Thompson. They were sentenced to be detained at Her Majesty's Pleasure, and were released on life license in 2001, with secret new identities.

David Dunning

Date November 24, 1993

Country UK

Why It's Key Jon Venables and Robert Thompson became the youngest convicted murderers in the United Kingdom for almost 250 years.

Fact A computer game featuring a CCTV image of James Bulger being abducted was withdrawn from sale by its distributors in 2007, following a complaint from James' mother.

Key Political Event
Zapatista uprising

On January 1, 1994, a previously unknown rebel group calling itself the Zapatista Army of National Revolution (EZLN) staged an attack in the main plaza of San Cristóbal de las Casas, the capital of the southern Mexican state of Chiapas. Their name recalled the example of Emiliano Zapata, a peasant leader who fought during the Mexican Revolution. The Zapatistas revealed themselves to the world on the day the North American Free Trade Agreement (NAFTA) took effect, attempting to call attention to the impact of trade policies on Mexico's poor rural population. The uprising was soon crushed by the Mexican military and the movement went on to seek alternatives to armed conflict.

Subsequent statements released by the EZLN have focused on non-violent solutions. Since 1994, the Zapatistas have consistently demanded comprehensive land reform and legal protection of indigenous peoples. Using "postmodern" tactics, they have positioned themselves as a major player in worldwide anti-globalization activism. Its chief spokesman, Subcomandante Marcos, believed to be a former philosophy professor, releases periodic communiqués via the Internet. Zapatistas have created autonomous communities in parts of Chiapas, attempting to implement more equitable economic arrangements through agricultural and craft collectives. Although few of the reforms they have demanded have been put into law, the activism of the Zapatistas has played a significant role in foregrounding the plight of Mexico's rural poor and forcing a debate on the consequences of globalization.
Charlotte Whittle

Date January 1, 1994

Country Mexico

Why It's Key The event marked the appearance of the most emblematic anti-globalization groups of the late twentieth century.

opposite Zapatistas gather for a convention in Chiapas.

Key Political Event
NAFTA comes into effect

In the wake of the 1989 Canada-United States Free Trade Area, negotiations on an agreement that would bring Mexico into the fold began in 1990. Given the insignificance of the commercial relationship between Canada and Mexico, the process was initiated mainly to serve the United States and Mexico's political and economic objectives. For a government, led by Carlos Salinas de Gortari, looking to break free from the economic volatility that strained the Mexican economy for most of the 1980s, the North American Free Trade Agreement (NAFTA) formed part of a wider Mexican reform agenda premised on free market ideals. Mexico embraced a North American destiny not necessarily shared by all as NAFTA's birth coincided with the beginning of the insurrection led by the Zapatista National Liberation Movement.

NAFTA came about in the United States amid fierce political debate, which eventually led Bill Clinton's administration to conclude soft side agreements on the environment and labor standards. With NAFTA, the United States aimed to bolster the stability and prosperity of its southern neighbor, and thus curb the flow of illegal migrants. However, more than ten years later, the issue of Mexican immigration remains at the forefront of American politics. On the global stage, NAFTA helped revive trade negotiations between the United States and the European Union, which culminated in the creation of the World Trade Organization (WTO), by demonstrating that the United States had a variety of free trade options.
Maxime Turcotte

Date January 1, 1994

Country USA

Why It's Key NAFTA created a Free Trade Area currently covering approximately 430 million people and more than a third of the world's economy.

Key Political Event
Rwandan genocide begins

The orgy of killing that swept across Rwanda in the spring of 1994 began with an explosion in the night: the crash of a plane carrying Rwandan President Juvénal Habyarimana and Burundi President Cyprien Ntaryamira on approach to the Kigali airport, most likely brought down by rocket fire and killing both leaders. It turned out to be the catalyst for the long-simmering rage of the Hutu tribe against the country's Tutsi minority to boil over into one of the worst acts of genocide in recorded history.

Armed with machetes and machine guns, Hutu militia fanned out across the country. On the first day, more than 8,000 Rwandans died. Two weeks later, the death toll stood at 112,000. At the end of the first month, it was 232,000. On May 17, when the UN first declared that what was occurring was "genocide," the body count was close to 500,000. In July, the Tutsi-led Rwanda Patriotic Front (RFP) captured Kigali, and the Hutu leadership, along with close to two million Hutu refugees, were in flight. In 100 days, more than 800,000 Rwandans had been killed.

In the following years, Rwanda has worked to recover from the mass slaughter of 1994. The country has a new constitution and is working to boost foreign investment. War-crimes tribunals have been ongoing since 1997. Despite much positive change, many survivors remain physically and emotionally scarred by the genocide, and thousands of women raped by militia now face a slow death from AIDS.

Heather Michon

Date April 6, 1994

Country Rwanda

Why It's Key The mass killing of close to one million Rwandans paralyzed the world community.

opposite Refugees line up for a Red Cross food delivery in Kigali, Rwanda.

664

Key Person
Osama bin Laden

Osama bin Laden was the son of one of the wealthiest men in Saudi Arabia, a distinction that gave him privilege and, for many years, protection. Born in Riyadh in 1957, within months of his college graduation in 1979 he was in Afghanistan fighting the Soviets. He arrived home, victorious, in 1989.

The devoutly religious bin Laden became a critic of the Saudi monarchy, especially after the Saudis aligned with the United States during the 1990–1991 Gulf War. After a period of house arrest, in 1992, he fled to Sudan. Sometime between 1992 and 1994, the Saudi government froze his financial assets.

Although he risked extradition and execution, he used his passport to enter the UK in 1994, establishing the Advice and Reform Committee in the London suburb of Wembley – really a multinational communications center for terrorist cells. Then, on April 9, the Saudi government announced that bin Laden's passport had been revoked on the grounds that "he committed acts that adversely affected the brotherly relations between the Kingdom of Saudi Arabia and some other countries," paving the way for the British to expel him.

Bin Laden quickly fled to Sudan, which requires no passports for Muslims. His investments in public works made him a popular figure with the people, but by 1996, the government seemed to be on the verge expelling him, and in May 1996, he left for Afghanistan. There, he and his followers holed up in mountains, where they allegedly remain today.

Heather Michon

Date April 9, 1994

Born 1957

Nationality Saudi Arabian

Why It's Key The move pushed bin Laden to Sudan and eventually to Afghanistan, where he began plotting wide-scale attacks on U.S. and Western targets.

Key Political Event
First democratic elections in South Africa

The last week of April 1994 marked a turning point for South Africa. This was the first time in the country's history that a multiracial, fully democratic election was held.

After Nelson Mandela's release from prison in 1990, he and Prime Minister F. W. de Klerk began work on an interim constitution for post-apartheid South Africa. Various representatives from the government, other political parties, and the country's liberation movements were brought together to begin negotiations in what was known as "The Convention for a Democratic South Africa" (CODESA). The process was an extremely fragile one, and discussions reached deadlock on numerous occasions. Racially and politically motivated violence escalated throughout the country during this period.

Despite these setbacks, a draft constitution was finally published on July 26, 1993, which provided for equal voting for all races, and an election date was set for April 27 of the following year. On the day, 85 per cent of the electorate turned out to vote. The African National Congress (ANC) was nominated into power with a majority of over 60 per cent, effectively ending five decades of apartheid and three centuries of white minority rule. Nelson Mandela, for many years a political prisoner, became president with de Klerk as one of his deputies. South Africa was immediately welcomed back into the international community and the new government began a process of development and reconstruction of the country.

Carly Fabian

Date April 27, 1994

Country South Africa

Why It's Key The first elections held in the country where all South Africans, regardless of race, were able to vote.

Key Political Event
Paula Jones files a lawsuit against Bill Clinton

In the 1980s, just one sex scandal was enough to sink the campaign of presidential candidate Gary Hart. But, in 1992 Bill Clinton survived allegation after allegation of sexual misconduct by women from his home state of Arkansas and was elected president. However, one woman who didn't come forward in the campaign, Paula Jones, was coaxed into the spotlight by a right-wing magazine, *The American Spectator*, which published her allegation that Clinton propositioned her in an Arkansas hotel room in its infamous "Troopergate" article in late 1993.

Although Jones was not fully identified in the story, she chose to file a lawsuit a few months later, just a few days short of the statute of limitations deadline. She found herself supported by conservatives opposed to Clinton's presidency, and acquired representation from

high-profile Washington lawyers. Unlike others who had accused Clinton of sexual misconduct, Jones, a young, married state employee, seemed stable and credible.

The trial moved slowly, with procedural and fact-finding motions receiving strident challenges from Clinton's lawyers, who argued that sitting presidents should not have to go through civil lawsuits while in office. A few months after the Monica Lewinsky allegations were made, the Supreme Court ruled that the case could go forward, and Jones settled for US$850,000 – almost all of it going toward legal fees – in November of 1998. Since then, Jones has largely disappeared from the spotlight, although she has expressed her disappointment that her trial didn't make her a greater celebrity, as it did for Lewinsky.

Martin Johnson

Date May 6, 1994

Country USA

Why It's Key Although this lawsuit was ultimately dismissed, it enabled the grand jury investigation that exposed Bill Clinton's affair with Monica Lewinsky, which led to his impeachment in 1998.

Fact After a judge decided that Bill Clinton's sexual history was relevant to the case, several women came forward to testify about their relations with Clinton.

Key Discovery
First genetically-modified food is sold

The now defunct company Calgene, Inc. produced the first GM food, the Flavr Savr tomato, in Davis, California, on May 23, 1994. Although modified with characteristics to make it more flavorsome and to ensure it had a longer shelf life, the tomato proved to be a commercial flop because it was essentially tasteless. Despite this unpromising start, scientists continued to utilize technology developed in the 1970s and 1980s that made direct manipulation of plant DNA possible. Plant cells that have their genetics transformed are then grown to produce the desired and marketable traits.

In addition to the Flavr Savr tomato, many other plants, such as corn, soybeans, and wheat, have been genetically modified for desirable traits, for instance to withstand weed killers, to be resistant to particular insect pests, or even to contain extra vitamins or a vaccine. Although the public in the United States and in Europe initially accepted GM foods, the outbreak of Mad Cow Disease in the United Kingdom led to a distrust of the government regulation of food safety. Advocates of GM foods claim that their use is a means of increasing food production and solving world hunger. Those against what they call "frankenfoods," argue that they have unforeseen ecological consequences. For instance, cross-pollination of GM and non-GM species may lead to the extinction of native plants and a decrease in biodiversity. As we still do not fully understand the impact of GM foods on economics and the environment, the debate is likely to continue.
Anna Marie Roos

Date May 23, 1994

Country USA

Why It's Key The introduction of the Flavr Savr tomato in American supermarkets was the first example of a food genetically modified (GM) to produce desirable qualities, such as longer storage times, ripeness and enhanced flavor.

Fact GM rice produced in the United States was boycotted by the European Union in 2006 because it did not contain "approved genes" for export.

1990–1999

667

Key Cultural Event
Channel Tunnel opens

The idea of a land bridge between England and France had been discussed for two hundred years. Traders and tourists on either side longed for an alternative to the unpredictable Channel crossing, which took as long in 1975 as it did in 1875. In England, though, many were reluctant to open their island fortress to the dangers of the European continent, be they Napoleon, Hitler, rabies, or illegal immigrants.

In 1981, political and technological conditions finally proved favorable; British Prime Minster Margaret Thatcher and French President Francois Mitterrand announced their support for a 31-mile tunnel from Folkestone, England to Coquelles, France. In addition to a record-breaking (and legacy-securing) feat of engineering, the privately financed, privately constructed, and privately managed project was to demonstrate the potential of free enterprise in the modern state. The demonstration was partly undermined when the tunnel proved to be the most expensive construction project ever undertaken, as well as one of the most delayed. In 1987, British and French engineers began tunneling from opposite shores and raced to reach the center point (the British won), and on June 6, 1994, the longest undersea tunnel in the world was opened to the public.

For the millions of people who use the tunnel every year, as passengers on Eurostar, or accompanied by their cars and trucks on the Eurotunnel shuttle, France, and England are now just twenty minutes apart.
Rachel Eley

Date June 6, 1994

Country UK/France

Why It's Key England and France, historic trading partners and rivals, were joined by a permanent land link for the first time since the Ice Age.

Fact At the time of its construction, the Channel Tunnel was the most expensive building project of the modern era. It cost UK£12 billion.

Key Cultural Event
O. J. Simpson arrested for murder

There was a time when Orenthal James (O. J.) Simpson, a.k.a. "The Juice," was celebrated as one of the most successful running backs in American football history. However, the brutal stabbing murders of his ex-wife Nicole Brown, and her friend Ronald Goldman on June 12, 1994, and the sensational events that followed, would eclipse much of Simpson's former sporting glory.

An immediate suspect in the murders, Simpson was ordered to report to the Los Angeles Police Department by 11 a.m., on July 17, 1994. He never showed. Later that night, police spotted a white Ford Bronco, belonging to Simpson's friend Al Cowlings, traveling south on Interstate 405. An hour-long, slow-speed chase ensued and was one of the most bizarre scenes ever broadcast live on network television.

What followed was a national obsession over what Western media called "The Trial of the Century." CNN's primetime host Larry King even said, "If we had God booked and O. J. was available, we'd move God." Simpson was acquitted of the murders in October 1995. However, in 1997, a civil jury disagreed with the judgment and awarded US$33.5 million, in wrongful-death suit, to the victims' families. In 2007, the Goldman family were awarded the distribution rights to O. J. Simpson's book *If I Did It: Confessions of the Killer*.

On September 14, 2007, Simpson again made headlines for the alleged armed robbery of sport memorabilia from a Las Vegas hotel room.

Annie Wang

Date July 17, 1994

Country USA

Why It's Key The trial was one of *the* most publicized criminal cases in U.S. history and highlighted deep-rooted racial tensions within U.S. society that would divide the entire nation along racial lines.

Fact Over 150 million Americans tuned in to watch the O. J. Simpson trial verdict, making it one of the most watched events in television history.

670

Key Political Event
Castro lifts restrictions on leaving Cuba

With the fall of Communism in the Soviet Union in 1989, Castro's government began to falter. He could no longer rely on his Soviet allies who had subsidized much of Cuba's economy, and by 1991, Cuba was suffering an economic crisis. Unemployment and inflation grew, and outdated equipment caused sugar and tobacco production to fall.

In an effort to tackle the problem, Castro adopted a quasi-free market economy and developed the tourist industry, He also urged the United States to lift the trade embargo it had imposed on Cuba since 1960. However, the U.S. government refused to negotiate until Castro ended his dictatorial regime, and by 1994, it had even tightened the embargo.

Castro remained equally stubborn, and threatened the United States. by lifting emigrant restrictions on his people, predicting an influx of Cubans onto American soil. The United States Administration was outraged, and warned Castro that it would not permit a repeat of the 1980 "Mariel Boatlift," in which Cuba had temporarily dropped restrictions and 120,000 Cubans had fled to America.

Eventually, the two nations signed an agreement, in which the U.S. agreed to admit 20,000 Cubans a year, if Cuba halted the mass exodus of refugees. For twenty years after the revolution, Castro had forbidden emigrants from returning, but now they were allowed to travel to Cuba without visas. But this was short-lived; by 1999, Castro had begun imposing a five-year ban on the return of those who had left without permission.

Mariko Kato

Date August 1, 1994

Country Cuba

Why It's Key This major exodus from Cuba into the United States resulted in a compromise between the two long-conflicting countries.

Fact In the same year, Fidel Castro's daughter sought asylum in the USA, causing him no little embarrassment.

opposite Protesters march against Castro's dictatorship in Little Havana, Miami, Florida.

Key Political Event
IRA announces end of violence in Northern Ireland

Although undoubtedly welcome after twenty-five years of bloodshed, the IRA ceasefire of August 1994 was greeted with reserve and suspicion in many quarters. The IRA statement announcing the ceasefire made it clear that they had not abandoned their goals, but rather were initiating a new front in their struggle. The lack of any indication of the permanence of the ceasefire led to fears that killing would be resumed should Sinn Féin (the IRA's political wing) not get its way.

The two years prior to the ceasefire saw both intense political movement and a surge in violence. The Hume-Adams declaration, by the leaders of the SDLP (the largest nationalist party) and Sinn Féin respectively, helped lead Sinn Féin out of the political wilderness. In December 1993, the Irish and British governments attempted to facilitate political dialogue through a joint approach known as the Downing Street Declaration. By October 1994, progress was being made as the Combined Loyalist Military Command, an umbrella group for unionist paramilitaries, similarly announced a ceasefire.

The political process, however, quickly became entangled in dispute as it became clear that deep divisions existed – even between the SDLP and Sinn Féin – with regard to the fundamental nature of the Northern Ireland conflict. The ceasefire ended in February 1996 when the IRA detonated a bomb at Canary Wharf in London. However a new ceasefire began in July 1997 and dialogue resumed.
Denis Casey

Date August 31, 1994

Country Republic of Ireland

Why It's Key After twenty-five years of violence, the provisional IRA announced a ceasefire in an effort to facilitate attempts to find a peaceful solution to the Northern Ireland conflict.

opposite **Celebrations follow the announcement of the end of violence.**

1990-1999

673

Key Cultural Event
Herrnstein and Murray's *The Bell Curve* published

The Bell Curve, the controversial bestselling book by Richard J. Herrnstein and Charles Murray, was first published on September 1, 1994. Its first key point, based on social Darwinism, is that intelligence has a bigger impact on a person's income, job performance, and the likelihood to commit crime than the person's social and economic background. In other words, in an equal opportunities society, intelligent people succeed on their own merit and the less intelligent ones remain in the lowest classes. Herrnstein and Murray's second claim is that there are racial differences in IQ, which are genetically caused. According to that claim, the Asian race has an IQ slightly superior to the Caucasian's because there are slight genetic differences between the two races, whereas there is a large difference between the Caucasian and African race.

The key points discussed in *The Bell Curve* caused a huge controversy shortly after the book's publication. Some people defended the book and some criticized it, saying that it supported scientific racism. Several esteemed scientists criticized the authors' methodology, claiming that they omitted facts and based their hypotheses on other people's research. Numerous books were subsequently written in response to *The Bell Curve*, including *The Bell Curve Debate* (1995), a collection of essays corresponding to the issues in Herrnstein and Murray's book. The controversy started by *The Bell Curve* still exists, and the scientific community is still debating whether the issues raised in the book are a valid basis for research.
Sonja Kudeljnjak

Date September 1, 1994

Country USA

Why It's Key *The Bell Curve* initiated an ongoing controversy on the overlapping of science, racism, and political correctness.

Fact The title of the book comes from the bell-shaped normal distribution of IQ scores.

Key Political Event
Arafat, Peres, and Rabin share the Nobel Peace Prize

The 1994 Nobel Peace Prize went to Yitzhak Rabin, Prime Minister of Israel; Yasser Arafat, the leader of the Palestine Liberation Organization (PLO); and Shimon Peres, the Foreign Minister of Israel. The two Israeli politicians and Arafat – previously mortal enemies – began to make overtures of rapprochement toward each other in the early 1990s, culminating in the Oslo Accords of 1993. These seminal talks, the first face-to-face diplomatic encounter of its kind between Israelis and Palestinians, saw Palestine recognize Israel's right to exist while Israel agreed to guarantee limited Palestinian self-rule in parts of the Gaza Strip and the West Bank.

For their leading role in orchestrating the Oslo Accords, Rabin, Arafat, and Peres were duly recognized by the Norwegian Nobel Committee, which stated in its accompanying press release that the three had "made substantial contributions to a historic process through which peace and cooperation can replace war and hate." However, while the Nobel Committee expected the Oslo Accords to usher in a period of peaceful fraternity in the Middle East, the agreement soon foundered, and Israel and the Palestinians soon returned to their previous attitude of mutual belligerence. Rabin was assassinated by an ultra-orthodox Israeli man in 1995. Toward the end of his life, Arafat found himself surrounded by Israeli tanks. The conclusion of Peres' acceptance speech – "We have reached the age where dialogue is the only option for our world" – proved to be either naïve or sadly premature.

Demir Barlas

Date December 10, 1994

Country Middle East

Why It's Key The Nobel Committee recognized Arafat, Peres, and Rabin for their groundbreaking work in advancing the cause of peace in the Middle East.

Key Political Event
Russian troops invade Chechnya

Towards the end of 1994, Russian troops invaded the former Soviet Republic of Chechnya, which had declared its independence shortly after the fall of the Soviet Union in 1991. Russia might have abandoned Communism, but not yet its ambitions in the Caucasus, into which Tsarist Russia first expanded in the eighteenth century. In the twentieth century, as in the eighteenth, Russia ran into stiff resistance from the hardy tribal people of the north Caucasus. Despite fielding a large mechanized army against Chechen leader Dzokhar Dudayev, a former Russian Air Force General, Russia made numerous tactical blunders against the Chechens, who emerged from the conflict with a reputation as one of the best small armies in the world. After losing men, morale, and materiel to the Chechen separatists, Russia withdrew in 1996.

The First Chechen War was a harbinger of struggles to come, as the once-secular national liberation movement of Chechnya rapidly evolved into a Muslim nationalist movement espousing jihad – or holy war – against Russia, echoing the nineteenth-century Imam Shamil rebellion. Chechnya proved to be a magnet for foreign jihadists, some of whom assumed high positions in the Chechen army, and added momentum to a Muslim transnational militancy that had begun over a decade earlier in Afghanistan. The First Chechen War hardened attitudes among both Russians and Chechens, whose spectacular and bloody clash of civilizations is now entering its third century.

Demir Barlas

Date December 11, 1994

Country Chechnya

Why It's Key Russia confronted Chechen separatism with a full-fledged invasion, signaling the renewal of age-old hostilities between Moscow and its Muslim subjects.

opposite Russian troops lead T-72 tanks towards the Chechen capital Grozny.

Key Political Event
Oklahoma City bombing

Today a park sits on the site of the Alfred P. Murrah Federal Building in memory of those who lost their lives there in a deadly terrorist attack. Just after 9:02 a.m. a truck concealing a massive homemade bomb exploded outside the building. Inside, office workers were starting their day and, on the second story, children were playing in the nursery. The effect of the bomb was devastating. One hundred and sixty-eight people, including nineteen children, were killed and five hundred injured as the front of the nine-story building collapsed. It took rescuers six weeks to recover all the bodies. Pictures of a fireman cradling the lifeless body of a baby symbolized the cruel loss of life.

At the outset, Middle Eastern terrorists were suspected of the attack but soon Timothy McVeigh, a thirty-three-year-old Gulf War veteran, attracted the attention of investigators when he was arrested for a traffic offense. Two days after the atrocity, McVeigh, along with friend Terry Nichols, were charged as suspects. Both had been soldiers in the U.S. Army. They opposed Federal authority and had extreme right-wing and militant patriot movement connections. Significantly, April 19 was the anniversary of the ending of the Federal Troops' siege at Waco where eighty Branch Davidians died. It was also Patriot's Day, the anniversary of the American rebellion against British authority at Lexington.

McVeigh was convicted of murder, conspiracy, and using a weapon of mass destruction. He was eventually executed in 2001. Nichols was sentenced to life in prison.
Lorraine Brownbill

Date April, 19 1995

Country USA

Why It's Key It was the worst peacetime terrorist attack in the USA until the attacks on the World Trade Center and the Pentagon in 2001.

Key Discovery
Wiles publishes proof of Fermat's Last Theorem

Andrew Wiles first learned about Fermat's Last Theorem as a ten-year old boy growing up in Cambridge, England. Famed French mathematician Pierre de Fermat had written the elegant little puzzle in the margins of a book in 1637. The theorem seemed so simple: could the equation $xn+yn=zn$ have a solution greater than the whole number 2? "I have a truly marvelous demonstration of this proposition," he wrote causally, "which this margin is too narrow to contain." Thus, mathematicians were off on a three-century-long quest to find Fermat's proof.

Wiles worked on the theorem through his adolescence, and again after receiving his PhD in mathematics from the University in Cambridge in 1980. Fifteen years later, he was a specialist in number theory on the faculty of Princeton University, still plugging away at Fermat in his spare time. Using the newest advances in number theory, he found the answer. In May 1995, he shocked the mathematics world by presenting a 150-page-long proof. Fermat's Last Theorem had been solved.

He is quick to point out that this is not the solution Fermat himself proposed: "It's a twentieth-century proof." His paper made him a rock star in academic circles, but Wiles admitted that he was a little sad to come to the end of his quest. "Fermat was my childhood passion. There's nothing to replace it," he said in an interview. "There is a sense of melancholy."
Heather Michon

Date May 3, 1995

Country USA

Why It's Key The solution to Fermat's Last Theorem solved a 300-year-old mathematical mystery.

Key Political Event
The Srebrenica massacre

The massacre at Srebrenica was the biggest mass murder in Europe since the end of World War II. A war crimes trial at The Hague would later describe it as "genocide."

The massacre took place at the height of a savage war between Bosnian Serbs and Muslims in the Yugoslav republic of Bosnia-Herzegovina. The Bosnian Serb forces had occupied more than half of the country and were accused of taking part in "ethnic cleansing" – forcibly removing non-Serbs from occupied areas to ensure Serbian domination.

The small town of Srebrenica was largely Muslim, but with a significant Serb minority. Although controlled by Muslim forces, the town was surrounded by Serb-held territory, and Serb commanders were anxious to destroy this pocket of resistance. However, the town had been declared a "safe haven" by the UN in 1993 and was theoretically protected from armed attack. Encouraged by this, tens of thousands had fled there from surrounding Serb-held areas.

In early July, 1995 with complete disregard for the UN, Serb forces began shelling the town. On July 11, Serbian troops entered the safe area and met with little resistance from either Muslim troops or the four hundred Dutch UN peacekeepers stationed there. Women and children were deported out of the area while all the men of fighting age were rounded up and imprisoned. Many of the prisoners were later shot and their bodies dumped in hastily dug mass graves. It is estimated that Serb forces executed more than 7,800 people.
Martin Sayers

Date July 11, 1995

Country Bosnia-Herzegovina

Why It's Key The massacre horrified the world and seriously called into question the UN's role in Bosnia.

Key Cultural Event
Combined DVD format announced

In the mid–1990s, over a decade had elapsed since VHS became the standard technology for home video viewing, and the desire to supplant it was approaching a crescendo. Many of the world's largest media companies, including Toshiba and Sony, were scrambling to be the pioneers of the next step. There was no question that the DVD, a form of optical disc storage that had already been popularized with the advent of the CD-ROM, had a mainstream future. But various companies were toying with their own particular notions of the DVD format, each of which contained different storage amounts and qualities of sound and image.

For movie studios and others in the entertainment business, the possibility of multiple DVD formats available on the open marketplace needlessly complicated distribution strategies. As Sony and Phillips began preparing one DVD format while Toshiba and Warner Bros. prepared another, whispers of a mounting technology war began circulating in the media. Finally, IBM interfered, eager to ensure that DVDs remained compatible with their optical devices, and convinced both sides to cooperate. Talks about the specific parameters of the new format began at various meetings and conventions, culminating in an announcement at IFA (a massive consumer electronics trade fair), outlining the market standard for DVD. With the capacity for several layers of data on each side of the disc, the DVD satisfied all concerned parties, leading to its wildly successful launch the following year.
Eric Kohn

Date September 1, 1995

Country USA

Why It's Key The combined DVD introduced the new generation of home video technology.

Fact The first DVD players became available for consumer purchase in November 1996.

Key Cultural Event
Million Man March

The march on Washington on October 16, 1995, was perhaps as controversial as it was praised. Proponents lauded the march's goals to improve the black community as a whole, but others chided its sole focus on black males – women were barred from marching, though organizers maintained that women played an important role in organizing the event.

The most controversial aspect of the march was arguably its organizer, Minister Louis Farrakhan, who has been seen as racist and anti-Semitic by many in and out of the black community. Several Christian ministers said they supported the premise of the march, but refused to participate under the direction of Farrakhan, the head of the Nation of Islam.

The march focused on such issues as poverty, crime, education, voter participation, and adoption.

Marchers were encouraged to prioritize their families, adopt black children, volunteer for tutoring and other programs in their communities, and to register to vote. Prominent black leaders including the Reverends Jesse Jackson and Al Sharpton, Dr Cornell West, and rapper Chuck D attended.

There remains a debate as to the success of the march. Organizers estimated a crowd of more than one million men, a figure that met the expectation at which the event's hopeful title hinted. Controversy ensued when the National Park Service later estimated the crowd total at 400,000. Voter registration among black males surged following the march, and many participants attested to becoming more community oriented as a result of the event.
Bethonie Butler

Date October 16, 1995

Country USA

Why It's Key Though controversial, the event largely sought to increase voter registration among black men, and it did – more than 1.5 million black men registered to vote in the year following the march.

opposite African-American men take part in the Million Man March to highlight the need for social improvement.

1990-1999

Key Political Event
Assassination of Yitzhak Rabin

When Yigal Amir assassinated Israeli Prime Minister Yitzhak Rabin at a peace rally in Tel Aviv, he aimed to kill both Rabin and the fledgling Middle East peace process. Rabin, prime minister since the surprise Labor electoral victory of 1992, had attempted to steer Israel toward peaceful dialog with its Arab neighbors.

Born in 1922, prior to the creation of the state of Israel, Rabin organized the defense of Jerusalem during the Israeli war of independence. By 1967, he was chief of staff of the Israeli army and his military leadership played a vital role in the Israeli victory of the Six Day War. Afterwards, Rabin opposed settling the newly occupied territories of the West Bank and Gaza Strip, believing they should be used as bargaining chips in any future political settlement. He subsequently became ambassador to Washington and turned to

politics, becoming prime minister from 1974–1977 and minister for defense from 1984–1990.

As prime minister during the 1990s, he entered secret negotiations with the Palestinian Liberation Organization (PLO), which resulted in the Oslo Accords of 1993–1994 promising self-government for Palestinians within the occupied territories. With King Hussein of Jordan, he also officially ended the forty-six-year state of war between their countries. For these actions his enemies likened him to Marshal Pétain: a war hero turned traitor. Although alternately both hawk and dove, his legacy is ultimately one of peace.
Denis Casey

Date November 4, 1995

Country Israel

Why It's Key The assassination of Israeli Prime Minister Yitzhak Rabin was an attempt to kill the fledgling Middle East peace process.

Key Political Event
Last Canadian residential schools close

Canada, no less than the United States, has a long history of institutionalized discrimination against its aboriginal population. The Canadian Residential School System, which officially closed down only in 1998, had a particularly spotted history. The system, designed to assimilate Canada's aboriginal tribes, exploited its students by putting them to work, provided an extremely low standard of education, and even covered up numerous crimes committed by teachers against students. Canada finally recognized the unfairness of the Residential School System in the late 1990s, capping nearly four centuries of imperialist education whose stated purpose was to Christianize and "civilize" large segments of Canada's native population. The Canadian government instituted reparations for former students of the system, but the conservative Tory party pointedly refused to apologize to the First Nations, the name given to the non-Inuit, non-Metis native peoples of Canada. The available reparations added up to between a few and several thousand dollars, based on the amount of years that a student had attended one of the schools.

Canada officially considers itself a rainbow republic, one that is equally open to all of its current inhabitants, but the record of the Canadian Residential School System constitutes an ongoing blot on that self-image. Horrible stories of emotional and physical abuse, up to and including murder, continue to emerge from the testimonies of survivors of the system.
Demir Barlas

Date 1996

Country Canada

Why It's Key The closing of the final residential school brought to an end to the systematic and brutal assimilation of First Nations people in education.

Key Political Event
Hamas suicide bombers in Jerusalem

On February 25, 1996, a suicide bomber from the Palestinian group Hamas detonated his payload on Bus 18 in Jerusalem, killing twenty-six people and wounding forty-eight. The attack, planned and carried out by the Izzeddine Al-Qassam Brigades – the military wing of Hamas – signaled the rise to international prominence of what had hitherto been an obscure militant group. Hamas, founded in 1987 with the aim of destroying Israel and replacing it with a Palestinian state governed under Islamic law, had carried out sporadic attacks on Israelis for several years, but it was not until the Bus 18 bombing that the group succeeded in a engineering a single high-casualty event and seizing a niche in the global consciousness.

The Hamas attack marked the true arrival of suicide bombing – previously a tactic perfected in Lebanon and Sri Lanka – on Israeli soil. Indeed, on March 3, 1996, Hamas struck the same bus line with a suicide bomber again, this time killing nineteen people. The attacks coincided with the rise of Islamist militancy among Palestinians who had hitherto responded to the largely secular influence of the Palestine Liberation Organization (PLO). In the subsequent decade, Hamas enjoyed rising fortunes in Palestine, where it joined the government and displaced the popularity of the PLO-affiliated Fatah party in 2005. In Israel and much of the West, however, Hamas garnered a reputation as a deadly terrorist organization unworthy of trust.
Demir Barlas

Date February 25, 1996

Country Israel

Why It's Key Hamas put itself on the map with a highly deadly terrorist bombing in Jerusalem.

Key Political Event
Truth and Reconciliation hearings commence

On April 1, 1996, the Truth and Reconciliation Commission (TRC) held its first public hearings to investigate the gross human rights violations – killings, abductions, torture, and severe mistreatment – that had occurred between March 1, 1960, and May 10, 1994. Chaired by Archbishop Desmond Tutu, the TRC was founded on the belief, as the then President Nelson Mandela expressed it, that "only the truth can put the past to rest." Conceived as supra-political, it undertook the investigation of violations perpetrated by state and liberation agents, and the apportionment of reparations to victims. Amnesty applications would be considered case-by-case, and depend on full disclosure, proof of political motivation, and proportionality.

Between 1996 and 1998, 7,112 perpetrators and over 20,000 victims testified, often face-to-face, in venues across the country. Specific sectoral hearings followed. Press attention focused on famous cases, such as Steve Biko's murder, and the hearings of apartheid politicians, security agents, and anti-apartheid activists – such as F. W. De Klerk, Eugene De Kock, and Winnie Mandela. Most senior figures in the apartheid regime refused to accept responsibility for crimes, and both sides attempted to block aspects of the hearings and the resulting report.

The commission granted amnesty to 849 of the 7,112 applicants; some of those denied amnesty have since been convicted in criminal trials. Its report eventually came out in 1998, condemning both sides for atrocities. While many argued that the TRC wrongly sacrificed justice, others praise it as a template for peaceful transitions in formerly oppressive societies.
Laura Pechey

Date April 1, 1996

Country South Africa

Why It's Key The South African Truth Commission, which went further than its equivalent European and South American predecessors, stands as the most important, controversial, and brave experiment in collective healing and democratic justice of the twentieth century.

Key Political Event
Russian troops withdraw from Chechnya

On May 27, 1996, after two years of brutal fighting in a war frequently described as Russia's Vietnam, Russian President Boris Yeltsin agreed to a ceasefire and promised to withdraw Soviet armed forces from Chechnya. The decision represented a humiliating turnaround for Yeltsin, who had claimed that the existence of an autonomous Chechen republic was an affront to Russian integrity. As the ferocious war continued, the Chechen capital city of Grozny was effectively burned to the ground. Despite being seriously outnumbered by superior troop numbers, equipment, and firepower, Chechen guerrillas waged a desperate war of attrition against the occupying Russian army, managing to inflict heavy and demoralizing casualties.

While the public initially backed Yeltsin's decision to invade, popular support for the war quickly faded, as casualty rates continued to rise, more and more Russians were taken as hostage, graphic images of the struggle were broadcast on television, and the conflict showed no sign of ending.

The ceasefire in May 1996 and a peace treaty signed later only represented a minor halt in the hostilities. When Vladimir Putin replaced Yeltsin, he renewed the offensive and the Second Chechen War began in August 1999.
Terence McSweeney

Date May 27, 1996

Country Chechnya

Why It's Key The withdrawal of Russian troops from Chechnya marked a victory, albeit brief, for the Chechen insurgents who had retaken the breakaway region.

Fact It is estimated that around 100,000 Russian and Chechen troops and civilians were killed in the conflict.

Key Cultural Event
Dolly the cloned sheep is born

Dolly looked and behaved like any normal lamb when she was born at the Roslin Institute in Edinburgh, Scotland. The circumstances surrounding her birth, however, were far from normal. Indeed, Dolly's birth reignited the flames of outrage that often accompany the idea of "cloning."

Cloning is not a modern phenomenon, and many forms have been developed over the years on all manner of organisms. Dolly was created via reproductive cloning: in order to create Dolly, udder cells were taken from an adult sheep, and the nucleus, or genetic material, was transplanted into a cell of a second sheep. The egg and cell were then electrically fused, and when it had developed into an embryo, it was implanted into a surrogate mother, who had a normal pregnancy and gave birth to Dolly.

Under the leadership of Dr Ian Wilmut, a team of researchers at the Roslin Institute had already cloned two lambs from embryo cells, yet the difference with Dolly was that she was cloned from adult cells. This was significant because this proved that genetic material from a specialized adult cell, such as the udder cell, could now be programmed to generate a new organism, whereas before, it was assumed that once an udder cell, always an udder cell.

Dolly died at six years old from a progressive lung disease, but not before she had six lambs of her own.
Kerry Duffy

Date July 5, 1996

Country Scotland

Why It's Key The birth of Dolly was the first successful cloning using adult cells.

opposite Dolly with her creator, Dr Ian Wilmut.

Key Cultural Event
Mehta's *Fire* is released and subsequently banned

When Deepa Mehta's *Fire* was first shown at the Toronto film festival in 1996, it received both critical and public acclaim. Lesbians, in particular, lauded the film for its overt portrayals of queer sexuality. Written, directed, and produced by Canadian-based Mehta, the film depicts the same-sex love affair that blossoms between two sisters-in-law, Radha and Sita, who have both been rejected by their husbands. Starring some of India's best performers, it won six prestigious awards worldwide.

When the film was released in India two years later, however, it provoked one of the most passionate and lengthy debates on homosexuality the country had ever witnessed. In December 1998, a small group of protestors, comprised principally of women from the Shiv Sena, the Hindu fundamentalist wing of the ruling

Bharatiya Janata Party (BJP), halted the screening of the film in theaters across the country. Protestors bought tickets to the screenings and once inside the halls, set fire to posters, destroyed furniture, and essentially banned a film that had been approved by India's stringent censorship board. These acts of destruction were construed as a necessary preventative measure against the proliferation of what Bal Thackery, leader of the Shiv Sena, has termed "a sort of social AIDS."

But while Hindu nationalists demonstrated against the film, civil rights organizations, women's groups and cultural bodies in India united to demand its continued screening. Legal battles were launched, newspaper articles published, and speak-out rallies organized, creating India's first public discourse on queer sexuality.
Bianca Jackson

Date September 6, 1996

Country India

Why It's Key The film and its ensuing protests highlighted same-sex sexuality in India, and resulted in the first public discourse on homosexuality in a country in which sodomy is still illegal under Section 377 of the Indian Penal Code.

Fact *Fire* is the first film in Mehta's "elements" trilogy, which also includes *Earth* (1998) and *Water* (2005).

Key Political Event
A world ban on nuclear weapons testing agreed

Seventy-one nations signed the Comprehensive Nuclear-Test-Ban Treaty (CTBT) on September 24, 1996, effectively ruling out all future atmospheric, exo-atmospheric, underground, and nuclear explosions.

The forerunner to the CTBT was the Partial Test Ban Treaty of 1963. Two of the nuclear powers – France and China – refused to sign, and the opening of the Nuclear Non-Proliferation Treaty (NPT) in 1968 became a key compromise measure.

The NPT limited the spread of nuclear weapons among non-nuclear states, signaling the desire for total disarmament in the future. Unfortunately, the lack of trust engendered by the Cold War meant that it was not until the collapse of the USSR in 1991 that progress was made.

Plans to convert the Partial Test Ban Treaty into a worldwide ban were backed by the UN in 1993. The treaty text and its two annexes took three years to draft before being formally adopted on September 10, 1996, at the United Nations General Assembly in New York.

Two weeks later, the treaty was signed by five of the eight nuclear weapons states. This symbolic act drew a line under the intensive period of nuclear weapons testing that had destabilized the middle of the twentieth century, with over fifty nuclear explosions recorded between 1945 and 1953.

Overseen by an international body based in Vienna, a sophisticated monitoring network today ensures ongoing compliance with the treaty. The CTBT must be ratified by all forty-four Annex 2 signatories before it comes into force, but the United States has yet to do this.

Jay Mullins

Date September 24, 1996

Country USA

Why It's Key The Comprehensive Nuclear-Test-Ban Treaty (CTBT) significantly limited the development of future nuclear weapons.

Key Cultural Event
Taliban seize control of Afghanistan

The origins of the Taliban's rise to power are shrouded in mystery. Legend has it that in the spring of 1994, neighbors from Mullah Omar's village of Singesar told him that a local Mujahideen commander had abducted two teenage girls and taken them to a military camp, where they were raped. In response, Mullah Omar gathered thirty Talibs and attacked the base where they freed the girls and hung the commander from the barrel of an old Soviet tank.

Originally starting out with a force of two hundred men, the Taliban quickly defeated local warlords, capturing the Afghan border town of Spin Baldak, the village of Takht-e-Pul, and the city of Kandahar in late October and early November of 1994. The battle for Kandahar lasted less than a week, and the Taliban were able to capture dozens of tanks, armored cars, military vehicles, and weapons, as well as six MiG-21 fighters and six transport helicopters, while only losing a dozen men.

In the next three months, the Taliban took control of twelve of Afghanistan's thirty-four provinces, with Mujahideen warlords often surrendering to them without a fight, and the "heavily armed population" giving up their weapons. On September 27, 1996, the Taliban captured Kabul soon after government forces abandoned the capital and effectively seized control of Afghanistan. Within hours, they commanded all key government installations – including the presidential palace, and ministries of defense, security, and foreign affairs – and proceeded to hang former President Najibullah and his brother from a tower.

Keith Leitich

Date September 27, 1996

Country Afghanistan

Why It's Key The Taliban's seizure of power laid the foundation for the rise of Islamic extremism in Afghanistan.

Fact The Taliban were one of the Mujahideen groups formed during the Afghan-Soviet War (1979–1989).

Key Cultural Event
Swiss banks hold property confiscated by the Nazis

During World War II, Jewish people persecuted by the Nazis tried to protect their savings by depositing their money in Swiss banks. Meanwhile, Swiss banks were also holding Nazi accounts, as well as helping Nazis to exchange the valuables taken from the Jews they had murdered for money.

Following the war, many Jewish survivors knew that their relations had opened bank accounts. However, the survivors had no access to account numbers or paperwork, and Swiss banks refused any access to accounts without death certificates. As millions had been murdered with no official records, there was no way for survivors or their relatives to access this money.

In April 2006, the U.S. Senator Alfonse D'Amato led Congress in a hearing about the accounts, and the question of Switzerland's morality during and after the war became a subject of international scrutiny. On Oct. 3, 1996, the first lawsuit was filed against Swiss banks on behalf of Nazi victims for US$20 billion, and centered over the amount of money that was involved. The Swiss banks maintained that they had settled the accounts regarding Jewish victims in payments to the Allies at the end of the war. However, Jewish organizations believed that up to several billions of dollars of Jewish money were being kept in Swiss banks. The lawsuit ended in a US$1.25 billion settlement in 1998. The money would be made available to the public, and Jewish survivors were able to access the money by submitting a claim to an international panel.

Anne Hsu

Date October 3, 1996

Country Switzerland

Why It's Key Swiss banks came under international scrutiny after being accused of cooperating with the Nazi regime and continuing to persecute the families of Holocaust victims.

1990–1999

689

Key Political Event
Bill Clinton defeats Bob Dole

In 1992, Bill Clinton became the first Democrat elected President since Jimmy Carter had won in 1976 in the wake of the Watergate scandal. Over the next four years, Republicans tried to blacken Clinton's reputation by accusing him of everything from sexual indiscretions to financial misdeeds. In 1994, a so-called revolution placed Congress in the hands of Republicans, many of them ultra-conservative newcomers. Clinton refused to be railroaded by the new Congress. When he faced re-election in 1996, Senate Majority Leader Bob Dole emerged as the Republican frontrunner and Clinton's chief opponent. The 1996 presidential campaign was the most expensive and one of the ugliest in U.S. history.

Clinton was charismatic, and his presidential record was clear. He had reduced the national debt by 63 per cent, and most Americans were economically better off than they had been since the 1980s. Clinton had strengthened the U.S. presence abroad while maintaining peace. Dole was hurt by his strong link to the tobacco industry. Polls revealed that he was heavily opposed by women, African-Americans, and young people. By April, a Clinton victory was considered a foregone conclusion.

On November 5, 1996, American voters proved the economy was still the issue, giving Clinton a clear victory. In the electoral college, which represents the states, Clinton triumphed over Dole 379 to 159. Clinton became the first Democrat to win re-election since 1944. After Franklin D. Roosevelt had won re-election in 1936, 1940, and 1944, a constitutional amendment limiting presidents to two terms had been passed.

Elizabeth R. Purdy

Date November 5, 1996

Country USA

Why It's Key Clinton's victory revitalized both the Democratic party and the political party system in the United States, and redefined American politics in a global sense.

Key Political Event
Labour wins the 1997 UK General Election

By 1997, the Conservative Party had been in government for eighteen years. However, since their last victory at the polls in 1992, John Major's government had been widely discredited by the devaluation of sterling, and subsequent withdrawal from the European Exchange Rate Mechanism on September 16, 1992 (commonly known as "Black Wednesday"). Over the course of the parliament, his government was further rocked by a series of scandals about MPs and ministers' private lives as well as deep internal divisions over Europe and the Maastricht Treaty.

The Labour Party had in July 1994 elected a new, young, charismatic leader in Tony Blair, who had successfully repositioned and relaunched his party as "New Labour." He was able to skilfully take advantage of the Conservatives' problems and convince the electorate that it was time for a break with the past.

When the election eventually came on May 1, 1997, it was clear that the Tories stood little chance of winning a fifth victory. However, it was the sheer scale of their defeat that took many by surprise. Labour won a majority of 179 seats in the House of Commons, their largest victory ever. The Conservatives scored just 31 per cent of the overall vote – its lowest share of the vote since 1832. With just 165 MPs returned at Westminster, they had no representation in either Scotland or Wales. The most successful political party in the UK had in the course of just one evening been reduced to a mere rump.
John Owen

Date May 1, 1997

Country UK

Why It's Key The election of Tony Blair in 1997 marked the Labour Party's biggest ever win at the polls and resulted in the Conservative Party's longest spell in opposition.

Key Cultural Event
Deep Blue defeats Kasparov

On May 11, 1997, Deep Blue, an IBM computer, became the first machine to defeat a reigning world chess champion in a formal match, consequently defining the way humans and technology relate.

Gary Kasparov, debatably the strongest player in chess history, had already beaten Deep Blue in 1996 and, disdainful of the ability of chess computers, welcomed a rematch the following year. Kasparov suggested that chess, as an intellectual struggle, was "species-defining," the perfect battleground to prove that computers could not "think" better than a human. For the 1997 rematch, IBM programmers, equally confident, had overhauled Deep Blue's processing power – it could now evaluate 200 million positions per second. The event took place in New York, gaining media coverage far beyond what two human opponents could command. With the scores level after five games, Kasparov lost the decisive sixth in just nineteen moves, uncharacteristically blundering in the opening. Crestfallen, Kasparov and his team accused the IBM delegation of cheating. Kasparov felt that at sporadic but key occasions in the games Deep Blue made counter-rational moves possibly contrary to objective chess rules but, paradoxically, profound strategically. This "creativity," Kasparov was averring, could have only come from human input. IBM programmers emphatically replied that this revealed the sophistication of their machine, but a refusal to a rematch, disallowing immediate scrutiny of the computer move logs, and a perhaps unusual jump in IBM's stock market value all helped lend the event an atmosphere of intrigue.
Michael Hallam

Date May 11, 1997

Country USA

Why It's Key Kasparov's loss showed that the best chess computer could beat the world's best chess player, and that technology could participate in traditional preserves of human intelligence.

opposite Kasparov's chess game against Deep Blue is watched in an auditorium via a TV link.

Key Cultural Event
Princess Diana dies in a car accident

Princess Diana was having a convivial time in the summer of 1997. She was divorced from Prince Charles, and was forging a life for herself outside the British royal family. At the end of August, she went on holiday in the Mediterranean with Dodi Al Fayed, son of millionaire businessman, Mohamed Al Fayed, and she was due to return to London on August 31 to spend time with her sons, William and Harry, before they returned to school.

The couple, who appeared to be engaged in a liaison, decided to spend a night in Paris before the princess flew back to London the next day. Their final evening, however, was marred by the constant attentions of paparazzi photographers, who were intent on getting a picture of the couple. This meant they chose to stay in the Ritz Hotel for dinner instead of going out as they had initially intended. After midnight, Dodi and Princess Diana waited with their bodyguard at the rear door of the hotel for a car to take them to Dodi's apartment. Henri Paul, assistant director of security at the hotel, was to drive them.

Pursued by photographers, the couple's Mercedes entered the Place de l'Alma underpass at high speed. It smashed into a pillar and hit the wall. Dodi Al Fayed and Henri Paul died instantly while the bodyguard was badly injured. Princess Diana suffered appalling injuries and was taken to hospital where doctors fought to save her. She died in the early hours of Sunday morning.

Lorraine Brownbill

Date August 31, 1997

Country France

Why It's Key Princess Diana was arguably the most famous woman in the world and her death heralded a turbulent period for the British monarchy, who were accused of not being in touch with the feelings of the British people who mourned her.

opposite A vast array of flowers and tributes for Princess Diana left at Kensington Palace.

Key Disaster
Severe forest fires in Indonesia

The "Southeast Asian Haze" spread fire-related particulate over a vast area throughout the second half of 1997, causing severe respiratory problems and compounding existing levels of air pollution.

Hospitals in Singapore experienced a 30 per cent rise in air-quality-related cases, and many poorer people were unable to protect themselves with facemasks and air conditioning units. Visibility was also drastically reduced, slowing down transport by air, land, and sea, as well as undermining agriculture, construction, and tourism.

The haze caused lasting damage to the atmosphere and biodiversity of Southeast Asia, and generated total costs estimated at US$9 billion in Indonesia, Malaysia, and Singapore. Damages to Indonesia were estimated at US$1 billion, with Malaysia and Singapore at US$0.4 billion. The arrival of the monsoon season finally helped to extinguish the fires. Coming off the back of similar incidents in 1991 and 1994, the 1997 Southeast Asian Haze led to the creation of the ASEAN Haze Technical Task Force for overseeing fire prevention and management measures across the region.

The exact causes of the fires remain unclear, but it is likely that the use of "slash and burn" techniques by Indonesian farmers contributed to its spread. It was later discovered that despite constituting only 30 per cent of the total area burnt, peat swamp vegetation played a key role in spreading the disaster to other types of terrain.

Jay Mullins

Date October 1, 1997

Country Indonesia

Why It's Key The "Southeast Asian Haze" choked vast swathes of the continent, causing colossal damage to the environment, economic activity, and public health.

Fact At its worst, the haze layer covered an area of over three million square kilometers and could be seen by satellites from space.

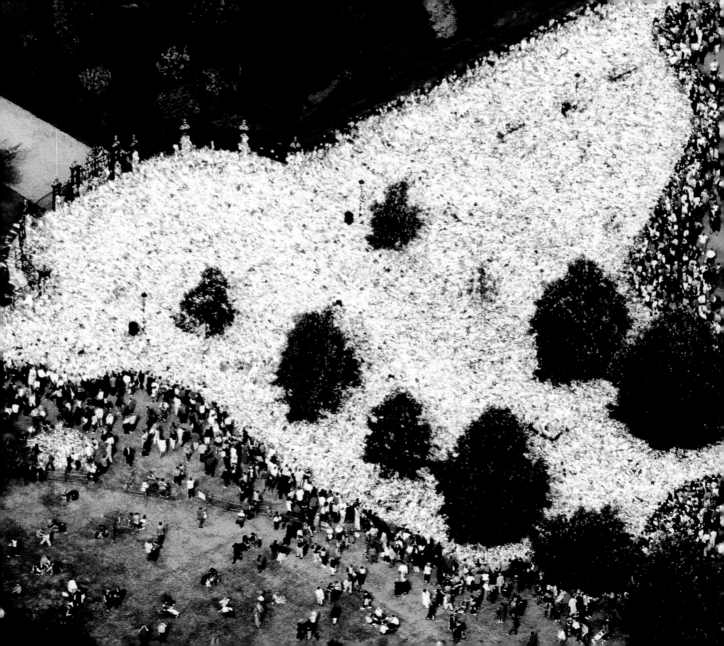

Key Cultural Event
Titanic is released

Based on the ill-fated 1912 maiden voyage of luxury cruiser RMS *Titanic*, the movie *Titanic* became a phenomenal commercial success upon its release in 1997. The fictional plot follows the intertwined fates of Rose Dewitt Bukater, a first-class passenger and socialite (played by Kate Winslet), and Jack Dawson, a third-class passenger and artist (played by Leonardo DiCaprio). When Rose, frustrated by her engagement to arrogant Caledon Hockley (acted by Billy Zane) attempts suicide, Jack stops her, and they begin a romance that is as brief and tragic as the voyage itself.

The making of the film was a colossal project for James Cameron. Even before he wrote the screenplay, he spent two years diving into the Atlantic Ocean to shoot footage of the real *Titanic*, which had sunk after hitting an iceberg. The filming with cast took six months, and many of the cast and crew, including Kate Winslet, caught the flu and suffered injuries. It was a lengthy epic at three hours and fourteen minutes, and was also the most expensive movie ever made, with a US$200 million budget.

Titanic opened in U.S. cinemas, taking in US$28 million on its first weekend, and stayed at number one for fifteen consecutive weeks in the U.S. box office. The film's success was echoed as it was released in other countries, and it won eleven Oscars in 1998, including Best Picture and Best Director, and seventy-six other awards worldwide. The movie holds the record as the highest-grossing movie of all time, at US$1.8 billion.
Mariko Kato

Date November 18, 1997

Country USA

Why It's Key *Titanic* became the highest-grossing film of all time.

Fact *Titanic* was written, directed, and co-produced by Canadian James Cameron, the creator of *The Terminator*.

opposite Leonardo DiCaprio and Kate Winslet in *Titanic*.

1990–1999

698

Key Political Event
The Kyoto Protocol

The Kyoto Protocol is a legal document in which the participating nations agree to reduce six greenhouse gas emissions, including carbon dioxide and methane, which are thought partly responsible for global warming. The overall aim of the agreement, to be achieved between 2008 and 2012, is to reduce emissions in thirty-six countries to 5.2% per cent below 1990 levels. The target reductions vary from nation to nation. For example, the European Union countries must reduce their omissions by an average 8 per cent while Canada's reduction target is set at 6 per cent.

By the time the Kyoto Protocol became legally binding in 2005, industrialized countries did not seem to be cutting emissions enough to reach their targets. Moreover, it suffered a major blow when President George W. Bush pulled the United States out of the agreement in 2001, saying that implementing it would damage the U.S. economy. His administration argued that the agreement was "fatally flawed" because it did not require developing countries like China and India to commit to reducing emissions. While developing nations who signed the agreement need not commit to specific target reductions, they must report their emission levels and develop national programs to help combat climate change. Participating countries can gain credits for actions that help the environment to absorb carbon, such as planting trees and soil conservation. Many climate scientists have doubts about how much the Kyoto Protocol can achieve, and reports issued two years after the treaty took effect indicated that most participants would fail to meet their emission targets.
Lorraine Brownbill

Date December 11, 1997

Country Japan

Why It's Key It is a global, legally binding step toward reducing greenhouse gas emissions in an attempt to mitigate the effects of global warming.

Key Cultural Event
Sensation Exhibition

The 1997 *Sensation* exhibition at London's Royal Academy attracted over 300,000 visitors, provoked numerous front-page headlines from press around the world, and forced the issue of art into a central position in the national and international consciousness that it had rarely occupied. The reason for such unprecedented mass awareness of a form of entertainment more usually the province of a niche few was not even ultimately the provocative works themselves, but rather the questions that they raised as to the nature of art and to notions of artistic freedom, as individuals and authorities internationally strove to censor and even ban the show.

The exhibition comprised works by Young British Artists from the collection of Charles Saatchi, and *Sensation* served to expose this new movement, shaped by the common intent of its artists to shock and give viewers pause through means that varied between the use of kitsch and irony (Marcus Harvey), exploring the line between art and pornography (Chapman Brothers), and the use of real animal and human substances as art-materials (Damien Hirst).

Particularly controversial works included Marcus Harvey's "Myra," reproducing the familiar image of the child-killer in a collage of children's handprints, and "Holy Virgin Mary" by Chris Ofili, depicting a black Madonna smeared in dung, with a cherub constructed out of pornographic images. It was this work that directly provoked Mayor Giuliani's crusade against the exhibition in New York, which in turn led to the cancellation of the exhibition by the National Gallery of Australia.

Alexandra Coghlan

Date 1997

Country UK

Why It's Key The new generation of young British Artists (YBAs) exhibited in the show invoked worldwide debates on censorship and the nature of art.

Key Disaster
El Niño affects world climate

Its devastating effects were felt across the globe from Peru to Borneo and from Kenya to California. In the freak weather conditions, lives were shattered, homes swept away, crops destroyed, and fragile economies battered.

The first indication of an impending El Niño event came with a marked increase in water temperature along the Pacific coast of South America. The El Niño phenomenon then developed to stir up the entire Pacific ocean-atmosphere system, deranging the weather systems of both northern and southern hemispheres. In strong El Niño years like 1998, the trade winds slacken or reverse; warm water is then forced eastwards where it evaporates, giving torrential rains over South America while the west Pacific faces drought conditions.

Of course many of the people affected by El Niño knew nothing of the science, but they knew the consequences only too well. It began in Peru where five or six inches of rain a day fell in places, rivers broke their banks, villages were swept away, and lakes appeared on what had been arid wasteland. In other parts of the globe, El Niño's effects were entirely opposite. There were droughts in Indonesia, forest fires in Malaysia, and scorching temperatures in Mongolia. Flooding affected central Europe while Madagascar suffered cyclones. In the United States, from California to Mississippi, mudslides and flash floods wrought havoc. El Niño had done its worst and 1998 turned out to be one of the strongest El Niño years in the twentieth century.

Lorraine Brownbill

Date 1998

Country Worldwide

Why It's Key The 1998 El Niño was the second strongest in the twentieth century and wrought havoc on lives and livelihoods across the world.

Fact 2,100 died and global damage caused by El Niño was over US$33 billion.

Key Cultural Event
Moonlight Maze hackers target the Pentagon

The so-called Moonlight Maze attacks, which began in 1998, were a series of successful attempts to gain access to secure government websites in the United States through the Internet. Computer hackers infiltrated restricted sites, such as the Pentagon, NASA, and the Energy Department, and it is believed that the hackers were able to search through thousands of sensitive files and documents, accessing information relating to military codes, weapon guidance systems, and maps of military installations, among other protected items.

The operations continued undetected for more than a year and were described at the time as the largest sustained cyber attack in the world. The highly organized computer hackers were traced to Moscow, Russia, but it is not known conclusively whether the attacks originated there. Russia has denied any involvement with the activities.

In the aftermath of the Moonlight Maze attacks and the events of 9/11, experts all over the world speculated that cyber terrorism had arrived and should be treated as a real and sustained threat to international companies and governments in the future. As a result, the Pentagon ordered US$200 million worth of new security technology, and President Bush ordered a US$1.5 billion increase in spending on nationwide computer and network security. In 2006, the American government created MAJCOM, a task force designed to protect U.S. cyberspace.

Terence McSweeney

Date 1998

Country USA

Why It's Key Cyber terrorism becomes a worldwide issue.

Fact Threats of cyber terrorism have been increasing since the 1990s; it has been reported that there are more than a thousand cyber attacks on the U.S. government every year.

Key Political Event
The devaluation of the Russian rouble

In the summer of 1998, Russia was hit by an economic crisis, which revealed the fragility of the Russian economy and highlighted the difficulties of the transition from a centrally planned economy to a free market system, less than a decade after the end of Communist rule and the establishment of the Russian Federation.

There were many determining factors in the crisis, which led to Yeltsin devaluing the rouble on August 17; each could be considered small in isolation, but when combined, they threatened to destabilize the economic infrastructure of one of the largest countries in the world. As early as March, when Yeltsin fired his prime minister and cabinet, warning signs were emerging. Declining demand for oil and other key Russian export goods, dependence on short-term borrowing, non-payment of taxes by industries, and an artificially high exchange rate saw foreign investors fleeing the Russian markets in the wake of the Asian financial crisis.

When inflation rates hit 84 per cent, several leading Russian banks were forced to close down. Yeltsin was forced to devalue the rouble on August 17, 1998, and he imposed a further moratorium on external debt. The devaluation affected people from all walks of life; many large businesses became bankrupt, and ordinary people saw their life savings reduced to almost nothing overnight.

While Russia recovered relatively quickly as demand for exports returned, Yeltsin's reputation was in a state of decline. Within two years he resigned and was replaced by Vladimir Putin.

Terence McSweeney

Date January 2, 1998

Country Russia

Why It's Key One of the most powerful countries in the world experiences a monetary crisis.

Key Cultural Event
The FDA approves Viagra

The creation of Viagra, the "little blue pill" that has revived the sex lives of men across the planet, involved hundreds of scientists and the accidental discovery of its sexual side effects. Originally, inventors Andrew Bell, Dr David Brown, and Dr Nicholas Terrett at the Pfizer offices in Kent in the UK discovered that the chemical compounds belonging to the pyrazolopyrimidinone class could be used to treat heart problems. Terrett then patented Sildenafil as a form of heart medicine in 1991, giving it the trade name "Viagra."

Trial studies of the drug in 1994 revealed that not only did it help the heart, but also increased blood flow to the penis, even in men who suffered from erectile dysfunction. Peter Dunn and Albert Wood, also Pfizer employees in Kent, then developed the nine-step process to synthesize a Sildenafil compound into a pill. On March 27, 1998, the Food and Drug Administration (FDA) approved Viagra as the first pill to treat impotence.

Within days of its release, Viagra became a worldwide phenomenon. Doctors wrote up more than 100,000 prescriptions for it per week at US$10 per pill in the United States alone. Just three months later, two million prescriptions had been given in the United States, and impotent men in other countries were paying hundreds of dollars for the pill on the black market. US$1 billion in sales were made in Viagra's first year of production, and the drug continues to sell successfully to impotent men everywhere.
Bianca Jackson

Date March 27, 1998

Country USA

Why It's Key The FDA's approval of Viagra gave impotent men a chance for an active sex life.

Fact A number of court cases have been brought against Pfizer as patients report negative side effects. Joseph Moran, a car dealer from New Jersey, filed a US$110 million lawsuit after the pill allegedly made him see blue sparks coming out of his fingers, causing him to black out and crash into two cars.

702

Key Political Event
The Good Friday Agreement

"Sunningdale for slow learners," quipped moderate nationalist Séamus Mallon, was the essence of the Good Friday Agreement signed by members of various political parties of Northern Ireland and the Irish and British governments in April 1998. Mallon's statement was more than a mere witticism, as the Good Friday Agreement reflected to a considerable degree the institutions envisaged by the Sunningdale Agreement of 1973.

The Good Friday Agreement was the result of a torturous political process that had been gaining momentum since the early 1990s. After numerous false starts, multiparty talks in Northern Ireland, chaired by former U.S. senator George Mitchell, began in earnest in 1997. Almost all major parties (a notable exception being the Democratic Unionist Party) and the two governments attended these talks.

The agreement reached provided for the creation of numerous institutions, such as a legislative assembly for Northern Ireland and a North-South ministerial council, to replace direct British rule. Referenda in both Northern and the Republic of Ireland accepted the agreement in May 1998.

Despite broad support, the agreement has been subject to sustained opposition from the outset by political and paramilitary forces. The most notable example of this was the Omagh bombing carried out by dissident republicans in August 1998. In spite of difficulties in implementing controversial elements of the agreement, it has, nonetheless, proved to be the beginning of inclusive and stable government in Northern Ireland.
Denis Casey

Date April 10, 1998

Country Republic of Ireland/UK

Why It's Key The Good Friday Agreement has provided the basis for peaceful, inclusive government in Northern Ireland.

Key Political Event
Pakistan and India test nuclear weapons

Between May 11 and May 13, 1998, India detonated five nuclear devices at its Pokhran underground site. Following these successful tests, India's regional archrival Pakistan detonated six devices of its own between May 28 and May 30, 1998. In doing so, Pakistan became the seventh country, and the first Muslim-majority nation, to conduct a successful nuclear test. Pakistan, which had been defeated by India in three wars since 1947, now had a credible deterrent to wield against its chief enemy.

Pakistan's strategic reasoning for joining the nuclear club was simple. India had had nuclear weapons since 1974 and, with its advantage in conventional forces, posed an existential threat to Pakistan. Though the United States, the European Union, and other world powers rejected this strategic calculus and condemned both India's tests and Pakistan's entry into the nuclear club, condemnation did not translate into international action against either country. Pakistan entered into a security partnership with the United States soon after the 9/11 attacks while the United States and India signed a civil nuclear energy cooperation pact in 2006. Despite a border conflict in 1999, India and Pakistan have not gone to war since 1971, perhaps proving that the advent of nuclear weapons in South Asia has rendered war unthinkable. Nonetheless, much of the global strategic community still worries that a Pakistani warhead will be stolen by, or deployed on behalf of, militant Islamists.

Demir Barlas

Date May 11, 1998

Country India/Pakistan

Why It's Key The emergence of a new player in the nuclear club raised the strategic stakes in South Asia and continues to generate fear and insecurity in the West.

Key Cultural Event
Microsoft accused of abusive monopoly

The accusations of an anti-competitive ideology from the twenty U.S. states were grounded in the Department of Justice (DOJ)'s questioning of Microsoft business practices in 1994. The DOJ reached a settlement with Microsoft that explicitly required them not to tie in competitive software such as the Microsoft Internet browser with the sale of Microsoft Windows packages.

The lawsuits in 1998, officially known as the *United States v. Microsoft*, came directly because Microsoft had continued to sell the Internet browser with Windows; now Windows 98 with Internet-focused features that arguably favored the Microsoft software. Microsoft claimed in their defense that the browser was a feature and not a product.

The prosecution of the DOJ judged that Microsoft had indeed manipulated the coding of software in order to damage the sales prospects of rival competition and maintain its corporate monopoly, as well as threatening PC manufacturers with the removal of Windows distribution licenses should they not include the Microsoft Internet browser as part of the package.

In 2001, the DOJ ruled that Microsoft was required to share its application interface with third-party companies until November 2007, and that Microsoft be split into one entity for Microsoft Windows and one for software. Despite many states filing appeals about the leniency of the punishment, many economic commentators saw this government intrusion into capitalist business practices as a dangerous watershed for the free market economy.

Greg Pittard

Date May 18, 1998

Country USA

Why It's Key Twenty U.S. states filed lawsuits against Microsoft alleging that they were abusing their monopoly of domestic computer sales, resulting in controversial government intrusion.

Key Political Event
President Suharto resigns

Born to a peasant family in Dutch-controlled central Java, Suharto always longed for Indonesian independence. When Japan invaded during World War II, he joined the Japanese militia against the Dutch, and after Japan's withdrawal in 1945, he joined the new Indonesian army. Suharto quickly became a leading military figure, heading the Indonesian National Revolution. By 1968, Indonesia gained independence, and Suharto had seized power from President Sukarno.

Over the next three decades, Suharto led an authoritarian militarist government under his "*Orde Baru*" (New Order) regime. He heavily stressed national security, and outlawed the Communist parties and ethnic Chinese, leading to many political purges and executions of Chinese-Indonesians. Thanks to his economic and industrial reforms, Indonesia's wealth increased, but it was largely distributed to Suharto's family members and business partners. Nevertheless, Suharto's strong anti-communist views won him the support of the West. Indonesia rejoined the UN, and continued its influential role in ASEAN.

Throughout his rule, Suharto deflected the issue of succession, but by 1997, the nation was suffering an economic crisis. By the time Suharto was elected to a seventh term in March 1998, university students were demanding democratic reform. In May, police shot six students during a demonstration, triggering two days of arson and looting in Jakarta in which some 500 people died. Suharto lost the support of political and military leaders, and on May 21, he resigned. Since then, charges of genocide against him have failed due to his ill health.
Mariko Kato

Date May 21, 1998

Country Indonesia

Why It's Key Suharto's controversial dictatorship remains a point of heated debate across the world.

Fact Like many Indonesians, Suharto has only one name. When he is discussed in relation to his religion, he is sometimes called Mohammed Suharto.

opposite President Suharto announces his resignation during a live broadcast on Indonesian television.

Key Political Event
U.S. Embassies bombed in Kenya and Tanzania

Three years before the world-altering events of 9/11, the al-Qaeda terrorist network headed by Osama bin Laden was indicted by the United States for two simultaneous attacks on its embassies in the East African capitals of Nairobi, Kenya and Dar es Salaam, Tanzania.

Both attacks came at 10:45 am local time when trucks loaded with explosives were detonated close to the embassies, killing at least 212 people in Nairobi and a further eleven in Dar es Salaam. Although most of the casualties were African, the attacks were aimed squarely at the United States and its foreign policy in the Middle East. Bin Laden himself made a series of bizarre accusations against the Clinton administration, claiming it had orchestrated the Rwandan genocide and had plans to partition Sudan.

President Clinton's response to the attacks was swift. Addressing the nation on primetime television, he gave the order for Operation Infinite Reach, a series of cruise missile strikes on suspected terrorist targets in Sudan and Afghanistan. One of the primary targets, the al-Shifa pharmaceutical factory in Khartoum, was suspected of producing VX nerve agent and having close ties to al-Qaeda. However, these claims were later shown to be unsubstantiated and could have resulted in the deaths of thousands of Sudanese civilians who were deprived of life-saving drugs.

Of the 21 people indicted by the U.S. for their involvement with the bombings, two were killed and ten have been captured. The whereabouts of the remaining nine, including Osama bin Laden, are still unknown.
Jay Mullins

Date August 7, 1998

Country Kenya/Tanzania

Why It's Key The attacks catapulted al-Qaeda into the public consciousness with Osama bin Laden placed on the FBI's Top 10 Most Wanted list.

FEBRUARY 20, 2006

www.time.com AOL Keyword: TIME

WHO'S BEHIND THE CARTOON MAYHEM? ■ BEING OBAMA

TIME

CAN WE TRUST
Google
WITH OUR SECRETS?

An exclusive inside look at the $100 billion empire that is dominating the Internet

BY ADI IGNATIUS

Google honchos, from top, Larry Page, Eric Schmidt and Sergey Brin

Key Cultural Event
Google founded

Stanford computer science graduate students Larry Page and Sergey Brin disagreed on most topics with strongly opinionated viewpoints. However, they found common ground when they started discussing the problem of computer information retrieval. From 1996 until 1998, Sage and Brin collaborated on perfecting an Internet search engine known at that time as Back Rub. Their improved search technology gained a reputation among university campuses.

In 1988, Page and Brin began searching for potential business investors. Unable to solicit interest from any large corporations, Page and Brin decided to start the company on their own. They raised an initial investment of nearly US$1 million and set up an office in a friend's garage. On September 9, 1998, Google opened its doors for the first time in Mountain View, California.

Today, Google is one of the most successful companies in the world. It provides not only one of the largest currently available Internet search engines, but it also has expanded to provide a wide host of online tools for organizing information, such as directions, mail, photos, and videos. Known for its relaxed and lively corporate culture, Google provides its employees with ample amenities and recreational facilities, including gyms, massage rooms, video games, pool tables, and ping-pong tables. The company also encourages initiative and creativity by allowing employees to spend 20 per cent of their work time on any Google-related projects they may be interested in. Google has changed the world by providing instantaneous and well-organized access to all types of information.
Anne Hsu

Date September 9, 1998

Country USA

Why It's Key Google opened its doors, providing what would become the world's largest search engine, and becoming a world-famous enterprise and corporate culture.

opposite The founders of Google make the cover of *Time* magazine.

1990–1999

707

Key Political Event
Mass graves found near Lake Radonjic

Years of ethnic tension preceded the Kosovo War, and spilled over into blind hatred and humanitarian atrocities. The predominantly Albanian-populated Kosovo had been vehemently calling for secession from the FYR since World War I, but until 1997, the protests and defiance had remained non-violent. In 1990, Kosovo's autonomy within the FYR had been revoked, and after years of unsuccessful peace protests led by the Democratic League of Kosovo under Ibrahim Rugova, pockets of radicals formed the Kosovo Liberation Army, which sought to threaten the government into action.

After minor attack,s the KLA's missions became more violent. In December 1997, the Serbian police responded by killing thirty Albanian civilians, becoming the first major violent act of the war. Emergency negotiations failed, and as the KLA grew in number,

they advanced further, claiming territories that were key to the nation's fuel supplies near Orahovac. All the Serbian men from the local village were reported missing and later found dead.

The war escalated to disaster when the FYR police found thirty-four bodies near Glodjane on September 9, 1998. Compounded by the findings of mutilated bodies of Serbian families two weeks later, the FYR secret police of Slobodan Milošević struck back with force, systematically attacking villages and immediately forcing 45,000 ethnic Albanians to flee to Albania and Montenegro. Approximately 300,000 were displaced from Kosovo, and widespread torture was enacted against those arrested by the FYR secret police, which saw the bodies slain by the KLA as justification for the atrocities.
Greg Pittard

Date September 9, 1998

Country Former Yugoslav Republic (now Serbia)

Why It's Key The bodies found by the police signaled a humanitarian emergency.

Key Political Event
The arrest of General Pinochet

General Augusto Pinochet had presided over the military junta in Chile until 1990, and during that time was suspected of ordering the killing of thousands of political opponents, who became known as "the disappeared."

While visiting Britain in 1998 for medical treatment, British authorities detained Pinochet after his extradition was requested by Spain, where he was being investigated over the deaths of Spanish citizens during his years in power.

The case provoked worldwide interest with human rights groups calling for justice for the thousands of people who had gone missing in Chile during the Pinochet years. However, Pinochet was in his eighties and in ill-health, and after two years of house arrest,

he was allowed to return home after a British court ruled that he was physically unfit to stand trial.

The aging general returned to Chile to be greeted by thousands of waving supporters. However, this popularity did not extend to the country's judiciary, and Pinochet was stripped of his immunity to prosecution and indicted on a series of charges. These related to murders and kidnappings of political opponents carried out in 1973 by a military hit squad called the "Caravan of Death."

Once again he was declared unfit to stand trial, but was ordered before the courts in 2005 on similar charges. However, Pinochet died on December 10, 2006, before he could be brought before a court.
Martin Sayers

Date October 16, 1998

Country UK

Why It's Key Pinochet's arrest showed that former dictators who were suspected of human rights abuses were no longer safe from international justice.

708

Key Political Event
"Land-For-Peace" agreement signed

It was the first time Yasser Arafat had ridden a bicycle for fifty years. With his security forces following, the sixty-nine-year-old Palestinian leader rode the pathways of the Wye River Plantation, his checked *keffiyeh* blowing in the breeze – a rare moment of fun in a long, hard week.

President Bill Clinton had invited Arafat and Israeli Prime Minister Benjamin Netanyahu to Maryland to try to restart the Middle East peace process, stalled for more than eighteen months. For the first four days, Palestinian and Israeli negotiators rehashed old grievances. Then followed four days of diplomatic door slamming and theatrics.

"We are going to stay here until we finish this," Clinton announced on Thursday morning. "We are going to finish it today, or we're not going to finish it."

Thus began "The Longest Day," a marathon twenty-one-hour negotiation session that resulted in the Wye River Memorandum. In the agreement, both parties affirmed their commitment to the 1995 Oslo II accords, which had mapped out a phased withdrawal from the Palestinian West Bank. However, withdrawals were dependent on the Palestinians meeting political benchmarks, with the United States playing a large role in monitoring their progress. Palestinians stood to win back two-fifths of their territory.

"In the end, after all the twists and turns and ups and downs, all their late and ultimately sleepless nights, both reaffirmed their commitment to the path of peace," Clinton said at the White House signing ceremony. "And for that, the world can be grateful."
Heather Michon

Date October 23, 1998

Country USA

Why It's Key The agreement restarted stalled Middle East peace negotiations.

Key Political Event
Gerhard Schröder wins German election

Helmut Kohl, the longest-serving German chancellor since Otto von Bismarck a century before, spent sixteen years (1982–1998) at the head of a majority coalition that included his moderately Conservative Christian Democrats, their Bavarian sister party, the Christian Social Union, and the small, free-market-oriented Free Democratic Party. Kohl rode the wave of German reunification in 1990 to renewed popularity, but scandals and persistently high unemployment later made him vulnerable at the polls.

In 1998, the Social Democrats, the major left-of-center party, chose a candidate for chancellor who could match Kohl's popular appeal. Reinforcing Gerhard Schröder's promises of change was the Social Democrats' firm commitment to their potential coalition partner, the small Green Party. The Greens,

founded in 1980 by environmentalists and peace activists, had never before come close to power. Their scruffy and strident leaders had seemed to pose a threat to the quiet respectability of German politics, which was oriented to the big business that found its home with the Christian Democrats and the big labor unions allied with the Social Democrats. The Greens still had a militant wing, committed to radical change, but the party's public face in 1998, and the expected foreign minister in a "Red-Green" cabinet, was Joschka Fischer, a former 1960s radical now widely respected even within the political establishment. Schröder's and Fischer's parties won a clear majority and went on to rule for seven years.

Brian Ladd

Date October 27, 1998

Country Germany

Why It's Key An election swept not only a new chancellor but also the new Green Party into power.

1990–1999

709

Key Disaster
Hurricane Mitch

Hurricane Mitch began as a tropical storm in the Caribbean Sea on October 22, but grew into one of the most devastating Atlantic hurricanes ever recorded. By October 26, winds near its center peaked at 180 miles per hour, leaving a trail of death and destruction in their wake. A slow-moving storm, it deposited historic amounts of rainfall – a major factor in the huge loss of life. In southern Honduras, for example, 25 inches of rain fell in 36 hours between October 29 and 31.

The countries that bore the brunt of the storm were Honduras, Nicaragua, Guatemala, and El Salvador with appalling numbers of dead and missing in each. Many unidentified victims were buried in mass graves making accurate estimates of the final death toll difficult. In Nicaragua, thousands died in floods and

mudslides. In Honduras, 70 per cent of the country's crops were destroyed. In El Salvador, 500,000 were made homeless. In Guatemala, 28 bridges and 31 highways were destroyed. The economic cost of Hurricane Mitch to these Central American countries was devastating. Indeed, the Honduran President claimed it destroyed fifty years of progress in his country. Hurricane Mitch went on to claim lives in Belize, Panama, Costa Rica, Jamaica, and Mexico before heading for Florida where tornadoes and winds still caused major damage.

Eventually, international debt repayments for the region were suspended and the United States put together a multi-million dollar aid package.

Lorraine Brownbill

Date October 29, 1998

Country Caribbean/Central America (the hurricane started in Honduras)

Why It's Key One of the deadliest and most powerful hurricanes on record in the Atlantic basin, the storm was the thirteenth tropical storm, ninth hurricane, and third major hurricane of the 1998 Atlantic Hurricane season.

Fact 19,000 people were killed and 2.7 million left homeless.

Key Political Event
USA and UK launch air strikes on Iraq

The Gulf War of 1991 ended with a ceasefire agreement requiring Iraq to comply with UN weapons inspections, under pressure of damaging economic sanctions. Initially, Saddam Hussein denied ever possessing weapons of mass destruction (WMDs), but inspectors discovered that Iraq had destroyed stockpiles of biological and chemical weapons at the end of the war, and was secretly trying to develop further WMDs through dual-capability research facilities. Hussein sporadically cooperated with and defied UN inspectors, torn between wanting the economic sanctions lifted, and wanting to uphold the appearance of a dangerous arsenal of weapons.

U.S. President Bill Clinton used air strikes a number of times to punish intransigence from Hussein. In 1993, the U.S. launched two attacks on Iraq, one in response to an alleged assassination attempt on former U.S. President George Bush. In 1996, the United States attacked again to keep Hussein from agitating a domestic Kurdish dispute. In November of 1998, Hussein outright refused to cooperate, eventually banning inspectors from Iraq. In response, the United States launched Operation Desert Fox on December 16, from airstrips in Kuwait. The UK sent fighter jets the next day, and the two nations carried out precision bombing against one hundred facilities over four days. The operation was not UN sanctioned, and domestic and international critics declared the offensive illegal and accused Clinton of deflecting attention from his impending impeachment in connection with the Monica Lewinsky adultery scandal.

David Anderson

Date December 16, 1998

Country Iraq

Why It's Key In a move eerily foreshadowing the Iraq War of 2003, the United States and UK joined forces, without UN sanction, to use military action instead of diplomacy against Iraq.

Key Political Event
Introduction of the euro

Europe learned from World War II: since 1945, the trend has been for closer integration to prevent any conflict like a world war from breaking out again by fostering closer political, economic, social, and cultural ties across the continent. The European Economic Community started with just six members from Western Europe in 1957, but by 2007, its successor, the European Union, stretched from the Atlantic to Russia, encompassing twenty-seven countries and 500 million people. A single European currency was aimed at securing this union irrevocably.

On January 1, 1999, this plan came to fruition, with the euro being introduced across eleven nations. The euro's first manifestation was electronic, allowing people in the Eurozone to bank in it and use it in travelers' checks. Although national currencies still existed, they were tied to the euro and so had no individual value. On January 1, 2002, coins and notes were introduced and the other currencies abolished; each country produces euros with its own national symbols on the back, but these are accepted across borders.

As an economic shift, it inevitably made business across Europe much simpler. But as a cultural change, it was initially unpopular in some countries, with claims that firms used it to inflate their prices. It quickly became accepted and will soon embrace most of the European Union (although the UK still firmly retains the pound), fulfilling its devisers' dream.

Josh Spero

Date January 1, 1999

Country Europe

Why It's Key The euro brought the ever-closer union of Europe to the pockets of its peoples in a fundamental and tangible way.

Key Cultural Event
West Nile virus outbreak in United States

Predominantly found in Africa, West Asia, and the Middle East, the West Nile virus is believed to have emerged over a thousand years ago, and is passed mainly through mosquitoes. However, it was only in 1999 that the first cases of West Nile were seen in the western hemisphere. The Center for Disease Control and Prevention (CDC) officially recognized the presence of the West Nile virus in New York in a press statement on September 30, 1999, after persistent outbreaks of encephalitis began the previous month. No one is certain as to how the virus came to North America. Many theories exist, including that the disease traveled through an infected migratory bird. Initially, the cases of West Nile virus were predominantly mild and sparse, but gradually the severity of the cases increased, with 149 cases and 18 fatalities reported over the next few years.

The situation worsened dramatically post-2001, with over 4,000 instances reported and 284 deaths. It was clear that in most cases of the disease, there were few to no symptoms, but those with weakened immune systems and the elderly experienced far worse effects – namely serious neurological damage and Parkinson's disease.

Since 2003, the death toll has risen by hundreds each year, and the problem has been fueled by infected blood transfusions. Despite research, there is still no known cure for the West Nile virus, which has made containment of the disease the national health services' priority. Treatment of patients has cost the government over US$200 million.

Greg Pittard

Date 1999

Country USA

Why It's Key The West Nile virus immediately spread throughout North America, killing hundreds of people and costing millions of dollars to government health funds.

Fact The West Nile virus was first isolated from a febrile adult woman in the West Nile district of Uganda in 1937.

Key Political Event
Clinton-Lewinsky scandal

When Democratic President, Bill Clinton, after months of denial, conceded in August 1998 that he had indeed had a sexual relationship three years earlier with twenty-four-year-old White House intern Monica Lewinsky, his aides hoped that it would bring an end to the investigation by independent prosecutor Kenneth Starr. However, in December the House Judiciary Committee proposed four articles of impeachment against the president, including charges that he had committed perjury before a federal grand jury and had obstructed justice in a previous civil case brought against him.

The president's troubles had started four years earlier when Starr began an inquiry into Clinton's land deals when he was governor of Arkansas. The investigation moved into the president's private life,

and the allegations that he had an affair with Lewinsky and then lied about it under oath in a previous sexual harassment case brought by Paula Jones. Lewinsky had also denied the affair but, by August 1998, after being offered immunity by Starr in return for a full testimony, she admitted that she had had sex with Clinton.

The impeachment trial lasted over a month with prosecutors claiming Clinton had disregarded the law and betrayed his oath of office to hide the affair. In February 1999, senators acquitted him of the impeachment charges of perjury and obstruction of justice by a vote of 55–45. Many senators did not feel that Clinton's actions constituted "high crimes and misdemeanors" specified by the Constitution as grounds for removal from office.

Lorraine Brownbill

Date 1999

Country USA

Why It's Key The fact that Bill Clinton had misled the American people and lied under oath about the affair resulted in him being only the second president in American history to face an impeachment charge.

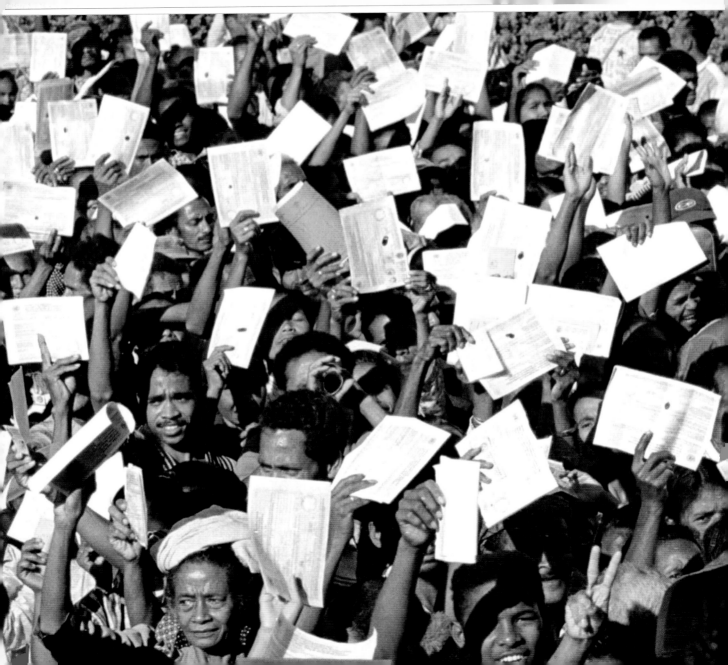

Key Political Event
The people of East Timor vote for independence

The island of Timor lies about 400 miles north of Darwin, Australia, across the Timor Sea. Controlled by the Portuguese since the sixteenth century, the people of the island's eastern half had grown into a placid colonial outpost. When the Portuguese decolonized in 1975, the Timorese proclaimed their independence, only to be invaded by neighboring Indonesia.

For the next quarter century, the Timorese lived under brutal Indonesian rule, with between 60,000 to 200,000 civilian deaths in 24 years out of a population of less than 700,000. In November 1991, Indonesian police killed 200 to 400 protestors trapped in a cemetery in Dili, an event that became known as the Dili Massacre.

The tragedy united Portugal, Australia, and the United States in favor of Timorese self-rule, and over the next eight years, there was increasing pressure for a peaceful solution. The independence movement quickly grew. Later that year, the UN convinced Indonesia to hold a referendum on the question of independence. On August 30, 1999, the Timorese went to the polls to choose between full independence, and becoming an autonomous Indonesian province. The vote wasn't even close: 78.5 per cent of voters chose independence.

The joyous occasion soon turned bloody: the Indonesian military launched a "scorched earth" policy of reprisals, leading to 2,000 civilian deaths and the destruction of 75 per cent of the country's infrastructure. The UN quickly approved a multinational stabilization force, called INTERFET, which kept order until the Democratic Republic of Timor Leste formally arrived on May 20, 2002. Peace and security remain elusive.

Heather Michon

Date August 30, 1999

Country East Timor

Why It's Key Independence after centuries of outside rule and the birth of the first new state of the twenty-first century resulted in huge massacres.

Fact Timorese peace activists Carlos Filipe Ximenes Belo and José Ramos Horta shared the 1996 Nobel Peace Prize for their work in gaining independence.

opposite Timorese voters gather outside a polling station.

1990–1999

721

Key Cultural Event
Boys Don't Cry released

The movies had showcased gender-bending characters before, but nothing came close to the haunting performance by Hilary Swank in *Boys Don't Cry*. Based on a real incident in Nebraska six years earlier, the movie starred Swank as Brandon Teena, a woman posing as a man, who successfully hid her true physical status for an extended time before the revelation of her secret led to her eventual rape and murder at the hands of outraged locals. The movie was released to great critical acclaim and built up a steady reputation. Its success ultimately paved the way for Swank to win an Oscar for her performance (Chloe Sevigny, as the woman that Brandon falls for, garnered a Best Supporting Actress nomination).

The phenomenal winning streak of the movie marked a major turning point in the history of independent cinema. Directed by first-time filmmaker Kimberly Bierce with the minor budget of roughly US$2 million, *Boys Don't Cry* made back its production costs many times over, gathering over US$11 million during the course of its theatrical run. It was a particularly surprising feat due to the graphic nature of the rape scene, which nearly resulted in the movie receiving an NC–17 rating (a marketing nightmare). While some people familiar with the source material contested the veracity of some details in the film, the provocative nature of the story was unavoidable. The movie wound up having a contemporary hook when a young man named Matthew Shepherd was murdered in a gay discrimination crime.

Eric Kohn

Date September 2, 1999

Country USA

Why It's Key The movie publicized the plight of many transgendered individuals, while showing that small-budget films could win Oscars as well as any others.

Fact Swank prepared for the role by actually pretending to be a man.

Key Political Event
WTO protest in Seattle

With the collapse of the Soviet Union and the end of the Cold War in 1991, the worldwide system of capitalism appeared to be virtually unchallenged. Scholars such as Francis Fukuyama declared "the end of history," arguing that the ideals of liberal democracy and the free market had triumphed over all possible alternatives. The vibrant economic growth of the 1990s seemed to bear out this idea, especially in the United Kingdom and United States.

It came as a surprise to many, then, when environmentalists in turtle costumes, black-hooded anarchists, and blue-collar union members hit the streets of Seattle, Washington to protest the meeting of the World Trade Organization, an international body that judges trade disputes between nations. A few radical participants clashed with police and broke the windows of stores like Starbucks, but most protesters were peaceful. The activists derided the WTO, the World Bank, and the International Monetary Fund for serving the interests of multinational corporations and making decisions without being elected by the people they affected. Meanwhile, critics likened the demonstrators to "flat earthers" who refused to believe the world is round; opponents of globalization, they said, failed to understand capitalism or offer a real alternative to it. In any case, "the battle in Seattle" inspired further protests at meetings of world financial institutions, notably in Washington, DC and Genoa, Italy, as activists worked to create a movement that questioned the consequences of globalization.

Alex Cummings

Date November 29, 1999

Country USA

Why It's Key A decade of political complacency in America ended when disputes over globalization broke out in the streets of Seattle.

722

Key Political Event
Yeltsin succeeded by Putin

On December 31, 1999, Russian president Boris Yeltsin dramatically resigned, leaving his Prime Minister, a relatively unknown Vladimir Putin, as the acting president of the Russian Federation, and making him one of the most powerful men in the world. Yeltsin's decline in popularity came about after a disastrous withdrawal from Chechnya, and continued and frequently drastic cabinet upheavals. These, combined with his eccentric behavior on the world stage, saw his public approval rating drop to almost zero.

Putin's rise from political neophyte and KGB intelligence officer in the 1980s to Kremlin aide, prime minister, and then president was meteoric. Yeltsin's expected opponents had been the renowned former prime minister, Yevgeny Primakov, and Moscow's mayor, Yuri Luzhkov, but both decided not to contest Putin in an election. He was then officially elected to the post on March 26, 2000.

While many expected Putin to respectfully carry out the wishes of the Kremlin elite, Putin's first actions as president marked him out as his own man. He sacked Yeltsin's daughter Tatyana Diachenko and several others who were closely associated with the former president.

Since 1999, Putin's impact on Russia has been considerable. Despite a presidency verging on autocracy and a sustained campaign of media suppression, he has enjoyed popular support at almost unheard of levels, presiding over a period of growth in the Russian economy and positioning Russia once again as a key player in world affairs.

Terence McSweeney

Date December 31, 1999

Country Russia

Why It's Key Vladimir Putin becomes the second president of Russia.

Fact Putin has a degree in law and a PhD in economics from Leningrad State University.

opposite Boris Yeltsin (right) waves a final farewell to the Kremlin as his successor, Vladimir Putin (left), looks on.

Key Cultural Event
Tobacco companies charged with civil racketeering

In 1994, Mississippi became the first American state to sue tobacco companies for monies spent on Medicare patients suffering from tobacco-related illnesses. The other forty-nine states followed suit, forcing tobacco companies to offer a settlement in 1998 of US$246 billion to be paid over twenty-five years. Five years later, Bill Clinton's Justice Department (DOJ) filed suit under the Racketeer Influenced and Corrupt Organizations Act (RICO), portraying tobacco companies as racketeers who had knowingly defrauded the public about the dangers of tobacco for fifty years. DOJ sought to recover US$280 billion in government funds that had been spent on medical treatment for federal employees, veterans, and Medicare and Medicaid patients. The government also wanted tobacco companies to pay for cancer research and stop-smoking programs.

As the case proceeded, a federal appeals court determined that RICO did not provide for forfeiture of illegal profits in civil cases. In 2007, U.S. District Court Judge Gladys Kessler found that tobacco companies had violated civil racketeering laws. She determined that they were continuing to defraud the public by hiding information about the effects of tobacco and were perpetuating their misdeeds by encouraging young people to buy their products. Because the appeals court had precluded a financial settlement, Kessler ordered tobacco companies to refrain from further racketeering, restricted efforts to make tobacco seem less harmful by deceptive advertising, and ordered acknowledgment of deception in newspapers and on television, web sites, and cigarette packages.
Elizabeth R. Purdy

Date 1999

Country USA

Why It's Key The Clinton administration succeeded in depicting tobacco companies as racketeers who had become rich spreading death and illness around the world, paving the way for a plethora of class-action lawsuits.

Fact According to the World Health Organization in 2006, the number of global deaths resulting from tobacco usage had risen to 4.9 million annually, an increase of 1.4 million in eight years.

Key Cultural Event
New millennium begins amid fears of Y2K

Around the world, billions of people celebrated as clocks struck midnight on the morning of January 1, 2000. The new era began in the Pacific Islands, with America being among the last to see in the New Year. In many countries the celebrations were the most spectacular ever seen with huge public firework displays starting at midnight, and public events such as parades taking place later in the day.

In the run-up to beginning of the the third millennium there had been worldwide concern that computer programs would fail due to the Y2K problem, or "millennium bug." This was due to the fact that in early computer program design, two digits were used to represent a year. It was thought that as the clocks turned to 2000, computer systems would revert to the year 1900 and therefore stop working properly. This

was potentially a major threat to large industries such as banks, utilities, and airlines. Many firms spent billions of dollars backing up their systems or upgrading their computers. But in the event, problems turned out to be very minor and there was no significant effect. Whether this was due to the preparations or owing to an overstatement of the problem still remains unclear, but to the relief of thousands, the new millennium began without a hitch.
Ros Bott

Date January 1, 2000

Country Worldwide

Why It's Key The New Year marked the end of the twentieth century and the dawn of the third millennium, symbolizing a turning point in history and causing worldwide celebrations.

Key Political Event
Britain restores the Northern Ireland parliament

Although the executive and institutions were restored three months later in May, Peter Mandelson (secretary of state for Northern Ireland) reintroduced direct rule through the Northern Ireland Act, which received royal assent on February 10, 2000.

The reason direct rule was reestablished was largely to do with the Irish Republican Army's (IRA) refusal to allow independent inspectors to visit their weapons dumps, which was the base of trust on which the Northern Ireland Assembly had been created. When talks between Sinn Féin (the political wing of the republican movement) and Ulster unionist parties broke down, Mandelson stepped in to bring back direct rule.

Prior to the June 1998 Assembly, three previous attempts at creating and sustaining an executive had been collapsed by the staunchest members of both sides, in 1973, 1974, and 1982. Until December 2, 1999, power rested in Westminster, and on February 10, 2000, Northern Ireland again was deemed unable to control her own destiny.

On May 30, the restoration of the executive gave ministers, chairmen, and deputy chairmen of governmental committees back their roles. There were two similar instances in the next six months, although the executive was suspended for only twenty-four hours on each occasion. The many decades of violent confrontation between the two factions has now largely ceased as a result of the power-sharing committee and the IRA's weapon decommissioning.

Greg Pittard

Date February 10, 2000

Country Northern Ireland

Why It's Key Decades of violence were to come to an end due to the power sharing executive.

Key Cultural Event Members of "The Movement for the Restoration of the Ten Commandments" cult die

In 1989, Joseph Kibwetere, a Ugandan schoolteacher and Catholic Church worker, attended a religious talk by Credonia Mwerinde, a former prostitute and beer merchant who claimed that the Virgin Mary told her to start a crusade to revive the Ten Commandments. Credonia convinced Joseph that the Virgin selected him to help, and he joined her and her two female associates, partly to give them credibility in a male-dominated society.

In 1992, Credonia and her comrades moved to Kanungu, where what began as a religious movement became a millennial cult called "The Movement for the Restoration of the Ten Commandments." The movement preached that on the eve of the year 2000, death, pestilence, famine, and war would come to everyone outside of the cult. People flocked to join, including ex-Catholic priests, local government officials, and police officers. Initiates were required to give their possessions to the cult, and members were prohibited from sex, medical care, makeup, soap, smoking, and drinking.

When, on January 1, 2000, doomsday did not arrive, members demanded their money back. The leadership responded by secretly and cruelly murdering groups of followers and burying them in mass graves, which were discovered later by investigators. The leaders promised the real doomsday would come on March 17, and on that day locked five hundred members in a chapel and ignited sulfuric acid and gasoline, causing an explosive fire which probably killed everyone rapidly.

David Anderson

Date March 17, 2000

Country Uganda

Why It's Key The event rivals the Jonestown Massacre as modern history's most horrific cult tragedy, with a total death toll of between 800 and 1,000 over almost four months. While Jonestown is believed to be a mass suicide, the Uganda tragedy is almost certainly mass homicide.

Fact Although the cult's leaders are believed to have died in the fire, whoever barred the doors from the outside is likely still alive.

Key Political Event
Zimbabwe siezes white farmers' land

From the very beginning of Zimbabwean independence, the redistribution of white-owned farmland to black farmers was a priority for President Robert Mugabe's government. The UK and other Western governments supported Mugabe's "willing buyer willing seller" program, which began in the 1980s to redress the inequalities of the past. However, the relationship between Zimbabwe and the governments funding the program began to break down in the 1990s after Mugabe removed the "willing buyer willing seller" clause. Land could now be taken regardless of whether the farmer wished to part with it, although he would still be compensated for his property.

The situation changed again in 2000, when a "fast track" resettlement program was announced on April 6, under which the government could acquire farmland for resettlement at any time, without compensating the owner. Implementation was disorganized and redistribution of the land haphazard, arousing widespread resistance from both farmers and members of the opposition, who alleged that land was only being allocated to Mugabe's cronies.

The commercial farming industry collapsed as large farms were taken over by inexperienced tenant farmers, and the country's staple and export crops were annihilated. The already struggling economy floundered and the population faced widespread famine, civil unrest, and violence. It had previously been known as the "bread basket" of Africa, but the implementation of the "fast track" land reform program meant that Zimbabwe was no longer able to feed itself.
Carly Fabian

Date April 6, 2000

Country Zimbabwe

Why It's Key This policy effectively destroyed the country's rich agriculture, severely weakened the economy, and caused much civil unrest.

Key Political Event
Sierra Leone hostage crisis

After 150 years as a British colony, Sierra Leone achieved independence in 1961. But the country was subsequently ruled by a succession of elite governments, which profited personally from its diamond trade, while the country remained in poverty. Dissatisfied with this corrupt and repressive government, Foday Sankoh created the Revolutionary United Front (RUF), a rebel guerrilla force, in 1991. Yet the RUF only worsened Sierra Leone's problems, launching attacks in an effort to take control of the diamond trade.

After a series of military coups, which saw the country fall into violent anarchy, the president, Ahmad Kabbah, and Sankoh formed a surprising peace agreement, apologizing for the atrocities committed previously. Although wary about the legitimacy of the settlement, the United Nations sent a peacekeeping force of 6,000 troops to the country to maintain order and curb violence, as the RUF continued to violate peace agreements. The UN proceeded to fight several pitched battles against the rebels, and after one such fight, 300 UN peacekeepers were taken hostage.

Sankoh, who had previously won amnesty and a seat in government, was held responsible. After he was captured in Freetown, the capital of Sierra Leone, the hostages began to be released. At the same time, sanctions were levelled against the RUF, and the UN Security Council banned the sale of so-called rough diamonds, which had played a large role in funding RUF activities throughout the civil war.

In 2002, Kabbah declared the civil war over, and agreed to begin war crimes trials.
Terence McSweeney

Date May 3, 2000

Country Sierra Leone

Why It's Key The hostage situation brought world attention to the worsening crisis in Sierra Leone.

Fact By 2002, Sierra Leone hosted the largest international peacekeeping force at that time: 17,500 troops.

Key Discovery
Genetic code is cracked

Although a rough draft of the human genome was first produced in the United States on June 26, 2000, the Human Genome Project was conducted at various research centers throughout the world, and was not completely finished until April 2003.

Our genetic code is made up of DNA (deoxyribonucleic acid), which is composed of four chemicals, called bases (abbreviated A, T, G, C). As these bases are repeated over and over again throughout our genome, the main goal of the project was to determine the sequencing of the bases. The order of the bases is important because it is the bases' code for proteins that provide instructions for the development of life and the diversity of species. DNA variations between species also offer a "history book" of how life on our planet progressed.

At the onset of the Human Genome Project, there was a debate as to whether the genetic information revealed should be made available without cost to the public. Some scientists feared the occurrence of genetic discrimination, or that those individuals who showed genetic susceptibility to a disease could face obstacles in attaining medical insurance or future employment. However, these fears seemed less imperative as private companies began to file thousands of patents on human genes. In a showdown between corporate and scientific interests, the international community decided to make the genome freely available. There continue to be legal questions as to whether past patents for human genes filed by private companies are valid.

Anna Marie Roos

Date June 26, 2000

Country USA

Why It's Key The identification of the 30,000 to 40,000 genes in human DNA helps us to understand human biology and to develop treatments for genetic disorders.

Fact The U.S. Human Genome Project was the first large scientific effort that at its onset addressed the ethical, legal, and social issues that would arise from its findings.

Key Disaster
Concorde crashes

Most of the passengers who boarded Air France Flight 4590 at Charles de Gaulle airport were holidaymakers looking forward to a luxury flight to New York before boarding a cruise ship bound for Ecuador. Two minutes after take off, the plane crashed and all 109 passengers and crew, and four people on the ground were killed.

Eyewitnesses reported that they had seen a fireball trailing from a left-side engine of the airplane during taking off. The French Accident Investigation Bureau later concluded that a piece of titanium debris, which had fallen from another plane, had started a catastrophic chain of events. The shard of metal shredded one of the plane's tires as it thundered down the runway. The tire burst, striking the underside of the plane's wing and rupturing a fuel tank, which ignited. It

was too late to abort take-off. The pilots fought to gain height to allow them to make an emergency landing at Le Bourget Airport. However, the voice recorder revealed pilot Christian Marty saying: "Too late... no time." Despite the crew's desperate efforts, they could not gain height, increase speed, or retract the undercarriage, and the plane crashed into a small hotel near the town of Gonesse, on the outskirts of Paris.

The crash was the beginning of the end for travel by Concorde and, although flights eventually resumed, after the 9/11 terrorist attacks in the United States there was a marked drop in transatlantic passengers. This, coupled with cost and environmental issues, led to the end of all Concorde flights.

Lorraine Brownbill

Date July 25, 2000

Country France

Why It's Key This was the first supersonic passenger airplane to crash and, although Concorde did continue to fly until 2003, it marked the beginning of the end for Concorde flights.

Fact The crash killed 109 people on board the aircraft and four on the ground.

Key Cultural Event
UN tackles poverty

In September 2000, member states met in New York for the United Nations Millennium Summit. The most pressing matter on the agenda was identifying goals in target areas to be accomplished by 2015. Approved by 189 nations, the eight Millennium Development Goals were: halving extreme poverty and hunger; achieving universal primary education; empowering women and promoting equality between men and women; reducing mortality for children under the age of five by two thirds; reducing maternal mortality by three fourths; checking the spread of diseases, with special attention to HIV/AIDS and malaria; protecting the environment through sustainable development; and providing financial assistance to developing countries through aid, trade, and debt relief. Because resources were limited in many developing countries, the United Nations worked closely with various international groups to help individual countries achieve the goals.

Although targets could not always be met by 2015, considerable progress has been made. Eradicating poverty was identified as the first MDG because poverty affects all aspects of life and often means the difference between life and death. Halfway through the target period, the 43 states that contain 60 per cent of the world's population had already halved extreme hunger and poverty. Great strides have also been made in enrolling children in primary school, increasing female literacy, improving health, providing safe drinking water and improved sanitation, and promoting economic development and stability.
Elizabeth R. Purdy

Date September 6, 2000

Country USA

Why It's Key International partnerships are essential for survival in developing countries that are unable to sustain their own populations, and these partnerships help to promote a stable global environment.

Fact Around the globe, more than a billion people subsist on less than US$1 a day, and four billion live on less than US$2 a day.

Key Political Event
Milosevic tried for war crimes

Slobodan Milosevic became President of Serbia in 1989 and immediately looked to assert his country's authority over the other member states of Yugoslavia. The result of this was the series of wars and conflicts that racked the Balkans for much of the 1990s. However, by the end of that decade, Milosevic's position was severely weakened, not least by the NATO bombing of Serbia, which ended the Kosovan war and damaged his strongman image.

By the time Milosevic called elections in September 2000, Serbia's economy was faltering and many Serbs were living in desperate poverty. Unsurprisingly, Milosevic lost the election but refused to recognize the opposition's victory. Hundreds of thousands of people took to the streets in protest and a national strike was declared, leading to Milosevic finally admitting defeat and stepping down as president. This was far from the end of Milosevic's problems. In 2000, he was arrested by Serbian police on corruption charges and subsequently handed over to the international war crimes tribunal at The Hague.

Milosevic's trial on charges of genocide and war crimes began in February 2002. He completely denied the allegations, alleging that the Serbs had been victims of a U.S. and European plan to break up the former Yugoslavia, and had simply been defending themselves. The trial made slow progress due to Milosevic's poor health, and on March 11, 2006, he was found dead in his prison cell after suffering a heart attack.
Martin Sayers

Date October 5, 2000

Country Yugoslavia (now Serbia)

Why It's Key The downfall and trial of one of the key players in the Balkan conflict signified the end of years of bloodshed in the former Yugoslavia.

Opposite **Slobodan Milosevic** on trial.

Key Cultural Event
Japanese government apologizes for leper colonies

On June 1, 2001, Japanese health minister Chikara Sakaguchi apologized to leprosy patients for a Japanese policy that had segregated them from society until 1996. After World War II, an international decree had called for the dismantlement of leper colonies after medical advances had deemed them unnecessary. However, in Japan, leprosy patients continued to be isolated under the 1953 Leprosy Prevention Law. They were confined in sanatoriums and forced to live in terrible conditions with little treatment. This law wasn't appealed until 1996.

On May 11, 2001, the Kumamoto district court ruled that the Japanese government must pay ¥1.82 billion to 27 plaintiffs. Though urged to appeal the court ruling, Japanese Prime Minister Junichiro Koizumi instead opted to issue an apology. In 2005, a committee revealed that the policy of colonizing leprosy patients was due to the unscrupulous relationship between Japanese business and bureaucracy, concluding that it was implemented by the Health and Welfare Ministry and the Japan Medical Association to secure larger budgets and keep doctors employed.

The leprosy scandal followed a string of other health-related controversies in Japan. One of the most notorious was the Health Ministry's failure to ban unheated blood products, despite knowledge of contamination risks. As a result, over 1,400 hemophiliacs were exposed to HIV. These scandals have been partly blamed on the hierarchical social structure in Japan, which makes criticism of powerful people and institutions difficult.

Anne Hsu

Date June 1, 2001

Country Japan

Why It's Key Found guilty of mistreating and colonizing leprosy patients, the Japanese government was forced to pay ¥1.82 billion in compensation.

Key Political Event
9/11 terrorist attacks

On the morning of September 11, 2001, nineteen young Arab men boarded four American commercial airliners. Unbeknown to the crew or passengers around them, the young Arabs belonged to a militant Islamic group called al-Qaeda, led by a man named Osama bin Laden. The men were terrorists; armed with knives, pepper spray, and basic piloting skills, they planned to hijack the planes.

At 8:46 a.m., American Airlines Flight 11, carrying ninety-two passengers and crew members, crashed into the North Tower of the World Trade Centre (WTC) in Lower Manhattan, New York. Shortly afterwards, at 9:03 a.m., a second commercial plane collided into the South Tower of the WTC. By noon that day, two more planes had dropped from the skies; one slamming into the Pentagon, and the other – apparently headed for the White House – into a field in southern Pennsylvania. International media outlets aired live coverage of the numerous attacks. The world watched horrified, as footage of people jumping from the burning buildings flickered across their television screens, and then, at 10:28 a.m., as the Twin Towers crumbled from the city's skyline forever.

Almost 3,000 people died as a result of the terrorist attacks of 9/11. The international community rallied behind the United States, one famous French newspaper headline reading: "We Are All Americans." President Bush declared a Global War on Terrorism, words that would shape the twenty-first century.

Annie Wang

Date September 11, 2001

Country USA

Why It's Key The attacks of 9/11 were one of the most devastating acts of terrorism on U.S. soil, and would mark the beginning of the international Global War on Terrorism.

opposite Suicide bombers fly planes into the towers of the World Trade Center.

Key Political Event
Anthrax attacks on the United States

Just a week after the events of September 11, letters containing anthrax spores were mailed to major media and political offices in the United States. The letters, addressed from New Jersey, contained anthrax in the form of a fine powder and the vehement messages "Death to Israel" and "Death to America." They were sent to the offices of ABC News, CBS News, NBC News, America Media Inc. and the *New York Post*.

On October 9, two further letters were sent to the Democratic senators Tom Daschle, of South Dakota, and Patrick Leahy, of Vermont. Fortunately, only Leahy's letter was opened. Out of the twenty-two people in total exposed to the spores, eleven inhaled the life-threatening variety, resulting in five deaths. However, dozens of buildings were contaminated, which propelled the Bush administration to spend hundreds of millions of dollars decontaminating postal facilities, US$1 billion cleaning up government buildings, and a further US$7 billion collectively on initiatives in chemical and drug research, and biochemical warfare.

Responsibility for the attacks was never claimed, so the origins of the anthrax remain unknown, despite early indications by the U.S. government of Iraqi and al-Qaeda involvement in the attacks. Debates over whether the anthrax was weaponized caused further controversy, and the implication of Iraqi activity alongside those responsible for 9/11 fueled political justification for U.S. insurgence into Iraq and the removal of Saddam Hussein.
Greg Pittard

Date September 18, 2001

Country USA

Why It's Key The anthrax attacks introduced a new and frightening form of terror, killing five people and triggering waves of panic across America.

opposite Buildings threatened by anthrax are decontaminated.

Key Political Event
Invasion of Afghanistan

Following the 9/11 attacks in 2001, U.S. officials quickly suspected the Islamic terrorist organization al-Qaeda, which had been implicated in numerous terrorist attacks on U.S. interests overseas since the early 1990s, including U.S. embassy bombings in Africa in 1998. It already had a history of small-scale holy war against the United States, and its leader, Osama bin Laden, publicly voiced support for the 9/11 attacks.

On September 18, 2001, U.S. Congress sanctioned the use of military force against those responsible for the 9/11 attacks, and on September 20, President George W. Bush used the phrase "war on terror" for the first time in a speech before Congress, naming al-Qaeda as the specific target, but also including "every terrorist group of global reach" as the broader enemy. Eventually, the term became the "Global War on Terrorism." Nations harboring terrorists were deemed as culpable as the terrorists, and on October 7, the U.S. government launched a military campaign against Afghanistan, where al-Qaeda was based.

The Taliban, Afghanistan's Islamic fundamentalist government, was ousted at the end of 2001 by U.S. forces and anti-Taliban rebels. The U.S. efforts to capture and kill al-Qaeda and Taliban leaders continued, though bin Laden escaped and al-Qaeda and Taliban forces proved difficult to defeat, extending the operation indefinitely. In 2003, the Afghanistan mission was taken over by NATO, after the United States expanded the War on Terrorism to Iraq.
David Anderson

Date October 7, 2001

Country Afghanistan

Why It's Key The invasion marked the beginning of the Bush administration's Global War on Terrorism, an approach to foreign and domestic policy characterized by heightened national security, including the use of punitive and preemptive military force in the Middle East.

Key Cultural Event
The iPod is born

In early 2001, Steve Jobs, the CEO of Apple Computer, noticed that although many companies had come out with digital music players, none of them was remotely desirable to the average consumer. He ordered his engineers to produce a better one, which he wanted on sale by Christmas that year. It had to be easy to use, gorgeous to look at, and powerful enough to hold an entire record collection in a jeans pocket.

With British industrial designer Jonathan Ive responsible for the machine's unique white plastic sheen, Jobs' team came up with the iPod, which, in its various incarnations, has now sold over 100 million units. Although it has countless competitors, it still dominates the market. Fashion designer Karl Lagerfeld reportedly owns seventy. The biggest change brought about by the iPod was that music no longer needed to

have anything to do with a physical object. Many iPod users rip all of their CDs to their computer, and then pack the CDs off to storage. Others bypass CDs entirely, using Apple's own iTunes online store to buy music as digital files. Still others use various illegal file-sharing services to download pirated music, sending conventional record labels into a panic from which they may never recover. Today, many children grow up barely aware that music was ever something you needed to buy in a shop and hold in your hand.
Ned Beauman

Date 2001

Country USA

Why It's Key With the launch of the first mass-market digital music player, Apple boss Steve Jobs forever altered the way that music is consumed.

Key Cultural Event
Enron goes bankrupt

Enron started as a small Texas energy company, but by the early 1990s it had become the United States' seventh biggest company. It was also one of the most admired, named "America's Most Innovative Company" six times by *Fortune* magazine. But despite posting startling financial results and seeing its share price climb to US$90, the company was in serious trouble. A series of complex partnership deals had deliberately removed US$500 million of Enron's debt from its balance sheet, and artificially inflated its financial position by over US$580 million between 1997 and the time of its collapse.

In October 2001, Enron stunned the market by announcing a US$638 million loss and write-offs totalling US$1.2 billion. The situation deteriorated rapidly and on December 2, the company filed for

the largest bankruptcy in U.S. corporate history. Enron's debts topped US$16 billion and its share price dropped to less than US$1, leaving banks, investors, and employees facing huge losses.

In 2002, the first Enron managers were charged with money laundering and fraud, and the audit firm Arthur Andersen was accused of having shredded tons of Enron documents, a charge that eventually led to its own collapse. In 2006 Enron's high profile CEO, Kenneth Lay, and his second in command, Jeffrey Skilling, were convicted of conspiracy, wire fraud, and other charges. In the wake of the Enron crash, the U.S. Congress passed the tough new "Sarbanes-Oxley" laws, which tightened the rules for auditors and made company directors criminally liable if they falsified their accounts.
Lynn Shepherd

Date December 2, 2001

Country USA

Why It's Key The crash of this stock-market superstar, amid allegations of fraud, caused tremors across corporate America.

Key Political Event
"Open Skies" Treaty

The United States ratified the "Open Skies" Treaty between the EU countries, and the United States and Canada in 1993, with the main aim of furthering transparency in the military matters of its members. It was originally conceived by President Eisenhower in 1955, but it was President George H. W. Bush who made the years-old concept a reality in 1989; however, it was not put into force until 2002.

There are five main recognized elements of the treaty: "territory," "aircraft," "sensors," "quotas," and "data availability." Under "territory," lands, islands, and internal and territorial waters are open to observation by other members, with flight safety the only viable reason for denial. The decision on "aircraft" used in any observation exercise is made by the state that is to be observed, being either their own or the observer's

aircraft. "Sensors" allowed on board are video, optical, panoramic and framing cameras, infrared line scanners, and a synthetic aperture radar. Collectively they enable day/night and all-weather capability and are available to all member states. "Quotas" of flights either taken or foisted upon are dependent on each nation's "Passive Quota," and the "data" from any flight is available to any member state, although they can only collect a portion of what is available due to the Passive Quota system.

Any changes to the treaty will be the result of a majority decision of the Open Skies Consultative Commission (OSCC), based in Vienna. The treaty is considered central in the fight against extremist acts, such as the 9/11 bombings in 2001.

Greg Pittard

Date January 1, 2002
Country Worldwide
Why It's Key The treaty established a regime of unarmed and unlimited aerial observation flights over the entire territory of its member countries.

Key Political Event
Indigenous peoples expelled from the Kalahari

The Kalahari Bushmen – also known as the San, the Kung, the Khwe, or the Basarwa – are perhaps the world's oldest indigenous peoples; in fact, some anthropologists believe them to be humanity's "genetic Adam," the people from whom we all descend. For centuries, they have lived their nomadic lifestyle in the harsh Kalahari Desert of modern-day Botswana. In 1961, as the British prepared to give up colonial possession of Botswana, they set aside the Central Kalahari Game Reserve, a piece of land the size of Denmark, for the Bushmen to live in perpetuity.

But beginning in the mid-1980s, the independent government of Botswana began looking into moving the Bushmen and their families off the Reserve and into settlements around the country. A 1985 study by the government concluded that they "had largely

abandoned their tradition, nomadic hunter-gatherer way of life in favor of a sedentary lifestyle." Between 1997 and 2002, 730 households were relocated to new settlements, and the government terminated shipments of supplemental food and water to those few who remained in the Reserve.

The Kalahari Bushmen deny that they agreed to resettlement, and charge the government with cultural genocide, carried out to mine the reserve for the diamonds that were discovered there in the 1980s. Life in the settlements has brought the tribe little but a life of alcoholism, poverty, and AIDS. In 2006, the Kalahari Bushmen won a court ruling stating that their removal was illegal, but the legal battle continues.

Heather Michon

Date January 28, 2002
Country Botswana
Why It's Key The fight of the Kalahari Bushmen to regain their lands has become a landmark in the fight for indigenous peoples and one of the longest legal battles in African history.

Key Cultural Event
Bollywood film wins Oscar

Lagaan was not the first Bollywood film to be nominated for an Oscar, but it was the first to win one, and is also the film that has done the most to popularize the genre in an age when English is the dominant language of the box office. Perhaps appropriately for a film that challenged the dominance of Anglo-American films, *Lagaan* is a story about mistreated Indian villagers who take on their British overlords at their own game: cricket. Aamir Khan, who also produced the film, plays the lead and won a Filmfare Best Actor Award for his role. *Lagaan* and its cast and crew went on to win more than forty awards, including the Academy Award for Best Foreign Language Film in 2002.

It cost £4.5 million, and has since grossed over £120 million worldwide. In the UK, it took £300,000 in its first four weeks and was among the top ten grossing films. *The Times of India* attributed the film's popularity with Western audiences to "its secular, inclusive brand of patriotism." Concentrating on its impact at home *The Hindu* said: "In its own way, *Lagaan* renewed the nation's hope and faith in itself."

Lagaan's success in India has been achieved in spite of Aamir Khan's naïvely signing a contract preventing him from releasing it for five years after its cinematic release. Nor is the film stranger to tragedy. Six months after the film was shot, its location – the villages connected to the city of Bhuj – was destroyed in an earthquake.

David Thorley

Date 2002

Country India

Why It's Key *Lagaan* became a box office sensation and forged a new place for Bollywood films in the UK and United States.

opposite Members of the *Lagaan* cast and crew at the Oscars.

Key Political Event
Religious riots in Godhra

Although the destruction of the Babri Masjid mosque in Ayodhya in 1992 prompted deadly sectarian riots across India, it was another dispute over the alleged birthplace of the Hindu deity Ram that incited the worst religious violence since Partition in 1947. The Sabarmati Express, bound for Ahmedabad, was filled with hundreds of Hindu activists returning from a pilgrimage to Ayodhya when the train was set on fire as it pulled out of a station in Godhra, a town in the western state of Gujarat, allegedly by a group of Muslim men. Fifty-nine people were burned alive in what one onlooker described as a "ball of fire."

However, the greater violence occurred after the fire in acts of retaliation. Though India's prime minister at the time, Atal Bihari Vajpayee, appealed for calm, riots enveloped the Hindu-majority state of Gujarat.

According to human-rights organizations, over 2,500 people were murdered – most of them Muslims – and over 100,000 of them were displaced, assembling in squalid camps around Gujarat. Schools and shops were shut in Godhra, and a curfew was implemented, with policemen ordered to shoot troublemakers.

In January 2005, Supreme Court judge Umesh Chandra Banerjee led an inquiry into the fire and found that it had not been started by Muslims at all, but had been an accident. However, the Bharatiya Janata Party (BJP), who ran the Gujarat state government at the time, rejected the railway ministry's findings. A separate inquiry into the riots has yet to reach its conclusions, but dozens of Muslims still remain under arrest for their alleged involvement.

Bianca Jackson

Date February 27, 2002

Country India

Why It's Key The riots at Godhra revealed the ongoing tensions between Hindus and Muslims over Ayodhya, and resulted in horrific religious violence.

Fact The burned-out shell of the Sabarmati Express still stands at the railway station in Godhra.

Key Political Event
Bethlehem church siege

The Church of the Nativity in Bethlehem is located on one of the holiest Christian sites, built over the spot where tradition says Jesus Christ was born. Constructed by Emperor Justinian I in 565 CE, it is administered by the Roman Catholic, Greek Orthodox, and Armenian Apostolic Churches, all of which have monastic communities around Manger Square. Located in the West Bank, it had struggled to keep above the Palestinian-Israeli fray, but in April 2002, found the war literally on its doorstep.

After a string of suicide bombings beginning in March 2002, the Israeli Defense Force (IDF) launched Operation Defensive Shield, the largest incursion into the West Bank seen since the Six Day War in 1967. On April 2, 2002, Israeli tanks were chasing a group of terrorist suspects through the streets of Bethlehem,

forcing about a dozen of them to take refuge inside the Church of the Nativity. Inside the church were more than 200 Palestinian civilians and at least 60 religious personnel, who were held hostage by the terrorists.

It was the beginning of a 38-day standoff between the Palestinians and the IDF. Despite a longstanding policy not to negotiate with terrorists, the Israeli government could not storm the church without international condemnation. Food, water, and electricity ran perilously short for the hostages and captors. In the end, the standoff was resolved peacefully, with 13 men exiled to Cyprus and 26 others banished to the Gaza Strip. But it was not without bloodshed: 11 people were killed, including the church's bell-ringer and a Franciscan monk.
Heather Michon

Date April 2, 2002

Country Palestine

Why It's Key The siege resulted in Israel capturing 13 of the 25 men on its most-wanted list.

Key Political Event
Jimmy Carter visits Cuba

On May 12, 2002, former U.S. president Jimmy Carter and his wife Rosalynn arrived in Cuba. Although not politically significant, the visit was of great symbolic importance because Carter was the first U.S. president in or out of office to visit Cuba since it had become Communist under Fidel Castro in 1959.

The relationship between the two countries had been rocky, particularly since the unsuccessful invasion of the Bay of Pigs in 1961 by United States-backed Cuban exiles. A year later, a possible nuclear war was averted when President John Kennedy faced down Russian leader Nikita Khrushchev and forced him to remove nuclear-tipped missiles aimed at the United States from Cuban military bases. However, while he was in office (1977–1981), Carter had made some attempts to normalize relations with Cuba.

Despite the widespread belief that Cuba was developing biological warfare, Cuban officials denied the allegation. During his trip, Carter paid an unofficial visit to a biological research center before meeting with Cuban dissidents and visiting schools. On May 14, Carter addressed the Cuban people in an uncensored television broadcast. Speaking in Spanish, he called for an end to one-party rule and asked that basic human rights be respected.

He also suggested that the United States end its forty-year trade embargo and allow more freedom of travel between the two countries. But six days later, Bush declared that the embargo would not be lifted until Cuba became more democratic.
Elizabeth R. Purdy

Date May 12, 2002

Country Cuba

Why It's Key In the midst of allegations that Cuba was developing biological weapons, the visit of Jimmy Carter, who travels the world on peace and humanitarian missions, offered some hope that future relations between the two countries might be less volatile and that Fidel Castro might take a softer line on human rights.

opposite Castro and Carter at a ball game.

Key Political Event
Moscow theater siege

When Svetlana Gubareva first heard gunshots during the middle of the musical production *Nord-Ost*, "my first thought was how well the director had worked such a clever stunt into the play." It took a few moments for Gubareva and the 850 other Moscow theater-goers to realize that the 40 masked attackers were not part of the show.

Demanding Russia's withdrawal from Chechnya, the terrorists lined the theater hall with explosives and prepared to wait the government out. Negotiators managed to win the release of 73 hostages over three days, but hundreds more remained trapped. Security experts realized there was little hope of a sneak attack on the massive building.

At 5 a.m. on the third day, some of the hostages heard a hissing sound. "They are gassing us!" Anna

Andrianova whispered into her mobile phone. "We're all going to be blown up." People began to fall unconscious. Half an hour later, security forces stormed the building, gunning down at least 33 terrorists in the next hour. As hostages were pulled into the snowy streets, it seemed like the operation had been a success. Within hours, the scope of the tragedy was clear: at least 129 hostages were dead from the mystery gas, others permanently disabled.

Russian officials have never divulged what gas was used in the rescue effort, nor given a plausible excuse for what went wrong. Four years later, a poll showed that only 9 per cent of Russians believed that the government was being honest about the operation.
Heath Michon

Date October 23, 2002

Country Russia

Why It's Key Called "Russia's 9/11" by some, the Moscow theater siege was used by the Russian government to crack down on Chechens around the country, while the botched rescue attempt eroded confidence in the Russian leadership.

opposite **Hostages are rescued from the Moscow theater siege.**

Key Political Event
Miss World killings

After the 2001 Miss World victory of Nigerian Agbani Darego, Nigeria seized its opportunity to host the 2002 pageant, deciding to spotlight the corruption-tainted country's tourist potential and boost its international image. Sadly, Miss World 2002 did not achieve this aim, and instead highlighted the ongoing, deadly violence between Nigerian Muslims and their Christian compatriots.

Tension was already in the air when, in early November 2002, the Miss World candidates arrived in Nigeria. Nigerian Muslims, incensed that the pageant was taking place during the Muslim holy month of Ramadan, went over the edge when, on November 16, journalist Isioma Daniel of Nigerian newspaper *ThisDay* wrote an article in which, according to local Muslims, she disparaged the character of Islam's Prophet

Muhammad by speculating that he would have personally welcomed the beauty pageant.

Daniel's remarks about Muhammad sparked riots in the city of Kaduna, in largely Muslim northern Nigeria, where the local offices of *ThisDay* were torched and street violence between Muslim and Christian gangs left scores of people dead. The 2002 violence demonstrated that some Nigerian Muslims were prepared to kill in order to forestall or punish any perceived criticism of Islam or the personality of its prophet, and that non-Muslim neighbors were willing to take up their end of the fight as well. In an ironic conclusion to the actual pageant, the Turkish Muslim contestant won the Miss World title.
Demir Barlas

Date November 22, 2002

Country Nigeria

Why It's Key The killings were a major example of the ongoing culture war between militant Islamists and non-Muslims in Nigeria.

Key Political Event
Iraq war protests

The UN contested the grounds for the imminent invasion of Iraq in 2003, with Secretary General Kofi Anan stating that the United States-led coalition removal of Saddam Hussein from power would be illegal. Nevertheless, the United States, UK, and Spain rationalized that Iraq could attack at any moment using weapons of mass destruction, and that they could not risk the danger any longer.

Serious protests began on September 12, 2002, with worldwide protests synchronized, including 200,000 attending a march in Washington D.C. Many of the organizational groups had been formed to oppose the United States war on Afghanistan. The protests were becoming more and more zealous because of the information leaks in the media at the time; beginning with the revelation that findings of Iraq purchasing

uranium for nuclear weapons were incorrect, yet these claims were continually used as justification for war.

Global protests were planned in unprecedented numbers after the report that Iraq did not have offensive naval capabilities, despite the Bush administration claiming that this was a serious threat. On February 15, 2003, large protests occurred across every continent and were officially the largest recorded in history. In the first four months of 2003, 36 million people worldwide are thought to have protested against the invasion of Iraq. The largest march was in Rome, which was attended by three million people.

Protests dwindled after war was declared, although they were vindicated after much of the evidence used to validate the invasion was discredited.
Greg Pittard

Date February 15, 2003

Country Worldwide

Why It's Key The protests on February 15 against the possibility of a United States coalition invading Iraq were the largest global protests ever recorded.

opposite Protesters against the Iraq war take to the streets.

Key Cultural Event
Vatican sexual abuse cover-up

Since the first criminal allegations of sexual abuse against members of the Catholic Church emerged in the 1980s, many had suspected that the Vatican was involved in systematically covering up the molestation and silencing victims. However, it was not until an American priest handed over a forty-year-old "blueprint for deception" to Texan lawyer Daniel Shea that the extent of the Church's subterfuge became clear.

The document, a sixty-nine-page Latin paper bearing the seal of Pope John XXIII, was sent to every bishop in the world in 1962, and outlined instructions for how allegations of sexual abuse should be dealt with the "strictest" secrecy. Threatening those who speak out about molestation with excommunication, the document also demanded that the victim take an oath of secrecy when making a complaint to the

Church, and that all allegations be stored in the secret archives of the Vatican. After discovering the document as part of his work for victims of abuse from Catholic priests in the United States, Shea handed it over to the U.S. authorities. It has since been pronounced as genuine by the Roman Catholic Church in England and Wales, and was identified as a "*Crimine Solicitationes*," or "instruction on proceeding in cases of solicitation."

According to the U.S. Conference of Catholic Bishops, the document was rendered null by later guidelines, in particular, the Vatican's 1983 Code of Canon Law. However, the Vatican sent a letter to bishops in May 2001 stating that the 1962 instruction was still in force.
Bianca Jackson

Date 2003

Country Vatican City

Why It's Key The document confirmed the suspicion that the Vatican was involved in covering up allegations of molestation, and victims around the world were given hard evidence with which to prosecute their abusers.

Fact As the document dates back to 1962, it undermines the Catholic Church's claim that sexual abuse in the Church is a recent phenomenon.

Key Cultural Event
SARS outbreak

Unlike the Spanish influenza epidemic of 1918, the multi-country outbreak of SARS did not become a full global pandemic, partly because of early warnings provided by several countries to the World Health Organization (WHO). The Canadian prototype Global Public Health Intelligence Network (GPHIN) Internet-based system proved its potential during this outbreak. Developed by the Public Health Agency of Canada, GPHIN collects "real-time" reports of public health around the world, tracking significant disease outbreaks, bioterrorism, natural disasters, and other issues related to health and safety.

The prototype GPHIN picked up Chinese-language accounts of atypical pneumonia as early as November 2002. It translated only headlines, and the first English-language account came through on January 21, 2003.

On February 26, SARS first spread from its point of origin in Guangdong, China, to Hanoi, Vietnam. The first Canadian cases were reported in March.

WHO worked to verify and monitor the outbreak, and on March 12, 2003, alerted the world to Severe Acute Respiratory Syndrome (SARS), a virus spread by sneezing or coughing in close contact with others. The organization reported over 150 cases in nine countries. By the end of the outbreak, SARS had affected more than 8,500 people in thirty countries, and caused some 900 deaths. Using what was learned from SARS, Canada upgraded its prototype to the CAN$2 million multilingual GPHIN II in November 2004.
Marie Powell

Date March 12, 2003

Country Canada

Why It's Key The World Health Organization's quick response to Severe Acute Respiratory Syndrome (SARS) helped to point toward ways to handle future global outbreaks of infectious disease.

opposite Woman suffering from SARS is treated in hospital.

Key Cultural Event
Brothel listed on stock exchange

In the state of Victoria, where the famed brothel The Daily Planet is located, the Prostitution Control Act of 1994 legalized prostitution in registered and licensed brothels. However, the world's "oldest profession" had been thriving in Melbourne for much longer than that. While John Trimble founded The Daily Planet in 1975, it was established on Home Street in Elsternick on the site of a previous "massage parlor" called Le Chateau.

From these humble beginnings, The Daily Planet has gone on to revolutionize the commercial potential of prostitution. Touted as the "largest and most exclusive bordello in the Southern Hemisphere," it has won several Australian Adult Industry Awards, and on May 1, 2003, it became the world's first brothel listed on a stock exchange. In preparation for floating its shares on a public stock exchange, The Daily Planet

turned to infamous Hollywood madam Heidi Fleiss to publicize the venture, calling her its international ambassador. The move proved prudent as the media all around the globe followed the event.

While buyers of shares were officially part-owners of the building, rather than the business itself, this didn't stop the opening day of trading on the Australian Stock Exchange from being extremely successful: over a million shares were sold and the original stock price doubled. However, its shares, which had at one time reached four times their original price, dropped in 2007 to remain steady at one quarter of their IPO (initial public offering).
Terence McSweeney

Date May 1, 2003

Country Australia

Why It's Key The Daily Planet was the first brothel to be floated on a stock exchange.

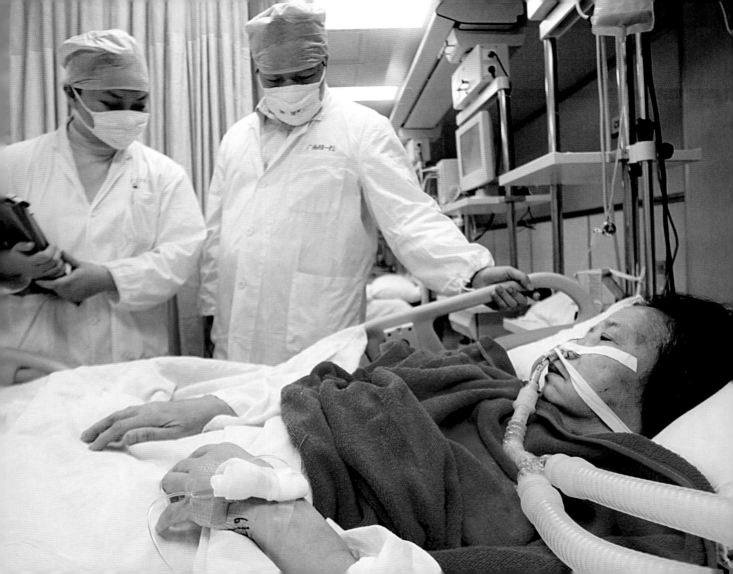

Key Disaster
Northeast Blackout

On Thursday August 14, 2003, at about 4 p.m. EDT, power plants in Ohio and Michigan began to report power outages. Also at that point, air conditioners and other electrical devices were draining power to beat afternoon temperatures of up to 87°F (31°C). A cascading outage caused the blackout to spread until it covered about 9,300 miles (24,000 km), and some 50 million people went without power across two Canadian provinces and eight Midwestern U.S. states. It affected air travel, street lights, subway trains, refrigeration units, and other aspects of daily life. Power remained out for up to four days in some areas of the United States.

Among other inquiries, a Canada-U.S. task force investigating the incident estimated more than 400 transmission lines and 500 generating units at about 260 power plants shut down. By April 2004, the task force reported Ohio-based FirstEnergy Corp's Eastlake plant triggered the cascade effect. Causes cited by the task force report included lack of understanding and support of the system, lack of monitoring and coordination to determine the severity of the incident, as well as inadequate tree trimming causing overgrown tree limbs to short out power lines.

The task force's 238-page report recommended setting up mandatory reliability standards and independent councils, upgrading equipment and maintenance, using backup generators in nuclear plants, and increased training and security, to prevent future widespread power outages.

Marie Powell

Date August 14, 2003
Country USA/Canada
Why It's Key It was the largest North American blackout in history.

758

Key Political Event
Saddam Hussein captured

While the Iraq War itself had splintered worldwide relations, the hunt for Saddam Hussein infused the debate with even more moral ambiguity. The Iraqi resistance had fallen within three weeks, and by April 9, Hussein had gone into hiding. Videos and audiotapes of Hussein surrounded by supporters and calling for a rejection of the U.S. occupation surfaced, but the coalition forces found no sign of his whereabouts.

However, a major breakthrough occurred when U.S forces shifted the focus of their hunt from Hussein's innermost circle to his more distant relatives and tribal allies, whom they believed Hussein had been lodging with. For over ten days, intelligence analysts interrogated multiple members of these tribes, until they were tipped off about the deposed ruler's hiding place. After nine months of searching, Hussein was finally found hiding in a tiny, blocked cellar, or "spider hole," under a farmhouse in al-Dawr.

Bewildered from months of being on the run, Hussein offered no resistance to the six hundred U.S. troops as they secured and removed him from his hideout, despite possessing a pistol. After he was DNA tested to ensure his identity and filmed in custody as proof of his capture, U.S. administrator Paul Bremer announced to journalists in Baghdad, "We got him."

Hussein was handed over to Iraq for an official trial for crimes against humanity, and the illegal use of chemical warfare. Hussein defied the court, but he was sentenced and then executed on December 30, 2006.

Greg Pittard

Date December 14, 2003
Country Iraq
Why It's Key The capture of Saddam Hussein was prematurely seen as an end to the Iraq conflict, but sparked controversy both in Iraq and in the West over the ethics of his subsequent trial and execution.

opposite Television footage of Saddam Hussein following his arrest.

Key Cultural Event
First black French newsreader

Black citizens in France had long suffered under-representation in the French media. While non-European immigrants constituted approximately 15 per cent of the French population, they were more vulnerable to poverty and unemployment than their white counterparts, and were regarded as an "invisible" social group. Efforts to promote the visibility of minorities were not wholeheartedly embraced, partly due to the French ideal of equality regardless of race or religion, which thwarted affirmative action.

But by the turn of the millennium, voices were gradually being raised. In 1998, 40,000 black people marched in Paris to commemorate the 150th anniversary of the end of slavery, and France won the soccer World Cup with a team with many black players. In early 2004, the High Council on Integration demanded that the government make it a condition of every broadcast channel to ensure immigrants are "fairly and properly represented."

Born in 1972 on Martinique, a Caribbean island, Audrey Pulvar worked for a Martinique TV channel before moving to a Caribbean network. In 2002, she was hired by state-funded company France Televisions, and in the following year appeared onscreen to report regional news. In September 2004, as part of the company's "positive action integration plan," Pulvar, aged thirty-two, became the first black newsreader to present the main evening news on national television in France. The editor of France 3's national news programs, Ulysse Gosset, claimed he hoped it would spark "a small revolution" in the world of French TV.

Mariko Kato

Date 2004

Country France

Why It's Key The appointment of a black newsreader caused a commotion in France and worldwide, even in the twenty-first century.

Fact Before Pulvar, black news reporters had only been seen in weather forecasts or regional news on French television.

Key Cultural Event
Abu Ghraib prison photos

When Sergent Joseph M. Darby of the U.S. Army's 372nd Military Police Company asked Specialist Charles A. Graner Jr. whether he could download some of the pictures Graner had taken during their time in Iraq onto his computer, he expected to find a travelogue. But what he discovered was photographs taken inside the prison at Abu Ghraib in which prisoners, mostly blindfolded Iraqi detainees, were being subjected to an array of physically and sexually sadistic acts. Naked prisoners were shown stacked in pyramids, led on dog leashes, and simulating sex acts, among other horrific forms of degradation.

Darby handed over the computer disk to a military investigator on January 13, and the Army immediately began a criminal investigation. But although the military informed the U.S. press that seventeen army personnel had been suspended from duty due to allegations of detainee abuse, the media did not pick up on the story until late April, a month after six soldiers had been charged with crimes including criminal charges of assault, cruelty, mistreatment, and indecent acts.

However, on April 28, 2004, the U.S. television program *60 Minutes II* aired the photographs, revealing to the world the atrocities that were occurring at the infamous prison. The public was outraged, and between May 2004 and September 2005, seven soldiers were sentenced to federal prison time. Graner was sentenced to ten years, while Brigadier General Janis Karpinski, who directed the prison at the time, was demoted to the rank of colonel.

Bianca Jackson

Date January 13, 2004

Country USA

Why It's Key Darby's revelation led to an investigation that outraged the world, and changed attitudes toward the war effort in Iraq.

Fact Many have branded Darby a traitor and a "rat," forcing him and his family to move towns and change jobs for fear of their lives.

opposite Photo of inhumane acts perpetrated in Abu Ghraib prison.

Key Political Event
CIA admits Iraq WMD claim was false

On January 28, 2003, U.S. President George W. Bush warned in a State of the Union address of Iraqi dictator Saddam Hussein's quest to manufacture nuclear weapons, and his possession of stockpiles of biological and chemical weapons. On February 5, U.S. Secretary of State Colin Powell declared that the Iraq Weapons of Mass Destruction (WMD) threat was fact, not assertion, before the UN Security Council, and on March 19, the United States initiated war against Iraq, according to President Bush, largely "to disarm Iraq."

The premise for the Iraq War was heavily criticized for being misinformed and even deceitful. UN Weapons Inspectors had been combing Iraq for WMDs since November 2002, finding nothing by March 2003. The United States' WMD accusations had some basis in reality, as Iraq had used chemical weapons in the

1980s against Iran and against a domestic Kurdish revolt; however, UN inspections in Iraq following the Gulf War of 1991 had destroyed countless WMD and facilities. But the Bush administration insisted that Iraq had reconstituted its WMD programs between the end of UN inspections in 1998 and their resumption in 2002, a claim never supported by evidence.

On February 3, 2004, Chief CIA Weapons Inspector David Kay admitted before U.S. Congress that "we were almost all wrong," about the WMDs. He turned over his inspections job to Charles Duelfer, who confirmed the absence of WMDs in Iraq in a comprehensive report released in October 2004.

David Anderson

Date February 3, 2004

Country USA

Why It's Key The admission confirmed international and domestic suspicions that the U.S. went to war against Iraq on a false premise.

2000–

Key Political Event
Taiwan hand-in-hand peace rally

More than half a century before the Hand-in-Hand Rally, the Taiwanese had suffered a violent massacre under the forces of the People's Republic of China. On February 28, 1947, the Guomindang government suppressed a Taiwanese uprising in which thousands of civilians were killed. This came to be known as the 228 Incident. During the White Terror period that followed, thousands more were killed or imprisoned. Fifty-seven years later, the Taiwanese were facing another threat from the People's Republic of China, who had deployed five hundred missiles along the main coast, targeted at Taiwan. Taiwanese President Chen Shui-bian proposed a referendum, and his people decided to show support.

The day of the peaceful protest was planned in commemoration of the 228 Incident on February 28,

now known as Peace Memorial Day, and was also only weeks before the Taiwanese presidential election. Two million Taiwanese formed a human chain over five hundred kilometers from the harbor at Keelung, Taiwan's northernmost city, to the southern tip in Pingtung County. Joined by other supporters from across the world, the Taiwanese civilians chanted slogans such as "Yes to Taiwan," "Oppose Missiles," and "Love Peace."

At one point during the event, participants "turned away" from the People's Republic of China, clearly appealing for Taiwan independence. When President Chen Shui-bian was reelected on March 20, he held a nationwide consultative referendum on the same day, regarding relations with the People's Republic of China.

Mariko Kato

Date February 28, 2004

Country Taiwan

Why It's Key The rally was one of the largest peaceful demonstrations of the twentieth century.

Fact The demonstration was inspired by Baltic Way, a human chain of two million people organized in the Baltic States in 1989.

Key Political Event
Madrid train bombings

On March 11, 2004, a series of bombs exploded within minutes of each other on four commuter trains in Madrid, killing 191 people and injuring 1,841. The government initially blamed the Basque separatist group ETA for the attacks, but on October 30, 2007, a Spanish judge found twenty-one people guilty, many of whom had strong ties to Islamic fundamentalist groups. Seven of the key suspects, including the "mastermind," Serhane ben Abdelmajid Fakhet, died in the attacks, and four of the accused disappeared before the trial.

Three central figures in the conspiracy received symbolic sentences of 40,000 years, and will serve the maximum of forty allowed by Spanish law. However, Osman Sayed Ahmed (known as "Mohamed the Egyptian"), the "link man" between the bombers themselves and international terror groups, was acquitted of all charges, sparking outcry across the country. For those convicted, charges ranged from forgery to murder, and several cells were implicated in the proceedings, including the Moroccan Islamic Combatant Group, to which the two suspected of carrying out the attack are thought to have belonged.

While the bombers' motives are not certain, many believe they were attempting to force a change of government in the elections scheduled for a few days after the attacks took place, and an eventual withdrawal of troops from Iraq. If so, they were successful: the Conservative Popular Party lost power to the Socialist Party, and troop withdrawals hastened in line with party policy made public in the run up to the election.

Greg Pittard

Date March 11, 2004

Country Spain

Why It's Key The bombings were the worst terror attack in Europe since the bombing of a Pan Am flight over Lockerbie, Scotland in 1988, which claimed 270 lives.

Fact The bombs consisted of ten backpacks filled with dynamite and nails.

2000–

Key Political Event
Ten new countries join EU

The acceptance into the European Union of the Czech Republic, Hungary, Poland, Slovakia, Slovenia, Latvia, Lithuania, Estonia, Cyprus, and Malta, eight of which were former members of the Communist Soviet bloc, brought varying reactions from across the international community.

In the incoming countries, throngs of people took to the streets, celebrating the promise of stabilizing their young democracies and of cultural and economic enrichment. The 15 EU members who had ratified their approval praised the progression of Europe, with introductory events held in Dublin, Ireland, which had held the 2004 presidency. The new 25-nation union was the world's biggest trading bloc, with a grain area growing by 50 per cent and an already world-leading agricultural production further increasing its influence on food prices and distribution worldwide. While the 15-member union accounted for 20 per cent of world trade, the expansion is expected to increase that number commensurately as the newer, less developed nations are mined for their resources and workforce.

But not everyone was pleased. Anti-globalization protests were held across Europe, their leaders drawing parallels with empires of the past and mourning the inevitable strong-arm tactics the increased power of the EU would engender, especially when trading to and from developing countries.

However, the incumbent EU president, Bertie Ahern, celebrated the end of any ill-feeling left over from the Cold War and the prospect of an "opening of minds as well as borders."

Greg Pittard

Date May 1, 2004

Country Europe

Why It's Key The expansion of the EU caused its population to grow by 28 per cent.

Fact The expansion extended the European Union to 25 nations and the population to over 455 million (the third largest in the world after China and India).

Key Political Event
Beslan school siege

The first day of school in Russia, the "Day of Knowledge," is supposed to be a joyous one. More than 1,200 teachers, students, and parents assembled in the gymnasium of School Number One in Beslan, Ossetia-Alania on the morning of September 1, 2004, ready to get the year off to a good start. When the first shots were fired, many children thought the balloons decorating the gym had popped.

Instead, thirty-two heavily armed attackers confronted the crowd and quickly gained control of the school. In the first hours of the siege, around twenty adults were executed, and the balloons and streamers were replaced with bombs and trip-wires. For fifty-six hours, the hostages sweltered in the stifling heat of the gym. Children and adults began to suffer from dehydration and heat exhaustion. Negotiations with

officials went nowhere. At around 1 p.m. on September 3, the terrorists accidentally detonated several bombs, caving in the gym wall and part of the roof. Thinking that an attack was underway, the gunmen began to fire wildly at hostages, who were desperately running for safety.

A few minutes later, police launched their own attack. When the dust settled, thirty-one of the attackers were dead, along with 186 children and 148 adults. More than 700 were injured. Among the survivors, the psychological scars have been slow to heal. "The ones who survived – we're not the same funny kids we used to be, we're serious now," said one young girl. "We're already grown-ups."
Heather Michon

Date September 1, 2004

Country Russia

Why It's Key The siege was one in a string of high-profile attacks by rebels within Russia.

opposite Survivors of the Beslan school siege.

Key Disaster
Asian tsunami

For millions of years in the Indian Ocean, the India plate had been gradually sliding under the Burma plate. On December 26, 2004, the tectonic plates finally gave way under the ocean some 160 km west of the Indonesian island of Sumatra.

An earthquake of 9.0 magnitude on the Richter scale occurred over an area spanning 1,000 km for over 500 seconds (the second highest ever to be recorded), triggering other earthquakes as far away as Alaska. It is estimated to have generated energy equivalent to 23,000 times that which was released by the atomic bomb dropped on Hiroshima in World War II. Moreover, it displaced huge volumes of water, causing the natural phenomenon known as a "tsunami." Within hours, deadly waves of heights up to 15 meters crashed onto the shores of eleven

countries in the Indian Ocean, as far-ranging as Africa and Thailand, drowning or sweeping people into the sea and destroying property.

A horrific aftermath followed, with corpses rotting in the tropical heat. With the lack of food and untreated injuries, health authorities feared a double increase in the death toll, and reverberations and aftershocks continued days after the disaster. The latest analysis by the United Nation puts the number of casualties at approximately 180,000 dead and 42,000 missing, including some 9,000 foreign tourists. A state of emergency was declared in Sri Lanka, Indonesia, and the Maldives, and a worldwide bid for humanitarian aid raised more than US$7 million.
Mariko Kato

Date December 26, 2004

Country Indonesia, Sri Lanka, India, Thailand, and others.

Why It's Key In terms of both magnitude and casualties, the Asian tsunami is considered the most destructive in history.

Fact The disaster was ranked ninth out of the ten deadliest natural disasters in history, measured in terms of estimated death toll. The 1931 Yellow River flood in China topped the list.

Key Political Event
The Orange Revolution

When Viktor Yushchenko began appearing in public in September 2004 with signs of a growing facial disfigurement amid accusations that government authorities had attempted to poison him, the political maneuverings and burgeoning social upheaval within Ukraine started to reach an intrigued global audience.

Yushchenko was the opposition presidential candidate for the Our Ukraine Party. Broadly Western-leaning, he had support from many constituencies of Ukrainian society and goodwill from Western administrations. Meanwhile, Viktor Yanukovych, the then prime minister, who was in favor of a close strategic relationship with Russia, pronounced state control and was accused of rigging the elections of November 2004.

Independent observers condemned various forms of electoral malpractice, intimidation, and multiple voting, and an outpouring of public dismay began developing revolutionary momentum. Thousands of protesters flooded Independence Square, central Kiev, wearing orange, the color of Yushchenko's party. Yanukovych supporters made counter protests, concerned their votes would be subverted by a popular rising. After thirteen days of protest and and civil disobedience, the Supreme Court ordered a re-election. Yushchenko won on December 26, polling just over half the vote. But the contest of the two Viktors had no absolute winner, and an ideological debate continues.

The Orange Revolution is emblematic of how many former Soviet bloc states are continuing to negotiate a political direction and economic and cultural place for themselves in a post-Cold War world.
Michael Hallam

Date December 26, 2004

Country Ukraine

Why It's Key The Orange Revolution involved millions of protesters and led to Ukraine's first ever democratic and freely elected President.

opposite Yushchenko supporters enjoy fireworks during a jubilation rally in Kiev on 28 December, 2004.

Key Political Event
Sri Lanka ceasefire breaks down

Sri Lanka remains mired in a civil war that began in 1983 between the separatist Tamil Tigers and the Sri Lankan government. The civil war has claimed tens of thousands of lives and continues to plague an increasingly impoverished and desperate populace. In 2001, the belligerents agreed upon a ceasefire that drew international recognition in 2002.

The Tamil Tigers – chastened by the post-9/11 possibility of U.S. military intervention or other decisive support on behalf of the Sri Lankan government – made overtures toward their erstwhile enemies in late 2001. The government proved responsive. In 2002 the two previously implacable opponents sat down at the bargaining table and achieved agreement in principle on a number of issues, the most important being the Tamil Tigers' abandonment of the idea of a separate Tamil state. But hostilities resumed in the wake of the Tamil Tigers' suspected assassination of Lakshman Kadirgamar, the Foreign Minister of Sri Lanka, on August 12, 2005. The Sri Lankan government did not remain passive in the face of this provocation, and renewed hostilities against the Tamil Tigers in 2006.

In 2007, the Sri Lankan government made significant headway against the Tamil Tigers in the southeast of the country, but the rebels remain active in their own right. It is tragically clear that, after two decades of active hostilities, neither side will surrender until the other is eliminated.
Demir Barlas

Date 2005

Country Sri Lanka

Why It's Key After a brief whiff of hope of a peaceful resolution, the long-running Sri Lankan civil war kept going apace.

Key Cultural Event
YouTube created

Social networking sites such as MySpace and Facebook have revolutionized the ways people relate each other, but few web creations have redefined the layman's relationship to information technology like YouTube. Its creators, Steven Chen, Chad Hurley, and Jawed Karim, were working at the e-commerce business PayPal when they formulated the idea for a video-sharing website.

While not a revolutionary concept, YouTube had a catchy name that reflected its appeal to the layman: allowing users to upload videos and interact with others through video content, it came across as a kind of do-it-yourself television. The first video, uploaded on April 23, 2005, proved the site's virtually boundless criteria. Titled "Me at the zoo," it showed a user doing just that. By the following month, the site was attracting roughly 30,000 users a day, with all sorts of content demonstrating users' willingness to respond to the open-ended structure. Such popularity quickly paved the way for Google's landmark purchase of the site in November 2006.

The legitimization of the site as a tool of political dialogue became clear when a Democratic presidential debate used questions submitted by YouTube in mid-2007, although its impact on national conversations had become apparent before then. *Time* magazine's person of the year for 2006 ("You"), reflected the site's impact on the role of the everyman in the larger conversation. Rather than marking the beginning of the end for television, YouTube gives us a sense for its future.
Eric Kohn

Date February 15, 2005

Country USA

Why It's Key The site revolutionized the role of the layman in international discourse.

Key Political Event
Uzbek troops open fire on protesters

On May 13, 2005, Uzbek government troops brutally suppressed a popular uprising in Babur Square in the city of Andijon. Following the massacre, Uzbek President Islam Karimov immediately linked the protests with Islamic extremists and international terrorism, a claim that was supported by the Russian and Chinese governments.

The uprising began over the trial of 23 men, who were senior employees of successful local businesses, accused of organizing an illegal religious extremist group called "Akramiya" to subvert the constitutional order. For several days leading up to the verdict, relatives, friends, former employees, and employees of the accused men gathered across the street from the court for organized silent protests, maintaining that the defendants had done no wrong. Prior to the verdicts being handed down, an armed insurrection broke out: friends and relatives of the defendants overran a number of police stations and seized weapons from a military garrison. From there, an armed crowd stormed the Andijon prison, where the defendants were being held, and freed as many as 500 prisoners.

The next day, crowds seized the provincial government building and called for negotiations with the government, but the talks quickly broke down. Soon thereafter, Uzbek government troops moved into Bobur Square and killed 100 or more armed insurgents and an unknown number of bystanders. By May 14, Uzbek government troops controlled the city center, though sporadic fighting continued in and around Andijon for another day.
Keith Leitich

Date May 13, 2005

Country Uzbekistan

Why It's Key The events in Bobur Square on May 13, 2005, significantly altered Uzbekistan's relationship with the United States, its onetime ally.

Key Political Event
Europe tackles people trafficking

World history is ridden with trafficking of human beings for prostitution, and matters were still grave at the end of the second millennium. In 2005, the United States State Department estimated that around 60-80,000 people were being trafficked across international borders each year. About 80 per cent were women and girls, and up to 50 per cent were minors.

Since the fall of the Iron Curtain in 1989, former Eastern bloc countries had been identified as major source countries of trafficking of impoverished women and children. Russian women were also reported to have been trafficked to countries such as China, Japan, and South Korea. Due to the Iraq War at the beginning of the twenty-first century, many Iraqi refugees were forced into prostitution in Middle Eastern countries. The United

States and the UK were also receivers of trafficked humans from various countries, and in 2006, Canada also faced the problem of modern-day sexual slavery.

Nations varied in their actions to stop human trafficking, but they were all called to attention in May 2005 by the Council of Europe, which adopted the Convention on Action against Trafficking in Human Beings. The convention saw those being trafficked as victims, not perpetrators, of crime, and gave them increased protection, including temporary residence permits. It opened for signature on May 16, and by October 2007, it had been ratified by ten countries and signed by twenty-seven other Council on Europe Convention member states.
Mariko Kato

Date May 16, 2005

Country Europe

Why It's Key The convention was an international call for action against human trafficking, which gained the support of many countries.

Fact Founded in 1949, the Council of Europe has forty-seven member countries and five observer countries, including the United States, Canada, and Japan.

Key Political Event
Turkey becomes energy hub

The Baku-Tbilisi-Ceyhan (BTC) Pipeline is a massive engineering project initially conceived at a meeting of the Organization for Security and Cooperation in Europe (OSCE) in 1999. It came online six years later, offering new oil from the landlocked Caspian Sea to an energy-starved world, and establishing Turkey as a major hub of energy distribution.

The pipeline, which is jointly owned by a consortium of oil companies that includes BP, the State Oil Company of Azerbaijan, and Chevron, runs 1,768 km underground from Baku, Azerbaijan to Ceyhan, Turkey by way of Tbilisi, Georgia. In taking this circuitous route, it allows the consortium to bypass both a newly assertive Russia and theocratic Iran in favor of their more pliable, Western-inclined neighbors. And with 1,076 km of the pipeline on Turkish territory,

the completion of the project marked the rising importance of Turkey as an important energy hub.

Already the site of age-old commercial shipping lanes such as the Bosporus and Dardanelles Straits, Turkey now had the Mediterranean port city of Ceyhan to serve as a hub of energy distribution. Ceyhan became the terminus of not only the BTC Pipeline, but also the Kirkuk (Iraq)-Ceyhan Pipeline, and the planned Samsun-Ceyhan Pipeline and Blue Stream Natural Gas Pipeline. With the completion of these projects, Turkey will become an indispensable global distributor of Central Asian and Russian energy, further leveraging its strategic position at the nexus of Europe and Asia.
Demir Barlas

Date May 25, 2005

Country Turkey

Why It's Key Resource-poor Turkey successfully leveraged its geographical position to become a hub of the emerging Central Asian energy market.

Key Political Event
Thirty-first annual G8 Summit

The thirty-first annual G8 Summit in 2005 was expected to be one of the most important in decades. The annual meeting between the UK, France, Germany, Italy, Canada, Japan, Russia, and the United States was set to hold discussions on crucial world issues, particularly the reduction of carbon emissions, the cancelation of Third World debt, and poverty in the developing world.

The Make Poverty History Campaign, the biggest anti-poverty campaign in history, placed pressure on the participating countries to generate solutions to worldwide impoverishment. Live 8 concerts were performed around the world in the lead-up to the summit to heighten awareness on Third World debt and AIDS, and were directly leveled at the eight leaders. This tension was amplified by demonstrations in the streets of Glasgow prior to the summit by those who were frustrated by the irony that many of the global issues being discussed at the forum were being caused or treated too leniently by the eight global powers attending. Conceivably the mass protests put enough weight on the G8 Summit to force them to acknowledge these concerns, with representatives from India, South Africa, China, Brazil, Mexico, and seven African nations invited to participate.

US$50 billion was pledged to the developing world by 2010, as well as a promise to make AIDS medicine universally accessible. However, the United States still refused to commit to the reduction of carbon emissions, and the disagreements over global warming and unnecessary military spending remain.

Greg Pittard

Date July 6, 2005

Country Scotland

Why It's Key The widespread pressure and protest generated by the summit indicated that the eight world leaders needed to take decisive action on urgent global issues.

Key Political Event
7/7 London bombings

On July 7, 2005, London was in high spirits. The day before, it had been chosen as the host city for the 2012 Summer Olympics. It was the first full day of the G8 summit, hosted by the UK, and people were still recovering from the Live 8 concert five days previously.

At 8:50 a.m., three bombs exploded within fifty seconds of each other on three Underground trains. A fourth was set off on a bus nearly an hour later, at 9:47 a.m. in Tavistock Square. The entire city's transport system was disrupted, and mobile phone networks reached their capacity and were forced to prioritize emergency calls. The suicide bomb attacks killed fifty-two people, and injured seven hundred.

A few days later, the police identified four Islamic extremist men from Leeds and West Yorkshire as the suicide bombers. In the following months, many speculations and accusations were made as to the network to which they had belonged, particularly regarding connections with al-Qaeda, not least because within hours after the attack, a statement claiming responsibility was posted on the Al-Qaeda website.

Following further attempted bombings in London on July 21, security across the country and the globe was raised to the highest alert status, particularly on public transport. Such efforts led to the tragic shooting of an innocent man, Brazilian Jean Charles de Menezes, the following day by Metropolitan Police. Nevertheless, such terrorist attacks made a major contribution to tighter border controls and terrorist laws that followed worldwide.

Mariko Kato

Date July 7, 2005

Country UK

Why It's Key The bombings were the deadliest attack on London since the air raids in World War II, and made an international impact.

Fact These acts of terrorism had been preceded by the plane attacks on the U.S. on September 11, 2001 and the Madrid train bombings on March 11, 2004.

opposite **Wreckage of the bus blown up in Tavistock Square.**

Key Disaster
Hurricane Katrina

Having already been a very bad hurricane season in the Atlantic, as the summer of 2005 drew to a close, little did people think that the worst was still to come. A Category 1 hurricane as it crossed southern Florida, Katrina grew in strength over the Gulf of Mexico before slamming 127-mile-an-hour winds into New Orleans, Louisiana, and the coastal cities of Mississippi and Alabama.

However, it was not the winds that caused the ensuing catastrophe. During the hurricane, the Gulf Coast at New Orleans – most of which is below sea level – was swamped by a storm surge. When the protective levees were breached, water rushed inland and 80 per cent of New Orleans city was flooded. The results were catastrophic: 1,500 deaths, billions of dollars' worth of damage, homes and businesses destroyed, jobs lost, crops flattened, tourism wiped out, environmental damage, and oil and gas production lost.

Before the hurricane struck, the mayor of New Orleans had ordered a mandatory evacuation. But many stayed behind. Around 20,000 people took refuge in the Superdome football stadium, but conditions after the flooding struck became intolerable and they, too, had to be evacuated. To add to the mayhem, lawlessness was rife, looters were being shot, bodies were floating in stagnant water, and disease broke out.

As scenes of desperate people struggling to survive in unimaginable conditions provoked outrage around the world, President Bush was accused of mismanagement and not reacting quickly enough.
Lorraine Brownbill

Date August 29, 2005

Country USA

Why It's Key It was the costliest disaster in U.S. history.

Fact 1500–1800 people died, with damages of US$300 billion and thousands of businesses and homes destroyed.

opposite Two survivors of Hurricane Katrina make their way to safety in devastated New Orleans.

Key Cultural Event
Outcry over Muhammed cartoons

On September 30, 2005, the Danish daily newspaper *Jyllands-Posten* published twelve cartoons of the Prophet Muhammed. They ranged in tone from one that showed the prophet walking along with a donkey to another that depicted him with a turban in the shape of a bomb. They'd been commissioned in response to a stand-up comedian and a children's author telling the newspaper they hardly dared bring up Islam in their work because of the political climate.

Although three of the artists received death threats in mid-October, the cartoons received little international attention until January 2006, when diplomatic protests arrived from Libya and Saudi Arabia. *Jyllands-Posten* produced a formal apology in response, but then several right-wing European newspapers decided to reprint the cartoons as a provocative gesture in support of free speech. This in turn led to angry protests around the Muslim world; the Norwegian and Danish embassies in Syria were set on fire, and dozens of people were reportedly killed by mobs.

There were claims of double standards on both sides. Muslims complained that Europeans mocked Islam in a way they would never mock Judaism, while Christians retorted that Europeans ultimately deferred to Islam in a way they would never defer to Christianity. Commentators wondered which was the more important value: politeness and respect, or free speech? That a cartoon could cause a worldwide storm shows how fraught the issues of integration and multiculturalism remain in today's Europe.
Ned Beauman

Date September 30, 2005

Country Denmark

Why It's Key Violent protests over a page of satirical cartoons forced the European media to reflect on its commitment to freedom of expression.

Key Disaster
Kashmir earthquake

The statistics almost defied belief: dead – 75,000; area affected – 30,000 sq km; population affected – 3.5 million; schools and colleges destroyed – 6,000. Behind the statistics were stories of unimaginable trauma and tragedy: children buried in collapsed schools, babies dying from cold, entire villages wiped out.

The earthquake's epicenter was 50 miles north east of Islamabad. Measuring 7.6 in magnitude, it killed over 73,000 in Pakistan and 1,300 in India, with the mountainous regions of Kashmir worst affected. Several towns were razed to the ground. Homes and public buildings were destroyed, and infrastructure, commerce and communications were brought to a standstill. Those who survived the initial earthquake faced the nightmare of hundreds of aftershocks, while the remoteness of the areas nearest to the epicenter, coupled with bad weather, meant aid agencies struggled to get relief to where it was most needed.

Hundreds of thousands of people were forced to face a Himalayan winter in tents with every day a struggle to survive. Pictures were beamed around the world of people rendered homeless, including children, the elderly, and the injured, making their way to safety across steep, rock-strewn mountainsides before the cold, further injury, disease, or death overtook them.

A week after the earthquake, hundreds of thousands in the most remote areas were still without food, water, and shelter. Inevitably, this increased the death toll. Eventually, aid poured into the region from around the world and the slow process of rebuilding lives and communities began.
Lorraine Brownbill

Date October 8, 2005

Country Pakistan/India

Why It's Key The scale of the catastrophe was enormous and, because of the geography of the area, lessons were learned about distributing aid and rebuilding lives in remote areas.

Fact The earthquake killed 75,000, and injured 69,000.

opposite Looking for survivors in the wreckage of the Kashmir earthquake.

2000–

775

Key Discovery
First face transplant

One of the most controversial and ambitious operations in reconstructive surgery, the face transplant had hitherto been banned on ethical and moral grounds. The expertise and knowledge to carry out the procedure had been in place for some years, but it was not until 2002 that the French ethical committee ruled that face transplants could be conducted only in exceptional cases; not only an aesthetic injury but also if the patient has difficulty eating and swallowing. The United States also had provisions put in place for such a procedure, but unlike in France, the opportunity had not arisen.

In May 2005, Isabelle Dinoire, a thirty-eight-year-old French woman, was savagely attacked by her pet dog after falling unconscious in her home. The horrific attack left her with extensive injuries to her face, and she was unable to eat or speak, living her life behind a mask. A perfect recipient for such a procedure, Dinoire underwent extensive counseling before the operation, and six months after the attack, with a suitable donor found, Professors Jean-Michel Dubernard and Bernard Devauchelle grafted tissue, muscles, arteries, and veins from the deceased donor onto Dinoire's face, and replaced her nose, lips, and chin.

Unlike what popular science fiction literature might suggest, Isabelle Dinoire did not take on the appearance of the donor, nor did she look like her former self. Rather, her new face is a "hybrid" of how she once looked and the face she received.
Kerry Duffy

Date November 27, 2005

Country France

Why It's Key A breakthrough in facial reconstruction, the operation provided hope for millions of patients with facial deformities.

Key Cultural Event
Turkish author tried for treason

When, in 2006, Orhan Pamuk became the first Turkish writer to win a Nobel Prize, reactions in his homeland were mixed. On the one hand, there was great national pride in Pamuk, who combines postmodern sensibilities with brilliant storytelling, and exhibits a profound understanding of the clashes between East and West and between religion and secularism. On the other hand, many Turks still could not forgive him for the earlier incident that had sent him into exile in the United States, fearing for his life.

In February 2005, Pamuk told a Swiss newspaper that "30,000 Kurds and one million Armenians were killed in these lands and nobody but me dares to talk about it," referring to the 1915 genocide by the Ottoman government. This event is still disputed in Turkey, and conservatives and nationalists viewed Pamuk's remarks as treasonable heresy. Pamuk was charged with "insulting Turkishness," which carries a significant prison sentence; but at the start of the trial, after he'd been pelted with eggs and stones on his way into the courtroom, he found himself acquitted.

At the time, Turkey was in talks to join the EU, and faced tremendous criticism from the international community for its laws about free expression, which see dozens of authors and journalists on trial every year. This criticism continued when it emerged that Pamuk had been freed on a technicality, not on principle, leaving Turkey's commitment to human rights still in doubt.
Ned Beauman

Date 2005

Country Turkey

Why It's Key The trial of Turkey's greatest living author for "insulting Turkishness" raised questions about the power of the EU to compromise with other cultures.

opposite Orhan Pamuk (right)

Key Cultural Event
Russia cuts Ukraine's gas supply

When Russia cut off gas supplies to Ukraine over a price dispute in January 2006, Europe braced itself for a new kind of "Cold War." Vladimir Putin's hard-line approach to the ex-Soviet satellite had underlined the West's increasing reliance on Russian fossil fuels, provoking grim predictions of rising heating bills and colder winters to come.

Since March 2005, Russia had been pressing Kiev to pay Gazprom the market rate of US$230 per 1,000 cubic meters for its gas imports, effectively quadrupling the country's expenditure on the fuel. Despite Russian protests that the price hike was purely an economic measure, Putin's troubled relationship with the pro-Western Ukrainian President Viktor Yushchenko raised suspicions of political subversion by the Kremlin. On December 29, Yushchenko rejected a US$3.6 billion loan from the Russian government that would have helped sustain Ukraine during the switchover to transactions at the market rate. On January 1, 2006, Russia cut supplies amid defiant claims from Ukraine's prime minister that the country possessed enough fuel reserves to cover the winter.

Immediate supply shortfalls were felt across Europe, with the old Soviet states most severely affected. The indirect threat to Europe contributed to a five-year deal being struck on January 4 that would see RosUkrEnergo, a joint-venture company, sell gas on to Ukraine for less than half the market rate. The outcome was hailed as a victory in Ukraine, where GDP rose by 6.2 per cent in the next ten months. In reality, the deal proved to be a face-saving measure for both sides.
Jay Mullins

Date January 1, 2006

Country Ukraine

Why It's Key The dispute highlighted Europe's over-reliance on Russian natural gas reserves.

Key Political Event
Hamas wins majority vote

Hamas is a Palestinian political party and military organization that emerged in 1987. It espouses a hard-line, Islamist philosophy, which calls for the destruction of the state of Israel and the establishment of an Islamic Republic in its place. Beginning as a resistance movement against the Israeli occupation of Palestinian territories, Hamas has used tactics including suicide bombings of civilian targets.

After the death of Palestinian leader Yasser Arafat, his secular Fatah party became increasingly unpopular, perceived as corrupt and unconcerned with the needs of ordinary Palestinians. Hamas became a popular alternative, particularly in light of its humanitarian efforts, such as the construction of schools and hospitals, the organization of welfare and education programs, and the facilitation of social services.

In the 2006 parliamentary elections, Hamas won a surprising victory over the ruling Fatah Party, winning 74 of 132 seats and 42.9 per cent of the vote. The election result was seen by many as disastrous for the Middle East peace process, given Hamas' hard-line stance against Israel and the fact that the party is considered an official terrorist organization by Canada, Japan, the United States, and the EU.

The victory also came at an immediate humanitarian cost for the Palestinian people, as numerous countries quickly cut off foreign aid until the Hamas government agreed to certain terms – such as renouncing terror and recognizing Israel. Politically and economically, Palestinians became increasingly fragmented and isolated on the world stage.

Justin Norris

Date January 25, 2006
Country Palestine

Why It's Key The surprising victory of this hard-line, Islamist, anti-Israel party led to Palestine's diplomatic isolation and heightened the conflict in the Middle East.

opposite January 27, 2006: Palestinian supporters of Hamas celebrate their electoral victory.

Key Discovery
Pluto loses planet status

In the known universe, size matters – but attitude matters more, according to the International Astronomical Union (IAU). During its ten-day assembly in Prague in August 2006, the IAU decided on a definition of "planet" that left only eight in orbit around the sun. On August 24, the IAU passed a resolution stating a planet has to be in orbit around the sun, be nearly round in shape, and "clear the neighborhood around its orbit." That knocked Pluto off the planet list, demoting it to the status of "dwarf planet" along with Ceres, orbiting between Mars and Saturn, and Eris (formerly "Xena" or 2003-UB313). The 2006 IAU resolutions call Pluto the prototype for a new category of "trans-Neptunian objects."

Clyde W. Tombaugh discovered Pluto on February 18, 1930 while searching for the cause of Neptune's orbital interruption. Charon, the largest of Pluto's three moons, was discovered in 1978. However, astronomers began reconsidering Pluto's status as a planet in the 1990s, when they discovered that it was part of the Kuipar Belt, an area full of small, icy, Pluto-like objects in the outer reaches of the solar system. Pluto had also been controversial because of its small size (about one-fifth Earth's diameter), composition, atmosphere, and unusual 247.7-year elliptical orbit, which is also synchronous with Charon.

However, the decision has been widely contested as only 424 astronomers voted, and some suggest that the decision to demote Pluto to a dwarf planet may be revisited at the next IAU meeting in 2009.

Marie Powell

Date August 24, 2006
Country Czech Republic

Why It's Key The decision left only eight planets in orbit around the sun, and set up new definitions of terms such as "planet" and "dwarf planet."

Key Political Event
North Korea explodes atomic bomb

On October 9, 2006, the Korean Central News Agency announced that the Democratic People's Republic of Korea had detonated a nuclear device at a site called Sangpyong-ri, near the coastal city of Kimchaek. The blast was estimated to have had an explosive force of less than one kiloton, but created seismic waves measuring 3.58 on the Richter scale.

Even though it is not known when North Korea launched its nuclear program, the North Korean nuclear weapons strategy is home-grown. It is believed that the North Korean Academy of Sciences, the North Korean Army, and the Ministry of Public Security initiated the nuclear weapons program sometime between the 1970s and the early 1980s, but it is only since the early 1990s, when it constructed a plutonium-producing nuclear reactor at Yongbyon,

that North Korea has been suspected of maintaining a clandestine nuclear weapons development program.

In 1994, the United States and North Korea signed the "Agreed Framework," whereby North Korea agreed to freeze its plutonium production program in exchange for fuel, economic cooperation, and the construction of two modern light-water nuclear power plants. Eventually, North Korea's existing nuclear facilities were to be dismantled, and the spent reactor fuel taken out of the country.

The international community's response to the nuclear testing was swift and unanimous. All five veto-wielding permanent members of the United Nations Security Council – including North Korea's close ally China – condemned the nuclear test.

Keith Leitich

Date October 9, 2006

Country North Korea

Why It's Key A nuclear-armed North Korea could provoke an arms race involving South Korea, Japan, and the People's Republic of China.

Fact Despite repeated warnings from the U.S., North Korea became the ninth country in the world to possess a nuclear weapon, joining the U.S., Russia, France, Britain, China, India, Pakistan, and Israel.

Key Cultural Event
Les Miserables breaks world record

As it marked the twenty-first anniversary of its debut in the West End, London, the musical Les Miserables broke the world record for the longest-running musical by completing 8,372 performances. It beat Cats – created by Sir Andrew Lloyd Webber, one of the most successful musical writers of all time – which had also run continuously for twenty-one years until May 11, 2002. Both Cats and Les Miserables were produced in the West End by theater producer Cameron Mackintosh.

Written by Alain Boublil and Claude-Michel Schonberg, Les Miserables is set in nineteenth-century France in the early moments of the French Revolution. It follows the fates of two men in deep conflict: parole convict Jean Valjean, a victim of miserable circumstances, and Javert, an officer of the law with

uncompromising principles of justice. Also featured is a tender love story between orphan Cosette and revolutionary student Marius. First performed by the Royal Shakespeare Company in October 1985, the musical was moved to the West End's Palace Theatre, where it played for more than 7,500 performances over eighteen years. In April 2004, it moved again to Queen's Theatre on Shaftesbury Avenue.

Seen by over 53 million people in 38 countries in 21 languages, Les Miserables is recognized as one of the most popular musicals in the world. The year 2006 was doubly celebratory for Mackintosh, who had also produced The Phantom of the Opera, which had become the longest running musical on Broadway in January with its 7,486th performance.

Mariko Kato

Date October 9, 2006

Country UK

Why It's Key Les Miserables is one of the world's most frequently performed and well-loved musicals.

Fact Les Miserables is based on the novel of the same title by French writer Victor Hugo.

Key Cultural Event
Pollock painting sells for record sum

When the story broke, in the November 2, 2006 issue of *The New York Times*, that Jackson Pollock's *No.5, 1948* painting had allegedly exchanged hands in a private sale between two mega-moguls, the news spread like wildfire. Pollock – widely considered one of the most important American artists of the twentieth century and a pioneer of the Abstract Expressionism movement – produced his most famous works during his so-called "drip period" between 1947 and 1950. Works from this period are highly sought after and rarely enter the public market. Even so, the fact that the painting had been sold was not what was making headlines around the world, but rather *how much* it had allegedly been sold for.

Quoting unnamed art "insiders," the article claimed that the music magnate and founder of Dreamworks David Geffen had sold the painting for an astounding US$140 million dollars to Mexican financier David Martinez. The figure exceeded the US$135 million Ronald Lauder, heir to the Estée Lauder cosmetics empire, had paid for Gustav Klimt's 1907 *Portrait of Adele Bloch-Bauer I*, making Pollock's *No.5* the most expensive painting ever sold.

Shortly after its publication, reports surfaced questioning the facts of the *NYT* article, and the alleged "buyer," David Martinez, released a public statement denying any ownership or involvement in the Pollock deal. The location of Pollock's *No.5* remains a mystery.

Annie Wang

Date 2006

Country USA

Why It's Key The exorbitant price demanded by Pollock's *No.5, 1948* reflected the rise of Abstract Expressionism as the new "popular" period in the art market.

Fact Pollock stopped naming his paintings in an effort to remove preconceptions by those viewing them. He chose instead to number them because he considered numbers to be neutral.

2000–

781

Key Political Event
Saddam Hussein is executed

The United States-led invasion of Iraq began in March of 2003. Iraq was seen as a threat to U.S. security, accused by the Bush administration of concealing, and attempting to develop, "Weapons of Mass Destruction." Within three weeks of the U.S. invasion, the Iraqi government collapsed, and Saddam Hussein went into hiding. On December 14, 2003, the U.S. military captured Hussein, and the former dictator was handed over to the new, American-backed, interim Iraqi government to stand trial for numerous counts of alleged "crimes against humanity." In November 2006, he was found guilty and sentenced to death.

The execution of Saddam Hussein was carried out on December 31, 2006. In a muted video clip released by the Iraqi government, Hussein is shown, dressed in black and appearing calm, as a noose is placed around his neck. This is where the official video stops, but a grainy amateur version showing the execution in its entirety soon surfaced in various media outlets.

The amateur footage appeared to be shot by a camera phone and, unlike the government video, the sound was left intact, allowing its viewers to hear the guards cruelly taunting Saddam just moments before his execution. The controversy sparked widespread international criticism of the execution, and heated moral debate over its unauthorized filming. It was widely expressed that basic respect for human life, and death, should be applied to everyone – even a murderous dictator.

Annie Wang

Date December 30, 2006

Country Iraq

Why It's Key The execution of Saddam Hussein signalled a major victory for the United States, and became hugely controversial after an amateur cellular phone video broadcast the entire execution on various media channels.

Key Political Event **Russian oil supplies to Poland, Germany, and Ukraine are cut off**

Russia's exports of natural resources, compounded by increasing oil and gas prices, have spurred its economic growth since the late 1990s and served as a tool of Russian political influence around the world. Because the EU imports more oil and natural gas from Russia than from any other single country, the economic relationship between these countries is crucial, with revenues from the sale of Russian oil and gas to the EU providing over 40 per cent of Russia's annual budget. Oil and gas produced in Russia are transported across thousands of kilometers of pipelines, before reaching Europe. The largest pipeline is the Druzhba ("friendship") line, which collects oil from the Urals and the Caspian Sea before traveling across Russia into Belarus where it forks, with one branch running west through Belarus and the other south through Belarus and Ukraine.

The 3-day lapse of oil supplies to the Druzhba line in January 2008 highlighted key economic and security issues within the EU and between the EU and Russia. On the surface, the cut was caused by a dispute between Russia and Belarus regarding transit taxes imposed by Belarus for oil passing through the pipeline. While the cut did not have serious economic repercussions for the EU, it reinforced the EU's dependency on Russian energy supplies. Such events have forced European leaders to re-examine the EU's energy policy, including exploring alternatives to oil and natural gas. The dispute also highlighted one of the many challenges Russia faces as it attempts to reassert itself internationally, namely the drawing on its energy resources as a potential source of political muscle.
Michael Wodzicki

Date January 8–11, 2007

Country Russia, Belarus, and the European Union

Why It's key The dispute between Russia and Belarus reinforced the European Union's (EU) dependency on energy supplies from Russia and forces the EU to rethink its energy policy.

Fact Russia is the world's second largest producer of oil and the world's largest producer of natural gas.

Key Political Event **Obama announces his presidential bid less than one month after Hillary Clinton**

In November 2008, Americans will elect a new President. This election will be different from any previous election: for the first time ever one of the candidates will be either a woman or a man of African-American descent. The race between New York Senator Hilary Clinton and Illinois Senator Barack Obama to become the Democratic Party's candidate for president has captured the attention and imagination of the American people and the rest of the world. In doing so, the race is irrevocably changing identity politics in America.

Many political analysts believe that Americans simply cannot conceive of what a woman president would look like. It was only 29 years ago that the first woman was elected to the U.S. Senate, rather than inheriting the position from a deceased husband or father, and according to the Inter-Parliamentary Union, America ranks 67th – between Zimbabwe and Turkmenistan – in terms of female representation in the senate. However, Obama, the self-proclaimed "skinny kid with the funny name," was also considered a long shot when he first announced his candidacy for president. Though the first African-American senator was elected in 1870, racism is still rife in American society, and right-wing extremists have targeted in particular Obama's Muslim heritage.

Though both Clinton and Obama are more than just representatives of their respective minority identity groups, their candidacies are a victory for liberalism in the United States, regardless of whether the Democrats are successful in the final election.
Michael Wodzicki

Date February 10, 2007

Country USA

Why It's key An Obama or Clinton nomination would be the first time that either a woman or African-American man is a candidate in an U.S. presidential election.

Fact: Obama and Clinton were not the only candidates who could have been potential history makers: Bill Richardson would have been the first Latino Democratic candidate.

opposite Obama (left) and Clinton

INDEX

784

797